The Slaves Who Defeated Napoléon

ATLANTIC CROSSINGS
Rafe Blaufarb, Series Editor

THE SLAVES WHO DEFEATED NAPOLÉON

Toussaint Louverture and the Haitian War of Independence, 1801–1804

Philippe R. Girard

THE UNIVERSITY OF ALABAMA PRESS
Tuscaloosa

Typeface: Bembo

∞

The paper on which this book is printed meets the minimum requirements of American National Standard for Information Sciences—Permanence of Paper for Printed Library Materials, ANSI Z39.48-1984.

Cover: Karl Girardet, "St. Domingue: Prise de la Ravine aux Couleuvres." In Pierre Lanfrey, *The History of Napoleon the First*. London, New York: Macmillan and Co., vol. 2, part 1, opp. p. 146.

Library of Congress Cataloging-in-Publication Data
Girard, Philippe R.
The slaves who defeated Napoleon : Toussaint Louverture and the Haitian War of Independence, 1801–1804 / Philippe R. Girard.
    p. cm. — (Atlantic crossings)
  Includes bibliographical references and index.
  ISBN 978-0-8173-1732-4 (cloth : alk. paper) — ISBN 978-0-8173-8540-8 (electronic)
    1. Haiti—History—Revolution, 1791–1804. 2. Haiti—History—Revolution, 1791–1804—Sources. 3. Haiti—History—Revolution, 1791–1804—Personal narratives. 4. Toussaint Louverture, 1743–1803. 5. Generals—Haiti—Biography. 6. Revolutionaries—Haiti—Biography. 7. Statesmen—Haiti—Biography. 8. Napoleon I, Emperor of the French, 1769–1821. I. Title.
F1923.G57 2011
972.94′03—dc23
                                                                    2011019639

Contents

vi / Contents

Illustrations

Acknowledgments

I received plenty of help during the many years I spent researching this book, starting with readers like my wife, Preble, and the anonymous reviewers of The University of Alabama Press. Most crucial was the warm hospitality provided by my family and friends who had the bad luck of living close to archival deposits. Among them were Nathalie and Emmanuel Blanc, Marcel Blanc and Michelle Berny, Ronald and Elizabeth Cook, Coralie Dedieu, Jacques and Marie-Madeleine Girard, Sophie and Guillaume Larnicol, and Nicolas Vercken. They have earned my eternal gratitude and a warning that future research projects might force me again to monopolize their couch. My research trips were funded in part by McNeese State University's Evelyn Shaddock Murray grant, Shearman grant, Joe Gray Taylor grant, and Violet Howell faculty award, the Library Company's PEAES fellowship, and a Gilder-Lehrman fellowship. I gratefully thank these institutions for their financial support. I would also like to single out employees of the Library Company of Philadelphia, the University of Florida's special collections, and the French naval archives in Vincennes for being particularly knowledgeable and friendly.

The Slaves Who Defeated Napoléon

Introduction

Cape Sámana, at the northeastern corner of the island of Hispaniola, was still a sparsely inhabited wilderness when on January 29, 1802, a small group of riders arrived at full gallop.[1] Their leader rode at breakneck speed, his aides-de-camp straining to keep up. His shining high boots, rich blue and crimson uniform, and tricolor feathers made a vivid contrast with his ebony-black skin under the vertical sun of the tropics. He was only 5'1", scrawny, his prognathous chin jutting under a toothless jaw, but six decades into an eventful life he radiated purpose and authority and he bore the military bicorne with an air of august dignity.[2] His name was Toussaint Louverture; he was a former slave; but he now governed in the name of the French Republic all of Hispaniola, the second-largest island in the Caribbean (present-day Haiti and Dominican Republic).

As he flew toward his destination, Louverture's thoughts probably drifted two thousand leagues across the ocean to Paris and his direct superiors. Eight years before, revolutionary France had emancipated most of the slaves in its colonies, but Louverture's increasingly autonomous rule had raised many eyebrows and he knew that his enemies were openly calling for his removal from office. Six weeks before he had learned from Jamaica that France had just signed a peace protocol with England, an important development that now made it possible for France to send a fleet to overthrow him.[3] The eventuality of his own demise had seemed distant at first, but when visiting the city of Santo Domingo a week before, Louverture had received a report from his spies that an expedition was ready to depart from Brest.[4] A few days later the news came that French warships had been sighted off Cape Sámana.[5]

The arrival of the French fleet was the reason why Louverture was now urging his horse—probably Bel Argent, his favorite mount—north and east. He had to see for himself how many troops France had sent to rein him in. If he was lucky, France had sent one lone agent onboard a lowly corvette, whom he would control as easily as he had controlled previous French envoys. But

1. Toussaint Louverture. Photographs and Prints Division, Schomburg Center, New York Public Library.

there was always the possibility that France might have used the suspension of hostilities with England to send several frigates carrying hundreds of troops. Louverture's large army would probably dominate them, but even a few hundred of Napoléon Bonaparte's soldiers were a force to be reckoned with.

The sight that greeted Louverture as the bay of Sámana finally came into view must have taken his breath away. Below him, lying at anchor, sailed three corvettes, eleven frigates, and ten *vaisseaux* (ships of the line), the largest warships of their time, each of them carrying upwards of one thousand sailors and troops. There was worse: far to the east, surging from the sea like monsters from the depths of hell, Louverture could see more vessels arriving, their sails seemingly blanketing the horizon from one end to the other. By

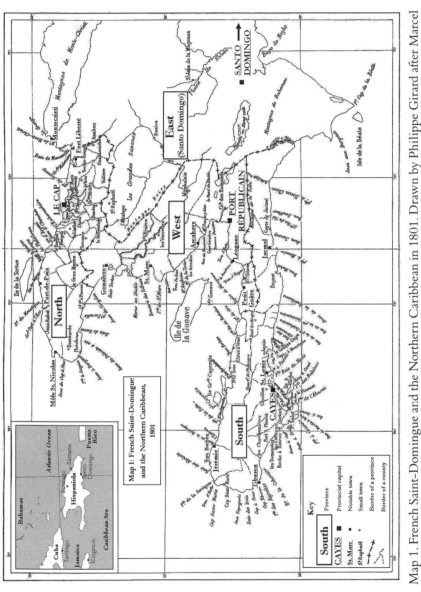

Map 1. French Saint-Domingue and the Northern Caribbean in 1801. Drawn by Philippe Girard after Marcel Mehl, "Carte de la partie française de Saint-Domingue," Ge B SH.146.2.9, Bibliothèque Nationale, Paris.

the time these reached Sámana a few hours later, the combined fleet totaled nine transports of various kinds, nineteen frigates, twenty-two of the massive *vaisseaux,* and over twenty thousand men and women.[6] Only God knew how many more stragglers were still on their way—and given the magnitude of the catastrophe befalling him, Louverture must have been tempted to abandon the Catholic version for the Vodou (voodoo) *bon dieu* of his Creole upbringing.

The fifty ships maneuvered to form three parallel lines and began ferrying hundreds of troops from one vessel to another, obviously in preparation for a landing. As night fell each ship lighted three fires to signal its position, and the scintillating armada, reflected on the Caribbean swells, now seemed three hundred strong under the myriad flickering dots of the starlit sky.[7] The force's size was evidence enough of Bonaparte's hostile intentions. "We must perish," allegedly said Louverture. "All of France has come to Saint-Domingue. They have been deceived, and they have come to seek vengeance."[8]

Louverture correctly guessed that the main landing would take place more than two hundred miles to the west in Cap Français or Cap (present-day Cap Haïtien), the largest city of the colony. Reaching Cap in time to warn its commander was of the highest importance. Should Cap fall intact, the French would have sufficient resources to mount a massive, coordinated offensive throughout Saint-Domingue. Louverture's rule, maybe even his life, would come to an end, but there was even worse to fear. Bonaparte had not sent two-thirds of the French navy solely to overthrow an elderly governor. His ultimate goal, Louverture suspected, was to restore slavery. If he was right, the freedom of four hundred thousand men, women, and children was at stake.

Egging Bel Argent down the hill, Louverture began galloping toward Cap. As a young slave, he had been entrusted with the care of the plantation's horses, and he was known as the best horseman in the colony; his entire life had prepared him for this very moment. In a desperate, headlong run, he flew west along the coast, racing the French fleet to Cap. If he won, he might successfully oppose the French landing and save both his rule and his people's imperiled freedom; if he lost, his entire world would come crashing down. The Haitian war of independence had begun.

～

To a contemporary audience, the land in which the Haitian Revolution took place brings to mind voodoo spells, Tontons Macoutes, and boat people—nothing worth fighting over. Two centuries ago, however, Haiti, then known as Saint-Domingue, was a sugar powerhouse that stood at the center of world trading networks. All the great statesmen of the time, from Thomas Jefferson to Bonaparte, spent much of their waking time, not worrying about an influx of Haitian illegal immigrants, but battling for a share of the colony's exports. Money, not surprisingly, was the reason. Contemporary Haiti might be the poorest country in the Western Hemisphere, but late eighteenth-century Saint-Domingue was the *perle des Antilles,* France's most valuable overseas colony, the largest exporter of tropical products in the world, and the United States' second-largest trading partner after England.

By the time Louverture witnessed the arrival of the French armada off Cape Sámana in January 1802, Saint-Domingue had been wracked by revolutionary turmoil for more than a decade. Political turbulences first erupted in 1789 when the aftershocks of the French Revolution reached Saint-Domingue and whites and free people of color began battling one another. The colony's half-million slaves remained seemingly docile at first, until they too revolted in 1791 and ravaged the rich plain surrounding Cap Français. The situation grew so dire that despite the reservations of the more racist planters, France opted in 1792 to enlist the support of the mixed-race *anciens libres,* whom colonial law had heretofore relegated to second-class status. Although of servile ancestry, they often owned slaves and plantations and most embraced the planters' side.

The support of free people of color had finally helped contain the slave uprising—without fully extinguishing it—when another seismic jolt hit Saint-Domingue. In 1793, following the advent of the Terror and the execution of Louis XVI, England and Spain declared war on France. Within months the English navy captured most of Saint-Domingue's western ports, including the administrative capital of Port Républicain (present-day Port-au-Prince), while Spain attacked the colony's northeast with the help of many rebellious slaves. Pressed on all sides, France's commissioner, Léger-Félicité Sonthonax, abolished slavery in a desperate bid to enlist the slaves in the struggle against foreign invasion. The bold move marked the first time a Western power had declared immediate emancipation in the New World (by comparison, England only abolished slavery in 1833, the United States in 1865, and Brazil in 1888). Sonthonax's revolutionary decree was confirmed by the French Convention in 1794 and extended to other French colonies like Guadeloupe. Four years after the beginning of its own revolution, France had become the leading advocate of racial equality and universal freedom in the Caribbean.

Emancipation was philosophically laudable, but it also proved militarily sound. Enlisting people of African descent, who formed the vast majority of the colonial population and were more resistant to tropical diseases than Europeans, meant that the French army could instantly field more soldiers in Saint-Domingue than any rival, even as France was unable to send reinforcements due to British mastery of the Atlantic. Among the converts to the French cause was Toussaint Louverture, who defected from the Spanish to the French army some time after the declaration of emancipation. With his help France pressured the Spanish and English armies mercilessly in years to come. With nothing to show for their efforts but wasted treasure and lives, Spain left Saint-Domingue in 1795, followed by England in 1798. Saint-Domingue was again in French hands, albeit without the slave labor system that had underpinned its agricultural wealth in prerevolutionary times.

The following years saw Louverture's progressive rise from general to states-man as he maneuvered to deport France's agents and have himself appointed governor in their stead. In a brutal civil war known as the War of the South, he also conquered the southern part of Saint-Domingue that had until then been controlled by one of his rivals, André Rigaud. By 1801, when Louver-ture invaded the neighboring Spanish colony of Santo Domingo (modern-day Dominican Republic), he found himself in control of the entire island of Hispaniola, concluding his meteoric rise from mere slave to master of France's richest colony. The first chapter of this book opens at this critical juncture, when the man who admirers and detractors alike were beginning to call the black Napoléon passed a constitution making him governor for life.

Meanwhile, in France, his white counterpoint debated whether Louver-ture, despite all his public declarations of loyalty to France, had de facto led the colony to independence (chapter two). After concluding that Louverture was indeed in open rebellion against the metropolis, Bonaparte prepared a massive expedition under the command of his brother-in-law, Victoire Le-clerc (chapter three), who crossed the Atlantic in the winter of 1801/2 (chap-ter four). Two years of bloody, desperate fighting ensued. At stake was not only Louverture's career but also France's colonial empire in the Americas, Louisiana, the supremacy of the English navy, the lives of forty thousand French soldiers, the liberty of four hundred thousand Dominguians, the in-dependence of Haiti, and, ultimately, whether the first successful slave revolt in the history of the world would survive. This struggle of epic proportions, in which lives were consumed by the thousands, is this book's main concern.

The French claimed that they had no intention of restoring slavery, while Louverture assured them of his loyalty to France, so the French landing in February 1802 was a confused game of bluff, made even more complicated by the need to assuage regional powers like Jamaica, Cuba, and the United States (chapters five and six). Within weeks the masks had fallen and Leclerc's and Louverture's armies battled in a bloody campaign that culminated in the epic siege of Crête-à-Pierrot (chapter seven). The French prevailed and Leclerc set out to reform the colony, while exiling Louverture to France under the suspicion that he was plotting a new uprising (chapter eight). But the Caribbean summer brought a yellow fever epidemic of unusual strength that decimated French ranks (chapter nine), and groups of runaway farm la-borers, convinced that France's ultimate goal was to reenslave them, launched a second uprising (chapter ten). When an increasingly despondent Leclerc retaliated by drowning thousands of people of color in the fall of 1802, most of the officers of color still loyal to France joined the ranks of the rebellion as well (chapter eleven).

Leclerc himself died in this hour of crisis, but his successor, Donatien de Rochambeau, having received new reinforcements from France, managed to retake all the major cities of the colony as 1803 began (chapter twelve). Pressure on French strongholds was light during these months, which Louverture's successor Jean-Jacques Dessalines spent battling with various rivals for the leadership of the rebel army (chapter thirteen). Meanwhile, in France, news of the disasters that had befallen the expedition led Bonaparte to reassess his imperial ambitions, sell Louisiana, and tighten the conditions in which Louverture was detained (chapter fourteen). Events in Europe, conversely, affected the situation in Saint-Domingue when war with England resumed and Rochambeau found himself under British naval blockade (chapter fifteen). Rochambeau's besieged forces eventually capitulated in November 1803 (chapters sixteen and seventeen) and in January 1804 Dessalines laid the foundations of the new state of Haiti (chapter eighteen). The disparate remnants of the French army found themselves scattered from Jamaica to Cuba, the United States, and Santo Domingo, from which the last survivors of the Leclerc expedition were expelled in 1809, an event that brought a final end to the Leclerc expedition (chapter nineteen).

Retracing such a titanic struggle is a difficult endeavor. Documents are numerous, almost overwhelmingly so; to make matters worse, they are written in four main languages (French, English, Spanish, and Kreyol), often in barely legible script, occasionally in cipher. Relevant sources are spread between twenty archives and libraries located in France, the United States, and Britain (see the bibliographic essay for a complete list of archival deposits). These practical constraints explain why until now no scholar had attempted to write a comprehensive, definitive history of the Haitian war of independence from an international perspective; in fact, completing this task took me far longer than the war itself lasted.

This work's main ambition is to employ the latest tools of the historian's craft, multiarchival research in particular, and to apply them to the climactic, yet poorly studied, last years of the Haitian Revolution. It relies primarily on contemporary French and Haitian military, commercial, and administrative sources such as letters and memoirs (women, rank-and-file soldiers, and lower-class Haitians left comparatively few documents and must often be studied through third-party accounts). This book's extensive archival basis will help correct the many factual inaccuracies that have plagued previous accounts and will present what evidence is available to settle such mysteries as what happened to Louverture's personal fortune. It will also help reassess the role of leading characters like the expedition's first commander, Leclerc, who was long presented in a positive light even though he pioneered the most notorious policies of his infamous successor, Rochambeau, including the use of man-hunting dogs.

Offering a reliable narrative of the Haitian war of independence, however, was only one of the goals of this study. Another was to move away from some previous scholars' obsession with the minutiae of guerilla warfare and offer instead a more rounded picture of these eventful times. Notable ambushes (such as Ravine-à-Couleuvres), sieges (such as Crête-à-Pierrot), and pitched battles (such as Vertières) must be covered as they marked important steps in the Haitian path to independence. But this book will also describe naval engagements with the British navy; civilian-military feuds for control of the colony; the role of U.S. merchants in supplying both parties in the war; diplomatic missions to Cuba, Jamaica, and the United States; and the lives of the plantation runaways, women, and children who have too often been ignored in previous accounts. This will be the story of barefoot freedmen ambushing Bonaparte's columns, but also of Rochambeau's mistresses, Italian child drummers, Jewish bankers in Kingston, Philadelphian weapons smugglers, Polish defectors to the rebel army, and African-born communities doggedly defending their independence from Bonaparte's and Louverture's generals.

When beginning this project, I assumed that the Haitian Revolution had all the ideological and racial tidiness one might expect from a slave revolt coupled with a war of independence. On one side would be black slaves yearning for freedom and nationhood; on the other would be racist white Frenchmen eager to preserve slavery and colonial rule. Little did I imagine that a kaleidoscope would have been a more apt metaphor. Late colonial Saint-Domingue was an Atlantic society at the crossroads of African, European, and Caribbean influences and was fragmented along racial, social, political, national, and gender lines. One could be black, white, or (according to the overzealous colonial chronicler Moreau de Saint-Méry) one of 126 combinations thereof. One could be a *grand blanc* (rich planter) or a *petit blanc* (poor white). One could be an *ancien libre* (person of color freed before the 1793 emancipation law) or a *nouveau libre* (newly emancipated slave). One could be a *Créole* (born in the colony), a *Européen* (born in France), or a *Congo* (born in Africa). One could be a *cultivateur* (farm laborer in the plains) or a *marron* (runaway living in the mountains). One, more commonly, could be a combination of all of the above and change one's affiliations depending on the issue du jour. Louverture's second, Jean-Jacques Dessalines, a former slave but also a plantation owner, fought with the rebel slaves in 1791–93, for Spain in 1793–94, for France in 1794–1802, against France from February to April 1802, and for France until October of that year, when he finally joined the rebel side for good. His complex trajectory was far from unusual. The only constant factor during the revolution, it seems, was greed, as officers, merchants, and planters of all colors battled ceaselessly for a share of Saint-Domingue's fabled wealth (other deadly sins from lust to wrath and envy were also frequently on display).

Race, which was long heralded as the main dividing line in Saint-Domingue, mattered in some instances (particularly in the war's closing months), but it was merely one of several components of one's identity. Many people of color fought on the French side until the very end of the war. Conversely, the rebel army included Polish and French defectors, was backed by the (itself multiracial) British navy, and was supplied by U.S. merchants, all of whom pursued ideological, strategic, and commercial goals that had little to do with race. Contemporary Haitians, who are predominantly black, will probably be surprised to read that many whites supported their independence and that a majority of the French army was composed of their colored ancestors until a few months before independence, but such is the historical record. In the end it may seem more effective to cast aside all attempts at categorization and study revolutionary Saint-Domingue as the sum of hundreds of thousands of individual histories—which is why I include extended vignettes on contemporary characters whose manifold lives fit no standard category. What grand unifying theory could otherwise account for Wladyslaw Jablonowski, the son of a Polish woman and a black father, who died fighting for white supremacy and French colonial rule on Bonaparte's behalf?

Even more novel will be this book's claim that the war did not necessarily oppose apologists and enemies of slavery. Contrary to popular belief, many members of the expedition (including Leclerc) opposed slavery; Louverture, by contrast, had owned slaves. Some white planters deluded themselves into thinking that slavery could be restored after a decade of revolutionary upheaval, while mountain runaways fought to disband the plantation system altogether, but most people in authority—whether black, mixed race, or white—fell in some intermediate category. Opposed to the concept of slavery as immoral or impractical, yet unwilling to let laborers leave plantations lest exports of sugar and coffee plummet, they embraced an intermediate system of forced but paid semifree labor. Even Bonaparte, who restored or maintained slavery in other French colonies in 1802–3, never openly advocated slavery in Saint-Domingue.

Previous works on the Haitian revolution often reflected their authors' racial, political, or national bias, so it might be pertinent to lay bare my own potential conflicts of interest at this juncture. As a twenty-first-century scholar, I have little patience for the racism and labor exploitation that under-pinned Bonaparte's colonial project in Saint-Domingue and can only rejoice at the thought that the former slaves won the war. As a white native of Gua-deloupe, however, I tend to view French imperialism in a more positive light than is customary among my academic colleagues, especially those of Haitian descent. As a thirtysomething educated French male, I am also prone to em-pathize with the young officers who died so far from the *patrie,* when other observers might look at them as greedy, oversexed monsters.

1

The Black Napoléon

Louverture and the 1801 Constitution

At 3 a.m. on Octidi, 18 Messidor year IX of the French Republic—Tuesday, July 7, 1801, in the Gregorian calendar—child drummers fanned around Cap Français to awaken the city's sleepy inhabitants with a peremptory drum roll.[1] It was early, even by the standards of the early rising inhabitants of the Antilles, but that day's festivities promised to be long and no one wished to be standing for hours in the oppressive afternoon heat of the Caribbean summer. By 5 a.m., the largely black contingents of the colonial army stood on the main square in orderly rows, their bright blue and red uniforms a reminder of the distant metropolis. They stood by detachments from the national guard, a more diverse unit drafted from the city's prominent citizens, including many *anciens libres*.

An hour later civilian and military authorities left the government house to join the troops lined on the plaza. Following the precise instructions established by Governor Toussaint Louverture, the trade commissioners marched first, followed by the naval administrators, the aldermen, the judges, the nine members of the constitutional assembly, and Louverture himself. His generals closed the march. This was an apt symbol: before Louverture, the civilian pillars of the constitution to be unveiled that day; after him, the real force behind his rule, the Dessalineses, the Christophes, and the Moyses, their ebony skin scarred by countless battles and the older wounds of the slave driver's lash. On one side, his administrators, most of them white; on the other, the upper echelons of his predominantly black army. "Constitutions are made of paper, but bayonets are made of steel," says one of these aphorisms so popular in the local Kreyol idiom.

Soldiers and bureaucrats gathered around the podium. "The deepest silence reigned," an unnamed chronicler wrote in the following day's *Bulletin Officiel de Saint-Domingue*. "Everyone awaited with impatience the reading of the text that would set the destinies of Saint-Domingue." The occasion called for slow, decorous pomp, for on that day the second constitution in Saint-Domingue's history was to be officially presented to its people.[2] No one could foresee that this constitution would be followed by another twenty-three in Haiti's turbulent political history and that half of the people present that day would be dead or in exile within three years. But everyone knew that metropolitan authorities had not been consulted on the matter and that First Consul Napoléon Bonaparte would react with fury when the news reached him that Louverture had single-handedly set up an autonomous government in France's richest colony.

The sun was now rising on the bay east of Cap, a bustling port with a short but rich history. It was not far from Cap that in 1492 Christopher Columbus had built Fort Navidad, the first European settlement in the New World. Pirates had later founded a haven in nearby La Tortue (Tortuga), before the French founded Cap itself in 1676. Blessed with a protected harbor and a large coastal plain, Cap was destined for a bright future. Destroyed by a fire in 1753, the city was rebuilt in stone, its streets paved, fountains and gutters built, and seventy-nine public monuments erected. Its eighteen thousand inhabitants, like the colony's population, were a mix of French-, Caribbean-, and African-born people of all colors whose differences were bridged by ties of labor, love, and commerce. The city reached its peak in the late 1780s, by which time it had acquired theaters, a learned society, freemason lodges, and the nickname of "Paris of the Antilles."[3]

To Louverture the city evoked different, more personal memories. One-third of all the Africans brought by French slave traders had arrived in Cap—almost as many in that city alone as the total number of slaves imported in the entire history of the United States. In 1790 a full nineteen thousand had landed there, more than the population of Boston.[4] The remains of the sickest among them, thrown overboard prior to landing, were still lying at the bottom of the glittering bay, just one mile from where Louverture stood on that early July morning. Louverture was a Caribbean-born Creole, but he may have learned of the horrors of the Middle Passage from his own father, who according to the oral tradition was the second son of an Arada (Ewe-Fon) chief in present-day Benin. Captured in combat (presumably by the neighboring warrior kingdom of Dahomey, a major exporter of African slaves), Louverture's father had been sold to a wealthy Dominguian planter, the Count of Noé. His son's constitution ceremony fittingly symbolized the family's unusual arc from political prominence to slavery and back.[5]

Louverture's own life had taken place within a short radius of Cap. The eldest of eight (or five) children, he was born on the Bréda plantation, a mere one league from Cap, around 1743. Louverture probably received an African name, but it has been lost to history. Instead, he was long known as Toussaint Bréda after his master's plantation (fellow slaves also dubbed him *fatras bâton,* or "contemptible stick," to mock him for his frail stature). The name "Louverture" (the opening) came much later, possibly as a result of his military exploits.[6] Like all Creole slaves, Toussaint's identity was thus an amalgam of French, African, and Caribbean elements, each one layered upon the other. Louverture's body may also have been a scarred palimpsest of his tumultuous life: African slaves often bore tribal scarifications as well as whipping and branding marks, and Louverture claimed that he bore scars from seventeen battle wounds.[7]

Louverture worked for a plantation manager, Bayon de Libertat, with a reputation for relative kindness, and he was unusually well treated as a slave. Assigned to the barn and stables, not the deadly sugar fields, he eventually rose to the position of coachman and unofficial veterinarian of the Bréda plantation. He married and learned how to read, neither of which was forbidden under the French servile code, the Code Noir, but both of which were rare among slaves.[8] Some authors claim that he joined Libertat's freemason lodge (as governor, he signed his name above a tell-tale succession of Masonic dots) and that he visited France as a slave, but evidence for such claims is scant.[9]

How distant those days now seemed! Starting in 1789, the whites of Saint-Domingue had begun endlessly debating the latest echoes from the French Revolution, oblivious to the fact that discussing the benefits of liberty and equality when surrounded by half a million people of color who outnumbered them twenty to one might set a dangerous example. It was in Cap that early in 1791 Vincent Ogé and Jean-Baptiste Chavannes had died on the executioner's rack for daring to demand equal citizenship rights for free people of color. It was around Cap that in August 1791 the slaves had revolted, ravaged the prosperous plain, and almost taken the city itself. Louverture had soon joined the revolt (or possibly initiated it), but following his usual Janus-like persona he had also seen Libertat's family to safety. It was Cap that had burned to the ground during a June 1793 quarrel between rival French officers and their black allies, and Cap where the French commissioner Léger-Félicité Sonthonax had abolished slavery later that year. It was also in Cap that Louverture had helped subdue the rebellious officer Jean-Louis Villatte in 1796, an episode that had launched the political career that now made him absolute ruler of Saint-Domingue.

~

Shortly after daybreak, the ceremony began and Bernard Borgella rose to speak. Like most of his colleagues in the constitutional assembly, he was white (the rest were of mixed race; none was black).[10] The racial imbalance might seem odd for a constitution that set the foundations for the future black state of Haiti, but loosening the ties that bound Saint-Domingue to France had long been the goal of white colonists like Borgella. Louverture had probably also calculated that the constitution would be a bitter pill for France to swallow and that it might look more innocuous if its authors were white. At any rate, Louverture had decided on all the crucial provisions behind the scenes, and many of the constitutional delegates were figureheads. Four hailed from recently conquered Spanish Santo Domingo and were unlikely to speak up; one had the good taste of dying before the assembly even gathered.[11]

Louverture also employed Borgella because he had the administrative and legal skills that eluded former slaves. He was merely one of a constellation of white advisers, priests, secretaries, and aides-de-camp that formed the backbone of Louverture's "black" regime. His director of fortifications, Charles Vincent, was white. So were his confessor Corneille Brelle, the comptroller general Joseph Bizouard, his private secretary Pascal, the administrator of public estates Joseph-Antoine Idlinger, and his paymaster and diplomatic envoy Joseph Bunel de Blancamp.[12]

Borgella's speech was a plodding paean to Louverture, "this extraordinary man . . . who rose like a phoenix from the ashes." Borgella knew his man. Louverture had immense intellectual gifts, particularly his keen political instinct; his one weakness was flattery. Another reason he employed so many whites may have been that he felt vindicated when planters who had once stood at the apex of Saint-Domingue's social and racial hierarchy waddled in the mud before him, the one-time slave whom only cattle would obey. As governor every town he visited was expected to greet him with triumphal arches, trumpeters, laurels, thrones, adulating crowds, gushing women, and orations comparing him to Spartacus, Hercules, Alexander the Great, and Bonaparte. A week after presenting the constitution, he would create a new region and name it after himself.[13]

After pausing for a second Borgella delivered a second speech, just as adulatory as the first, then began to read the entire constitution, article by article, in its original French.[14] In the audience, many people of color only spoke Kreyol or their native African language; regional dialects would predominate in France for another century, so many lower-class whites spoke limited French as well.[15] One can only sympathize with their boredom as the ceremony proceeded, for hours, in the legalese version of a language they barely understood. But even someone with a full command of French could not fully understand the constitution, since many of its clauses were elaborate smoke screens meant to appease potential objections from the metropolis. The preamble meekly "proposed" the text "to the French government" for approval when it had already been discussed, ratified, and implemented, and would be published before France ever had a chance of asking for modifications. Louverture, the preamble further explained, had played a minimal role in drafting the constitution, which contradicted the historical record but gave him plausible deniability should the text incur the wrath of the metropolis. The first article stated that Saint-Domingue was a "colony, which belongs to the French empire" to better disguise the fact that the constitution turned the island into a virtually autonomous dominion.

The constitution was carefully phrased to avoid offending its metropolitan audience, but it was also meant to take effect in Saint-Domingue, where the black majority was more concerned with individual freedom than national independence. Most Dominguians were *nouveaux libres* who had only been freed officially with Sonthonax's 1793 decree of emancipation, which had then been confirmed by a 1794 law and the 1795 French constitution; in the areas of western and southern Saint-Domingue that were under English occupation at the time, slavery had survived until 1798.[16] But Bonaparte's 1799 constitution had vaguely specified that colonies would be governed by distinct laws, which seemed to imply that he did not recognize colonial subjects as full-fledged French citizens and that he might restore slavery one day. Louverture thus preemptively enshrined the sacred principles of citizenship and emancipation in his 1801 constitution in case France ever chose to forsake them. "There can be no slaves on the territory; slavery is forever abolished," the third article read. "All men are born, live, and die free and French." In the crowd even those who spoke little French understood the words. The same idea was expressed three times in as many sentences. They were free.

To the people of color known as *anciens libres,* emancipation was a secondary issue since they had already been free before the revolution; many had in fact owned slaves. Foremost on their minds were the discriminatory laws that had curtailed their rights in the prerevolutionary era. In 1792, after much hesitation, the French National Assembly had extended full citizenship to free people of color, but the *anciens libres* knew that the more conservative whites still rankled at the idea that miscegenational bastards could be their equals. The constitution's next clause, also formulated in three different ways, was intended to appease their fears. "Every man, whatever his color, has access to all jobs. The colony makes no distinction except for virtue and talent. . . . The law is the same for all, whether it punishes or protects." They were equal.

Louverture could easily relate to the slaves' main concerns because he had been one himself. A less widely known fact was that he had been emancipated before 1776 (a rare feat for a black male) and that he qualified as an elite *ancien libre* whose political and social interests were distinct from those of the black majority. There was a third, final aspect to his prerevolutionary life, known only to himself and a few close relatives, and that would remain unknown to the rest of the world for almost two centuries: after his emancipation, Louverture had purchased slaves of his own.[17] Such was the secret to Louverture's inordinate ability to rule Saint-Domingue's fractious population: during the first half century of his life, he had been successively a slave, a freedman, and a slave owner.

Hopefully, only the French-speaking planters were listening to Borgella by this point. Despite the previous clauses guaranteeing liberty and equality, the sixth article of the constitution explained that the colony's wealth stemmed from exports of tropical produce and that one could not allow the plantations to whither for lack of workers. "Our plantations," Louverture allegedly said, "are our gold mines."[18] The two biggest sources of government revenue were the export tariff on tropical crops and rent from publicly owned plantations, so allowing former slaves to stop working would have led to his regime's collapse.[19] On a more personal level Louverture needed laborers for the many estates he had acquired during the revolution and that dotted the colony from the plain of Cap to Gonaïves and Ennery.[20] His generals were not forgotten; Dessalines was rumored to earn one hundred thousand francs a year from each of his thirty-two plantations, which if true meant that the former slave was one of the richest men in the world.[21] Rich, that is, if he and Louverture could find workers for their sprawling estates.

Land in Saint-Domingue had long had little value in and of itself; labor mattered far more. For much of the eighteenth century, royal officials had given away concessions, free of charge, to all those who promised to provide the workers.[22] By 1789 French assets in Saint-Domingue amounted to the fantastic sum of 1.5 billion livres, 1.1 billion of which was human property, by far the biggest investment of a typical planter.[23] A planter's wealth was thus measured in scores of slaves, not acreage, a concept that Louverture and his followers could easily grasp when in underpopulated West Africa a chief's prominence also depended on the number of subjects under his control.[24]

The legal status of plantation laborers was the most explosive issue facing Louverture, his predecessors, and his successors, regardless of the color of their skin. Emancipation had been such a defining moment for the black population that restoring slavery was a political impossibility. But letting former slaves do as they pleased would have resulted in utter ruin for the colony since most dreamed of carving out large estates into small plots devoted to subsistence agriculture, when tropical crops such as sugar required heavy investments that only large plantations could sustain. Sonthonax, the great emancipator of 1793, had solved this delicate matter by creating an intermediate labor status between those of slave and freedman. These so-called *cultivateurs* (cultivators) were paid a portion of the crop for their labor and could not be whipped, but they could not quit their job and pursue alternate employment. Soldiers, planters, and servants were exempt from field duties, but everyone else (which predominantly meant young black women) had to work on plantations whether they wished to or not.

When in power Louverture maintained Sonthonax's cultivator system, in part because like many Creole house hands he had a deeply ingrained disdain for African-born field hands. He even tied cultivators to their plantations for life (when Sonthonax had only required three-year contracts) and essentially turned cultivators into serfs, a status that had fully disappeared in metropolitan France with the French Revolution.[25] Louverture also reduced the cultivator's pay from one-third to one-fourth of the crop, and even then fell behind on payments. As of July 1800, Pierre Baptiste, Louverture's godfather and the manager of his sugar plantation at Héricourt, wrote in his hesitant French that he urgently needed cash "because the cultivators are always pestering me about their pay." Baptiste himself had not been paid for thirty-one months.[26]

Unfortunately, the young male cultivators best suited for the rigors of sugarcane cultivation were in short supply after a decade of war. No census is available, but anecdotal evidence shows that one hundred thousand people had died during the revolution thus far, or 20 percent of the prerevolutionary population, most of them men.[27] Desperate for laborers, Louverture tried in 1801 to obtain the return of slaves who had followed their master into exile in the United States, but the request was likely to take time.[28] Allowing the population to grow by natural means—pregnant women were no longer forced to work in the fields and the birth rate was on the rise—would take even more time, which the aging Louverture did not have.[29]

Finding workers had always been a struggle in a colony with a *negative* natural growth rate of 5 percent per year, so Saint-Domingue's rapid population growth before the revolution had largely stemmed from French immigration and imports of African slaves. With this in mind, Article 17 of the 1801 constitution called on "the Governor to take all acceptable measures to encourage and favor the augmentation" of the number of farm laborers through the "introduction of cultivators." The words were so carefully chosen as to be meaningless to the uninitiated. What Louverture had in mind was no less than the restoration of the Atlantic slave trade, which had largely disappeared from French colonies along with slavery itself. Ever since 1799 Louverture had secretly inquired whether British slave traders would be willing to sell some of their human cargo along the coast of Saint-Domingue, and in the fall of 1801 he would send his diplomat, Bunel, to Jamaica for the same purpose.[30] Louverture, the son of a survivor of the Middle Passage, could always rationalize his collaboration with slave traders by pointing out that the slaves would be given the semifree cultivator status upon their arrival. But the fact remained that he was seeking a Faustian bargain with purveyors of African flesh, English ones to boot.

~

"The state of war," explained Article 34 of the constitution, "creates a state of abandon and malaise in the colony." Before the revolution, Saint-Domingue had been at the center of the Atlantic economy, exporting tropical produce to North America and Europe while importing slaves from Africa, foodstuffs from New England, luxuries from France, and cattle and bullion from Spanish colonies. But a decade of naval warfare with England had severed most links to France, and the outbreak of the Quasi-War with the United States in 1798 had brought an abrupt end to the U.S. trade as well. Famine and financial ruin were such a possibility that the article entrusted Louverture with the authority to take "whatever measures are necessary to assure the colony's food supply."

As was the case with many other clauses of the constitution, the article merely rationalized Louverture's existing policies. For years he had conducted an elaborate and largely secret diplomacy to secure Saint-Domingue's access to the vital U.S. market. In November 1798, he had contacted U.S. President John Adams to obtain an exception to the embargo that Congress had recently imposed on France. Within eight months U.S. merchants had returned to Dominguian ports, bringing with them much-needed arms and ammunition. Louverture had even managed to convince the U.S. Navy to attack his rival, André Rigaud, in probably the first U.S. attempt at regime change overseas.[31]

A commercial agreement with the United States could always be justified in light of the colony's dire need for foodstuffs, but in May 1799 Louverture had also signed a secret convention with France's archenemy Great Britain. Afraid that British cruisers operating out of Jamaica would attack his merchants at will, Louverture had promised not to sponsor slave revolts in Jamaica in exchange for British acquiescence to the U.S. trade.[32] Louverture had proven true to his word and had even leaked the details of a French plan to invade Jamaica and free its slaves. Louverture's crucial assistance had ensured that the planned uprising never took place; Jamaica's slaves would not be freed until 1833.[33]

Louverture's foray into the largely white world of international diplomacy had proved a success. Saint-Domingue's trade bounced back, as did the colonial economy, and Louverture even began to hope that England might come to his rescue should France ever try to topple him.[34] Incredibly, he managed to conduct such treasonous negotiations without openly breaking with France, whose government was too preoccupied with the European war to protest openly when it learned of the various secret treaties.[35] For a man raised as a mere slave, Louverture's ability to establish and maintain such a complex web of international alliances was a testament to his political genius.

~

After Borgella finished reading the constitution, Louverture rose to deliver his own oration. He was more comfortable with Kreyol metaphors than the flowery style used in contemporary French rhetoric, but on this very special day he more than rose to the occasion. His speech, at any rate, was brief, which by itself was a great quality when the shortening shadow at Borgella's feet indicated that noon was not far off. "Whatever your age, your social status or your skin color," he reminded his audience, "you are free, and the constitution that was presented to me today will forever secure that liberty." But, he admonished his followers, citizenship brought duties as well as rights—a leitmotiv in French revolutionary discourse—and the inhabitants of Saint-Domingue would have to live up to the obligations of freedom. Public servants, he said, "may probity and righteousness guide your actions." Soldiers, he added, "act with discipline and subordination." Cultivators, he concluded, "avoid sloth, the mother of all vices!"

There, however, was the rub. The constitution wishfully announced that plantations would become "the tranquil asylum of an active and stable family" in which planters and cultivators would collaborate as if they were fathers and children (which, given the planters' promiscuous habits, they occasionally were). But no matter how often Louverture enjoined cultivators to work, his admonitions fell on deaf ears.[36] Cultivators, who had grown up in a colonial world in which to be free meant to be idle, associated field labor with slavery and resisted it to the utmost. Not even the prospect of earning a fourth of the crop would draw laborers to the fields when they could feed their family with minimal labor in Saint-Domingue's fertile soil. Most African laborers, observers noted despondently, lacked the European drive to accumulate material goods and felt no need to earn a salary.[37]

Being a chief, Louverture knew, was a thankless job. He dedicated every waking hour to the welfare of the colony, only to be criticized by illiterate field hands who did not understand the public good. Just two months before, cultivators in Cayes had revolted, and Louverture had found himself obliged to use force after moral suasion had failed.[38] Whipping had disappeared with slavery, but cultivators were now hit with a club. Dessalines, who served as inspector of agriculture in the western province, was particularly feared and demanded that white and black managers of underperforming plantations be publicly beaten, while randomly chosen cultivators were executed as an example for others.[39] Louverture always asked Dessalines to fulfill such distasteful tasks so that he could claim after the fact that his subordinate had exceeded his orders, but in 1801 he promoted Dessalines to division general in a sure sign that he viewed his harsh labor practices as essential to the plantations' renaissance.

Louverture's rule in Saint-Domingue, however benevolent, was a dictatorship. His constitution called for an elaborate system of elections (Article 23), but Louverture's word, not Jean-Jacques Rousseau's general will, had the force of law. In a nod to Charles-Louis de Montesquieu, the constitution specified the domains of the legislative, executive, and judicial powers (sections 7, 8, and 9), but in practice every public servant, judges included, answered directly to Louverture, and he had the right of life and death over his subjects.[40] That summer, when one of his relatives stole a bag of silver from his dresser, Louverture ordered the courts to inflict the death penalty instead of the prison sentence provided by the law. The offender was executed in public to prove that no one, however close his relationship to Louverture or minor his crime, was beyond his reach.[41]

Bonaparte, who had just seized power in a coup d'état, could hardly criticize Louverture's heavy-handed style of government. Three provisions of the constitution, however, were likely to be controversial in Paris. Articles 28 and 30 made Louverture governor for life with the authority to appoint his own successor, and Article 77 specified that the constitution would be implemented before France had a chance to approve it. The metropolis's right to appoint and dismiss colonial governors and pass colonial legislation was thus wholly ignored. Nowhere did the constitution declare outright independence, but its various clauses meant that Saint-Domingue was now an autonomous polity loosely bound to the mother country.

"Long live the French Republic and the colonial constitution!" Louverture exclaimed as he concluded his speech. All the forts guarding the bay responded with a thunderous twenty-three-gun salute. A twenty-one-gun salute was a customary display of respect; French gunners usually added a twenty-second shot when honoring the Republic. By awarding himself a twenty-third shot, Louverture signaled—with a big bang—that Saint-Domingue's governor now stood one step above France.[42]

～

The officials hurried to the tribune to give Louverture a congratulatory accolade, but the ceremony was not yet over. Fouqueau, the president of the tribunal, explained that he too "wished to express the public's satisfaction" with Louverture's enlightened rule. Another long, adulatory monologue followed as Fouqueau thanked Louverture for bringing peace and prosperity back to the colony.

To secure the backing of metropolitan authorities, Louverture liked to emphasize that under his rule Saint-Domingue was as prosperous as it had ever been.[43] But the glowing statistics published on his orders were routinely falsified, and the reality was less reassuring. In the once-prosperous north, the plantation economy had almost completely collapsed after the slave revolt of 1791 and the emancipation decree of 1793. The south had been ravaged in the 1799–1800 civil war, while the Artibonite region had greatly suffered in an 1800 flood. Saint-Domingue, in its first period of relative peace in a decade, was now beginning to recover, but the dizzying heights of 1789 were still far off. Exports of tropical produce, which had fallen from about 230 million pounds in 1789 to a mere 4 million pounds in 1795, were back to about 70 million pounds, or one-third of the most prosperous year on record.[44]

Such numbers reflected the partial recovery of the coffee sector, but the sugar industry, the most lucrative in colonial times, remained in shambles. Sugar had once been the specialty of the environs of Cap, where Louverture had grown up, but the area had also been the epicenter of the slave revolt; a person who visited the once-prosperous plain in 1799 described it as a "pitiful desert."[45] Production of refined white sugar had almost ceased, while that of unrefined brown sugar remained limited for lack of mules, mills, and workers.[46] Louverture's own sugar plantation at Héricourt produced a paltry profit of 6,520 francs in 1800–1801 (despite investing 3,000 gourdes, or about 25,000 francs, to repair the water mill), when a well-run sugar plantation before the revolution could net hundreds of thousands of francs a year. Louverture's other plantations were far from prosperous as well.[47]

To bring sugar plantations back to their previous splendor would require an immense infusion of cash, which the colony currently lacked. Also needed were the specialized skills that eluded a coachman like Louverture, a tile-layer like Dessalines, a waiter like Christophe, or the *anciens libres* who had typically made their fortune in indigo and coffee. Convinced that the white planters' capital and know-how were essential to the recovery of the sugar plantations, Louverture encouraged white deportees to return to the colony, even though the black rank-and-file resented the presence of their former owners, and French law banned the return of aristocratic exiles (or émigrés).[48] Many planters, though uncomfortable with the idea of serving a former slave, pragmatically supported him because they saw him as a forceful general who would put their laborers back to work, not a revolutionary French hothead like Sonthonax. That Louverture was suspected of fomenting independence was an added benefit, since many planters had long harbored similar ambitions.

More than race or politics, the main source of conflict between black officers and returning white planters was thus the ownership of the colony's plantations. During the revolution, colonial authorities had confiscated the estates of planters who had fled the slave revolt because they fell under a French law punishing counterrevolutionary émigrés.[49] The colony had then leased the plantations to well-connected friends of the regime, Louverture and his officers foremost among them, who had no interest in allowing owners to recover their property. Even though he welcomed their expertise, Louverture thus confiscated virtually all the profits when owners sent managers to represent their interests, and even those planters who returned in person found it hard to recover their estate outright.[50] Planters privately grumbled over their declining status, but few dared lament their fate too loudly in a military dictatorship run by their economic rivals.

One such plantation owner, Michel-Étienne Descourtilz, has left us with a revealing account of his arrival in Saint-Domingue under Louverture's reign.[51] A native of eastern France, Descourtilz ostensibly traveled as a budding natural historian eager to study the fauna of the New World. But his wife came from a family of Dominguian planters, and by heading to the Caribbean he most likely hoped to recover the valuable plantations held by his Creole relatives. Leaving his wife and child in France, Descourtilz sailed with his mother-in-law, Mrs. Rossignol-Desdunes, on an unusual and harrowing honeymoon cruise that took them from Charleston to Santiago de Cuba before they finally reached Port Républicain on a leaky privateer in April 1799.

The planters Descourtilz met in Saint-Domingue all told a similar story. Many cultivators had fled to the woods, never to return. The few laborers who remained devoted their time to their individual gardens and refused to work in the sugar fields. The brother of Descourtilz's wife even faced assassination attempts from his mixed-race half brother, who probably hoped to appropriate his father's entire estate after killing the legitimate heir. For Descourtilz, recovering the family's plantations that had been confiscated by the state took much time and effort, and colonial officials never reimbursed the profits generated during the owners' long exile. Descourtilz remained in Saint-Domingue, where he would personally witness the crucial events of the next few years, but like many of Louverture's white allies he was mindful to behave in a manner appropriate to the new economic and racial order.

～

Following Fouqueau's speech, all the dignitaries proceeded to the cathedral for a formal *Te Deum*. Louverture was notoriously devout, and during mass some mention must have been made that Article 6 of his constitution established Roman Catholicism as the sole religion of the colony. As governor, Louverture persecuted Catholicism's main rival in Saint-Domingue,

Vodou, which to orthodox Catholics was a heretic cult fusing Catholic saints with the gods of Benin and the Congo.[52] Vodou was also historically associated with rebellion, including the 1791 slave revolt that had begun the Haitian Revolution, so Louverture had solid political grounds to ban the night-long rites of possession. Generally, Louverture viewed religion as a means to cement his political power and strove to put the Church firmly under his control. When a bishop had arrived from France in March 1801, Louverture had refused to recognize him because he had not personally selected him, and in his constitution he made sure to reserve for himself the right to appoint colonial priests (Article 8).[53]

Given Louverture's overt use of religion for political purposes, whether his embrace of Catholicism was heartfelt remains an open question. Many of Louverture's critics described his piety as a mere facade at odds with his sexual life and bloody political record.[54] One of his modern biographers is also convinced that Louverture (like many Haitian statesmen) privately worshiped Vodou even as he persecuted its followers.[55] Gauging one's spirituality two centuries after the fact is more faith than science, but Creole *anciens libres* like Louverture were some of the most devout Catholics in the colony, and there is no reason to question that, with religion as with other issues, he was genuinely drawn to the European model. Haitian worshipers are pragmatists who switch from Catholicism to Vodou depending on the circumstances, and Louverture's spiritual journey seems to fit the pattern. At the height of his power, when he ruled Saint-Domingue in collaboration with the planter hierarchy, he had every reason to seek the support of the French god. Only later, in 1802 when the French government turned against him and the planters abandoned him, would Louverture trample a crucifix to punish the god who had failed him.[56]

After mass Louverture and his entourage retired to the government house, where a banquet had been set up for six hundred guests. In stark contrast with the French gourmet tradition, Louverture was a frugal man whose grocery lists included few luxuries besides wine, *taffia* (cheap rum), charcuterie (cured pork), and many candles for his late-night working sessions.[57] Always afraid of being poisoned (a paranoia he shared with prerevolutionary planters), he drank spring water and bottled wine and ate unprepared foods like bananas unless a trusted old woman was present to cook a stew before his eyes.[58] The banquet was thus more a way to put his power on display than an occasion to indulge. Before the revolution the arrival of a colonial governor had been marked by a parade, adulatory harangues, a grand mass, and a reception at the government house with a fawning elite.[59] Louverture, who had most likely witnessed such events firsthand, must have felt the need to follow the time-honored rituals step by step on the grandest day of his life.

Louverture's receptions fell into one of two categories. His *petits cercles* (little circles) were audiences opened to all, black cultivators included, during which Louverture, dressed in the attire of the white planter (white cloth and madras handkerchief), received and belittled supplicants seeking government positions. By contrast, *grand cercles* like the July 7 reception were formal affairs reserved for the colony's elite.[60] On such occasions, after all guests had gathered in their best attire, Louverture would make a grand entrance to the sound of an orchestra. Wearing his dress uniform, he would address each guest in turn, treating upper-class white women to a respectful *madame* (madam) while women of color had to satisfy themselves with a mere *citoyenne* (citizen)—thus perpetuating discriminatory forms of address that had belittled free people of color such as himself in the prerevolutionary era.[61] He particularly appreciated the quaint politeness of ancien régime aristocrats, and after a particularly well-crafted compliment he would turn to the black officers following him and urge them to "try to learn these manners and how to introduce yourself the proper way. This is what you get from being raised in France; my children will be the same."[62]

Thinking of his children can only have brought back bittersweet memories for Louverture. He had fathered eleven, five of whom had survived Saint-Domingue's atrocious infant mortality rate.[63] In 1796 his two eldest sons, Isaac and Placide, had gone to school in Paris. Having one's offspring educated in France, a hallmark of the landed elite in prerevolutionary times, was a source of pride for Louverture. But with time he had begun to fear that his bold steps toward colonial autonomy might have adverse consequences for his sons. He had repeatedly demanded that they be sent back but to no avail. They had become hostages.[64] He even seems to have attempted to have his sons kidnapped from their school and repatriated.[65]

As was common in the Creole world of his time, Louverture also relied on an extensive kinship network. His brother Pierre had fought, and died, earlier in the revolution. His other brother Paul and nephews Charles Belair and Moyse were generals in the colonial army. His cousin Felix was a battalion chief. According to the oral tradition, two of his nephews served as his aides-de-camp (Thimotée Dupont and Bernard Chancy), and his nieces married the generals Dessalines and André Vernet.[66]

Black Dominguians typically preferred common-law unions (*plasaj*) to official marriages, but there again Louverture espoused the European standard. Long before the revolution he had married Suzanne Simon-Baptiste, and as governor he railed against the colony's lax morals and forced several of his collaborators to marry their mistresses. Many of his contemporaries mocked his prudishness as hypocritical since he himself kept mistresses in all corners of the colony; but Louverture's numerous dalliances with the wives and daughters of powerful men, more than a form of sexual gratification, must have been political acts.[67] In prerevolutionary times a master's ability to have intercourse with his slaves had been highly symbolic of the control he exerted over his human property, so taking white mistresses was a powerful way for Louverture to underscore his authority.[68] Conversely, the planters' sexual demands had been a painful reminder of the male slaves' powerlessness, so Louverture's affairs may also have been a form of personal vindication for a man whose favorite son, Placide, was of mixed race.

Louverture's relationship with white society was complex. White planters had owned him and freed him; he now emulated and humiliated them. Even as he embraced most of the French colonial model, Louverture suspected that white planters could never be fully loyal to him. To a white woman who asked him to be her son's godfather as a token of her affection, he replied that whites would only love him "if I had their skin; but I am black and I know their hatred for us. . . . After I die, who knows if my brothers will not be re-enslaved? White colonists are the enemies of the blacks."[69]

The inscrutable, towering Louverture was a hard man to befriend; his peculiar position at the juncture of African, Creole, and European influences further isolated him, leaving him as a white man in a black man's skin, feared but not loved, alone and lonely. His nephew addressed him as "governor" in his letters; his own brother used the deferential *vous*.[70] Aside from his wife and sons, only four people seem to have ever been close to Louverture, all of them white, and even they could not be certain that they had truly pierced Louverture's armor. The first was Étienne Laveaux, the general responsible for Louverture's rise to power and a man he called "my dear father"—only to send him back to France at the earliest opportunity.[71] Another was his secretary Pascal, who dared call Louverture "my good friend" in his letters—but who confessed in a report that even he could not claim to know Louverture's innermost thoughts.[72] A third was his former master, Libertat, whose life Louverture had saved during the slave revolt; and yet, when Libertat returned from exile, Louverture refused to embrace him and reminded him curtly that "there is today more distance between you and me than there was in the past between me and you."[73]

The most unusual of Louverture's white confidants was a young teacher named Mialaret, who had come to Saint-Domingue in 1789 at a time when the colony was seen as a promised land flowing with milk and molasses. Mialaret had landed in Port-au-Prince alone, aged fifteen, with only the shirt on his back and no skill other than his education. He had also arrived on the eve of the biggest slave revolt the world had ever seen, but he was a lucky man who survived years of fighting when many others did not. One of his many close brushes with death came when he was captured by Louverture in

1794 and earmarked for execution. But Suzanne Louverture reminded her husband that their sons needed a tutor, and the young teacher spent the next few years in the Louverture household. Louverture's lack of education left him insecure in his dealings with educated whites and *anciens libres,* and he often barged in during class time to learn a thing or two without stooping to become a young man's pupil. Louverture's reading was plodding, his writing even worse, and he relied on white secretaries for his abundant correspondence. But afraid that they might betray his thoughts he often asked several secretaries to draft the same letter, then awoke Mialaret at odd hours to help him read the various versions and ensure that they matched. The two spent many a night, their heads drawn close, as they pored over the tiny script by the flickering light of a candle. So close was their relationship that Louverture refused to free Mialaret when his sons left for France, probably unwilling to let go of a man who had seen him in so many unguarded moments.[74]

Louverture's relationship to his black ancestry was as tortured and convoluted as his love-hate relationship with whites. Having grown up in an increasingly bigoted Saint-Domingue, he bitterly resented any hint of racism, but black freedmen like himself had eagerly copied white mores, and for all their anger at white racism Louverture and his fellow *anciens libres* often recycled colonial prejudices against lower-class African-born slaves.[75] As governor, Toussaint-the-scion-of-the-ancien-régime purchased African laborers from British slave traders, while Louverture-the-former-slave posted two sentinels to guard a monument dedicated to the law of emancipation.[76] Louverture could invoke the ideals of the French Revolution in formal French speeches, such as the one presenting the constitution, then make clever use of Kreyol metaphors when addressing cultivators.[77] A few years before, when a mob had come to insist that whites be exiled from Saint-Domingue, Louverture had calmly mixed wine with water, then asked the onlookers to separate the two ingredients. "Impossible," they had answered—which was Louverture's point exactly. In his mind, white and black Saint-Domingue were irreversibly linked.[78]

Louverture's personal library was that of the typical educated European, replete with translations of classical works.[79] His favorite author was Guillaume Raynal, the historian of European colonialism who after recounting the horrors of slavery had famously asked, "where is he, this new Spartacus, who will encounter no Crassus?" Ever since his mentor Laveaux had brought his attention to this passage, Louverture had become convinced that he was the black Spartacus of the prophecy.[80] He was not the only one to think that he was destined for great things; his contemporaries, enemies included, all agreed that he stood out from the cadre of black chiefs that had emerged from the slave revolt, that he was "astonishing," "extraordinary," and "truly a great man."

"I must admit," grudgingly wrote a racist critic, "that Toussaint is a glorious exception to the inferiority of his race."[81]

Only one other man could match the torrent of superlatives routinely heaped on the governor of Saint-Domingue: the first consul of France, Napoléon Bonaparte. Both were conservative sons of the revolution, land-bound islanders, peace-seeking warriors, pragmatic Catholics, puritanical womanizers, and administrative geniuses. The parallels were obvious—to anyone, that is, but Bonaparte himself. As governor, Louverture was supposed to address his official correspondence to the minister of the navy and colonies, but eager to be recognized as one of the world's greats he often wrote directly to Bonaparte. The first consul would not lower himself to write to a mere colonial administrator and instructed his minister to draft all replies in a slight that deeply hurt Louverture's pride. When receiving yet another letter signed by Bonaparte's underling, Louverture would push it away, unread, muttering to his visitors "keep on, this is nothing . . . minister . . . valet!"[82]

Bonaparte's aloofness rankled Louverture; it also worried him. Rumors swirled that the French government was not as pleased with his actions as official dispatches claimed and that Bonaparte was secretly thinking of removing him from office. Louverture had all outgoing mail searched in an attempt to quell bad accounts of his reign, but there was always a risk that damaging reports had slipped through the censor's net.[83] A constitution could not as easily be swept under the rug; in the days to come, Louverture would have to inform the government of his bold move in the most innocent way possible, lest his adversaries point to the constitution as proof that he was moving toward independence. One hour after noon Louverture ended the reception and dismissed his guests. The ceremony presenting the constitution was over; the battle to get it approved in France had just begun.

As he looked for a person who might convince France to acquiesce to his constitution, Louverture turned to Charles Humbert de Vincent, an old colonial hand who had defended him in Paris many times before.[84] Vincent had first come to Saint-Domingue in 1786 as a French-born lieutenant of the engineers, then had quickly risen to commander of the colony's fortifications. Paid a sizeable twelve thousand francs a year and married to the daughter of a planter, he seemed destined for financial success until the onset of the slave revolt forced him and his family into exile. He regained his position as director of fortifications in 1796, but the revolutionary period was a frustrating and lonely time otherwise. His wife and children stayed in France, and his white colleagues died one by one of tropical fevers, including a younger namesake who may have been his brother.

Despite his past as a creature of the ancien régime, Vincent understood that the 1791 slave revolt had altered the racial order in an unalterable way, and he served Louverture loyally. After Louverture deported French commissioners in 1796 and 1798, Vincent went to Paris to defend his superior's decision. Time and again he urged the government not to resort to force, so convinced was he that a French expedition would be decimated by fevers and that former slaves would massacre the remaining white planters if France ever sent a large army.

Vincent's eagerness to defend both Saint-Domingue and France's interests brought no rewards. While combing through the archives of the Ministry of Navy in Paris, he found no trace of his military records and realized that decades of dutiful service had been lost to some bureaucratic mishap. In an age famous for twenty-year-old generals, he was still a mere brigadier chief, a rank he had obtained in 1797 and that had yet to be confirmed by Paris. Worse, as Vincent and other French envoys returned to Cap in 1800, they were surrounded by a mob of cultivators, physically abused, and even treated to three mock executions (engineering such incidents to intimidate his opponents was Louverture's favorite ploy).[85] Even life was only marginally better than death; sick and lonely, denied the basic funds needed to discharge his duties, he again and again pleaded to be sent back to France.

Early in July 1801, Louverture sent Vincent to Gonaïves for a few days (presumably so that he would not witness the ceremony in Cap), but Vincent soon learned of the constitution's main clauses and he courageously warned Louverture that he was making a mistake. A colony simply could not write its own constitution, he explained; he was further horrified to learn that Louverture intended to print the document before Paris even had a chance to approve it and to send a copy via regular mail. Better to send a handwritten copy, as if individual clauses were still being discussed, and ask a trusted envoy to defend the document in person. Louverture was not used to being criticized in this manner. The constitution could not be reversed, he snapped. He felt "carried by some occult force that he could not resist." "I took flight to join up with eagles," he also allegedly said. "I must be careful when flying back to earth; I can now only sit at the top of a rock, and this rock must be the constitution that guarantees my power for as long as I will live among men."[86]

After he left Louverture's office, Vincent could only think of the disasters ahead. Bonaparte would surely react with fury upon receiving the constitution and send a punitive expedition. Blacks would massacre white planters before falling to the might of the French army, which would then be ravaged by fevers. Vincent visited all the influential citizens of Cap—Louverture's secretary, Pascal; the constitutional delegates Gaston Nogérée and Jean-Baptiste Lacourt; the black commander of Cap, Henri Christophe—in the hope that they might sway the headstrong governor. Probably fearing for his own future, Christophe expressed his opposition to the constitution and offered to support France if it ever planned to remove Louverture by force; but he could offer little more than sympathy for now.[87]

Despite his initial outburst Louverture was sufficiently astute to understand that it would be wise to heed the advice of a man who knew the inner workings of the French government better than anyone in the colony. After thinking the matter over, he wrote a letter to Bonaparte in which he claimed that the constitution had been forced upon him by an overeager assembly and that he now "hastened to send it to you to seek your approbation."[88] Concerned that a copy of the constitution might reach France before he had a chance to make his case, Louverture carefully limited the distribution of the printer's initial run, and so for much of the summer it was virtually impossible to obtain a copy of the text that had been presented with so much fanfare on July 7.[89] Louverture then summoned Vincent and told him that he would personally carry four copies of the constitution to France, along with the submissive letter to Bonaparte. Vincent remained unconvinced and boldly described the constitution as a "manifesto against the government" that was tantamount to independence. "I know that everyone wishes me ill and that my children will never inherit what little I have amassed," Louverture replied angrily.[90] He then darted out of the room through a back door, jumped on a horse awaiting him, and rammed it through a crowd of petitioners who had come to see him.

Concerned that Louverture might punish him for his frankness, Vincent abruptly left the colony a few days later with a copy of the constitution.[91] During a stop in the United States, he met the French ambassador, Louis-André Pichon, who described the text as a "masterpiece of impertinence" and warned that Louverture was now in "open rebellion against France."[92] Pichon's anger was a sure harbinger of Bonaparte's own reaction, so Vincent fired off a series of urgent letters, in terms stronger than he would have dared to use in person, to urge Louverture to reconsider his constitutional ambitions.[93] Vincent also noticed with concern that U.S. newspapers had already obtained leaked copies of the constitution and had reproduced the text in toto.[94] The entire eastern seaboard was abuzz with rumors that, one score and five years after the United States had broken ways with England, Saint-Domingue was now the second European colony in the hemisphere to have achieved independence.

That Louverture's ultimate ambition was nationhood was a widely held view among contemporary U.S., French, and English observers, and to this day many modern historians, anti-imperialists in particular, see Louverture as the father of Haitian independence.[95] Assessing the intentions of the secretive Louverture is a difficult endeavor, but he most likely did not intend to take such a step. He already enjoyed near-complete autonomy and had little to gain from a clean break with France. He had, however, much to lose. His two sons lived in Paris as hostages; his black subjects were unwilling to forsake France, the sole European power to have embraced emancipation; and he was unwilling to throw himself at the mercy of Great Britain and the United States, two slave-owning powers with which he had recently encountered diplomatic difficulties.[96] Cautious, devious even, Louverture was not the man for stirring calls for rebellion. Incremental steps toward autonomy, obscured by elaborate smokescreens and followed by loud claims of loyalty to France, had always been his preferred strategy, and he saw no reason to alter a method that had been crowned with success. Louverture never advocated independence, not even when Bonaparte sent an expedition to oust him—not even when he was captured and left to rot in a French cell.[97]

The stern letters that Vincent had sent from the United States convinced Louverture that he could not be counted on to defend the text in Paris. He thus sent a second white envoy, the constitutional delegate Nogérée, along with another letter to Bonaparte to "destroy the calumnies spread by my enemies."[98] Louverture's letter in hand, Nogérée rushed to the United States, trying to reach France before Vincent could besmirch the constitution.[99]

As Vincent and Nogérée sailed away, Louverture did not remain idle and launched a series of reforms intended to revive the colony. He was everywhere. "His movements are very rapid and uncertain," wrote the U.S. commercial agent in Cap.[100] He was rumored to be in Port Républicain, when he was in Saint-Marc. He was sighted in Gonaïves, then Cap again. In one week he crisscrossed the mountains between the two main cities of the colony, presumably inspecting his own plantations at Ennery in the process, all the while continuing to issue new laws at a frantic pace and negotiating with the British and U.S. consuls.[101] "The most salient aspect of general Toussaint's character," wrote his secretary Pascal, "is the desire to command to others."[102] "Cabinet work, which could have been alien to his kind, political schemes, and boundless activity are for him a pleasure as sharp as enjoying a meal or possessing a woman would be to most men. . . . Seeing everything for himself, crossing the colony like lightning, answering 100, 200, 300 letters in a day, are for him an ecstasy, a need."

In less than a month (July 18–August 12), Louverture initiated, then personally approved, eighteen major pieces of legislation. He made Catholicism the official religion of the colony and called on fathers to recognize their illegitimate offspring. He set up new territorial divisions, courthouses, and municipal councils and devised a harsh new criminal code. He gave debtors additional time to reimburse their debts and reorganized the colony's finances. He tried to auction off state-owned plantations and prevent the return of some émigré owners. He regulated public notaries and title offices, then he began the monumental task of documenting property deeds destroyed during the war. By the time he issued a law regulating the formal dress of colonial administrators (down to the fabric and color of knee britches), he had thoroughly transformed a colony long known for its chaotic legal system.[103]

Louverture's legal achievements were remarkable for a former slave with no formal education. They were also unlawful, since the authority to legislate in the colony lay with France's civilian agent in Cap; but it was a long time since Louverture had reduced the power of the agent to shreds.

∼

As of 1801, the French agent in Saint-Domingue was a longtime colonial administrator named Philippe Roume de Saint-Laurent. A white Creole from Grenada, he had once supported slavery on the pragmatic ground that the French economy needed colonies, which could not exist without slaves. Like many others he adapted his views to revolutionary realities, and by 1796 he had become a fervent proponent of abolition on the equally pragmatic ground that France needed black freedmen to fight its wars in the Caribbean.[104] He eventually married his colored mistress and proudly described himself as the "husband of a mulattress, the father of a quadroon, and the son-in-law of a negress."[105]

Despite his planter background, Roume was thus known as a moderate figure when he was appointed as French agent in Cap in 1798. He hoped to slowly gain Louverture's trust and gently nudge him in a direction conducive to French interests, but Louverture immediately sent mobs to threaten Roume, only to call them off in an unmistakable sign that the agent would only survive at Louverture's discretion.[106] Over the following months, Roume's concessions failed to assuage Louverture, and the relationship between the two men quickly soured. When Roume learned in 1799 that Louverture was negotiating with the British, he firmly warned against such treasonous talks.[107] Louverture retaliated by confining Roume to his house as a virtual prisoner and contacting him only when he needed the agent to give his official seal of approval to a decree.[108] In 1800 Louverture sent five thousand cultivators to bully the agent into authorizing the takeover of Spanish Santo Domingo, then locked him up in a chicken coop when Roume dared contact the Spanish governor.[109]

Roume's health declined markedly in 1801, and Louverture, prodded by Vincent and Pichon, began to fear that the agent might die in prison.[110] Unwilling to provoke France just as he was trying to get his constitution approved, Louverture ordered Roume freed as a gesture of goodwill; the agent and his multiracial family embarked for the United States in early September.[111] Freeing Roume was a risky move that left him free to inform the

French government of the abuse he had endured for almost two years, but Roume, after the emotional and physical toll of captivity, had lost much of his combativeness. Even after he reached New York he dared not detail all the intelligence he had gathered in captivity, so paranoid was he that the long arm of Louverture would reach him in exile.[112] His letters became increasingly long, rambling, or outrightly incoherent.[113] At the risk of performing an ex post facto psychiatric examination, only one conclusion is possible: Roume had lost it.

In six weeks Louverture had sent three French administrators to the United States, and, ultimately, France: the director of fortification Vincent, the constitutional delegate Nogérée, and the agent Roume (to hedge his bets, he also sent his diplomat Bunel to England).[114] All three were white and carried with them stunning news of Louverture's imaginative rewriting of the imperial bond. All three, however, were opponents of slavery, and two of them opposed a French expedition altogether. If they made it past British cruisers, they would successively reach France in the next two to three months and argue, Louverture hoped, against any use of force. It would take another few months before the French government sent its official reply and Louverture learned whether he had managed once again to claim extensive political autonomy without severing all links with France. All he had to do was wait; his future was now in the hands of his rival among history's greats, first consul of France, Napoléon Bonaparte.

2

The White Toussaint

Bonaparte's Decision to Invade Saint-Domingue

For Napoléon Bonaparte, as for Toussaint Louverture, 1801 marked the apex of a career that had brought him from obscurity to international fame in less than a decade. Born in Corsica shortly after France acquired the island, Bonaparte only bore French citizenship through an accident of history—just like Louverture. The scion of lesser nobility from the provinces, he would never have risen above the rank of junior artillery officer had the French Revolution not broken out and allowed him, as it did Louverture, to fulfill his extraordinary potential. From the siege of Toulon to the campaign of Italy, one success followed another. The campaign of Egypt was a notable setback, but Bonaparte sneaked back to France before his name could be tainted with defeat, toppled the Directory, and took the head of a triumvirate with the Cesarean title of first consul of France.

The Consulate showed Bonaparte at his best, triumphant yet devoid of the hubris that would mar the later empire. When he forced his way into office in 1799, the *chouan* uprising was still festering and France's armies were on the defensive, but Bonaparte quickly turned France's military fortunes around. More impressively he showed that he was not only a fighting general but also a ruler with a knack for solving ancient squabbles with astonishing speed and elegance. His capacity for work was enormous; his attention to detail, unparalleled. Letters streamed in from all corners of Europe; day and night, replies came with detailed instructions on the most trivial subject. For a decade France had been torn by religious controversies; Bonaparte negotiated a Concordat with the pope. The ancien régime's legal system had been a Byzantine hodgepodge of local customs since medieval times; he began work on the Code Civil that still governs French law. In September 1800 the United States agreed to a peace at Mortefontaine; he obtained Louisiana from Spain a month later; Portugal, then Austria, sued for peace early in 1801. England would surely have to follow. He was the master of France; in those days it meant most of Europe as well.

Alas, the sorry state of the French colonial empire marred an otherwise splendid year. U.S. merchants largely monopolized the commerce of France's colonies, while the French merchant fleet lay ruined. In the Indian Ocean colonies of Île de France (Mauritius) and Bourbon (Réunion), white planters were in a state of open rebellion. Martinique was under English occupation. In Guadeloupe French agents and officers of color quarreled continuously, and in Saint-Domingue Louverture kept fighting internal enemies instead of the British.

Despite his reputation as a continental warrior, Bonaparte never lost sight of France's overseas possessions and began seeking advice on colonial matters within weeks of his 1799 coup d'état.[1] Particularly worrisome was the state of the empire's crown jewel in Saint-Domingue, which seemed to be rapidly marching toward independence. Some of his advisers favored appeasing Louverture; others urged him to remove him from office by force. In the end he did both, initially hoping to ally himself with Louverture, then embracing military action when he became convinced of his disloyalty. For two equally strong-willed statesmen to clash with each other was probably preordained; but the decision-making process that led Bonaparte to launch the ill-fated Saint-Domingue expedition was a long and tortuous one, worth recounting here.

∼

Many standard histories posit that Bonaparte launched the expedition primarily to appease Caribbean planters eager to recover their plantations and their slaves.[2] The theory is largely based on Bonaparte's own recollections in St. Helena, where he claimed that the constant *criailleries* (loud whining) of colonial supplicants were to blame for his decision to invade Saint-Domingue.[3] "When the peace [of Amiens] was signed," he also remembered, "the old settlers, the merchants, and the speculators buried me under all sorts of demands."[4]

Or did they? Bonaparte, his secretary wrote in reference to the Saint-Domingue expedition, "was not the kind of man to decide on a war based on deliberations in the *Conseil d'État* [his advisory council]," and it is hard to imagine such a self-driven individual let a few whining planters shape the future of the French empire.[5] By blaming some outside influence for a decision he took on his own, Bonaparte was simply trying to shed all responsibility for the disastrous outcome of the expedition, confirming John F. Kennedy's adage that "victories have a thousand fathers, but defeat is an orphan."

That Joséphine Tascher de la Pagerie, the daughter of planters from Martinique, is to blame for pushing her husband to invade Saint-Domingue is another much-repeated historical canard.[6] The story of the beautiful woman who launched a thousand ships across the sea has Homeric appeal, but it is historically inaccurate. Louverture saw to it that Joséphine's plantation in Léogane was cultivated in her absence, giving her no financial incentive to wish for his removal.[7] According to her memoirs, she warned her husband *not* to attack Louverture, and she made no reference to a restoration of slavery in her letters.[8] By 1801 her centers of interest had shifted from young lovers to botany, and the few requests she ever made regarding Caribbean affairs were for exotic plants to be shipped to her greenhouses at Malmaison.[9]

Other colonial exiles were more active, but contrary to Bonaparte's later claims they were not all archconservatives rooting for a return to prerevolutionary institutions. The Dominguian legist Médéric Moreau de Saint-Méry, now employed as French resident in Parma, was famous for a massive work in which he described Saint-Domingue's prosperity before the revolution, but other colonial experts were less nostalgic about the days of slavery. Shortly after the 1799 coup, when Bonaparte's minister of the navy invited various Saint-Domingue exiles to offer their advice on colonial issues, former slave owners like François Page and Paul Alliot-Vauneuf argued *against* an expedition because they thought it impossible to force blacks soldiers back into slavery. Other participants, like Louis Dufaÿ and Jean-Baptiste Belley, advocated the use of force, but they could hardly be suspected of doing so out of nostalgia for servitude: they were the white and black deputies sent to France in 1793 to obtain the abolition of slavery.[10] Later that month the former planter Louis Rallier advised the minister of the navy to support Louverture, just as Léger-Félicité Sonthonax, the emancipator of 1793, urged him to send a sizable force to Saint-Domingue.[11] The most extreme suggestion—for Louverture to be put to death for colluding with the British enemy—was put forward by Étienne Mentor, a black deputy.[12]

For planters and former slave owners like Page to reconcile themselves with the idea of black rule might seem surprising, but conservative colonial thought had always been characterized by its pragmatism. French planters had not gone to Saint-Domingue to build a city upon a hill, a grand experiment in social engineering; they had gone there to make a lot of money, by any means necessary. When told that slavery was an insult to the ideals of the Enlightenment, colonial writers answered that slavery was the only practical way of growing crops in the tropics.[13] Conversely, when the slave revolt grew into an overwhelming force, planters like Page (and Charles de Vincent, Philippe Roume, and Louverture) accepted emancipation as an immutable element of the new colonial order. In a detailed scholarly work he published for Bonaparte's benefit in 1801, Page confessed that he had once embraced slavery. But he also explained that the genie of emancipation was now out of the bottle and that defeating Louverture's vast army was unthinkable when colonial authorities had failed to disband tiny bands of plantation runaways in the past.[14] He was not the only planter to adapt his views to circumstances.[15]

Colonial lobbyists sent Bonaparte an endless flow of handwritten memoirs, but their policy prescriptions ran the gamut from liberal to reactionary. Some memoirists thought that France could restore the status quo ante, slavery included, and called for a large-scale expedition, but many others were convinced that restoring slavery was immoral, unfeasible, or both; some even favored restoring the old system of white indentured servitude.[16] At any rate most of these reports, still accumulating dust at the French National Archives, show no indication of ever being read. They probably had no more influence over governmental policy than liberal salon hostesses like Madame de Staël and Julie Talma or the famous abolitionist Henri Grégoire and his Second Society of the Friends of the Blacks.

Far from being a cohesive group dedicated to reactionary causes, the colonial lobby included many individuals sent by Louverture to defend his record. Aware that the French government would devise its policy on what little intelligence reached Paris, Louverture prevented his enemies from leaving the colony and regularly sent agents to France to denounce his metropolitan critics.[17] In 1799 he dispatched to Paris his secretary Pascal, who published testimonies favorable to Louverture and silenced unflattering reports. "This way," he proudly reported, "public opinion is shaped. . . . We trounced [our enemies] and are now masters of the battlefield." In a fitting footnote to the diverse, confused nature of the colonial "lobby," Pascal was actually an *agent double* who privately advocated Louverture's overthrow even as he officially defended him.[18]

To give greater credence to the colonial lobby theory, some historians have instead focused on the holdovers from the old Bourbon empire who during the Consulate regained prominent positions in the Ministry of the Navy and the Conseil d'État, where they could theoretically have steered Bonaparte's policies toward a conservative agenda.[19] Among them were Charles Pierre Claret, Comte de Fleurieu (Louis XVI's minister of the navy); Eustache Bruix (a Dominguian planter and former minister of the navy); Vincent Viénot de Vaublanc (another Dominguian planter); Laurent Truguet (former minister of the navy); Jean-Baptiste Guillemain de Vaivres and François Barbé de Marbois (former *intendants,* or financial ministers, of Saint-Domingue); Daniel Lescallier (former governor of Réunion); and Pierre Malouet (former governor of Guiana).

Their role, however, was complex. A colonial connection did not always equate with reactionary views, and administrative veterans of the old empire, like exiled planters, supported a wide variety of policies. At one extreme stood ancien régime apologists like the *fructidoriens,* who had been exiled to Guiana under the Directory for their views. Among them was Malouet, who after the 1793 emancipation had moved to London to beg the British government to invade Saint-Domingue and restore slavery. Back in France under the Consulate, Malouet defended the restoration of slavery in the Conseil d'État and denounced the black race's domination of the Caribbean in his *Collection de mémoires sur les colonies* (1802).[20] But other officials with privileged access to Bonaparte had far more progressive records. Truguet, who had personally known Bonaparte since the 1793 invasion of Sardinia, wrote four reports opposing both slavery and an expedition in 1799–1800. Lescallier had supported attempts to employ freedmen on Guiana's plantations and was a card-carrying member of the Second Society of the Friends of the Blacks. The minister of the police Joseph Fouché, who had flirted with communism during the revolution's radical days, also opposed the restoration of slavery in meetings of the Conseil d'État.[21]

Pulled apart by these conflicting influences—rather than steadily encouraged by a lobbying juggernaut of racist planters—Bonaparte constantly hesitated between conciliation and confrontation. In November 1799 he ordered that a three-thousand-man expedition be readied at once; a month later, he sent Vincent to reiterate France's trust in Louverture. Work continued on the expedition, which went through a variety of commanders and slowly grew to 3,600, but it remained blocked by British squadrons and was at any rate too small to conquer Saint-Domingue.[22] Meanwhile, the minister of justice was working on a possible restoration of the slave trade.[23] As 1800 turned into 1801, after years of manifold lobbying by planters and colonial experts of every political shade, Bonaparte still had to decide what he should do with the formidable governor of Saint-Domingue.

∽

Information provided by Louverture's minions and conservative exiles was by nature biased, so Bonaparte was more likely to be swayed by reports he obtained directly from his own representatives in the Caribbean. His agent in Cap, Roume, was under tight surveillance so Bonaparte's best informants were the French agents in Santo Domingo, Antoine Chanlatte and François-Marie Périchou de Kerversau. Both made a compelling case for Louverture's removal, not because they longed for the glory days of slavery, but because they were patriotic officers convinced that Louverture was a traitor to the Republic. In the end their warnings about Saint-Domingue's slow slide toward independence made more of an impression on Bonaparte than the conflicted debates on emancipation in Parisian circles ever did.

Kerversau was the heir to an old noble family from Brittany, and he, like many of his class, had defended Louis XVI and incurred the wrath of

Robespierre. After narrowly escaping the guillotine, he wisely volunteered for colonial duty and headed for Saint-Domingue. Luckier than Vincent, he was quickly promoted to brigadier general, then French agent in Spanish Santo Domingo. The position put him first in line to become governor of the colony, which Spain had ceded to France under the 1795 treaty of Basel; however, Santo Domingo had never been officially transferred, and in the interim it remained under the rule of a Spanish governor.[24] His new position also gave Kerversau an opportunity to build an extensive intelligence network that kept him abreast of Louverture's every move. He established private channels to Louverture's secretary Pascal and his treasurer Joseph Idlinger, learned of Louverture's negotiations with the British from his brother-in-law, and forwarded this information to his superiors in remarkably detailed reports.[25]

Despite his social background, Kerversau was neither a racist nor an advocate of slavery. In Spanish Santo Domingo, he employed freedmen in French privateers and was personally appalled when the British navy sold captured black sailors as slaves.[26] Upon hearing a rumor that Bonaparte was considering restoring slavery, he warned that "no portion of the French territory can be soiled with slavery ever again."[27]

Kerversau's urgings focused solely on Louverture's dubious loyalty to France. He had initially been impressed by Louverture's intelligence and political finesse, but after Louverture exiled the agent Gabriel d'Hédouville in 1798, Kerversau began to fear that Louverture's good nature had been perverted by the circle of sycophants comparing him to "the new Spartacus predicted by Raynal" and "General Bonaparte."[28] When Hédouville's successor, Roume, was also sidelined, Kerversau concluded that French agents would always be ignored unless they were "backed with powers and forces able to command obedience and respect. This is my opinion; I know many others would disagree."[29] This letter, dated February 1799, was Kerversau's first allusion to a possible French expedition. It was far from the last. Kerversau became convinced that Louverture's ultimate goal was to obtain independence in collusion with France's Anglo-American foes.[30] This he dared say overtly in a letter to Louverture, after which Louverture angrily summoned him to Cap and Kerversau, fearing for his life, fled for France with his child, relatives, and nine-months-pregnant wife.[31] Chased by British and U.S. cruisers, he took refuge in Puerto Rico, where he continued to send ever-longer reports that stridently denounced Louverture as a traitor.

Kerversau's successor as French agent in Santo Domingo was Antoine Chanlatte. Always mindful of one's *limpieza de sangre* (purity of blood), Spanish authorities initially resented the presence of a mixed-race officer.[32] They need not have worried: Chanlatte was a supporter of Louverture's rival André

Rigaud, and like Kerversau he promptly attacked Louverture as a dangerous Anglophile in his letters to Paris. In the spring of 1800, when Louverture sent the white general Pierre Agé to take over Spanish Santo Domingo, Chanlatte incited a Spanish mob to attack Agé's small column, forcing Louverture to put his plans on hold.[33]

Unable to find a way to France, Kerversau returned to Santo Domingo just as Louverture, still smarting from Agé's failed mission, announced his intention to take over the colony by force of arms despite Paris's formal orders to the contrary. The Spanish governor made halfhearted attempts to defend the colony, but his troops were ill trained, outnumbered, and probably unwilling to risk their lives to protect a colony that was legally France's, not Spain's. The invasion was swift and complete.[34] Louverture justified his illegal move by referring to alleged cross-border raids by Spanish slave catchers, but capturing all of Hispaniola's ports to thwart a potential French invasion was a more likely motive.[35] In fact, he does not seem to have even abolished slavery in Santo Domingo itself.[36] Fearing for their safety, Chanlatte and Kerversau promptly fled the colony; by the time they reached France in September 1801, the expedition they had advocated so many times in their reports was fast becoming a reality.

⁓

Bonaparte prided himself on being a pragmatic ruler after a decade during which Frenchmen had guillotined one another in the name of grand political *idées*. As news from the Caribbean reached him from all directions, he distilled the mass of advice fed him by the fractious colonial lobby to two policy options: "To consolidate and legalize the regulations respecting labor established by Toussaint, which had already been crowned with the most brilliant success"; or to send an expedition to overthrow him.[37] The latter option struck Bonaparte as thoroughly impractical at a time when French ports were blockaded by superior British squadrons. With favorable weather and a lot of luck, a small fleet could sneak out to Ireland or Egypt, but the large-scale, continuous shipments required to restore white rule in Saint-Domingue were out of the question as long as Britannia ruled the waves. Slavery apologists be damned, Bonaparte thus concluded that it was in the government's best interest not to risk entire regiments in an expedition that was doomed before it could even set sail. "I inclined to the former scheme," he later remembered, because it was "most conducive to the influence of [the French] flag in America. With an army of twenty-five to thirty thousand blacks, what might I not undertake against Jamaica, the Antilles, Canada, the United States itself, or the Spanish colonies?"[38] France should renew its commitment to emancipation, he explained in 1800, because "this island would go for England if the blacks were not attached to us by their interest in liberty."[39] "They will produce less sugar, maybe, than they did as slaves; but they will produce it for us, and will serve us, if we need them, as soldiers. We will have one less sugar mill; but we will have one more citadel filled with friendly soldiers." Years later in St. Helena, as Bonaparte mulled over the failures of his reign he noted regretfully that his first intuition had been the correct one.[40]

Bonaparte's plan to use Dominguian freedmen for offensive actions in the Caribbean was not as revolutionary as it seemed. In 1793–94, Spain and England had taken over many French colonies (often with colored regiments of their own), but revolutionary France had mounted a successful counteroffensive by using the most effective weapon in its arsenal: the power of ideals. With little more than the 1794 law of emancipation at his disposal, the French agent in Guadeloupe, Victor Hugues, had enlisted local slaves, retaken the colony, beaten back a second British invasion, then raided the Lesser Antilles at will. Black slaves were more resistant to tropical diseases and typically represented 90 percent of the population of a Caribbean island, so enlisting them instantly shifted the balance of power in France's favor, albeit at the cost of destroying the traditional plantation system. Even as some planters and bureaucrats lobbied Bonaparte to remove Louverture from office, he received a deluge of memoirs urging him to use Saint-Domingue's black army against targets as varied as Trinidad, Jamaica, Louisiana, Newfoundland, and Nicaragua.[41] These ambitious plans can only have appealed to Bonaparte's penchant for colonial adventures.

Louverture was energetic, courageous, and crafty, characteristics that annoyed Bonaparte but also earned his respect because they so closely mirrored his own temperament.[42] Rather than fight him openly—a policy that was impossible given British mastery of the seas—Bonaparte sensibly concluded that he should direct Louverture's ambitions in a direction compatible with French interests. Despite the rough treatment Louverture had meted out to Vincent's delegation a year before, Bonaparte thus decided in February 1801 to send another group of French agents to Saint-Domingue. "Do not give Louverture any cause for complaint, but guide and direct his efforts toward order, tranquillity, and a revival of agriculture," he instructed the putative colonial prefect. Soon, he hoped, "black legions" could be unleashed on the British empire.[43]

On March 4, 1801, after he had settled on a policy of collaboration with Louverture, Bonaparte drafted a personal note to the governor of Saint-Domingue. The letter, written in an elaborate script and bearing an autograph signature of the first consul above a bright wax seal, was sure to please its recipient, who had complained so often of having to deal with mere ministers. "Citizen," Bonaparte wrote, "I have read the various letters you sent me, along with the proclamations you made. I am ordering the minister of the navy to appoint you as captain general of Saint-Domingue. The government could not have given you a greater proof of its trust." Rebuild the plantations and organize your army, he ordered. "Soon, I hope, elements of the army of Saint-Domingue will contribute in your region to further the glory and possessions of the Republic. I salute you affectionately."[44]

At this moment in history, the white Toussaint and the black Napoléon were in near-perfect agreement. Both wished to revive exports of plantation crops through the semifree cultivator system. Both planned on maintaining a significant black army in Saint-Domingue. Louverture was more likely to use his troops to maintain internal order than to launch risky ventures overseas, but Bonaparte's personal letter would likely have alleviated many of his fears regarding French intentions. Had Bonaparte also sent Louverture's sons back to Saint-Domingue—the other request he had made in the letter he had sent with Vincent—the two men could have sealed an alliance immensely beneficial to them and to their people.[45]

Alas, after thinking the situation over, Bonaparte decided not to send the letter. On March 29, 1801, Louverture was fired from the French army. The new agents, slated to depart on April 10, never left. A month later preparations for an expedition began in earnest.[46]

⁓

Bonaparte was constantly juggling multiple negotiations at once, so events in faraway Russia and India may have contributed to his sudden change of heart. In January 1801, Bonaparte had learned that Czar Paul was on the verge of invading British India. Such an operation would have made the alliance with Louverture particularly appealing, as it opened the possibility of a worldwide, two-pronged assault on Great Britain's two most valuable colonies. But Paul's assassination that March halted Russia's mobilization efforts and lessened the appeal of simultaneously invading Jamaica with Louverture's army. March 1801 was also the month when in England the warmongering Premier William Pitt gave way to the more accommodating Henry Addington, who began mentioning a possible cease-fire. Should these overtures lead to a lasting peace—still a distant prospect at the time—the value of Louverture's army would diminish considerably. Conversely, peace with England would allow Bonaparte to ship an expedition to the Caribbean.[47] To paraphrase Carl Von Clausewitz, his policies changed so that he could continue war by other means.

Another crucial factor explaining Bonaparte's change of plans was the information gap prevalent in the age of sail. In the Caribbean, frequent sailings and the reliable trade winds made for a one-way journey of one to three months, and an ingenious visual telegraph system allowed Bonaparte to send a simple message from Paris to the main Atlantic port of Brest, four hundred miles away, in a matter of minutes. But ever since the outbreak of the war with England sailings had become rare and ships carrying official correspondence had been routinely intercepted (to this day, the British National Archives are a prime source on French colonial policy). Many letters were sent via New England as U.S. merchants acquired a dominant share of the colonial trade, but even this circuitous route became unreliable when the Quasi-War with the United States erupted in 1797 (which explains why the U.S. National Archives are another rich documentary source).

Given the fast-paced nature of revolutionary politics on both sides of the Atlantic, Louverture and Bonaparte were both devising intricate policies based on information that was woefully out of date. Louverture's contacts in France had warned him in 1800 that an expedition was on the verge of sailing to take over Spanish Santo Domingo, and from there to attack Saint-Domingue.[48] The alleged invasion was merely a decoy to facilitate the departure of reinforcements destined for Egypt, but it convinced Louverture to seize Santo Domingo before France could land troops in that colony. Conversely, Bonaparte drafted his March 4, 1801, letter to Louverture under the assumption that his orders not to take over Santo Domingo, issued a few months earlier, had been obeyed, when Louverture had in fact already invaded the colony.[49] By the time Bonaparte wrote his friendly letter, Louverture was summoning an assembly to draft a constitution that would surely enrage the first consul when he would hear of it—in October 1801.[50]

Had he known of Bonaparte's favorable mood, Louverture would have been tempted to cultivate his friendship by adopting conciliatory policies. Instead, on February 12, 1801, he wrote defiantly that he had just completed the invasion of Santo Domingo and that his troops would soon "be just as good as any European troops"—a thinly veiled warning that he stood ready to fight off any French invasion. That same day he mailed a second letter in which he announced that he had jailed the agent Roume for opposing the invasion. Both letters were addressed directly to Bonaparte, when etiquette dictated that he write to the minister of the navy.[51] Also on February 12, Louverture sent a third letter, addressed to his sons Isaac and Placide, in which the usually stoic governor allowed his emotions to run free. "I kiss you with all my Heart and remain your good father for life," he wrote ruefully.[52] His somber tone probably stemmed from the knowledge that he was on a collision course with Bonaparte and that he might never see his sons again (Louverture and his sons would actually be reunited one year later almost to the day—but they would come with twelve thousand French troops).

Louverture's three letters left on board the corvette *Enfant Prodigue* and arrived in early April.[53] There is unfortunately no account of Bonaparte's reaction upon reading them, but one can easily extrapolate from his standard reading habits. Bonaparte often read at his desk, leaning back on his chair, while his secretary tried to guess the content of his correspondence by decoding his nervous ticks: when receiving bad news, Bonaparte instinctively poked the arm of his chair with a pocketknife to calm his nerves.[54] In a defiant, even threatening, tone, Louverture's letters each announced one grave act of insubordination—the invasion of Santo Domingo and the imprisonment of the French agent—and Bonaparte's reading of each one was presumably punctuated by a stab of the knife.

Given the sudden turnaround in Bonaparte's policies in March–April 1801, Louverture's impudent letters and the events they announced were likely the single most important factor in convincing Bonaparte of Louverture's fundamental disloyalty. Six months later, when it came time to justify the expedition to the French public, Bonaparte's official newspaper reproduced both letters, along with Louverture's July 1801 constitution.[55] These documents had nothing to do with the economic losses inflicted on French planters by the 1794 law of emancipation, and instead underscored Bonaparte's overarching fear that France's most important colony was on a path to independence. Even as he claimed in his memoirs that he had sent the Saint-Domingue expedition at the insistence of the planter lobby, Bonaparte always aimed his sharpest piques at Louverture for kicking out one French agent after another, "negotiating with the English, both directly and secretly," and generally being a traitor to France.[56] Such accusations, which had been a staple of Kerversau's reports for two years, gained credence when they were confirmed by Louverture's own actions in the spring of 1801.

After fleeing from Santo Domingo, Kerversau and Chanlatte had sailed back separately to make sure that at least one would reach France if the other was captured. They did not land until September 1801, months after Bonaparte had abandoned his plan to ally himself with Louverture, but their arrival did much to harden his views. Chanlatte wrote several incriminating reports on Louverture and published a pamphlet in which he concluded that "many years will pass before blacks [of full African descent] become civilized. In their hands, freedom is a dagger with which they will self-destruct."[57] For his part, Kerversau sent a voluminous memoir summarizing years of intelligence on Louverture's duplicitous behavior, which earned him a personal encounter with the minister of the navy a week later. Another endless report ensued, followed by an executive "summary" that went on for twelve pages, then yet another stream of reports.[58] Kerversau never called for the restoration of slavery (and in fact criticized Louverture for imposing too harsh a labor system); instead and as always, he emphasized Louverture's wobbly patriotism in words that deeply influenced Bonaparte.[59] Two days after Kerversau's briefing, Bonaparte urged his minister of foreign affairs to conclude a peace with England as soon as possible because "each day is precious."[60] Plans for a Saint-Domingue expedition now switched to a new stage: active political planning.

~

Bonaparte was not the man for small ambitions. The Saint-Domingue expedition, sparked by fears that Louverture would lead Saint-Domingue to independence, eventually turned into a vast plan to bring the French colonial empire back to the prosperous state it had enjoyed on the eve of the French Revolution. Born in 1769, Bonaparte was old enough to remember the imperial golden age of the 1780s, when French colonies had dominated Europe's sugar and coffee markets. Since then, British and U.S. frigates had chased the French navy from the Caribbean, Anglo-American merchants had taken over France's colonial trade, and French exports to the colonies had plummeted from 110 million francs in 1789 to a paltry 200,000 francs in 1801.[61] In the age of sail, warships depended on merchantmen to train able seamen, so the loss of the colonial trade also spelled doom for Bonaparte's navy. By 1801 British blockades had become so tight that the main military port of Brest found it hard even to ship out small coastal grain traders.[62] If Bonaparte hoped to ever match the one-hundred-thousand-man British navy (which was a prerequisite for any invasion of England), he needed a functioning merchant navy, and thus an outlet for French commerce overseas.

For a brief period in 1798, Bonaparte had hoped that he could make good France's losses with Egypt, which "was to supply the place of Saint-Domingue and the Antilles."[63] But bad news from the Orient reached him in rapid succession in the summer and fall of 1801, culminating with the capitulation of the French expeditionary force in August 1801.[64] As his eastern dreams vanished in the desert, the pendulum of Bonaparte's ambitions shifted back west and he soon began preparing plans for Guadeloupe, Martinique, Tobago, and Louisiana in addition to Saint-Domingue.

Never a visionary in economic matters, Bonaparte envisioned a restored empire organized according to eighteenth-century mercantilist theories. These held that a government's main economic goal was to obtain a trade surplus, which could best be achieved by growing export crops in the tropics. To ensure that colonies only existed to benefit the metropolis's commerce, a variety of trade restrictions (known in France as the *exclusif*) limited the colonies' ability to trade with anyone but the mother country. As he drafted his plans for Saint-Domingue, Bonaparte specified that U.S. merchants would eventually be banned per mercantilist orthodoxy to the benefit of French merchants.[65] Jean-Baptiste Colbert, Louis XIV's colonial minister and the father of the *exclusif,* could not have agreed more; the clamors of Creole planters, who had long complained of such trade restrictions, were once again ignored.

The *exclusif*, however, had its limitations. Before the French Revolution, France had proved unable to ship the requisite amount of supplies to its colonies, and foreign merchants had penetrated the Dominguian market through legal loopholes and outright contraband. It was particularly difficult to feed the colony from France at competitive prices when the North American cornucopia loomed so close. Bonaparte thus came to the conclusion that France should find a local source for the foodstuffs that its Caribbean colonies, being single-mindedly devoted to the production of cash crops, so sorely needed. He eventually set his eyes on Western Louisiana (which France had ceded to Spain after the Seven Years War) as a potential breadbasket for his revived Caribbean empire and asked that the colony be returned back to France in the secret treaty of San Ildefonso (1800). Louisiana was a colonial backwater and a drain on the Spanish treasury, but in Bonaparte's plan it would supply French colonies with flour, cattle, and timber and thus alleviate the need for U.S. imports.[66] In October 1801, just as the Saint-Domingue expedition was ready to depart, Bonaparte began pressuring the Spanish ambassador for the immediate transfer of Louisiana.[67]

Bonaparte's often surreal colonial dreams have led a recent historian to describe his imperial policies as a form of "colonial dementia" that bore no connection with reality.[68] But the plans he made in 1801 meshed into an ambitious, coherent plan in line with two centuries of French colonial thought. The restoration of direct French rule in Saint-Domingue, combined with smaller expeditions to other Caribbean colonies and the retrocession of Louisiana, would create a massive, integrated French empire stretching from the Maroni River in French Guiana to the Missouri River in northern Louisiana. Colonial rebirth, in turn, would end the economic slump in French Atlantic ports, train a new generation of sailors, and, ultimately, help man the dominant French navy that would undertake an invasion of England. The very future of France as a world power now depended on the expedition of Saint-Domingue.

~

As Bonaparte's imperial vision took shape, one important element of his colonial policy remained in flux. Before the French Revolution, "no colonies without slavery" had been the motto of conservative thinkers who insisted that only African laborers could withstand the heat and tropical fevers of the Caribbean. As he debated how to rebuild the prerevolutionary empire, Bonaparte thus had to decide whether to maintain or discard the 1794 law that had formalized the abolition of slavery in Saint-Domingue.

Seen from today's perspective, Bonaparte was a racist. As a young student at the military academy of Brienne, he had taunted a mixed-race classmate (who, strangely enough, later fought in the Saint-Domingue expedition). He also treated Alexandre Dumas, the Saint-Domingue-born mixed-race general best known as the *grand-père* of the writers Alexandre Dumas *père* and *fils,* with utter contempt.[69] To Bonaparte, race trumped nation and he expressed his sympathy for the Martinique planters who had welcomed a British invasion rather than free their slaves.[70] As he prepared his plans for Saint-Domingue, he inserted a clause stating that white women who had committed the ultimate racial transgression of "prostituting themselves" with officers of color should be deported to France.[71]

Because of Bonaparte's racial views and his closeness to reactionary figures like Malouet, most scholars have assumed that he had from the outset a well-articulated plan to restore slavery in Saint-Domingue.[72] Bonaparte, however, was a complex man whose ties to abolition were as ancient as his racial prejudices. He had grown up on an island, Corsica, that for centuries had been victimized by slave raids launched by Barbary pirates. Like Louverture and Kerversau, he had read approvingly the works of the abolitionist historian Guillaume Raynal; unlike them, he had actually corresponded with their author.[73] After seizing power in 1799 he accordingly assured the population of Saint-Domingue that "the sacred principles of liberty and equality will never suffer any change" and reiterated his abolitionist stance, both publicly and privately, in May 1800, January 1801, and again in his March 1801 letter to Louverture.[74]

Bonaparte never expressed in writing any intention to restore slavery in Saint-Domingue, and instead continued to express his commitment to emancipation even after deciding to overthrow Louverture. In November 1801 he drafted a proclamation, to be distributed as the expedition landed in Saint-Domingue, in which he assured former slaves that they would remain free. That same month he told the parliamentary chambers that in Guadeloupe and Saint-Domingue "all are free; all will remain free" and that he had only dispatched an expedition to Saint-Domingue because its "submission" to France had come under question. Also in November Bonaparte wrote his minister of foreign affairs that his goal was not "commerce and finances" (that is, slavery) but to "crush the government of the blacks."[75] Several authors insist that Bonaparte drafted secret instructions asking the general in charge of the Saint-Domingue expedition to restore slavery. These instructions did exist, but they actually stated that the French Republic would never put "back in irons" men it had recognized as free and that blacks would merely be disarmed and sent back to work as "free cultivators."[76] That fall a budget proposal for the Ministry of the Navy noted that some possible expenses, such as the cost of "renewing the trade in forced cultivators from the coast of Africa," would depend on future political decisions.[77]

All these proclamations of abolitionist faith may seem odd, or even deceitful, considering that Bonaparte was simultaneously considering maintaining slavery in other colonies like Martinique and Santo Domingo, but Bonaparte, ever the pragmatist, saw no contradiction in adapting his policies to match each colony's profile. Here was a practical man who in 1798 had freed slaves in Malta, then condoned slavery in Egypt, in both cases to gain the goodwill of the Egyptian population.[78] His 1799 constitution had specified that French colonies would be governed by distinct laws, a clause often thought to be a prelude to the restoration of slavery in all colonies, but that actually enabled him to maintain slavery in some colonies while others remained free.[79] Bonaparte accordingly planned to allow the planters of Santo Domingo to keep their slaves, even as abolition remained the norm in nearby Saint-Domingue, because "the French government's guiding principle is to govern peoples according to their habits and customs."[80] In early March 1801 he reiterated his promise that blacks would remain free in Saint-Domingue (where they were dominant) while abandoning plans to impose the emancipation law in Réunion, where white planters had vowed to secede rather than free their slaves.[81] An October 1801 letter explained that slavery would be maintained in Martinique (where it had never been abolished), then went on to explain that in Saint-Domingue the government's goal was merely to "enforce the rights of the metropolis."[82]

This realist policy made sense to a man for whom ideology mattered less than practicality. It was particularly suited for Saint-Domingue, where Louverture's harsh labor rules offered an alternative—the cultivator system—to the slavery/emancipation dichotomy that could allow a revival of agriculture without resorting to slavery itself. The plan's only weakness was that it made no provision for black public opinion. To a Dominguian cultivator, Bonaparte's contrived policy seemed illogical: how could a country enslave some of its colonial subjects while keeping others free? The attempt to pursue distinct policies in neighboring colonies, particularly in Saint-Domingue and Guadeloupe, would eventually spark important doubts about Bonaparte's ulterior motives and do much to undermine the Saint-Domingue expedition.

∽

By October 1801 Bonaparte had made a firm decision to remove Louverture from office. He had long hesitated before reaching this conclusion, but the takeover of Santo Domingo, the imprisonment of Roume, and the briefings of Kerversau had convinced him that Louverture's ambitions needed to be checked as soon as a fleet could leave French ports. Nothing seemed capable of derailing his plans when a messenger arrived from Saint-Domingue with yet another letter from Louverture. It was the director of fortifications Vincent.

After leaving Cap in July with copies of Louverture's constitution, Vincent had stopped in the United States and Spain, and he only met Bonaparte in Joséphine's residence of Malmaison on October 8.[83] Some histories of the expedition suggest that Bonaparte made the decision to remove Louverture from power at that very moment, when Bonaparte, "almost instantly, and through a fit of ill humor," suddenly opted for war upon hearing of the constitution.[84] This is inaccurate; Bonaparte had given up on Louverture six months earlier, and he met Vincent one day *after* instructing the minister of the navy to begin active military preparations for the expedition.

Vincent, as so often in his career, was in the wrong place at the wrong moment, but he nevertheless set out to convince Bonaparte to forgo his plans by listing the disastrous events likely to occur if he proceeded with the expedition. Five-sixths of the white population of Saint-Domingue had died or left the island, leaving few local allies to enlist, while Louverture could count on a large army, "defensive works in all possible landing sites, extensive fighting experience in this theater, unknown hiding places," and "strong ambush tactics." His men could spend an entire month without being resupplied; during the recent invasion of Santo Domingo, they had marched over twenty-five miles a day through forested mountains, a pace so strenuous that the infantry had been forced to slow down to allow the cavalry to keep up. Vincent's concluding remarks, preserved in a notebook now housed in Rouen's public library, were apocalyptic. "Saint-Domingue cannot be conquered. . . . An enemy one cannot see, who lives off nothing, sleeps where he wants, is full of strength. A destructive climate. The army will die of hunger and thirst after landing."[85] Better, Vincent insisted, to do as Louverture wished: to send back his two sons along with a letter and a promotion to flatter his ego.

Bonaparte was not a man easily scared away by military difficulties. Far from swaying him, Vincent's visit and the new constitution he brought along only confirmed Kerversau's warnings that Louverture was fast moving toward independence. "This gilded African!" Bonaparte allegedly erupted. "I will not rest until I have torn the epaulettes off every black in the colonies."[86] The quote may be apocryphal, but the anger was real. Years later in St. Helena, Bonaparte remembered that the constitution had left him "outraged. . . . From that moment there was no longer room for deliberation: the black chiefs were ungrateful and rebellious Africans." It was now "impossible to establish any system" with black officers as he had once hoped.[87]

Convinced that his native France would lose entire armies while fellow colonists succumbed to racial war, Vincent wrote a long memoir reiterating his concerns a week after his frustrating encounter with Bonaparte. He then again met Bonaparte to caution him that the expedition would put France's best troops "at the mercy of the British navy and of the climate of Saint-Domingue."[88] Bonaparte would not budge. I "predicted the Saint-Domingue's expedition unhappy fate," Vincent later recalled. But "Bonaparte had no doubt of victory."[89]

Despite his private misgivings, Vincent remained a faithful soldier and patriot. Realizing that the expedition would sail anyway, he urged Louverture in a letter to submit without a fight and shared his considerable expertise with French military planners in the likely eventuality that Louverture would choose to fight.[90] He sent plans of the fortifications French troops would encounter and revealed the location of possible stashes of weapons. He listed the guerilla tactics used by black soldiers, down to their war cry, and the ways to counter them. He described the kind of light uniform best suited to the Caribbean climate and, rightly predicting that Louverture would burn the towns, suggested that the expedition bring tiles and timber to rebuild houses. His memoirs and letters, often overlooked because they have since been sold to the University of Florida, were long, detailed, and invaluable. "When one goes to Marmelade via the hills," he explained, "one will find on the right hand side an old drunken white in charge of guarding the cannon on the small hill, and who will be happy to be relieved of his duties without a fight."[91] But Vincent's advice for war received no more attention than his urgings for peace, and the general in charge of the expedition proceeded to commit many of the blunders Vincent had so presciently warned against.

The only payment Vincent ever received for his principled stand was poverty and banishment.[92] The slave revolt had already ruined the plantations he and his wife owned in Saint-Domingue; the Ministry of the Navy now refused to pay his salary arrears under the pretext that he had served a rebellious governor. He was shipped off to Elba, off the coast of Italy, to oversee the tiny island's defenses, and with plenty of time to devote to literary pursuits he began working on—appropriately enough—a tragedy. He continued to serve in the French army, but it was a full eighteen years before he was promoted from *chef de brigade* to acting *maréchal de camp*. Despite the injustice of being punished for being the bearer of bad news and sound advice, Vincent served Bonaparte loyally until his downfall and returned to Elba in 1812 to shore up the island's fortifications against a possible invasion.

Still, occasionally, history has a way of providing some higher justice. When Bonaparte was first overthrown in 1814, he was exiled, of all places, to the island of Elba. Upon arriving in beautiful Porto Ferraio, he took up residence in the home of the director of fortifications—Vincent's house.

3

Eve of a Battle

Planning the Leclerc Expedition

FALL 1801

As Napoléon Bonaparte began the titanic task of preparing the expedition of Saint-Domingue, his first priority was to strike diplomatic agreements with the Caribbean's dominant naval powers, England and the United States, without whose support the French fleet could not reach its theater of operations or sustain itself once it got there. This delicate diplomatic task was entrusted to the minister of foreign affairs, Charles-Maurice de Talleyrand-Périgord, a slippery, opportunistic bishop-turned-politician whom Bonaparte would one day describe as "shit in silk stockings." Particularly adept at charting a course through the revolution's stormy waters, Talleyrand had secured a position in all the regimes that had ruled France since Louis XVI (except for the radical Convention) and would continue doing so until his death in 1838. He was occasionally treacherous, but Bonaparte appreciated his ancien régime flair and kept him as one of his closest advisers for most of his reign. The two met every day for about an hour, usually in the evening to accommodate Talleyrand's night owl schedule. Together they made and remade the map of Europe.[1]

Talleyrand's first task was to obtain enough supplies for the expedition from the United States. In theory, the Napoleonic army lived off the countryside, foraging as it went, in order to increase its mobility. But Saint-Domingue's plantations focused primarily on export crops like coffee, and French troops would be heavily reliant on imported foodstuffs (growing local produce such as yams and plantains would have been a simple alternative, but white colonists had always insisted on eating bread, and Bonaparte preferred to risk exposing his troops to famine than deprive them of French cuisine).[2] The French merchant navy, devastated by years of naval warfare, was incapable of shipping enough supplies, so U.S. merchants would initially have to provide the republican Eucharist of flour, wine, and gunpowder.[3]

Enlisting U.S. commercial support was no easy task. Since 1798 France and the United States had fought the Quasi-War, a conflict caused, ironically, by Talleyrand's own wrongdoing during the Directory. Talleyrand negotiated a peace agreement with the United States at Mortefontaine in September 1800, but U.S. merchants continued to express misgivings about feeding sailors and soldiers they had so recently fought. Many openly favored Toussaint Louverture, who had dutifully protected U.S. ships from French privateers during the Quasi-War.

Luckily for Talleyrand, in March 1801 the Francophile Virginian Thomas Jefferson entered the Executive Mansion and U.S. politics shifted just as Bonaparte began preparing the Saint-Domingue expedition. Compared with the Massachusetts-born John Adams, who had favored the commercial interests of New England merchants over those of southern planters, Jefferson seemed likely to be more sympathetic to France's colonial interests. Like all southern slave owners in the wake of the Gabriel slave conspiracy, Jefferson had ample reasons to fear the example of a society ruled by rebellious slaves.[4] This was a president Talleyrand could do business with.

The young French ambassador to the United States, Louis-André Pichon, brought up the matter of the Saint-Domingue expedition during his first encounter with Jefferson and was pleased to report that Jefferson had compared Saint-Domingue to "another Algiers in the seas of America" in reference to the piratical Barbary states.[5] "There is no support for Toussaint in the United States," Jefferson rather incorrectly stated. "Isn't his example dangerous for two-thirds of the states?"[6] Informed of the conversation, Bonaparte and Talleyrand optimistically told the commander of the expedition that Jefferson had pledged to supply the French army while "starving" Louverture (he had not) and that all logistical problems were solved.[7]

But Jefferson, the slave-owning advocate of liberty, held views on human bondage that were as convoluted as Louverture's and Bonaparte's. By the time Talleyrand received Pichon's report, Jefferson had already changed his mind. After taking a second look at his predecessor's policies, he concluded that Louverture had dutifully protected U.S. commerce and that assisting a French imperial resurgence would complicate the United States' own plans to expand into Louisiana.[8] As cynical as it might sound, an ideal scenario for the United States was for France to get bogged down in a bloody Saint-Domingue quagmire, which would give Bonaparte and Louverture no opportunity to direct their ambitions to the North American continent and plenty of reasons to buy U.S. gunpowder.

Five months after their July 1801 meeting, Jefferson thus summoned Pichon and asked disingenuously, "Why not declare the island independent, under the protection of France, the United States, and England?"[9] A baffled

Pichon explained that it was much too late for such policy reversals; at that very time, the largest squadron in the French navy was preparing to leave Brest for Saint-Domingue. Bonaparte, moreover, would never have acquiesced to the independence of France's most valuable colony, especially under the tutelage of its Anglo-American rivals.

Jefferson's second thoughts boded ill for the future. By January 1802 the French expedition, still under the impression that Jefferson wholeheartedly supported its mission, was days from landing in Saint-Domingue. Meanwhile, Secretary of State James Madison instructed the U.S. commercial agent in Cap to adopt a policy of "strict neutrality," by which he meant that he should make no effort to combat U.S. contraband to Dominguian rebels.[10] The misunderstanding was to create much acrimony in the days after the French landing.

～

In the fall of 1801, even as Bonaparte prepared to launch the largest overseas expedition of his reign, English squadrons blockaded all the ports from which the fleets were supposed to sail. He either hoped that the expedition would miraculously sneak past the English blockade (as he had done when he had left for Egypt while Horatio Nelson was courting his mistress in Naples), or, more likely, he was supremely confident that peace with England would come soon.[11]

In the end Bonaparte relied on peace, not Lady Emma Hamilton. "The equinox is coming and each day is precious," he told Talleyrand in September, before informing him that a European peace absolutely had to be signed by the first *décade* (week) of Vendémiaire so that war could begin in the Caribbean.[12] The reliable Talleyrand did not disappoint him and on October 9, 1801, exactly on schedule, the London preliminary articles of peace called for a temporary suspension of hostilities between France and England. Even though a permanent peace treaty had yet to be negotiated and war might resume at any time, Bonaparte decided to launch the long-awaited Saint-Domingue expedition at once. This was a massive gamble that Bonaparte felt he had to take given the expedition's narrow window of opportunity. Caribbean expeditions traditionally left in late fall, after hurricane season and the equinoctial gales of the North Atlantic, but early enough that troops could campaign before the onset of summer and its deadly fevers. Louverture would also build up his defenses as soon as he knew of the peace preliminaries, so the expedition would have to reach Saint-Domingue before he could be informed of the massive military build-up taking place in French ports.

Eager to proceed with the expedition, Bonaparte asked the British for their cooperation immediately after the peace preliminaries were signed.[13]

The two countries had just concluded a bitter decade-long war, which it-self had followed a century of almost continuous imperial rivalries, so the English were wary of allowing such a massive fleet to leave French ports. Marcus Rainsford, an English citizen who had spent several weeks in Saint-Domingue in 1799 at a time when France was planning an invasion of Jamaica, warned his government that the French could easily shift targets and attack British colonies once they reached the Caribbean.[14] Another well-informed observer, James Stephen, predicted that the expedition was doomed to failure due to the same problems—distance, terrain, and disease—that had plagued Great Britain's own disastrous invasion of Saint-Domingue in the 1790s. However, should France decide to attack Jamaica instead, Brit-ain's most valuable Caribbean colony would be lost since the small squadron in Port Royal could not be counted on to stop a large French fleet a few hours' sailing away.[15]

Informed of English hesitations Bonaparte presented the expedition as a clash of civilizations and argued that England and all other slave-owning powers could only benefit from the downfall of Louverture's black regime. As a sign of good faith he also provided detailed lists of the ships being read-ied in Brest, an important piece of intelligence that the British had previ-ously only obtained through espionage. A master of the hard sell, he finally added that given the expedition's tight schedule any delay would force him to cancel it altogether and return to the policy he had favored until March 1801: use Louverture's army for offensive operations in the Caribbean.[16]

The threat was credible enough that the English soon gave in. "The two governments share the same interest," Prime Minister Henry Addington told the French negotiator in London. "We both want to destroy Jacobinism, es-pecially that of the blacks."[17] "Toussaint's black empire," the instructions to the governor of Jamaica went, "is one amongst many evils that have grown out of the war—and it is by no means our interest to prevent its annihila-tion."[18] Still concerned by the magnitude of the expedition, the British re-quested that the French send their warships *en flûte* (disarmed), but Bonaparte retorted that this was an insult to national honor and that most ships would leave with their full complement of guns. At any rate, the suave Talleyrand reassured his British interlocutors, the French fleet was "by no means in a condition to meet an enemy," while that of its Spanish ally (which provided six transports) was "in so wretched a state as to be truly despicable as ships of war."[19] Not fully convinced the British prepared a large squadron to match the French fleet ship for ship and instructed the governor of Jamaica to give no logistical assistance to the expedition.[20]

Talleyrand could be proud. In a few months of intense diplomatic ac-tivity he had obtained U.S. and English support for the Saint-Domingue expedition—or so he thought. Only the future would tell whether relying on former enemies to supply one's army overseas was a wise proposition.

~

After ironing out a few diplomatic kinks Bonaparte shifted his focus to the myriad logistical tasks associated with the mammoth expedition. For the previous two years he had repeatedly ordered his navy to prepare a fleet for Saint-Domingue, only to put such plans on hold due to staffing problems, the British blockade, and his ever-changing policies. The first order to ship out had come as early as December 1799, countermanded days later when he had decided to send Charles de Vincent, only to be followed by new orders to prepare a Caribbean fleet in January 1800. Delayed multiple times, the fleet had eventually been rerouted to Egypt when Bonaparte had chosen to ally himself with Louverture, only to be held up in Toulon.[21]

After these uncertain, confused beginnings, the genesis of the Saint-Domingue expedition can be traced back to a May 4, 1801 order to prepare a 3,600-troop expedition in Brest.[22] Coming shortly after Bonaparte had turned against Louverture, the squadron was most likely intended as the first installment of a force that would grow once peace with England was secured. Immediately after the peace preliminaries were signed, Bonaparte ordered that 6,000 troops be ready to sail from Brest by October 20, with 5,600 troops to follow from Le Havre, Lorient, Cádiz, and Rochefort. Including later reinforcements, he planned to assign an impressive 17,800 troops to this one theater.[23]

The expedition was a major test for Bonaparte's new minister of the navy, Denis Decrès, who took his position just days before the preparations began in earnest. Decrès was a pliant sycophant, but he found the courage to warn Bonaparte that up to twenty thousand men arriving all at once might be needed to defeat Louverture's sizable army, and in a flurry of new orders Bonaparte began adding yet more troops and ports to the ballooning expedition. Another sixteen hundred troops would sail out of Vlissingen (a.k.a. Flushing) in the Netherlands, one thousand from Brest, and five hundred from Rochefort, while squadrons in Le Havre, Lorient, and Cádiz, scheduled to depart at a later date, would leave with the main fleet. Vincent met Decrès and Bonaparte just then, and Bonaparte must have been moved by his apocalyptic warnings because a day later he changed his plans once more. The combined fleets, now carrying fifteen thousand troops, were not sufficient, so Bonaparte ordered the three-thousand-man Toulon fleet, which he had just earmarked for the Indian Ocean, rerouted to Saint-Domingue. An additional three thousand men would leave Brest as soon as feasible.[24]

Bonaparte also tapped his allies. The Netherlands provided sailors, ships of the line, and food for the squadron leaving from Vlissingen. Five Spanish ships of the line and a frigate marooned in Brest were incorporated into the main fleet, while another squadron sailed out of Cádiz.[25] As the cost of the expedition passed 3.3 million francs for the Brest squadron alone and the perennially empty Napoleonic treasury borrowed from the following year's budget to meet current expenses, Spain was also asked to bankroll part of the expedition.[26] The obedient allies received little for their efforts: as negotiations for a permanent peace took place in London, Bonaparte adamantly refused that France cede an inch of its empire, but he generously offered Dutch Ceylon and Spanish Trinidad to the British.

By November 1801, when Talleyrand obtained Britain's approval for the expedition, it had mushroomed to a seven-port, forty-three-thousand-man behemoth, half of them sailors. Transporting the army mobilized two-thirds of the serviceable units in the French navy, including twenty-eight of its large ships of the line (*vaisseaux*) and dozens of frigates and corvettes.[27] No expedition of that size would ever again leave French ports while Bonaparte ruled.

~

The troops about to embark belonged to the most effective fighting force of its time, one fashioned by a decade of revolutionary warfare. During the French Revolution the nobles and foreign mercenaries of the old Bourbon army had given way to young bourgeois volunteers who fought well because they did so for *liberté* and *nation,* not king and country. The introduction of the military draft had also dramatically increased the size of the French army, slated to total 320,000 men in 1802 despite the peace with England. Instead of drilling professional troops into obedient tin soldiers, innovative tactics encouraged citizen-soldiers and officers to display initiative on the battle-field, while the creation of the *demi-brigade* (an independent fighting force that is the ancestor of the modern division) made for a mobile, versatile force. This army, which had repeatedly humiliated the great powers of Europe, was the formidable force about to be thrust upon Louverture.[28]

A large portion of the first wave of soldiers sent to Saint-Domingue came from the Army of the Rhine, an elite corps known for its attachment to revolutionary principles. Their commander, Jean Moreau, was an opponent of Bonaparte's 18 Brumaire coup who would later be involved in a plot to overthrow Bonaparte, so many contemporaries alleged that he selected Moreau's troops for colonial duty as part of a cruel ploy to rid himself of his rival's supporters.[29] This conspiracy theory, however, is ahistorical. Bonaparte was still on cordial terms with Moreau in the fall of 1801.[30] Had he truly designed the expedition to weaken his enemy, he would have entrusted it to Moreau himself, or to another critic like Jean-Baptiste Bernadotte (who helped organize the expedition but never left with it). Another famous Moreauist,

Joseph Hugo, was the only officer in his unit *not* to go to Saint-Domingue—thankfully for French literature, since a year later his wife gave birth to the famed Victor Hugo, whose vast opus includes *Bug Jargal,* a novel set during the Haitian Revolution.[31] Instead, Bonaparte awarded the overall command to his brother-his-law and insisted that his favorite sister and nephew follow him to Saint-Domingue, hardly the hallmark of a suicide mission.

Bonaparte selected units for their bravery, not their political leanings. To limit casualties, governmental memos advised him to send crack veterans, not raw draftees or sickly foreign deserters, and among other magnificent troops the Brest fleet carried the 5th light demi-brigade, a unit to which Bonaparte was particularly attached (the Toulon and Cádiz squadrons, scheduled to arrive after the first landing, brought comparatively weaker units like the German battalion).[32] Only in later months, when it became clear that units routinely suffered staggering rates of attrition in the Caribbean climate, would Bonaparte send a preponderance of disposable troops such as deserters and foreigners. The expeditionary army's sole weakness was that it included many demi-brigades of the line, units of heavy infantry that were more suited for standard pitched battles than for the mountainous terrain and guerrilla warfare of the Caribbean.

The elite troops sent to Saint-Domingue were led by a distinguished roster of generals that included no fewer than one lieutenant general, ten division generals, seventeen brigadier generals, and twenty-six adjutant-commandants. Their names read like a who's who of the French army, from Charles Dugua and Pierre Boyer (who had served with Bonaparte in Egypt) to Jean Boudet (a brother in arms from Marengo). Many had extensive colonial experience. Boudet, Pierre Thouvenot, and Edmé-Étienne Desfourneaux had served in Guadeloupe; Philibert Fressinet and François Watrin in Saint-Domingue; and Donatien de Rochambeau in Martinique and Saint-Domingue. François de Kerversau, whose knowledge of Santo Domingo was unparalleled, returned with the expedition at Bonaparte's personal request.[33]

Colonial duty was normally an unpopular assignment, but in late 1801 there was a wealth of qualified officers eager to join the expedition because peace had closed off alternative theaters in Europe. So numerous were the volunteers that there were not enough units to accommodate them all and that left many officers as supernumeraries.[34] Saint-Domingue's fabled wealth was another strong incentive. Jean Hardÿ, a noted general who had gained his first major promotion on the battlefield of Valmy, was typical of the many officers dreaming of glory and riches. He had vowed never to set foot on a ship after almost dying on his way to invade Ireland in 1798, but captivity in England and a nasty wound had left him penniless. Like many others, he volunteered for the expedition primarily to make money. Writing to his pregnant wife, he explained that he hoped, "after my return, to have acquired, through licit means, enough to guarantee your well-being, along with that of our children."[35]

The lower ranks of the French army were far less enthusiastic. The draft was a five-year, unpopular institution, and 27 percent of the young men called to duty in 1801–5 dodged the draft.[36] Contrary to their officers, who received a 50 percent pay increase overseas and had the means to invest in a plantation, soldiers had little to gain financially from colonial duty.[37] Police reports prepared in the winter of 1801–2 indicated that the French population was remarkably lukewarm toward the expedition and even pessimistic about its likelihood of success.[38] French sailors, who knew the ravages of tropical fevers better than most, were busy seeking medical exemptions.[39] One of these sailors, Jean-Jacques Audubon, should have been eager to serve since he was a native of Cayes in Saint-Domingue. But his brief service as a cadet in the French navy had left him seasick and unhappy, and he left the navy on the eve of the expedition. Drafted again in 1806 he fled to the United States, where he shot birds instead of humans and achieved recognition as the famed naturalist John James Audubon.[40]

The veterans of the Army of the Rhine were superb troops, but their republican spirit could be a liability in the long run. The expedition's goals were to deny Saint-Domingue the right to self-determination, and, many suspected, to reenslave its people, so there was a real risk that idealistic commoners, willing to risk their life in defense of liberty, would be poorly suited for a war waged on behalf of aristocratic planters. Sooner or later the peasants who formed the bulk of Bonaparte's army were bound to notice that Saint-Domingue's planters were not unlike the feudal lords they had fought during their own revolution.

Officers of color presented a unique quandary when selecting the units that would compose the army of Saint-Domingue. White colonists were prone to accuse mixed-race individuals for every disaster that had ever befallen Saint-Domingue, and existing contingency plans called on Bonaparte to rely on a white-only force.[41] But just as the expedition began taking shape, significant numbers of officers of color landed in French ports. They had fled Saint-Domingue after the defeat of Louverture's rival, André Rigaud, a mixed-race goldsmith and general who was eager to avenge himself and immediately offered his services upon landing in France.[42]

As often, Bonaparte remained impervious to the pleas of the colonial lobby and welcomed officers of color in French ranks. He had successfully used ethnic minorities in the campaign of Egypt, and in his view mixed-race *anciens libres,* who had a long and proud military record in Saint-Domingue, would be essential allies in a war against black upstarts.[43] He treated Rigaud with

Table 1.
French and foreign units scheduled to leave in late 1801.

Unit name	Port of departure					
	Brest (Adm. Villaret)	Brest (Adm. Gravina)	Rochefort (Adm. Latouche)	Lorient (Adm. Delmotte)	Toulon (Adm. Ganteaume)	Cádiz (Adm. Linois)
General staff	71	5	25	18	11	6
Unattached officers	31		8	5		87
1st regt. of foot artillery					161	
3rd regt. of foot artillery	82					
4th regt. of foot artillery	158	84				
8th regt. of foot artillery	77		73	52		
6th regt. of horse artillery	41		192			
Artillery train	146	40	23			
Sappers	659	374				
5th light demi-brigade	874	438	360			266
11th light demi-brigade	58					
15th light demi-brigade					542	
19th heavy demi-brigade			382			
21st heavy demi-brigade					29	
25th heavy demi-brigade				792		
30th heavy demi-brigade		586				
31st heavy demi-brigade	590					
38th heavy demi-brigade	992					
56th heavy demi-brigade			506			

68th heavy demi-brigade			850			
71st heavy demi-brigade	461	116				
74th heavy demi-brigade					540	
79th heavy demi-brigade	229	347				
90th heavy demi-brigade			470			
Legion of the Loire	275		614			
Expeditionary legion	343				988	746
Land artillery workers	2	9				
Naval artillery workers	23					
German battalion						819
Squadron of the Loire	151					
19th regt. of chasseurs	159					104
1st regt. of hussars	26					
Total	5,448	1,999	3,503	867	2,271	2,028

Grand total: 16,116 (plus 1,119 civilian administrators, family members, and domestics)

Source: Jean–Baptiste Guillemain de Vaivres, "Extrait d'un état adressé par le commandant en chef de l'armée navale de Saint-Domingue . . ." (Feb. 20, 1802), CC9/B23, Archives Nationales, Paris. *Note:* Totals adjusted to correct mathematical errors in the original.

respect—allegedly saying in reference to his war against Louverture, "I blame you for only one thing, not to have been victorious"—and maintained him in his rank, presumably so that he could use him for his future plans.[44] Against the wishes of his entourage he announced his intention to exploit racial enmity between *noirs* (blacks) and *mulâtres* (mulattoes), which he viewed as the primary cause of the War of the South.[45] He personally asked that Rigaud be enlisted in the expedition, and Rigaud gathered dozens of his supporters in Rochefort. Among them were Alexandre Pétion and Jean-Pierre Boyer, two lesser officers destined to become presidents of Haiti.[46]

Bonaparte also sent many other officers of color who had run afoul of Louverture during his controversial rise to power. Antoine Chanlatte, Kerversau's colleague in Santo Domingo, came along. So did Jean-Louis Villatte (whom Louverture had expelled in 1796), Jean-Baptiste Belley (the first black deputy ever admitted to the French National Assembly), Kayer (who left on Hardÿ's staff), and the Martinique-born deputy Étienne Mentor. The black officer Jean-Pierre Léveillé had developed a particularly strong antipathy for Louverture, partly because his brother had been killed on Louverture's orders.[47] At its creation the army of Saint-Domingue was not an all-white force bent on racial war but a composite group in which political and personal enmities often trumped one's racial affiliation.

~

Given the physical impossibility of monitoring the theater of operations from Paris, selecting an able commander was essential to the expedition's success. Various generals were considered at one time or another, but Bonaparte rejected them all and, one day after ordering Decrès to proceed with the expedition, he selected a twenty-nine-year-old general with the promising name of Victoire (victory) Emmanuel Leclerc.[48] He was a rather odd choice as he had never served overseas, a background that spared him from the ideological baggage that often weighted his colonial colleagues but also left him wholly unaware of the unique society he was destined to rule. This alone should have disqualified him for such a delicate mission, especially given the widespread availability of more experienced generals like Rochambeau, Desfourneaux, and Kerversau.

Bonaparte's preference for the inexperienced Leclerc probably stemmed from his penchant for employing family members and administrators, however flawed, whom he knew well (like the mediocre Decrès and the treacherous Talleyrand). Bonaparte's association with Leclerc went back to his campaigns in Italy and was unusually intimate.[49] One day Bonaparte had surprised Leclerc during a most private moment. He had spent some time observing the officer's technique hidden behind a folding screen; further inquiry had revealed that Leclerc's partner was none other than the beautiful Pauline Bonaparte.[50]

"Paulette," as he called her, was Bonaparte's favorite sister, but he was also aghast that her many romantic trysts had brought dishonor to the family clan. Leclerc was the most acceptable of her many lovers—more so than the old bureaucrat Louis Fréron, whom Pauline had recently left at Bonaparte's in-sistence—so after witnessing Leclerc's gallantry firsthand Bonaparte insisted that they be married at once. His wedding present was a promotion to briga-dier general. By sending Leclerc to Saint-Domingue, an assignment likely to be financially rewarding, Bonaparte was offering a prosperous future to the young couple.[51]

Summoned to Paris on October 8, Leclerc was only officially selected as captain general of the army of Saint-Domingue on the twenty-third.[52] The delay reflected Leclerc's hesitancy about the distant assignment, which he tried to decline by arguing that he could not leave his unmarried sister Aimée alone in France. Bonaparte did not object to the notion that a woman needed male supervision, but he cleverly ordered that another man be in charge. "To-morrow, your sister will be married," he replied. "I don't know yet who the husband will be, but she will be married, and well married."[53] (General Louis Nicolas Davout turned out to be the lucky man.)

Faced with Bonaparte's insistence, Leclerc ultimately concluded that the assignment was the most lucrative he could ever obtain in peacetime. The position of captain general carried a yearly salary of one hundred thousand francs, plus twenty-three thousand francs of living expenses and a seventy-five-thousand-franc stipend for travel costs, in addition to the business op-portunities that would surely open up in Saint-Domingue.[54] By comparison, Leclerc's immediate superior, Decrès, only made eighty thousand francs a year.[55] Even a short assignment could make him one of the richest men in France. No profit was too small; Leclerc apparently enlisted his four-year-old son Dermide as a cabin boy for the Atlantic crossing to secure the 9 francs monthly retainer (a stratagem that also gave his son some official sea time should he ever join the naval profession).[56] Leclerc's brother also came with the army.[57]

Leclerc's utter ignorance of colonial affairs made him overconfident, even cocky. Before the expedition set sail, Charles Malenfant, a Saint-Domingue planter who no longer saw slavery as a realistic proposition, tried to warn Leclerc about upcoming difficulties. "The blacks are not the same as they were 19 years ago," he explained, using the neutral term *noirs*. Using the more derogatory *nègre* (Negro), Leclerc replied that his enemies would "drop their weapons as soon as they see an army."[58] Oblivious to the fact that the French invasion of Egypt had ultimately ended in disaster, Leclerc added that the French infantry had made little work of the famed Mameluke slave-soldiers at the Battle of the Pyramids. He then shifted the conversation to Louverture's alleged fortune, which seems to have been his main center of interest all along. Contempt for their enemy was common among colonial newcomers in Leclerc's army.[59]

Leclerc would mature during his short stay in Saint-Domingue, but as of November 1801 he came across as a brash fop. Blue-eyed, with light brown hair, he bore a passing resemblance to Bonaparte and often aped his physical tics in the hope of stealing the first consul's aura.[60] Before his departure, he purchased a massive 237-volume encyclopedia and works on agriculture, geography, war, and Saint-Domingue—many of which, intriguingly, could also be found in Louverture's library.[61] Depending on one's perspective, he was either a humanist in the best tradition of the Enlightenment or a mediocre student cramming the night before an important exam. If so, he hardly deserved an *A* in geography. Mistaking the hilly, forested terrain making up much of Saint-Domingue's interior for the sand dunes of Egypt, he asked that a regiment of dromedary riders be sent with the expedition.[62]

~

Bonaparte was also busy brushing up on colonial affairs as he devised a strategy for victory. He met Vincent and Kerversau, ordered urgent reports on the history and current state of the French empire, consulted colonial archives dating back to the ancien régime, and asked for up-to-date collections of maps and plans.[63] As former commander of the expedition of Egypt, which had mobilized three hundred ships and fifty-four thousand men, Bonaparte could also have drawn valuable lessons from his own experience. Among other mistakes Bonaparte had landed in July, without adequate food and water but with heavy woolen uniforms, and had lost fifteen hundred men to dehydration and diarrhea in a four-day period. His army had then defeated the Mamelukes only to be slowly weakened by disease, guerilla warfare, and lack of naval support.[64] And yet Bonaparte went on to repeat many of the same mistakes in Saint-Domingue. He also completely ignored the precedent set by Great Britain's failed attempt to invade Saint-Domingue in 1793–98, even though the two expeditions eventually followed similar trajectories. When Jean-Baptiste Lapointe, a mixed-race officer who had fought in British ranks, correctly warned Bonaparte that one hundred thousand men would be needed to defeat Louverture, he dismissed the number as fantastic.[65]

Having studied the situation as best he could, Bonaparte summoned his secretary on October 29 to draft Leclerc's secret instructions. The two worked late into the night, finishing with a hot chocolate to calm Bonaparte's sensitive stomach, and the following day Bonaparte handed the document to Leclerc while telling him that he had "a nice opportunity to get rich. Go, and do not tire me anymore with your endless requests for money."[66] Leclerc's instructions—Bonaparte's roadmap for victory in Saint-Domingue—were an elaborate multitiered plan under which Leclerc was to publicize his intention to collaborate with Louverture so as to land his troops safely, then deport all black officers at a later stage. Leclerc would then restore the old colonial order, mercantilist trade restrictions included, except in one crucial area: Leclerc's "political goal in the French part of Saint-Domingue" was to have "free black cultivators."[67]

Bonaparte's plan, relying more on deception and collaboration than brute force, showed that he had heeded Vincent's and Lapointe's warnings even as he publicly dismissed their direst predictions. By refusing to embrace reactionary goals like slavery, he hoped to attract many of Louverture's officers to the French side, a distinct possibility according to the latest intelligence reports. Rigaud predicted that Louverture's subordinates would desert him in droves if the French expedition was large and impressive enough, and Louverture's secretary, Pascal, said as much in a secret memoir.[68] Bonaparte also received a report by the agent Philippe Roume that a "furious storm was brewing" and that Louverture's African-born black cultivators were only waiting for Bonaparte's support to revolt.[69] "All of this leads me to think," Bonaparte joyfully wrote Leclerc, "that the obstacles you will have to face will be less important than we feared."[70] To further isolate Louverture from the Dominguian rank and file, Bonaparte wrote a proclamation in which he emphatically promised, in both French and Kreyol, that "regardless of your origins and your skin color . . . you are all free and equal. . . . Don't believe those who tell you that white people want to put you back into slavery."[71]

Increasingly hopeful that force might not even be needed to restore French authority, Bonaparte prepared a letter to Louverture a few days after he finished his public proclamation. In it he denounced Louverture's constitution as "contrary to the dignity and sovereignty of France," but he also reminded Louverture that France was the only country to recognize "the freedom of the blacks" and promised money and honors if he collaborated with Leclerc.[72] The letter marked the second time, after the aborted March 4 letter, that Bonaparte had written directly to Louverture. Judging by the continued preparations for the expedition, Bonaparte was intent on removing Louverture from office at any cost, but he left open the possibility that Louverture would bow out gracefully against a pledge to keep his people free.

Bonaparte also heeded Vincent's suggestion that sending Louverture's sons Isaac and Placide ahead of the expedition might help mollify their father.[73] The two boys had been studying in France since 1796 and were now attending the Collège de la Marche, a school that was a miniature version of the colony and also hosted the sons of the colonial officers Rigaud, Belley, and Léveillé; the orphans of white planters massacred in the slave revolt; and Roume's stepson. Louverture's children thrived under the stern but loving regimen of the defrocked *abbé* Jean-Baptiste Coisnon, and within a few years they acquired a solid grounding in the sciences, classics, and French, which they proudly displayed to the minister of the navy in yearly ceremonies.[74] As rumors about the expedition spread in the fall of 1801, Isaac could not help but "worry when seeing the military preparations aimed at their country."[75] But he was convinced by reassurances that none of this military build-up was aimed at his father and even penned a poem in Bonaparte's honor that showcased his fine command of the French language, if not his political sense.[76]

Ô toi dont la valeur commande à la victoire	O you, whose valor brings victory,
Et dont les grands desseins ont mérité la gloire	Whose great ambitions deserved glory,
Jeune et vaillant héros, l'éclat de la grandeur	Young and valiant hero, your grandeur,
Du beau jour qui nous luit, augmente la Splendeur.	Of the shining day, increases the splendor.

One weekend in November, Isaac, Placide, and Coisnon went to the Tuileries Palace to meet Bonaparte and Leclerc. The Tuileries was in central Paris, not far from the Collège de la Marche, but nineteenth-century Parisians rarely left their neighborhood, and this must have been the first time the boys caught a glimpse of the center of French power. Bonaparte began the meeting by asking Coisnon, rather impolitely, which of the two boys was truly Louverture's (Placide was the mixed-race son of Suzanne Louverture). "Your father is a great man, who rendered great services to France," Bonaparte said as he turned to Isaac. "You will tell him that I, first magistrate of the French people, promise him protection, glory, and honor. Do not think that France intends to bring war to Saint-Domingue: the army I am sending there is not destined to fight this country's troops, but to reinforce them."[77]

After quizzing Isaac on mathematics, probably to check on the quality of Coisnon's instruction (the French government paid the boys' tuition), Bonaparte dismissed the two children. The following day they were summoned again to attend a grand reception organized by Decrès where they met Leclerc; Vincent; the future prefect of Saint-Domingue, Pierre Bénézech; the famed explorer Louis de Bougainville; and all the luminaries of the French colonial hierarchy. The befuddled boys were presented with superb armor and military uniforms and were treated as esteemed guests. They then left for Brest, where they would depart for the island of their youth and reunite with a father they had not seen for five years.

~

By mid-November, the Saint-Domingue expedition was nearly ready. Bonaparte had seriously envisioned such an expedition for six months, but the bulk of the preparations had taken place since he had received word of the London articles of peace in early October. In a little over a month Bonaparte and his administration had equipped an entire fleet, drafted Leclerc's instructions, married off his sister, secured English acquiescence, and generally performed all the tasks associated with sending twenty thousand troops and as many sailors to the other side of the Atlantic. The planning was a bureaucratic feat that was all the more amazing considering that the entire administration of the Ministry of the Navy, in this age of fiscal parsimony, consisted of a mere 160 employees.[78]

Bonaparte's plan, however, overlooked crucial logistical, political, and epidemiological factors. The navy struggled to find enough flour for the Brest squadron, so departing warships were issued the standard six-month supply of rations, leaving them unable to spare any supplies for the army after the landing.[79] This left Leclerc at the mercy of the United States and Jamaica, two former, and possibly future, enemies. Bonaparte had devised an elaborate political strategy to isolate Louverture from Saint-Domingue's population of color, but eager to enrich a close family member he entrusted its implementation to a general who was woefully unprepared for the task. Last and most crucially, Bonaparte failed to anticipate how yellow fever, a disease that had decimated many a European army in previous centuries, would ravage the expedition. His plan was to land the army in wintertime and defeat Louverture within weeks, but he made no provisions for the eventuality that the fighting might drag on into the summer and cost him an army.[80] Bonaparte, who had experienced a major epidemic in Egypt and had grown up on an island whose coastal areas remained virtually uninhabited until World War II because of malaria, should have known better.

Once the last preparations were complete, Bonaparte told Leclerc and his staff to leave at once. The wife of General Hardÿ, who stayed in Paris on account of her pregnancy, was terrified lest the cruel sea or tropical fevers orphan her child before it was even born (the notorious reputation of Creole seductresses was probably also on her mind). But her husband assured her that fighting would be minimal, reminded her of their dire need for cash, and, as all good husbands should, dismissed the Creole women's sensuous ways as a myth.[81] Pauline would have loved to play the role of the (not so faithful) Penelope with Mrs. Hardÿ, but Bonaparte rejected her demand. "How could my brother be so cruel as to send me into exile amongst savages and snakes?" Pauline complained.[82] This was to no avail; Bonaparte had heard rumors that Pauline had become suspiciously attached to a Parisian actor, and probably also remembered how his own wife, Joséphine, had cheated on him while he was campaigning in Egypt.[83] He insisted that Pauline leave with the expedition. But thousands of young men accompanied the Leclercs and forcing Pauline to follow her husband proved quite ineffective in the end. Leclerc would spend the next six months defending both the colony and the marital bed from rival officers—only to lose both wars.

4

King of the Tropics

The Atlantic Crossing and the Moyse Uprising

The city of Brest is built on cascading hills that converge on a river, the Penfeld, bordered on both sides by piers and naval entrepôts. During the Napoleonic era, as today, Brest was primarily a military port whose activity ebbed and flowed with the fortunes of the French navy (its dreary weather was a more reliable feature, then as now). As of 1801 the city's ships were under the command of Admiral Louis-Thomas Villaret de Joyeuse, whose long maritime service had already taken him from India to the Antilles (his brother, a brigadier chief in the artillery, also left with the expedition).[1] Given the French navy's poor record during the revolutionary wars, however, Villaret had acquired much of his naval experience in a long string of naval disasters, most notably when he had lost seven ships of the line at the "Glorious" First of June in 1794. When asked what he thought of the expedition, one old tar replied, "Nothing good . . . Villaret is in charge. . . . I have sailed with him for ten years, and he never brought us anything but bad luck."[2]

A great honor though it was, Villaret's command brought its lot of logistical headaches. The main challenge, compounded by Bonaparte's many changes of plans, was to find enough room for the hundreds of soldiers daily streaming into Brest. Ships of the line were extraordinarily jammed even in normal circumstances and were rather poor candidates to serve as troop transports. But the ruined French merchant fleet could supply few transports, and Bonaparte was eager to give his military crews some much-needed sea time after a decade of English blockades. Villaret's captains were thus instructed to find some room—somewhere between the seventy-four large guns, naval stores, and six hundred men found on a typical ship of the line—to accommodate an additional two hundred, four hundred, or even seven hundred men per ship, or double the regular complement.[3]

By mid-October, with considerable difficulty, Villaret had managed to fit six thousand troops and their equipment on board his ships when he received word from Paris to make room for sixteen hundred more. Running short of options he stripped some ships of the line of their cannon, which rendered them useless as weapons platforms but freed precious square feet of deck space.[4] The change was made all the more necessary by an acute shortage of able sailors, which had already forced him to draft local fishermen.[5] A week later more troops reached Brest, and Villaret hastily pressed into service three decommissioned ships of the line.[6]

By the time October turned into November, the men who had embarked when Bonaparte had first instructed Villaret to prepare an expedition had been on board for six months, most of them without shore leave to avoid desertion. Half a year they had sat one next to the other on a deck with a mere five to six feet of headroom, sharing their tight quarters with the pigs and chickens that would feed them en route. Half a year they had smelled the noxious effluvium rising from the bilge. One by one they began to die—of typhoid, colic, and fevers, and all the diseases associated with dampness and tainted food.[7]

Cold, rain, and even death could be endured with stoicism, but to French soldiers navy food was simply beyond the pale. Due to food shortages in Brest, some sailors dipped into their naval reserves before they even set sail and found themselves forced into a monotonous diet of salt meat and sea biscuit. The latter, molded into a round shape that had not been manufactured for years, were suspiciously stale. The wine was even worse. Captains were clamoring for an investigation into naval procurement, which Villaret refused to do because, he explained disarmingly, "they are right."[8]

The eight thousand troops who had embarked on the Brest squadron by November 2 were far from alone. Ships also had to accommodate sailors, civilians, and the officers' large entourages. Villaret's staff alone numbered fifty-two officers, and civilian administrators like the colonial prefect, Pierre Bénézech, brought their own retinue of clerks. To these Leclerc would soon add his own aides-de-camp, servants, and a personal poet. Another 328 officers with no unit to command enlisted as supernumeraries.[9] Room also had to be found for the army's equipment, including thirty-two siege pieces, 62,300 barrels of gunpowder, 600,525 cartridges, and 120,000 flint stones. These were barely loaded when eighty fretful horses and three mules arrived in Brest with orders to embark them too (thankfully, Leclerc's dromedaries never reached Brest).[10]

The expedition had raised hopes that white planters would regain the economic prominence they had once enjoyed; so many opportunists flocked to Atlantic ports to travel on the government's dime and join in the expected gold (or rather sugar) rush. Louis Bro, the son of a Parisian lawyer, had no ties to the tropics, but he had a lifelong passion for the military profession and desperately wanted to be a part of the greatest adventure of his time. He found a spot on the *Duquesne*.[11] Alfred de Laujon, a lawyer who had spent six years in Saint-Domingue during the colony's heyday, also seized this opportunity. Despite several close brushes with death during the revolution, he had fond memories of the colony's riches and was eager to return, especially since his wife had recently become pregnant and family finances were tight. He boarded the *Scipion* in Lorient.[12]

Ships of the line, generals, and gunpowder: one might expect such martial terms to apply to an adult, male-only world, but numerous women and children could be found on the overcrowded decks of the French men-o'-war. Many officers, starting with Leclerc, brought their family; so did some soldiers. Of 641 passengers in the Brest squadron, 103 were wives, 59 children, and another 214 were various individuals of undetermined sex and age.[13] In addition to these civilians, a typical ship of the line employed dozens of teenage officer trainees (*aspirants*) and cabin boys (*mousses*). Despite their young age they were expected to serve in the midst of battle, as did the children employed by the army as drummers and fifes to set the marching pace during infantry assaults. A contingent of female cooks (*cantinières*) and prostitutes was also de rigueur. Shortly after leaving Brest the captain of the *Patriote* even discovered a female stowaway who had sneaked on board disguised in sailor slops to follow her lover bound for Saint-Domingue.[14]

By the middle of November, after a hectic month of preparations, the Brest expeditionary fleet was ready. All that was now required, an increasingly frustrated Villaret wrote repeatedly to his superiors in Paris, was for Victoire Leclerc to deign to leave the capital and take up his command.[15]

∼

The best account of Leclerc's last days on French soil was drafted by Jacques de Norvins, an aristocrat and émigré who in November 1801 was working as secretary for the prefect of Paris when his brother introduced him to Leclerc. Taken by the excitement surrounding the expedition, Norvins volunteered on a whim to follow Leclerc as his secretary. "Do you have any financial interest there?" inquired a dumbfounded Leclerc. "None," Norvins answered untruthfully. "I leave so that I can follow you; I would never do it with someone else." Only when the meeting was over did Norvins contemplate the magnitude of his decision. He left anyway to pursue "curiosity and danger" (and wealth), but he announced his decision to his mother in a letter so that he would not witness her angst in person.[16]

Pauline, who was prone to motion sickness, was the first of the Leclercs to leave Paris so that she could travel in short stages. Leclerc and Norvins caught up with her two days later in Rennes, at which point they entered a region,

Brittany, that was as alien to most Frenchmen as Saint-Domingue itself. Norvins could not help but being struck by the locals' "primitive idiom" (Briton, a Celtic language), faith in "priests and sorcerers," and their profound hatred of a republican government they had fought as *chouan* royalists just months earlier.[17]

Excitement was palpable when the small group finally reached Brest on November 18. Norvins met Isaac and Placide Louverture—"aside from their color, they were like two young Frenchmen"—as well as Coisnon, who had once been his teacher. He also visited the *bagne,* where French criminals sentenced to hard labor performed the port's most arduous tasks in conditions eerily similar to slavery. Little of that bothered leading officers, who spoke loudly of the riches awaiting them and boasted that "they had not volunteered for Saint-Domingue simply for a change of scenery."[18] With an eye to the deadly fevers awaiting them, a few of Leclerc's generals debated whether they should set up a *tontine* (a common purse to which everyone would contribute, with the proceeds to go to the last survivor), but they quickly dropped the macabre idea.

Had Leclerc reached Brest in the summer of 1801, he could have witnessed the first demonstration of a newfangled invention called the submarine (which Bonaparte rejected as thoroughly useless in naval warfare). Instead, he was treated to the impressive sight of the 110-gun, three-decked *Océan,* his and Villaret's flagship. Leclerc and Pauline took over a spacious 900-square-foot cabin that boasted elaborate woodwork, golden carpeting, and silk drapes to filter the sun from a private balcony; the poop deck above, normally destined for short-range carronades, was refurbished as a garden for Pauline's additional comfort.[19] Accommodations for lesser individuals were far more spartan. With its full crew the *Océan* carried a staggering 1,200 people, not including 500 troops and passengers and a company of rats so familiar that they always traveled on the same ship. One of the *Océan's* passengers was none other than Pauline's old lover, Louis Fréron, who had been appointed as subprefect of Cayes and was scheduled to travel with his former mistress and her current husband (Fréron found the arrangement unnerving and left on a later ship).[20]

The narrow channel linking Brest to the open ocean, beset by high tides and submerged rocks, was singularly difficult to navigate in the age of sail, so tacking against the wind was a quasi-impossibility with dozens of bulky ships of the line manned by raw sailors. The winds were favorable at first and Villaret pressed for an immediate departure. But Leclerc refused to leave Brest until he had received the cash promised by Bonaparte and a despondent Villaret had to resign himself to the fact that "the sails will go up when the piasters go in."[21] It was only on the twenty-second that the officers received three months' pay (soldiers only got one) and that Leclerc announced that the fleet could finally set sail.[22] Strong westerly winds appeared just as he gave the go-ahead.[23]

Jean-Baptiste Lemonnier-Delafosse, one of the restless sailors on the fleet, blamed all these delays on Pauline, who had allegedly held up the entire fleet because she would not abandon Paris and its nightlife. This was a misrepresentation of her role, but his analysis of the delays' military implications was more accurate. Rejecting lower-deck rumors about former slaves' poor military skills, Lemonnier feared that the weeks spent waiting for the Leclercs might give Toussaint Louverture enough time to prepare his defenses and extend the campaign into the summer months when tropical fevers would cost many a man his life.[24] He was right: a prompt departure in early November, followed by a short one-month crossing, would have brought the expedition to Cap in early December, when Louverture's army, roiled by a major cultivator uprising and unaware of the European peace, could hardly have mounted an effective defense. The missed opportunity was one of the expedition's many "what ifs."

By early December, the expedition was still bobbing impatiently in the harbor, the ships' prows facing west and inimical winds. Knowledgeable sailors feared that the westerlies, which dominate in Brittany, might last for weeks or months. Worse, the swell picked up on the eighth and soon turned into a winter gale. Several vessels broke their cables and began drifting in the middle of the night. Sick, tossed about in the jam-packed ships, the less-seasoned passengers must have wondered whether their first sea journey would end before they had even cast anchor, but the storm died down before the fleet could be too damaged.[25]

Finally, on December 13, after twenty days of unfavorable weather, the winds subsided then shifted to the northeast. At dawn the following day the ships set sail at long last and one by one they filed through the channel of Brest.[26] Aside from Villaret's flagship *Océan*, Norvins' *Patriote*, Bro's *Duquesne*, and Lemonnier's *Mont Blanc*, the squadron included vessels bearing proud revolutionary names like *Révolution* and *Jean-Jacques Rousseau* and five Spanish ships of the line. After weeks of frustration the sight of the Brest squadron as it broke into the open Atlantic was awe-inspiring. "The weather was magnificent," Lemonnier remembered. "Frost, lit by the sun, transformed the ship's sails into immense drapes of silver."[27]

As French shores sank below the horizon, some men looked forward to a life of adventure in a sensuous isle; others worried what would happen to the wives and sweethearts they had left behind. "Farewell, seductive Emilie / I leave for foreign shores" lamented a naval purser with a taste for poetry. "I know that my sincere heart / Will always cherish these sweet knots / But

Table 2.
French and foreign ships composing the squadrons of the first expedition (November 1801–January 1802).

Squadron	Date of departure	Ships of the line	Frigates	Corvettes	Transports
Brest (Adm. Louis–Thomas Villaret de Joyeuse)	Dec. 14, 1801	Cisalpin Daulo? (Sp.) Duquesne Gaulois Guerrero (Sp.) Jean-Jacques Rousseau Jemmapes Mont Blanc Neptuno (Sp.) Océan Patriote Révolution San Francisco de Asís (Sp.) San Pablo (Sp.) Wattigny	Furieuse Nécessité Précieuse Syrenne Soledad (Sp.)	Cigogne Diligente	Fidèle Fraternité Recouvré Danaé
Lorient (Adm. Jean-Louis Delmotte)	Nov. 6–Dec. 22, 1801	Scipion	Cornélie	Apollon Mignonne Rhinocéros	
Rochefort (Adm. Louis-René de Latouche-Tréville)	Nov. 6–23, 1801	Aigle Argonaute Duguay-Trouin Foudroyant Héros Union	Clorinde Embuscade Franchise Guerrière Uranie Vertu		Bayonnaise

Toulon (Adm. Honoré Ganteaume)	Dec. 28, 1801–Jan. 29, 1802	Banel Constitution Dix-Août Indivisible Jean Bart Swiffsure	Créole		Badine Mack
Cádiz (Adm. Charles-Alexandre Linois)	Jan. 18–24, 1802	Desaix (ex-Pelayo) Intrépide San Genaro	Indienne Libre Muiron		
Vlissingen (Adm. Andries Hartsinck)	Jan. 4, 1802	Ajax (Ne.) Brutus (Ne.) Jean De Wet (Ne.) Neptune (Ne.)	Poursuivante		
Le Havre (Capt. François-Jacques Meynne)	Jan. 8, 1802 [stopped in Cherbourg; left Jan. 13]		Infatigable Valeureuse Comète Revanche	Serpente Bacchante	
Total		35	21	9	5

Source: "État des troupes parties de France pour Saint-Domingue" (ca. 1806), F/5B/67, AN; "État des troupes de l'armée expéditionnaire de Saint-Domingue . . ." (Feb. 20, 1802), BB4 162, Service Historique de la Défense (Département de la Marine), Vincennes.

will you remain faithful / When I am away from your eyes?"[28] The Leclerc expedition had finally embarked on its rendezvous with destiny thankfully unaware of the fact that most of the people on board would be dead within a year.

~

Although mostly known for his victories on land, Bonaparte sailed more than any other French statesman and always displayed a keen interest in a naval profession he had once considered for himself. Unfortunately, he was not as gifted a naval strategist as a military one (only the northern tip of Corsica has anything resembling a naval tradition), and he often imposed unrealistic deadlines on his admirals, as if one could deploy fleets with the exactitude of marching infantry columns. He instructed the main squadrons of Brest, Lorient, and Rochefort to leave on the same day, meet near Belle Île, off the Atlantic coast of France, and proceed to Saint-Domingue en masse to achieve tactical surprise.[29] The vagaries of wind and sea decided otherwise.

Villaret dutifully veered south after leaving Brest and joined the Lorient squadron, but the good weather did not last long. As the fleet plied the Bay of Biscay in vain search of the Rochefort squadron, another winter gale arose, accompanied by a thick fog. Lemonnier watched in horror as the massive *Océan,* its lower yardarms dipping into the waves, running ten knots despite reefing all sails, almost crashed into his *Mont Blanc* for lack of visibility. Older ships like Bro's *Duquesne,* which had been brought back from retirement due to the shortage of transports, were suffering even more, their poorly jointed hulls leaking at a steady rate. The fleet would normally have headed west to escape the dangerous proximity of the French coast, but Villaret grimly held his station to fulfill Bonaparte's orders.[30]

His search was hopeless; Louis-René de Latouche-Tréville's Rochefort squadron had bypassed the first stop to avoid the storm and headed straight for the Canary Islands.[31] After needlessly waiting for seven days, Villaret headed west without the Spanish flagship *Neptuno* and Bro's *Duquesne,* which had rerouted to Spain to repair persistent leaks. A second stop in the Canary Islands, which Latouche had already left, proved just as pointless, and in the end the multiple rendezvous points cost unnecessary hardships and precious time while failing to ensure a joint arrival.[32] Bonaparte blamed Decrès for the blunder, then proceeded to give equally unrealistic orders in the run-up to Trafalgar.[33]

Once the first few days' storms and seasickness had subsided, the expedition settled in a routine made quarrelsome by army-navy feuds. French soldiers were prone to look down on their naval colleagues, whose poor performance in the revolutionary wars stood in stark contrast with the army's many victories on land. In typical fashion, Norvins snickered at the crass ignorance of the sailors of the *Patriote,* many of whom (who hailed from Brittany, Provence, Malta, or Sweden), could not properly pronounce the name of their own ship in French. Angry to be mocked by landlubbers, sailors answered in kind and fistfights were common.[34] The upper echelons were no better. Villaret still fumed at the unfashionable tardiness of Leclerc, who criticized Villaret's insistence on making all the stops required by Bonaparte, and the two commanders, whose collaboration was essential for a successful landing, were close to blows by the time they reached Hispaniola.[35]

Having failed to find Latouche's squadron, Villaret's fleet slowly plodded across the Atlantic at the pace set by slow units like the *Océan.*[36] Seas remained heavy; the *Océan* alone lost one man each on New Year's Eve and New Year's Day, neither of whom could be rescued from the frothy waters. Well aware that the success of the expedition depended on a joint arrival, Villaret organized his fleet in three parallel lines and insisted on a close formation. This was a difficult endeavor for ships of varying speeds traveling in choppy waters, and captains constantly sent flares to reveal their position and avoid bumping into one another. Also to preserve secrecy, Villaret sent his light units to chase every distant sail—U.S. merchantmen in particular—that might spot the fleet and warn Louverture.

Villaret's efforts were for naught. By January 17, a mere eight ships still sailed with the *Océan,* down from thirty-two when the Brest and Lorient squadrons had joined up, and U.S. gazettes had already published reports of an encounter with a mysterious westbound French fleet.[37] The rest of the fleet was spread across the Atlantic, as were the five squadrons sent from other European ports and whose fate remained unknown. Villaret was not even sure where his own ship was. Calculating one's longitude was a notoriously difficult task without an accurate watch, and when the captains compared their logs on the twenty-eighth, their calculations varied from 67'26 to 68'10—a worrisome inexactitude since they could make landfall any day now and might crash into Hispaniola if the coast was nearer than expected.

It was customary for sailors to organize a ceremony honoring the king of the tropics on a pollywog's first crossing of the Tropic of Cancer, so the fleet's arrival into warmer waters provided memoirists with plenty of colorful material. Surrounded by other sailors dressed as Neptune, slaves, and the Devil, the *Roi Tropique,* shivering in the balmy weather despite wearing heavy furs, held court on the main deck and warned newcomers that they should be baptized before entering his tropical realm. All, from grenadiers to generals, would be thrown into a big bucket of water unless they paid a bribe to be sprinkled instead. The penniless and the penny-pinchers took the plunge; others paid up. Lemonnier, who traveled on the *Patriote* with the 5th light demi-brigade, reported that the crew had collected 80 gold louis from the many newcomers on board their ship. The top brass must have been stingier, because the much larger *Océan* only yielded 50 louis. Drinking, dancing, and general merriment followed. Many sailors took this opportunity to get tattoos to protect themselves from death (black soldiers carried talismans for the same purpose, but Catholic and Vodou spells proved equally ineffective on the battlefield).[38]

Unbeknownst to the sailors rejoicing in the tropics, most of the other fleets were only setting sail at this time. The Havre squadron left on January 8, only to stop in Cherbourg due to bad weather.[39] The Toulon squadron got under way on January 9, one month behind schedule, and endured such a choppy crossing that the ships never opened their gun ports to give some fresh air to the troops huddled inside.[40] Embroiled in seniority disputes with his French colleague, the Dutch admiral commanding the Vlissingen squadron also did not leave until January. To make up for the delay, Decrès ordered that the squadron head straight for Saint-Domingue, but the hardheaded Dutch, who received a percentage of food expenditures and stood to profit from a long crossing, insisted on spending a month in the Canary Islands. The anxious French officers on board only reached Cap a full fifty-seven days after the fighting began.[41] The Cádiz squadron fared better, reaching Saint-Domingue a few days after the main fleet.[42]

The *Banel,* a Venetian ship of the line that Bonaparte had seized during his Italian campaigns, had the most eventful journey of all. Added to the Toulon fleet despite fears that she was not seaworthy, she was caught in a winter storm and foundered off the Algerian coast on January 15. Half of the seven hundred troops and crew survived the wreck, only to be robbed and captured as soon as they reached the shore. The "Moors," as French accounts described them, seemed particularly interested in the *Banel's* women and children, most likely because concubines and domestic servants, not male cultivators, were the most prized slaves in the Muslim world. With some irony the would-be colonists thus found themselves at risk of being enslaved on the Barbary Coast, where Muslim potentates routinely forced captured infidels into servitude well into the nineteenth century. Most of the *Banel's* passengers were released when Bonaparte threatened war, but local traditions hold that at least one of the nine women on board remained as the concubine of a local chief. Renamed Mama Binette, she is still considered a holy woman by local Muslims, her well-kept mausoleum a most unlikely memorial to the now-forgotten Leclerc expedition.[43]

∽

Unaware of the massive fleet about to leave Brest, in October 1801 Toussaint Louverture left on a three-week tour of Saint-Domingue's southern province.[44] He stopped in Saint-Marc to attend the marriage of Jean-Jacques Dessalines, an often cruel general who in a union of fire and water chose to wed a gentle, merciful woman named Claire-Heureuse (clear-happy). Nuptial festivities went on for days, but the hard-working governor left at 4 a.m. to inspect neighboring plantations. The groom, who served as inspector of cultivation in the western province, followed along, leaving guests to party on their own.

Meanwhile, in Cap, the city's commander, Henri Christophe, noticed on the evening of October 21 that something odd was afoot. Unknown soldiers were reported in the barracks; mysterious gatherings were taking place in the streets. As Christophe rode his horse into the pitch-dark streets to investigate, a musket ball whizzed by. Christophe charged on and captured the aggressor, a man called Trois Balles (three bullets), who under torture revealed the names of his co-conspirators. Christophe spent the rest of the night arresting suspicious individuals and disbanding barricades. So effective was he that many white inhabitants of Cap only learned when they woke up that a plot intended to kill them all had just failed.

The respite was short-lived. On the twenty-third, reports arrived from the countryside that plantation laborers had risen in revolt throughout the northern plain. Marching to the rallying cry of "death to all whites," the rebels had killed three hundred white planters. Christophe promptly defeated the main body of the rebels in Pont Rouge and arrested the commander of Limbé, Joseph Flaville, for showing a suspicious lack of energy. Rumors that the conspiracy was the brainchild of General Moyse, Louverture's adoptive nephew and likely heir, can only have added to Christophe's enthusiasm since the two held rival commands in the plain of Cap.[45]

Contrary to many officer feuds, the Moyse uprising was not merely a dispute over territory and spoils, but a true ideological struggle over the meaning of the Haitian Revolution. Louverture, Dessalines, Christophe, and many other black officers satisfied themselves with nominally freeing the slaves while taking over plantations for themselves. This, however, was too incomplete a transformation in the eyes of many cultivators who hated the plantation system, even one that benefited black officers. Appalled by Louverture's recent overtures to Jamaican slave traders, some plantation laborers even feared that he might restore slavery.

Moyse was the rare officer sympathetic to the cultivators' cause. "I cannot convince myself to be the executor of my own color," he explained as he refused to enforce his uncle's harsh labor code.[46] He never had a chance to articulate his long-term goals, but he probably intended to dismantle large estates and legalize small-scale farming, after which Saint-Domingue would become a republic of independent black yeomen and Moyse—Moses—would set his people free.[47] History would show that he was the precursor of the modern Haitian state.

For Louverture, after three years of personal rule and adulatory speeches, the revolt was a rude reminder of his own unpopularity and a direct challenge to his plans for the revival of Saint-Domingue's economy. Because he had often engineered fake popular demonstrations in the past, many theories circulated that he was the true force behind the uprising, but his actions after he learned of the revolt abundantly proved that his anger was genuine.[48] After calling on his allies in Jamaica for military assistance, he ordered Dessalines, who had committed many of the labor abuses that were the root cause of Moyse's ire, to crush the revolt.[49] Christophe had largely subdued the rebellion already, but in a wrathful honeymoon Dessalines massacred a quarter of Plaisance's cultivators as he moved north.

Louverture entered Cap on November 4, still fuming at the thought that his own nephew had rebelled against him. As he reached the main plaza he formed the troops in a square and angrily reminded them of their ingratitude. It was a sign of Louverture's extraordinary authority and courage that he dared face the armed throngs, virtually alone, with only the power of his words to whip them back into shape. One by one he ordered the officers who had plotted against him to denounce themselves; one by one they stepped out of the ranks and, on his command, killed themselves on the spot. Joseph Flaville, Trois Balles, and the other main conspirators were ripped to shreds with grapeshot in the middle of the square. To Vodou devotees, the usually composed Louverture, who always delegated his bloodiest work to Dessalines, must have seemed transfigured, as if possessed by a vengeful *lwa* (spirit). Louverture and Dessalines then toured the area to decimate rebellious plantations and execute Vodou priests, often using the messy bayonet instead of guns. The number of black cultivators executed after the uprising reached two thousand in the plain of Cap alone, and possibly five thousand overall.[50]

Moyse insisted on his innocence, but Louverture ordered him jailed in Port-de-Paix while he assembled a court-martial in Cap. The presiding officers hesitated to judge Moyse without giving him a chance to defend himself, but at Louverture's insistence they promptly rendered a unanimous guilty verdict. In a last display of courage, Moyse personally gave the firing orders to the squad that shot him.[51]

Had Christophe not nipped the uprising in the bud, it would probably have spread throughout the colony. Louverture's fury grew as he fully realized the magnitude of the threat he had so narrowly avoided. On November 14, three weeks after the uprising, another twenty suspected conspirators were shot in

Cap, and Louverture warned that he was not finished yet.[52] Ten days later, in a bitter speech addressed to the population of Cap, he railed against the people "without religion or morals" (Vodou followers) who were responsible for the revolt. In a likely reference to his adoptive nephew, he also dwelled at length on the duties of parents and children. Parents neglected to educate their offspring, Louverture fumed, so boys turned to vagrancy, daughters to prostitution, and towns like Cap were untrustworthy havens of thieves and libertines; the lazy cultivators of the countryside were scarcely better. After he was done calling his listeners laggards and whores, Louverture listed a set of punitive measures, including a law sentencing persons of color who made statements that might alter public order to the death penalty.[53]

The Moyse uprising must have left Louverture overwhelmed with raw feelings of sadness and anger. Having failed to understand the deep yearning for land ownership among the black masses, he had found himself obliged to kill his own nephew. Moyse was a trusted associate whom Louverture had used in difficult assignments like the invasion of Santo Domingo and whom he had recently promoted to division general, a rank only Dessalines had achieved. Just four months before, Louverture had sent heartfelt condolences upon the death of Moyse's son, and it is highly possible that Louverture had selected him as his successor, as the 1801 constitution gave him the right to do.[54] Now it was Louverture who would outlive Moyse.

Another close associate had died. Bayon de Libertat, the plantation manager under whom Louverture had spent the first four decades of his life, was among the three hundred planters massacred during the uprising. Louverture could be coldhearted at times, but Libertat had manumitted him, and his death must have affected him deeply.[55] Louverture's brother Pierre had died eight years before; his other brother Paul was in Santo Domingo; his two sons were hostages in Paris. For the aging Louverture, absolute power was a realm of near-absolute loneliness.

∼

International developments were another source of irritation for Louverture, who despite courting the British and U.S. governments throughout 1801 had yet to seal a defensive alliance when the Moyse uprising broke out.[56] The new U.S. president, Thomas Jefferson, had proved a difficult partner. He had recalled the U.S. consul in Cap—a close supporter of Louverture who rented his own residence from the governor—and replaced him with Tobias Lear, a failed businessman who had volunteered for the job primarily to make money. Lear bore the neutral title of "commercial agent" and had come with no letter of introduction, prompting Louverture to complain that "his color was the cause of his being neglected, and not thought worthy of the usual attentions."[57] Both Jefferson and Lear were slave owners; Louverture also learned that some U.S. captains had abused their trading privileges by abducting black Dominguians and selling them in the U.S. South.[58]

The British had proved even more difficult, seizing many of his ships on technicalities and even carrying out raids on Saint-Domingue soil despite a 1799 treaty of nonaggression.[59] The British navy would be Louverture's first line of defense in the event of a French invasion, and he labored ceaselessly for a new treaty despite his growing anger. But the negotiations proceeded slowly because a new governor sent to Jamaica died before he could take office.[60] It was not until November that a treaty was finally ready—only to be cast aside when the new governor of Jamaica abruptly canceled all negotiations and his consul in Port Républicain asked all British citizens to evacuate Saint-Domingue.[61] Louverture soon learned the reason for this sudden turnaround. Something even more horrible than war had taken place in Europe: peace.

In the weeks that had followed the Moyse uprising, Louverture had prevented U.S. merchants from leaving Cap for fear of sparking a panic in U.S. ports.[62] As planned, U.S. newspapers only reported on the uprising after it had been safely contained, but the embargo had the unintended effect of cutting off all incoming news at a critical time. News of the London peace preliminaries reached the United States by November 11 and Jamaica by the twenty-ninth, but it was not until early December that Jamaican envoys informed Louverture that for two full months the war had been over in Europe.[63]

The peace could not have come at a worse time. To defend white planters targeted by the Moyse uprising, Louverture had alienated the black laborers who would be his primary supporters in the event of a French invasion, only to learn as the last firing squad finished its ghastly chore that France was now free to attack him. That Bonaparte had failed to notify him of the peace preliminaries was a singularly bad omen, and a British agent described Louverture as "exceedingly depressed."[64] In a bizarre speech delivered in Port Républicain, Louverture first denied rumors that France was sending an army with "liberticidal" goals, then, shifting to this very eventuality, warned that he stood ready to fight. "A good child must show submission and obedience to his mother," he explained in reference to the colonial bond. "But should the mother become so denatured as to seek the destruction of her child, the child must obtain vengeance, God willing. Should I die, I will die as a brave soldier, as a man of honor; I fear no one."[65] Weeks later came reports that Bonaparte was indeed readying an expedition.[66]

Some authors have written that Louverture, who had heard many times before of a possible French expedition, brushed off the latest peace scare and neglected to build up his defenses.[67] In fact, he immediately went to work on a defensive strategy, a domain in which his keen political sense and long experience gave him a distinct edge over Bonaparte and Leclerc.[68] In their planning the French made almost no reference to the failed Spanish and British invasions of the 1790s because they were convinced that they could easily prevail where their despised rivals had failed. Louverture, by contrast, viewed the upcoming conflict as a continuation of a decade-long struggle for colonial autonomy and drew valuable lessons from previous European failures. White troops had proven particularly vulnerable to tropical fevers, guerilla warfare, and reliance on imported food and troops. Louverture incorporated these lessons—the very ones Bonaparte had overlooked—into his own strategy.

Louverture's plan was to station troops in all major ports of the colony and to contest a French expedition from the outset. Defending Saint-Domingue's long coastline would likely be difficult, but even if they prevailed the French would only conquer a mound of ashes. Louverture's subordinates were under orders to burn everything as they retreated to the mountains, where they would live off local crops grown by female cultivators. They would then wage a war of ambushes that could be considered a success as long as French casualties mounted and the fighting dragged on. The coup de grâce would come with the summer, when the French, short on food and decimated by fevers, would have to leave or die.[69]

Six years before the Peninsular War, in which the term *guerrilla* was coined, Louverture had perfected the principles of partisan warfare. One hundred years before the twentieth century's great wars, he was also preparing for a total war, in which indoctrination and economic warfare would be as essential to victory as the fighting itself. Louverture had refused to publicize Bonaparte's many commitments to emancipation and planned to appeal to the laboring classes by claiming that the French had come to restore slavery.[70] In a revealing letter he explained in considerable detail how a local commander should secure the printing press, an essential tool in a propaganda war.[71] He also paid particular attention to his supplies. The revival of the colonial economy allowed him to buy twenty-five to thirty thousand guns from U.S. merchants, which joined the large stockpiles accumulated during a decade of fighting.[72] U.S. historians have failed to find much evidence in U.S. mercantile records that U.S. merchants supplied Louverture, but French-language sources leave no doubt. In June 1800 his treasurer, a French administrator named Jean-Baptiste Vollée, wrote Louverture that a Captain Daniels had arrived from Baltimore with five hundred barrels of flour. "He also brought in the greatest secrecy—and this is the reason why I am writing myself—21 barrels of corn containing 294 small casks of powder." Vollée added that the ship's owner, who owned a gunpowder factory, was eager to send more.[73]

European observers unanimously described Louverture's troops as a hardened, disciplined lot. Contrary to an oft-repeated Haitian claim, there is little evidence that prominent Haitian revolutionary generals like Henri Christophe were veterans of the colored battalions that had fought in the American Revolution.[74] Instead, many drew on the military traditions of prerevolutionary runaway communities—and, ultimately, African warriors.[75] All had also acquired extensive military experience during the decade-long Haitian Revolution. They were largely immune to tropical diseases, knew how to live off the countryside, and were deeply committed to their freedom. Their tactical skills still left much to be desired in a conventional pitched battle, but they were mobile, enduring troops who were well suited for the insurrectionary war that Louverture envisioned.

Contemporaries generally estimated Louverture's professional army at 20,000 troops (out of a pool of 60,000 men able to bear arms), but such numbers are subject to caution.[76] Louverture and his officers were known to pad army rosters for personal gain, so on paper Louverture's army amounted to fifteen demi-brigades of 1,500 men, when he had at most thirteen demi-brigades of 1,200 men. Declaring artificially high salaries for his unpaid, and occasionally nonexistent, troops allowed Louverture and his treasurer to demand a 16.5 million francs appropriation for an army that cost only 4.5 million and spirit away the budget surplus to build up a war chest. Vollée (stolen) truly deserved his name.[77]

In February 1801 Louverture had ordered that a gendarmerie be put together, but local municipalities, which were expected to pay for and quarter the force, had dragged their feet. When the gendarmerie of Fort Liberté was finally operational in December 1801, it only amounted to two officers and nineteen soldiers, enough to maintain order but too few to repel an invasion.[78] In July Louverture had also ordered that all men from fourteen to fifty-one years of age be enlisted in a national guard, but it is not clear how combat-ready such units were by early 1802.[79] When he learned of the European peace, Louverture began aggressively recruiting men and requisitioning horses for his standing army, but like Bonaparte he faced permanent draft dodging on the part of an unenthusiastic citizenry. In one drill only 10 percent of the cultivators rushed to army headquarters when the alarm was sounded.[80]

While Bonaparte, in Paris, debated whether to send officers of color with the expedition, Louverture, in Cap, wondered what to do with Saint-Domingue's white population. He deported the Creole general commanding

Table 3.
Toussaint Louverture's army (estimate).

Unit	Location	Size
Division of the North (Henri Christophe)		
2nd colonial demi-brigade	Cap and Limbé	1,200
5th colonial demi-brigade	Fort Liberté	1,200
9th colonial demi-brigade	Port-de-Paix	1,200
Guides		300
Artillery and gendarmerie		900
Division of the South and West (Jean-Jacques Dessalines)		
3rd colonial demi-brigade	Port Républicain	1,200
4th colonial demi-brigade	Saint-Marc, Jérémie	1,200
7th colonial demi-brigade	Arcahaye	1,200
8th colonial demi-brigade	Cayes	1,200
11th colonial demi-brigade	Cayes	1,200
12th colonial demi-brigade	Cayes	1,200
13th colonial demi-brigade	Port Républicain	1,200
European battalion	Cayes	250
Guides		300
Artillery and gendarmerie		900
Honor guard	Port Républicain	1,800
Division of the East (Augustin Clervaux)		
1st colonial demi-brigade	Sámana	1,200
2nd colonial demi-brigade	Santiago	1,200
10th colonial demi-brigade	Santo Domingo	1,200
Guides		200
Artillery and gendarmerie		400
Recap		
Division of the North		4,800
Division of the South and West		11,650
Division of the East		4,200
	Total	20,650 troops

Source: Pamphile de Lacroix, *La révolution de Haïti* (1819; reprint, Paris: Karthala, 1995), 284.

Fort Liberté, François Pageot, but he also hoped that some idealistic French officers would side with him and kept Pierre Agé, the commander of Port Républicain, in his post.[81] White planters were a more problematic group. In a long speech Louverture reminded them of all that he had done for them and begged for their loyalty, but he also sent two planters to prison for gloating that French troops would soon restore slavery and, weeks after executing Moyse for plotting to massacre white planters, he told his officers to be ready to kill all white civilians as soon as the French landed.[82] In an unusually personal moment he told his colleagues of a white man who had humiliated him as a slave, and whom he had killed when the 1791 slave revolt had offered him the opportunity to settle old scores.[83] Massacres may also have been designed to cement the loyalty of his subordinates, who could hardly defect to the French side after killing white planters.[84]

As the Moyse uprising had made painfully clear, the main flaw in Louverture's defensive strategy was that he faced many enemies within his own camp. He sought to reconcile himself with mixed-race individuals, but it would take time before they forgot or forgave the brutal repression that had followed his victory over André Rigaud during the War of the South. In Grande Anse, an area where white and mixed-race planters shared ancient family ties, white planters and *anciens libres* agreed not to sound the alarm cannon at the arrival of the French troops so as to give the local black cultivators no time to take up arms.[85] The intentions of the plantation runaways living in the mountains were equally uncertain, and Louverture asked his 13th demi-brigade to closely monitor the Maniel group led by his longtime rival Lafortune.[86]

Intriguingly, Louverture still thought at this late stage that he might reach an agreement with Bonaparte. Early in 1802 he sent the white planter Merceron the Elder with a letter in which he again asked Bonaparte to draft a personal note and send back his sons. "Make him comprehend that in losing me he will lose . . . not only Saint-Domingue but all the West Indian colonies," he told Merceron.[87] Merceron never reached his destination (and would have arrived much too late at any rate), but Louverture's hopes for last-minute deal-making are fascinating in retrospect given Bonaparte's own hesitations. Weeks before the first clash of arms, the two statesmen were closer to reconciliation than one might think.

By January 1802, one month after learning of the European peace, Louverture was ready for a French invasion (though he could be concerned about the loyalty of many of his subjects), and he left for Santo Domingo to deliver his instructions to his brother Paul, who was in charge of the local garrison.[88] Overall, France's excellent troops and superior tactics made Leclerc's army the odds-on favorite in any standard encounter with Louverture's. Bonaparte's long-term planning, however, was poor, so ultimate victory was likely to rest on the rebel side should the war drag on for months or years, as Louverture hoped. France's ability to prevail quickly, prior to the onset of the deadly summer months and any renewal of hostilities with England, would make or break the expedition. Ultimately, Saint-Domingue's future would hinge on a few weeks' fighting in early 1802.

5

Parley

The French Landing

On January 29, 1802, after forty-six days at sea, the main French fleet sighted Cape Sámana at the northeastern tip of Hispaniola. Sailors and troops scurried about the decks excitedly, eager to catch their first glimpse of the fabled isle whose verdant fronds undulated with the trade winds above the turquoise waters. Forty-four years later, the sailor Jean-Baptiste Lemonnier-Delafosse could still remember each detail of this wondrous day. "Every morning, the fleet sailed closer to the shores of Saint-Domingue, which exhaled, at dawn, the thousand scents of a bouquet that one could smell but not see.... Delicious perfumes in comparison with the deleterious emanations from our ship!"[1]

As Sámana Bay came into view, Admiral Louis-Thomas Villaret de Joyeuse realized that the Rochefort squadron had preceded him there; so had many of the ships, like Jacques de Norvins' *Patriote,* that had lost contact with the Brest fleet in the mid-Atlantic.[2] Villaret was relieved to learn that most of the ships under his command had made it across the ocean safely. But the staggered arrivals also meant that despite all Villaret's efforts to preserve secrecy, Toussaint Louverture might have learned of the French arrival in time to take defensive measures (he was in fact observing the fleet's maneuvers in person).

Surrounded by a seemingly invincible armada, Victoire Leclerc did not share Villaret's concerns. Upon learning that officers of color had just rebelled in Guadeloupe, he boasted that he should have made a quick stop on that island, where he would have subdued the uprising in a mere week or two.[3] According to Louverture's memoirs, Leclerc learned of his presence in Sámana but was so intent on taking the colony by force that he refused to let Louverture's sons disembark and give peace a chance.[4]

The following week, which saw multiple landings in Cap and other cities of the colony, was destined to become the most eventful and hotly debated period in the expedition. Depending on their agenda, authors have alternatively blamed Leclerc or Louverture for the breakdown of negotiations and the outbreak of fighting. But Leclerc's mission was to replace Louverture in office, while Louverture's abiding goal was to prevent such a thing, and it is hard to see how events could have unfolded amicably when two men competed for a single post. The only question left open-ended was whether the French would prevail quickly enough to avert the destruction of the main ports.

Military matters were further complicated by the fact that the troops on both sides served the same republic and that no one wished to take the responsibility of launching an unprovoked assault on fellow Frenchmen. Leclerc thus courted a fight while pretending to negotiate to defuse the concerns of the black cultivators. Meanwhile, Louverture secretly urged his subordinates to resist any landing while obfuscating his role to avoid declaring himself in open rebellion with France. The result was a complicated game of bluff in which everyone spoke of peace while marching unstoppably toward a tragic end.

Considering that time was of the essence, the French campaign began quite leisurely. The fleet wasted three precious days transferring troops from one ship to the other in preparation for the various landings because units had been embarked pell-mell in Brest. In all, the short trip from Sámana to Cap took five days (by comparison, Bonaparte had taken Alexandria twelve hours after landing in Egypt).[5] François de Kerversau and Charles de Vincent had submitted detailed contingency plans before his departure, but it was in Sámana that Leclerc suddenly requested some last-minute advice on how to overcome Cap's defenses.[6] It was also in Sámana that Villaret realized that he had somehow forgotten to embark pilots familiar with the port of Cap, an incredible snafu considering that the city was his main strategic objective.[7]

The blunder became even more evident when the French fleet finally reached Cap, only to realize that the buoys marking the entrance to the port had been taken away.[8] Leclerc, whom Bonaparte had instructed to take Cap in one day to prevent it from being burned, insisted on an immediate landing despite the risks of hitting unmarked reefs. But Villaret, in the cautious attitude typical of this era's French navy, replied that he would not risk a contested landing without pilots under the converging fire of Cap's formidable forts. Interservice rivalry and basic incompetence meant that the landing in Cap now depended on the goodwill of the black commander of Cap, Henri Christophe.

Born on an English island (probably Grenada or St. Christopher), Christophe had once worked as a waiter at a Cap inn and had a sophisticated, cosmopolitan demeanor that made him far more popular in Western accounts than the unpolished Dessalines. A rich plantation owner known for the magnificent parties he threw in his Cap mansion, he had a vested interest in averting the destruction of the city. The only issue likely to sway him was slavery. Although often described as an *ancien libre,* Christophe was a recently freed slave with a genuine attachment to the 1794 law of emancipation, and Vincent and Philippe Roume had identified him as the black general most likely to support Louverture's overthrow if individual freedom remained the norm.[9]

Informed by a U.S. merchant of the French fleet's arrival two days before it reached Cap, Christophe initially rejoiced and prepared to welcome the French troops with open arms. By the time the fleet sighted Cap, however, he had become overtly hostile, summarily executing a white officer and ordering his gunners to fire on a French cutter that had sailed too close to shore. A likely reason for his sudden change of heart was that Louverture, who had raced Villaret's slow-moving fleet ever since witnessing its arrival in Sámana, had reached Cap just in time to ensure his subordinate's loyalty. Louverture would later insist that he was absent from Cap during the French landing to reject any responsibility for the events that took place there, but his taste for deception and the general chronology say otherwise. Several reliable witnesses place him in the city.[10] Grocery bills dated January 31, 1802, also suggest his presence. Ominously, his last purchase was burning oil.[11]

Louverture's alleged absence considerably complicated Leclerc's mission, since his orders were to open negotiations and he had no one to talk to. Christophe compounded the problem when he notified Leclerc that he was under strict orders not to let any fleet sail into the port without Louverture's personal go-ahead, which might take a few days as the governor was out of town. Leclerc abruptly answered that all the forts should be evacuated at once or he would treat Christophe as a rebel and land fifteen thousand troops while another twelve thousand attacked nearby cities (both numbers were exaggerations).[12]

The threats failed to sway Christophe. Leclerc's aide-de-camp, sent on shore to deliver Leclerc's peremptory response, noticed that during their meeting Christophe made frequent visits to a nearby room to consult a mysterious interlocutor and surmised that Louverture was monitoring the negotiations behind the scenes. Probably at Louverture's demand, Christophe begged Leclerc to wait another two days and warned that he would contest a French landing otherwise.[13]

A more astute or obstinate officer than Leclerc would have seen through the ruse and attacked at once. In Fort Liberté, which 1,800 French troops were simultaneously approaching, Donatien de Rochambeau bypassed preliminary negotiations and immediately proceeded with the attack. The channel leading into the bay of Fort Liberté and the city itself were defended by several powerful forts, but Rochambeau landed six hundred crack troops of the 5th light demi-brigade to clear out the approaches to the bay. As they neared the fort of La Bouque, the French assured their opponents that they were "your brothers, your friends, who bring you liberty," only to end their short-lived attempt at battlefield political discourse when the fort's defenders opened fire.[14] The French stormed the first ring of fortifications with characteristic élan and quickly overwhelmed the defenders. In the nearby battery of l'Anse, a sergeant sneaked into the fortified perimeter alone, but so determinedly that the entire garrison, convinced that he must have been the vanguard of a larger force, fled before him. With the entrance to the bay cleared, the French naval squadron, five ships strong, sailed into the bay in a compact mass. After firing a broadside into one last fort towering above the city, the ships veered sharply to fire the rest of their cannon, then launched their shallops before the land batteries could respond. The troops stormed the fort, and the garrison fled with such haste that it did not have enough time to burn the town. Lemonnier, who sailed in the fleet, could be proud. Twelve French soldiers and two officers had died, including Rochambeau's nephew Alphonse-Louis de la Châtre, killed gloriously while leading the assault on La Bouque; but the city had fallen intact in a matter of hours.

News from the landing in Fort Liberté hardened Leclerc's and Christophe's stance. French troops had found written orders from Louverture (probably left as he made his way to Cap) to resist any French landing, thus confirming Leclerc's suspicions that Christophe had no intention of ever allowing the French ashore. Christophe, for his part, complained that Leclerc was negotiating in bad faith, speaking of peace while storming nearby cities. Sensing that Cap stood on the brink of ruin, city notables formed a delegation in a last-ditch attempt to reach a negotiated settlement. At its head was the Martinique-born black mayor of Cap, César Télémaque. He had once been a slave servant in Paris (where Leclerc's secretary, Norvins, had met him as a child), but he had been free for most of his adult life, was married to a Frenchwoman, and was an out-and-out Francophile.[15] Christophe remained deaf to his supplications, as did Leclerc when he met him offshore, and after a most fruitless night the Télémaque delegation rowed back to the distant shore for one last, equally ineffective attempt to mollify Christophe.

War it was, but Télémaque's example showed that the loyalty of Cap's population of color was far from assured for Louverture. On his way to meet Christophe, Leclerc's aide-de-camp had purposely dropped a packet containing copies of Bonaparte's proclamation, which reiterated France's commitment to emancipation and had a marked impact on black public opinion. To counter its effect, Christophe gathered his troops to warn them that Bonaparte's reassurances notwithstanding the French had come "to ravish their freedom."[16] He also locked the gendarmes and national guardsmen inside their barracks, probably for fear that the many urban *anciens libres* among them would side with the French. In a clear sign that he intended to make good on his threats to torch the city, Christophe distributed combustibles and emptied his own house of valuables. A flood of armed blacks from the provinces streamed into the city, some of them moved by fears that the French had come to restore slavery, others attracted by the promise of an open city ripe for looting.

Now convinced that Christophe was only stalling for time, Leclerc finally decided to attack and would have done so at once had a strong land breeze not pushed the French fleet several miles alee. Drawing from the plan of attack prepared in Sámana, Leclerc thus chose to land west of the city while Rochambeau rushed from Fort Liberté to the east. The planners had identified the bay of Acul as the most convenient landing site (as had Bonaparte in his instructions), but a mysterious captain named Toulouze approached Leclerc with information that a better spot could be found in Port Margot farther west. Toulouze was actually a white supporter of Louverture who had proposed the alternate site because it was distant and difficult to access, but Leclerc fell into the trap.[17]

Early on the fourth, Leclerc led a flotilla of small units westward while a sulking Villaret remained near Cap with the ships of the line, whose draft was unsuitable for amphibious operations. Officers familiar with the coast, still unaware of Leclerc's change of plans, watched incredulously as his flagship frigate sailed past the bay of Acul. It took hours before the fleet reached the Limbé dock near Port Margot, then many more hours to ferry the troops to the shore, particularly distant in this spot. Leclerc could consider himself lucky that local defenders offered limited resistance, because the frigates were too far to offer covering fire, and a gun battery defending the dock could easily have decimated landing parties. Only 2,400 men had landed by the morning of the fifth, when an increasingly anxious Leclerc, realizing that he was wasting valuable time, ordered them to head for Cap at once.

The area had been hit hard by the repression that had followed the Moyse uprising, so the French found local supporters as soon as they made their intentions clear. Scores of armed cultivators initially fought back, convinced that they were facing "Spaniards and Englishmen who had come to kill them all" (probably a rumor spread on Louverture's orders).[18] Leclerc urged his overeager troops to show mercy, and many locals, unwilling to die for the unpopular Louverture, quickly surrendered when they learned the identity of their opponents. "When we took up arms with Moyse against the whites, didn't the governor exterminate us?" exclaimed a cultivator. "Why doesn't he resuscitate Moyse, if he wants to fight the whites!"[19] Louverture, probably on his way to Port-de-Paix after his surreptitious stop in Cap, found few friends in the area. Near his plantation at Héricourt, he bumped into the first lines of the division of Jean Hardÿ and was almost killed when a bullet hit his horse. Caught with only a few members of his personal guard, Louverture prudently retreated after a half-hour firefight that could have changed the course of the war on its very first day.[20]

Meanwhile, Villaret, still aghast by Leclerc's accusation that he lacked daring, learned from the U.S. commercial agent in Cap that the forts guarding the port had been left unguarded.[21] He immediately sent two of his ships to challenge the forts, and the main gun decks were cleared in record time as Norvins (on the *Patriote*) and the lawyer Alfred de Laujon (on the *Scipion*) watched in awe. The two 74s discharged a few thunderous broadsides and the forts "more or less fell into the sea, with their cannons and a few corpses," Norvins remembered.[22]

Mistaking the distant sound of broadsides for a general naval assault, Christophe ordered Cap set ablaze. Houses, including Christophe's own, were set on fire; boiling sugar poured into the streets while overheated barrels of rum blew up with a hundred-proof roar. Public buildings were particularly targeted: three times, Christophe's men set the Providence Hospital on fire, only to see the flames extinguished by the sick and the infirm. The destruction culminated when the arsenal, loaded with gunpowder, exploded in a blast that shook the entire city to its foundations and tipped over most of the houses spared by the fire. André Rigaud's mixed-race followers, whom Leclerc had left on the frigate *Vertu* and who were convinced that they would be deported if the landing went well, watched happily as flames rose in the distance. "Now, we won't go to Madagascar," one officer of color exclaimed happily.[23] If the rest of the colony followed Cap's example, Leclerc would need all the help he could get.

Seeing that the city was aflame, Villaret rushed his fleet into the port as soon as the morning breeze picked up early on the sixth. Most army troops were with Leclerc, so the landing parties were an odd mix of civilians and sailors. Laujon and Norvins, dressed like pirates, landed with the rest, only to be met by throngs of children calling them "*papa blan.*"[24] They conquered what was left of the city while Christophe's men retreated to the interior. Then, like true pirates, they proceeded to loot what little had survived the fire.

Leclerc was still nowhere to be seen. The day before the city was taken, he reached Acul, where he should have landed a day before, only to pause to give his freshly debarked troops some time to catch up. As night fell the red glow that engulfed the horizon showed that Christophe had made good on his threats and that Leclerc had failed to save Cap. Adding insult to injury the army's vanguard ran into Norvins and other French sailors when it finally reached Haut du Cap on the sixth, thus giving a fitting conclusion to a week of army-navy infighting. The only silver lining was that a thousand civilians from Cap, who had been sent to Haut du Cap to be executed, had taken various detours through the hills (possibly with Christophe's tacit approval) and were still alive when the French navy entered Cap.

Leclerc could only survey the devastation as he finally reached the city later that day. Ninety percent of Cap lay in ruins, leaving only sixty houses standing; the cost to U.S. merchants alone was estimated at three hundred thousand dollars in burned cargo.[25] Louverture's scorched-earth policy, so central to his long-term strategy, had met its first success: the colony's commercial center, far from providing the expedition with the bulk of its resources, would be a major drain on its finances as it struggled to rebuild. Norvins found Cap a depressing city once the exhilaration of his pirate raid had worn off. The expedition's plethoric top brass commandeered the few surviving houses, so Norvins spent his first night inside a half-demolished house and awoke to the acrid smell of charred coffee, caramel, and burning rum. Scouring the city for two of his relatives he knew to be living in Cap, he learned that one of them, stabbed by a trusted black servant during the landing, was dead.[26] As for Laujon, who had kept fond memories of his stay in prerevolutionary Saint-Domingue, he was treated to the nightmarish sight of "corpses amidst the rubble" and "half-burned bodies with arms, legs, and heads peeking under masses of stone."[27] Cap had burned in 1753; the surrounding plantations had gone up in flames during the 1791 slave uprising; it had burned again in 1793 during some French officers' feud. After their narrow brush with death, the inhabitants set up tents against the stone walls still standing amid the smoldering ruins and began rebuilding their city yet again.

A humbled Leclerc, unsure how to tell the first consul that the Paris of the Antilles lay in ruins before his eyes, waited three days before he wrote to Minister of the Navy Denis Decrès about the landing, and even then only made a passing remark about the fire. Eager to spread the blame for the expedition's first disaster, he accused sailors of "insubordination" and "looting," criticized Villaret as "irresolute," and described U.S. merchants as "veritable Jews with whom one cannot reach a decent deal."[28] He then set out to conquer the rest of the colony.

～

In the days that followed the landings in Cap and Fort Liberté, Leclerc received the first reports on the various military operations that had taken place elsewhere in Hispaniola. Most of them had been one-sided French triumphs, though Leclerc did not know whether he should rejoice at the good news or fear that his colleagues' success would reflect badly on his own unsatisfactory record.

François de Kerversau had been tasked with the capture of the city of Santo Domingo, where he had once served as agent. To complete this difficult mission he was only given two unarmed frigates, one cannon, and 450 men when the city was ringed by stone fortifications flecked with one hundred cannon and garrisoned by 1,200 troops under Louverture's brother Paul. Short on troops, Kerversau relied on ruse. He pressured Paul so mercilessly to let his troops land that the irresolute general, whom Louverture had instructed to resist a French landing during his recent visit, wavered and sent couriers to ask his brother for further instructions. Louverture replied that Kerversau should not be allowed ashore at any cost; but he also drafted a second, bogus letter, which the courier was to show French soldiers if he ever was questioned, urging Paul to collaborate with the French. The courier was intercepted and Kerversau cleverly showed Paul the second letter. Paul must have had his doubts about his brother's sudden change of mind, but the letter was authentic and the local Spanish population restless. He thus made his submission against the solemn promise that slavery would never be restored in Saint-Domingue.[29]

The second-largest city in Spanish Santo Domingo was Santiago, whose defense Louverture had entrusted to Augustin Clervaux. A light-skinned, French-educated officer, Clervaux was disinclined to fight his countrymen, as was Guillaume Mauviel, an ambitious French cleric still upset that Louverture had refused to appoint him as colonial bishop a year earlier. Forced to choose between Louverture and the French Republic, Clervaux quickly surrendered at Mauviel's urging.[30] With Santiago's submission, the French had now taken the entire Spanish part of the island—two-thirds of Hispaniola—without firing a shot. Kerversau was even able to send Paul Louverture's black troops to Leclerc, along with 1 million francs in cash.

Meanwhile, three thousand troops under Jean Boudet neared Port Républicain, Saint-Domingue's second-largest city. Following the agreed-upon procedure, Boudet sent his aide-de-camp with Bonaparte's proclamation and a letter demanding that French troops be permitted to land. Dessalines was out of town at the time, leaving the white general, Pierre Agé, in charge, but a light-skinned battalion chief, Louis Lamartinière, stripped him of his command and refused to allow the French to land until Dessalines' return.

Having quickly exhausted his diplomatic options, Boudet prepared to attack. The town's main fort, recently reinforced with six hundred troops, should have been able to resist any French assault, but the garrison was led by a mixed-race general who had never forgiven Louverture for his war against Rigaud and promptly surrendered. Once the fort was secured French troops proceeded up the coast to the Léogane gate, where they told the defenders that they "had come with the olive branch of peace."[31] This garrison, which included many of Louverture's elite *guides,* chose to fight, forcing the French to trade the olive branch for sharper-edged implements. They took the redoubt sword in hand under the covering fire of the naval squadron and secured the city in a matter of hours with a mere twenty-five dead. The defenders who did not join the French side left to join Dessalines, taking Boudet's envoy, Agé, and three hundred white hostages with them. Port République had been captured intact, and its treasury yielded a windfall in cash for the French officers. A large cache of Louverture's letters was also seized, as was his secretary Pascal, who was promptly sent to Cap to reveal what he knew of Louverture's plans.[32]

With all of Hispaniola's main ports in French hands, Leclerc next set his sights on Port-de-Paix, a sizable city west of Cap and a jumping-off point to the strategic port of Môle Saint-Nicolas and the island of La Tortue. Vincent had warned that it was well defended by land and sea, but as usual Leclerc ignored the contingency plans drafted in Paris and sent Jean Humbert with twelve hundred men, one ship of the line, and two frigates to take the city by force. Port-de-Paix was under the command of the black general Jacques Maurepas (a.k.a. Morpas), whom an admiring French subordinate later described as "good-looking, gentle, sensitive to fashion, splendid in all ways," and an ardent Francophile.[33] But his patriotism took second place to his personal allegiance to Louverture, and he proved to be one of France's bravest adversaries. When Humbert sent two parliamentarians with Bonaparte's proclamation, Maurepas kept them hostage, and Humbert had to ask the fleet to force its way into the port. A barrage of hot shot, unfavorable winds, and—as always—a lack of qualified pilots forced the ships to retreat and spend the night tacking offshore. Maurepas used the short respite to send women, children, and white prisoners to the interior, then burned the town and retreated to a fortified plantation as Humbert's troops landed the following day. When an overzealous Humbert pressed the assault over soggy trails littered with booby traps, Maurepas inflicted a heavy loss of two hundred men on the attackers. Survivors limped back to town, harassed by female skirmishers along the way, and Humbert barely managed to hold on to what remained of Port-de-Paix while Leclerc rushed reinforcements from Cap. This was the first time that the expeditionary army had been defeated in combat.[34]

∽

With the exception of Port-de-Paix, Louverture's army had lost one city after another without much of a fight and often without any destruction; that Port République had fallen intact particularly saddened him. "What a pity that a traitor lost the town and that our orders [to burn the town] were ignored!" lamented Louverture in a letter to Dessalines. "Try, by any means, to burn the city; it is built in wood; it is only a matter of sending a few faithful emissaries. . . . Don't forget that until the rainy season rids us of our enemies our only resources are fire and destruction."[35] Meanwhile, always careful to hedge his bets, Louverture wrote to Leclerc that the Franco-French fighting had been one tragic misunderstanding and asked—seriously, it seems—that the money taken from the Port Républicain treasury be sent back to him.[36]

Standing in the ruins of Cap, Leclerc could not dismiss Louverture's overtures outright. A halfhearted effort at diplomacy would help his standing with Bonaparte, who had hoped that Leclerc would attract local commanders to his side and might be displeased to learn that he had instead courted a fight that had resulted in the burning of Cap. A round of negotiations, even if unsuccessful, might also convince the population of color that the French did not come as conquerors. Bonaparte's proclamation and a similar one issued by Leclerc had resonated so well with Dominguians that Leclerc had already been able to form three companies of black troops in Cap. Leclerc could also use a short pause to give the other squadrons sent from France enough time to reach Cap. He had spread a rumor that he had 40,000 men at his disposal when he only had 9,400—600 of whom were already sick or injured. But his enemies would soon do the math for themselves, and he had read reports that Louverture's forces totaled 17,000. He thought it best to open negotiations with Louverture, which would surely fail, then launch an all-out campaign a few days later once his army had regrouped.[37]

Two weeks after his arrival in Saint-Domingue, Leclerc thus summoned Louverture's sons and assured them that his one desire all along had been "to get along with your father. . . . It is necessary for you to bring him the letter from the first consul, so that he knows my intentions and how highly I think of him."[38] Accompanied by their tutor, Jean-Baptiste Coisnon, the children left hurriedly in the middle of the night, riding all day through the wilds of northern Saint-Domingue, whose sharp colors and exotic scents must have awakened faint memories from their youth. Coisnon, who in a few months had been thrust from his teaching pulpit to an unfamiliar war zone, must have been less reassured, but he was an abolitionist who genuinely prayed for a peaceful outcome to this crisis.

It was late in the evening when the group reached Louverture's plantation at Ennery, where the boys reunited with a loving mother they had not seen for more than five years. Louverture arrived the following day, embraced his children fondly, and then got down to business. Coisnon had brought with him Bonaparte's November 18 letter, in which he had promised "freedom" to black Dominguians and "consideration, honors, fortune" to Louverture if he remained loyal to France.[39] The letter, enclosed in a vermeil box and adorned with a ribbon of silk and the republic's seal, was one of the two things Louverture had so ardently desired; the other was to be reunited with his sons. Louverture read and reread the letter with evident relish, but the statesman in him knew better than to assume that all was well. Bonaparte's offer of peace stood in stark contrast with the conduct of his brother-in-law, Louverture complained to Coisnon, and he could hardly submit to its terms while French troops were fanning out across the colony, conquering everything in their path. He vanished into the dark of night to work on his response. He had been with his children for two hours.

By morning time a white planter named Granville, whom Louverture had spared to use as a courier, brought Louverture's response to Ennery. The curt message criticized Leclerc for his aggressive behavior and demanded a cessation of hostilities before negotiations could begin. The boys brought the letter to Leclerc, who claimed that he could only organize a cease-fire in Cap because other units were too far to be reached. Louverture should order a general cease-fire of his own and come to Cap in person to negotiate, Leclerc explained. If Louverture complied, he could keep his fortune and rank.[40]

Isaac and Placide once again hiked across the mountains to meet their father, but the tone of their second encounter was far less congenial than the first's. Sensing a trap, Louverture refused to go to Cap and replied that he could hardly submit "to an expedition led by several white generals, as well as Rigaud, Pétion, Boyer, Chanlatte, all my personal enemies."[41] After assembling the troops protecting him at Ennery, he told them that only war could secure their freedom. "General," the troops yelled back, "we shall die with you."[42]

The only outstanding question, Louverture told his sons, was whether they would side with "their fatherland or their father."[43] One can only imagine the turmoil raging in the boys' hearts as they saw their native island at war with their adopted nation. On one side stood their teacher and surrogate father; on the other was their formidable father, whom they genuinely loved but who had massacred many white civilians, a fact Granville had explained in graphic detail when they had returned to Cap. In the end, Placide, the light-skinned elder stepson, chose war in his adoptive father's camp; the younger Isaac, though biologically closer to Louverture, opted for France. As often in the conflict, one's actions did not always match one's racial affiliation, and a dumbfounded Haitian historian later switched around the two sons' war records to better support his simplistic understanding of Haiti's racial politics.[44] That same day, word reached Louverture that his brother Paul had surrendered to Kerversau and now fought on France's side.[45] War had torn the Louverture family apart.

～

Throughout the negotiations, Leclerc expected that diplomacy would fail and that full-scale operations would soon begin. As he rejected Louverture's call for a general cease-fire—under the spurious excuse that he could not contact his own troops—he ordered his generals to continue their military operations, particularly in the south. The region had been Saint-Domingue's last frontier at the outset of the revolution, but its relative backwardness had spared it most of the destruction inflicted on the more developed north, and it was now the richest coffee-growing area in the colony.

Eager to deny the province's riches to his enemies, Louverture had sent his nephew and aide-de-camp to deliver a letter to the commander of Jérémie, Jean-Baptiste Dommage, in which he urged him to convince the black cultivators that the French had come to restore slavery. Dommage was to defend what he could and burn the rest. As for the white planters, Dommage had *"carte blanche,"* a pun that in Louverture's circuitous style meant that he wanted them dead.[46] Louverture's plans, however, quickly went awry. A traditionally Francophile province, the south had also been the site of the bloody civil war between Louverture and Rigaud, and like the areas at the epicenter of the Moyse uprising, its inhabitants disliked their governor far more than the metropolis. An officer of color loyal to France captured Louverture's letter before it could reach Dommage, who promptly rallied to the French side when two ships of the line appeared in Jérémie. His troops, who were given two months' salary in advance, did not complain.[47]

Dessalines, whose traditional command was in Saint-Marc, was expected to flee north after he learned of the fall of Port Républicain. Instead he headed for the mountains to his south, circled around his enemy's position undetected, and late on February 9 burst into Léogane, a prosperous town a few miles southwest of Port Républicain.[48] There he gave a vehement speech to the garrison and ordered their chief to defend or burn the city. When he left two days later, Dessalines could reasonably hope that Léogane, which had delayed Louverture's army for months during the war with Rigaud, would halt the French advance. But French soldiers backed by a naval squadron reached Léogane immediately after Dessalines' departure, and though faced with a seemingly impregnable fortified hill in Cabaret Carde they quickly overwhelmed the defenses with a coordinated assault of heavy and light troops. The rebels fled to the hills and Léogane was retaken with the loss of only three French soldiers. The French also captured a rich convoy carrying the town's treasure, but the town, including the nearby plantation owned by Joséphine Bonaparte, went up in flames.[49]

Dessalines, who had conquered the south on Louverture's behalf during the war against Rigaud, intended to keep marching southwest and ravage the entire region after he left Léogane, but Boudet beat him to Petit Goâve, blocking the main road to the west.[50] From there, Boudet sent two ships of the line to Cayes, whose commanding general, Jean-Joseph Laplume, had received orders from Dessalines to burn the town. But Laplume had once belonged to one of the communities of plantation runaways that were at odds with Louverture; when a French envoy promised him that slavery would not be restored and that he could keep his military rank, he quickly switched sides. He brought with him 3 million francs from the local treasury; he also proved to be one of France's most dedicated black allies.[51]

The loss of Léogane, Jérémie, and Cayes, combined with a complete lack of success in convincing southerners to join his cause, obliged Dessalines to veer southeast.[52] His destination was Jacmel, a quiet port nested at the end of a picturesque bay that Dessalines knew well as the site of the longest and bloodiest siege of the War of the South. Panic struck the city when its old tormentor arrived on the eleventh, the ruins of Léogane still smoldering behind him. Dessalines immediately announced to the white population assembled on the main square "that he declared war on them, that he would unleash the blacks on them, that he already saw death on their face, and that they were in his eyes mere cadavers already."[53] But the black commander of Jacmel, Dieudonné Jambon, was a moderate who had promised white inhabitants that he meant them no harm, and he courageously refused to second Dessalines' plans. In an abrupt shift, Dessalines then consented to spare white civilians if they agreed to write a letter insisting that they preferred to live under Louverture's rule (Dessalines probably intended to use the letter, along with his kind treatment of Jacmel's civilians, in the ongoing propaganda battle for the colony's hearts and minds). The population complied and Dessalines left that night and headed north. His personal guard in tow, he went from plantation to plantation, preaching revolt along the way, only to be chased by angry mobs trying to capture him. Dieudonné, who seems to have weighed his options carefully in these unstable times, sent some of his black troops to fight the French in Léogane so as to satisfy Dessalines and rid himself of his most troublesome troops. Then, as soon as Dessalines had reached a safe distance, he allowed local whites to rearm, distributed Bonaparte's proclamation, and announced that he was on France's side after all.

Dieudonné's about-face completed the French conquest of the south, which had required few troops and, with the exception of Léogane, had brought the entire region under French rule with minimal destruction. Oddly, there seemed to be a negative correlation between the size of a French unit and its likelihood of success. Generals with too many troops at their disposal, like Leclerc and Humbert, were always tempted to fight their way in, sometimes with disastrous consequences. Officers backed by minimal forces, like Kerversau, were more prone to encourage Louverture's subordinates to abandon him, which they were often inclined to do due to personal grievances. Not only did such negotiations cost Leclerc no lives or money; they actually added to the French army and treasure as entire units abandoned Louverture. Leclerc, however, drew a different conclusion from these unexpected successes: all-out war was now possible.

~

As reports of the submission of the south reached Cap, Leclerc brought an end to his negotiations with Louverture and prepared to launch large-scale operations in the island's interior. His diplomatic mission a failure, Coisnon prepared to return to France. He brought with him the ten-year-old son of Clervaux, a way to reward his father for his prompt submission in Santiago, but also to ensure his future loyalty. "If you are still alive," Coisnon wrote mournfully to Isaac and Placide before he set sail, "remember that you have a second father in France who will help you if you need it."[54]

Leclerc's belligerence was further spurred by the arrival of several fleets whose fate had long been uncertain. The Toulon squadron sighted Cap on February 11 with 4,000 troops and four ships of the line. The Cádiz squadron, under Charles-Alexandre Linois, followed on the seventeenth with 1,900 troops (including a battalion of Germans) and three ships of the line.[55] As Linois prepared to enter the pass of Cap, he noticed that no pilot or buoys were there to guide him—even though a week had passed since the port had been captured—and signaled for a sharp turn. The Intrépide veered as ordered, but the Desaix and the San Genaro, encumbered with foreign troops and passengers, stayed on course too long and hit submerged reefs. The San Genaro threw all its guns overboard and the tide lifted it to safety the following day; but the Desaix was declared lost.[56]

Sailors, always sensitive to fate, consider it bad luck to change a ship's name; the superstitious were vindicated. Initially named the Tyrannicide, the Desaix had been rebaptized in 1800 when Bonaparte had visited Brest (naval authorities had feared that the ship's name would be interpreted as a commentary on the dictator's recent coup).[57] Cables, sails, passengers, and everything that could be salvaged were ferried to shore, but the sinking hull disappeared into the multicolored ballet of the reef's tropical fish. Villaret, who had just informed his superiors of the burning of Cap, sat down for the second time in a week to report some embarrassing news.[58] The Desaix, a 74-gun ship of the line whose upkeep had cost the French government a sizable 386,000 francs the previous year, was no more.[59] Amazingly, another ship was damaged off Cap a month later, also for lack of pilots.[60]

The young adventurer, Louis Bro, whose arrival had been delayed when a leak had forced the Duquesne to refit in Spain, reached Cap with the latest squadrons. Days after the fire he could still see columns of smoke rising from the coast. "The city and the plain are ruined," he wrote his father. "It is a deplorable sight." Despite the destruction, he remained enthusiastic about

the expedition's prospects and decided against joining the civilian administration after realizing that "the only thing that people respect here is the
army."[61] Leclerc, who knew some of Bro's relatives, offered him a generous
rank of brigadier colonel in his personal guard and Bro enlisted on the spot.
An equally eager Norvins insisted that Leclerc employ him as a traveling secretary so that he could witness the fighting in person.[62]

When the deadline for Louverture's submission expired, Leclerc declared
him and Christophe as outlaws (though not Dessalines, possibly to divide the
black camp). With an eye to public opinion he promised that he had come to
preserve the cultivators' freedom and that soldiers who deserted Louverture
would be welcomed into the French army.[63] Equally eager to get the black
masses on his side, Louverture replied with his own proclamation refuting
Leclerc's point by point and declaring *him* an outlaw.[64] Some white planters,
who had experienced firsthand the reality of colonial war for the previous ten
years, begged Leclerc to reconsider his decision to open the campaign, to no
avail.[65] Leclerc, whom Bonaparte had instructed to open military operations
within two weeks of the landing, seemed invigorated by the onset of war and
grandiosely added that he would not take off his boots until he had captured
his enemy.[66] One can only hope that his promise was an empty boast. For
the next seventy-two days, through hills, heat, mud, tropical downpours, and
musket fire, Leclerc would find himself waging a campaign much longer and
harder than anything he had ever anticipated—all of which he would have
to do while negotiating with his neighbors to ensure that his army would be
fed and paid.

6

Supply and Demand

Leclerc's Diplomacy with the United States, Cuba, and Jamaica

While the French fleet had battled its way into Cap, John Rodgers had watched its progress with the keen eye of the military man. Rodgers was a veteran of the young U.S. navy, famous for his role in the capture of the French frigate *Insurgente* in 1799. Despite his heroic record he had been taken off active duty when the Quasi-War had ended and the nickel-pinching Jefferson had cut the navy's budget by two-thirds. Forced to embark on a peacetime career in the mercantile business, Rodgers had left Baltimore in December 1801 for a destination that was familiar to many merchants on the Atlantic seaboard: the United States' second-largest trading partner, Saint-Domingue.[1] Rodgers had landed in Cap just as news of the European peace had reached the Caribbean. British merchant ships had promptly left for Jamaica, but U.S. merchants had remained in Cap and had found themselves front and center during the French landing. While Henri Christophe's men had searched the burning streets of Cap for civilians they could kill, one U.S. merchant had profited from the confusion to steal cash from the victims, but Rodgers had courageously remained on shore to save women and children.[2]

The presence of U.S. merchants like Rodgers—at least twenty U.S. ships could be seen in the bay—presented Victoire Leclerc with a dilemma that would puzzle him for months. On the one hand he desperately needed neutral merchants to feed his army, since French ships had arrived with minimal supplies (many of them rotten or missing) and the granaries of Cap had burned alongside the city. On the other hand he was leery of trusting foreigners who had supplied his enemy for years and whom Napoléon Bonaparte wanted out of the colony at the earliest opportunity.[3] Aghast by venal traders willing to feed one army after arming its opponent, yet unable to bypass the omnipresent U.S. commercial fleet, Leclerc embraced an erratic and ultimately unsuccessful policy: he would buy from U.S. merchants while expressing his displeasure with constant petty vexations.

U.S. merchants were equally unsure whether they should celebrate or lament Leclerc's arrival. War could be good business at a time when the European peace had brought stagnation to U.S. ports, but Toussaint Louverture had protected U.S. merchants, and he was genuinely popular in northern ports.[4] That Bonaparte was suspected of planning to restore slavery was an added irritant to the merchants from Philadelphia, whose large Quaker community was a hotbed of abolitionist sentiment. The U.S. commercial agent in Cap, Tobias Lear, also suspected that France would take possession of Louisiana as soon as it had secured Saint-Domingue and privately hoped that Leclerc would become mired in military difficulties so as to protect the United States' continental ambitions.[5] The pattern—mutual antipathy balanced by mutual need—remained the norm throughout Leclerc's tenure.

Leclerc immediately set the tone. A week after landing, he restricted foreign trade to Cap and Port Républicain to limit smuggling and ordered all U.S. ships in Cap embargoed and searched to ascertain whether they were carrying gunpowder hidden in flour barrels (some did).[6] Given the scarcity of food in Cap, embargoed U.S. merchants hoped to sell their cargo at a premium, but Leclerc set arbitrary prices and forced them to accept bills of exchange for lack of cash. Leclerc's requisitions were consistent with standard French military practice, but they were deeply unpopular with U.S. businessmen whose notions of political economy came from Adam Smith's theories on supply and demand, not Thomas Aquinas's views on fair price and the public good.[7] Bills of exchange, whose value fluctuated with the issuer's credit worthiness, were particularly unattractive since Bonaparte was infamous for not paying his bills on time and his notes were selling for less than fifty cents on the dollar in U.S. ports.[8] In following weeks U.S. merchants were also forcibly enrolled in the local national guard—a duty that ran counter to a national aversion for a standing army—then submitted to another unpopular embargo after a March 20 raid by Christophe.[9]

When the embargo took effect, Rodgers and another merchant, Anthony Davidson, were the only U.S. nationals allowed to leave Cap as a reward for helping French civilians during the burning of Cap (the poorly informed Leclerc was probably unaware that Rodgers had fought in the Quasi-War or that he had warned Christophe of the arrival of the French fleet). The two broke the news of the French landing in the United States.[10] Public opinion was already incensed by rumors of a French takeover of Louisiana, so Leclerc's requisitions soon sparked a wave of recriminations in Atlantic ports. The Caribbean-born Alexander Hamilton, though a close friend of an officer who fought in the expedition, urged readers of the *New York Evening Post* to boycott the ports of Saint-Domingue in retaliation for French commercial restrictions.[11]

Unaware of the uproar his abrasive treatment of U.S. merchants would cause in the United States, in February Leclerc sent one of his generals, François Watrin, to Philadelphia to borrow money and buy supplies.[12] Watrin probably expected success since Philadelphia was replete with Saint-Domingue exiles, and the richest man in the United States, Stephen Girard, was a French-born banker with extensive commercial ties in the Caribbean. Watrin hired another famous French-born entrepreneur, Victor Dupont de Nemours, to help him float one million francs worth of bonds, but so bad was French credit that no one would buy French bonds, even when sold by Dupont, even at a 50 percent discount. In fact, not even Dupont wanted them; he had already loaned two hundred thousand francs to the French embassy, most of which had never been paid back. In the end Dupont only managed to place a paltry six-thousand-dollar note, and Watrin headed back to Cap empty-handed.[13] By what kind of "unconceivable negligence," the French ambassador Louis-André Pichon boldly asked Charles de Talleyrand, had the government "sent such a considerable army with a sword, but no money?"[14]

Although young (he had been appointed ambassador at age twenty-nine), Pichon had spent a decade as a diplomat in the United States. The many letters he sent to Leclerc that spring thus gave the inexperienced general a refresher course on the U.S. government's close ties with the Louverture regime.[15] Pichon added that securing a reliable food supply was critical to the expedition's success and that Leclerc should nevertheless strive to maintain good relations with the United States, but his prudent advice was undermined by the French consul in Philadelphia, Charles François Liot, who held a grudge against Louverture for taking over his wife's plantations in Saint-Domingue.[16] In his letters, Liot described the Americans' "indecent joy" upon learning of Louverture's opposition to the French landing and warned Leclerc that some merchants were preparing to sail to Saint-Domingue with hidden stores of ammunition.[17]

The biting articles published in the Federalist press and Liot's letters reached Leclerc in April. Failing to grasp the concept of a free press (Bonaparte had banned newspapers that did not toe the government line), Leclerc saw the articles as official U.S. policy. Convinced that Lear was intentionally inciting U.S. merchants not to loan him money, Leclerc declared that there was no reason why a U.S. diplomat should even be present in a French colony and pronounced him persona non grata. On April 17, Lear left Cap to pursue an eventful diplomatic career that would later take him to Algiers to negotiate a treaty with Barbary pirates.[18] Leclerc insisted that U.S. merchants were still welcome (he reduced tariff barriers and began paying cash), but exiling the U.S. commercial agent was a strange way to send this message.[19]

Rodgers and Davidson returned to Cap in April 1802. They had left the city as heroes, but they returned to a radically different environment and were sent to prison as soon as they landed. "I was conducted to a cell, much resembling an oven," Rodgers wrote, where "I succeeded an unhappy wretch, whose body had been conducted to a more peaceable cell—namely his grave but a few hours previous to my being made his successor." The merchants were kept prisoners until Davidson paid a substantial bribe, at which point they were released under the condition that they set sail immediately "and not land again, under pain of death."[20] Leclerc refused to explain the charges held against them, but one may surmise that he blamed them for spreading ill will in U.S. mercantile circles. Upon returning to Cap, Rodgers had had an altercation with a French veteran of the Quasi-War, so his past as the captor of the *Insurgente* may also have caught up with him. Rodgers left Saint-Domingue and eventually returned to the U.S. navy; like Lear, he headed for the Barbary Coast, where he covered himself with enough glory for six U.S. warships to have been named after him.

Rodgers and Davidson's incarceration, which violated all U.S. concepts of due process and coincided with Lear's expulsion from Cap, was the most severe dispute to affect an already frayed French–U.S. relationship.[21] Leclerc's overt hostility to U.S. merchants was understandable given their past support for Louverture—not to mention Bonaparte's constant demands that he restore the old *exclusif*—but it was a perilous policy when sixty of the sixty-seven merchant ships present in Cap in March 1802 hailed from the United States.[22] These provided the colony with most of its income since French merchants, operating under a preferential tariff, paid few taxes.[23] Pichon repeatedly urged Leclerc to respect "a country that is your sole source of subsistence" and that had recently gone to war to avenge French exactions against U.S. commerce. "Take these people the way they are," he also wrote. "All they want is to make money."[24] The advice was sensible, but Leclerc accused Pichon of defending U.S., not French, interests and asked for his dismissal. Eventually recalled to France, Pichon was fired from the diplomatic service in disgrace.[25]

⌒

Money, just as food, was essential to the success of a costly expedition fought on the far side of the Atlantic. During their wars with France the British had developed a modern system of government debt, supplemented after 1799 by the creation of the income tax; they were thus a well-financed foe, and many Dominguians remembered the British invasion of 1793–98 fondly because of the occupiers' free-spending ways.[26] Bonaparte, by contrast, hated both new taxes and a large national debt (which had been the immediate causes, he might have remembered, of the American and French revolutions). He thus wanted war to pay for itself, which in practice meant that his allies and his vanquished enemies were expected to help finance the French empire. Given the wealth of prerevolutionary Saint-Domingue, Bonaparte was confident that the Leclerc expedition would sustain itself, and he sent Leclerc off with a minimal cash stipend, which he obtained by asking Spain for money and raiding a fund earmarked for war invalids.[27] Leclerc would raise the bulk of his funds locally—or so hoped the optimistic Bonaparte, who had once hoped, and failed, to finance the invasion of Egypt in that manner.[28]

Louverture's scorched-earth policy immediately undermined Bonaparte's optimistic financial plans. Leclerc's army levied taxes, raided local treasuries, and seized rebel generals' assets, but production and export taxes on tropical produce (the main sources of colonial revenue) plunged when plantations in the north and west were set afire.[29] By April 1, Leclerc estimated that he needed over 4 million francs a month to feed his army and govern the colony, or 53.5 million francs a year including one-time rebuilding costs, when the ravaged colony could only provide 14.8 million. He thus asked Bonaparte and Decrès to send close to 39 million francs over the next twelve months, one-third of it in cash.[30] The staggering sum must have horrified government accountants: a mere 5 million francs had been allocated for the colony for Year X (1802), and Leclerc's demand amounted to one-third of the annual budget of the Ministry of the Navy.[31] Just as Leclerc was writing his letter, Denis Decrès explained from Paris that Bonaparte wanted to cut costs and was hopeful that Leclerc had found enough cash in Louverture's coffers to finance the expedition on his own.[32] In all Leclerc would only receive 10.3 million francs during his tenure as captain general.[33]

While he waited for an answer to his demand for funds, Leclerc faced a significant budgetary shortfall, which he bridged with various short-term expedients such as postponing the payment of his troops' salaries (a winning strategy, since most of them died over the next six months). He also turned to the colonies of France's Spanish ally, which could draw on the silver mines of Peru and Mexico and minted most of the coins used in the cash-starved Caribbean. Immediately after the landing in Cap, Leclerc thus sent the civilian administrator François Lequoy-Mongiraud to Cuba with a request for two million francs and a thousand men. Cuba's plantation system had grown rapidly in recent years, as had the risk of a slave revolt, so its governor proved eager to help contain labor unrest in Saint-Domingue. Mongiraud could also count on the support of Federico Gravina, the Spanish admiral who had sailed with the Brest fleet (and later fought at Trafalgar), and the intendant of Cuba, an admirer of Bonaparte who kept a portrait of the first consul in his office. Within days the colonial council loaned the requisite two million francs; Cuba also sent food and Havana's arsenal, the only modern refitting facility in the Caribbean, helped repair French ships damaged during the crossing.[34] Overjoyed by Havana's generous loan, Leclerc immediately requested an additional three million francs, while sending a frigate to pick up another million in Veracruz. He also asked an officer to purchase three thousand mules and six hundred horses in Caracas, prepared a mission to Cartagena, and bought cattle in Santiago de Cuba.[35] Soon countless French envoys could be found sailing the Caribbean Sea in search of Spanish gold.

Mongiraud had been entrusted with a second, more delicate mission: to buy five hundred bloodhounds specifically trained to chase down black rebels.[36] France's use of man-hunting dogs during the Haitian Revolution was the most disturbing crime in this singularly cruel conflict and is still vividly remembered in Haiti today. Leclerc's successor, Rochambeau, is usually blamed for the policy, but Mongiraud's mission clearly shows that it was initiated by Leclerc at the very outset of the expedition. Bonaparte had not mentioned war dogs in his instructions, so Leclerc must have come up with the idea on his own, possibly by reading Guillaume Raynal and Bartolome de Las Casas's histories of the Caribbean during the Atlantic crossing, both of which noted (with horror) that conquistadors had used dogs to great effect against the native Tainos.[37] The use of canine units in the recent Maroon War in Jamaica and the role they played in chasing slave runaways in Cuba were also well known in the colony.[38]

Leclerc's interests in cold cash and war dogs are testimonies to the general's hard edge. But he was also the product of the Enlightenment, and his envoys spent considerable time and energy collecting scientific specimens of the local flora and fauna (possibly in imitation of Bonaparte, who famously had brought 167 scholars with him to Egypt). Asked by a local naturalist to help recreate Saint-Domingue's famed learned society, Leclerc petitioned Paris for six botanists.[39] He also instructed a French captain sent to Veracruz to bring back "a few stuffed and living birds and animals of this country," while panthers, monkeys, and parrots arrived from Cartagena.[40] Some of these exotic animals served to grace Pauline's residence near Cap, while others, including a striped cat and a caiman that traveled on the *Conquérant,* continued their journey all the way to France along with human deportees in the summer of 1802.[41] The most unusual specimen was a manatee sent to the Paris Museum of Natural History in May. Leclerc did not explain how his sailors had managed to load the portly, ten-foot mammal on board their ship, but he did provide an interesting tidbit of information drawn from personal research: manatees taste just like beef.[42]

~

Every story set in a Caribbean isle must have a buried treasure. This one is no exception, since Bonaparte's plan for financing the expedition rested partly on his brother-in-law's ability to find Louverture's alleged personal fortune. "You have no idea how much money is stolen in the administration, and how much land and cash some chiefs have," an anonymous colonist explained in May 1802. "Toussaint and Dessalines would be the richest individuals in Europe. . . . There must be enormous sums stashed somewhere in preparation for a war with France."[43]

According to several contemporaries, in the days that followed the French landing Louverture hid his treasure on his Héricourt plantation, or possibly the mountains of Grand Cahos. The scenario is plausible since Louverture visited both locations during the period, but estimates that put the treasure at dozens, or even hundreds, of millions of francs seem wildly excessive given the scarcity of specie in the colony. The typical story went on to specify that Louverture shot all the workers who had helped him bury the loot and that no one knew the treasure's exact location but him (or his wife, who according to an alternate theory was the one who hid the money).[44] Despite all his efforts Bonaparte never managed to goad Louverture into revealing where he had hidden his treasure, so its location—or even existence—remains the expedition's most tantalizing mystery to this day.

Piecing together the fate of Louverture's alleged treasure with archival sources is exceedingly difficult, not least because those who knew the most about its location were also most likely to remain silent or lie. Still, one can reach a few conclusions, starting with the fact that there were two distinct treasures, Louverture's and the colony's, which are too often conflated in existing accounts. Louverture and his wife were wealthy individuals whose assets consisted largely of land and tropical crops, along with the sums that the notoriously tight-fisted Louverture had saved from the three-hundred-thousand-franc salary he had awarded himself in his constitution. The colonial government had its own, far larger, sources of income, which it obtained primarily from rents and taxes on tropical crops and exports and that were typically paid in kind, not in cash.

Most government funds were taken over by the French as they landed. Leclerc obtained 2.3 million francs in the south and east of the colony, which he used to finance his army. While fighting in the Grand Cahos, Donatien de Rochambeau also found a large sum hidden on the Magnan plantation. Neither Rochambeau's find (amounting to 600,000 francs) nor the 3 million francs that Jean Boudet found in the treasury of Port Républicain were mentioned in the financial report that Leclerc submitted to Bonaparte in April 1802, so one can safely assume that the funds disappeared into the pockets of French officers—and, ultimately, those of the British captains who looted French ships as they left Saint-Domingue in late 1803.[45] According to Louverture, officers of color such as Henri Christophe also stole some of the colony's funds, whose total value he put at 11.7 million francs.[46]

To these funds must be added those that Louverture had sent overseas for safekeeping after rumors of impending war had reached Saint-Domingue. One of Louverture's white aides-de-camp, Augustin d'Hébécourt, left with a considerable sum of money before the French landing, but he was arrested in Santiago de Cuba, sent back to Cap, and eventually deported to France, and one can only wonder what happened to the funds Louverture had asked him to convey.[47] Leclerc also arrested another of Louverture's white associates, his paymaster Joseph Bunel, whom he suspected of preparing to send vast sums to the United States (Bunel insisted that Christophe had emptied the Cap treasury before the French landing and that he had no government funds in his trust).[48]

One last theory—particularly popular in contemporary Haiti—holds that in December 1801 Louverture sent a Gonaïves merchant named Caze with six million francs to Philadelphia, where it was appropriated by the French financier Stephen Girard.[49] Louverture was indeed very close to a Cap merchant named Jean (or Jean-Paul) Caze, but documents show that after Caze tried to send some of his own money to Philadelphia he was arrested on Leclerc's orders and stripped of his funds.[50] Girard thus probably never had a chance to steal Louverture's treasure—though, if he did, he put it to good use. He died childless and willed all his money to a private school for destitute children, Girard College, that to this day continues to serve a diverse group of students, several of whom must be descendants of the white and black Dominguians who settled in Philadelphia after the Haitian Revolution.

Most of the funds mentioned in contemporary documents were probably part of the colonial treasury, not Louverture's personal fortune. According to Louverture he only possessed 250,000 francs in 1802, a figure that seemed suspiciously small to Bonaparte but probably accurately described the *cash* amounts available to him. Louverture and his wife owned or rented a dozen plantations near Cap, Gonaïves, and Léogane (along with a house in Cap), so their wealth was tied up in real estate. Their plantations, like others in the colony, had suffered extensively during the revolution and had barely begun to recover by 1802.[51] A detailed inventory of Louverture's plantations in the spring of 1802 found little of value besides two carriages, a handful of mules, and a few bags of coffee.[52] The buildings themselves probably went up in smoke during the destructive fighting of the following year, because Isaac Louverture only obtained thirty-five thousand francs when he tried to reclaim his parents' estate in the 1820s.[53] Convinced that Louverture must have hidden money somewhere, in ensuing decades countless hopefuls dug holes and appealed to St. Anthony (patron of lost objects) and his Vodou colleagues in a vain attempt to find Louverture's lost riches.[54] None of them struck gold, but they came far closer to unearthing his fortune than they ever realized. As a planter, Louverture did keep his valuables hidden underground: for he was rich primarily with land.

The fate of Louverture's personal fortune says a lot about the Dominguian economy. In 1802 as in Spanish colonial times, young men flocked to Hispaniola to seek quick windfalls in gold, when the colony's wealth stemmed primarily from agriculture and its riches were right there for anyone to see: sugar mills, land, and laborers. Hilliard d'Auberteuil, one of the best analysts of the colonial economy, liked to explain its inner workings by citing Jean de la Fontaine's *Le laboureur et ses enfants,* a famous fable that seems to have been familiar to Louverture.[55] The poem starts as an elderly farmer gathers his children and tells them that a treasure is hidden on the family estate. The greedy heirs fan across the land, digging everywhere but finding nothing—until the following year, when the well-tilled earth yields a bumper crop.

D'argent, point de caché. Mais le père fut sage	(There was no cash hidden anywhere. But the father was wise
De leur montrer avant sa mort	To show them before his death
Que le travail est un trésor.	That work is a treasure.)

And so it was with Louverture's legendary treasure, which consisted of land and workers, not gold. Unfortunately, the Haitian Revolution destroyed most of the colony's plantations and killed half its population, and only ashes now remain of Saint-Domingue's fabled wealth.

~

In its haste to surprise Louverture, the Leclerc expedition had sailed before a comprehensive peace treaty between England and France could be finalized. The spring campaign thus unfolded in an uncertain diplomatic environment, made all the worse by the fact that echoes from the tense negotiations unfolding in Amiens reached the Caribbean with the usual one- to two-month delay. The *perfide Albion* would likely sever vital sea lanes from France should the nascent peace founder, so maintaining good relations with Jamaica was one of Leclerc's foremost priorities from the time he landed in Cap in February 1802.

British authorities also had much to fear from a resumption of war, which might incite Leclerc's large army to head for Kingston instead of Cap. "The loss of Jamaica would be complete ruin to our credit," wrote the British secretary of war, before claiming that a French invasion of Jamaica would be even worse than a landing in Britain itself.[56] Prodded by an anxious Parliament, the British admiralty had decided in the fall of 1801 to send a large fleet to Caribbean waters to match the French squadrons sent to Saint-Domingue, but the usually diligent British navy completely failed in its mission. The British fleet did not leave Britain until early February, while the ships of the line already on theater were not deployed until the middle of that month, so the Leclerc expedition reached Cap before any British capital unit had even set sail.[57] Worse, the light units deployed near Saint-Domingue to spot unusual activity somehow managed to miss the large incoming French squadrons, and with all British nationals evacuated from Saint-Domingue the British were wholly unaware of the momentous events unfolding nearby. In the end, the admiral in charge of the Jamaican squadron only learned of the French landing when the French frigate *Cornélie* paid him a courtesy call on February 18 to inform him that dozens of French warships had been in Caribbean waters for a month.[58]

With the British navy temporarily outgunned and outsmarted, defending Britain's largest sugar colony lay solely on the shoulders of the commander of Jamaica's armed forces, Governor George Nugent. There was, however, little that he could do. Employing black soldiers resistant to local fevers seemed to him the only sensible defensive strategy, but the planters who dominated the island's legislative council were adamant that blacks not be armed, and Nugent spent his tenure locked in sterile political battles instead of military preparations.[59] To meet the threat of French invasion, Nugent thus resorted to the time-honored strategy of letting Britain's enemies annihilate each other. If only Louverture could offer a determined resistance, he privately hoped, the French would have little opportunity to attack Jamaica.[60] Within a week, as he received word of the fighting in Cap, he left Spanishtown on a sightseeing excursion, followed by a two-month tour of the island's militia, effectively banking that Louverture's army would protect Britain's crown jewel during his absence.[61]

In retrospect, an invasion of Jamaica was the best use that could have been made of Leclerc's large force, but this scenario was never on Bonaparte's or Leclerc's agenda. In the letter he sent onboard the *Cornélie,* Leclerc insisted that he harbored no ill intent against Jamaica (he also argued that the British would be well served to contribute supplies to an expedition that would benefit all white colonial powers in the region, but in Jamaica as elsewhere the oft-used reference to a clash of civilizations convinced no one; national interests far outweighed race in the region).[62] Because the oversize crews of the ships of the line gobbled inordinate quantities of food, Leclerc sent most large warships back to France shortly after their arrival and only kept shallow-draft frigates and corvettes that were well suited for coastal surveillance but that would be outclassed in any engagement against a British squadron.[63] Decrès, concerned that his costly ships of the line were deteriorating rapidly in tropical waters, concurred and asked that even more large units return to French ports.[64]

So quickly did Leclerc repatriate his fleet that by March 1802, when news reached the Caribbean that negotiations in Amiens had taken a wrong turn and that war might resume at any time, the French navy was no longer in a position to threaten Jamaica. A British captain, who sailed the HMS *Nereide* to Cap under false pretenses to spy on French forces, noted gleefully that French ships were "infamously dirty" and in no condition to meet an enemy because many crewmen were doing combat duty on shore.[65] The admiral in charge of the Jamaican station thereafter concluded that Jamaica was safe as long as the French had "ample employment in Saint-Domingue."[66] Within weeks, with the belated arrival of reinforcements from England, his squadron ballooned to twenty-eight ships of the line and thirty-two small units, while the French fleet shrank to four ships of the line and twenty-two small units.[67] For France the window of opportunity to take over Britain's largest sugar colony—and free its slaves in the process—had passed. Leclerc even began to fear that the British might now be the ones planning to attack their neighbor.[68]

While Nugent and Leclerc eyed each other suspiciously across the Windward Passage, their spouses engaged in a gentler round of muslin diplomacy. Nugent's wife, Maria, was the daughter of a loyalist family from New York that had left the United States after this country's independence. Genuinely in love with her husband (a fact worth noting in an age where marriage was as much a social alliance as a union of hearts), she had followed him to Jamaica, but adapting to his new posting had proved difficult. She disliked being surrounded by "blackies" and found the local white planters promiscuous, cruel, and uncouth.[69] She was also terrified by the deadly tropical fevers and was devastated that, four years into their marriage, she had yet to become a mother (she was actually pregnant, though she did not know it yet).

In this context the sophisticated Pauline Bonaparte must have struck Lady Nugent as a soul mate. The two exchanged letters and gifts throughout 1802 despite the ups and downs of French-British relations. Maria was particularly fond of the fashionable Parisian dresses that Pauline shipped her on a regular basis. These were rather risqué by British standards, but all eyes trained on Maria when she wore Pauline's gowns during the governor's balls, and she described every trim in minute detail in her journal. Pauline's brother was often described as an incestuous monster in British propaganda, and the two women stood on opposite sides of a yawning national divide. But individuals are defined by many allegiances, class and gender foremost among them, and the two upper-class women from Manhattan and Corsica found much common ground despite the bitter rivalry opposing their adopted isles. Men, however, are from Mars, and Pauline's husband chose to spend the spring of 1802 fighting it out in the mountains of Saint-Domingue instead of exchanging diplomatic niceties with his enemies.

7

Ash and Iron

The Spring Campaign

FEBRUARY–APRIL 1802

For Victoire Leclerc and other French generals, the beginning of military operations brought an end to three frustrating weeks during which their actions had been constrained by the competing demands of politics, diplomacy, and the navy. Now that the bulk of the troops had landed and that Toussaint Louverture had been clearly identified as an enemy, the familiar business of war—marching columns, sieges, and maneuvers—could finally take over. After the arrival of the squadrons of *Toulon* and Cádiz and the defection of several colonial officers, the expeditionary army outnumbered Louverture's at 16,116 troops (see table 4).[1] This, newcomers thought, was more than enough to achieve a quick victory against colonial troops that they viewed as an "incompetent rabble" that would never stand its ground in conventional combat.[2] Jean Hardÿ, the general who had left his pregnant wife to secure a fortune in Saint-Domingue, described the troops under his command as first rate and predicted that Louverture would be defeated within a month, well before the rainy season. A few areas of the colony might then have to be pacified, but "this would not be difficult."[3]

Louverture probably did not share the French generals' giddiness. He was a political and strategic genius, but his tactical record on the battlefield, the claims of his admirers notwithstanding, left much to be desired. Throughout the Haitian Revolution, he had struggled to win decisive victories despite benefiting from overwhelming numerical superiority. He had obtained his most notable victories by turning on his allies (Spain in 1794) or negotiating with his enemies (England in 1798), and Rigaud's hopelessly outnumbered forces had almost defeated him in the War of the South. At the arrival of the French expedition, Louverture had tried to hide from his adversaries, only to lose control of the coastal areas in a matter of days. With his remaining forces, concentrated near Port-de-Paix (under Jacques Maurepas), Cap (under Henri

Table 4.
French and foreign units that arrived during the spring campaign (February–May 1802).

Name of unit	Date of arrival	Troops who survived the crossing	Port of departure	Ship
5th light demi-brigade 11th light demi-brigade 31st demi-brigade of the line	Feb. 3, 1802	7,000	Brest	Villaret squadron
56th demi-brigade of the line 68th demi-brigade of the line 90th demi-brigade of the line	Feb. 3, 1802	3,000	Rochefort	Latouche squadron
Legion of Saint-Domingue 19th light demi-brigade 28th light demi-brigade 74th demi-brigade of the line	Feb. 11, 1802	4,000	Toulon	Ganteaume squadron
German battalion Legion of Saint-Domingue 19th regt. of chasseurs	Feb. 17, 1802	1,900	Cádiz	Linois squadron
98th demi-brigade of the line 8th regt. of artillery	March 29, 1802	2,100	Havre and Brest	*Comête* *Zélé* *Tourville*
7th demi-brigade of the line	April 3, 1802	1,500	Vlissingen	Hartsinck squadron

Total: 19,500

Source: Armée de Saint-Domingue, "État général des troupes arrivées dans la colonie" (ca. July 1803), CC9/B23, Archives Nationales, Paris.

Christophe), Port Républicain (under Jean-Jacques Dessalines), and Gonaïves (under himself), he planned to run and hide again, this time in the mountains; he even took all the maps of the colony with him to make it harder for his foes to find him.[4] His last hope was that the broken terrain of the *mornes* (hills) would slow down French troops long enough for the summer fevers to kill his enemy in his stead.

Given the position of Louverture's forces, Leclerc organized his army into five main divisions that would converge into the interior in a strategy of mass envelopment. Hardÿ was entrusted with the main force, which would march from Cap to Dondon with Leclerc and push Christophe's men south. The division of Edmé-Étienne Desfourneaux would cover his right flank, moving from Acul to Plaisance and Gonaïves, where it would face Louverture, while Donatien de Rochambeau's division would leave Fort Liberté and follow the border with Santo Domingo to St. Raphaël to ensure that no enemy escaped eastward (François Kerversau also instructed his troops to seal the border). Meanwhile, Jean-François Debelle's troops would chase Maurepas from Port-de-Paix and move inland to Gros Morne, while Jean Boudet, operating out of Port Républicain, pushed Dessalines up the Artibonite region.[5] Even if Louverture's men managed to fall back, they would eventually be trapped in a central location, forced into a conventional battle, and decisively crushed. Alfred de Laujon, the court notary, compared the campaign to a giant *battue:* a hunt where one would force a prized stag into a corner, then move in for the kill.[6]

The French set off from their positions on February 17, and within a day the three main divisions of the north had taken Plaisance, Dondon, and St. Raphaël. Hardÿ's division moved particularly fast; its general (whose name translates as "daring") always at the forefront. In Gonaïves he led the assault across a river as Christophe retreated before him; in Ennery he defeated Louverture and captured a considerable depot of guns and ammunition. This was the second time, after the landing in Limbé, that Hardÿ had encountered and beaten Louverture, but frustratingly he again managed to escape.[7] The hilly terrain and unexpected resistance took a heavy toll on French troops as they advanced. "One must have seen this country to realize the kind of difficulties we encounter at every step," Leclerc reported. "I never saw anything comparable when crossing the Alps. . . . The rebels hide in the impenetrable woods bordering the valleys, then retreat to the hills when pressed."[8]

Farther west, Debelle arrived in Port-de-Paix on the nineteenth to reinforce Jean Humbert's battered forces. He brought with him troops from the Toulon squadron, who had endured a particularly unpleasant Atlantic crossing and were sent into combat within days of reaching Saint-Domingue.[9] As Debelle's division set out to attack Maurepas the following day, a tropical

Map 2. The Spring 1802 Campaign. Drawn by Philippe Girard after Marcel Mehl, "Carte de la partie française de Saint-Domingue," Ge B SH.146.2.9, Bibliothèque Nationale, Paris.

downpour broke out and the main assault force, struggling to keep its footing on soggy slopes, failed to carry the defenses. A second column that was supposed to turn the main enemy position reached its destination behind schedule and the uncoordinated assault failed.[10] For the second time in a week the French army had faltered before Maurepas, forcing Hardÿ and Leclerc to divert their path to Gros Morne to come to Debelle's assistance. They were about to attack when Maurepas, seeing himself surrounded, promptly surrendered against a promise that he would keep his rank in the French army. Maurepas' decision was probably also motivated by news that the commander of nearby Jean Rabel, egged on by the mountain chief Lubin Golart, had revolted against him.[11]

Despite continuous fighting, Rochambeau's division reached Ennery on the twenty-second, in the very heart of Louverture's domain. His favorite plantation was in the area, as were his wife and other family members, so he chose to make a stand in Ravine-à-Couleuvres (garden snake canyon), a valley hemmed in by steep cliffs and dense woods. After obstructing the only trail with obstacles, he positioned hundreds of grenadiers and dragoons to block the way out of the ravine, while recently drafted cultivators took position in the woods to harass the French as they proceeded up the trail. Rochambeau's forces attacked anyway and a primal melee ensued as the two forces, which had little artillery at their disposition, battled it out in gritty hand-to-hand fighting. French losses must have been heavy given the strong defensive position, but French and Haitian sources offer wildly different estimates of the forces involved in the battle, and it is impossible to offer an authoritative estimate of the casualties suffered on either side. There is even some disagreement as to who won the encounter, though Louverture was forced to pull back and, by commonly accepted standards, lost the engagement.[12] He even narrowly escaped death when he passed near a French post and one of his guides was killed by his side.[13] Many of his men, concluding that his cause was forlorn and that Napoléon Bonaparte's formidable legions were invincible, began deserting his army.[14]

～

"All the inhabitants think that Louverture is lost . . . and that we are masters of the colony," wrote Leclerc from Gros Morne on the twenty-seventh. He added, "and I share their opinion," then, in a first display of doubt, crossed out the phrase and went on to cite a litany of problems instead. His troops had bypassed numerous gatherings of armed cultivators in their rapid march south, which sooner or later would have to be subdued. Louverture, though defeated three times, remained as elusive as ever. He had burned Gonaïves and many other cities as he retreated, and supplies were scarce. Overall, ten days of combat had cost Leclerc 600 dead, 1,500 wounded, and 2,000 sick, and he urgently asked for 12,000 troops so as to save "the first colony in the world" and "decide if Europe will keep colonies in the Antilles."[15]

Just as Leclerc was summarizing the beginning of the campaign for Bonaparte's benefit, one of the officers also present in Gros Morne, Adjutant-Commandant Achille Dampierre, was updating his diary. Dampierre said nothing of the grand maneuvers that preoccupied Leclerc; he was a fighting officer who saw the campaign, not as flags and pins on a map, but as a daily grind of marches and ambushes. His unit had left on February 17 with the Desfourneaux division and had begun receiving hostile fire before it had crossed its first river, then again at regular intervals for the next five miles. Skirmishes had abated near Limbé where there were fewer trees by the road, but the lull had proved temporary. Soon the towering outline of a fort had appeared atop a mountain pass. For lack of draft animals, French troops had been forced to hand push cannon up the pass, all the while clearing the trail of obstacles and dodging fire from the fort. They had carried the position, but all the officers who had led the assault had been killed or wounded. More skirmishes had accompanied the march down to Limbé, where the troops had spent two days shivering under the torrential rains that followed the onset of the campaign. They had then resumed their difficult slog south, their clothes drenched with lukewarm sweat and rainwater, fighting every step of the way and losing eighty dead and 220 injured in the two-day march from Limbé to Gros Morne. Only then had Dampierre found enough time to update his journal.[16]

Further down the line of military hierarchy, war acquired yet another dimension, one in which ambushes were merely one of many hardships caused by the unfamiliar climate and terrain. The tropical rains and steamy heat of the Caribbean came as a shock to the veterans of the Army of the Rhine. Mosquitoes, scorpions, the giant crab spider, and centipedes—all of them deadly—were other unpleasant novelties.[17] Saint-Domingue's landscape, fashioned by millions of years of geological activity at the edge of the Caribbean tectonic plate, was a labyrinth of ravines and *mornes,* and the French found themselves fighting in mountainous ranges with the foreboding names of *Grand Cahos* (great chaos) and *Pensez-y-bien* (think twice about it).[18] Less than a third of the colony had even been mapped; the rest remained terra incognita to the very French government that claimed the land as its own.[19] Moreau de Jonnès, a young lieutenant in the French army, gave a vivid account of the reality of war seen from the lower officer level:

> The art of war was limited to the use of one's legs. . . . Martial prowess consisted in climbing an escarpment, cross a rivulet that had flooded into a tempestuous torrent, sink mid-thigh into the fetid mud of the mangrove, suffer from the sting of cacti and the thousand spiny shrubs of the Antilles, wear clothes constantly wet with sweat, rains, and rivers, and sleep on damp soil, without protection from the cold nights. . . . We could not sleep, even though we were always exhausted, because as soon as we closed our eyes, we were swamped by clouds of flies.[20]

Poor planning only added to the challenging environment. Despite André Rigaud's warning that Louverture would destroy carriages and kill mules, the expedition had brought no spares and soldiers had to carry all their equipment on their back and harness themselves to mortars like beasts of burden.[21] Napoleonic armies normally lived off the countryside when the wagon train fell behind, but most granaries had been torched on Louverture's orders, soldiers were reluctant to sample the local fruit out of a mistaken belief that these caused yellow fever, and food supplies were insufficient.[22] Despite Vincent's advice, no one had thought of bringing rain jackets, sun hats, and tents, so troops wore a heavy woolen uniform that was unsuited to the heat of the plains, slept on the cold, soggy ground of the mountains, and fell sick to heat stroke and common colds. Four thousand shoddy pairs of shoes had been found in the ships' holds when contractors were supposed to have provided four times that number, so soldiers trod barefoot through mangroves and spiny thickets.[23]

There is unfortunately no firsthand account of the campaign written by an army private, but the New York Public Library holds a manuscript written by the sailor Jean-Baptiste Lemonnier-Delafosse, who was sent to shore to assist Rochambeau's division. His nominal goal was the capture of Sainte-Suzanne near Grande Rivière, but one would be hard-pressed to identify operational objectives from his confused account. His tribulations began when he and a fellow sailor left their column to satisfy a bodily function, only to get lost and spend the following days hiding in the woods, terrified that the rebels might capture and torture them. The fog of war was made worse by the fact that black troops fought on both sides and that Lemonnier never quite understood who was a friend or foe. "This new kind of war, where we never saw the enemy, perplexed officers and soldiers," he wrote. "It was like going back to school; we understood nothing to it."[24] The sailors eventually encountered a friendly column, only to get lost again and endure another trek in which they battled mosquitoes and chiggers. After thirteen days they headed back to Fort Liberté, where Lemonnier, his right leg lacerated by a piece of shrapnel, halted his brief and bewildered career as an infantryman.

The children and women trudging along army columns, exposed to the same terrain and dangers because the war knew no defined boundary, also remain voiceless. Army cooks and quartermasters (*cantinières* and *vivandières*) rarely appear in the documentary record, while soldiers' spouses were only mentioned after their husbands died and they prepared to recross as widows the ocean they had so recently navigated as wives.[25] Children were also numerous; one German battalion listed twenty-three of them for a mere twelve officers and thirty-eight grenadiers.[26] So many were there, in fact, that the army eventually had to set a quota of two *enfants de troupe* (child mascots) per company. The number did not include children ten and above, who were old enough to enroll as fife or drummer, or those who, upon reaching the ripe old age of twelve, had to enroll as regular soldiers.[27] This was an army of children and teenagers, led by generals, Leclerc included, who were often in their twenties.

For the French army, Caribbean warfare was as confounding as the region's flora and fauna. The term *guerrilla war* had not yet been coined so contemporaries spoke of an "Arab war" in reference to the campaign of Egypt (another apt description was the "black Vendée").[28] Making matters worse, Bonaparte had sent few of the light skirmishers who would have been suited to the terrain.[29] French military doctrine normally called for columns of heavy infantry to spread out before charging against enemy positions, but they could not deploy in the narrow mountain trails and the rebels chose to attack un-suspecting troops from hidden positions on a column's flanks. "These Arabs of Saint-Domingue only attack laggards and those who are lost," complained a brigadier-chief. "When they actually attack a column . . . they know where to retreat because they know the area perfectly."[30] Despite the difficulties of the campaign, morale remained high at first. "Had Leclerc promoted all those who conducted themselves with bravery," wrote his chief of staff, "there would not be a single private left in the army."[31]

French soldiers were prone to criticize the rebel way of war as unfair and cowardly because they did not conform to European norms, but they were consistent with tactics that African-born rebels and veterans of the earlier years of the Haitian Revolution had experienced since their youth. African wars, very common due to the continent's political fragmentation, often aimed at capturing slaves rather than territory and thus typically consisted of short campaigns and raiding parties. African warriors' tactics and weapons had proved sufficiently effective against their European foes for most of Africa not to be colonized until the late nineteenth century.[32] Guerrilla tactics had also served the rebels well since 1791. At the beginning of the Haitian Revolution, rebellious slaves had proved highly vulnerable to the disciplined fire of a professional army in the open, but they had quickly switched to a war of nightly raids and arson that had allowed them to defeat their French owners, Spain, and then England.

Louverture had tried to drill his army in the European style during his tenure as governor, but he quickly reverted to the rebels' default mode when the lopsided routs of Port Républicain and Cap demonstrated the limita-tions of his troops in pitched battles.[33] "Obstruct trails, throw corpses of horses into springs; destroy and burn everything," he instructed Dessalines.[34] The strategy made good use of the rebels' strengths. In colonial times slaves had learned to supplement their meager diet with local fruits and roots, wild game, or even carrion, and they could live off far more limited resources than their opponents.[35] The French "have done amazing things during the wars they fought in Europe," Louverture told his troops. "But under this burning climate, you have one advantage: you can stand fatigue better."[36]

Even less is known of rebel soldiers than of their French counterparts, ex-cept that they were a diverse group, composed of individuals born on three continents and whose general profile one can reconstruct by using prerevolu-tionary demographic data. On the eve of the Haitian Revolution, two-thirds of black Dominguians had been African-born, so many rebels were survivors of the Middle Passage. French traders had first imported slaves from Sene-gambia before shifting their focus to the Bight of Benin and the Congo, and no fewer than one hundred tribal groups (or "nations") had been represented on Saint-Domingue plantations. Natives of the Congo had been most numerous (representing 34 percent of slaves), but one also encountered Bambaras, Igbos, Yorubas, Louverture's Ewe-Fon brethren, and every ethnic group from Mauritania to Mozambique.[37] All these groups were presumably represented in the rebel army, in addition to Creoles born in Saint-Domingue (like Louverture), natives of the British Caribbean (like Christophe), and, more surprisingly, white Frenchmen. During the battle of Ravine-à-Couleuvres, a battalion chief pointed out with some befuddlement that his men had killed a member of Louverture's personal guard and that he was "a Frenchman from La Rochelle."[38] Dessalines also sent some Frenchmen to reinforce a unit in Mirebalais.[39]

The correspondence of Louverture's generals makes frequent references to women and children accompanying rebel units.[40] This should come as no surprise: men had outnumbered women on slave ships and plantations, but ten years of war had disproportionately affected young males, and women formed a majority of Saint-Domingue's population by 1802.[41] Such women abided in part by the gender norms of their tribal group, which did not always preclude military service since women served as soldiers in African polities like the kingdom of Dahomey (present-day Benin).[42] Women had participated in the slave revolt since its beginning in 1791, and their military role only grew with their demographic weight.[43] Louverture initially planned to give women mere logistical roles like growing food while entrusting the heavy fighting to his professional, male army, but desperate for troops as entire demi-brigades abandoned him he increasingly resorted to hastily drafted farm laborers as the campaign progressed.[44] Judging by the composition of the labor force in plantations of the era, a majority of these armed cultivators—Louverture's last line of defense—were black women, half of them born in Africa.

⁓

To incite Louverture's supporters to switch sides, Leclerc treated civilians with respect and promised repeatedly that he had not come to restore slavery.[45] His proclamations had their intended effect, and within days of landing in Cap he was able to raise several companies of black soldiers, enlist the local national guard, and employ some black guides. By April 1, six weeks after the campaign had begun, he had a total of seven thousand colonial troops fighting for him, or as many as the number of European troops still fit for duty.[46] By the end of the campaign there would be more troops of color fighting for France than against it.

Many local commanders in the northern region joined the French side from the outset of the campaign. Makajoux, the commander of Pilate, quickly defected, as did Jolicoeur in Port Margot, Louis Dau in Acul, Jean-Pierre Dumesnil in Plaisance, and a dozen others.[47] Each of them commanded a town and the adjoining countryside, so their support was essential to help control swaths of territory that French troops had no time to garrison as they maneuvered to encircle Louverture. Motives for defecting to the French side ranged from disaffection with Louverture's rule to the idealistic tone of Leclerc's proclamations. Many expected the French to win and wished to be on the victor's side; one black officer also cited his opposition to wanton acts of arson, probably because he owned plantations. But the most significant factor was an order by Leclerc that declared all assets belonging to rebel officers as forfeit.[48] Economic sanctions would have been an empty threat during the 1791 slave revolt, when the rebels did not even own their own bodies, but colonial officers were now members of the propertied elite, with much to lose in case of a defeat.

Among the converts was a black officer with the unique moniker of Gingembre Trop Fort (ginger too strong), who commanded the city of Borgne (one-eyed man). Gingembre's unusual name stood out even in a colony led by a Toussaint Louverture (All Saints Day the Opening) and whose place names ranged from Sale Trou (dirty hole) to Tiburon (shark). Although only 4'8" tall, Gingembre cut a commanding figure with his long spurs, large earrings, and oversized saber.[49]

Gingembre's tortuous itinerary in the early weeks of the war was typical of the difficult choices that local officers had to make as they attempted to balance their racial affiliations, economic self-interest, and the ever-shifting balance of military power in a given region.[50] Gingembre had received orders from Louverture to fight incoming French troops and, if forced to retreat, take white hostages and burn everything. He dutifully assisted Maurepas during the battle for Port-de-Paix, but he was clever enough to simultaneously notify the French that he was thinking of surrendering (Félix Dépassé, commander of Borgne's national guard, also offered his services to the French while massacring white civilians). Sensing an opportunity for promotion, Gingembre's subordinate Joseph Casimir spared Borgne and appealed to the French, who rewarded him by promoting him to city commander. In a matter of days Borgne's three leading military figures had all divided their allegiances in an attempt to salvage their careers.

Gingembre spent ten days fighting under Maurepas, then switched sides after Maurepas' own surrender. Professing his newfound loyalty for France, he returned to Borgne and insisted that "interim commander" Casimir step down.[51] French commanders probably had some doubts about his loyalty, but they needed local strongmen like Gingembre to maintain order, and he regained his former command despite Casimir's grumbling. Knowing what the French wanted to hear, he immediately announced that his first goal as restored commander of Borgne would be to get cultivators back to work on their plantations.

Unwilling to forgive Gingembre for the fires and massacres he had so recently condoned, white civilians were panic-stricken when he returned to town. They immediately accused him and Maurepas of plotting to rejoin rebel ranks at the first opportunity and of facilitating the escape of several rebels accused of killing plantation owners. Still hopeful that he might regain his command, Casimir eagerly joined the public outcry against Gingembre. Deluged with letters from the various factions in Borgne, military authorities in Cap officially sided with the powerful Gingembre, though one suspects that in private they shared the planters' misgivings. With people of all shades fighting on both sides of the conflict—all of them wearing the French uniform, since Louverture had not declared independence and his troops marched under the tricolor—the war was a complex tangle in which an individual's ideals and ambitions were as significant as his racial affiliation.

Farther south in Port Républicain, Pamphile Lacroix was also contemplating his career options. Born in 1774 to a lawyer from Provence, Lacroix had followed the typical itinerary of a bourgeois officer during the French Revolution. Luckier than his brothers (two of whom died in combat), he had gradually ascended the ranks of the French army under the tutelage of such generals as Jean Moreau. But by 1801 he had been an adjutant-commandant for two years and he began to fear that he would obtain no further promotions as long as peace prevailed in Europe. After some hesitation he embarked on the Leclerc expedition with the purely self-interested goal of making brigadier general.[52] Lacroix was unusually literate and impartial; thankfully for later generations of historians, he survived the Leclerc expedition, published a masterful history of the Haitian Revolution, and left two thick personal files in the army archives in Vincennes that are another invaluable resource on the Leclerc expedition.[53]

Lacroix served as Boudet's chief of staff in Port Républicain, where he spent much time trying to convince Louverture's followers to abandon the rebel side. The arrival of large French contingents and the prompt submission of the south were strong incentives to defect. So was the fact that the French generally treated deserters and prisoners well.[54] As he freed a captured black officer, Lacroix gave him a set of Bonaparte's proclamations and urged him to tell his old unit "the way the French from Europe welcome the French from Saint-Domingue" and emphasize that "we are serving the Republic" when "their chiefs only speak of freedom to serve their interests and obtain the labor of those poor cultivators they used to hit with clubs."[55] Lacroix's case proved so compelling that within a few days he was swamped with deserters and had to stop distributing army rations for fear of attracting thousands more recruits.[56]

When the spring campaign began, Boudet left Lacroix and a few troops to guard Port Républicain while he marched north to join Leclerc's other divisions. Boudet's troops captured Arcahaye, then Saint-Marc, but they found little but ashes and corpses. After his failed attempt to ravage the south, Dessalines had returned to his traditional command in Saint-Marc, which he set ablaze—starting with his own luxurious mansion—before it could fall to French hands. Two hundred French civilians also fell victim to his wrath.[57] Instead of continuing north to join Louverture, the unpredictable Dessalines then turned back south toward Port Républicain. An anxious Lacroix wondered how he would defend the city with eight hundred troops and the sailors from the naval squadron when Lafortune and Lamour Derance came to offer their services. Heading groups of runaway cultivators who profoundly disliked plantation-owning officers like Dessalines, they helped save Port Républicain for France. Dessalines fell back on the Mirebalais region, killing all the cultivators he encountered in his rage.[58]

Dessalines failed to convince inhabitants of the west and south to follow him, but he did manage to shake their trust in the French army. Many of the officers of color who had rallied to France's side had done so based on Leclerc's reassurances that he had no intention of restoring slavery. Dessalines and Louverture countered with a propaganda offensive that described Leclerc as the stooge of the planter lobby, leaving many people of color unsure whether they should support Dessalines, who had abused them in the recent past, or the French, who had done so throughout the previous century. Visibly troubled by Dessalines' charges, a black brigadier chief named Paul Lafrance took Lacroix aside and asked him in tears whether "you are here to restore slavery? Whatever happens, the old Paul Lafrance would never do you any harm. . . . But my daughters, my poor daughters . . . slaves . . . Oh! I would die of grief."[59] Gaining, or losing, the support of countless black officers like Lafrance and Gingembre—by convincing them that their ideals or their self-interest would be better served by siding with France—would decide the eventual outcome of the evolving conflict.

～

Michel-Étienne Descourtilz, the naturalist who had sailed to the Caribbean during Louverture's heyday to recover his wife's plantations, was still in the colony when the Leclerc expedition landed in February 1802. Living in north-central Saint-Domingue, at the bull's eye of Leclerc's envelopment maneuvers, he found himself caught in the midst of epochal events, which

he later related in a rare, if atrociously written, account of the spring campaign as seen from a civilian's perspective.[60]

Descourtilz was in Gonaïves when Louverture, cornered by converging
French columns, stormed into town atop his stallion. Betrayed by his subordinates and abandoned by his creator, Louverture rode directly into the church,
smashed a crucifix, and torched the building in a sacrilegious gesture that was
a pivotal moment in his spiritual life. As Spanish auxiliary and French governor, he had made frequent displays of piety; from February 1802 until his
death he never again appealed to the European god who had failed him.

"With a low, threatening voice and ferocious eyes" (or so wrote Descourtilz), Louverture then announced that he would kill all white plantation
owners—and left abruptly.[61] Louverture rarely oversaw massacres in person
so as to deny any personal responsibility, but he tacitly approved his subordinates' actions, and in at least one letter Dessalines asked him for his express
authorization before executing a group of white prisoners.[62] Jean-Baptiste
Vollée, Louverture's white financier and a loyal supporter, was immediately
shot—possibly so that he could not reveal the whereabouts of the colonial
treasury—while black soldiers forced Descourtilz and other white notables
to turn over their valuables.[63] This step, which preceded most massacres of
civilians during the war, suggests that financial gain was as powerful a motivator as racial hatred for the average Dominguian. The rebels then took the
survivors inland to Petite Rivière, where they were jailed for days in a tiny,
suffocating cell.

Dessalines, who had earned a reputation for cruelty in countless massacres of Dominguians of all colors, arrived in Petite Rivière at that critical
juncture, still fuming at his failure to retake Port Républicain. Thankfully,
so did his wife, the gentle Claire-Heureuse, who hid Descourtilz under her
bed to protect him from her husband's wrath. He was still cowering there
when Dessalines entered the room to discuss the fate of white civilians with
his officers. The more moderate among them expressed their reluctance to
kill the innocent along with the guilty, but Dessalines reminded them of the
atrocities committed by the planters during the slavery era and quickly silenced their doubts with generous servings of *taffia* (rum). His officers still
saw Saint-Domingue as a combination of individuals, each of them characterized by their unique moral foibles, but Dessalines no longer made any distinction between "good" and "bad" planters. He had already reached a point
in his ideological development where he saw Saint-Domingue as a combination of racial and social groups engaged in a battle for supremacy. Even then,
when Descourtilz's hiding place was discovered, Dessalines agreed to spare
Descourtilz on account of his medical expertise. The story of the husband
discovering a man hidden under his wife's bed sounds almost too theatrical

to be real, but the respite awarded Descourtilz rings true: engineers, doctors, priests, and secretaries often survived the Haitian Revolution because they had skills that were uncommon among former slaves.

That same night, soldiers fanned across Petite Rivière to massacre the white population, the more hesitant among them constantly prodded by *taffia* and Dessalines' potent reminders of slavery. Several times Descourtilz neared death only to survive when he showed the tools of his trade or a former patient vouched for him. Others were not as lucky. Descourtilz made particular note of "impaled pregnant women" and "children neutered with bad scissors," gory details that mirrored those found in accounts written by white captives during the 1791 slave uprising.[64] Then, as later, sexual crimes, particularly those committed against white women, struck white observers as the most vivid insults to the racial and social order; then, as later, acts of cruelty against civilians seemed intended as payback for the slave masters' own sexual crimes.

Despite popular anger at the alleged plan to restore slavery, race remained a porous dividing line, and Descourtilz noted that Dessalines' wife, a black nurse called Pompée, and several mixed-race individuals treated him humanely in the days that followed the massacre at Petite Rivière. Promoted to director of the rebel army's ambulance system, Descourtilz even boasted that "my success in curing the injured promptly turned me into an important character."[65] He thus followed Dessalines' mixed force of soldiers and cultivators as they marched into the *morne* of Grand Cahos, massacring, burning, and leaving a trail of ash and blood behind them.

Another white prisoner caught in the massacre of Petite Rivière was Mialaret, the tutor of Louverture's children. The incredible streak of good luck that had seen him through the Haitian Revolution seemed to have finally run out. "A woman" (probably Claire-Heureuse Dessalines) appeared one night by Mialaret's cell to free him.[66] Eluding his pursuers, Mialaret managed to reach the coast, where he boarded a French ship, only to be attacked by a pirate ship from the nearby lair of Providence; marooned on a parched, deserted island; saved by a passing U.S. merchant ship; and returned to France in 1804, fifteen years after he had left as a teenager. Mialaret's eventful life later took him to Elba, where he met Louverture's fallen rival, and Louisiana, where he seduced the orphaned heiress of a plantation. The marriage proved unhappy, not least because Mialaret emancipated many of his wife's slaves, but it produced a daughter who married the famous French historian Jules Michelet and wrote the story of her father's unusual revolutionary journey.

Some details of Descourtilz's and Mialaret's narrow brushes with death were probably exaggerated for dramatic effect, but the massacres they witnessed were all too real. In the two-month spring campaign, about three thousand white civilians perished, or 10 percent of the prerevolutionary white population, leaving only ten to twelve surviving whites in some *quartiers* (counties) by the time the fighting subsided.[67] French columns advancing through the Grand Cahos encountered many an example of Dessalines' revenge. Marching with Leclerc along the Artibonite River, his secretary, Jacques de Norvins, saw caimans feasting on human flesh, then the scorched remains of hundreds of civilians in Verettes. Lacroix witnessed the same ghastly scene when he crossed the town on March 9.[68]

> The butcher who committed this act had shown no compassion for either sex or age. . . . Girls, their breast torn apart, looked as if they were begging for mercy for their mothers; mothers covered with their pierced arms the children slaughtered on their bosom. . . . Our men were so brave that this horrible sight, far from frightening them, only made them more ardently desire to strike their enemy. One of the detachments volunteered to fight while we were still visiting the carnage; never have I seen anything comparable to the ardor they displayed in their task.

Creoles were all too familiar with such cruelty, which they had inflicted and witnessed many times before and during the revolution, but racial warfare came as a shock to French soldiers. Some elite Frenchmen and most colonists were racist in the modern, biological sense of the term, but "scientific" racism had yet to take hold in metropolitan France, where the term *race* was often used interchangeably for what one would call today *social class* or *region of origin*. With a mere five thousand people of color in all of France (most of them in Paris or Atlantic ports), most of the soldiers in the expedition had probably never even seen a person of color until they embarked for Saint-Domingue.[69]

The French soldiers' color-blind outlook may explain why they behaved with remarkable restraint in the opening weeks of the expedition—and why their attitude changed as colonial prejudices and the brutality of war sank in. By March 1802, a month after the initial landing, atrocities against white civilians were routinely followed by retaliatory massacres; in one notorious case the Hardÿ division summarily executed six hundred prisoners accused of killing one hundred civilians. Following yet another massacre of civilians, a British captain visiting from Jamaica saw French soldiers line up two hundred black prisoners at the edge of a ready-made grave before shooting them all methodically. The second massacre may well have been Hardÿ's handiwork as well, since his division was in the area at the time. Neither of them, it goes without saying, was mentioned in the letters he sent to his wife.[70]

By the end of February, Dessalines headed one of the last organized units in Louverture's once-proud army. Facing him were the divisions of Hardÿ, Rochambeau, Boudet, and Desfourneaux, all of them rapidly closing on his position. Not one to surrender, Dessalines chose to make a stand in Crête-à-Pierrot, a fort overlooking the Artibonite River, not far from the town of Petite Rivière where Mialaret and Descourtilz's companions had met their end.[71] The area had once been a flourishing plain, but by March 1802 it was a war-torn wasteland crisscrossed by a few elderly survivors.[72] The fort itself dated back to prerevolutionary times and had been expanded by the British in the 1790s. Vincent had mentioned it in one of his memoirs, but Leclerc, uninformed as always, confessed that he did not know of the fort's existence until he had to take it in a siege that marked the climax of the spring campaign.[73]

There were two ways to capture a fort. One could dig trenches and lines of circumvallation, starve and bomb the garrison, and generally follow the rules of eighteenth-century manuals on siege warfare. Alternatively, one could storm a fort without lengthy preparations, banking on the fact that it was garrisoned by inferior troops lacking discipline and marksmanship— the very prejudices the French held against colonial troops. The latter tactic had worked well in Fort Liberté, Port Républicain, and Léogane and fit the French taste for élan, so no one saw any need to alter it as the campaign neared its apex.[74]

First on the scene was Debelle. Eager to make up for his unsatisfactory performance in Port-de-Paix, he charged against the fort on March 4 before the other columns could join him. The assault failed miserably, leaving two generals injured—including Debelle—and three hundred troops dead. Dessalines personally led a sortie to exploit the advantage, but the fighting soon became confused as Dessalines' men, still wearing the French uniform, encountered the black troops of Maurepas' 9th demi-brigade, now fighting on the French side. After he was almost killed by one of his own captains, Dessalines returned to the fort to await the next French assault. Much to his annoyance, Louverture and Christophe stopped by in the days that followed and commandeered several hundreds of his men to replace those they had lost to desertion. This left him with a mere 1,200 troops to face the bulk of the French army.

Leclerc and the Boudet division arrived a week later to reinforce what was left of the Debelle division (now headed by Leclerc's chief of staff, Charles Dugua, following Debelle's injury). They brought with them the 13th demi-brigade, a colonial unit led by Alexandre Pétion, one of the mixed-race officers who had come with the expedition. Before the French could attack,

Dessalines opened the gates of the fort and told the sick and the cowardly that they should leave at once. "These gates are lowered for those who are not willing to die," he announced. "The friends of the French should go while they have the opportunity, because they can only expect death here."[75] He then took a barrel of gunpowder, grabbed a torch, and warned that he would blow up the fort if his men failed him. A French negotiator approaching the fort was swept away by a cannonball by order of Dessalines, who also killed a black agent who entered the fort with a copy of Leclerc's proclamation hidden in his ponytail. The red flag went up on all corners of the fort. Surrender was not an option.

These details were related by Louis Boisrond-Tonnerre, the scion of a wealthy dynasty of mixed-race southern planters, who despite his background was an admirer of Dessalines who glorified his every move. The only other source on what took place inside the fort suffers from the opposite bias, since it was written by the naturalist Descourtilz, still a prisoner of the rebels. According to his account, Dessalines' men tortured six of the French prisoners taken during the first assault, drank their blood, and ate their hearts in a ritual that may have been religious in nature, or an act of revenge, or the product of hunger—or simply a story made up by Descourtilz to emphasize his captors' barbarity. His version of Dessalines' speech, however, is consistent with the general's usual style. "Do not lose your heart," he told them in Kreyol. "Whites from France cannot resist Saint-Domingue's men. They will walk, walk, and then stop. They will get sick and die like flies. Listen attentively: if Dessalines surrenders to the French a hundred times, he will betray them a hundred times.... After this, Dessalines will set you free."[76]

When the French launched their second assault at dawn, led by Boudet in person, Dessalines' troops defended themselves with an intense barrage of artillery. The women in the fort took an active part in its defense, particularly Marie-Jeanne Lamartinière, the wife of the battalion chief who had contested the French landing in Port Républicain. The French got as far as the moat and seemed on the verge of taking the fort when Dessalines ordered one last discharge of artillery that wounded Boudet and finally broke the back of the French assault. Harassed by continuous cannon fire and a sortie by some of the defenders, French troops hastily retreated down the hill, and Leclerc and Dugua had to intervene to prevent an outright rout. Both were injured in the action, bringing the count of French generals wounded in the siege to five, including the captain general himself.

Dugua and Boudet's injuries forced Lacroix to travel from Port Républicain to take over their divisions, which had suffered a total of seven hundred casualties. The command, which came with a coveted promotion to brigadier general, surely pleased Lacroix, but the troops he now led must have been par-

ticularly shaken. Those under Debelle had participated in the difficult capture of Port-de-Paix and two costly attacks on Crête-à-Pierrot; their commanding general had been replaced twice in a week.

The fate of the wounded at Crête-à-Pierrot must have been particularly
wrenching, not only inside the fort (where Descourtilz was the only source
of medical care), but also outside, where French military surgeons were constrained by the limitations of an age that did not know of germs, infections,
and anesthetics. There is no detailed account of the treatment of the wounded
during this siege, but one can extrapolate from another battle, fought later that
year, in which a cavalry officer had his arm shot through by a bullet. After riding his horse back to Cap—wounded soldiers were expected to walk to the
nearest aid station in the Napoleonic era—the officer waited three hours before local doctors bandaged his arm. A surgeon stopped by later, but unwilling to offend his colleagues he did not undo their bandage until a day later,
when he finally set the broken bone almost thirty hours after it had been shattered. The surgeon did little more thereafter than install a catheter to drain the
pus from the swollen arm and monitor the wound for any sign of gangrene,
while the patient's immune system, for a full fifty days, fought off a massive
infection that might have turned into septicemia had the patient not acciden-
tally shifted his arm one day. A piece of cloth and a shard of bone—probably
the root cause of the infection—fell from the wound and the patient recovered soon after. He had been so well treated by contemporary standards that
the surgeon wrote a lengthy account of the case in the colony's medical journal to boast about his success.[77]

Human frailty added to the primitive state of medicine. Bonaparte had
shut down medical schools on the eve of the expedition, leading to a 50 percent drop in the number of army surgeons between 1801 and 1804. Leclerc,
for his part, had left the army's medical supplies in Brest because he deemed
them subpar, so his doctors spent the entire campaign without proper equipment. Louverture's scorched-earth policy also meant that the sick and the
wounded often lay on the ground, in the open.[78] One can only imagine the
appalling scene near Crête-à-Pierrot given the massive number of casualties
sustained during the siege. Corpses from both armies were left to rot in place,
and a Haitian historian who visited the battle site four decades later noted
that it was still strewn with the skeletons of fallen foes whose bleached, intertwined bones had finally found amity in death.[79]

Leclerc turned thirty on March 17. When he had sailed to Saint-Domingue,
he had probably not expected that he would celebrate his birthday—his last—
at the foot of an impregnable fort, injured, amid the moans of the amputees
and the mutilated bodies of hundreds of civilians and soldiers. A few days

later he sent his brother back to France and asked Bonaparte, for the first of many times, to be recalled.[80]

After two unsuccessful assaults, Leclerc concluded that the fort would have to be taken in a more traditional manner and left for Saint-Marc to fetch artillery pieces. He also called on the Hardÿ and Rochambeau divisions to join the siege. The two generals were supposed to wait for artillery support, but Rochambeau chose to attack immediately, possibly on account of a rumor that Louverture had hidden his treasure inside the fort. The rank and file, "infuriated by the notion that they would have to mount a siege against such enemies," also itched for another try.[81] Rochambeau sent his division up the hill; it returned with three hundred fewer men a few hours later. "And so," wrote a despondent Lacroix, "Crête-à-Pierrot, in which there were fewer than 1,200 men left, had already cost us over 1,500 casualties, with nothing to show for it."[82] Finally chastened by the three deadly assaults, the army hunkered down and adopted the conservative tactic it probably would have used from the outset had it not underestimated its adversary: blockade and bombardment.

The lull allowed Dessalines to repair Crête-à-Pierrot and build a second redoubt on a nearby hill.[83] He entrusted the main fort to Brigadier Chief Magny while Lamartinière took over the redoubt, his wife Marie-Jeanne still by his side. After urging them never to surrender or evacuate unless they received his ring as a coded signal, Dessalines then abandoned his subordinates to their fate (the oral tradition claims that Dessalines could make himself invisible and travel to and from the fort at will).[84] Boisrond holds that Dessalines left so that he could gather more supplies, but Descourtilz's accusation that Dessalines was afraid of the upcoming bombardment is more credible; in an uncharacteristic display of weakness, he wrote Louverture that he had abandoned his post due to a terrible migraine.[85]

Crête-à-Pierrot was the first time that French and rebel troops lived in close quarters for a sustained amount of time. They faced each other across a battlefield strewn with cadavers, but the lines were close, assaults frequent, and French troops learned much about the political ideas of their opponents—which, they discovered, mirrored their own. The white prisoners in the fort included a band of musicians whom their captors ordered to play "La Carmagnole," a famous revolutionary song that called on true patriots to hang aristocrats. Lacroix's soldiers looked at each other in befuddlement as the familiar stanzas streamed across no man's land. They were the army of Moreau; no one had ever called them "aristocrats" before. "Our soldiers glanced at us," remembered Lacroix, "as if to say: 'Were our barbaric enemies right? Were we no longer the soldiers of the Republic? Had we become servile instruments of politics?'"[86] Many of them must have reflected on the fact that the aristocratic planters bayoneted on Dessalines' orders were not so different from the noble lords they had guillotined during the Terror.

Identifying one's true enemy was made all the more difficult by the fact that the French presented themselves as the liberators of the oppressed cultivators and that they fought alongside the colored demi-brigades of Maurepas and Pétion. When an elderly black couple caught near the fort was accused of espionage and summarily whipped, Lacroix ordered his men to free the accused, one blind, the other deaf. Their backs bent by old age, they slowly walked away, only to break into a victory dance as soon as they were out of range. They were indeed rebel spies on their way to Crête-à-Pierrot to deliver Dessalines' ring—the signal that Magny and Lamartinière could evacuate.

The French opened a steady bombardment when Leclerc returned with siege pieces on March 22 and the situation quickly became desperate inside the fort, where Descourtilz struggled to tend to the many wounded while food, water, and bandages ran out. After one hundred defenders died in a matter of hours, Magny proposed to end the siege with a dramatic mass suicide that would have provided an interesting counterpoint to the tragic last stand of the rebels from Guadeloupe in Matouba that same spring. His troops sensibly insisted on trying to escape, and though they were surrounded by a ring of French units that outnumbered them ten to one, half of the garrison sneaked through enemy lines in the dead of night in what Lacroix described as a "remarkable *fait d'armes.*"[87] After Descourtilz informed Leclerc that the fort was unguarded, French troops finally seized the position and massacred all the wounded who had been left behind, most likely in revenge for the losses suffered during the siege and the massacres of civilians that had taken place nearby.

The siege was a public relations embarrassment for Leclerc. He had sacrificed 2,000 troops to capture a fort manned by 1,200 rebels, half of whom had escaped, when everyone had been convinced of the French army's superiority in standard set pieces like a siege. The many officers who had flocked to the French side when it looked the strongest—people like Gingembre— might be tempted to return to Louverture's side if they concluded that he might win after all. Lacroix noted ruefully that cultivators, invigorated by the heroic defense of Crête-à-Pierrot, ambushed French columns with renewed energy because "we no longer inspired moral terror."[88] Christophe wrote excitedly that such a retreat "was well worth a victory" and that his dispirited troops had been overjoyed when he had told them how "those who were inspired by the powerful zeal of liberty had so thoroughly humbled their enemies."[89]

Fearful of the consequences the bloodbath of Crête-à-Pierrot might have in the larger battle for popular support, the French did their best to hide their losses. During the sorrowful march back to Port Républicain, Boudet ordered his officers to leave large gaps between the ranks so that no one could notice how much the division had shrunk in a few weeks. Leclerc published a triumphant account of the siege in a local newspaper, and equally worried by Paris's reaction he told his generals to lie about the number of soldiers under their command, "as he was already doing himself in his official reports."[90] To explain why he only had 7,500 men still fit for duty, Leclerc vaguely referred to an unspecified number of soldiers who had fallen victim to "arson, murder, and fatigue," not combat.[91] The crude propaganda deceived no one. Local civilians, Anglo-Americans, and Bonaparte quickly learned of the appalling slaughter at Crête-à-Pierrot, which remained the war's most notable battle until Vertières eighteen months later.[92]

⁓

In its haste to bring a quick end to the campaign, the French army had sliced through central Saint-Domingue, throwing all opposition aside but never stopping long enough to establish any lasting control over the countryside. As popular resistance revived in the aftermath of Crête-à-Pierrot, armed cultivators raided recently conquered areas at will, and French officers in the south reported anxiously that the colonial officers who had recently surrendered might change their minds once they realized how few white troops garrisoned the vast region.[93] Louverture concluded that he could undo recent reverses by sparking popular uprisings in the French's unprotected rear, a tactic probably inspired by his rival Rigaud, who had used it to devastating effect during the War of the South. Louverture thus slipped through French lines and headed for Port-de-Paix, only to run into Maurepas' 9th colonial demi-brigade and realize that they now fought on France's side. Although surrounded by hostile troops, Louverture lost none of his usual composure and dared them imperiously to fire at their commander. Time stood still as troops hesitated over whether to shoot or obey the fallen governor, until someone opened fire and Louverture had to find refuge in flight.[94]

Louverture miraculously escaped—yet again—but he was injured in the engagement, and his hope of disrupting Leclerc's strategy of envelopment by seizing Port-de-Paix was shattered by Maurepas' defection. His beloved horse was also killed under him during his hasty retreat, while his and Dessalines' sons were captured around the same time. Cut off from many subordinates in the chaos of the unfolding campaign, Louverture only now learned that some family members, such as Jean-Pierre Louverture, had defected to the enemy.[95] Louverture sent yet another agent to incite southerners to rebel, but he failed to overturn the locals' deep-seated antipathy. He was, increasingly, alone.[96]

It was a sign of Louverture's desperation that in April 1802 he appealed to Sylla, Sans Souci, Makaya, and Petit Noël Prieur, who headed groups of plantation runaways that were active near Ennery and Cap.[97] They could inflict significant losses on columns of French soldiers, but begging bands of African-born rivals to drop rocks from mountaintops was probably not what Louverture had had in mind when two months before he had headed an army of up to twenty thousand hardened veterans that made the governors of all nearby colonies tremble.

Christophe was more successful than Louverture in threatening their enemy's unsecured rear. While the French army was distracted by the siege of Crête-à-Pierrot, he backtracked to the rich plain of Cap, where he burned many valuable plantations and enrolled thousands of their cultivators. He went as far as a hill overlooking the city of Cap, from which he aimed a 12-pounder at the government house on March 18. The city was only weakly garrisoned since Leclerc had sent virtually every soldier into the interior, but sailors from the Cap squadron helped establish a defensive line and Christophe's assault, along with a second one ten days later, achieved little beyond rebel casualties.[98]

Cap, the main entryway for U.S. supplies and French reinforcements, could not be allowed to fall. Realizing that his aggressive plan of action had put a strategic port in danger, Leclerc hastily ordered the Hardÿ division to march to Cap. This took Hardÿ's troops on a long, difficult trek through central Saint-Domingue. After battling their way through countless ambushes mounted on Louverture's orders, they ran into Christophe's own troops as they left Dondon and were caught between two rebel forces. Short on cartridges the division was nearly annihilated and lost over four hundred men getting to its destination.[99] Once so confident in his letters to his wife, Hardÿ now described the campaign as "horrible, with much fatigue and deprivations." "War in this country is a terrible business," he added soon after.[100]

~

The campaign had now degenerated into a bloody, confused stalemate. Although militarily superior overall, the French could not control all areas of the colony at once, while Louverture could not entertain any reasonable hope of victory in the near future after losing so many men to desertion and combat. Like two aging boxers in an indecisive bout, the French and the rebels battered each other mercilessly, yet remained unable to inflict the blow that would knock out their enemy.

Christophe, whose conduct during the French landing in Cap had been equivocal, was particularly tempted by French promises of amnesty. Accustomed to a sophisticated lifestyle in Cap, he begrudged the unpleasantness of life on the run and was "tired," he explained, "of living in the woods like a brigand."[101] After his first raid on Cap, he contacted the city's new French commander, who foolishly rejected his overture. The demoralized Hardÿ proved more amenable, and after his difficult trek to Cap he promised Christophe a sizable reward if he agreed to surrender. Christophe did not dignify Hardÿ's offer of a bribe with a response and insisted that the one vital question at stake in the conflict was that of emancipation.[102] Troubled by persistent reports about the strength of the planter lobby in Paris, he would not surrender unless he received a formal reassurance that universal freedom would remain the cornerstone of French law. Leclerc yielded and on April 25–26 he issued two important documents: a public proclamation promising that he would draft laws based on the twin principles of "liberty and equality"; and a decree canceling Christophe's outlaw status, thus allowing him to regain his plantations.[103] Christophe must have trusted Leclerc, because he soon visited Cap to meet him in person, then sent his eldest son to be educated in France.[104]

Christophe's submission was an unpleasant surprise for Louverture, whom Christophe had continued to meet and serve even as he secretly corresponded with Leclerc. What Christophe did not know was that Louverture had also been secretly preparing the ground for his own surrender since early April, when the arrival of 3,600 reinforcements from France must have convinced him that the campaign was unwinnable.[105] After four hundred of the newcomers were captured, Louverture chose not to send the prisoners to Dessalines to be massacred and instead treated them well—better, in fact, than Bonaparte's corrupt pursers, since the hungry, barefoot troops now received beef and shoes.[106] Louverture also freed the French officer captured during the landing in Port Républicain so that he could deliver conciliatory letters to Boudet. But Louverture boldly asked that Leclerc be recalled to France as a precondition for his capitulation, and these early negotiations soon collapsed.[107]

Christophe's submission a few weeks later only put more pressure on Louverture to end the war. He later claimed that he could easily have won the spring campaign and only surrendered to prevent further bloodshed, but his situation was perilous in the extreme. Christophe had defected with 4,000 armed cultivators and 1,500 troops, and soon revealed the location of Louverture's secret stashes of weapons.[108] Short on ammunition, Louverture's soldiers were now reduced to melting lead and making cartridges by hand.[109] Dessalines was the only officer of note still on Louverture's side, and even he lost many men to desertion when he was taken with a bout of sickness in the aftermath of the siege of Crête-à-Pierrot. Louverture confessed to Dessalines that he was considering surrendering, but his indomitable subordinate angrily rejected such treacherous talk and privately made plans to put Louverture under arrest. Backtracking, Louverture immediately assured Dessalines that he had no intention of seeking a cease-fire. He then left to do just that.[110]

On April 29 an envoy sent by Louverture secretly traveled to Cap and negotiated an agreement under which all rebel generals and soldiers would be pardoned and reincorporated in the French army if they stopped fighting.[111] After two and a half months of combat and thousands of deaths, the cease-fire reestablished an equilibrium eerily similar to that prevalent before the onset of general war: two large forces of European and colonial troops that cohabited uneasily while claiming to serve the same republic. Weeks of fratricidal conflict had achieved no discernable purpose. White civilians were particularly outraged to learn that at Louverture's request the bloodstained Dessalines had been included in the general amnesty.

Well aware that Bonaparte's instructions were to deport black officers, not rehire them, Leclerc explained apologetically in his reports to Paris that the cease-fire was a temporary measure dictated by difficult circumstances. His military situation was indeed as delicate as Louverture's. After weeks of campaigning, Saint-Domingue remained so insecure that Leclerc returned to Cap by ship after the capture of Crête-à-Pierrot to avoid Hardÿ's fate. By that time the campaign had cost his army five thousand dead and as many sick and wounded, or half of the forces that had arrived from France. Leclerc attributed most deaths to imaginary diseases to conceal his losses at Crête-à-Pierrot, but he knew that spring was almost over and that tropical diseases—real ones—would soon ravage his army. Upon learning that Bonaparte had also sent an expedition to Guadeloupe, he also began to fear that the reinforcements he was so urgently requesting would be diverted to other theaters. News that peace negotiations in Amiens were going poorly was another reason to worry. The fleet sent from Britain had finally reached Jamaica, while most of Leclerc's ships of the line had returned to Europe, so France's naval superiority was a distant memory. Informed (falsely) by the governor of Jamaica that he had fourteen thousand men at his disposal, Leclerc could even fear that his land forces were outmatched as well.[112]

Forced by mutual exhaustion to an agreement they both resented, Louverture and Leclerc arranged to meet in person on May 7 on a plantation outside Cap to finalize the cease-fire. On the sixth, Leclerc was dining in the harbor when he learned that Louverture had come to town a day earlier than expected (most likely to forestall any French plan to capture him). Louverture came with several dozen members of his guard, who followed him with drawn sabers wherever he went, and looked more like the defiant leader of a victorious army than a vanquished foe begging for mercy. The white population, still mourning the losses of the spring massacres, looked at him with suspicion, anger even. "This is human nature for you," Louverture told Hardÿ as they rode into town. Not long before, "I saw these people groveling at my feet."[113]

Leclerc rushed to shore to meet Louverture, and the two generals had a long, rancorous interview while Leclerc's secretary, Norvins, listened. Faced with Leclerc's litany of complaints regarding his recent behavior, Louverture deflected all criticisms by claiming, as was his habit, that controversial events were none of his doing. "The blacks" had insisted on fighting the French; "Christophe" had burned Cap; "Dessalines" had killed white civilians. Ever more modest, he declined Leclerc's offer to continue serving in the French army to help control the cultivator population because he was "too old, too sick; I need to rest in the countryside." Besides, he added with a hint of mockery, "when I told the blacks to work on plantations or fight in the demi-brigades, they obeyed me. They should obey you, since you hold a rank higher than mine."[114]

After concluding peace, the two generals broke bread—almost. Afraid of being poisoned, Louverture waited until the end of the meal before accepting a block of gruyere cheese, cutting thick slices from all sides, and eating the center. Sitting sullenly, he refused to even talk to his brother Paul, who had lost Santo Domingo without a fight.[115] Further down the table, Norvins asked his more talkative neighbor Dessalines, now back in the French army, why he had killed so many civilians. "Because Louverture ordered it," Dessalines answered. "He was my chief, I had to obey him. Leclerc is my chief now: if he asked me to kill Louverture, I would do it."[116] Aside from Louverture, Leclerc, and Dessalines, guests included Christophe, Pétion, and Jean-Pierre Boyer. In retrospect, Norvins noted, all six officers (in that order) had, or would, rule Haiti between 1798 and 1843. Had Leclerc seized this opportunity to capture all colonial officers as they made their submission, as Bonaparte's instructions specified, the course of Haiti's history would have been radically different; but Leclerc felt too weak to take such a bold step at the time.[117]

Louverture left Cap the following day and headed for his plantation in Ennery, where he planned to bide his time until the summer fevers gave him back the advantage he had lost on the battlefield. When his cultivators accused him of having abandoned the cause, he told them not to worry because "your brothers are still under arms, and all black officers kept their rank."[118] Members of his personal guard stayed in Cap, where Leclerc employed them as guides in French units, thus unwittingly providing Louverture with a network of spies with which he would follow the dramatic decline of the French army over the next few weeks.[119]

Despite the many hurdles that still lay ahead of him, Leclerc could look back on the recent past with pride. In less than three months he had conquered all of Saint-Domingue, when Spain and England had never controlled more than swaths of the colony during their years-long campaigns. Aside from the botched landing in Cap and the bloody siege of Crête-à-Pierrot, he had conducted a swift, effective campaign in difficult terrain against an enemy that, at the time of the initial landings, outnumbered his army two to one. Shortly after Louverture's submission, he learned that England and France had finally signed a peace in Amiens and that he could now bank on both internal and international amity.[120] He immediately began to work on the political reforms that would occupy him for the remainder of the spring.

Hardÿ, whose ardor for war had ebbed considerably during the campaign, was glad to report to his wife that peace was finally upon him. Many of his colleagues took the opportunity to redirect their energy toward the famously seductive women of Saint-Domingue, but he assured his wife that they had made "no impression" on him. On May 17, two weeks into the peace, he learned that his wife had just given birth to a son. "Tell me what his name is, and who is the godfather," he wrote in a tone of joy tinged with melancholy. "I tenderly hold you against my heart, as well as my three dear children. I will remain yours for the rest of my life."[121] Hardÿ did remain faithful to his wife until his dying breath—but that moment came much earlier than expected. Ten days after writing the letter, he contracted yellow fever and died in a few hours. His remains, interred in the citadel of Cap (which was renamed Fort Hardÿ), never saw France again.

8

Lull

Love, Loot, Labor, and Louverture's Exile

In the spring of 1802, as fighting ceased and exiled planters began to return to Saint-Domingue, a young Philadelphian going by the name of Mary Hassal landed in the ruins of Cap in the company of her sister and brother-in-law.[1] Beautiful and articulate, she was destined to live a tumultuous love life, which she would then relate in *Horrors of Saint Domingo, in a Series of Letters Written by a Lady in Cap Français* in an elegant, witty English prose not unlike Jane Austen's.

An avid chronicler of all things French and sentimental, Hassal was particularly intrigued by the sexual mores of the women of the colony. "The Creole ladies have an air of voluptuous languor which renders them extremely interesting," she marveled. "The *faux-pas* of a married lady is so much a matter of course, that she who has only one lover, and retains him long in her chains, is considered as a model of constancy and discretion."[2] In France, too, Saint-Domingue was known as the place to go for early death, easy money, and casual sex—a curious combination of Sheol, Babylon, and Gomorrah—and the sensuous reputation of the Creoles was on everyone's mind as the twenty-thousand-strong, predominantly male expeditionary force settled in Saint-Domingue.

Judging by prerevolutionary accounts, there was some truth to Saint-Domingue's reputation for libertinage. White and black men outnumbered women before the revolution, so marriage was relatively rare and extramarital intercourse commonplace. It did not help, either, that the slave system gave female slaves little leeway to reject their master's advances. So common was master-slave intercourse that after a century of French colonial rule the mixed-race population was rapidly approaching the white population in size. To these societal factors, contemporary medical theory added that a tropical climate encouraged sexual activity.

Central to the archetype of the libertine colony was the woman of mixed racial descent, or *mulâtresse*. Although many of these women made their living as entrepreneurs, white male authors often castigated all *mulâtresses* as kept women and conniving seductresses eager to trap innocent planters in a web of seduction. A mixed-race woman named Zelica was the main character in a later work by Hassal, who also noted that *mulâtresses* were so attractive that white women lobbied for a law preventing them from wearing elaborate adornments in a vain attempt to make them less appealing to their husbands.[3] One author even sees male fascination for *mulâtresses,* many of them the daughters of the planters' dalliances with their black slaves, as inherently incestuous.[4]

Hassal's letters from Cap dwelt at length on Pauline Bonaparte, technically not a Creole but nevertheless the native of a fair-weathered isle with a reputation for amorous penchants. Pauline found burned-out Cap dull and dreary; with Victoire Leclerc off to fight Toussaint Louverture in his muddy boots, there was little left for her to do, and she fell back on an old hobby of hers, one that involved dashing young men, preferably of military rank. The first time that Hassal paid a visit to Pauline in her mansion overlooking Cap, she found her in "a room darkened by Venetian blinds" where the idle Pauline lay reclining on a sofa in the indolent manner of the luscious Creoles. Barely acknowledging Hassal's presence, she "amused General Boyer, who sat at her feet, by letting her slipper fall continually, which he respectfully put on as often as it fell" (getting one's feet caressed by a slave was a favorite pastime of female planters).[5] Hassal voluntarily left the scene ambiguous in her letter, but in a later book she clearly hinted that the two were lovers and that "the presence of General Boyer was considered by Madame Le Clerc as an ample consolation for the absence of her husband."[6]

There were several Boyers employed in the expedition. The fetishist mentioned here was Pierre Xavier Boyer, who had served under Bonaparte in Italy and Egypt, reached Saint-Domingue shortly after the main squadron (he was with Louis Bro on the leaky *Duquesne*), and took over as commander of Cap when Leclerc left on the spring campaign. "The general in chief left his wife in Cap and asked me to guard this precious jewel," Boyer remembered fondly. "She was the sister of the first consul, the most beautiful person of her time."[7] Boyer was clearly not unhappy to see his superior mired in a lengthy campaign and wrote Leclerc to delay his return to Cap, supposedly to give him more time to install wallpaper in Pauline's apartments.[8]

Hassal had her share of tropical trysts, most notably a tumultuous affair with Leclerc's successor. As often with the individuals who lived through these eventful years, her life seemed too strange to be true—which, in fact, was the case. Despite its title, Hassal's *Series of Letters* was a work of fiction, written by a French woman whose real name was Leonora Sansay.[9] Hassal/ Sansay also authored *Zelica, the Creole,* a lesser known novel set during Saint-Domingue's dying days, and *Laura,* a romantic novel that she misleadingly presented as "a faithful account of real occurrences" in Philadelphia.[10]

Hassal-Sansay's fictional writings could easily be dismissed as historical sources, were it not for the fact that the love triangles depicted in her novels were inspired by actual events that she had personally witnessed. Like the heroines of her three novels, the real-life Hassal/Sansay had lived and loved in Philadelphia (where she had become romantically involved with U.S. Vice President Aaron Burr), only to depart for Cap at the instigation of her enraged husband and live through the Leclerc expedition. Details mentioned in her works are often consistent with primary sources and add much depth to a documentary record overly tilted toward military operations. Her writings are an essential, if perplexing, historical source: memoirs *à clef* disguised as a romantic novel pretending to be a history. Such layered sources, part fiction and part fact, are not uncommon when it comes to the Haitian Revolution, whose historians must learn to navigate a world constantly shifting between myth, distortion, fiction, and, at long last, history.

Although primarily preoccupied with titillating anecdotes on the sexual life of rich, idle Creoles, Hassal/Sansay's writings also emphasized an oft-forgotten dimension of the Leclerc expedition: that the white planter elite that allegedly lobbied so hard for an expedition actually resented the presence of a French army on Saint-Domingue's soil. One reason for the planters' growing discontent, she argued, was that French officers, their ears still buzzing with fantastic tales of colonial license, began a concerted assault on the virtue of the colonists' wives shortly after wresting the colony from Louverture's hands. Many officers in Leclerc's immediate entourage indeed married into planter families within months of arriving in Saint-Domingue, and the beautiful month of May, wedged in between a spring of war and a summer of disease, bristled to the sound of romantic escapades.[11]

For members of the Leclerc expedition, the Creoles' legendary wealth was as potent a draw as their renowned charms. Marrying the rich heiress of a plantation had been the dream of every penniless newcomer in the prerevolutionary era, one far easier to attain now that a decade of revolutionary violence had dramatically increased the supply of well-endowed widows. Some colonists even alleged that French officers had only halfheartedly tried to protect male planters during the massacres of the spring campaign because "this left them many widows they could marry."[12] There might have been some truth to their suspicions. A French officer described his wife-to-be as "citizeness Renaud, widow of Derval, landowner in the counties of Jacmel and Léogane."[13] Another noted with evident relish that a planter "died this morning at ten and left without any relatives or friends his *demoiselle,* who is very pretty."[14]

For women of all colors, matters of love were also intertwined with practical considerations. Before the revolution planters trying to get colonial authorities on their side had often married off their daughters to prominent bureaucrats and officers, so marriage might have been a way for female planters to mitigate the effects of Leclerc's increasingly dictatorial regime. For their part, female slaves, who knew that resistance was futile because laws banning the rape of a slave were not enforced, had occasionally used sex as the most likely path to emancipation.[15] Women of color were thus conditioned to view intercourse with a white man as a form of social promotion and may have yielded to the advances of their French suitors to obtain power or land. Hopeless romantics aside, love in the time of malaria was a most businesslike affair.

~

Three Gs brought French officers to Saint-Domingue (gold, girls, and glory), and in Hassal/Sansay's books accounts of naked greed came a close second to tales of steamy affairs. In prerevolutionary times, most French settlers had come with the ambition of becoming a rich absentee owner, a dream that was still alive in 1802 and that explains much of the behavior of the French officer class. "The professed intention of those who have come with the army is to make a fortune," Hassal/Sansay noted, "and return to France with all possible speed, to enjoy it."[16] Even Jacques de Norvins, who claimed that he had volunteered to follow Leclerc on a whim, sought a printing contract once he reached Cap and speculated in coffee. "Send me money," he wrote family members, "and I will quickly double the investment."[17] Lying on the number of rations, conning planters, stealing from plantations: any occasion to make a quick franc was employed.[18] Rich Creoles were often the victims of such abuses. Raymond Labatut, a planter who owned much of La Tortue, was fined for failing to prevent an insurrection on this island, while a relative of the future prefect of Louisiana, Antoine Laussat, was jailed for refusing to pay another planter's debts.[19]

Leclerc complained that "many of the people who came to Saint-Domingue did it so that they could amass ingots," but he was hardly a model of integrity himself.[20] "I have no time to try to make a fortune here," he explained to Bonaparte in a letter—before asking him for the island of La Gonâve (west of Port Républicain) that he hoped could secure him two hundred thousand francs a year.[21] As captain general, he single-handedly raised the pay of naval officers by 30 percent, awarded army officers additional rations and meal indemnities (in addition to 50 percent extra pay), and added one hundred thousand francs to his already considerable salary. Meanwhile, the egalitarian principles of a republican army notwithstanding, soldiers had to make do with their regular pay, which they received months in arrears if at all, and feed themselves with a meager ninety centimes daily allowance (sex was also far from egalitarian: the officers who so eagerly pursued widowed planters instructed privates not to have intercourse with cultivators for fear it would disrupt plantation work).[22]

Paul Aldebert Henry Valete was one among the many French officers whose interest in the expedition was primarily monetary.[23] In 1801, when rumors of an expedition to Saint-Domingue had first surfaced, Valete was a thirty-six-year-old unemployed brigadier chief whose salary had just dropped to 125 francs a month. His half-pay could not finance the lifestyle of a Parisian cavalry officer married to a noblewoman from Provence, nor could it secure adequate dowries to ensure that his four daughters married well. The Saint-Domingue expedition, when Valete heard of it, thus seemed like manna from heaven, and he ceaselessly lobbied the ministry of war for an appointment. He did not manage to leave with the initial fleets, but he secured a spot on a ship scheduled to bring reinforcements in March 1802.

The delay gave Valete three months to finalize his business plans while his colleagues fought it out in the mountains of Grand Cahos. He offered his acquaintances to be their business agent in Saint-Domingue, tapped an elderly aunt for an inheritance, collected old debts, and sold his library. This gave him a starting capital of 8,000 francs, which he planned to invest in sundry items, sell them in Saint-Domingue for sugar and coffee, and double his investment in a four-month round trip. Feverishly adding numbers on scraps of paper, he calculated that reinvesting profits would secure him a fortune of 1,395,311 francs within six years, at which point he would return to France "rich as a Creole," as the expression went. He could also buy shares in slave ships if slavery was restored, which according to statistics he had gleaned in various books could bring a return of 4 million francs on a 2.8-million-franc investment within sixteen months. That few of his numbers added up did not seem to dampen Valete's enthusiasm: he left for Brest in high spirits, confident that he was about to procure a bright future for his family.

Valete seemed genuinely excited by his Caribbean adventure, but his wife and children found the prospect of his long absence hard to fathom. Valete had barely left for Brest when two of his daughters, in the round handwriting and hesitant spelling of young children, sent plaintive letters asking their *"cher papa"* if he still loved them.[24] Lonely and short on money, his wife, Désirée, moved to a small apartment and skipped meals to save enough to pay her daughters' music instructors. By March, when news of the burning of Cap reached France, she began fearing that her husband's financial plans had been ruined along with the city and that their sacrifices might come to naught. But it was too late to desist by then; Valete left Brest on March 29 for Port Républicain, where he took a post on Rochambeau's staff and set to work on his financial plans.

Embezzling army funds and soliciting kickbacks paled in comparison with the profits one could derive from plantation agriculture. Before the revolution slave owners could make a profit of five hundred to two thousand francs per worker per year, or well above one hundred thousand francs for an average-size sugar plantation. Even when balanced with the enormous start-up costs, the return on investment was 8 to 10 percent a year, a significant figure in a protoindustrial age and enough to guarantee its owner a princely income for life.[25] Purchasing a sugar plantation, whose total value often exceeded half a million francs in prerevolutionary times, was beyond the means of most French officers, but there was a way to dramatically reduce ownership costs. Revolutionary law called for the confiscation of the assets of émigrés (ex-iled aristocrats), so the many planters who had left the colony in 1791–93 to escape the slave revolt had seen their plantations confiscated in their absence. The *domaines*, the administration that had taken over their estates, controlled as many as two-thirds of the colony's plantations by 1802, which it rented out to private entrepreneurs who could make a fortune with someone else's land as long as the lease was set low enough.[26]

Despite the alleged influence of the planters' lobby, Bonaparte's instructions made no change to the policy of confiscating émigré estates, and French officers began making note of promising plantations as soon as they landed in Saint-Domingue.[27] Leclerc put the *domaines* under the supervision of the colonial prefect, even though (or because) he viewed him as a venal bureaucrat.[28] With a level of detail that amply proves the importance the colony's hierarchy attached to plantation ownership, the *domaines* immediately began a systematic census of the plantations under its control.[29] Leading officers then divided the spoils, and Leclerc put aside one sugar plantation for himself. Pauline's lover, Boyer, took two coffee plantations, Louis-René de Latouche-Tréville three, and Donatien de Rochambeau outdid everyone with no fewer than eight leases spread between sugar, coffee, and cotton.[30] It was easy for an influential officer to insist on an artificially low rent, and an administrator estimated that 500 of the *domaines*' 607 plantations in the south had been leased for a quarter of their actual value. Officers did not even pay the reduced rates and instead billed the government for the cost of the repairs.[31] One such plantation was described as leased "well below its value. The buildings are considerable, generally in good repair, the fields vast and well maintained. . . . The current owner is making complaints."[32]

Metropolitan officers, Creole planters, and black officers may have come from three different continents, but they shared a common predilection for land farmed by others, and the estates of the émigrés were a politically explosive issue. French officers eager to lease sequestered estates found themselves at odds with the estate's owners, many of whom began to return in 1802 and asked for their property to be returned, and with colonial officers, who had no intention of giving away the leases they had obtained under Louverture.[33] In the end the need to assuage officers of color trumped the property rights of white colonists, and Leclerc promised that loyal colonial officers would keep their leases while making it difficult for planters to recover their estates.[34] The fires set on Louverture's orders during the spring campaign had also burned many notarial records and property deeds, so an expedition allegedly organized to help planters recover their plantations actually dispossessed many of them of their estates for good.[35]

The rebels' scorched-earth policy, following on ten years of revolution and neglect, had been comprehensive, and Leclerc, who had read Louverture's overoptimistic reports on the colony's economic revival in Paris, was taken aback by the sorry state of most of Saint-Domingue's plantations.[36] Bringing ruined estates back to their former splendor would require a massive injection of cash, since equipment and livestock on sugar plantations often cost one hundred thousand francs and the total value of agricultural assets in Saint-Domingue (including slaves) had topped one billion francs before the slave revolt.[37] Despite warnings by a knowledgeable author that rebuilding Saint-Domingue's plantations would cost anywhere from forty million to four billion francs, the ever-optimistic Bonaparte had completely ignored the financial side of the colony's revival in his planning.[38] He eventually had to issue regulations postponing debt payments to give the planters some financial breathing room while the colony rose from its ashes, thus denying French merchants and bankers any opportunity to profit from the expedition in the near term.[39]

Despite the extent of the damage the mood among people eager to tap into Saint-Domingue's wealth remained optimistic in the spring of 1802. The French and British governments terminated welfare payments doled out to Saint-Domingue refugees to incite them to head back to the colony, and exiled planters returned in large numbers. When compared with the thirty-one thousand immigrants who had come from France in the entire eighteenth century, the dozens of thousands of troops, planters, and adventurers who landed in Saint-Domingue in 1802 represented an unprecedented migration.[40] Refugees brought what cash they had left after ten years of exile, and investors were confident that the colony was on a path to recovery.[41] Leclerc offered generous terms to all those who wished to help rebuild Cap, and the city slowly began to recover from the fire.[42] Eager to rebuild its merchant fleet, the government also urged French merchants to head for Saint-Domingue.[43] So many ships answered the call that by summertime the price of imported goods plummeted in Cap and many merchants had to sell their wares at a loss.[44]

～

The revival of the plantation economy could not occur without a large, docile labor force, whose legal status was the single most complicated issue facing Leclerc as he shifted his focus from war to domestic reforms. Many cultivators had fled to the woods during the campaign, and plantations were woefully short of workers.[45] Leclerc ordered plantation managers and cultivators to return to the countryside as soon as the fighting ceased, but this was merely a stopgap measure while he settled a debate that was central to the future of the colony's black population: whether slavery should be restored in Saint-Domingue.[46]

Leaving the philosophical and economic merits of slavery aside, Leclerc's decision-making process derived largely from his uncertain military situation. The reinforcements trickling in from Europe could not make up for the thousands of casualties he had suffered during the spring campaign and the many more soldiers who would die of fevers over the summer, so he knew that he would remain reliant on the loyalty of colonial troops for the foreseeable future. Some planters deluded themselves into thinking that black cultivators preferred the stability of the servile state to the uncertainties of freedom, but Leclerc was (rightly) convinced that a restoration of slavery would incite a popular uprising and push *nouveaux libres* officers like Henri Christophe to defect.[47] Even Leclerc's white troops might not stand for a restoration of slavery: with the exception of old colonial hands like Louis-Thomas Villaret de Joyeuse, many members of the expedition were idealistic republicans who equated the former black slaves with the oppressed French peasants of 1789 and the colonists with aristocratic landlords. Louis Fréron, Pauline's former lover and the new subprefect of Cayes, even told his black guests at a dinner party that he would sooner fight with the rebels than help restore the ancien régime.[48]

Given his tenuous hold over Saint-Domingue, Leclerc was careful not to inflame political passions with ill-advised talk of human bondage. After the landing he distributed proclamations that emphatically embraced emancipation (though slavery remained the norm in Santo Domingo, where it had never been abolished).[49] When Joseph, the slave of a U.S. merchant in Cap, jumped ship in early April, French authorities granted him his freedom despite the recriminations of his owner.[50] Later that month Leclerc formed an advisory council to help him draft a labor code, and at Christophe's insistence he specified that it would be based on "liberty and equality."[51] Much to the dismay of the more racist planters, the council included persons of color as well as whites, and Christophe participated in the deliberations.

The labor code preoccupied Leclerc for much of the month of May, as evidenced by a series of handwritten drafts that are now housed at the University of Florida. The phrase, "without cultivation, no colonies," found at the head of the first draft disappeared from later versions, probably because Leclerc had been told that it was too reminiscent of the old planter motto, "without slavery, no colonies." Instead, draft number three explained that he would reject both the excesses "of the Ancien Régime, when the poor slave had no recourse" and the demagoguery of radical firebrands like Léger-Félicité Sonthonax.[52] The actual wording of the articles changed as Leclerc compulsively wrote and rewrote the law, but all versions embraced a middle road, and the finished code mirrored Louverture's own cultivator system. This was no coincidence; Leclerc had asked Louverture for advice and requested copies of his labor regulations to serve as a template.[53] "I will more or less follow Toussaint's labor code, which is very good," he wrote Decrès. In fact, he added, "it is so strict that I would never have dared to propose one like this on my own given the current situation."[54] Leclerc's labor code, made public on May 15, maintained a strict labor regimen inspired by military discipline while guaranteeing cultivators their freedom and a salary.[55] In the long term, Leclerc explained in his correspondence to Paris, his ambition was to disarm the population, disband the colonial army, and return to France; he would not personally restore slavery.[56]

Several authors claim that the council assembled by Leclerc was dominated by reactionary planters who openly talked of restoring slavery.[57] In fact, its membership was diverse, Leclerc's commitment to emancipation well known, and on June 13 the council issued a carefully balanced report that described slavery as "anathema" in the current political context but forced labor a necessity in a tropical climate. The labor regulations proposed by the council were thus nearly identical to those favored by Louverture and Leclerc.[58] At any rate, the influence of the planter council was nil. The main goal of the expedition was to restore French authority overseas, so Leclerc, unwilling to see a colonial council claim quasi-sovereign powers as previous ones had done in 1790 and 1801, insisted from the outset that it had no legislative authority and published his labor code one month before the colonial council issued its recommendations. When the council began complaining about tax rates, he imposed a wartime contribution of thirteen million francs, then disbanded the council altogether.[59]

The colonial council's demise was one step in a progressive shift toward military dictatorship. Bonaparte had specified in his instructions that Saint-Domingue would be administered by a triumvirate consisting of a captain

who had much to fear from the competing claims of their fathers' illegitimate offspring.

The outbreak of the French Revolution in 1789 made the status of the *gens de couleur* the colony's most contentious issue. Bonnet, who had access to the latest newspapers from France, debated with his friends whether the principles of the Declaration of the Rights of Man applied to mixed-race individuals like himself, while leading free-colored planters went to Paris to lobby for full citizenship rights. Many white Creoles rejected this notion as preposterous, and the two communities jockeyed for political prominence with increasing animosity despite the fact that slave ownership gave them common economic interests. It was not until the 1791 slave revolt had proven the fallacy of fighting fellow planters that whites granted all *gens de couleur* legal equality in exchange for their support in helping to put down the revolt. Even then, conservative white authors continued to describe them in terms more vicious than they ever used against rebellious black slaves, and the young Bonnet was almost lynched by a white mob in Port Républicain.[69]

The revolutionary era was also the period when Bonnet joined the military profession. He spent the 1790s serving under various mixed-race southern officers and in 1795 traveled to France to denounce rival black officers like Louverture as traitors to the republic. He later fought in the War of the South, only to flee to Santiago after André Rigaud's defeat.[70] By that time France had grown weary of the black generals it had once supported, and Bonaparte decided that Rigaud and his mixed-race supporters, whose social profile was identical to that of white planters, would be essential allies in the upcoming war. Shortly after the French landing, two frigates traveled to Cuba to pick up Bonnet and several hundred pro-Rigaud exiles. They arrived in Saint-Marc in March 1802.[71]

Leclerc should have made extensive use of the *anciens libres* given their long-standing association with France, but he was torn between the competing demands of the colony's various constituencies. Some white planters, whose hatred for their mixed-race rivals had not ebbed with the revolution, spread rumors that they were secretly planning to revolt.[72] The return of Rigaud's party also threatened to upset the privileged position that black officers had enjoyed since their victory in the War of the South, after which they had confiscated the estates of their foes. In March, Rigaud wrote to the black commander of Cayes, Jean-Joseph Laplume, to demand that his sequestered plantations be returned, and Laplume, who had personally leased some of these plantations, predictably complained to Leclerc. Laplume's prompt submission had greatly facilitated the French takeover of the south, so Leclerc sided with him in the feud and ordered Rigaud and his family deported to France. Before May was over, Rigaud was back in France while the French government, unsure how to treat an officer who had committed no specific crime, tried to sort out the particulars of his case.[73]

Anciens libres were particularly prominent within the national guard, the heir to the prerevolutionary colonial militia. Initially meant as a part-time auxiliary force composed of all free Dominguians (including whites), the militia had in practice encompassed few white planters, who preferred to focus on more remunerative activities.[74] Many *anciens libres* guardsmen thus had decades of experience catching plantation runaways or fighting in mountainous areas, missions closely related to the counterinsurgency operations that baffled the heavy demi-brigades of the line of the main expeditionary force. But Leclerc ordered the national guard disarmed in May, instantly losing a precious auxiliary.[75]

Leclerc, whom Bonaparte had instructed to employ mixed-race individuals against Louverture's predominantly black army, thus did the exact opposite, exiling Rigaud while maintaining Laplume, Christophe, and Jean-Jacques Dessalines in their rank. "This is a bold tactic," he explained apologetically, but he was certain that he had "become the master" of Dessalines' mind and that he could use him in the upcoming disarmament campaign then arrest him at a convenient time.[76] His hopes proved completely misplaced. Black officers defected anyway, Rigaud's exile and other vexations pushed mixed-race individuals into open revolt, and within a year Bonnet had gone from supporter of the expedition to adjutant general in the rebel army. Bonaparte generally refrained from criticizing his brother-in-law during his exile in Saint Helena, but he did fault him for two mistakes. The first was to fall victim to local prejudices against the *gens de couleur,* when he should have courted their support. The second was his failure to deport black officers immediately after the end of the fighting.[77]

~

In his secret instructions to Leclerc, Bonaparte had specified that as soon as Leclerc secured a foothold in Saint-Domingue, he should deport white women guilty of sexual involvement with officers of color, Louverture's white supporters, and, crucially, all black officers above the rank of captain. Rigaud's exile, far from being an isolated incident, was thus one element of a vast plan of deportation initiated by Bonaparte himself and that Leclerc only partially implemented.[78] The plan was not without precedents, since Britain and Spain had relocated black auxiliaries to Florida and Honduras after their failed invasions of Saint-Domingue, and France would continue to use its colonial empire as a dumping ground for political deviants for the rest of the century.[79]

There is no record showing that Leclerc ever prosecuted the white mistresses of Louverture. Pamphile Lacroix' memoirs relate that, after capturing Port Républicain, he and Jean Boudet began sifting through Louverture's records and in a secret box "found hair braids of all colors, rings, golden hearts struck with arrows, little keys, souvenirs, and a multitude of love notes that left no doubt as to the immense success the old Toussaint had enjoyed with the ladies."[80] Despite Bonaparte's instructions, Boudet and Lacroix burned the mementos, threw the ashes at sea, and the damning evidence vanished in a double ordeal by fire and water. This act of disobedience may have stemmed from simple gallantry; but interracial intercourse had been a grave transgression for white women in prerevolutionary times, so destroying all evidence of the women's closeness to a former slave may also have been intended as a necessary step on the way to restoring the old racial order.

Leclerc was more diligent in deporting the white administrators of Louverture, only a few of whom, such as Joseph Idlinger, kept their position. Bernard Borgella, Étienne Viard, and Philippe Collet, the authors of the 1801 constitution that had so enraged Bonaparte, were deported to France, where they were put on trial and eventually acquitted (Borgella's mixed-race son remained in Saint-Domingue, where he became a noted general after independence). Leclerc's staff also hunted down other signatories of the constitution. Augustin d'Hébécourt, a French officer who had served Louverture so loyally that he had been nicknamed the "black white," was also deported to France, where he was jailed in the castle of Ifs. Louverture's supporters were often Creole planters, so their deportation can only have added to the local elite's growing discontent, especially since Leclerc took their disgrace as an excuse to confiscate their assets.[81]

A prominent victim of the white purge was Joseph Bunel de Blancamp, a person often described as mixed race in the English-language literature, but who was in fact a white merchant whom Louverture had employed as commercial agent and diplomatic envoy (his wife, Marie Bunel, also a merchant and possibly Louverture's mistress, was a black *ancien libre*). When Leclerc learned, shortly after the landing in Cap, that Bunel had represented Louverture in his treasonous negotiations with the United States and Jamaica, he ordered Bunel put under arrest. For the cash-strapped Leclerc, financial considerations were also at play, since Bunel had served as Louverture's paymaster and he was told to give one million francs or be shot. The sentence was never carried out, but Leclerc kept Bunel prisoner throughout 1802 and confiscated his stores, ship, and funds. In the end Leclerc's brusque treatment of the Bunels, which culminated in November 1802 when his wife Marie was arrested as well, needlessly earned the expedition two powerful enemies. Marie and Joseph Bunel had been slave-owning merchants who epitomized the white and free-colored elite that Leclerc could easily have co-opted. Instead, they fled to Philadelphia, where they eventually sponsored contraband runs to equip the rebels of Saint-Domingue.[82]

To fulfill the third, most crucial component of Bonaparte's deportation plan, Leclerc wrote Decrès that he intended to deport as many as two thousand officers of color employed in the colony.[83] Only a fraction of that number actually left Saint-Domingue, and their names must have come as a surprise to Bonaparte. In addition to Rigaud, Leclerc exiled several officers, like Martial Besse and Jean-Baptiste Belley, who had sailed with the expedition. Bonaparte must have wondered why they came back in disgrace just a few months after he had dispatched them to Saint-Domingue, when the generals they were supposed to overthrow still drew a salary from the colonial treasury.[84]

Leclerc's reliance on his former opponents had its skeptics, starting with the Creole planters in Hassal/Sansay's *Zelica* who gathered nightly at the house of the heroine's husband to express their concern that Leclerc had become the "dupe" of black generals who were only waiting for the upcoming summer fevers to destroy his army.[85] Similarly, after Jacques Maurepas defected to the French army, a flurry of complaints streamed into army headquarters, all of them warning that Maurepas was secretly encouraging cultivators to resist. In a partially ciphered letter to Leclerc, Edmé-Étienne Desfourneaux reported that "many individuals of [Maurepas'] district tell me that [this general is unhappy to serve under] us [and that] he describes as [traitors] those who [rallied to our side]."[86] Dessalines' bloody record and late submission made him even more suspect. Two weeks into the peace, Donatien de Rochambeau detached a battalion of the reliable 5th (white) demi-brigade to Dessalines' headquarters and instructed its commander to discreetly spy on the general, write a report on his intentions every *décade* (ten-day week), and send it by sea to avoid any risk of interception. Units of colonial troops that had deserted Dessalines in the past, and were thus unlikely to collude with him, were also stationed in the area.[87]

Despite his suspicions Leclerc never deported Louverture's most prominent subordinates, largely because he did not feel strong enough to do so given the growing ravages of yellow fever.[88] Instead of Christophe and Dessalines, whose names had become synonymous in France with the burning of Cap and the massacres of white planters, Leclerc's deportations primarily targeted minor rebel officers, not all of them black. Pierre Agé, the white general who had commanded Port Républicain under Louverture, was sent to France. Sixteen members of Louverture's staff (three of them white) were sent to Guiana, where they were held on the island that would later become the site for France's infamous *bagne*. Leclerc refused to deport Maurepas—but he exiled his white superior, Desfourneaux, for being too close to Creole planters.[89]

Most Saint-Domingue deportees, along with those sent from Guadeloupe and other French colonies, traveled on returning warships and landed in military ports such as Brest, Toulon, and Cádiz. From there they headed for destinations as varied as Bonaparte's home isle of Corsica (where they built roads as forced laborers), Mantua (where they joined a battalion of black pioneers), Toulon (where they dived on wrecked warships), and the Fort de Joux (a prison fortress in eastern France). Spread between Corsica and Elba, Île du Diable, Île de Ré, Île d'Aix, and Belle Île, the Caribbean exiles eventually charted a gulag archipelago that stretched from the Americas to old Europe.[90]

As the deportees reached European ports, French administrators were puzzled by the fact that most of the exiles arrived without documentation to explain why they had been expelled.[91] A frigate sent in June carried a typically motley group of sick and overage soldiers, war widows, twenty-five prisoners held in irons for unspecified reasons, and another seventeen individuals each of whose name was accompanied by cryptic notes in Leclerc's handwriting, such as "Cappe—thief" and "Ferragean—many crimes."[92] These individuals had clearly left in disgrace, but their punishment might range from early retirement on half-pay to house arrest or execution depending on their crime, and judges could not decide on an appropriate sentence when the entire prosecution rested on a handful of words (in his instructions, Bonaparte had left open the possibility that black officers deported from Saint-Domingue would keep their rank if they agreed to serve in Europe). For lack of evidence some legal proceedings were limited to French jailers asking their prisoners to explain the reason for their deportation, then freeing them or reincorporating them into the army after they predictably insisted on their innocence.[93] An early batch of two hundred deportees, who spent three months waiting in Brest for authorities to decide their fate, were less lucky. Unscrupulous captains used the delay to sell some of the prisoners to departing slave traders, and they headed back to the Caribbean in what, for some, may have been their second experience of the Middle Passage.[94]

⁓

While the overwhelmed Leclerc juggled diplomacy, finance, agriculture, and the overarching fear that his black subordinates might be disloyal, the man who had done the same thing for the previous three years lived in semi-retirement on his plantation at Ennery, along with his sons Isaac and Placide.[95] For Louverture, who disliked Cap, Ennery was a haven of peace and quiet to which he retired when the demands of government grew too strenuous.[96] Not coincidentally, Ennery was also located near one of the last foci of rebellion still festering in near-pacified Saint-Domingue, Mapou, where Sylla and a group of runaway cultivators refused to lay down their arms.[97]

After an ineffectual round of negotiations, Leclerc sent Achille Dampierre, the adjutant-commandant who had led the difficult march from Cap to Gros

Morne in February, to dislodge Sylla with a mixed force of European and colonial troops. Mapou was a well-fortified camp, with a palisade surrounded by hidden booby traps, and Dampierre found the assault singularly difficult. His men "had to cross ditches covered with leaves, and whose bottom was strewn with nailed planks and thorns that could pierce even shoes, and climb steep rocks by holding onto tree roots, while the enemy threw enormous rocks from the summit." As often in communities of African runaways, women participated in combat, and Dampierre was struck by the "ferocious screams of joy of the women, which redoubled every time they saw one of our men fall injured."[98] Sylla's camp was finally taken, but the defenders fled and their leader remained at large. Louverture had declined to provide any help during the assault and was suspected of inciting Sylla's resistance behind the scenes. Cultivators' attacks on local French troops and a suspicious explosion that almost killed a French battalion chief were also thought to be his handiwork.[99]

It was in this context that early in June two of Louverture's letters were intercepted. They were addressed to Jean-Pierre Fontaine, one of his aides-de-camp whom Leclerc had so imprudently taken on his staff. "I heard that Leclerc, in La Tortue, is in very bad health, and I want you to keep me informed of this matter," Louverture instructed him. "We need w[eapons] from New England. . . . Tell Gingembre [Trop Fort] that he should stay in Borgne and make sure that no cultivator works there."[100] "Providence has come to save us," he also joked in reference to La Providence hospital in Cap, where the first cases of yellow fever had been diagnosed.[101] Various authors have claimed that the letters were forgeries designed to inculpate Louverture, but Leclerc described them as genuine in his own correspondence and there is no reason to doubt their authenticity when they are consistent with Louverture's long-term strategy for victory.[102]

If the letters were indeed forgeries, their author would have to be the man from whom Leclerc obtained much of his damning intelligence: Jean-Jacques Dessalines. Louverture had overseen his entire career, promoting him from obscure guide to division general, yet it was his former protégé who most stridently accused his mentor of fomenting a new revolt.[103] Contemporaries often described Dessalines as a brute, but he was destined to outsmart every one of the generals fighting over the colony, and his denunciation showed him at his most cunning. By inciting the French to arrest and deport Louverture, he ensured that the position of leader of black Saint-Domingue was now open for the taking.

Leclerc could not ignore the mounting evidence proving Louverture's intention to renew the uprising, but he proceeded cautiously for fear that cultivators around Ennery might revolt to defend their leader. In conversations with the French battalion chief commanding the local garrison, Louverture had explained that he had "no trust in the French," and he clearly could not be seized by surprise when he had displayed so much wariness during his recent visit to Cap.[104] After asking Dessalines to arrest Louverture, which the wily general declined to do, Leclerc delegated this difficult task to the French general Jean-Baptiste Brunet.[105]

Brunet first tried to gain Louverture's trust by expressing his intention to settle in Saint-Domingue and asking Louverture if he could provide some advice on plantation management. "Therefore, General," Brunet concluded, "you may look at me as a neighbor, and thus as a friend."[106] Louverture welcomed his overtures and began to confide how saddened he was by Leclerc's refusal to trust him, "after all my devotion to him and to the public good."[107] Brunet seized the opportunity to invite Louverture to discuss the matter in person; bring your wife along, he added disingenuously.[108] (Louverture's memoirs tell a slightly different story: that Brunet stationed a large number of French troops near Louverture's plantations to spark incidents and incite him to ask Brunet for redress.[109]) Either way, after spending one month in relative obscurity, Louverture was eager to be consulted on a matter of state, however trivial, and exclaimed triumphantly "look at these whites. They are so sure of themselves, they think they know everything, and yet they have to consult old Toussaint."[110] Pride, one of his few weaknesses, proved to be his undoing.

The day set for the encounter ticked by, and as evening approached, Brunet concluded that Louverture had sensed a trap and would never come. He had even begun considering a daring raid to seize Louverture when the old general unexpectedly appeared.[111] After reaching the Georges plantation with a small guard of twenty men, Louverture left his troops outside the main house to meet Brunet inside. Unwilling to perform such a dishonorable task as arresting a fellow officer during friendly talks, Brunet absented himself during the conversation and sent his squadron chief to arrest Louverture in his stead. Alone and defenseless, Louverture surrendered his sword without a fight (Brunet had doled out many bribes—including four thousand francs to Dessalines and his entourage—so Louverture's guards may have been complicit in his arrest).[112] French troops then ransacked Louverture's residence to find clothing and jewels, bringing this inglorious episode of French military history to a fitting end. Leclerc also seized Louverture's plantations in following days, but he was disappointed when a detailed audit yielded little of value.[113]

Brunet could only marvel at how easy it had been to seize the famously prudent Louverture.[114] For the first and only time in his life, Louverture trusted his opponent, a momentary lapse of judgment that has puzzled his admirers ever since. He was immediately taken to the frigate *Créole* in Gonaïves, whose captain he famously warned that "by striking me, you have merely cut the tree of black liberty in Saint-Domingue. But it will spring back up from its roots, for they are many and deep."[115] The authenticity of the quote is subject to caution, but the words aptly merged the French and Creole traditions that defined Louverture: planting a tree of liberty was a standard feature of revolutionary festivals in France, but it could also evoke the *mapou* tree of Vodou rites.

The *Créole* next headed for Cap, where Louverture spent three days brooding while preparations were made for his exile. He carried with him the letter in which Brunet had proposed to meet him as a "sincere friend," which he must have read and reread while wondering how he could have fallen for Brunet's simple trap. Boyer, who hosted Louverture during his stay in Cap, noticed that he refused to eat (probably for fear of being poisoned) and that he seemed terrified at the idea of going on a ship, which is understandable given that he had never sailed in his entire life and may have suspected that he would be drowned.[116] His wife, niece, and sons were all captured in turn and the whole family embarked on a ship of the line named—of all things—*Le Héros*.[117] They sailed on June 15, bound for Brest and a lifelong exile. Fontaine, the recipient of Louverture's letters, and Gingembre, who was cited in one of them, were deported to Corsica later that month on board Bonaparte's favorite frigate, the *Muiron*.[118]

As the *Héros* sank under the horizon, Leclerc braced himself for the general uprising that would surely follow the exile of Saint-Domingue's formidable governor. Days ticked by; a few gatherings took place, which quickly evaporated after two lesser chiefs were arrested and shot; one of Louverture's former mistresses tried to assassinate Leclerc; but, much to Leclerc's surprise, little else happened. Colonial troops stayed mum; only Sylla continued his lone, desultory insurrection.[119] The absence of popular anger confirmed, seven months after the Moyse uprising, that Louverture had simply grown unpopular after three years of absolute power. He was long described more positively in France and the United States than in his native country, and it took over a century before Haitians realized that their country had produced one of history's greatest figures.

Louverture's former subordinates, barely disguising their glee, congregated in Cap soon after his exile. Seeing 120 officers of color massed around the dinner table, Boyer leaned over to Leclerc and whispered that now might be the time to capture the colonial army's entire leadership in one fell swoop. Leclerc hesitated, then decided against it, still unsure of the aftershocks that might follow Louverture's arrest.[120] He had already declined to capture Dessalines and Christophe when they had come to make their submission a month before, and it was the second time that he had failed to act on Bonaparte's orders. He would never face such an opportunity again, for within three months Dessaline's and Christophe's demi-brigades would be virtually the last remnants of Leclerc's once-mighty army.

9

Mal de Siam

The Yellow Fever Epidemic

Summer 1802

The spring of 1802 was an exciting time for a young doctor like Joseph-André Hugonin to practice his trade. Born in the French Alps, he had studied medicine in Grenoble, then Paris, along with mathematics, "because they straighten out one's thoughts and elevate the soul," and philosophy, an important discipline in a profession "where one makes decisions on life and death."[1] After teaching in Toulon and Marseille and serving in the Army of Italy, he had volunteered on the spot when hearing of the Saint-Domingue expedition. His lifelong ambition was to write a treatise that would unify the competing disciplines of medicine and surgery, and he was eager to study the poorly understood field of tropical pathology. Caribbean doctors often looked down on their metropolitan colleagues, especially young ones with grand theories and no practical knowledge of tropical diseases, but the revolutionary army revered youth—nary a soul in the Leclerc expedition was above thirty—and Hugonin was entrusted with the directorship of Les Pères, the military hospital of Cap.

The outbreak of fighting in February 1802 soon brought a steady stream of wounded soldiers to Les Pères. Hugonin cared for no fewer than 166 patients in the month of Ventôse (February–March), many of them suffering from bullet wounds and ensuing infections, which he treated by draining pus and amputating the most worrisome cases. He also cared for a roomful of feverish patients, whom he subjected to the era's cure-all, bloodletting, accompanied by laxatives and emetics. Judged by the standards of his time, Hugonin was a good doctor, and he was proud to report that only nine of his patients had died during his first month in Saint-Domingue, most of them of tetanus, gangrene, infections, and blood loss.[2]

Much of this was familiar territory for Hugonin. He and his colleagues were always on the lookout for unusual parasites specific to the Caribbean, such as the chigger, a tiny flea that burrowed into the sole of barefoot soldiers; elephantiasis, which manifested itself by grossly swollen legs and scrotum; and the Guinea worm, which local women of color extracted from one's skin by slowly wrapping the worm around a needle. The most spectacular case that year involved an officer who complained of unbearable itching inside his nose until further inquiry revealed that the patient had a nest of tiny worms swarming inside his nasal cavity. The worms opened a path to his mouth, where they fell one by one until, a terrifying eleven days and 150 worms later, the officer finally recovered.[3]

All of these ailments paled in comparison with the scourge of the Antilles, yellow fever, whose aliases were almost as numerous as its victims and included *mal de Siam, yellow Jack,* and *vomito negro.*[4] Even though it was also called *maladie du pays* (disease of the area), yellow fever was not native to the Caribbean and had been introduced from Africa in the sixteenth century. Yellow fever had decimated the white indentured servants initially sent to man sugar plantations, so this slave-introduced disease, ironically, was the main reason planters had shifted to an overwhelmingly black laboring force—along with a major factor in black Dominguians' successful bid for emancipation.

The intensity of the yellow fever epidemic of 1802 came as a surprise to Napoléon Bonaparte, but the risk of disease was well known to knowledgeable observers, and many of the critics who had warned against the expedition, like Charles de Vincent, had done so because they knew that a white army could not survive long in the tropics.[5] Yellow fever had killed many more planters and soldiers during the colonization of the Caribbean than slave revolts and war ever had, most recently in the 1790s, when it had ravaged the French troops sent to subdue the slave revolt and Britain's own invasion army; it was also common knowledge that up to half of European newcomers typically succumbed during the so-called seasoning process (the rest acquired lifelong immunity and longtime Creoles were famously exempt). The fever's mode of transmission, however, was poorly understood, and a contemporary aptly described it as "a disease, whose origin is uncertain, its cause unknown, its symptoms equivocal, and its effects all the more terrible since we have yet to discover how to prevent, stop, or combat them."[6]

In light of these known risks, the medical aspects of the Leclerc expedition were rather poorly thought out. Before leaving, Victoire Leclerc asked for enough medical supplies to care for six thousand patients, but he declared the drugs unfit for human consumption and left his entire pharmacy in Brest, along with many of his health officers.[7] He issued orders to start organizing hospitals immediately after the landing, but such necessities as buildings, food, and nurses were in tight supply and the wounded endured substandard care throughout the spring campaign.[8] Well aware that the onset of summer would mark the beginning of a deadly epidemic for which the medical service was woefully unprepared, soldiers and administrators counted down the days with a sense of dread. "What I fear is disease," Denis Decrès wrote in March, "and I am anxious to hear what you have to say about the impact of the climate."[9] By the time his letter had crossed the Atlantic, Decrès' worse fears had already been realized.

Yellow fever first struck in late April in Cap, where it had most likely been introduced from British Jamaica. Kingston was already affected by April 20, when James MacNamara of the HMS *Cerberus* left for Cap, where he noted that the French had four thousand wounded in their hospitals, but as yet no victims of epidemic disease.[10] When accounting for yellow fever's three- to five-day incubation period, the first individuals infected by British sailors would have begun to die in the last days of April, which is when yellow fever made its first appearance in the city. If MacNamara indeed brought yellow fever to Saint-Domingue, as seems likely, he killed more French troops and sailors than Horatio Nelson ever did and played a central role in crushing Bonaparte's colonial ambitions. In less than two weeks, Leclerc wrote, the epidemic made "frightening progress throughout the army," but April was far from the cruelest month.[11] By early May, two hundred men were being admitted every day and hospitals were overwhelmed. The frightful yellow fever epidemic of 1802 had begun and would eventually claim more lives in peace than the spring campaign itself.

The fever found a particularly fertile ground in Cap. The sudden influx of thousands of Europeans devoid of immunity, many of them huddled in town because the countryside was wracked by revolt, provided the virus with an abundance of potential victims living in close proximity. Taking an evening stroll was a favorite pastime for local Capois, a custom that exposed passersby to the mosquitoes for which dusk was also the main social hour. The half-ruined city, built at the foot of a hill, was infamous for its hot, stagnant air and became a muddy cesspool as soon as the rainy season began, providing a perfect breeding ground for mosquitoes. For lack of tents Leclerc's soldiers typically bivouacked in the open, leaving them particularly vulnerable to nighttime critters.

Army hospitals, their air heavy with the moist heat of the approaching summer and the rank smell of death, quickly became a hellish concentrate of squalor and suffering. Les Pères had not burned during the landing in Cap, but several walls had collapsed when the arsenal had exploded, and it was in terrible condition. It was also vulnerable to rebel raids, occasionally forcing doctors to spend the night defending their patients sword in hand.[12] In this and other hospitals, the sick and the wounded usually shared two communal rooms, so none of the horrific effects of yellow fever—neither blood nor diarrhea nor vomit—could be hidden from incoming patients, who were taken to the beds recently vacated by their unlucky predecessors in the midst of the moans and cries of the dying. Most people spent a few days in such horrid conditions before they left for the cemetery, but Les Pères was where Hugonin lived, slept, and worked. This was also the place where, in the tenth year of the French Republic, he died of yellow fever.[13]

Victor Bally, the army doctor who delivered Hugonin's eulogy, did not describe his end in any detail, probably because they were childhood friends and it was too painful to relive the agony of the "companion of my youth and a friend of my heart."[14] But descriptions of the disease abound and one can easily retrace Hugonin's final hours. Yellow fever first manifested itself with a violent bout of fever, accompanied by a painful headache surging right behind one's eyes. The headache rarely lasted, but it soon gave way to acute suffering in the kidneys, vomiting, and wild thrashing about as patients strained to find a position that lessened the pain of their burning skin. They also sweated abundantly and constantly complained of thirst. A terrifying aspect of the disease was that it was rarely accompanied by delirium; patients remained lucid until the final moment of agony and were able to chart the progress of their disease, compute their chances of survival, and get a glimpse of their future suffering by looking at their bedmates.[15]

Doctors often noted a lull around the third to fifth day, though the virus was such a potent strain that year that many patients did not last that long. For a few hours the fever abated, the pain lessened, and patients began hoping that they might survive the disease after all. In some cases they were right, and they embarked on a slow recovery that put them back on their feet after several months of convalescence. In most cases (80 percent according to Leclerc), the symptoms returned with a vengeance and the malady entered its last, climactic phase.[16] Skin turned a bright yellow that gave *yellow Jack* its first name; a constant stream of foul-smelling black blood oozed from the nose and mouth, accompanied by diarrhea and vomiting, also black, which explains why Spaniards referred to the disease as *vomito negro*. Lying, exhausted and terrified, in the blood-soaked, rumpled sheets, patients then drew their final, halting breath. Hugonin was twenty-five.

~

Bally was luckier than his childhood friend and lived until the end of the expedition, by which point he had risen to the directorship of the colony's hospital system. The epidemic of 1802 gave him unparalleled experience in the field, which he tried to share by founding a "journal of medicine, surgery, and natural history" with a few colleagues in January 1803.[17] The journal aimed at publishing research findings sent by the colony's doctors in the hope that their combined expertise might help prepare the medical service for the likely return of the epidemic in the summer of 1803. Bally found no cure, but his journal has left us with a detailed picture of the way he and his colleagues struggled to make scientific sense of the biblical plague that had befallen them.

Another interesting source on the French medical service are the deliberations of the health council that Leclerc set up in May 1802 to seek medical advice. Composed of prominent health officers like Bally, the health council quickly responded with a report that described the terrifying symptoms of the disease, presented its causes, listed possible cures, and suggested prophylactic measures. As often with contemporary medical prose, the report was clear, well organized, convincing, and false.

The disease, most doctors concurred, was miasmatic in nature. Having noticed that yellow fever struck hardest in humid, low-lying areas like swamps, they concluded that it was caused by poisonous vapors called miasmas. The recent heat wave had unleashed the "noxious air one breathes near the burned-out houses that serve as public latrines . . . the smell of cadavers improperly buried in the cemetery . . . and the stagnant water in the streets that turns into a poisonous cloacae."[18] The "Paris of the Antilles" was indeed a foul-smelling city. Visitors approaching the town were first met by the cemetery, where forty thousand badly interred corpses shared a small lot, often forty to a tomb, then a dock by the river that was a favorite spot for defecating, followed by an empty meadow used for dumping trash, an open-air butchery, and a swamp. The overwhelming stench of rotting horseflesh also wafted from a pier used as equine dumping ground.[19]

The miasmatic theory was the most reputed of its time, but other hypotheses had their supporters. Many medical experts, noting that the fevers only struck during the warm season and predominantly affected people from cold climes, blamed the change of temperature instead. Drawing from humoralism, a medical school going back to Hippocrates, they posited that switching abruptly from a cold to a warm climate upset the balance between the blood's four "humors" (basic substances) and forced it to expand brutally, thus explaining the fever's infamous black vomit. The more consensual doctors embraced both theories plus a few others as they claimed that people became sick when they did not sweat enough, got drunk, ate fresh fruit, slept around, or worried too much. A few people sensed that the disease might be contagious, but critics answered that some people had been in close contact with soiled sheets for months and had never gotten sick.[20] It was not until 1881 that Carlos Finlay of Cuba discovered that yellow fever was a virus transmitted via certain species of mosquitoes, and 1900 before he was proven right when a U.S. occupation army conducted a full-scale experiment to rid Havana of mosquitoes and yellow fever instantly disappeared—as did malaria, which is transmitted by another type of mosquito.

Local doctors, who looked down on their metropolitan colleagues and refused to participate in the health council's deliberations, generally advocated limited treatments for yellow fever patients, but army doctors like Bally were proactive types who did not despair of finding a cure. The council thus listed a variety of drugs that might prove effective, along with baths, purgatives, emetics, enema, and possibly bloodletting, though this reliable standby seemed to hasten the death of the severely weakened yellow fever patients. Over the next six months, Bally dutifully tried these cures and many others. Quinine, which was effective against malaria, proved useless against yellow fever. Bloodletting, a misbegotten panacea that had killed countless patients in history, should theoretically have restored a balance of humors, but Bally abandoned it when experience showed that it killed nineteen out of twenty patients. He then turned to vesicatories (plasters designed to create blisters), which he applied at various spots of the skin, then poured mercury onto the raw wound, sometimes in conjunction with bloodletting. A four-year-old went through three of these barbarous treatments, accompanied by a variety of internal drugs. The child died within twenty-four hours, leading Bally to conclude that radical methods might not work after all. Desperate for help, he and others turned to the folk remedies of women of color, such as rubbing the sick with lemon juice in the hope that the acid would counter deadly vapors. These failed too. In a rare case of professional humility, Bally concluded that "there is no known method to neutralize the miasma.... It is beyond our reasoning and analyses."[21]

Yellow fever proved equally deadly in the other hospital of Cap, La Providence, which had been built in 1775–76 with funds obtained from a tax on manumissions—including, possibly, Toussaint Louverture's, who was freed around that time.[22] When Dr. François took over the hospital and asked Bally for "a method that had at least in a few cases been crowned with success," Bally responded that there was none; nothing, neither cold baths nor ammonia, had worked. Not one to be stumped, François amped up doses, then, convinced that a deficient nervous system was the root cause of the disease, proposed "heroic remedies" (read: life-threatening) such as applying red-hot "fire buttons" on various spots of the skull in the hope that this would shock the brain into reacting, a terrible ordeal he justified with a deluge of Latin quotes worthy of a medieval quack.[23]

It is easy in retrospect to laugh at the doctors' crass ignorance, but most of the health officers sent to Saint-Domingue were considered experts in their time, and the expedition's chief surgeon, doctor, and pharmacist had all been selected for their extensive experience in the Caribbean.[24] Even today, doctors have no cure to offer a yellow fever patient aside from preventing dehydration with a saline solution and starting a transfusion if blood loss becomes life threatening (as Bally had noted, bloodletting is counterproductive). These, however, can only lessen the symptoms, not kill the virus itself, and doctors can do little but watch as it destroys the patient's liver and kidneys and kills, as yellow fever still does today, 15 to 50 percent of those affected (a preventative vaccine now exists).

Prophylactic measures designed to protect those still healthy offered greater hopes of success, then and now. The health council, Bally, and other supporters of the miasmatic theory proposed to station troops on windy hilltops to keep them away from miasma-infested lowlands. Advocates of the humor theory countered that troops should travel in multiple stages from Europe, land during the winter months, and first reside in cool areas to give their blood a chance to expand gradually. The few proponents of the contagion theory advocated garrisoning troops in isolated barracks, preferably away from the towns.[25] Although based on erroneous premises, these measures would have been effective anyway as they would have put soldiers away from mosquitoes and the sick. Proposals that the streets of Cap be cleaned, the dead buried properly, and the swamps drained would also have done much good, while helping combat other common afflictions like typhoid and diarrhea.

In the report it drafted at Leclerc's request, the health council noted that despite insisting for two months that Cap be cleaned up nothing had been done yet. It reiterated its demands for better hygiene in the report and further asked that troops be stationed on hilltops, but Leclerc replied that he was not happy with the council's conclusions and would not act on its recommendations.[26] The council begged again two weeks later that "stagnant waters" in the streets be drained and the cemetery moved, still to no avail.[27] Leclerc's only solution to the epidemic was to ask for veterans of the Egyptian campaign under the misguided belief that they would be immune to hot-weather diseases.[28] Leclerc did not give any explanation for his refusal to implement the council's recommendations, so one is left to wonder whether he objected to the cost of the clean-up campaign or whether he feared that stationing troops in the interior would expose them to the risk of being defeated piecemeal by guerilla attacks. Either of these obstacles paled in comparison with the cost, both financial and human, that the epidemic eventually inflicted on the expedition, so the failure to implement simple prophylactic measures was possibly Leclerc's greatest error as commander in chief. It was only in late August that he began stationing fresh troops on hills near Jérémie to "season" them.[29] In time, Leclerc also built a hospital in La Tortue, where the sick could be quarantined and enjoy the dry, windy climate of the island, but his slow, incomplete response to the epidemic remains inexplicable since the rest of his correspondence clearly shows that he was watching his army waste away in the climate with considerable alarm.

In all fairness, Leclerc did implement the recommendations of the health council for one person: himself. In mid-May, as the epidemic began reaching worrisome proportions in Cap, he complained of unspecified ailments and headed for La Tortue. He brought with him Pauline, who displayed great interest in rural black culture and attended a *chica,* a pulsating dance similar to Vodou rites of possession.[30] Upon his return to Cap, Leclerc established his residence on a plantation located on one of the windswept hills overlooking Cap, while his men suffered and died in the moist squalor below.[31]

Another sign of malign neglect was the condition of the hospitals, which remained badly underfunded even after the spring campaign had lain bare their woes. In Port Républicain, the hospital director was so short on funds that he could not buy brooms to sweep the floor or carrots to make soup.[32] Several hospitals (including Cap's Les Pères) lacked a roof, so the sick slept on rotten mattresses under the frequent downpours of the rainy season.[33] Hospitals in forgotten corners of the colony were even worse. In Port Margot, a visiting general found a ramshackle building in which a single doctor cared for six hundred patients. The wounded were devoured by worms and parasites and one hundred patients had died the previous week for lack of food and basic care. The general commandeered fifty troops to serve as nurses, but they cannot have been too qualified since he described them as "prison rejects whom we cannot employ as soldiers."[34] In Fort Liberté, it was not lack but total absence of care that proved deadly when all the doctors of the military hospital died, as did the two naval surgeons sent from the ships in the port, and the sick were left to fend for themselves.[35]

Embezzlement only added to an already tragic situation. In the midst of the epidemic French generals spent over 48,000 francs of public monies to redecorate their residences in Port Républicain with crystal chandeliers and mahogany nightstands, while the local hospital had to make do with a few dozen old mattresses whose price was too low to be worth recording.[36] Pauline and Victoire Leclerc spent 175,000 francs redecorating their residence above Cap, while the budget to completely renovate Les Pères and build a pharmacy and two new wings came to a modest 58,000 francs.[37] Unscrupulous hospital employees stole the effects of yellow fever victims, administrators diverted public funds, and Leclerc eventually privatized the administration of hospitals in September in the misplaced hope that this would improve the service.[38] Judging by Bally's urgent requests when he became director of the health service, hospitals were still woefully underfunded in the summer of 1803, more than a year after the first outbreak of disease.[39] The long record of negligence confirms that despite the limitations of nineteenth-century medicine the yellow fever epidemic of 1802 was partly a man-made disaster.

~

In the summer of 1802, while thousands of soldiers lay dying in the hospitals of Cap, French readers of the government mouthpiece, the *Moniteur Universel,* could easily be forgiven for thinking that the expedition was going as well as it could. After the main squadron had left Brest, the *Moniteur* had published an article by a Saint-Domingue colonist claiming that the death rate in the hospitals of Cap was typically lower than in Parisian hospitals.[40] A few months later, the *Moniteur* had published one of Leclerc's letters; the tone was predictably upbeat since every pessimistic sentence had been expurgated from the original.[41] On June 13, another letter by Leclerc explained that Louverture was under arrest and that losses caused by the fevers were minimal (Leclerc had actually written that yellow fever was now decimating his army to the tune of thirty soldiers a day).[42] A month later, at a time when Leclerc's estimate of daily losses had jumped to one hundred for Cap alone, an anonymous "publicist" wrote that the fevers had proven "less pernicious than one could have feared" and that the army was already fully seasoned.[43] Letters sent from soldiers stationed in Saint-Domingue were routinely intercepted, so the only yellow fever epidemic ever mentioned to the readers of the *Moniteur* was the one that struck U.S. cities that year.[44]

Wartime propaganda, then as in every other conflict, had two main purposes: to minimize military setbacks, but also to educate the public on the rationale for the war. The *Moniteur* accordingly described how Louverture had jailed the agent Philippe Roume, Henri Christophe had refused to allow French troops to land, Jean-Jacques Dessalines had massacred civilians, and Louverture had plotted to renew the insurrection. For those more interested in hard cash than patriotic outrage, the *Moniteur* also regularly published statistics on France's once-lucrative trade with Saint-Domingue. Few of those were articles in the modern sense of the term; instead, the *Moniteur* reproduced primary documents such as Leclerc's dispatches that looked impartial but were actually carefully edited to justify the war.[45]

Frenchmen hungry for a colorful account fleshing out the events listed in the *Moniteur* could refer themselves to René Périn's *L'incendie du Cap,* which appeared shortly after news of the landing reached France. The hastily published book was of very low literary quality, but its imaginative mix of fact and fiction created a vivid narrative of black brutality. With its fast, heavily accentuated style, the book seemed meant to be read aloud in the street rather than enjoyed at leisure. "In your impenetrable hills, you think that you can escape the vengeance of the first nation in the world?" a typical passage went. "You are deceiving yourself, cruel people! We vanquished the whole universe. We will appear, and you will be no more!"[46] Even illiterate buyers could get a good grasp of its content by looking at the enclosed engraving of the landing in Cap, which showed savage black warriors setting the well-built city on fire, while orderly rows of French troops arrived to save imperiled white women. Other books by Félix Carteau and Louis Dubroca followed before the spring was out, but they were more polished and presumably intended for a more educated audience.

This crude propaganda deceived no one, not least the popular classes that formed the bulk of Bonaparte's army (draftees were theoretically selected by lot, but the rich often hired a replacement to serve in their stead).[47] As early as March 1802, when the first triumphant reports on the landing appeared in the *Moniteur,* the French public anxiously noted that Cap had burned and that Louverture had a large army. A month later rumors about heavy battle casualties were circulating, and the mixed-race students in Jean-Baptiste Coisnon's school speculated that the rebels might win after all.[48] By early July, a British spy wrote, Brest was buzzing with "the most distressing accounts of the ravages of the yellow fever at Saint-Domingue and Martinique."[49] Soldiers invoked health problems to avoid being sent to the Caribbean, sailors deserted as soon as they learned of their destination, and a few draft riots even erupted.[50]

Public opposition to the expedition was problematic given Leclerc's urgent pleas for reinforcements. To give greater weight to his requests for troops, Leclerc sent much of his early correspondence with Bonaparte's brother, Jérôme, whom the first consul had sent to Saint-Domingue to give him some naval training and fashion him into a Napoléon of the seas. But Jérôme, who hated all things maritime, quickly found himself at odds with his naval superiors and Leclerc sent him back to France to get rid of him while passing on important letters. Jérôme returned to France in record time, but Bonaparte sent him back just as quickly, and Jérôme reappeared in Cap in April, only to be sent back to Paris once again with more demands for troops.[51]

After he was informed of the difficult landing in Cap, Bonaparte assured Leclerc that he would send reinforcements to help subdue the "brigands" and issued detailed orders to gather a second expedition to Saint-Domingue. Probably aware of the limitations of the *Moniteur's* propaganda efforts, he insisted that the troops not be told of their destination until they had already left France. Orders for more reinforcements followed when news of the bloodbath at Crête-à-Pierrot reached him in late May.[52] Ships of the line had returned from Saint-Domingue in poor repair, so many reinforcements traveled on a hodgepodge of small military and commercial vessels that left piecemeal over the next few months.[53]

Table 5.
French and foreign units that arrived during the yellow fever epidemic (June–October 1802).

Name of unit	Date of arrival	Troops who survived the crossing	Port of departure	Ship
2nd expeditionary battalion	July 2, 1802	1,600	Brest	*Pélagie Conquérant*
7th light demi-brigade 11th light demi-brigade Legion of Saint-Domingue	Aug. 1, 1802	1,300	Toulon	*Formidable Annibal*
83rd demi-brigade of the line	Aug. 12, 1802	650	Brest	*Intrépide*
3rd light demi-brigade	Aug. 18, 1802	2,000		*Vautour* and convoy
Polish legion 8th demi-brigade of the line	Sept. 11, 1802	2,570		*Laudy* and convoy
98th demi-brigade of the line	Sept. 15, 1802	200	Havre	*Vigilant Argus*
4th battalion of gunners	Sept. 18, 1802	512	Ile de Ré	*Egyptienne*
86th demi-brigade of the line	Sept. 20, 1802	227		*Prudent*
Unspecified	Oct. 1, 1802	522		*Le Jeune Aristide*

Total: 9,581

Source: Armée de Saint-Domingue, "État général des troupes arrivées dans la colonie" (ca. July 1803), CC9/B23, Archives Nationales, Paris.

All too aware that reinforcements would land in the midst of the deadly summer, Bonaparte often selected disposable troops like convalescents and foreigners, not the crack units that had sailed with Leclerc.[54] To his minister of war, who asked what should be done with a group of eighty foreign deserters stranded in a recruiting depot in Le Havre, Bonaparte replied that they should be sent to Saint-Domingue. A month later Decrès asked again what should be done with the group, which he described in pitiful terms as virtually naked, covered with scabies, and "followed by forty or fifty women and seventy or eighty children living in dire misery." Again Bonaparte replied that they should embark and that "the number of women and children should not be viewed as an obstacle."[55] Another group of foreign deserters, released from British jails following the peace of Amiens, were sent to Saint-Domingue before they ever had a chance to return home.[56] Upon seeing the haggard men and women stumbling out of the latest troop transports, Leclerc complained that he was getting the "refuse" of the army, including a sixty-six-year-old general named David Tholosé.[57]

∽

In the summer of 1802 a naval cadet named Christophe Paulin de la Poix de Fréminville was waiting impatiently in Brest for his chance to leave for the Antilles. Fréminville was an aristocrat who lost little love on the French Revolution, but he was fascinated by the flora and fauna—and *femina*—of the tropics, and he had initially hoped to embark with the first expeditionary fleet. Delayed several times, he finally left in July on board the ship of the line *Intrépide* with 650 troops, as many sailors, twenty criminals, fifteen fortune-seekers, and the son of Donatien de Rochambeau.[58]

On the same ship was Gicquel, a noble who had enrolled in the navy at age ten in 1794. Gicquel had already traveled to Saint-Domingue earlier that year, only to sink off Cap along with the *Desaix,* and he wrote of his eagerness to "better know the Antilles, where I had been wrecked twice but whose charms I had never had a chance to experience." Finding "glory and profit" was also on his agenda.[59]

Yet another hopeful aristocrat on the *Intrépide* was the young Armand de Vanssay, who had once thought of prepping for the elite military school of Polytechnique, only to conclude that he could gain more advancement in a few months' service in the Caribbean than years of mathematical drudgery in Paris. His mother, who had grown up in Saint-Domingue and knew of its deadly fevers, was mortified by his decision, but he countered that it would give him an opportunity to check on their relatives' plantations and that the entire family would benefit from his service overseas. In May he secured her teary approval and headed for Brest, assuring his brother Achille (who also planned to head for the colony as a merchant) that this voyage was "absolutely necessary for advancing in the military career. It would be pure madness otherwise."[60]

After a short crossing of thirty-three days, the *Intrépide* reached Cap on August 12. Fréminville was a hopeless romantic, so his first glimpse of "the high mountains of Saint Domingue ... covered with green forests" and "eternal flowers never wilted by winters" left him with an indelible impression.[61] A closer look proved less enthralling. Cap was in the midst of an epidemic so intense that the population dumped corpses unceremoniously in the streets in the dead of night, to be buried en masse before dawn broke. The dying were often mixed in with the dead in the confusion, and there were a few reports of freshly interred individuals rising from their graves, long before horror movies popularized the zombie phenomenon.[62] Nighttime burials were designed to hide the extent of French losses, but the rebels were not deceived and timed their attacks to coincide with new peaks in mortality, yelling to the city's defenders, "you whites, you will all die!"[63]

The gaping holes that the epidemic had left in army ranks soon convinced Leclerc to tap the navy for reinforcements. Drafting sailors squandered away France's small supply of able seamen, but Leclerc was desperate for troops and he felt that he could hardly leave thousands of young men idling off shore when fighting raged on land.[64] After their arrival, Gicquel and other sailors from the *Intrépide* were thus sent on a small barge to guard a river near Cap, where constant rebel attacks and bouts of fever soon killed fourteen of seventeen fellow midshipmen. "I spent one month there, burned by the sun during the day and awakened every night to repulse attacks," Gicquel remembered in horror. "These were bloody, sinister fights that cost me many men, and where the greatest difficulty was to distinguish between the blacks fighting on our side and those who had become our enemies."[65]

The constant parade of anonymous corpses was depressing enough, but Fréminville and his contemporaries were particularly struck by the number of prominent victims. So was Vanssay, who had left with a thick pile of recommendations, only to learn upon reaching Saint-Domingue that virtually all his contacts were dead. Jean Hardÿ and Jean-François Debelle, who had been at the forefront of the spring campaign, died soon after the epidemic began, as did thirteen of the sixteen people who shared Hardÿ's house and another division general, Jean-Denis Le Doyen. One of Leclerc's dispatches notified Paris that the elderly Tholosé had landed with the latest reinforcements, then, in a postscript, that he was already dead. Charles Dugua, Leclerc's immensely fat and immensely popular chief of staff, passed away in October to everyone's sorrow. The administration also paid a heavy price. Pauline's old lover Louis Fréron died, along with three other subprefects. Grand Judge Despeyroux died. Colonial Prefect Pierre Bénézech died, as did his children, brother, and wife.[66] All told, twenty-seven division generals, brigadier generals, and adjutant-commandants, including seventeen of the thirty-six who landed in February 1802 and five of the eleven sent with the reinforcements that summer, died in Saint-Domingue, most of them of yellow fever. The Leclerc expedition, not Borodino nor Waterloo, was the single costliest event for general officers in the revolutionary and Napoleonic era.[67]

According to old-timers, not even during the British occupation had the fever been so deadly. The three priests who had come from France with bishop Guillaume Mauviel all died in the summer of 1802, even though they had been in the colony for over a year.[68] In Jamaica, too, the fever took a heavy toll, and the governor's wife, Maria Nugent, noted with angst in her diary that this year had turned out to be "more than usually sick."[69] The fever also prevailed in Cuba, where the *San Genaro,* which had headed to Havana for repairs after being damaged with the *Desaix* off Cap, lost half her crew to fevers and desertion while waiting for her hull to be patched.[70] U.S. ports involved in the Saint-Domingue trade were also affected, as were the Lesser Antilles, both French and English. A battalion of five hundred troops that traveled via Guadeloupe had shrunk to 250 men by the time it reached Saint-Domingue.[71]

In the absence of quarantine orders (the disease was not deemed contagious), the epidemic quickly leaped from one port to another, especially those situated near *esters* (swamps and mangroves teeming with mosquitoes). Port Républicain, the second-largest city in the colony and a notoriously unhealthy spot on account of its swamps, was still fever free as of May 11, when the frigate *La Franchise* arrived from Jamaica with an outbreak of yellow fever on its hands. Despite the obvious risks of contagion, port authorities allowed twenty sick sailors to head for the hospital and an epidemic ensued.[72] Arcahaye was struck in June; by early July, the south was no longer immune either.[73] By August only Santo Domingo and Môle Saint-Nicolas were free of the disease, but the latter was deemed so healthy that a large hospital was built to accommodate the sick from other areas, and it soon experienced its share of misery as well. Santo Domingo was hit later that month; in a few days, half the small garrison had left for the hospital or the cemetery and their commander, François de Kerversau, wondered how long the epidemic could possibly last when it had already killed off so many of its potential hosts.[74] And yet more victims there were: the reinforcements Leclerc had urgently requested during the spring campaign poured in throughout the summer of 1802, dying as quickly as they landed, like so many sacrificial oxen driven up to the altar.

After a brief stay in Cap, the *Intrépide* was sent to Port Républicain, where Fréminville took up residence at the house of a "beautiful Clarence" and predictably became infatuated with "her little childlike hands and her cute feet, which only the charming Creoles of our French colonies possess." But the epidemic proved as bad there as in Cap, and Fréminville snickered that many of the "gold-diggers" who had embarked on the *Intrépide* (fearless) to make a fortune were soon "green with fright."[75] They were not alone. Soldiers and officers, who thought nothing of attacking an enemy redoubt under a hail of musket fire, viewed yellow fever with sheer terror. Even those spared by the fever lived with the nagging sense that they would be next. After attending the funeral of yet another general, Lacroix pointed an English visitor to three other graves "ready dug for the next one that should drop off," while Leclerc's secretary, Jacques de Norvins, who dined at his table, remembered the awkward feeling whenever servants discreetly removed the plate of a guest who would not make it to dinner that night.[76]

Gallows humor was a common defense mechanism. Upon seeing a group of seven officers pass by, Norvins bet with a friend how many would be alive within four days' time (correct answer: one). Two weeks into the epidemic, the officer Achille Dampierre could cite the name of a friend who had died on each of the days it had lasted and regularly took "melancholy walks" to the cemetery of Cap. But he also concluded that the only way to overcome grief was to "shield oneself with a good dose of insouciance" and learn to "laugh at everything, even a *de profundis*."[77]

During the expedition to Egypt, disease and combat had caused widespread discontent among Bonaparte's troops within one month of the landing, and the morale of the army of Saint-Domingue followed the same rapid downward curve.[78] One can only imagine the state of mind in units like the 7th demi-brigade of the line, whose 1,395 soldiers were down to 83 survivors and 107 sick by September, or the 11th light, which only had 163 men and 201 sick left out of 1,900.[79] In late May two soldiers stepped out of the ranks during a parade in Cap and declared that "they would neither be shot, or massacred by the negroes, if it was the intention of the French government to get rid of the army in that way" (an allusion to the rumor that Bonaparte had purposely selected Jean Moreau's followers for colonial duty).[80] Preferring to choose the hour of their own death, they blew out their brains on the spot. By July Leclerc noted that "consternation" reigned among his men.[81] Rations and salaries were distributed sporadically, if at all, and he began to fear that his army, unpaid and ravaged by disease, might mutiny.[82] By late August some soldiers were so distressed that, indifferent to the risk of punishment, they complained aloud to their superiors about their plight.[83]

It was in this context that word arrived from Paris that Bonaparte wished to become first consul for life and that a plebiscite should be organized to ratify his decision. The vote, which took place in late August in Saint-

Domingue, was far from democratic since soldiers signed an open log and their military superiors—starting with Bonaparte's own brother-in-law—instructed them to vote *oui*.[84] It was thus an indication of the troops' dissatisfaction that at least two soldiers summoned enough courage for a Gallic *non*. When their officer tracked down their signature and summoned them for a talk, the soldiers explained that "Bonaparte was the one who had made them come here and that they did not like him."[85] Their superior tried to reason with them but eventually chose not to punish them. After six months of near-constant fighting and four months of epidemic, he may have agreed with them in private.

There was everything to fear about fear itself, since doctors held dejection as one of the causes of the fever. Generals thus urged soldiers to be cheerful in the midst of despair, but doctors also warned against rum and women, while Leclerc cut down the wine allowance to save money, so troops had little cause for rejoicing overall.[86] To boost morale, forts were renamed after generals who had succumbed to the fever, doctors received promotions and bonuses, and (probably at Pauline's urging) Leclerc made a special request that the government care for the widow and children of her old paramour, Fréron. Bonaparte also earmarked fifty spots in the military *lycée* of the Prytanée for the sons of deceased officers, starting with Hardÿ's.[87] Despite their admonitions, doctors were just as saddened as everyone by the constant presence of death, and Bally's journal, published in the aftermath of the epidemic, was filled with references to the "sad memories" and the "horrors" of the months past.[88] Leclerc insisted that new doctors should be selected for their strong morale, "which is necessary given the painful feelings they experience, everyday, in the midst of the dead and the dying," but happy or not, health officers were exposed to contagion on a daily basis and no fewer than 119 doctors and pharmacists died in 1802.[89]

It was upon reaching Port Républicain that the *Intrépide* began to experience its first cases of yellow fever. The victims' bodies were dumped at sea, but despite such measures yellow fever spread like wildfire in the overcrowded warship. As many as twenty-five sailors fell ill each day, three-fourths of the crew eventually became ill—including Gicquel, Vanssay, and Fréminville—and the *Intrépide* lost 320 men in sixteen days.[90] Her fate was not unusual. Captains returning to France wrote dramatic reports of crews ravaged in a matter of weeks, leaving nearly empty ghost ships that were completely debilitated before they ever had a chance to fire a single cannonball. A merchant ship from Bordeaux lost forty of its forty-eight passengers within eight days of casting anchor in Cap; a single cabin boy survived in a Swedish merchant, which had to be auctioned off. The ship of the line *L'Aigle,* which had arrived with the Rochefort squadron, lost a man each day she spent at anchor in Cap, the corvette *Bacchante* lost 84 sailors out of a crew of 109, and the *Goéland* went through two entire crews.[91] None of the captains' prophylactic measures, neither perfumes nor smoke, succeeded in ridding the ships of the deadly miasmas.

Patients had little faith in doctors' ability to provide a cure. When he first felt the dreaded chills, Fréminville headed to a hospital on shore, but it struck him as derelict even after the spartan conditions of a man-o'-war. So thick were the clouds of mosquitoes that he had to light a fire to smoke them out, a measure aimed solely at his personal comfort but that probably saved him from being infected by his bedmates (Fréminville responded to quinine and had probably contracted malaria, not yellow fever).[92] Also sick with fevers, Gicquel left his barge and headed back to the *Intrépide* for treatment. The naval doctor prescribed a variety of drugs, but Gicquel discreetly dumped the potions overboard, survived, and eventually confessed the peccadillo to his doctor, who kept mentioning him as his lone success story.[93] The ship's surgeon also declared the drugs offered by his colleague "useless! I am doomed. I recognize how vain and ridiculous our science is!" and died three days later.[94]

Distrustful of doctors whose only remedy was to "bleed people white" (Norvins' words), many Frenchmen resorted to women of color in their hour of despair. Norvins relied on a young *mulâtresse* who threw away the drugs prescribed by his doctor and gave him baths of water perfumed with orange peels, a remedy she had learned from her black mother. Norvins was pleased to note that he survived whereas his doctor died two days later.[95] Vanssay, who for eight days teetered between life and death, attributed his survival to the "women of color who managed to save my life."[96] Women of color, who had long served as midwives on plantations and had a large repertoire of folk remedies, served dutifully during the epidemic, and many patients praised their kindness. The army at first instructed soldiers to be treated in army hospitals, but the failure of European doctors to provide any effective cure soon forced it to repeal the ban, and in the end even army hospitals employed women of color as nurses for lack of white volunteers.[97] Using colored personnel in the midst of a black rebellion presented obvious security risks, and the ever-suspicious naturalist Michel Descourtilz claimed that he overheard two black nurses plot how they would alter drug prescriptions to kill the French soldiers under their care; but hospitals, desperate for personnel, continued to employ black nurses, all the while keeping them under close watch to ensure that they had no contact with rebels on the outside.[98]

By the fall of 1802 the once-mighty squadron of Cap was down to three ill-maintained ships of the line, each with a third of their regular complement, forcing their captains to complement the overwhelmingly white crews they had brought from European ports with people of color.[99] Employing colored sailors was common practice in Caribbean waters, but more unusual was the French navy's heavy reliance on captured rebels, many of whom manned the very ships deporting them to France. Asked to support a military operation in St. Louis, the *Intrépide* embarked one hundred black prisoners to man the capstan and raise anchor, then more prisoners a week later when the operation proved costly in human lives. By the end of the year, the *Intrépide,* which had left Brest with a six-hundred-strong crew, was making do with one hundred and sixty sailors and forty black prisoners.[100] As the practice spread and security concerns grew, Leclerc specified that colored sailors could not constitute more than a third of a crew, but in practice the proportion was often much higher. One captain only had seven white sailors left on his brig; another commanded six white and two hundred black or mixed-race sailors.[101]

Contemporaries noticed that ships were not affected by yellow fever when they were out at sea (that is, beyond the reach of coastal mosquitoes), so the devastating losses in the French navy could easily have been averted by sending the ships on long cruises, a method that would have had the added benefit of giving the inexperienced crews some sea time. Decrès warned Leclerc that "a navy [at anchor] is only a source of costs and disasters," while Louis-René de Latouche-Tréville, a competent sailor who took over the Saint-Domingue station after Admiral Villaret's departure, also begged Leclerc to send his ships on cruises.[102] But Leclerc ordered the navy to remain in the main ports, no matter how heavy losses were, and passed several decrees to combat desertion in the navy. Many warships never left port except to transport the sick to the hospitals of La Tortue and Môle, a practice, Latouche complained, that spread the epidemic to the few ships still healthy.[103] There was no military rationale for keeping large ships of the line after the signature of the peace of Amiens, so one surmises that Leclerc, who shared the Napoleonic army's characteristic contempt for the navy, simply wanted sailors to face the same risks soldiers did. He treated the navy as a junior service, and Latouche asked repeatedly to be sent back to France because he resented being at the beck and call of a general young enough to be his son.[104]

Several passengers of the *Intrépide* were among the lucky few allowed to return to France. Gicquel set sail after six months in the tropics, but his bad luck continued and he went on to witness an incredible streak of naval disasters, from the battle of Trafalgar to the infamous 1816 wreck of the *Medusa*.[105] Fréminville left in November, and after a long career in the navy he spent his retirement years writing a scholarly treatise on his favorite pastime—which, much to his wife's dismay, was cross-dressing.[106] The young Vanssay, whose dreams of fortune and promotions had disappeared along with his health, followed in July 1803, by which point war with England had resumed. He miraculously made it past two large English squadrons, but like most returning officers he was poorly treated by Bonaparte.[107]

Equally eager to flee the killing fields of Saint-Domingue, members of the army deluged Leclerc with requests for leaves of absence, but these were much harder to come by in a land-bound force. After he secured the promotion to brigadier general that had brought him to Saint-Domingue, Pamphile Lacroix wrote Paris that he had found all the "military glory" he could ever hope for and was now eager to leave a colony "where staying is becoming daily more odious on account of my health."[108] But Bonaparte accused him of cowardice and ordered him to stay put.

In practice, the only way for an officer to leave the island honorably was to serve as an envoy, as Jean Boudet did in October when he was sent to France to beg Bonaparte for reinforcements.[109] Officers vied desperately for such positions, including the young adventurer Louis Bro, once so enthused by the military profession, then furious at himself for "getting onboard that damned galley," and finally elated when he managed to be assigned to one of the diplomatic missions to the Spanish Main (Bro later returned to Saint-Domingue and was wounded at the battle of Vertières).[110]

Members of the health service also had good reasons to long for healthier climes. Early in June 1802, as Hugonin was in agony in Les Pères, the hospital's pharmacist, Bonamy, asked Leclerc for a permanent leave of absence because, he explained bluntly, the hospital "smells like death. . . . All I could hear last night in nearby rooms were the death rattles of three moribund soldiers." Leclerc lambasted Bonamy as a "coward" in the army's daily newspaper (a powerful accusation in an institution built on honor), but he left out an interesting tidbit of information. The same day he had received Bonamy's infuriating letter, Leclerc had drafted a pressing letter of his own to beg Paris to send him back to France.[111]

This was Leclerc's third such letter in a week, and far from his last. The month of Prairial, though only seventeen days old, had already cost him two thousand dead, he explained. His administrators were "crooks," some generals "idiots," and the latest reinforcements "scum"; daringly, he even directed his share of criticism to his superior, Decrès. Convinced that his "languishing state" would surely lead to his death, he plaintively pleaded for his recall.[112] Leclerc's oft-made requests became an open secret in the colony, a fact that cannot have improved his troops' sagging morale.[113] Concerned about the health of his wife and son, Leclerc also urged Pauline to leave the colony, but she refused, saying, "here I reign like Joséphine does in Paris, I am the first lady."[114] Contrary to her husband, she remained steadfast throughout the epidemic. After all, she liked to remind her interlocutors, she was a Bonaparte.

Late in August the number of victims finally began to decline and the survivors rejoiced that the epidemic might end with the summer. But it was back in full force within days and September proved as costly as previous months, probably because it coincided with the arrival of various units not yet exposed to the disease.[115] French reinforcements continued to land throughout the winter, and the army never reached a point where the virus had run out of potential hosts. In October, 289 soldiers died in La Providence, another 271 followed in November, 301 in December, 323 in January, and 240 in February; all of them were listed as "feverish."[116] This left the army precious little time before the return of the warm season and with it the likely outbreak of a new epidemic.

It is easy for a historian, looking at two-hundred-year-old columns of statistics on a microfilm reader, to forget that each number stood for a human being, whose life and ambitions were wiped out in a few days' time by an invisible foe, as were the lives of the wives and children who had followed the army of Saint-Domingue. Among the victims was Joseph Arné of the 68th demi-brigade, who in October 1802 died in Port Républicain of yellow fever, as his wife had before him. They left behind two orphans, one in the care of a relative in France; the other, age seven, alone in an unfamiliar war zone where she had lost both her parents to a terrifying malady. What became of the girl is anyone's guess.[117]

Relatives who had stayed in France were safe from the fever, but they spent their days in anxious agony for lack of reliable news; as late as 1803, despite the clamor of military families, the French government had yet to publish a complete list of the officers (let alone soldiers) who had died the previous year.[118] Those families that had been notified had received little to account for their loss, making it difficult to follow rituals of nineteenth-century mourning when these typically entailed being in the physical presence of the dead relative.[119] "I cannot begin to explain the pain I felt upon losing my son," the grieving mother of a squadron chief wrote in February 1803.[120] She had merely been handed a short notification, and she begged for a death certificate, an account of her son's last wishes, and some small memento to remember him by.

Estimating how many people died during the epidemic is more art than science. Sailors, civilian administrators, and national guardsmen—more than ten thousand individuals altogether—were not always included in army rosters, and keeping track of colonial troops was virtually impossible as they switched from being enemies to allies and back over the course of the year. Overwhelmed doctors had no time to keep accurate records; there was no officer left to take the roll in some units; the army's payroll office closed shop when all its employees fell sick or died; and commanders were reluctant to report losses so that they could collect salaries for deceased soldiers.[121] So bad was the record keeping that Lacroix, who moved from Port Républicain to Santiago after his request for leave was denied, did not know how many soldiers served under his new command. Neither did Latouche know the number of sailors—and, more surprisingly, ships—on his station. Leclerc only had access to the casualty lists from Cap and multiplied available figures by four to get a rough estimate of the mortality colony-wide and hence the size of his army.[122]

What numbers are available must take into account Winston Churchill's quip about lies, damn lies, and statistics. Leclerc's early reports were purposely misleading as they alternatively minimized losses (to discourage the rebels) or exaggerated them (to ask Paris for reinforcements). He put the death toll at 160 men a day in July and August for the city of Cap alone, a rate that when extrapolated to the colony would have killed 70,000 people over the course of the epidemic, or twice the number of troops sent to Saint-Domingue that year. At the other extreme, one of his aides-de-camp cited a suspiciously low 14,000 dead as of September, probably for the benefit of his British interlocutors.[123] More convincing estimates put total deaths at 22,000 to 24,000 troops and sailors out of 34,000 who had reached Saint-Domingue by October 1802.[124] Official reports point to slightly smaller totals (15,000 to 20,000 soldiers out of 29,000 to 32,000), but they are often incomplete and may have overlooked some categories of individuals.[125] The two hospitals of Cap left rosters of the patients who died under their care that total 5,800 names, also consistent with a death toll for the colony above 20,000.[126]

Determining how many of these deaths are attributable to disease is another complicated matter. Leclerc's letters variously wrote that he had 11,000 (or 13,800) European troops still alive around May 1, which meant that the spring campaign had cost him 6,200 to 9,000 of the 20,000 soldiers who had sailed with the first expedition. He tended to blame all his losses on sickness, not combat, but hospital records in Port Républicain at the end of the campaign list 60 percent of the patients as wounded, and one can safely assume that 4,000 to 5,000 Frenchmen died in combat or related wounds that spring.[127] Leclerc also mentioned the loss of 11,700 soldiers and 5,000 sailors from early May to mid-September, the vast majority of whom must have died of yellow fever since relatively few French soldiers were involved in combat operations during that period.[128] Using the more conservative estimates, of the 35,000 soldiers and sailors who went to Saint-Domingue in 1802, at least 15,000 (or 43 percent) had died of yellow fever by November, 3,000 (or 8 percent) had died of other diseases, 5,000 (or 14 percent) had died in combat, and at least 6,000 (20 percent) were in the hospital or convalescing. Most of the surviving sailors had returned to France, leaving about 4,000 soldiers fit for duty. The numbers do not fully sustain Leclerc's constant refrain that yellow fever single-handedly wiped out his army, but disease did kill or incapacitate at least 70 percent of all the forces sent to Saint-Domingue that year and left him with a force too small and demoralized to mount offensive operations until the arrival of a new batch of reinforcements in the winter.

For an army to be decimated by disease was not a novel phenomenon in history. Disease far outstripped combat casualties in virtually every war until the twentieth century and often dramatically altered the course of history, most famously when Hernán Cortés and Francisco Pizarro conquered Mexico and Peru with a few hundred men, Amerindian allies, and smallpox. It was only too natural, then, that the era of European colonization of Hispaniola, which had begun when European diseases had wiped out the native Tainos, would end when African diseases wiped out French colonizers.

French generals and memoirists often dwelt at length on the epidemic to minimize their opponents' accomplishments. "The rebels would not be an issue, if they were our only enemy," wrote Kerversau after underlining that the French army had prevailed in almost every military encounter.[129] This argument is only partly convincing. Yellow fever was a fact of life in the Caribbean, and it was up to French generals to adapt to its constraints, just as they had to take into account other factors like terrain, distance, and fortifications. Bonaparte and Leclerc chose to downplay the risk of an epidemic even after experienced officers had amply warned them, whereas Louverture developed his strategy around the certainty that an epidemic would break out in the summer of 1802. Some rebels, such as the nurses who mixed up medications or the colonial officer who failed to prepare barracks so that white troops would sleep in the open, even strove to compound the fever's effects.[130] Guerilla warfare, by making it dangerous to station garrisons in the mountainous interior, also bottled up European troops in a few overcrowded ports, where the death rate was highest. That the epidemic broke out at the worst possible moment was thus not the consequence of the rebels' good luck, but the result of a decade of experience acquired watching previous European forces waste away in the climate, and the rebel victory was as legitimate as the Russian triumphs against Napoléon I and Adolph Hitler in the icy winters of 1812 and 1942.

The oldest among the rebels could also remember the day, back in the middle of the previous century, when Makandal had foreseen that Saint-Domingue's slaves would be set free by disease.[131] Makandal was a Maroon rebel who in the 1750s devised a vast conspiracy to poison the whites of Saint-Domingue, only to be denounced and arrested. In January 1758, when Louverture was about fourteen years old, Makandal was brought to Cap to be burned at the stake as a public warning to the city's many slaves, and a large, multicolor crowd gathered to witness his final moments. Many of his supporters secretly hoped that he would magically escape, since Makandal was a holy man (his name meant "sorcerer") who claimed that he could transform himself into a *maringouin* (mosquito) at will.

As a fire was lit under him, Makandal struggled against the approaching death. So strong was he that he actually broke free of the pole, the slaves shouted "Makandal sauvé!" (Makandal is free!), and the authorities had to vacate the plaza to restore order. Makandal was then thrown back onto the pyre and executed as planned, but the slaves, who had not witnessed his death, remained convinced that he had flown away before the flames could devour him and that he would one day return to free his enslaved kin. For half a century thereafter, two generations of slaves hoped for the second coming of Makandal. French sons of the Enlightenment laughed off such superstitions, but the epidemic that broke out in the summer of 1802, ravaging French invaders while sparing black rebels, proved that Voltaire was no match for Vodou. For it was a mosquito—the *Aedes aegypti,* to be precise—that wiped out Bonaparte's army and helped fulfill Makandal's dream of a free Haiti.

10

Faux Pas

The Maroon Uprising

Early in June 1802 Victoire Leclerc prepared to implement the third phase of Napoléon Bonaparte's instructions: confiscating the weapons of all cultivators and irregular units. The disarmament campaign, if successful, would secure France's control of the countryside and force laborers back to work, but the tone of Leclerc's correspondence was surprisingly somber as he repeatedly complained about the low quality of the latest reinforcements, the lack of cash, and the first cases of yellow fever. He also took this opportunity to make one of his many demands to return to France, hardly a sign of optimism.[1]

As Leclerc well knew, the disarmament campaign was a massive undertaking. In addition to the arms already present in Saint-Domingue at the outbreak of the slave revolt, France had sent thousands of guns with Léger-Félicité Sonthonax in 1796, the British had left an ample supply when they had evacuated in 1798, Toussaint Louverture had bought thirty thousand guns from U.S. merchants in 1800–1801, and estimates of the total number of guns in the colony went as high as one hundred thousand.[2] Sonthonax, then Louverture, had told former slaves that their guns were the best guarantor of their freedom, so disarmament was likely to instill fears among cultivators that the French had ulterior motives.[3] In Trou d'Enfer (hell hole), over one thousand cultivators warned that they would "rather die than give away their weapons."[4] Leclerc first ordered those least likely to resist, the white planters and the national guard, to turn in their weapons—which left planters vulnerable just as Leclerc told them to return to the countryside—then, in early June, he prepared to do the same with the much larger cultivator population.[5]

The magnitude of the task was made clear in a report prepared by the division controlling northwestern Saint-Domingue. "The area under Brigadier Chief Parnaugeon has yet to be disarmed," the report began. "We need to proceed with caution so as not to send back into the woods the cultivators who have returned. Their behavior leaves much to fear since nothing ties them to the land; their huts were burned, as were their crops." In a nearby area where most cultivators had not yet returned to the plantations, disarmament would be even more problematic and violence, such as "hitting people with sticks to make them confess how many guns they own," would be required. As for Môle and Port-de-Paix, the largest towns in the region, disarmament would depend entirely on the goodwill of Jacques Maurepas, whose loyalty the report doubted. The list of areas yet to disarm went on, along with an assessment of the requisite number of European troops: two hundred men to garrison Gros Morne; seven hundred in Marmelade; fifty for the Horlenweck plantation alone.[6] Such numbers, quite extraordinary for a relatively minor corner of the colony, far exceeded the manpower at Leclerc's disposal in the midst of the yellow fever epidemic.

Bonaparte had instructed that colonial troops be disarmed along with cultivators, but Leclerc did not think that he could do both at once and instead introduced a plan to incorporate colonial troops into the expeditionary army. Drawing from the revolutionary precedent of the "amalgam," when the professional soldiers of the old royalist army and the bourgeois volunteers of 1792 had merged into single units, Leclerc chose to dissolve the colonial regiments into the demi-brigades brought from France. The official goal was to combine the best of the French army (where there were many qualified officers and administrators) and the colonial army (which had an abundance of hardened troops), but incorporation also made it easier to control, and ultimately disarm, colonial troops once they ceased to exist as independent units.[7] Leclerc also recreated a gendarmerie to help maintain order on plantations and composed in equal parts of European troops, colonial troops, and Louverture's own gendarmes—some of them veterans of the *maréchaussée,* which had fulfilled a similar mission in colonial times.[8]

Every petty commander had claimed grandiose titles during the slave revolt, and the expedition had come with its own plethora of supernumeraries, so Saint-Domingue's armed forces were astonishingly top heavy. Incorporation, by sharply reducing the number of demi-brigades, had the added benefit of giving Leclerc an excuse to dismiss countless officers of color. Some colonial officers whose unit was disbanded were demobilized with the lowly rank of first-class captain, while others were grouped into the *compagnie d'élite* (elite company), a corps that despite its name was a dumping ground for surplus officers.[9] Even those who kept their rank found themselves under the authority of the white officers of the receiving unit, who were systematically considered senior to their black colleagues.

In another move likely to spark popular discontent, Leclerc ordered cultivators back to work just as he launched his disarmament campaign.[10] His labor code was based on Louverture's, but the Moyse uprising had shown the extent of popular opposition to plantation work, even under the semi-free cultivator system, and recreating large estates manned by hundreds of obedient workers was a tall order after ten years of revolutionary upheaval. Louverture had banned the sale of small plots, but many squatters had divided vacant fields into individual gardens, and returning planters hesitated to push their legal claim for fear of being killed.[11] Some colonial officers (presumably not those who had obtained leases from the *domaines*) supported the cultivators' cause; so did the young men who formed the lower ranks of the colonial army, many of whom had formed common-law unions with *cultivatrices*.[12]

Even Leclerc's relatively benign labor code restricted the cultivators' freedom in ways they found unacceptable when they had spent a decade building new lives outside the plantation world. Cultivators could not leave their plantation without a passport and ran the risk of being sentenced to hard labor simply for going about the countryside unauthorized.[13] Also to stabilize the labor force, the code stipulated that cultivators could not get married without the express consent of their planter. Jean Michel, a battalion chief in Cap Rouge, accordingly contacted the employer of his long-time partner, but when the planter refused to agree to the marriage, Michel began to wonder whether rumors on the "liberticidal projects" of the French were true. Jean-Pierre Lindor, another *ancien libre* living with a black cultivator, feared that his wife and their seven children might be torn from him if she was forced to return to her plantation of origin. Marie-Jeanne Rénoult, who had established herself as an urban market seller during the revolution, complained of being sent back to her former plantation when she now saw herself as a businesswoman.[14] None of these individuals was as well known as Jean-Jacques Dessalines or Henri Christophe, but the bulk of the colony's population consisted of anonymous cultivators and troops like Michel, Lindor, and Rénoult, whose aspirations could not be dismissed without consequences.

Louverture had faced similar resistance when implementing his labor code, which he had overcome by authorizing Dessalines to resort to extralegal violence. French officers also concluded that the mild penalties specified in Leclerc's labor code would not force people to work, but overcoming the cultivators' apathy required methods likely to spark even more unrest.[15] In one of several similar cases afflicting the comparatively quiet county of Jérémie in the southern province, a black man named Pierrot repeatedly tried to kill the manager of his plantation, presumably to avoid being sent back to work. A gendarme was sent to arrest Pierrot, who promptly tried to knife him. Pierrot was sentenced to be whipped as a punishment, which, far from cowing him, prompted him to incite local cultivators to revolt. The next logical step would have been to execute him, but this would have submitted Pierrot to a penalty more severe than those allowed under the Code Noir that had once regulated slavery.[16]

Planters had routinely ignored legal provisions protecting slaves in pre-revolutionary times, and as plantation work resumed, some planters paid little heed to Leclerc's regulations. The planters' favorite instrument was the whip, even though it was now illegal, and as a symbolic reminder of slavery, its use had far-reaching political implications. In August a cultivator entered Jérémie completely naked, his back bloody with the deep cuts carved by the lash. The officer in charge did not have the presence of mind to send him quietly to the hospital, so the cultivator began showing his wounds to all who would look, warning that "whites cut up Negroes and will restore slavery."[17] His fate quickly became the talk of the town, where slavery had only been abolished with the British evacuation of 1798. A plot to kill all the whites of the town narrowly failed soon after.

Chains were also associated with slavery in the popular imagination. Before the revolution, black women accused of abortion had been forced to wear a thorny iron collar until they delivered another child for their master, and the tight, heavy chains used as punishment had occasionally maimed a slave for life. Louverture's use of chain gangs had helped spark the Moyse uprising, so when a French general placed an order for chains, Leclerc fired back that "one can never speak of chains in the colony. The very word scares the blacks. . . . My mission here is as political as it is military."[18]

Faced with the return of their former owners, the disarmament campaign, and the strict labor code, cultivators began to wonder whether all these events were coincidental or preliminaries to their reenslavement. Time and again Leclerc assured them that their freedom was not imperiled, but planters openly debated the merits of restoring slavery, oblivious to the fact that their imprudent habit of discussing politics in front of their laborers had already helped spark the 1791 revolt. In June a planter in Cap bumped into one of his former slaves (now an officer), tore off his epaulets, and told him that it was time to go back to the fields. Afraid of political repercussions, Leclerc sentenced the planter to be put in the stocks, bearing a sign that read "partisan of slavery," on Cap's main square, where the jeers of the *marchandes* (black market women) guaranteed maximum publicity among the black population.[19]

Aptly guessing that the peace of Amiens would precipitate a public debate on whether slavery should be maintained in the colonies that France had recovered from Britain, Leclerc also urged his superiors in Paris not to make any public declarations in favor of slavery—or even publish racist jokes—for fear of the impact these would have in Saint-Domingue.[20] Unfortunately for

Leclerc, just as he was trying to convince black Dominguians that he had no intention of ever restoring slavery in Cap, his brother-in-law, in Paris, was considering this very measure for the rest of the French empire.

⌒

The spring of 1802 saw several significant developments that could potentially upend the colonial debate in Europe. With the peace of Amiens, England agreed to retrocede all the French colonies it had conquered during the previous war, including some where slavery was still in effect. Meanwhile, reports reached Paris that French expeditionary forces had landed in Saint-Domingue and Guadeloupe and promptly vanquished their opponents. These events, the thinking goes, emboldened reactionary activists, whose intense lobbying pushed Bonaparte to restore slavery throughout the empire.[21]

The actual picture is much blurrier. Two critical biographies of Louverture published that year, by Cousin d'Avallon and Jean-Louis Dubroca, focused solely on his lack of patriotism, and Dubroca even described the 1794 law of emancipation as an "invaluable gift of liberty."[22] In a follow-up to his 1801 treatise, François Page merely advocated "slavery, whenever it is possible; and freedom, whenever it is necessary," by which he meant that France could not realistically restore slavery in Saint-Domingue.[23] Other authors refrained from laying out too reactionary an agenda because they were unsure of the general public's reaction. Barré de Saint-Venant, a former planter whose *Des colonies modernes* described the aftermath of emancipation in apocalyptic terms, did not publish a third volume on a possible restoration of slavery for fear of a public backlash. In his *Soirées Bermudiennes,* Félix Carteau overtly favored a restoration of slavery, but well aware that such a proposal would be controversial he sat on the manuscript from 1798 to 1802 and only published it when he sensed that the course of the revolution was about to reverse itself. Louis-Narcisse Deslozières also advocated a return to slavery in his *Egarements du nigrophilisme,* but his book only came out in March 1802, and it is unclear how much impact it had on policy making.[24] Given the fractious nature of the colonial lobby, in 1802 as in 1801 slavery remained a debate that only Bonaparte could settle.

In 1802 as in 1801, Bonaparte did not see the debate over slavery as an either/or dichotomy, but as a compromise that changed according to local circumstances. When the preliminary articles of peace had been signed in London, he had announced his intention to keep slavery in the colonies, like Martinique and Réunion, where it had never been abolished, and emancipation in others, like Guadeloupe and Saint-Domingue, where the 1794 law had taken effect. The peace of Amiens changed nothing to this graduated approach. Many authors have written that Bonaparte restored slavery on May 20, 1802, but the law passed on that day merely *maintained* slavery in the

colonies where it already existed, restored the slave *trade,* and vaguely specified that the government would decide on "a healing system that will vary
according to circumstances" for the colonies where slavery had been abolished.[25] Saint-Domingue's future, then as before, remained up for grabs.

Bonaparte had designed the two parliamentary chambers of the Consulate
as rubber-stamp legislatures that would back all his decisions, and to ensure
even greater compliance he dismissed dozens of his liberal enemies in March
1802. Despite the purge the May 20 law passed by relatively slim majorities
in each chamber, showing an unexpected level of opposition to Bonaparte's
decision to maintain slavery in Martinique.[26] If Bonaparte ever decided to
restore slavery in Saint-Domingue, it would not be because overwhelming
political pressures had forced him in this direction.

At Denis Decrès' behest, the May 20 law was followed by a series of discriminatory decrees that drastically curtailed the rights of citizens of color.
Among other things, Decrès obtained that officers of color would no longer
be sent to the Caribbean, and in September he cancelled all public funding
for Jean-Baptiste Coisnon's multiracial colonial school. Children of color, on
whose education so much money and effort had been lavished, were kicked
out and drafted as drummers in the army.[27] In the long run, Decrès hoped,
Saint-Domingue's cultivators would voluntarily submit to an outright restoration of slavery.[28]

Because of the overall arc of French colonial policy that year, scholars
usually assume that Bonaparte had a clear plan to restore slavery in Saint-
Domingue. But he actually never sent Leclerc any firm order to that effect. Slavery seemed to have his preference, since he restored it wherever he
could, but the military situation in Saint-Domingue was so delicate that it
called for a unique approach (he even briefly considered creating a new race
in Saint-Domingue through mandatory multiracial polygamy).[29] In the end
Bonaparte decided that Leclerc, being on the scene, was the only person able
to judge what was militarily and politically feasible, and on May 21 he instructed Decrès to inform Leclerc of the law passed a day before and to re-
affirm the government's trust in "whatever measures [Leclerc] will take to re-
assert the rights of the metropolis."[30] The conservative Decrès probably had his
own thoughts on the matter, but he dutifully wrote Leclerc that the continuation of slavery in Martinique "had nothing to do with Saint-Domingue. You
know what is good and what will suit the government. You alone, being on
the spot, can calculate what can most advantageously be obtained."[31]

In the summer of 1802, a few months after he had sent large expeditions
to France's various Caribbean possessions, Bonaparte judged that the time
was ripe to renege on some of his earlier promises and fired off a series of
letters to colonial officials. On July 13 he authorized Antoine Richepance

to restore slavery in Guadeloupe, and a month later he instructed Victor Hugues to prepare to do the same in Guiana.[32] One might thus have expected that the letters he sent to Leclerc on July 1 and 22 would say something of a possible restoration of slavery in Saint-Domingue, but these merely repeated Bonaparte's long-standing demand that black officers be deported. "Rid us of these gilded Africans, and there will be nothing left for us to wish," he wrote.[33] His last letter to Leclerc, dated November 27, announced the arrival of large reinforcements with which France could retake the offensive in the winter of 1802/3, yet despite this considerable commitment of resources Bonaparte merely described Leclerc's ultimate goal as "restoring tranquility in this beautiful and vast colony."[34] Bonaparte would probably have welcomed a restoration of slavery in Saint-Domingue if it could have been done cheaply and easily. This, however, was a big "if," and Bonaparte trusted his brother-in-law to follow the policy most conducive to French interests. If France were ever to restore slavery in Saint-Domingue, Leclerc—not Decrès or Bonaparte—would be the one making this momentous decision.

Contrary to oft-repeated claims that Leclerc was about to restore slavery, he did not see it as a realistic proposition, at least in the short term. Faced with pockets of armed resistance and a deadly epidemic, he was in no position to forsake emancipation in the summer of 1802, a fact that his correspondence makes abundantly clear. On July 6 he forwarded a copy of his labor code and added that "I know what the colony needs, but I also know when we can implement it."[35] The cryptic comment was possibly referring to the future restoration of slavery, but the rest of the letter, which described the epidemic's terrible toll and his increasing reliance on colonial troops, explained how unrealistic any harsh measure was in the current context, and he even proposed to encourage white farmers to settle in Saint-Domingue so that the colony would no longer have to rely exclusively on a black labor force. The last letter he ever sent Bonaparte, in October 1802, set out a tentative schedule: finish the disarmament campaign by winter's end (for which he needed twelve thousand men at once); do nothing during the summer of 1803 (while receiving another three thousand men to make up for losses to fevers); then "accomplish your goals" in the winter of 1803/4 if he received an additional fifteen thousand men.[36] Leclerc must have doubted whether Bonaparte would ever commit the massive numbers of troops he deemed indispensable. At any rate, he insisted that he would not stay through another summer and that it would be up to his successor to implement whatever plans Bonaparte had for the long term. Leclerc's sense of honor and personal preference for individual liberty probably also weighed on his mind. "Do not think of restoring slavery here for quite some time," he wrote Decrès after hearing of the May 20 law. "I think I can do everything so that my successor can implement the decisions of the government, but after issuing numerous public proclamations to guarantee the freedom of the blacks, I do not want to contradict myself."[37]

Committing oneself to emancipation in Saint-Domingue while maintaining or restoring slavery in nearby islands seemed contradictory, so many people in Bonaparte's entourage advised him to take a uniform approach. The former minister of the navy, Pierre Forfait, favored a blanket resumption of slavery throughout the Caribbean, while, at the other extreme of the political spectrum, the former agent Philippe Roume thought it best to extend emancipation everywhere, Martinique included.[38] Bonaparte, however, thought that he could compartmentalize his policy and instructed Richepance to keep his plans for Guadeloupe secret to avoid spreading alarm in Saint-Domingue.[39] It remained to be seen whether such crude attempts at deception would be sufficient to convince Dominguians that the situation in nearby French colonies had no bearing on their own future and allay fears that they were next in the first consul's black book.

∼

Four hundred miles southeast of Saint-Domingue, in the heart of the Lesser Antilles, Guadeloupe lies below the cloud-wrapped cone of the Soufrière volcano, its two main islands spread out like the wings of a tropical butterfly. France's second-largest sugar producer after Saint-Domingue, Guadeloupe also experienced much turmoil during the French Revolution, which, as in its larger neighbor, stemmed as much from ideological quarrels and clashing personal ambitions as it did from racial hatred. Chaos first erupted in 1792 when royalist planters sought to exile the envoys of the revolutionary republic. A year later slaves revolted in Trois-Rivières, not to demand their emancipation, but to rid the island of aristocratic planters agitating for independence. Given the slaves' attachment to French revolutionary principles, colonial authorities naturally turned to them during two 1794 English invasions and freed them in exchange for military service. The tactic paid off when the invasions were repulsed and the black citizen-soldiers of Guadeloupe became the most powerful army in the Lesser Antilles.[40]

Guadeloupe had regained a modicum of stability when in October 1801 officers of color exiled the colony's captain general. As he learned of the rebellion, Leclerc immediately feared that Bonaparte would divert future troop shipments to Guadeloupe, and in April he sent Boudet and two hundred men to Guadeloupe in the hope that they could strike an agreement with the rebellious officers and forestall any need for a larger French force.[41] Unbeknownst to Leclerc, Bonaparte had also heard of the recent upheavals, and a 3,500-strong expedition led by Antoine Richepance was already on its way. As in Saint-Domingue, many officers of color rallied to the French side after it landed, while others suspected that it had come to restore slavery and revolted under the motto "liberty or death." Rebel colonial units, which could not maneuver as easily as their Dominguian counterparts did in the vastness of Hispaniola, waged a conventional war that promptly ended in defeat and mass suicide. But communities of runaways continued to wage a guerilla war in the mountains of the Basse Terre, and combat and yellow fever had cost Richepance over half his forces by the end of summer.[42]

In July 1802 Richepance implemented a series of ominous reforms that took away the cultivators' salary, reestablished the use of the whip, and restored old distinctions between *nouveaux* and *anciens libres*.[43] In an effort to rid the island of potential troublemakers, he also loaded 1,500 rebels on board a small squadron bound for the Spanish Main, where he hoped that some could be sold at a profit (the men were dressed in loincloths to pass them off as African-born slaves). Authorities in Cartagena saw through the ruse, so some frigates next headed for New York and the U.S. slave market. They hit Pedro shoals off Jamaica, stopped in Kingston for repairs, and rerouted for Cap on the advice of Governor George Nugent, who probably hoped to exacerbate Saint-Domingue's already combustible situation. Once in Cap a few rebels swam to shore, bringing with them news of the brutal restoration of French authority in Guadeloupe. The frigates were immediately sent away to the United States, Corsica, and Puerto Rico, but not before the story of Guadeloupe's plight had spread throughout the colony.[44]

The incident could not have taken place at a more unfavorable time for Leclerc. Desperate to stem the swelling rumor that slavery would soon be restored throughout the French empire, he had hidden the text of the May 20 law, but slave traders had come to Saint-Domingue to offer their services, and everyone knew that the slave trade had resumed.[45] Reports that the forces sent to Tobago and Martinique had maintained slavery in these islands would soon follow.[46] Leclerc's attempts to restrict the flow of information even backfired when rumors spread that the May 20 law contained a clause restoring slavery in Saint-Domingue, when it did not.[47]

Eager to strike a truce with the Maroons and to secure the loyalty of troops of color still serving on the French side, Richepance never officially restored slavery, but his harsh policies convinced everyone in Saint-Domingue, Leclerc included, that he had, and panic swept the black population. Alfred de Laujon, who had found a position as court clerk in Port Républicain's tribunal, was inundated with *nouveaux libres* desirous to purchase their freedom from their former master in case slavery was restored and *anciens libres* wishing to notarize documents proving their free status (a return to the prerevolutionary order should not have affected the latter, but many *anciens libres* were "libres de savanne" whose freedom had never been registered to avoid paying the manumission tax, and they were afraid of losing their freedom to a legal technicality).[48]

By early August Leclerc morosely informed Bonaparte that the (alleged) restoration of slavery in Guadeloupe had completely undermined his mission. "My moral ascendancy is now destroyed," he wrote, so "now that your plans for the colonies are well known, if you want to keep Saint-Domingue, you need to send a new army."[49] The disarmament campaign, he informed Decrès, would have to rely solely on force.[50] In much of the north, localized uprisings turned into a general rebellion, and had it not been for the timely arrival of reinforcements from France Leclerc confessed that he would likely have lost the colony.[51]

For the black population of Saint-Domingue, the last few weeks' events had awakened a deep, primal fear that their freedom was at stake in the conflict. Captured rebels now died "with incredible fanaticism," wrote Leclerc. "They laugh at death. Women are the same."[52] Colonial officers like Dessalines still served in the French army, so this exponential growth in popular resistance took place almost entirely within the lower ranks of the black population, more specifically within a group often overlooked in accounts of the Haitian Revolution: the mountain Maroons.

～

In the center of Port-au-Prince, on the Champ de Mars plaza that borders the presidential palace, several statues commemorate the heroes that made it possible for Haiti to exist as a nation. Dessalines features prominently; so do Christophe and Louverture. For a country to honor its founding fathers is to be expected—monuments dedicated to Thomas Jefferson and George Washington also dot the National Mall in Washington, DC—but one of the statues on the Champ de Mars is more unusual. It depicts a black man blowing into the conch shell that slaves used to spread the message of revolt, and whose name is purposely left ambiguous. This statue, known as *neg mawon* or *marron inconnu* (unknown Maroon), is dedicated to the anonymous, unsung heroes of Haiti's slave revolt.[53]

Maroonage dated back to the earliest days of European colonization, when a Taino named Henri escaped from his Spanish *encomendero* (lord) and created the first Maroon community in the mountains of Bahoruco (the term *Maroon,* or runaway slave, comes from *cimarrón,* or wild animal). The Tainos soon succumbed to European diseases, but as slavery grew in the eighteenth century black Maroon communities sprang up along the ill-defined border between Saint-Domingue and Spanish Santo Domingo, including Henri's old haunts in the Bahoruco Mountains, as well as in Jamaica and Surinam. Maroon communities rarely harbored more than a few hundred runaways, but they were well entrenched and colonial authorities eventually signed treaties allowing the Maroons to live autonomously as long as they did not raid plantations or accept new runaways. This made them the first independent black polities in the Caribbean.

Studies on the exact prevalence of Maroonage on the eve of the Haitian Revolution are conflicting, but the phenomenon certainly involved thousands of runaways a year, most of whom lived in towns and coastal plains and relied on enslaved friends for survival.[54] Borders between the world of the plantation slaves and that of the Maroons were accordingly porous. Two of the leaders of the 1791 uprising, Dutty Boukman and Jean-François Papillon, were former Maroons. During the Haitian Revolution, cultivators and soldiers were quick to flee to the woods when discipline on plantations or in the army grew too oppressive, and much to Louverture's annoyance dozens of thousands of individuals experienced the life of the Maroons.[55] In addition to the small prerevolutionary communities, Maroon groups thus came to encompass, at least temporarily, a large section of Saint-Domingue's laboring class.

What truly distinguished the Maroons from the rest of the colonial population was not that they lived in the mountains but that, contrary to colonial and metropolitan officers, *anciens libres* and white planters, and obedient cultivators, they did not aspire to lease, own, or work on plantations. Rejecting the French economic model of large-scale agriculture, they dreamed of growing subsistence crops like yams and cassava on their own plots, an attractive, if unambitious, alternative to the slavery by another name favored by every other group in Saint-Domingue. By putting individual freedom above economic expediency, they articulated the most radical agenda of all the groups vying for the colony, one that eventually prevailed in Haiti. They were the true rebels of Saint-Domingue.

Because they were often at odds with the colored elite, the Maroons were long ignored in the Haitian historiography of the revolution. Classic historians like Beaubrun Ardouin and Thomas Madiou, who favored the sophisticated *anciens libres* and, to a lesser extent, colonial officers like Dessalines, relegated the Maroons to the far corners of the war of independence as uncouth barbarians whose indiscipline delayed independence. Even C. L. R. James's *Black Jacobins,* an influential work inspired by black nationalism, downgraded the Maroon leaders to "nameless petty chieftains" who led "bands" of rebels while describing Louverture's subordinates as "generals" leading "armies" even when they had fewer men under their command.[56] It was not until the works of Jean Fouchard and Carolyn Fick that historians finally began to acknowledge the Maroons' contribution to the Haitian Revolution. Their role was particularly notable in the summer of 1802, when the colonial army fought on the French side and Maroons provided the only significant opposition to French rule.

Incorporating the Maroons into the larger narrative of the Haitian Revolution is a necessary but daunting task. Maroons were illiterate to a man, purposely led a life of seclusion, and did not leave a single firsthand account of their lives. Because they did not serve in the French army (though they occasionally fought as allies), there is little trace of their service in military archives. All that we can learn about them must be gleaned from third-party accounts, which are usually scanty and disparaging.

Contemporary sources alternatively referred to the Maroons as *Congos, Guinéens,* or *Africains,* suggesting that they drew their ranks primarily from the African-born population, as was already the case before the revolution. Their world thus abided largely by social norms they had brought from Africa, and which can be extrapolated from what is known of newly imported slaves before the revolution. Prerevolutionary chroniclers made a sharp distinction between Creole and *bossale* (African-born) slaves, the former serving primarily as domestics and skilled workers, the latter as artisans or more often field hands (and thus as cultivators during the revolutionary era). Creole slaves typically prided themselves on their cultural affiliation with their French masters and despised Congos fresh off the ship, virtually naked except for a "tanga" hiding their genitals, their bodies covered with ritual tattoos and scarifications, branding marks, and the various mutilations inflicted as a punishment for running away.[57]

Africa's great diversity notwithstanding, most slaves came from a handful of linguistically and culturally homogenous areas, and many managed to spend their lives alongside members of closely related "nations" (tribal groups). Many tribal practices thus survived the trauma of the Middle Passage and helped shaped the cultural milieu in which New World slaves operated, as well as that of Dominguian Maroons, whose communities were often composed of members of a single nation.[58] That French management styles left slaves free to organize their spare time also made it easier for the Congos to maintain their cultural practices than their brethren in the U.S. South. All chroniclers noted the Congos' passion for games imported from Africa, such as stick fights, and for dancing the *chica* or the *calenda* to the sound of the *bamboula* (drum), banjo, and calabash rattles; each tribal group had brought its own moves, and rivalries between dancers of distinct nations were common. Dominguian slaves also organized their quarters in the African style, with a circle of huts surrounding a central square, a pattern most likely repeated in Maroon communities. Families of cultivators typically gathered at night in a single *ajoupa* (hut) "naked and crouching," wrote the naturalist Michel Descourtilz, "some talking, the oldest speaking in Guinean language, others singing some air from a dance, while the youngest fed the fire with dried cow dung to smoke out mosquitoes."[59]

African-born slaves longed to return to "Guinea" (Africa), a term still synonymous with heaven in contemporary Vodou. Reversing the Middle Passage was a daunting journey that few Maroons undertook, but the faithful knew that the deceased joined a parallel world of spirits and ancestors in Guinea and that death was the easiest way to reunite with long-lost relatives. Newly arrived slaves were thus notoriously prone to suicide. During the revolution, Europeans similarly noted that black rebels showed no fear of death, either in combat or on the scaffold (they did fear mutilation and dismemberment, because they joined the world of spirits inside their mortal envelope; the guillotine erected in Port Républicain in 1793 was immediately destroyed as cruel and unusual punishment).[60]

Vodou, a syncretic religion mixing elements of Islam, French Catholicism and mysticism, and African spirit worship, was typical of the Congos' Afro-Caribbean world (few Creoles practiced it, at least openly).[61] Renegade Catholic priests, many of whom had supported the slave revolt in 1791, could often be found within Maroon camps and likely contributed to this religious medley. The cult of the snake *lwa* (spirit) Damballah, for example, which Descourtilz witnessed, was popular in West Africa, but it also had its Catholic pendant in St. Patrick, who had gone to Ireland as a slave and allegedly chased serpents from the island.

Rebel slaves embraced Vodou from the outset of the 1791 revolt, not least because it claimed to protect its followers from pain or even death, and its appeal remained strong in 1802 despite Louverture's efforts to preach Catholicism. The Maroon leader, Lamour Derance, was described as "devoted to all the superstitions of the Africans."[62] Another leader "held a white dog by a ribbon and bore dirty trinkets, hairs, sheep tails, etc." during an attack.[63] Yet another named Gilblas was hanged while wearing his talisman to convince his followers that no magic could obviate France's wrath.[64] The Maroons' terrifying war cries, which often appear in French accounts, may also have been spells designed to protect them from harm.[65]

To historians and ethnologists, contemporary Vodou is a fascinating field of study because its expansive body of myths contains cultural artifacts dating back to the days of the Haitian Revolution. Vodou practices, in the words of the historian Joan Dayan, are essentially "ritual re-enactments of Haiti's colonial past."[66] Among many other examples, the *parler langage* (speak language) that Vodou priests still use to summon the *lwas* consists of a jumble of sentences in African languages and is the closest thing to a recording of the voices of eighteenth-century slaves a historian will ever encounter.[67] The *lwa* of maternal love, Erzulie Dantó, is a persecuted black woman, while the *lwa* of romantic attachment, Erzulie Freda, is a coquettish *mulâtresse;* the contrast between the two is undoubtedly a legacy of sexual politics on colonial plantations. *Bossale,* a term once used to describe newly imported slaves, now refers to newcomers being initiated into Vodou. The *zombie* phenomenon may be a metaphor for the way masters once turned their slaves into unthinking automatons or a new take on the word *vumbi* (ghost) that the Congolese used to describe the white slave traders who had come to take them to the underworld. The most effective countermeasure against *loups-garous* (werewolves), monsters who take off their skin at night to roam the countryside, is to spray the shed skin with salt, pepper, or lemon juice so that they cannot put it back on, a method that coincidentally mirrors the tortures planters inflicted on their slaves after whipping them raw. However problematic as a historical source, Vodou rites are thus a rare window into the slaves' experience and paint a worldview dominated by the distant memory of Africa and the hatred of slavery.

Maroon women abided in part by gender norms imported from Africa, the most unusual of which, to European and Creole observers, was their participation in combat. Even though his own wife had fought with him at Crête-à-Pierrot, Louis Lamartinière was struck by the "prodigious quantity of women" he found in a Maroon camp he overran in August 1802, at a time when he was fighting on France's side.[68] Most Maroons escaped to the woods, but three men, five women, and three children chose to jump to their death from a cliff rather than surrender. Women were often listed as prisoners, possibly because they had family obligations and could not run away as easily as men did, but also because they were at the forefront of many attacks.[69] A French officer also warned his subordinate to "watch for the wives of the cultivators, as they are usually the ones who spy for the rebels and who talk them into revolting."[70]

Maroon communities were always persecuted by the powers that be and were in a constant state of war readiness. They fought a guerilla war of ambushes and arson, coordinating their assaults to the sound of the conch shell. Their armament was often primitive, but they made up for their lack of formal military training with a great dedication to the cause.[71] Despite the belittling labels of "chiefs" and "bands," Maroon leaders were recruited from the large population of African-born cultivators, and their groups could be thousands-strong during the revolution. In parallel to the colonial army of Louverture and Dessalines, Saint-Domingue was thus divided between numerous local Maroon leaders whose names often betrayed their African birth (Yayou, Sanglaou, Gilles Bambara, Sermangai).[72] Maroon groups were typically decentralized, each warrior pledging personal allegiance to a specific chief (often belonging to the same tribal group), who only collaborated with other leaders if he chose to, and a general in the colonial army marveled how Lamour Derance had to gather an "assembly of the chiefs" before making any decision.[73] Estimating the total number of Maroon leaders in the colony at a striking two thousand, Leclerc was happy to note that they never coordinated their actions, otherwise his shrinking army would have been overwhelmed by a massed attack.[74]

In the north, Maroon leaders included Makaya, Noël Mathieu, and Va Malheureux (go poor man).[75] Some, like Lubin Golard near the town of Jean Rabel, had initially welcomed French invaders who fought their nemesis Louverture.[76] Others, like Sylla near Ennery, had defended their independence jealously and refused to lay down their arms during the May armistice.[77] Most were actively resisting French rule by June, when Leclerc launched the disarmament campaign and forced cultivators back to work. The most powerful of the northern leaders was Sans Souci (no worry) near Grande Rivière, who had submitted to the French after the landing, only to join the uprising after they tried to arrest him.[78] Christophe and Sans Souci had a long history of enmity that far predated the Leclerc expedition, and the black general (now fighting on France's behalf) tried hard to capture the Maroon leader throughout the summer. "If Sans Souci was a soldier," Christophe complained, "I could reach him, but he is a cowardly and cruel brigand, who has no qualms about killing those he suspects; he knows when to flee, and covers his retreat by leaving only a desert behind him."[79]

Farther south, the most prominent Maroon leader was Lamour Derance. He had always resented Louverture's strict labor regimen, had sided with André Rigaud during the War of the South, and had launched a raid near Jacmel in December 1801 upon hearing of the Moyse uprising. He had thus welcomed the French as the enemies of his enemies and helped Pamphile Lacroix repulse Dessalines' dangerous counterattack against Port Républicain in February 1802. Rigaud's exile troubled him, however, and at the end of spring he left for the mountains to sulk and wait. The disarmament campaign convinced him to join the rebellion, and by July he was raiding Léogane and the plain of Cul de Sac around Port Républicain with a considerable party.[80] Derance also presided over a loose constellation of rebel groups headed by such leaders as Lafortune, Jean Marie, Laroze, and Jacquet.[81]

The enmity between colonial generals and Maroon leaders was real, but the Maroons' embrace of free labor and African cultural practices appealed to many privates and noncommissioned officers in the colonial army. Like slaves and runaways before the revolution, soldiers and Maroon rebels thus lived interconnected lives, and it was not uncommon for the lower levels of the colonial army to join the Maroon world. On June 20, a few weeks after Leclerc introduced his unpopular plan to incorporate colonial units into

French demi-brigades, the roster for a battalion of the 9th colonial demi-brigade showed that only four of thirty petty officers were willing to serve. All the others had disappeared into the woods, resigned, or called in sick. Desertion was also high among privates, and much of the demi-brigade found its way into Sylla's group.[82]

It was even possible for more notable black officers to cross the thin line separating the colonial army from the Maroon world. Jean-Pierre Léveillé had come to Saint-Domingue with the Leclerc expedition, but by May 1802 he was mentioned as one of the Maroon leaders operating near Sylla's stronghold in Mapou. The documentary trail is limited, but Léveillé's profound hatred for Louverture (who had killed his brother) probably explains why he refused to rejoin the colonial army as long as Louverture's acolytes were still employed. He was also described as poorly educated and probably felt culturally closer to African-born Maroons than to elite *anciens libres*. Captured in June, Léveillé managed to escape (probably with the help of sympathetic colonial soldiers) and Dessalines spent the rest of the summer chasing him. It was only in 1803 that Léveillé made his peace with colonial officers and rejoined their forces in the south, by which point he had completed a full circle from the world of the plains to that of the mountains and back, a journey that seems to have been surprisingly common among the black rank and file.[83]

～

Despite growing hostility among the black masses, Leclerc plowed ahead with his disarmament campaign, which was a prerequisite to reestablishing any lasting control of the colony but proved as difficult as he had expected. His generals proceeded county by county for lack of troops, often merely pushing rebels from one area to another, and they only found a fraction of the massive quantities of guns thought to be in the colony. Throughout, the Maroons staged surprise attacks, burned plantations, and then hid in the woods when pressed.[84] This forced the French into a massive counterinsurgency operation that relied primarily on brute force. "I am just back from Marmelade and St. Michel, where I acted just as you requested," Jean-François Debelle wrote at the beginning of the campaign. "One needs to use strength when talking to these people, because they view mercy as a sign of weakness. Wherever I go, I spread terror."[85]

The insurgency grew in July along with the rumor of a French plot to restore slavery, forcing Leclerc to ramp up the repression. In June he had ordered his officers to shoot Maroon leaders and imprison rebel cultivators, a relatively restrained policy. In July he adopted the much stricter rule that Maroons of any rank found with weapons in their hands should be shot, women included. A new criminal code stipulated that anyone resisting public authorities was liable to be shot, and rebels were executed daily in Port Républicain and Cap. No legal proceedings preceded these executions, martial law having been reinstituted.[86]

A few French officers were uncomfortable with the blanket use of executions, but those who treated the rebels with undue leniency could be exiled or see their plantations confiscated, and ambitious officers quickly learned to draft martial reports.[87] One officer who did not seem troubled by the expedition's violent turn was Pauline's dear friend Pierre Boyer, whose reports reveled in tales of brutality. "Everything is going well here," he wrote from Port-de-Paix. "Since tomorrow is Sunday [market day], and all the blacks will come to town, I hanged fourteen of them to the gates of the city for all to see, including five women. . . . Maurepas is surprised to see a sweet-looking white like me execute blacks as I do, and he tells me that with two weeks of this regimen I will be feared and obeyed."[88]

Daily executions of prisoners failed to dampen the ardor of the Maroon rebels, so violence rose yet another notch. By August, finding an undeclared gun on a plantation was sufficient to shoot the plantation's manager and gang drivers. Hanging, which had been pioneered by Boyer, was generalized because it seemed to make more of an impression on those who witnessed it. The first gallows went up in Port Républicain on August 11 to execute ten Maroons, and hanging quickly spread to the surrounding countryside.[89] As had long been the case in Europe, gallows were often erected on a high spot so that they could be seen from afar, and prisoners were hanged on market day to make an impression on visitors from the countryside.[90] Delighted to see that his practices had become standard operating procedure, Boyer scolded subordinates who did not hang rebels with sufficient abandon.[91]

The island of La Tortue had long been a rare quiet spot on Saint-Domingue's northern coast, and Leclerc had even spent a few days there in May to rest with Pauline. The turbulent summer, however, did not spare the once-faithful isle, and in June a first cultivator uprising destroyed most of its plantations. Leclerc accused Raymond Labatut, a white planter whose own property had remained suspiciously unscathed, of encouraging the revolt and sentenced him to pay a fifty thousand francs indemnity, with more cash to be taken from the cultivators' salary.[92] A month later, after Leclerc ordered that the island's population be disarmed, a second, larger outbreak broke out in which local cultivators massacred French convalescents sent from the mainland. One of the officers of color sent with the expedition, Martial Besse, was sent to put down the revolt, but when he chose to negotiate with the rebels Leclerc exiled him to France for his lack of firmness. Finding a less restrained officer did not take long. Boyer was stationed in nearby Port-de-Paix and rushed to crush the uprising in La Tortue with characteristic fury, killing the entire adult black population according to one account.[93]

Boyer's correspondence was intercepted by the rebels, who thus ignored nothing of his passion for hanging and nicknamed him "Boyer le cruel."[94] Leclerc, however, found nothing to fault with his record and assigned him the disarmament of Moustique. Boyer entered the area in high spirits on August 13 and soon crushed all opposition. He left behind him a trail of twitching corpses, but his superiors were pleased with the result.[95]

With time Boyer and other generals learned that the most effective counter-insurgency tactics were to divide one's forces into small, mobile columns (which the French called "colonnes mobiles" or "colonnes infernales" in reference to the *chouan* uprising), position them along likely routes of escape, then launch a coordinated assault; such maneuvers were often described as a "chasse" or "battue" because they resembled an animal hunt.[96] When possible, food crops like banana trees were also destroyed to force hungry Maroons to leave their mountain lairs. Prisoners were then tortured to learn the location of the weapons. Some reports also proposed to hold all black cultivators in fortified compounds to better control them, a technique later used in similar conflicts like the Cuban war of independence (*reconcentración*), the Mau Mau uprising (emergency villages), and the Vietnam War (strategic hamlet program).[97]

Such tactics proved effective, and given enough time and men the French army would likely have prevailed; but the toll of the yellow fever epidemic grew in tandem with the insurgency, and by late July Leclerc found himself short of troops. When La Tortue revolted on the twenty-second, he was able to spare a few men, but when nearby Port-de-Paix followed a day later, he had none left to counter the latest outbreak. Another uprising involving over six hundred armed cultivators immediately followed in Gros Morne, which the local commander tried to contain with a mere twenty-five gendarmes and eighteen German troops before having to fall back.[98] From then on French commanders continuously clamored for troops that Leclerc did not have. There was little to expect from European reinforcements, who succumbed to yellow fever as soon as they landed, so Leclerc turned to the one group he could count on to fight the Maroon rebels: the colonial army.

≈

Using black troops in a campaign aimed at subduing black rebels had its drawbacks, since sympathizers could smuggle ammunition to the rebels or tip them off before upcoming raids. Duplicity was also suspected in the suspicious escapes of the Maroon leaders Makaya, Charlot, and Léveillé.[99] So little did the French trust their colonial allies that in late August the garrison of Port Républicain introduced a password to recognize friend from foe. The first password was revealing: "hypocrisy."[100]

Leclerc, however, thought it impossible to do without colonial troops as long as yellow fever ravaged his European army. Within a week of announcing his plan to incorporate colonial units into French demi-brigades, he reported that he only had 10,000 European troops still fit for duty, when he would have needed 25,000 to overwhelm and disarm colonial troops. Thousands of reinforcements landed in the following weeks, but the cost of the epidemic was such that his overall strength remained the same on July 6; by late August, despite another 3,850 reinforcements, Leclerc estimated that he would soon be down to 5,000 men able to bear arms. Responding to Decrès' latest demand that he deport black officers, Leclerc explained that he could not possibly comply when they were the only ones still able to march against the Maroons.[101] Using colonial troops also seemed a sensible way to reduce French losses since it was believed that strenuous marches in the heat of the day caused yellow fever (white troops were sent to march after dusk, which had the unintended effect of exposing them to mosquito bites).[102]

After dismissing three-fourths of the black officers when he merged French and colonial units in June, Leclerc was thus forced to rehire many of them a month later. Even Jean-Pierre and Paul Louverture found themselves back in France's employ.[103] Colonial officers insisted on being paid cash, so Leclerc scrambled to find enough funds by selling his flour stockpile and borrowing against customs revenue (French troops, whose loyalty was more assured, were paid months in arrears, if at all).[104] Leclerc immediately threw colonial units into the disarmament campaign, usually pairing black generals with the Maroon leaders they were known to despise. Christophe thus chased Sans Souci, Makajoux went after Sylla, and Maurepas and Dessalines pursued their rivals near Port-de-Paix and Plaisance.[105] As a test of loyalty Leclerc systematically assigned colonial officers to the most dangerous missions. By the end of the month he still had little trust in Maurepas, but he concluded that Christophe and Dessalines "are doing well, I can even say that I owe them a lot."[106]

Dessalines threw himself headlong into his first mission. Asked to disarm La Brande, he captured everyone—women, children, and men—and gave no quarter to those found with weapons in their hands. "I hanged a few of them and shot the others," he proudly reported, "and I hope that ten years from now La Brande will remember the lesson I taught them."[107] His French colleagues were impressed. "For seven days, Dessalines had been hunting the brigands of La Brande the way one hunts wild beasts. He has shot, clubbed, and hanged on a daily basis."[108] Soon the French were giving him orders to "exterminate the brigands to the last man" in nearby Pilate and Plaisance and employing him wherever the depleted French garrisons had been forced to halt the disarmament campaign.[109] "For Dessalines to show up in Le Pendu [the hanging man] would do more to force armed rebels to surrender than a column of 200 men," an officer wrote.[110]

Despite Dessalines' zeal, some of Leclerc's subordinates objected to employing a man who weeks earlier was massacring white planters. Edmé-Étienne Desfourneaux and Donatien de Rochambeau, two officers closely aligned with the Creole planters, kept Maurepas and Dessalines under close watch, and in July Rochambeau forwarded to Leclerc an intelligence report listing Dessalines as one of several "false, deceitful men, plotting new crimes, who should urgently be arrested."[111] He constantly harassed Dessalines, even shooting six of his subordinates, and an exasperated Dessalines eventually warned Leclerc that he would sooner resign than continue serving under Rochambeau.[112]

Called in to arbitrate the feud, Leclerc brushed aside Rochambeau's concerns and put Dessalines under the command of Jean-Baptiste Brunet (Desfourneaux was deported to France around the same time).[113] Another general who questioned Dessalines' loyalty only had thirty-six European troops left in his division, so French losses were probably the main reason why Leclerc felt he had no other choice but to continue employing Dessalines.[114] At any rate, his new superiors were full of praise. "Dessalines works like a God," Brunet's chief of staff told Brunet, who reported to Leclerc that "Dessalines is doing wonders."[115] Soon Dessalines was given his own division, and Leclerc wrote to Bonaparte, partly in horror, partly in awe, that he was using Dessalines as the "butcher of the blacks."[116]

Dessalines' French critics and Haitian admirers, equally unable to comprehend how Dessalines could serve on France's side at a time when uprisings were breaking out everywhere, have often concluded that he was actually playing a double game, claiming to attack Maroon camps to obtain guns and supplies from the French army, which he then surreptitiously gave to his opponents.[117] This was unlikely since the French kept Dessalines under tight surveillance and found nothing specific to reproach him for until the end of September. It was also unnecessary because the French were down to their last reserves and Dessalines could easily have overwhelmed them if he had switched sides at the height of the epidemic.

Dessalines' attitude only makes sense if one studies revolutionary Saint-Domingue, not as a binary world in which blacks fought whites, but as a multifaceted society in which class mattered as much as skin color. Dessalines looked at his opponents not as members of a fellow race—Africans of different tribal backgrounds have markedly different physical characteristics—but as an alliance between the Maroon rebels who had rejected Louverture's authority and the reluctant cultivators he had punished as Louverture's inspector of cultivation. In the event of a French defeat, Dessalines could hope to become ruler of Saint-Domingue, so the disarmament campaign must have struck him as a golden opportunity to eliminate future opposition to his rule. This was probably what he had in mind when he hoped that "ten years from now" the people of La Brande would remember his visit. At the rate the French were dying, there would be no European troops left in ten months, and the main issue was not whether Saint-Domingue would be ruled by blacks or whites in a decade's time, but whether it would be ruled by plantation-owning generals or mountain-bound Maroons.

This conniving plan, if true (Dessalines obviously never couched his thoughts on paper), showed a singular ability to project himself in the future and weigh the various political factions in Saint-Domingue. Leclerc did not suspect that Dessalines could hatch such a complicated plot because Leclerc viewed him as a bloodthirsty beast firmly under French control. He should have been more careful: the last person to employ Dessalines as a thoughtless executioner had been Leclerc's predecessor Louverture, now living in exile because he had been betrayed, much to his surprise, by a seemingly brutish general named Jean-Jacques Dessalines.

11

Revolt

The Defection of the Colonial Army

The ship of the line *Intrépide,* on which Christophe de Fréminville had sailed to Saint-Domingue, also brought a brigadier general named Wladyslaw Jablonowski. Fréminville described him as "Japanese," but he actually belonged to the even more exotic category of mixed-race Poles. Born in Dantzig to a white mother and a black father, Jablonowski had studied at the military academy of Brienne, where one of his classmates, a young Corsican named Napoleone Buonaparte, had taunted him on account of his mixed racial ancestry. Jablonowski had served the Bourbon army, then his native Poland, before reintegrating the French army in 1797, where he had risen to the rank of general and commander of the 2nd Polish legion.[1]

Left unemployed by the 1801 peace preliminaries, Jablonowski looked at the Saint-Domingue expedition as a way to resume his career. Polish nationalism aside, he asked for French citizenship so that he would no longer have to fight "for a secondary power," and despite his racial background, he volunteered to serve in the Caribbean as there was no other theater of operations available in peacetime.[2] Health problems prevented him from leaving with Leclerc, but he found a spot on the second wave of reinforcements. When he finally got his deployment orders in May 1802, he hurriedly married a Parisian named Anne Barbe Lenot, and in July the newlyweds embarked for the Caribbean. Upon reaching Cap, Jablonowski was quickly transferred to Saint-Marc to help put down an insurrection that had sprung up in the western province's mountainous interior. It was an indication of the ravages of yellow fever that his superior had to rummage through three different demi-brigades to form a meager one-hundred-man column under his command.[3]

Rebellions were a common sight in the turbulent summer of 1802, but the uprising facing Jablonowski was qualitatively very different. Rumor had it that it was inspired by Charles Belair, Toussaint Louverture's nephew (or possibly illegitimate son) and putative heir. Belair had fought Victoire Leclerc in the spring campaign, joined the French army after Louverture's submission, and was one of those colonial officers whose loyalty was essential to Leclerc's ability to complete the disarmament campaign. His defection marked the first time a prominent officer of the colonial army had revolted since the spring of 1802.[4]

Like his uncle, Belair was a cautious man who urged the troops and cultivators in his district to revolt, yet refused to openly endorse their actions for fear that they might fail. But his superiors had long-standing doubts about his loyalty and immediately suspected his complicity when his close associates and troops joined the rebellion. Jean-Baptiste Brunet ordered Belair to rush to Cap and beg for Leclerc's forgiveness, but remembering how Brunet had treacherously captured his uncle he refused to comply, even as he continued to insist on his innocence.[5]

Belair made one egregious mistake: he rebelled alone, without coordinating his efforts with other generals of the colonial army, and in the words of a French officer was "an idiot, because he has no means or strength."[6] In sharp contrast with the downcast mood prevailing during the yellow fever epidemic, the French reacted with calm to a revolt they were confident they could quell. They sent converging columns under Jablonowski and the Parisian cavalryman Paul Valete, both of whom had recently arrived; they also made extensive use of local figures whom Belair had failed to enlist, including the white and mixed-race Creoles François Pageot and Faustin Répussard and the colonial officers Bazelais, Gabart, and André Vernet, all of them subordinates of Jean-Jacques Dessalines.

Haitian historians find it particularly hard to make sense of Dessalines' actions during the Belair uprising, when he not only failed to lend Belair the support that could have helped him succeed but also expressed to Brunet his "ardent desire" to help quell the revolt.[7] His apologists have gone to great lengths to rationalize his actions by claiming that his behavior was part of a multilayered conspiracy to help Belair by fighting against him, or simply rejecting outright the abundant evidence proving Dessalines' collaboration with the French army.[8] In fact, the key to Dessalines' behavior was a simple, straightforward clash of personal ambitions. Louverture was now in exile, as were likely heirs like his sons and André Rigaud, so the two main candidates to take over Louverture's mantle were Belair and Dessalines, two rivals whose relationship had long been strained.[9] Dessalines cleverly used the Belair uprising to rid himself of his most dangerous opponent while proving his loyalty to France, a tactic that was nothing new to a man who had previously demanded Louverture's exile and who would soon write to Leclerc to denounce his colleagues Henri Christophe and Jacques Maurepas as traitors.[10]

Faced with the combined might of France's army and his local rivals, Belair stood no chance of success. Within days his wife, Sanitte, was found hiding in a tuft of tall grass, Belair surrendered, and the couple was sent to Cap on the poorly named ship *Liberté* to be judged. Given Belair's ambiguous attitude during the uprising, there was no firm evidence of his guilt, but Dessalines insisted that Belair and his "ferocious wife" should be severely punished for their "acts of barbarism," and on October 5 a court-martial sentenced them both to death.[11] Sanitte Belair, a forceful woman who was considered as much a leader of the revolt as her husband, was sentenced on her own account. The court transcript indicates that he was shot and that she was decapitated, but according to the oral tradition, she insisted on being shot so as to die like a true warrior.

Despite their tragic end, the Belairs could find some solace in the thought that they had outlived one of their foes. On the morning of September 29, barely a month after he had landed in Saint-Domingue, an attack of gout had claimed Jablonowski's life. "I sacrificed everything to follow my dear Jablonowski," his wife wrote in despair. "I loved him. . . . All was destroyed in an instant. Grief overwhelms me."[12] Jablonowski was only one of twenty-seven general officers destined to die in Saint-Domingue, but his sacrifice was arguably the most pointless: he had given his life to fight fellow people of color for another country's colony on behalf of a racist classmate.

~

Jablonowski was far from the only Pole to serve and die in Saint-Domingue. Deluged with Leclerc's pressing demands for reinforcements, yet hesitant to send good troops as long as the epidemic lasted, Bonaparte increasingly turned to foreigners for colonial service—Germans, Swiss, and most notably Poles.[13] Their country annihilated by three successive partitions, Polish nationalists had joined the French army in large numbers during the revolution, eventually forming entire demi-brigades in the hope that their service would convince France to support their claim to nationhood. Instead they were used as disposable tin soldiers in a distant theater, where far from fighting for their independence they died on behalf of a foreign empire.

The first Polish unit earmarked for colonial duty was the 3rd demi-brigade of the line, which in April 1802 received orders to ship out from Italy.[14] Composed of 2,400 Polish troops and officers, twenty-six butchers and bakers, nineteen Italian servants, fourteen *femmes de troupe* (cooks and prostitutes), four *enfants de troupe* (child mascots), and four doctors, the demi-brigade was a diverse lot. The ships that received them were equally varied; only two French warships could be spared, so the demi-brigade embarked on a flotilla of small merchantmen purchased as far away as the United States, Denmark, and Russia.

The one sentiment uniting this disparate force was its reluctance to serve. For fear that the Poles, who had not been paid for eighteen months, might mutiny, two French demi-brigades monitored their departure; as an added precaution, the Poles were not told of their destination until they were out at sea. Only at this point did the troops, many of whom thought that they were going home given the recent peace of Amiens, learn that they were headed west by south, not east by north. A few officers, enthralled by the allure of the Indies, spoke enthusiastically of seeing "people of colors other than white" and eating "pineapples, as abundant as potatoes in Poland."[15] But many others failed to see the relevance of colonial warfare to the cause of Polish independence and asked to be relieved of duty, only to be confined on board during stopovers to prevent desertion. One persistent captain escaped twice, only to be sent to a disciplinary battalion and dispatched to the colonies a third time.[16]

After leaving Tarento on May 15, the fleet endured a particularly long and unpleasant journey. A storm immediately broke out and wrecked the ship carrying most of the supplies. The survivors sailed again a few days later from Livorno and, after further stops in Spain, Africa, and South America, finally reached Saint-Domingue in September. By this time the troops had spent six months on board ships so overcrowded that one-third of the passengers had spent the entire crossing outside for lack of room below decks. Two days after its arrival Leclerc sent the entire demi-brigade into the maelstrom of war.[17]

Polish troops had served bravely on all the battlefields of Europe, but in Saint-Domingue they were unanimously decried as third rate. Accustomed to pitched battles (the 3rd was a regiment of the line), the Poles understood nothing of guerilla warfare and within weeks of their landing complaints about their shortcomings piled up in French headquarters. Poles could not withstand the heat; they were too slow; they could not charge up the hills. They spoke no Kreyol, and often no French as well, so an officer complained that during a rebel attack "I had to grab them by the arm to bring them to their post" because they could not understand simple instructions.[18] Another officer even asked to get his colonial troops back because he found it easier to fight the Maroons with former slaves than Slavs.[19] "The Poles are abominably bad for the kind of war we are waging here," his sympathetic superior concurred.[20]

The Poles' linguistic limitations often proved disastrous on the battlefield. Two weeks after the 3rd demi-brigade landed in Cap, Leclerc sent its third battalion to support an operation against the Maroon leader Sans Souci. As part of a general sweep on Grande Rivière, the battalion's third company was to proceed from Borgne to Port Margot. Or so thought the Poles; their actual destination was Saint-Georges, but the fine points of Haitian geography were lost in translation. The company's black guide was better informed and set off in the right direction, but when ambushes began to multiply, the Polish captain accused him of purposely leading the column astray and shot him for treason. Now guideless, the column lost its way in a maze of ravines, its jagged itinerary marked by the mutilated bodies of stragglers. Six survivors made their way back to French lines after a weeklong trek, a 90 percent death rate.[21] Other columns only did marginally better, and Leclerc concluded dejectedly that "the Poles, though brave, are too slow and are getting slaughtered by the blacks. The combat of 15 September cost me 400 men."[22]

Some French officers were quick to attribute the Poles' poor record to national defects, but it more likely reflected their unwillingness to serve Bonaparte's political agenda. The Poles could not shake the impression that they might be Saint-Domingue's Russians, fighting aginst some Caribbean boyar's serfs. The yellow fever epidemic, which regained in intensity after they landed, only added to their discouragement. Between combat and disease, by the middle of October the demi-brigade's first battalion only had 147 survivors (plus 341 sick) out of the 984 men who had landed on September 2. A month later the number of soldiers still fit for duty had dropped to eighty. On the first anniversary of the battalion's arrival, only six officers and fourteen soldiers were still listed as alive. Liberating Kraków by way of Cap had proved costly for the sons of Polonia.[23]

～

With his army bleeding to death from the thousand cuts of skirmishes and disease and the number of European troops fit for duty down to four thousand, Leclerc announced in September that he would halt the disarmament campaign for lack of troops.[24] But Pandora's jar could not be closed tight. The rebellion continued to fester and Leclerc even had to take the field in person for the first time since the spring campaign to assist in a counterinsurgency operation.[25] The war went on, forcing Leclerc to look ever more desperately for troops. Most of the French units that had landed with him had long since succumbed to war and disease, foreign reinforcements had proven subpar, and the loyalty of colonial units was increasingly becoming questionable. There remained only one untapped military resource in the colony: white and *anciens libres* colonists, a valuable group well versed in mountain warfare, largely immune to local diseases, and already present in Saint-Domingue.

Militia service had been highly unpopular with white planters before the revolution, but eager to halt a rural insurgency that threatened their plantations, colonists regularly petitioned military authorities for the right to form local militias in 1802.[26] Distrustful of the colonial elite, Leclerc had instead ordered all planters disarmed and confiscated the ammunition of existing national guard units.[27] It was thus at the behest of Donatien de Rochambeau, a general more attuned to the demands of the Creoles, that Répussard, a colored planter from Verettes, revived his town's national guard in August. Composed of local planters, both whites and *anciens libres,* the Verettes guard proved particularly effective at hunting the Maroons of the Artibonite over the following weeks. Revealingly, it was Répussard who captured Belair on September 10.[28]

Répussard's *fait d'armes* and the disastrous Polish assault on Saint-Georges were probably on Leclerc's mind when he announced on September 18 that he had decided to rebuild the national guard to supplement his dwindling army. Composed of merchants and planters between the ages of sixteen and fifty, the guard would include men of color as well as whites of all nationalities (U.S. and British merchants formed their own units). Leclerc initially planned to revive the national guard solely in Cap, but faced with clear evidence that guardsmen were the only alternative to black colonial troops he immediately opted to do the same in Port Républicain, then in every major town of the colony (Spaniards were also drafted in large numbers in Santo Domingo).[29] Military necessity had finally overcome his deep aversion for aristocratic colonists.

Asking local planters to help defend their own property saved the expedition from immediate defeat that fall. Coastal cities were filled with planters who had fled rural violence, so by late October the national guard formed the bulk of urban garrisons.[30] Military disdain for civilians notwithstanding, guardsmen fought well and proved particularly well suited for counterinsurgency operations. Répussard constantly asked to be sent chasing rebels in the mountains, an essential task that French and Polish troops only undertook reluctantly. When rebels took over Verettes in late October, he also managed the remarkable feat of escaping to Saint-Marc over the mountains with the town's entire civilian population, women and children included, and all his supplies.[31]

By the fall of 1802, with Polish infantrymen; Basque and Maltese sailors; Spanish, U.S., and English guardsmen; planter militias; German battalions; colored colonial troops; occasional Congo allies; and even a French soldier or two, the "French" army in Saint-Domingue had become a military League of Nations. When he was reassigned to yet another command that September (Fort Liberté), Pamphile Lacroix noted that the garrison had been reduced to a single French officer backed by fifty colonial troops. He brought with him a foreign battalion composed of Bonaparte's various European allies and proceeded to raise a national guard among the town's Creoles and draft sixty Spanish cavalrymen from nearby Montecristi, thus rounding up a composite force that now employed two Frenchmen, including himself.[32]

This patchwork of alliances should have called for a moderate policy aimed at courting all of France's partners. A careful approach was all the more desirable since, six months into the expedition, significant segments of Saint-Domingue's black population remained opposed to the revolt. Accounts abound of cultivators denouncing rebels or extinguishing fires because they refused to see their house destroyed or lose their share of a plantation's profits.[33] In the Brunet division, officers were under standing orders to treat black laborers as potential allies, but the increasingly bitter Leclerc had finally lost his faith in people of color and chose this moment to launch a month-long orgy of carnage.[34]

~

As September progressed, reports of black desertion or treachery landed on Leclerc's desk with increasing frequency. Small groups of three, four, or ten soldiers and gendarmes regularly disappeared in the dead of night, only to reappear a few days later in rebel ranks, and some colonial officers were widely suspected of equipping the rebel army with supplies drawn from French arsenals. Sympathetic soldiers and cultivators regularly informed rebels of upcoming French offensives, and captured rebel leaders sent to headquarters under armed guard had a suspicious tendency to escape on the way.[35] Even seemingly loyal allies could not be trusted. Two days after visiting the only sugar plantation still functioning near Cap, Leclerc's secretary, Jacques de Norvins, was surprised to learn that the friendly cultivators he had just met had risen in revolt. All, young children included, had played the part of the trusted servant admirably, as had Norvins' own domestic, who absconded to the rebels around that time.[36] Such events forced Leclerc to reassess his long-standing reliance on colonial troops, whom he no longer saw as essential allies but as rebels in the making.

Judicial procedures hardened noticeably as a result. Back in February an officer had taken the trouble of setting up a military tribunal and bringing in witnesses before punishing a suspected arsonist, and later that spring Leclerc's administrators had spent considerable time drafting plans for colonial tribunals.[37] The start of the disarmament campaign in June and the reinstatement of martial law in July had radically simplified judicial processes, but there remained the principle that punishment should stem from individual guilt. Orders from headquarters instructed officers in the field to summarily execute anyone found with a gun, but the death penalty, however liberally applied, was still meant as payback for a crime.[38] The army's September 9 order of the day, which instructed soldiers to hang all *conducteurs* (plantation foremen) in areas plagued by insurrection, even those not overtly supporting the uprising, marked a momentous shift toward collective responsibility.[39] Soon all cultivators in a plantation where a single criminal act had taken place were executed, and in the colonial army entire units were held responsible for the defection of a single soldier.[40] "I will be obliged to destroy . . . a large part of the cultivators who, having become accustomed to banditry over the past ten years, will never agree to work," Leclerc wrote Decrès on the seventeenth. "I will wage a war of extermination, and it will cost me many lives."[41] This was the first of several such references to a policy of blanket executions in his correspondence.

The exponential growth in the number of suspects was reflected in the way prisoners were put to death. Until July the primary form of execution had been the firing squad, a penalty clearly military in nature. At Boyer's instigation, August had been the month of hanging, in the hope that this frightful death would intimidate those hesitating to join the revolt. Starting in September, drowning eclipsed all other modes of execution because it was the most efficient way to execute prisoners on an industrial scale. Dozens, hundreds, and eventually thousands of avowed rebels and suspicious individuals were embarked and thrown at sea.[42] In a troubling harbinger of a later genocide, some prisoners were also gassed with sulfur in the holds of French ships.[43]

Some of Bonaparte's critics blame him for the horrors committed in Saint-Domingue, but his instructions had merely asked Leclerc to deport black officers to France, not massacre entire colonial units, let alone wage a war of "extermination" against black cultivators.[44] Caribbean deportees arriving in Brest were not drowned but carefully vetted before—at worst—being sent to jail. André Rigaud's relatives even received back pay for the time they spent in Saint-Domingue.[45] No one—not even Louverture—was executed no matter how great his transgression. Some liberals like Madame de Staël even described black massacres of soldiers and civilians as legitimate retaliation for the horrors of slavery.[46] After hearing troubling reports that unarmed prisoners had been drowned in large numbers, Denis Decrès expressed his hope that these were merely "rumors" spread by the English press or individual "acts of vengeance" performed in the heat of combat.[47] Bonaparte's intention, he reminded his addressee, was to deport the worst culprits to Corsica.

As seen from Paris, there were strong economic motives to show mercy to Dominguian rebels. The colony's wealth lay primarily in its labor force, which planters had brought from Africa at tremendous expense, and experts had long warned that "a territory without population . . . is useless."[48] In 1800 several authors had justified their opposition to an expedition by pointing out that a war could only be won by killing off most of the cultivators, an economic heresy that would deprive the plantations of their valuable work force.[49] As they heard of the large-scale massacres taking place in Saint-Domingue, government officials began fearing that these would add to the

Danse de Negres à S.t Domingue.

2. The population of color in Saint-Domingue was torn between three cultural influences: French, African, and Creole, which were apparent in manners of dress and pastimes. J. Granveur Laroque, "Danse de nègres." In Lacques Grasset de Saint-Sauveur. *Encyclopédie des voyages, contenant l'abrégé historique des moeurs, usages, habitudes domestiques, religions, fêtes.* Paris: Deroy, 1796, 5: plate 18.

already gigantic expenditure of rebuilding the plantations and that Leclerc was destroying the colony in order to save it.[50] If all that France ever recovered was a sparsely populated wasteland, it might as well have concentrated its efforts on Santo Domingo—or Louisiana, or Guiana, or any vacant piece of land in the vast, underexploited Western Hemisphere.

The decision to ramp up violence, contemporary documents show with great clarity, was taken locally by Leclerc and his officers in response to the military difficulties they experienced in the field. Atrocities were most common in the north and west, the areas wracked by constant uprisings, less frequent in the quieter south, and almost nonexistent in the forgotten east. Lacroix, whose district of Fort Liberté stood on the border with Santo Domingo, tried to secure the loyalty of his diverse force by such peaceful measures as giving colonial troops enough food and wine.[51] François de Kerversau, stationed farther east in the city of Santo Domingo, was also notable for his moderation.

The level of violence in a given district was also directly related to an officer's ideological outlook. Leclerc's abolitionist chief of staff, Charles Dugua, was opposed to atrocities, and according to some accounts, tipped off colonial units about to be massacred.[52] Records of the division of the republican general Bertrand Clauzel never mention any atrocities, not even in the circuitous style often used by French officers when alluding to such unfortunate events.[53] The oral tradition in Haiti also claims that Polish units refused to massacre colonial troops.[54] In the navy some captains discreetly released prisoners earmarked for drowning in other parts of the colony to avoid a task that was, in the words of the sailor Jean-Baptiste Lemonnier-Delafosse, "unworthy of the French name, even though the victims were only negroes."[55]

In a small society like Saint-Domingue, personal connections often trumped racial antagonism. In Port Républicain, Captain Jurrien recognized among the prisoners slated for execution an officer of color he had fought in a duel twelve years earlier. Finding it dishonorable to kill a rival who had behaved with courage during their previous encounter, Jurrien had him shipped secretly to France. Also in Port Républicain, Admiral Louis-René de Latouche-Tréville noticed that in a passing shallop a black man named Pierre Michel was flashing the distress signal of freemasons. He invited the brother on board his ship, where in the privacy of his cabin he performed the secret sign of a master mason. Latouche arranged for Michel to go to Brest.[56]

In the area immediately surrounding Cap, where the military situation was direst and Leclerc's orders harder to evade, such instances of mercy were rare and French policy became oddly schizophrenic. Suspicious of all people of color, the army slaughtered rebels and civilians on a large scale—but to conduct such operations the French army needed troops, which it drew largely from colonial units given its own losses to yellow fever. Inspire "terror," "give no mercy," "kill everyone on the spot": such were the instructions to a French commandant sent to put down the latest uprising.[57] But to do so he was given a detachment of the 6th demi-brigade, a colonial unit. How long troops of color would witness wholesale massacres before they defected was the question on which the future of Saint-Domingue now hinged.

∽

Before and during the revolution, the French army in Saint-Domingue had been multiracial, and it would likely have remained that way had it not been for the one-two punch that struck the colony in the summer and fall of 1802. The first shock (the rumor that Bonaparte intended to restore slavery) convinced many Maroons and cultivators to rebel over the summer. Most colonial units remained in French service until October, and it was the generalization of French atrocities that finally pushed them into open rebellion.

The official rationale for mass executions was to dissuade troops and cultivators from supporting the rebels, but violence completely failed to make an impression on the population of color. Already in prerevolutionary times, chroniclers had noted that slaves stoically endured the worst torments, a trait they attributed to a thick skin that allegedly sheltered them from pain, or, more convincingly, to the belief that death would bring them back to Africa.[58] Compared with the tortures inflicted during that period, Leclerc's relatively humane forms of executions must have come across to former slaves as gently quaint; even mass drowning, which Louverture had employed during the War of the South, was nothing new.[59] Love of liberty also bred fortitude. Confident that enslavement was worse than death, and that death itself would take them back to "Guinea," the rebels marched to the scaffold with quasi-jubilation. "We all want to die," a rebel leader boasted.[60] "One hundred and seventy-six [deserters] were embarked at Jacmel for Port Républicain," Leclerc wrote in awe. "Of this number, 173 strangled themselves on the way, the battalion chief at their head. There you see the men we have to fight!"[61]

Aside from inciting the rebels to treat their own prisoners with equal savagery (gouging out a prisoner's eyes was Lamour Derance's trademark torture), French atrocities only had one noticeable effect: to push loyal colonial troops to defect, since Leclerc was executing the innocent as readily as the guilty and the odds of being killed by the French army seemed greater when serving under it than against it.[62] Desertion in colonial units, already a nagging issue since rumors on a possible restoration of slavery had gained credence, increased markedly in the last days of September after Leclerc instituted the principle of collective responsibility. Supposedly safe corps were no longer immune, and on September 27 fifteen officers of color from an elite company defected in a single night. In Plaisance, the entire 5th colonial demi-brigade, prodded by its own officers, refused to respond to orders. Even Lacroix, who had tried so hard to endear himself to the garrison of Fort Liberté, reported that his colored troops and guardsmen had begun deserting in droves.[63]

Leclerc eventually concluded that colonial officers were simply biding their time until the end of fall, when the epidemic would have broken the back of the French army and they would defect en masse. Leclerc's only hope was for large reinforcements to arrive before they could bring their plan to fruition, but when a particularly large rebel group neared Cap in early October he became convinced that the moment of reckoning had come. Desperate for a few weeks' respite, he warned in a proclamation to colonial troops that defecting at this time was "madness. . . . Don't you know that the cruel epidemic . . . has ceased? . . . Don't you know that a new army, as large as the one that already landed in Saint-Domingue, is on its way?" The proclamation would have been more effective had it not included a companion text addressed to French soldiers that said nothing of reinforcements and merely predicted that the epidemic would soon cease.[64] On October 12, Leclerc also threw a ball in a last-ditch attempt to woo colonial officers, but the latest news from France put a serious damper on the party. Bonaparte, rumor had it, had told abolitionists to start wearing black as a sign of mourning. The anecdote swept around the room, leaving everyone convinced that a wholesale restoration of slavery was imminent. "I am an *ancien libre*," Augustin Clervaux told his hostess, Pauline Bonaparte. "But should there be any plan to restore slavery, I would immediately join the ranks of the rebels."[65]

In this volatile situation any incident could push wavering officers over the edge. In Cap, it was the arming of the national guard, which took place on October 13, that was interpreted as a prelude to the disbanding and possible execution of all colonial units. That night, Clervaux and Alexandre Pétion joined the rebellion. Their troops manned large segments of the French defensive line in Haut du Cap and planned to rely on the 6th colonial demi-brigade, garrisoned within Cap itself, to take the city by surprise. But Clervaux lost his nerve and Cap was narrowly saved. Pétion and Clervaux only attacked Cap later that day so as to prove their mantle to the Maroon leader Petit Noël Prieur, who questioned the legitimacy of born-again rebels who had spent the previous months harassing him. But by that time Leclerc had hastily assembled surviving French troops, the national guard, and U.S. merchants, and the defensive line held firm. As a security measure Leclerc also ordered the entire 6th colonial demi-brigade held on board ships in the harbor.[66]

Pétion and Clervaux's defection was a severe blow for Leclerc. Pétion was one of the mixed-race officers who had arrived with the expedition in February, eager to avenge Rigaud's defeat in the War of the South. Clervaux, a French-educated quadroon, had been a member of the court-martial that had recently sentenced the Belairs to death and had served so loyally that Bonaparte had promoted him to brigadier general.[67] For mixed-race *anciens libres* like them to abandon the French side did not bode well for the loyalty of the remaining black officers.

Christophe was now the only prominent colonial officer still on the French side in the plain of Cap. A genuine supporter of French rule, he had just sent his nine-year-old son to be educated in France, but rumors of an impending restoration of slavery were starting to take their toll.[68] "If your skin was the same color as mine, you might not be as trusting as I am," he told the general taking his son to France. "The blacks of Saint-Domingue are getting worried because they have heard of the decree of 30 Floréal [May 20]."[69] Pétion and Clervaux's desertion—which, if the recent past was any lesson, would prompt Leclerc to punish their colleagues still in French service— forced Christophe's hand, and on the sixteenth of October he joined the rebellion, fully aware that his decision would cost him his son. Left to fend for himself after Jean-Baptiste Coisnon's colonial school lost its funding,

François-Ferdinand Christophe died at an orphans' hospital in Paris in 1805. More than a decade later, by which time General Christophe had become King Henri I of Haiti, he remained a heartbroken father whose official historian continued to make references to the prince's lonely death in France.[70]

Christophe immediately headed for the camp of Prieur, who was so outraged to see his old tormentor switch sides that he threatened to kill Christophe on the spot. It took all of Pétion and Clervaux's diplomacy to cool the men's tempers and organize a joint attack against their common French enemy.[71] The rebels made a second attempt against Cap's defenses, probably with the help of the Maroon leader, Makaya, and Louverture's brother, Paul, who left the French army around that time.[72] Once again the defensive cordon around Cap remained as the last barrier protecting the once-mighty expeditionary army from complete annihilation. Throughout the night, as one assault followed another, Leclerc oversaw the town's defense in person, switching from one hot spot to another and encouraging his troops as he went.[73]

Convinced that his exhausted garrison could not hold out much longer against the rebel waves, Leclerc ordered the guns spiked and the ammunition dumped into the harbor.[74] He also asked his secretary, Norvins, to take Pauline and their son Dermide to a ship in preparation for an evacuation. Seeing this, Cap was seized by a panic and civilians scurried everywhere in the darkness in a mad rush to find a spot on departing ships. Only Pauline remained calm and refused to leave the pier because, she told Norvins, "I am Bonaparte's sister and I am not afraid of anything."[75] Norvins, she explained, should simply kill her if she ever ran the risk of being captured by the rebels. With dawn came news that Leclerc had miraculously repulsed the assault, and Pauline cheerily doubled back to meet her victorious husband, her regal poise worthy of a Bonaparte.

∾

The rebellion of all colonial units near Cap marked the start of the deadliest weeks of the war of independence. Convinced that he could no longer trust anyone, Leclerc ordered the entire 6th colonial demi-brigade thrown overboard, the largest such massacre to date. Twelve hundred corpses descended into the azure waters, including the brother of Clervaux and the wife and children of Paul Louverture.[76] "Men, women, and children were continually seen floating in the harbour," wrote an English observer. "No trial was wanted; the color condemned them."[77] Gruesome scenes ensued as hundreds of corpses, their face turned a diaphanous white after a few days' stay in the water, washed up on shore. For weeks the inhabitants of Cap refused to eat fish, until executioners learned to dump their victims farther out at sea.[78]

Leclerc spared the mixed-race members of the national guard, who had helped save Cap during the recent attacks, but the population of color lived in terror. Guy Bonnet, the supporter of André Rigaud who had returned from Santiago de Cuba during the spring campaign, was now living in Cap, where he found himself in the midst of a murderous pogrom. Together with Nicolas Geffrard, another *Rigaudin* on the run, he hid in the house of two sympathetic *mulâtresses* while gendarmes hunted for men of color to be used, depending on the circumstances, as recruits or victims.[79]

Despite the racial undertone of the latest massacres, financial criteria played an important role when selecting victims. "What kind of men did we drown in Saint-Domingue?" asked a French general. "Blacks taken prisoner on the battlefield? No. Conspirators? Even less. No one was ever tried." "For a slim suspicion, a report, an equivocal word, two hundred, four hundred, eight hundred, up to fifteen hundred blacks were thrown at sea. . . . On 28 Frimaire [December 18], three mulatto brothers fought on our side, two of them were wounded, yet despite their service they were drowned on the twenty-ninth. They were rich, and two days after their death their beautiful house was taken over by the local general."[80]

With the defection or execution of most colonial troops, Leclerc could no longer afford to garrison all the cities along the northern coast, and he ordered his subordinates to regroup in Cap, Môle, and La Tortue.[81] Lacroix evacuated Fort Liberté during the night of October 16. Lemonnier, still using braces because of the injury he had sustained during the spring campaign, managed to find a spot on the lone brig earmarked for the evacuation, but others drowned as a shallop, overcrowded with panicky civilians, tipped over. More died a few days later when a merchantman from Nantes, unaware that the city was now in rebel hands, cast anchor in Fort Liberté, only to see its entire crew massacred.[82]

After a major rebel assault on Port-de-Paix narrowly failed on the twenty-first, Leclerc also ordered French troops stationed there to evacuate, taking with them all colonial units so that they could be drowned in Cap.[83] The leading colonial officer in town was Jacques Maurepas, whom the French had long suspected of disloyalty. Maurepas also happened to be rich, so his most dedicated critic was a French general who owed him money and hoped to take over his considerable fortune after his death.[84] Maurepas agreed to embark for Cap in the hope that he would be exiled to France, but his trust proved misplaced. As soon as their ship reached the harbor, Maurepas and some family members were thrown overboard and drowned.[85] Stories later emerged that he had also been whipped like a slave and his epaulettes nailed into his shoulders, but these details may have been added by later historians eager to give his martyrdom a Christ-like aura, complete with scourging and crucifixion. Either way, his tragic end was a stern reminder to all remaining colonial officers that they only had two options left: to defect or to die.[86]

With all notable colonial officers in the northern province dead or in open rebellion, all eyes trained on the western province and Jean-Jacques Dessalines. His critics' repeated allegations that he was a traitor had taken their toll and by the end of September Leclerc had serious doubts about his loyalty. "Dessalines, who had never thought of rebelling, is now considering it," he wrote Bonaparte. "But I know his secret, he won't escape me."[87] Eager to assuage Leclerc's doubts, in late September Dessalines launched one of his signature assaults on a Maroon camp near Ennery, brutally killing women and children after flushing them from the woods, and his immediate superior concluded that Dessalines genuinely wished to help pacify the countryside because "he cannot do otherwise. The blacks dislike him after all he did to them."[88] Dessalines also met Leclerc to quell unfavorable rumors and even proposed to return to France with him.[89]

His protestations of loyalty notwithstanding, Dessalines' behavior in the following days became increasingly suspicious. He was supposed to go to Marmelade after meeting Leclerc in Cap, only to disappear for two days and resurface in Grand Bois, where he claimed to have been sidetracked by his eagerness to pursue the rebels.[90] Meanwhile, he made thinly veiled warnings that the growing number of victims of French repression (which included one of his cousins) might push him into revolt.[91] In the aftermath of Pétion and Clervaux's defection, he wrote to reiterate his "devotion to France," but also to lament the latest executions. "I was told that all the elite companies in Port Républicain were embarked! . . . One of my nephews, age 18, was hanged!" he wrote on the day of the second attack on Cap. "See how much I have suffered; but I will not revolt nonetheless."[92] Two explosive decrees by Bonaparte confiscating the property of generals who had taken arms against France during the spring campaign may have reached Saint-Domingue around that time, further angering a large landowner like Dessalines.[93]

On October 20 and 22, two French attempts to apprehend him left Dessalines no choice but to defect.[94] And yet in a move no doubt inspired by Louverture's own calculated ambiguity when he had abandoned the Spanish army in 1794, Dessalines managed to remain uncommitted for another few days so as to capture unsuspecting French cities by surprise. He sent one of his subordinates to attack Gonaïves, then another who was to pretend that he had come to rescue the town so that he could get past French lines. He also arranged to take Saint-Marc with the collusion of the colonial unit garrisoned inside, but the French learned of the conspiracy in time and shot all colonial troops on the spot.[95] It was not until October 24, after the failure of the assault on Saint-Marc, that he finally wrote a letter to make his defection official and explain his motives. Commitment to emancipation was waning in France, he explained, and in Saint-Domingue officers of color were randomly executed. "I am French, a friend of my country and liberty, and I cannot sit idly while such atrocities are committed."[96] His list of grievances, which could easily have been written by any of the colonial officers who defected that month, could be summarized in two words: slavery and atrocities.

Dessalines' defection sparked another wave of mass executions throughout the colony. "War has become very simplified, it pits whites against blacks," Latouche wrote to a captain in Port Républicain on October 16. "I took measures to ensure that prisoners no longer bother us, and I encourage you to do the same."[97] Executions in Port Républicain had only averaged three to five a day, but on the twenty-sixth, shortly after Dessalines' desertion became known, 165 black prisoners were sent at once to the pontoon ship used for executions. After that date, groups of forty to fifty captives were dispatched on a daily basis, and a British merchant in Cap estimated that between Port Républicain and Jacmel fifteen hundred people had been shot, drowned, or suffocated in the last week of October alone.[98]

Orders to exterminate colonial troops went to all provinces of the colony, whether they had been plagued by desertion or not. Jérémie had witnessed its first uprising in September, but it had been quickly contained, and the situation, as in much of the south, was far from catastrophic. The town's black commander, Jean-Baptiste Dommage, was nevertheless arrested on suspicions that he was supporting the rebels and was hanged in Cap a few weeks later. As with Maurepas, economic motives may have played a role since the greedy general Louis d'Arbois promptly took over Dommage's command and estates.[99]

Despite the difficult military situation, there were still officers who disagreed with Leclerc's murderous agenda. To Kerversau, Leclerc's headquarters wrote in October that the prisoners in Santo Domingo's jails should "all be shot, without exceptions" and, most chillingly, that even the youngest among them, who had "nursed on a criminally guilty milk," should be drowned at once.[100] These included the children of rebels recently deported from Martinique, one of whom Kerversau had adopted into his household.[101] Kerversau explained to his friend Lacroix that military affairs in Santo Domingo had not reached a point where one would have to resort to such "cruel extremities," and he did not carry out the executions (Leclerc had just fallen sick, so Kerversau may also have banked that he might die).[102] The colonial prefect wrote a strongly worded letter insisting that Kerversau execute all armed blacks as ordered, but Kerversau dragged his feet for another ten days. Finally, on November 16, a corvette arrived from Cap with strict orders to embark all black troops at once, and Kerversau ran out of excuses. "Tomorrow, no black troops will remain," he wrote pensively to Lacroix. "I cannot write more at the moment. Doing one's duty can be cruel at times."[103]

Leclerc's personal journey during the nine months he spent in Saint-Domingue was remarkable. When he landed, he was a naive idealist attached to revolutionary principles and a brash fop desirous to make a quick fortune; only later did he comprehend the magnitude of the task he had undertaken. Courageous when he faced human foes, he looked at yellow fever with sheer terror, and over the summer his correspondence acquired a somber, plaintive tone as he realized that any additional day in the colony might cost him his life. The epidemic turned him into a recluse and a hypochondriac; barricaded in his private residence, he regularly complained of ill-defined fevers and wrote to Decrès that "it is too cruel to live as I do."[104]

Leclerc also grew increasingly frustrated by France's refusal to give him the means to win the war. Despite his frequent requests for cash, Bonaparte continued to insist that the expedition pay for itself, and Leclerc continually had to tap neighboring colonies for loans. In October alone, he sent an agent to Havana to collect prize money owed to French privateers, begged the Dutch governor of Curaçao to make a loan of three hundred thousand gourdes, and borrowed sixty thousand Jamaican pounds from a Jewish banker in Kingston.[105] That Bonaparte was hardly more forthcoming with decent troops put Leclerc in an impossible situation. Had France sent ten thousand men in a single shipment as he had requested, Leclerc complained in late September, he would not have had to continue employing colonial units of dubious loyalty.[106]

In this difficult context, by the middle of September Leclerc's letters began to show symptoms of what a psychiatrist might diagnose today as depression. "During this cruel malady," he wrote Decrès, "I only sustained myself through sheer moral strength." But the restoration of slavery in Guadeloupe had ruined any chance of success and all in all he had "not had a single day of satisfaction" since arriving in Saint-Domingue.[107] His letters to Decrès became abrupt and rude, and in late September he suddenly announced that he would no longer report to the minister of the navy, his direct superior.[108] The colony "is threatening to collapse and bury me with it," he wrote the minister of war a few days later.[109] "Ever since I arrived here, all I saw were fires, insurrections, murders, the dead and the dying," he wrote Bonaparte. "My soul is wilted, no thought can distract me from these hideous scenes."[110]

Leclerc's dejection may explain his increasingly pitiless edge. On September 17, he had written of the need to wage a war of "extermination" against the rebels. Three weeks later he openly considered a general massacre of virtually the entire adult black population of Saint-Domingue, rebel or not—what a later age would call a genocide. "Here is my opinion on this country. We must destroy all the negroes in the mountains, men and women, keeping only infants less than twelve years old; we must also destroy half of those of the plain, and leave in the colony not a single man of color who has worn an epaulet. Without this the colony will never be quiet."[111] In prerevolutionary times observers had often noticed that colonial newcomers were initially appalled by the cruel treatment meted out to the slaves, only to become as heartless as any old colonist in six months' time; Leclerc's trajectory fit the pattern perfectly.[112]

October brought two painful blows. The general rebellion in Cap shattered what little hope Leclerc still entertained that he could keep the colonial army on his side until the arrival of reinforcements from France; and a rumor reached him that a handsome general, Jean Humbert, had caught Pauline's expert eye. Leclerc, who already had unrelated disagreements with Humbert, promptly sent him back to France in disgrace, telling Norvins bitterly that "you are the only one here who never cheated me."[113] Bonaparte refused to employ his sister's lover in the French army for most of the following ten years, and, bored and broke, Humbert finally left for Louisiana, where he earned Andrew Jackson's praise for his heroic service during the 1815 battle of New Orleans.[114]

Betrayed by colonial and French officers alike, Leclerc crossed the last limit separating him from insanity during the October attacks in Cap. Something snapped in him; he was now a broken and bitter man, all too eager to abandon the colony to some apocalyptic finale. He appeared "panic struck," wrote an English observer, and his "mind evinced a considerable degree of agitation."[115] "Leclerc was without energy," Mary Hassal wrote, "tormented by jealousy for his wife, deceived by his officers, impos'd on by the black chiefs," and thought only of abandoning the colony to its fate.[116] To Norvins, he proposed to embark secretly with a handful of officers, let someone else take over the captain generalcy, and retire in the forest of Villers-Cotterêts in his native France. "My finances are of no interest to me anymore," he explained. "La Gonâve [the island Bonaparte had promised him] will go the way of Saint-Domingue."[117]

Leclerc's last contribution to the expedition took place in the early hours of October 16, when he personally oversaw the defenses of Cap during the second rebel attack. No bullet hit him that night, but six days later he began complaining of a severe fever and soon experienced all the familiar symptoms of yellow fever. Some contemporaries attributed Leclerc's malady to the moist heat of the battlefield, and to some extent Leclerc's malady was indeed connected to his service that night.[118] For months he had remained isolated in his residence above Cap, and there is no indication that he ever visited a hospital. This self-imposed quarantine was probably the reason why he survived while the rest of his army shivered and died below him. The October 16 battle marked the first time in months that he spent an extended period of time in Cap, this during the mosquito-friendly nighttime hours. He fell sick six days later, which corresponds to yellow fever's incubation period, and it is tempting to think that in the heat of battle a tiny mosquito had inflicted the mortal blow. If so, one can only imagine that she was a reincarnation of the Maroon rebel Makandal, who finally obtained his revenge forty-four years after his fiery demise.

Early on the twenty-second, Leclerc summoned the army's chief doctor, Dr. Peyre, to complain of a violent headache, kidney pain, and a sore throat. Peyre gave him sugary water perfumed with orange flowers, but by nighttime Leclerc was delirious with fever, and he remained violently sick throughout the twenty-third. He recovered some strength over the following days and even proposed to take a tour of Cap to silence rumors that he was dying, but Peyre warned him that yellow fever often abated momentarily on the third day and that it would be advisable to rest. Leclerc thus spent the twenty-eighth at his desk, "sad and pensive" as he perused the various dispatches informing him that Dessalines had abandoned him.[119] As expected, the recovery was temporary and Leclerc collapsed on the twenty-ninth. The following day's symptoms—violent fever, thirst, diarrhea, and vomiting—left no doubt as to the ultimate outcome. On November 1, yellow fever reached its horrifying climax as black blood and vomit poured out of every orifice of Leclerc's body, and his skin turned a bright yellow. Early on November 2, the Catholic day of the dead, he drew his final breath.

In an ancient Corsican ritual, Pauline sheared her beautiful hair and laid it on her husband's corpse. Her mourning may have been sincere, but observers dismissed it as theatrical performance given her recent conduct. "Madame Leclerc, who had not loved him whilst living, mourned his death like the Ephesian matron," snickered Hassal/Sansay.[120] "With hard private duty she had worn every officer of the general's bodyguard, and handsome aide-de-camp, off their legs," added a visiting British captain.[121]

The army's propaganda machine, which had hidden the gravity of Leclerc's "mere indisposition" from the troops, made every effort to portray his sudden death in a positive light.[122] He had "succumbed to the sorrows, sacrifices, and exhaustion of his constant struggle for your prosperity," the *Gazette Officielle* informed its readers on November 3, and "there is no doubt that victory is awaiting you."[123] But the young and dashing Leclerc was a popular general and it is far from certain that dreams of victory were foremost in the minds of the melancholy soldiers as they lined up along the streets of Cap later that day, where to the mournful tune of a cannonade, four generals, five aides-de-camp, and eight grenadiers carried the coffin to the docks, where it was transferred to a black-draped shallop of the *Swift Sure*.[124]

Alone among the dozens of thousands of French people who died in this war, Leclerc's body was embalmed and repatriated to France. The aides-de-camp who escorted him, though undoubtedly moved by their leader's untimely death, cannot have been displeased to have found an excuse to leave the forsaken colony (his honor guard represented one-third of all home leaves granted that fall).[125] The Leclercs' fourteen domestics also came along; intriguingly, despite Leclerc's recent talk of racial extermination, only half of them were white.[126] Pauline was adamant that the *Swift Sure* take the direct route to Brest so as to return to Paris faster, but Latouche insisted that she head for Toulon lest the barely seaworthy ship founder in the rough seas of the North Atlantic. Latouche carried the day, Pauline spent the return voyage sulking, and the nine-week crossing, with heavy seas and short supplies, was far from pleasant. Finally, on December 29, the *Swift Sure* reached the Mediterranean coast of France and an elated Pauline announced that she would bypass quarantine and land at once.[127]

Decrès was hardly heartbroken upon learning of the death of a general who had consistently criticized him (and whose widow he immediately proposed to marry), but for the sake of governmental propaganda Bonaparte insisted that Leclerc be eulogized as a hero. A grandiose, thirty-thousand-franc funeral mass was organized in Marseille, where Leclerc had left fond memories earlier in his career. To avoid giving additional publicity to yellow fever's terrible toll, his body was then whisked away through small roads to Villers-Cotterêts, where he had hoped to retire, and his family erected a discreet monument.[128] His heart was taken to Paris, where it remains in a storage room of the Museum of the Army, a stone's throw from Bonaparte's own grandiose tomb.

The Consulate proved so successful at aggrandizing Leclerc that to the present day he enjoys a flattering, and largely undeserved, reputation in the French and Haitian literature as a tragic hero (the only one who did not fall for government lies was Bonaparte, who in his memoirs underlined Leclerc's strategic mistakes).[129] Leclerc's limitations as a captain general were in fact notable. He was thoroughly unfamiliar with Saint-Domingue's environment and in the first few months of his tenure made a variety of mistakes—from botching the landing in Cap to alienating *anciens libres* and colonists—that had disastrous military consequences. His attachment to emancipation was laudable, but it was overshadowed in the last weeks of his life by his genocidal plans. Many of the most notorious policies of his reviled successor—from gassing prisoners to employing man-hunting dogs—were initiated under him, and there is no reason to believe that if he had lived another year he too would not have turned into some sadistic monster. Dying in one's prime has its perks.

Pauline found ways to overcome her husband's death, both financially and emotionally. Leclerc's estate was estimated at the surprisingly small sum of eleven thousand francs, but the amount did not include shipments of colonial crops that Leclerc had sent to France or the salary supplement he had awarded himself.[130] His fortune must have been sizable, because half a century later distant German relatives were still clamoring for a share of his estate.[131] Pauline also obtained a generous pension from her brother, and exactly a year after losing her husband (the minimal delay under the law) she remarried the vexingly effete, but delightfully rich, Prince Camillo Borghese.[132]

12

Reprieve

Rochambeau and the French Counteroffensive

WINTER 1802/3

At dawn on November 2, 1802, four hours after Leclerc passed away, a ship left Cap for Port Républicain to fetch the new captain general of the army of Saint-Domingue.[1] Leclerc's successor was the commander of the western province, Donatien-Marie-Joseph de Vimeur de Rochambeau, an aristocrat who bore one of the most illustrious names in the Americas. His father had commanded French forces during the American Revolution, where Rochambeau himself had fought as a young aide-de-camp before serving as governor of the Windward Islands, Saint-Domingue, and Martinique in the 1790s (the son of Admiral François de Grasse, who had commanded French naval forces during the American Revolution, also served in the Leclerc expedition).[2] Rochambeau was one of those few individuals who personally witnessed the three great revolutions of the era, in the United States, France, and Saint-Domingue. Judging by his private correspondence, now housed at the University of Florida, the experience had left him with a vast network of friends within the planter milieu.[3]

Rochambeau had initially been selected as Saint-Domingue's captain general, only to be made Victoire Leclerc's second, possibly because Napoléon Bonaparte preferred not to give the overall command of the expedition to a man who was the epitome of the old colonial order.[4] In his reports Rochambeau had a tendency to slip back from the Republican calendar of the French Revolution to the Gregorian calendar of the popes; he also often wrote of Port-au-Prince and Fort Dauphin, when these cities' names had been republicanized to Port Républicain and Fort Liberté during the revolution.[5] Leclerc had been careful not to chain prisoners for fear of drawing parallels with slavery, but Rochambeau reinstituted the *corvée* (chain gang) in Cap and under his rule police reports listed the *nègres* (literally "niggers") who had attacked their *maître* ("master") as if the year had been 1788, not 1802.[6] When a slave belonging to a U.S. merchant had fled to Saint-Domingue in the spring of 1802, Leclerc had insisted that he should be freed; a year later, when a similar incident involved runaways from the Turks and Caicos, Rochambeau ordered them returned to their British owner.[7]

For Bonaparte and Leclerc, determining *whether* slavery should be restored in Saint-Domingue had been a long, tortured process; for Rochambeau, determining *when* it should be restored was the only point in discussion. On the first of January 1803, he enumerated to Denis Decrès the measures he deemed indispensable for the regeneration of Saint-Domingue. Number one on his list of New Year's resolutions was a brutally clear goal: "to proclaim the enslavement of the blacks."[8] Like many conservative thinkers, he thought that blacks preferred the servile state to the uncertainties of freedom, so in his view restoring slavery might even convince some rebels to return to their plantations. Neither Decrès nor Bonaparte ever responded directly to his repeated demands that slavery be restored, but there is little doubt that given the opportunity Rochambeau would have taken that step. In preparation for this moment he personally authenticated a manumission certificate for a black *nouveau libre* with the interesting name of Marianne (possibly his mistress) so that her freedom could not be put in question once slavery was restored.[9]

Rochambeau's conservative views were well known to Creole planters who applauded his promotion as a clean break from "the folly and Negrophilia of [Leclerc] and the Jacobin generals who surrounded him."[10] Conversely, Rochambeau was unpopular with many of the generals who had come with the Leclerc expedition because his aristocratic name and ties to the ancien régime were anathema to their republican ideals. Leclerc had repeatedly asked for Rochambeau to be replaced, and after his death some officers debated how they could arrange for a more liberal figure to be appointed as captain general in his stead.[11]

While Rochambeau made his way to Cap, the colonial prefect, Hector Daure, took over as interim captain general, fully certain that the colony was on the verge of collapse. "Troops are wholly discouraged, the white population of the island universally terrified," he wrote the day after Leclerc's death.[12] The defense of Cap was in the hands of a ragtag group of soldiers, sailors, foreign merchants, and assorted civilians. Of the thirty-four thousand European troops and sailors who had landed since February, twenty-four thousand had died and seven thousand were sick, leaving only three thousand able-bodied Europeans (not counting guardsmen) to defend the entire colony. Six months of war and disease had wiped out entire units. The 28th light demi-brigade was down to forty soldiers; the 3rd, to six; the 7th, to five.

Some demi-brigades had become so skeletal that the last surviving troops were incorporated into larger corps and the flags of the defunct units shipped back to France.[13]

The economic situation was equally desperate. The rural insurgency had forced many planters to flee to Cap for safety, and thousands of destitute civilians were relying on the army for rations. French garrisons had evacuated northern towns so suddenly during the last, panicky days of Leclerc's tenure that they had left their stores behind them and food was in short supply. U.S. ships could not make up for the shortfall because Daure had imposed a two-week trade embargo to stem news of the colony's latest woes. As a result, soldiers only received two biscuits a day and some people could be seen roaming the plain of Cap in a desperate attempt to scavenge sugarcane stalks despite the risk of capture and torture.[14] Burdened with thousands of sick and civilians, the army spent 3 million francs a month doling out food and salaries. Meanwhile, exports of tropical goods were in freefall due to the insurgency, as were customs revenues, and the army only collected half a million a month in taxes. The soldiers' pay was three months in arrears and private contractors clamored for three million francs in unpaid bills.[15]

So critical was the colony's situation that some overeager U.S. and Jamaican newspapers, unable to get reliable information because of the trade embargo, informed their readers that the expeditionary army had already evacuated and that French rule had come to an end.[16] The news was premature, but barely so, since in the north and west of Saint-Domingue, France only controlled a minority of the territory it claimed as its own. A dozen cities from Fort Liberté to Port-de-Paix had been evacuated, so on the northern coast the army only held on to Cap, Môle, and La Tortue with 3,300 troops and guardsmen, plus 5,000 sick. In the west, the French had left Gonaïves, Ennery, Verrettes, and Arcahaye and defended Jacmel, Saint-Marc, Léogane, and Port Républicain with 2,300 troops (including the national guard), plus 2,000 sick.[17] The situation in the south was superficially better, since the region had only witnessed some sporadic rebel activities and the French still held on to most towns. But French contingents were reduced to a single battalion at half strength and southern planters feared that the rebels would strike as soon as they realized the weakness of their enemy.[18]

Such was the situation when Rochambeau reached Cap around November 10. In retrospect, one understands why no officer challenged his accession to the supreme command. Serving as captain general in such hopeless times was hardly an enviable task.

∽

Rochambeau's most urgent priority was to find enough troops to defend the few areas still under French control. Two brigadier chiefs rushed to Paris, Guadeloupe, and Martinique to beg for immediate reinforcements, while Rochambeau asked the governor of Cuba for one thousand Spanish troops and tried to enlist twenty-nine crippled foreigners stranded in Puerto Rico.[19] Over the next few months he repeatedly asked Paris that three large expeditions of ten thousand men reach Saint-Domingue at regular intervals in 1803, each of them grouped in compact masses so that they could be employed in a combined offensive.[20]

No meaningful help could be expected for months, so in the interval Rochambeau made do with what army he had. It included a remarkable number of people of color despite Leclerc's policy of mass drownings, which Daure had continued during his short tenure. Colored sailors represented at least one-third of the crews in Môle; the French commander of Santiago was still employing black troops; the black officers Paul Lafrance and David Troy defended the Mirebalais area for France; and in Jacmel people of color formed the bulk of French forces until May 1803.[21] In Saint-Marc, the main dividing line was not race but social occupation since planters served eagerly on the French side while merchants of both races were ready to "sell themselves to Dessalines, just as they had under Toussaint."[22] People of color remained in French employ even in Cap, where Rochambeau created a unit of colored pioneers, employed one colonial company of artillery, and allowed *anciens libres* to serve in the national guard.[23]

The influence of the multiracial national guard was particularly strong in the southern province, where there were only 250 French soldiers and 200 Poles against 860 guardsmen and gendarmes.[24] The black general, Jean-Joseph Laplume, retained his title in Cayes, officers of color commanded cities as notable as St. Louis and Petit Goâve, and throughout the region people of color played as prominent a role in containing the rebellion as they did in fostering it.[25] In one typical incident eleven rebels went to a plantation in Plymouth to incite cultivators to join the rebellion, only to be thwarted when a foreman refused to embrace the rebel cause and ran to the authorities. By the time a squad of soldiers reached the plantation, the cultivators had themselves captured most of the rebels, whom Laplume ordered shot. Judging by the documentary record, the episode seems to have played out almost entirely within the population of color.[26]

Luckily for Rochambeau, his pleas for troops were answered much faster than he could ever have anticipated. Leclerc had sent pressing requests of his own for months, so early in November (just as, unbeknownst to him, Leclerc died in Cap) Bonaparte ordered Decrès to send large reinforcements over the next two months. He first planned on sending 3,900 troops, then 5,600, then raised the number to 9,500 a month later when he heard of the defection of colonial units.[27] By February 1803, by which time news of Leclerc's death had reached France, the total number of reinforcements sent or scheduled to be sent was nearing 16,000, and Decrès told Rochambeau that he would soon have all the means at his disposal to go on the offensive. "It will be quite pleasing," he added wistfully, "to finally have a chance to report some good news about Saint-Domingue to the First Consul."[28]

After sending 20,000 troops with Leclerc, then 9,400 reinforcements over the summer of 1802, the winter of 1802/3 marked the third time in a year that Bonaparte had sent an army to Saint-Domingue. As part of his ambitious plan to rebuild the French colonial empire, he had also sent 3,600 troops to Guadeloupe, 2,670 to Martinique, 1,227 to India, 585 to Guiana, 300 to Réunion, and 201 to Senegal.[29] Such large contingents were a marked effort on his part and probably the most that could be mustered without leaving France's European borders dangerously unguarded during the tenuous peace with England. The one weakness of the plan was that despite Rochambeau's demands and Bonaparte's orders, Decrès expressed his inability to assemble large naval squadrons and sent the troops piecemeal as ships became available. Soldiers thus arrived haphazardly, making it difficult for any military commander to mount a coordinated offensive akin to Leclerc's spring campaign.[30]

The quality of the troops was also uneven. Bonaparte sent some regular French units such as the 86th demi-brigade of the line, but Rochambeau complained that they were led by "old wigs"—elderly, incompetent officers sent to the colonies in lieu of retirement.[31] Of much lesser value were some disciplinary units of deserters, a battalion of assorted foreigners (including English sailors), and six hundred Swiss from the 3rd Helvetic demi-brigade—only seven of whom would ever return to their Alpine homeland.[32] Of 244 European troops who reached Jacmel in May 1803, the town's commander complained, half were Poles, the rest raw French recruits who in many cases had never fired a gun in their lives.[33] These troops cannot have been too motivated because Bonaparte specified that the latest reinforcements should be locked on board ships and kept unaware of their destination to prevent desertion.[34]

The single largest unit to ship out that winter was the 2nd Polish demi-brigade, which left Genoa in January 1803 to join the unhappy, low-performing survivors of the 3rd. Judging by the divisionary rosters, the rank and file were mostly Polish nationals (along with a smattering of Czechs), the drummers came from all corners of Europe, and as befits national stereotypes the shoemaker was Italian. Interestingly, two Frenchwomen served as *fusillers* (riflewomen) in the unit. As with the 3rd, the one element unifying the diverse group was lack of motivation. Captain Fadzielski of the 1st Polish demi-brigade had no intention to "travel to empty countries and fight with the

Negroes for their own sugar" and was thus relieved when he learned that his demi-brigade would not ship out.[35] Less pleased was the commander of the 2nd, who chose to abandon his command and disappear rather than head for Saint-Domingue.

Another unenthusiastic newcomer was André Guimot, a twenty-four-year-old medical student from Douai who had initially volunteered for colonial service to secure wealth and a promotion to second-class surgeon. But as he waited for a ship in Brest in the summer and fall of 1802, Guimot learned from returning sailors of hard fighting and heavy losses and by October he was thoroughly alarmed. "For three months," he wrote a friend, "the public papers have told us that the epidemic is over, and just recently they claimed that the *Tourville* had not lost a single man. But everyone in Brest knows that the *Tourville* lost 100 crew members on her way back from Saint-Domingue, and returning officers tell us the most horrible stories."[36]

It was by then too late to opt out of the expedition, and in October Guimot left Brest on board the *Industrie,* a private ship commissioned by the government because of the dearth of transports. She was small at 250 tons, but she was nevertheless loaded with over eighty officers, women, and passengers in addition to her regular crew. Sixty-four people shared the main cabin, which measured a mere thirty-two feet by fifteen feet. The ship also carried chickens, geese, ducks, twenty-four pigs, and as many sheep, which made for noisy companions since they were not fed to save on provisions. The ship, Guimot noted with some perplexity, had been built as a slave trader and was scheduled to head for the coast of Africa as soon as it had left its white cargo in Saint-Domingue.

The Atlantic crossing of the *Industrie* was unpleasant, the seas heavy, the passengers sick. Worst of all was the captain's wife, Mrs. Dh . . . , a feeble woman who had been advised to follow her husband under the theory that the sea air and tropical climate would somehow improve her health. Her doctor had apparently not noticed that she was pregnant and would have to deliver her child at sea. Labor began in the midst of yet another frightful storm; "the delivery was quite long," Guimot noted laconically.[37] The child survived, but his mother died shortly before the ship crossed the Tropic of Cancer, where in a break with tradition no Roi Tropique celebrations were held. It was thus with much relief that on November 28, 1802, Guimot sighted the port of Cap, after a dreadful six-week crossing that was considered uneventful for the time.

Guimot's first impression of Cap was traumatic. The epidemic had killed many more people than Bonaparte's newspapers would admit (including, he learned, Leclerc himself), and eight months after the burning of Cap the city was still a ruin under siege. "All that remains are the walls of the houses, a few

Table 6.
French and foreign units that arrived during Rochambeau's counteroffensive (November 1802–March 1803).

Name of unit	Date of arrival	Troops who survived the crossing	Port of departure	Ship
86th demi-brigade of the line	Nov. 25, 1802	1,425		Sagesse and convoy
49th demi-brigade of the line	Dec. 8, 1802	451		Alexandrine Républicain
Unspecified	Dec. 14, 1802	100		Calypso
7th demi-brigade of the line (detachment)	Dec. 17, 1802	226	Via Guadeloupe	Colombe
Free battalion 7th light demi-brigade	Jan. 2, 1803	1,007	Toulon	Duquesne Sybille
20th demi-brigade of the line 23rd demi-brigade of the line	Jan. 27, 1803	1,001	Toulon	Indomptable Mont Blanc
3rd Polish demi-brigade	Feb. 1, 1803	185	Toulon	Deux Amis
Foreign battalion	Feb. 10, 1803	314	Havre	Rhin
60th demi-brigade of the line	Feb. 26, 1803	623	Toulon	Aigle
110th demi-brigade of the line	March 3, 1803	1,183	Havre	
14th light demi-brigade	March 3, 1803	739	Toulon	Atlante

2nd Polish demi-brigade (1st battalion)	March 10, 1803	643	Genoa	*Fougueux*
2nd Polish demi-brigade (2nd and 3rd battalions)	March 29, 1803	1,659	Genoa	*Argonaute* *Héros* *Vertu* *Serpente*
Depot from various corps	March 29, 1803	88	Brest	*Diligente*
3rd Swiss demi-brigade	March 30, 1803	632		*Redoutable*

Total: 10,276

Source: Armée de Saint-Domingue, "État général des troupes arrivées dans la colonie" (ca. July 1803), CC9/B23, Archives Nationales, Paris.

of which have been re-roofed," he wrote. "Blacks and brigands spare none of the whites they capture, gouging out their eyes or . . . occasionally bleeding them like pigs."[38] By the time Guimot reached his destination in Cayes late in December 1802, the excitement that had initially led him to volunteer for the expedition was long since gone. And yet it would be the military performance of young men like him that over the next few weeks would decide whether Saint-Domingue would remain a French colony or not.

~

Despite the sense of panic prevailing in the immediate aftermath of Leclerc's death, the undermanned French garrisons managed to hold on to the cities still under their control relatively easily. The French army had found it hard to pursue rebels into forested hills, but once the fighting moved to fixed positions in the plains the tables turned and it began to inflict heavy casualties on rebel assailants with minimal losses on its side. In Cap, the commander of the artillery, Bertrand Clauzel, established blockhouses (fortified turrets), a tactic borrowed from the British occupation of Saint-Domingue and that proved highly effective over the next thirteen months.[39] On October 26, an attack on Cap was repulsed, as was another on November 4 and yet another on the sixth. Throughout, the French made up for their small numbers with murderous artillery fire at close range, which the rebel army could not answer in kind because it lacked specialized gunners and cannonballs of the proper caliber. Dejected after losing so many men for no gain, the rebels withdrew after burning Haut du Cap, and the exhausted defenders of Cap awoke on the seventh to find that their enemies were gone.[40] The rebels probably next headed for Môle, because on the eighteenth this city suffered a major assault, which in a new tactic involved using cultivators as human shields. The garrison, though largely composed of the sick and invalids, held firm and the rebels, caught between the fire of the main line and that of advanced posts, paid a heavy price.[41]

François Watrin, the young general who had replaced Rochambeau as commander of the western province, died of yellow fever just as quickly as he took up his new command, but the rebels proved equally unsuccessful in this region.[42] In Saint-Marc, the civilian population rejected orders to evacuate and pressured the French commander to stay put. After executing the colonial troops who refused to be disarmed, he reinforced fortifications and enrolled planters who had evacuated from the interior. Jean-Jacques Dessalines fought like a "jean-foutre" (dumb ass), a French officer proudly wrote after Dessalines was forced to retreat on November 2.[43] The rebels next launched a major assault against Léogane. They made their way into the center of town, but they did not know how to use the cannon they had captured during the fighting and had to retreat to the main fort by the sea. Reinforcements soon rushed in from nearby Port Républicain, and faced with a combined land and naval assault the rebels had to abandon the fort as well.[44] François Pageot also repulsed numerous attacks on Jacmel even though many of the planters who had taken refuge in the town were people of color, as was much of the town's garrison, and he doubted their loyalty. The largest assault took place on February 16, 1803, when five rebel columns led by the most notable rebel leaders in the area launched a surprise nightly attack. The rebels were well prepared but failed miserably. Three of their officers were killed, as were many attackers; no French defender was even wounded.[45] After these various reverses the rebels chose not to attack Port Républicain and instead divided themselves into small bands that burned plantations in the plain of Cul-de-Sac. Only weeks before, they could reasonably have thought that they were on the verge of taking control of the entire colony; they were now back to an inconclusive war of ambushes and arson.[46]

Saved from immediate annihilation, Rochambeau sent his army on the offensive as soon as the first reinforcements began to arrive late in November 1802. A large, combined campaign was unthinkable due to the haphazard nature of troop shipments, so he opted to retake individual cities every time a new unit arrived from Europe. His first objective was Fort Liberté, the port he had captured during the initial landings. On December 1, Clauzel and one thousand men of the newly arrived 86th demi-brigade promptly retook Fort Liberté without a single casualty while its not-so-courageous commander Toussaint Brave (a.k.a. Toussaint Daut) fled to the mountains. The French later retook the nearby cities of Laxavon and Ouanaminthe, thus reestablishing the land route to Santo Domingo. Brave twice attempted to retake Fort Liberté in April 1803, failing both times despite the assistance of allies inside the city.[47]

The arrival of over one thousand troops in early January gave Rochambeau another chance to regain some strategic breathing room, this time on Cap's western flank. His plan was for Clauzel to retake Port-de-Paix and the smaller cities nearby so as to reestablish contact with Môle and protect the hospitals of La Tortue. One of the two ships of the line serving as transports, the ill-fated *Intrépide,* maneuvered too close to the coast and broke its rudder, a mishap that may have been caused by the fact that the ship, down to 139 sailors after being ravaged by yellow fever, was simply undermanned. But the *Duquesne* fared better and landed its troops under the nose of the fortress of Port-de-Paix, whose poorly aimed fire whizzed harmlessly above the ship's rigging. Clauzel quickly retook Port-de-Paix, forcing François Capois-la-Mort, the most notable officer of color in the area since Jacques Maurepas' death, to retreat to the mountains.[48]

All the main population centers along Saint-Domingue's northern coast were now back under French control. The only cause for irritation for Rochambeau was that his son Philippe, a midshipman in the navy, had been on the *Intrépide* during her incident. He switched to the luckier *Duquesne,* but even then showed no aptitude for things maritime. Constantly seasick, he eventually transferred to the 5th light demi-brigade and embarked on a military career that would take him all the way to Moscow during the 1812 campaign of Russia.[49]

~

French-held towns housed individuals of multiple racial and political shades, so the enemy within was as dangerous as the army at the gates, and Rochambeau's military counteroffensive unfolded in tandem with security measures aimed at suspected rebel sympathizers. His treatment of enemy prisoners was often cruel, and to this day Rochambeau is remembered, often exaggeratedly so, as a sadistic butcher whose vicious reign epitomized the worst excesses of French colonial rule in Saint-Domingue. Rochambeau "did not share [Leclerc's] kindness," a memoirist wrote in a typical mischaracterization of Leclerc's record. "Shortly after he took over, war became atrocious."[50] Rochambeau actually killed fewer prisoners than Leclerc, and to some extent his bad reputation is undeserved. What gives him a unique place in the rich annals of human cruelty is that he executed his victims in a manner that remains shocking two hundred years after the fact.

Rochambeau's tenure began auspiciously enough. After reaching Cap he deported some black prisoners to France, a practice Leclerc had long since abandoned.[51] He also spared several people of color destined to be drowned, including the black wife of Toussaint Louverture's paymaster, Marie Bunel, who was freed after spending a month on a ship on Leclerc's orders. Some female rebels continued to be executed, but in another sign of mercy the commander of Môle decided that prisoners with young infants would be employed as nurses in the city's hospitals instead of being killed.[52]

A month into his command, Rochambeau wrote to Decrès that he thought it essential to "destroy, or deport, black or mulatto generals, officers, soldiers, and planters, in totality."[53] The words sounded harsh, but it is worth noting that, contrary to Leclerc, Rochambeau excluded cultivators from the list of his victims, and even then did not put his policy into effect. In late February, after again expressing his intention to "exterminate" prominent people of color, he added that he would only do so after the arrival of large reinforcements.[54] In the meantime, drownings continued, but they affected relatively small groups. In a five-day period in December, for example, twenty-six people were "embarked" in Cap (usually a euphemism for drowning), a far cry from the thousands of victims killed in Leclerc's final days. A brief description of their crime accompanied each name, when Leclerc had long since stopped bothering about individual guilt.[55]

Like many of his Creole friends, Rochambeau feared and hated liberal whites and mixed-race *anciens libres* far more than black cultivators, and his executions did not solely target black rebels. He particularly despised the impoverished *petits blancs,* whom he described as the "refuse of society," and settled scores with colonists known for their past support for Louverture.[56] Three of the twenty-six individuals "embarked" in December, for example, were whites accused of helping Moyse and Louverture massacre white planters; twelve were mixed-race individuals. Rochambeau had once supported the rights of free people of color, but as captain general he increasingly embraced the fanatical hatred of *ancien libres* that was characteristic of some local planters.[57] Prominent mixed-race individuals were particularly targeted in the south, officially because they abetted the rebellion, but more likely to confiscate their estates.

Rochambeau had a bizarre, almost playful approach to death. In a cruel prank designed to play on racial enmities, two prisoners—one black, one of mixed race—were told that the one who would hang the other would be spared (the black man, who was the first to volunteer, was then appointed as chief executioner and nicknamed "Tombaret").[58] An elaborate, witty slang also arose to describe the barbaric modes of execution employed under Rochambeau's rule. Drowning a prisoner became known as "giving a codfish a bath," while drowning many at once was "netting a big prize." A person being hanged was "promoted" or "ate hemp salad," while one shot by firing squad had his or her "face washed with lead." Most troublingly, the victim of a "hot operation" was burned at the stake, one who "rose in dignity" was crucified, and one who "descended into the arena" was devoured by dogs.[59] A few officers, like Louis d'Arbois in Jérémie, eagerly followed Rochambeau's lead and devised sadistic tortures of their own, but Republicans like Clauzel generally found such methods objectionable.[60] Even for Charles Malenfant, an old-time colonist who had witnessed both ancien régime slavery and revolutionary violence, the atrocities of the Rochambeau era were too much. "My pen cannot retrace such horrifying crimes," he wrote in his history of the Haitian Revolution before moving on.[61] And yet retrace these crimes we must, for the exactions committed under the reign of Rochambeau played a central role in hardening the rebels' stance and remain an important part of the Haitian collective memory to the present day.

A famous case involved three black prisoners caught while trying to set a plantation on fire. The attempted arson, along with the fact that the suspects were blamed for atrocities committed against French prisoners, called for an appropriate punishment, and a pile of *bagasse* (dry sugarcane stalks) was erected on St. Louis square in Cap for their benefit. As a crowd watched agape, the men were tied to three poles arranged in a triangle and the tinder lit under their feet. "In less than two minutes," recalled the sailor Jean-

Baptiste Lemonnier-Delafosse, the bodies of two of the prisoners "burst up, their skin cracked, and the fat, oozing from the flesh, fed the fire that was eating them. Their arms and legs contracted, and after some horrific screams their mouth spouted some white foam and cavernous sounds broke from their chest." The third prisoner, who was upwind, was still unscathed and yelled in Kreyol to his companions that "they did not know how to die, and that he would show them." After loosening his bonds, he sat down in the flames and burned without uttering a single moan. The incident also made a great impression on Mary Hassal, who used it in two of her novels.[62]

In another gruesome episode, sixteen officers of the colonial gendarmerie were rowed to an islet in the bay of Montecristi where, one by one, they were crucified by the shore and left to die. Their cruel end is only known to us through the nineteenth-century historian Thomas Madiou, whose account is occasionally inaccurate, but this particular episode rings true. It is not hard to imagine that a French officer, at a time when elite education consisted largely in studying the classics, would resort to the penalty earmarked for rebellious slaves in Roman times, or that a playful Deist would find it topical to crucify his enemies in a bay named after another famous rebel sentenced to die on the cross. If Madiou's account is correct—and there is no reason to believe that it is not—this must have been a long, painful death for the sixteen officers lined up along the shore like agonizing pietàs, whose gnarled, statuesque bodies testified to the horrors of the Haitian Revolution under the reign of Rochambeau.[63]

Making sense of such grotesque scenes is difficult unless one analyzes Rochambeau's tenure as the last of three successive stages in the expedition, each of them characterized by a unique form of violence. Despite some rapes and summary acts of revenge, the spring campaign had largely been a traditional clash between two armies vying for territorial control and whose excesses would not have been out of place on European soil. By the fall of 1802, however, the war had become a revolutionary struggle over ideals, and entire groups identified by their social or political characteristics—such as cultivators and colonial units—had succumbed in episodes eerily reminiscent of the Loire drownings during the Terror. Rochambeau's accession to power, finally, saw the rise of a colonial form of violence, one often characterized by bizarre excesses as imperial agents, fighting an alien enemy far from the eyes of public opinion, gave free rein to their most deviant fantasies. Rochambeau's horrific tortures were familiar to the colonists, who had broken countless slave rebels on the rack in the fall of 1791, and to the veterans of the expedition of Egypt, who had seen the Arab assassin of Jean-Baptiste Kleber burned and impaled in 1801. But cruel and unusual punishments had been banned in France since 1789, and to a metropolitan audience Rochambeau's monstrous tortures seemed alien and ancient, as if drawn from some medieval dungeon.

~

As the colonial economy spiraled downward in late 1802, bringing tax and tariff receipts down with it, the army's financial difficulties showed no sign of abating. The army treasury showed a pitiful balance of 3,055 francs and 17 centimes in late November, and despite occasional windfalls it hovered near zero throughout the winter.[64] In an exasperated tone that evoked Leclerc's own frustrations with Bonaparte's lack of financial foresight, Rochambeau repeatedly complained that he was only receiving a fraction of the 1-million-franc monthly shipment that had been promised to him, forcing him to deal with "usurers."[65] Even with the governmental subsidy, the colony would have had difficulties meeting monthly expenses of three million francs at a time when tax receipts had plunged to a mere two hundred thousand francs.[66]

Rochambeau's solution to the fiscal shortfall, like Leclerc's before him, was to borrow large sums from foreign lenders, leaving for later the issue of repaying the loans or addressing the colony's long-term financial viability. In the winter of 1802/3, he sent multiple agents to Jamaica, the United States, Veracruz, Cartagena, Caracas, and Havana.[67] When counting Leclerc's previous missions, some Spanish imperial outposts saw up to half a dozen French envoys in a year's time, each of them eagerly demanding large contributions of Spanish silver.

The most notable of Rochambeau's agents was a brigadier general named Louis de Noailles, who like Rochambeau was the veteran of three revolutions, having fought for the cause of U.S. independence at the battle of Yorktown, offered to abandon his aristocratic privileges during the famous night of August 4, 1789, then fled back to the United States after the Terror had claimed his wife's life. His Anglo-American connections were the main reason he was selected for an ambitious mission that was to take him to Jamaica, Cuba, and the United States to make pressing demands for thirty million francs.[68]

Noailles' first stop was Kingston, where he was supposed to borrow up to ten million francs from private investors like the Jewish banker Alexander Lindo, who had already loaned sixty thousand Jamaican pounds to the colony.[69] But diplomatic faux pas made for a tense visit. Exporting specie was a sensitive issue in mercantilist days, and the British were irate that the first installment of Lindo's loan had been loaded without consulting local authorities.[70] In a deliberate snub, the admiral of the station forced Noailles to wait for days before allowing him to land, and Governor George Nugent, who had just been informed that war with France might soon resume, proved equally uncooperative.[71] Noailles' boasts that the French intended to "hamstring" the rebels by killing a large part of the black population also had a way of appalling Nugent and his wife, whom Naoilles met on Christmas Eve.[72] Despite Noailles' insistence that Rochambeau's long-term plan to restore slavery would benefit all colonial powers in the region, Nugent refused to grant Lindo the status of official French representative in Jamaica or consent to any other cash shipment.[73]

Nugent was convinced that the matter of French loans had been brought to rest, but Noailles actually convinced Lindo to loan an additional seven million francs, half of which was secretly exported to Saint-Domingue in the first months of 1803.[74] Why Lindo agreed to gamble such a large sum remains unclear. He was a Francophile who had supplied André Rigaud during his war against Louverture, and he was close to a French Jew who had been executed while trying to spark a slave revolt in Jamaica in 1799.[75] But he was also a well-established Kingston businessman who regularly met with the governor, and like so many individuals of this era he may simply have been a complex, self-driven character primarily motivated by money (he stood to collect a 12 percent profit on the loan and was also made the French army's leading supplier).[76] Lindo's financial hopes, however, went unmet. As rumors of a possible war with England grew more persistent, Rochambeau stopped paying interest on the Lindo loan, which Bonaparte himself refused to recognize, and Lindo never recovered the massive investment he had made in the expedition of Saint-Domingue.[77]

Noailles next headed for Havana. His argument that Saint-Domingue's neighbors should help "save the colony or risk perishing with it" made an impression on the security-conscious Spanish governor of Cuba, the Marquis of Someruelos, who within days offered 123,000 gourdes in addition to the 445,000 he had already loaned Leclerc.[78] But Noailles, consistent with Rochambeau's admonition that Spain was a subject state of France and his own dismissive view of Cuban society, did little to reward Someruelos's generosity. Ignoring Spain's strict trade restrictions, he made plans to import eight thousand contraband slaves into Cuba to earn extra cash, while the captains who had brought him to Havana under diplomatic flag surreptitiously sold their black servants. Smuggling was nothing new in the region, but Spanish authorities were terrified that imported black Dominguians might preach revolt to their Cuban brethren and saw these breaches of diplomatic protocol as a serious affair.[79] The ensuing controversy strengthened the position of the *intendant* of Cuba, a personal enemy of Someruelos and an opponent to the pro-French line, and in February 1803 previously forthcoming Cuban authorities arrested all black Frenchmen present in Cuba and threatened to expel other Frenchmen as well.[80] The abrupt shift may also have been inspired by the undiplomatic conduct of French envoys in other Spanish colonies, since the officer in charge of purchasing mules in Cartagena illegally exported cash, while his successor displayed the revolutionary tricolor in a multiracial, lower-class neighborhood that was a hotbed of social unrest.[81]

As the Franco-Spanish dispute grew more acrimonious, Someruelos sent Francisco de Arango y Parreño, a well-educated bourgeois from Havana, to Saint-Domingue to complain about French smuggling and, more importantly, to assess whether the French could win the war and reimburse their debts. Aware that a negative report would ruin French credit, Noailles advised his superiors to treat Arango well and assure him that with Spanish financial assistance French victory was assured. Arango's official report, however, was apocalyptic. The French army could only prevail by exterminating the black population and turning the colony into a "desert," he explained. As for the state of the plantations, "the quill is falling from my hands, as I begin to draw the sad description that can currently be made of what was not long ago the most flourishing and richest colony in the world."[82] His depiction was largely accurate, but Arango also had his own reasons to favor abandoning Saint-Domingue to its fate. A determined Cuban booster, he ambitioned to spark an economic boom in his own isle and viewed his visit to Saint-Domingue primarily as an opportunity to spy on Cuba's main economic rival—with great success, since with his help Cuba soon turned into the great sugar powerhouse of the nascent century.

Before his departure Arango signed a vague convention in which he made no firm financial pledge, and based on his advice and Noailles' various slights Cuban authorities stopped sending any more cash to their beleaguered allies.[83] According to his instructions, Noailles' journey was supposed to end with one last stop in the United States (where he would borrow 10 million francs from private merchants), but he never completed the last leg of his journey. He most likely would have failed anyway, since the country was in an uproar over French ambitions in Louisiana and another of Rochambeau's envoys obtained nothing.[84] Overall the sums obtained in the winter of 1802/3 were substantial, amounting to 11.5 to 21.4 million francs depending on sources.[85] But the poor treatment meted out to the few individuals willing to help finance the expedition and Bonaparte's atrocious record for paying Saint-Domingue's debts had thoroughly ruined the colony's credit by the end of spring 1803.[86] From then on, Rochambeau's army fought with an empty purse.

⤳

During his lengthy stay in Havana, Louis de Noailles learned that Leclerc had once made inquiries about acquiring slave-hunting dogs, and he immediately began to explore the benefits of obtaining some teams for the army of

The Mode of exterminating the Black Army, as practised by the French.

3. Mass drowning by the French army. The presence of dogs in the water was unlikely, though Thomas Madiou made a similar claim in his history of the revolution. J. Barlow, "The Mode of exterminating the Black Army as practised by the French." In Marcus Rainsford. *A Historical Account of the Black Empire of Hayti.* London: Albion Press, 1805.

Saint-Domingue. The use of dogs as combat auxiliaries had a long history in the Caribbean, most famously in Spain's and Britain's wars against Tainos and Maroons, and they were remarkably well suited for the counterinsurgency operations waged in Saint-Domingue. Although his instructions said nothing on the topic, Noailles thus took it upon himself to request four hundred dogs from the governor of Cuba. In February 1803, a first shipment of two hun-

The mode of training Blood Hounds in St. Domingo, and of exercising them by Chasseurs

Published as the Act directs, July 4 1805, by J.L. Cundee, Ivy Lane, Paternoster Row.

4. French war dogs. J. Barlow, "The mode of training Blood Hounds in St. Domingo, and of exercising them by Chasseurs." In Marcus Rainsford. *A Historical Account of the Black Empire of Hayti.* London: Albion Press, 1805.

dred dogs left with their Cuban conductors for Cap, where they were destined to become the main actors in the most notorious of Rochambeau's crimes.[87]

The dogs reached Cap on March 1. Decorated with feathers and silk strands, the massive, growling beasts cut a fearsome appearance. Most of the current dog breeds did not appear until the Victorian era, so the dogs were variously described as bulldogs, Newfoundland dogs, mastiffs, or bloodhounds, and were most likely assorted mongrels selected for their size and aggressiveness. The mood among the populace of Cap was accordingly jubilant, and it was immediately decided that a demonstration would be held in a makeshift amphitheater built, of all places, in the cloister of a former convent. Like the crucifixions of Montecristi, the scene had obvious classical parallels, and the attendees probably thought of themselves as latter-day Romans disposing of their criminals in an entertaining fashion (less enthusiastic attendees may have wondered instead whether they had become Neros executing Christian martyrs). Pierre Boyer, who had hanged rebels with so much fervor during the disarmament campaign, was front and center and according to some accounts even offered his own black servant as a sacrificial lamb for the experiment.

The dogs, who had been starved on purpose, entered the arena and approached the hapless, bound victim as the crowd watched intently. Slowly, they sniffed and circled; then they walked away. Like Sainte Blandine, the famous martyr of Lyon, it seemed that the prisoner would be saved by divine intervention when Boyer jumped into the arena, tore open the man's stomach, and the scent of blood finally awoke the dogs' appetite (Lemonnier, who witnessed the scene, holds that the dogs never approached to eat the prisoner and that he was eventually spared).[88] Despite the first experiment's mixed success, similar executions regularly took place thereafter in front of the government house in Cap, much to the annoyance of local residents who complained about the noise. Madiou even claims, less convincingly, that dogs swam about French shallops to devour prisoners as they were drowning.[89]

The dogs' primary purpose was to assist counterinsurgency operations, not satisfy the mob's appetite for blood, so most of them were divided into squads of twenty-five and assigned to army divisions. Using dogs was "indispensable," Rochambeau's chief of staff explained apologetically to a metropolitan correspondent. Rebels often hid in the bushes, allowed French columns to pass by, then attacked them by surprise in the rear, so the only way to locate them was to use hounds "trained to chase maroon Negroes."[90] "This tactic may seem inhuman at first," he added, but "the dogs will so terrify the brigands that they will quickly surrender."[91]

A new uprising in La Tortue quickly gave the dogs an opportunity to prove their worth. The island's breezy climate was considered salutary for yellow fever patients, and despite two major insurrections in the summer of 1802 it had become home to a network of sixteen hospitals hosting 2,500 convalescents. In the night of February 17, after the French recaptured nearby Port-de-Paix, cultivators and soldiers crossed the channel on board small barges, attacked La Tortue's hospitals by surprise, and massacred the patients in a carnage that particularly unsettled the French.[92] The director of hospitals was found lying on a beach, badly injured. The island's leading planter, Raymond Labatut, was captured, and though he eventually managed to escape his wife remained in rebel hands; adding insult to injury, a French officer then accused him of conspiring with the rebels in order to seize his estates.

An unlucky Pamphile Lacroix, who had just been transferred to La Tortue to rest, found himself at the heart of the insurrection. He managed to flee with an injured grenadier, but the pair spent seven days wandering through the island's rocky hills before they made their way to Cap. Lacroix's brother was killed in the uprising, and he was so thoroughly shaken by the experience that he finally obtained a pass to return to France. Although he would serve loyally in the French army for another thirty years, his greatest achievement was his 1819 history of the Haitian Revolution, the best written by any veteran of the expedition. The book quickly glanced over the Rochambeau period, which clearly its author found too painful to retrace.[93]

Informed of the events in La Tortue, Rochambeau sent three hundred troops under the French officer Ramel to crush the uprising. Ramel managed to save some white survivors, but after three weeks of fighting the rebels were still active and Rochambeau fired him for his lack of vigor.[94] His replacement, Boscu, left with twenty-five of the newly arrived dogs. According to his detailed orders, the dogs were to be kept strictly segregated from the mixed-race guardsmen for fear that they might become accustomed to the scent of black skin. Curious observers were also told not to feed the dogs, possibly to avoid poisoning, but more likely to keep them hungry for human flesh. "For the dogs to acquire taste, it will be necessary to give them bait before you unleash them," Boscu's cryptic orders went. "Squadron Chief L'Allemand will tell you what is meant by bait."[95]

The dogs proved far less formidable than their reputation. Communicating with their Cuban drivers was difficult, and the dogs, surrounded by allies and enemies of all colors, were simply overwhelmed and confused by Saint-Domingue's complex racial politics.[96] Capois-la-Mort, who had come from Port-de-Paix to oversee the insurrection, escaped to the mainland unscathed, bringing with him two hundred cultivators, whose recruitment had been one of the main reasons for the attack. Within weeks there were more raids on the island.[97]

The uprising in La Tortue coincided with a major insurrection in the southern province, forcing Rochambeau to shift his attention to this previously quiet corner of the colony.[98] In February 1803, he announced his intention to move his headquarters to his old command in Port Républicain to oversee the next phase of military operations. He had to delay his departure when the rebels twice attacked Cap, but a second, larger rebel offensive broke out in the south and despite the pleadings of the civilians of Cap, Rochambeau left on March 17. From then on most of the reinforcements from France were rerouted to the southern province.[99] Bad news awaited

Rochambeau upon his arrival in Port Républicain. A column of reinforcements that had imprudently chosen to walk to Cayes instead of traveling by ship had been ambushed and decimated.[100] In Petit Goâve, an officer of color, Lamarre, had finally grown weary of the exactions of Louis d'Arbois and turned over the city to the rebels despite the admonitions of his superior, another officer of color still loyal to France.

Rochambeau immediately sent six hundred troops to retake Petit Goâve. The force included many members of his honor guard and was led by the Swedish officer Netherwood, who was particularly motivated since Rochambeau had promised him a Creole bride as a prize for retaking the town. Lamarre torched the town and retreated to the main fort, and when an over-eager Netherwood attacked the fortified position his forces were devastated by enemy fire and had to fall back. Noailles' secret weapon again proved a dud as fifty dogs turned around in the heat of battle and attacked the retreating French troops. Netherwood's leg was shattered in the assault and he died a month later; in all, fifteen officers were killed or wounded, along with 150 soldiers, a fourth of the attackers and the biggest tally in a French attack since the siege of Crête-à-Pierrot. The frigate *Franchise,* overloaded with casualties, returned mournfully to Port Républicain, where Rochambeau ordered that the wounded wait until nighttime to disembark to hide the extent of the disaster.[101]

A week later, when a French force encountered resistance while landing in Arcahaye, the memory of Petit Goâve was still so fresh on everyone's mind that the troops quickly reembarked, the ships fired a few broadsides from the safety of the sea, and everyone returned to Port Républicain before incurring any casualties. A French captain, noting that an inordinate number of rebels were present on shore, was pleased to report that the naval bombardment had been deadly. What he did not know was that an important rebel gathering was about to take place in the city, and that a successful assault would have given the French a chance to capture Dessalines and all his major lieutenants.[102]

Despite the frustrating setback in Petit Goâve, the arrival of more reinforcements from France (the 2nd Polish demi-brigade landed in March) incited Rochambeau to mount his most ambitious operation to date, a vast sweep through the southern province designed to end recent rebel operations in the area. To that effect he put together a division of two thousand men, divided it into four columns of five hundred men each, and instructed them to leave from Abricots, Dame-Marie, Les Irois, and Tiburon at the western extremity of the province, then roll up the narrow peninsula in a concerted effort to push the rebels past Grand Goâve and Baynet. The columns proceeding along the southern and the northern coasts would receive continuous support from the navy, while the two making their way through the mountain ranges of the interior would employ squads of dogs to locate rebel nests. The French would then establish a defensive cordon to prevent further incursions into the south.[103]

The expedition was a lamentable failure. D'Arbois was supposed to lead one of the columns in person, but he delegated the task to a local guardsman, and orders that all four columns proceed in tandem were disregarded. As always, the Poles lacked daring and mobility, and in the oppressive heat of a Caribbean May they inched their way at a glacial pace through the mountains while being decimated by ambushes. Nicolas Geffrard, the general commanding all rebel forces in the south, had plenty of time to attack one enemy after the other, and in a tactic that would have made Bonaparte proud, he defeated his superior enemy piecemeal before it had time to join in a single mass. The campaign ended in recrimination and chaos, and losses must have been heavy because French reports gave no precise figure.[104]

As always the dogs made no difference in combat. "They always ended up cowering between their driver's legs whenever they heard a gunshot," a French officer recalled.[105] "After I was induced to try this new type of recruits, I bought a large quantity of dogs in Cuba at tremendous expense," Rochambeau later wrote with irritation. "We tried them once or twice in combat, they proved worthless, they bit no one, and from then on we did not use them because they were perfectly useless against an enemy bearing a firearm."[106]

Despite the dogs' unsatisfactory record, Noailles continued his purchases and in May 1803 proudly reported that he had just bought three hundred beasts of the best quality. The French agent in Havana was less impressed and described them as "street dogs" gathered in a huff to justify the large sums earmarked for their purchase.[107] The latter assessment was probably more accurate since 105 dogs in a first shipment of 184 died in the short crossing to Cap. The remaining one hundred dogs left on the schooner *Diligente,* only to be captured by a British warship, thus providing a fitting conclusion to a most wasteful expenditure of money.[108]

Despite their minor role as executioners and combatants, Noailles' dogs quickly acquired an oversize importance in the popular imagination. To Rochambeau's many detractors, the dogs became a vivid symbol of his atrocities, more so than execution methods like drowning and hanging that killed many more rebels. There was something in the use of animals to hunt and rip apart human beings that was considered thoroughly inhumane, even in a revolution that saw the use of every torture imaginable by man. Geffrard, for one, explained that he had joined the rebels because they had "trained dogs to drink the human blood of two or three of our brothers every day in Cap."[109] Dessalines similarly compared the French to "cannibals" and in a reference to Spain's Taino victims wrote that "for the second time in the history of our unhappy isle, dogs were feeding on its children."[110]

By the time Dessalines made this comment in September 1803, history was fast exacting some culinary justice. The tightly besieged French towns were increasingly subject to famine, and throughout the colony starving French garrisons had begun eating every animal they could get their hands on.[111] Many of Rochambeau's fearsome man-eating beasts, it seems, ended their futile career as military chow.

~

The southern campaign marked the last time that the army of Saint-Domingue marched on the offensive. As the spring of 1803 drew to a close, the rebels resolved internal squabbles, and with the renewal of the naval war with England most of the reinforcements promised by Bonaparte never reached Saint-Domingue. French fortunes, which had briefly revived, never recovered.

In the short term the recapture of the ports on the northern coast provided an important morale boost to the French army while diminishing the rebels' ability to import contraband. Economically, however, it made little long-term sense. These cities only existed as outlets for the sugar plantations of the plains and the coffee plantations of the hills, which could not produce anything as long as they were threatened by raids staged from the mountains, and colonial experts had long warned that controlling the colony's interior was the key to any lasting victory. Critics also argued that Rochambeau should have sent the reinforcements he had received in November 1802 to the plain of Port Républicain and the southern province—the only areas still producing tropical goods and paying taxes at the time—instead of launching meaningless expeditions to recapture burned-out ghost towns like Port-de-Paix.[112] By the time Rochambeau had shifted his attention to the southern province, a major uprising had already taken place and a valuable province had been lost. "I cannot understand the blunder he just made," a French general wrote. "He retook Port-de-Paix, Jean Rabel, places where there are only ashes, while abandoning the south, the region that provides us with our only resources."[113] C. E. P. Wante, who had replaced Louis Fréron as subprefect of the southern region, similarly complained that for too long generals had "deliberated instead of acting, temporized instead of marching," and that their incompetence had allowed the rebellion to take hold.[114] The criticism must have hit the spot, because Rochambeau fired him soon after.

In French accounts, explanations for the achievements and limitations of

Rochambeau's counteroffensive usually emphasized factors like his choice of targets and the poor quality of the latest reinforcements. But French officers often ignored that the main reason why they had been able to retake a few towns that winter was that Dessalines had spent the period fighting, not the French, but rival rebel factions in a successful attempt to fashion a unified army under his control.

13

Unity Is Strength

Dessalines and the Unification of the Rebel Army

Jean-Jacques Dessalines' defection brought to the fore a general who, despite his prominent rank, had long been dismissed by his rivals as a half-civilized brute.[1] Although often described as Caribbean-born in the literature, Dessalines was a *bossale* (African-born slave) according to most contemporaries, who also made note of his tribal scarifications and halting Kreyol. His African birth put him below native Dominguians in the colonial pecking order, as did the fact, according to some sources, that he had suffered the indignity of belonging to a black freedman. And yet it was this social nonentity who eventually rose higher and further than the many better-born rivals who had underestimated him.

An obscure slave, Dessalines played no leadership role in the 1791 slave revolt, but his courage in the field eventually convinced Toussaint Louverture to enroll him as one of his guides. Dessalines' fortunes grew with those of his mentor, and by 1801 he had become a division general, a rank only Louverture and Moyse had achieved. But Louverture only looked at him as an executioner and gave him missions—such as punishing Rigaud's followers after the War of the South, enforcing discipline among black plantation workers, and massacring white civilians during the spring campaign—that required more brawn than brains. Dessalines' long record of violence also made for a lengthy list of personal enemies among all segments of the population.

Dessalines was feared and hated, but he was not respected. He seemed uncouth when compared with many of his colleagues, and his enemies alleged that he was content as long as he had killed someone that day. Other accounts noting his personal bravery, limited intellect, and love of dancing played into contemporary stereotypes of lower-class blacks as fundamentally harmless individuals who could turn violent when left unchecked, but who were otherwise docile instruments if well led. That Dessalines was the man who eventually outsmarted every rival in the competitive political environment of the Haitian Revolution must have come as a surprise to many of his contemporaries.

Given Dessalines' personal hatred for Donatien de Rochambeau (under whom he had served during the disarmament campaign), everyone expected him to launch an all-out assault on French positions immediately after he joined the rebellion. The French camp, still reeling from the shock of Leclerc's death, braced for the incoming storm as November 1802 began—only to be surprised when rebel attacks proved small and uncoordinated and Dessalines largely disappeared from sight. The relative calm allowed the embattled French to retake a few towns over the following winter, but it kept the most astute observers off balance: what could Dessalines be doing?[2]

Dessalines was actually busy fighting his most dangerous enemies—but they were neither white nor French. The exile of Louverture and the deaths of Moyse and Charles Belair made it relatively easy for Dessalines to claim the overall command of former colonial units, but two important groups still had to be won over. First were the mixed-race supporters of André Rigaud whose memories of Dessalines' bloody record during the War of the South were still vivid; second were the Maroons who remembered him as the man who had implemented Louverture's strict labor rules and seconded France's disarmament campaign. The Maroons' opposition was particularly significant since they could draw from the large cultivator population and represented four- to five-sixths of all rebel forces in every region of the colony.[3] They were also traditionally unruly and unorganized, so fashioning the disparate rebel groups into a national army—by the power of his word or the tip of his sword—was a difficult task that would consume most of Dessalines' time over the following months.

～

Clashes between colonial officers and Maroon leaders erupted in the northern province immediately after the defection of Henri Christophe, a general who like Dessalines was disliked for his role in the disarmament campaign.[4] Christophe's enemies included the Maroons' acknowledged leader in the north, Sans Souci, along with his subordinates Petit Noël Prieur, Makaya, Jacques Tellier, Va Malheureux, and the imaginatively named Cacapoule (chicken shit). Bad blood from the previous summer was compounded by the fact that most Maroon leaders were African-born *bossales,* when Christophe and many of his colleagues were Caribbean-born Creoles who looked down on the Maroon bands as uncivilized mobs. Strong words were exchanged, Prieur refused to share his supply of gunpowder, and Sans Souci and Christophe almost came to blows when the former requested the overall command of all rebel forces in the north.[5] Making matters worse, Bertrand

Clauzel in Cap cleverly concentrated his artillery fire on sections of the rebel line manned by Maroons to confirm rumors that Christophe was deliberately assigning his allies to the more exposed sectors.[6]

The animosity was such that Dessalines had to personally intervene. In January 1803, he moved north to apportion the various commands and decided that Christophe would command the Dondon area—whose cultivators promptly revolted and twice ran Christophe out of town. Dessalines himself must have been unpopular with Sans Souci's followers, since the disarmament campaign had occasionally brought him to the northern province and weeks before his defection he had been fighting the Maroon groups of Gagnet and Jacques Tellier near Plaisance.[7]

Probably acting with Dessalines' assent, Christophe eventually invited Sans Souci to iron out their differences face to face, only to capture and assassinate him and his lieutenant Makaya during the parley. So ignominious were these murders that Prieur broke with the rebel army and killed Louverture's brother Paul in retaliation. Dessalines then launched a full-scale military offensive that forced Prieur and his Maroon followers into the mountains, where they remained for much of the remainder of the war.[8]

Sans Souci's assassination left the Maroons unable to challenge Dessalines' leadership of the rebel forces in the north, but the French army, informed by its spies of the recent clashes, exploited the rebel-Maroon divide to cement its otherwise tenuous hold on Cap. At Rochambeau's demand, a black officer, Louis Labelinaye, wrote to six Maroon leaders to denounce Christophe as a "tyrant" and promise that the "French government's principles [on slavery] have not changed."[9] The French also established a market outside Cap, where Maroons flocked to sell provisions and coffee, thus greatly alleviating the penury of food in the city.[10] By the summer of 1803, Rochambeau's chief of staff was pleased to note that "Congo" allies served as scouts in the army and "fight loyally and courageously in our ranks."[11] That they continued to do so until the very end of French rule was testament to the intensity of class warfare within the black population.

∼

Dessalines' success against Sans Souci left him free to focus his attention on the isolated and restive southern province. Traditionally respectful of French authority, mixed-race southern planters had rejected Louverture's calls to arms after the French landing; even the cultivators had proven remarkably quiescent. Given Dessalines' infamous record during the War of the South, only flagrant political errors on France's part could possibly push southerners into Dessalines' arms—which is exactly what happened. Leclerc's rash decision to deport Rigaud in the spring of 1802 had been most impolitic, but his lack of finesse paled in comparison with that of Rochambeau and his minions, whose greed, cruelty, and bigotry never yielded to the obvious necessity of conciliating natural allies.

The most striking incident was a bizarre ball organized by Rochambeau in March 1803 that stands out even by the war's peculiar standards. After he moved his headquarters to Port Républicain, Rochambeau threw a party for local notables that unfolded normally until, at the stroke of midnight, women of color were led to a nearby room, dimly lit and draped in black. Four coffins had been laid out, each topped with a human skull, while funeral chants added to the macabre atmosphere. Rochambeau relished the women's terror for a few moments, then informed them that they had just attended the funeral of their loved ones (who, depending on the sources, were actually in the coffin or were executed the following day).[12] When Rochambeau later returned to Cap, he also reinstituted racial segregation in theaters.[13]

Some French officers, most notoriously Louis d'Arbois in Jérémie and Berger in Cayes, enthusiastically embraced his racial agenda, while those who objected were silenced or exiled.[14] Within a month of taking over, Rochambeau sent back to France Charles Desbureaux, the French commander of the south and a moderate who employed people of color and refused to engage in indiscriminate massacres.[15] The black general and former Maroon Jean-Joseph Laplume, who had served France faithfully since the landings of February 1802, initially replaced him, but his rank and long record of service were no protection against the growing swell of intolerance. Rochambeau first ordered that no officer of color be allowed into the colony, then, in March 1803, announced that all positions of authority in the southern province would henceforth be held by white officers only. "It is high time the white color dominates everywhere," his chief of staff wrote.[16] Laplume was exiled in May 1803, his departure further dividing southern Saint-Domingue into two unbridgeable camps, with whites dangerously isolated on one side of a yawning racial chasm. Napoléon Bonaparte must have disagreed with such dangerous racial policies, because he treated Laplume honorably and awarded his widow and nine children a generous pension when Laplume died in Cádiz shortly after his arrival.[17]

Rochambeau's antipathy led to fears among the mixed-race population that his ultimate intention was to kill them all, an allegation largely founded in fact.[18] "The white color is now waging a war against the two others and the colony needs to <u>molt</u>," Rochambeau explained to Denis Decrès. "Otherwise we would need to wage a new war every two or three years. Maybe my ideas are not popular in France and the government finds them too extreme. But I am on the scene, I am used to this horrid colony, and my plan is the only one that can take it safely to port."[19] "Molting" (*faire peau neuve*) was an interesting expression, which according to Rochambeau's chief of staff meant that it would be necessary to kill "all negroes, negresses, and men and women of color above the age of ten."[20] The plan would have brought the colony back to the most sorrowful days of Leclerc's rule, but Decrès' opposition and a lack of troops forced Rochambeau to put his plans on hold, and for the time being he limited himself to persecuting or deporting a few prominent people of color.[21]

Officially, hostility between white and mixed-race colonists stemmed from the latter's origin as "the children of debauchery" (Rochambeau ipse dixit), but racial slurs and accusations of bastardry were often an excuse to wage economic war against a rival class of landowners.[22] Upon taking office, Rochambeau announced his intention to confiscate the plantations of rebel officers, after which his officers and administrators jockeyed for an opportunity to lease sequestered plantations.[23] But the best preserved estates were located in the south, where they had been leased to officers of color still serving on the French side. An administrator warned Rochambeau that canceling such leases would "particularly affect men of color, a number of whom are still loyal to our cause," but the lure of quick riches proved hard to resist.[24] In a typical case a mixed-race brigadier chief, Nérette, was accused of advocating a revolutionary agenda after he was seen wearing a red scarf around his head. The scarf turned out to be a home remedy against a bad toothache, but the French officer reporting the incident nevertheless recommended that he be dismissed from his command. The fact that Nérette owned a remarkable three sugar and four coffee plantations near St. Louis was probably the root cause of his sudden disgrace.[25] After learning that the commander of Jacmel, Dieudonné Jambon, also leased seven plantations, Rochambeau launched an ambitious survey of all land titles to identify colored officers who operated a plantation without valid property titles.[26]

In an intriguing form of a reverse Oedipus complex, mixed-race Dominguians had long rejected the black ancestry of their mothers while emulating their white fathers, particularly in the south where most white and colored families shared time-honored ties. The exactions of Rochambeau and his acolytes thus struck the *anciens libres* as an incomprehensible rejection of their innate Frenchness. "I must have been confused with our common enemies," a battalion chief complained after being sent to a prison ship in Cap. He was a mixed-race officer who had served in Europe and surely could not be assimilated "with a race so alien to our principles and so different from our skin color," he wrote in reference to the black rebels.[27]

And yet for all their reluctance to part with the *belle France,* mixed-race individuals found no other option but to defect when their wives were sexually abused, their assets seized, and loyal officers executed on the flimsiest evidence. After d'Arbois drowned Bardet, a mixed-race Francophile who had helped the French secure Fort Bizoton during the landing in Port Républic-ain, his brethren in Petit Trou deserted the French army en masse. In Cayes, another drowning incident pushed the mixed-race officer and rich planta-tion owner Jean-Louis Férou into the rebel ranks, when his natural inclina-tion would have been to support the colonial order.[28] As French exactions multiplied, so did defections (including a major plot in Port Républicain in January 1803), which in turn justified another round of summary execu-tions.[29] As rumors that Rochambeau planned to exterminate the mixed-race population gained credibility, many southerners came to a stunning conclu-sion: they might be better off under Dessalines.

Dessalines, his reputation as an advocate of black domination notwith-standing, was a practical man who employed mixed-race individuals like the southern planter Louis Boisrond-Tonnerre in his inner circle. Eager to bring the *anciens libres* into the rebel fold, he cleverly fanned their fears by claiming in a proclamation that Leclerc had once showed him a French plan to "slaughter all the mulattoes, even nursing infants."[30] He then delegated the actual task of spreading the revolt in the south to the mixed-race officer Nicolas Geffrard, a native of Cayes and a man with great military skills (he had once made a living as a wild boar hunter). He, like Guy Bonnet, was a former supporter of Rigaud, but while hiding together during the October 1802 massacres in Cap, they had witnessed enough atrocities to reject France for good. Geffrard headed south to unite the various rebel groups operating in the area, while Bonnet became his liaison to Dessalines.[31] His mission of reconciliation succeeded beyond anyone's expectations, and in January 1803 a black southerner composed a rebel song to trumpet the new alliance to the French enemy.[32]

Et bien, ces mulâtres	So, these mulattoes
Dits lâches autrefois	You once called cowards
Savent-ils se battrent	Don't they know how to fight
Campés dans les bois?	Entrenched in the woods?
Brave Dessalines	Brave Dessalines
Dieu conduit tes pas.	God leads your actions.
Geffrard en droite ligne	The straight-shooting Geffrard
Ne te quittera pas.	Will not abandon you.

By the time Geffrard recruited Férou in March 1803, he had brought most notable commanders in the southern region, including some Maroon lead-ers, under single leadership. Geffrard met various setbacks when attacking French-held towns given the rebels' limitations in siege warfare, but his mere presence encouraged France's colored allies to defect, and he wreaked havoc in the once-quiet southern countryside. His crowning achievement was the failure of Rochambeau's May 1803 southern campaign, which gave proof, if any was needed, that he had been most imprudent in adding yet another group to the long list of his enemies.[33]

~

Dessalines' southern strategy unfolded in parallel with simultaneous efforts to gain control of the western province. His main rival in the area was Lamour Derance, a Maroon leader with extensive support among the black masses. The rebel-Maroon feud was partly a clash of personal ambitions, since both Derance and Dessalines ambitioned to become general in chief of all rebel forces. But it also reflected a genuine cultural divide between Dessalines' professional forces and a Maroon "army" composed of loosely coordinated bands grouped according to African tribal affiliations.[34] Dessalines had served as Louverture's inspector of cultivation in the western province, and he struggled to rival Derance's (or even France's) popularity among the black rank and file. Most cultivators of the plain of Cul de Sac rejected his calls to revolt, and as late as May three to four thousand black women were heading to the markets of French-held Port Républicain each Sunday with cartfuls of poultry and provisions.[35]

Just as he had with Louverture, Leclerc, and Sans Souci, Dessalines proceeded cautiously and deceptively. He initially recognized Derance as his military superior, and in February their allied forces collaborated in a joint attack on Jacmel. Meanwhile, behind the scenes, he prepared to overthrow Derance by wielding the carrot and the stick.[36] In the Cul de Sac, he staged raids to force hesitant cultivators to join the rebel side while also funding popular *bamboulas* (night-long dances). When the most openly hostile of Derance's lieutenants, the commander of Arcahaye, refused to assist him during an assault on Saint-Marc, Dessalines attacked him and gave his command to his ally Alexandre Pétion. The show of force was then followed by a round of diplomacy aimed at Derance's other subordinates, and in May 1803 commanders from all corners of the western and southern provinces (except Derance) congregated in Arcahaye. Given the secrecy surrounding the Arcahaye conference, frustratingly little is known of the important negotiations that unfolded there, but Dessalines must have been convincing because the assembled leaders unanimously recognized him as supreme commander. They also agreed to keep their defection secret from Derance for now.[37] To seal the newfound alliance, Dessalines staged a flurry of attacks from Léogane to Mirebalais and sent two columns (dubbed "*infernales*" after the Vendée uprising) to destroy everything of value in the Cul de Sac, the last area of the colony still producing tropical goods now that Geffrard had ravaged the south.[38] "Coupez têtes! Brûlez cases!" was his motto ("Cut off heads! Burn houses!").[39]

Rochambeau's southern offensive, launched around the same time, indirectly helped Dessalines since the campaign's sole achievement was the capture of the Maroon stronghold of Maniel. Defeating a group that had lived in virtual independence for one hundred years was a notable achievement, but the Maniel Maroons supported Derance (who used their camp as an ammunitions depot and a shelter of last resort), and the French victory could not have come at a better time for Dessalines.[40] Derance was now weak and isolated; all that was needed was for a trap to be set.

By July 1803, Geffrard's own efforts at unity had been successful enough for Dessalines to visit the south for the first time since Rigaud's defeat. The significance of the *anciens libres'* turnabout cannot be overestimated. The War of the South had been Saint-Domingue's Civil War, and to embrace Dessalines' party was as momentous a move for a mixed-race southerner as it would have been for a Georgian planter to vote for a black Republican three years after Sherman's March. The local population remained suspicious, but Dessalines came with a bevy of promotions, and the mood in Camp Gérard, where the gathering took place, was celebratory. Dessalines confirmed Geffrard as commander in chief of the rebel forces in the south and promoted him to division general to reward him for his political and military successes. Férou and a few others were made brigadier generals and commanders of the yet-to-be-conquered coastal towns. Dessalines also incorporated three Maroon groups into a new colonial demi-brigade led by the Maroon leader—and now colonel—Gilles Benech.[41]

Probably informed of the rebel gathering, the French commander of Jérémie begged Férou to return to the French fold, warning that Dessalines, "once your executioner . . . keeps the heart of a tiger and dreams of tearing you to pieces."[42] Given d'Arbois' many previous crimes in the area, the appeal failed to sway Férou, and it was Dessalines who drafted the response in a lively prose probably penned by his secretary, Boisrond. The letter made a vivid description of "cities turned into forests of scaffolds" and "ships ringing with the wail of the victims held inside" to explain Férou's decision to defect. Then, in a passage that nicely summarized the filial dilemma at the heart of their experience, it concluded that mixed-race individuals had finally understood how their woes had come "from those you call their fathers, and that more natural links connect them to their mothers."[43] Oedipus was king again.

Getting back to the immediate business of the rebel gathering at Camp Gérard, Dessalines switched from French to Kreyol to address the assembled throngs. Well aware of his unpopularity in the region, he assured his audience that "if I blindly followed Louverture during the civil war, it is because I thought that his cause was liberty. . . . Brothers, let's forget the past, let's forget these horrific times, when deceived by the French we fought one another." According to the account, the crowd yelled back "war to the death against the whites," and unity was sealed on the altar of a common hatred for Louverture and, allegedly, the white race.[44]

The successful meeting in Camp Gérard convinced Dessalines that it was now time to finish off the last of his domestic rivals. In typically Machiavellian fashion, he offered the leadership of all rebel forces in the western province to an overly trusting Derance, who headed for the plain of Cul de Sac to claim his command. A trap was awaiting him. The unit he had come to review was actually under orders to capture him, and Derance's career, like Louverture's and Sans Souci's, ended with a rather inglorious, but very effective, breach of the officer code of honor. Derance's death in captivity further sullied the entire episode, but for Dessalines the ends justified the means.[45] Nine months after leaving the French army, he had fathered a rebel army united under a single leadership: his own.

~

The task facing Dessalines as he shifted his attention from internal unity to the war against France seemed insurmountable: defeating the Napoleonic army, a feat that would take a series of Europe-wide coalitions another eleven years to accomplish. His first order of the day was to give some semblance of military posture to the disparate rebel units, whose courage was undisputed but whose marksmanship and field tactics left much to be desired. The defection of most colonial demi-brigades in the fall of 1802 brought a core of veteran troops to the rebel side, along with a cadre of officers with a decade or more of military experience. Within days French reports noted that rebel attacks now involved former soldiers "fighting with order" in addition to the usual retinue of rampaging cultivators.[46] Over the following months, Dessalines equipped Maroon groups once loyal to Sans Souci and Derance with guns and pikes, drilled them regularly, and by the spring of 1803 Rochambeau's chief of staff estimated that armed cultivators were militarily equivalent to regular troops. Using a page from the Maroons' book, Dessalines also built mountain redoubts in case Bonaparte sent another expedition and the rebels were once again pushed on the defensive.[47]

The rebel army combined the best of European-style field tactics with the guerrilla methods that had proven their worth during the revolution. Arson and raids ravaged rural areas, making the French financial plight desperate by June 1803. Capturing coastal French towns proved more elusive, but in their attacks the rebels displayed an increasingly elaborate grasp of field tactics. After French artillery forced the rebels to fall back during a February 4 attack on Cap, the French unleashed their cavalry on the retreating forces. Carnage would normally have ensued, but the rebel infantry formed into squares, an effective countermeasure that required great coordination on the part of the troops (Bonaparte had won the Battle of the Pyramids in that manner). During another attack in Jacmel, the rebels brought with them ladders and ox hides to get past the palisades and thorny bushes circling the town. The attack failed, but clearly the rebel army was a far cry from the slaves who in 1791 had thrown themselves headlong on artillery pieces in the belief that one could stop cannonballs with talismans.[48]

Leclerc's war of "extermination" and Rochambeau's "molting" plan failed to eradicate Saint-Domingue's large population of color, but they further dented the number of adult males, and finding enough able-bodied soldiers was becoming a veritable issue for Dessalines by 1803.[49] The shortage gave growing importance to female combatants, who were eager to serve because the twin threats facing the population of color—genocide and slavery—affected them as much as anyone else. Some female cultivators, holding their child by the legs for emphasis, told a French officer that they "would prefer to dismember their infant than see him enslaved."[50] Even children, a Spanish visitor wrote in horror, "amuse themselves by injuring dead or expiring whites with their little sabers."[51] Staying aloof from a conflict that knew no precise front line would have been difficult anyway: in Jacmel, four women of color were captured as they fled the city to reunite with their husbands, while others who stayed behind were executed in retaliation for their husbands' desertion.[52]

Women fought in person when mountain strongholds were attacked, but the main rebel columns were predominantly male and women usually served in ways that reflected their place in the colony's social and sexual spheres. As under Louverture, they dominated the field of logistics, grew food, and carried supplies, ammunition, and heavy guns; Claire-Heureuse Dessalines even owned a barge to trade salt along the coast. Female market sellers were noted smugglers of war contraband and traded food and sex with French soldiers in exchange for ammunition, which they hid underneath their skirts as they returned to the countryside to fetch more provisions.[53] These countless suppliers remained anonymous, only achieving some form of collective recognition in the semimythical character of Défilée (a.k.a. Dédée Bazile), who according to Haitian folklore was a *vivandière* (quartermaster) in Dessalines' army. Another popular figure, the Vodou spirit Marinèt Bwa-Chèche, originated as a female soldier who allegedly fought by Dessalines' side.[54]

As market sellers, prostitutes, and nurses, women of color had unparalleled access to French camps; the French even used them as messengers when negotiating with rebels.[55] Women navigating the porous border between the

French and the rebel worlds were thus also active in the fields of sabotage and espionage, which became crucial as the war shifted to a series of inconclusive sieges. Intelligence provided by female spies on conditions inside French towns was particularly useful as it helped the rebels attack in the midst of an outbreak of disease or target posts weakened by desertion.[56]

Well aware that the multiracial, multinational, politically fractious coastal towns teemed with rebel sympathizers, the French developed a set of countermeasures, most of them aimed specifically at women of color. Hospitals were first asked to isolate nurses; Rochambeau then ordered all women of color to justify why they resided in French towns or face being sent to prison.[57] As Cap faced several rebel attacks in February 1803, an order went out to "force all women back in their houses, especially *négresses*," followed two weeks later by a thorough search of the "petite Guinée" (the black quarter) that led to the arrest of several black women.[58]

Equal-opportunity access to the revolutionary struggle also meant equality in death. In a typical case, Henriette, a mixed-race woman from Cap who had tried to abscond to the rebels, was hanged at Place Cluny, the city's market square, as a warning to female market sellers.[59] The French also banned black dances for fear that Vodou rituals might serve as a cover for conspiracies, and the ensuing repression affected both priests (*houngans*) and priestesses (*mambos*). A *houngan* and a *mambo* were arrested in Cap for organizing a rite of possession and were hanged in their full regalia in an attempt to prove that Vodou talismans offered no protection. Other *mambos* were burned with their idols.[60]

In a break with Louverture's land-bound outlook, Dessalines increasingly brought the war to the seas as well. The rebels' main weapon was the barge, a small vessel that Rigaud had employed during the War of the South. Barges could be propelled by oars or sails, giving them a distinct edge when larger, ponderous merchantmen found themselves becalmed and defenseless near the coast. French crews were heavily reliant on prisoners of color of uncertain loyalty, and white captains found the barge attacks particularly unnerving. In one famous incident the merchant brig *Virginie* was attacked by seven rebel barges just as it reached Port Républicain in March 1803. With the wind in their favor, the rebels boldly pounced within sight of the city, whose population watched helplessly as the ship was overwhelmed and captured. The episode cost French commerce four hundred thousand francs and the lives of several of the ship's passengers, including two children.[61] This and similar incidents incited the commander of the Saint-Domingue station to make pressing requests in Paris and Kingston for small warships suited for coastal surveillance.[62] This flotilla scored some successes as it grew in size, but the resumption of the war with England soon brought an abrupt end to his efforts, and the barges remained a major threat to French cabotage until the end of the war of independence.

The most problematic issue facing Dessalines as his army grew in size was to provide it with the sinews of war. The disarmament campaign had barely dented the colony's plentiful stocks and a French report estimated that there were on average two guns for each rebel; but finding enough gunpowder and cartridges was difficult.[63] Colonial officers helped themselves from French arsenals as they defected, but these supplies did not last as Dessalines battled both France and his Maroon rivals and he soon faced acute supply problems. In the south, the troops of Geffrard and Férou were neither paid nor fed nor clad, and the cavalry of Geffrard used sabers made from barrel iron rings. Some rebels even fought with sticks and stones.[64]

Like Louverture before him, Dessalines turned to U.S. merchants, the most daring of whom visited areas of the west and south distant from the main French squadrons to exchange tropical crops like coffee for gunpowder, weapons, even prefabricated barges. The contraband trade was an open secret: the *Gazette of the United States* wrote that the French army was in desperate straights whereas "coffee and sugar were cheap on the coast and a pair of pistols or a musket would fetch two hundred weight of either from the blacks."[65] Smugglers included disenchanted Frenchmen like Joseph Bunel, for whom contraband took on the form of a personal vendetta after the cruel treatment Leclerc had inflicted on him and his wife. After being deported to France, Bunel headed to the United States, where he wrote to Dessalines that he had incited merchant friends in Baltimore to ship some supplies and that he was eager to do the same.[66]

Despite the peace of Amiens, British merchant and military ships also headed for Saint-Domingue, where the French often noticed newly manufactured British guns in rebel hands.[67] Their motives ranged from high politics to simple greed and racial loyalty. The commander of the Jamaican squadron, concluding that a protracted conflict would leave the French too overwhelmed to entertain any design on Jamaica, made no effort to prevent Jamaican smugglers from making the short run to southern Saint-Domingue. The captain of the corvette *Suriname* must have been motivated primarily by profit since he sold gunpowder to both the French and the rebels besieging them in Jacmel. John Perkins, the only mixed-race post captain in the British navy and a veteran of the Haitian Revolution's early years, also sold contraband in Tiburon.[68] By the spring of 1803, the French noted that the rebels used their guns unsparingly, a sure sign that they had solved their supply problems.[69] The French, besieged on land and soon to be blockaded by sea, could only wish that they could say the same.

∾

By placing most rebel groups under his command, Dessalines had composed an army; but he had not fashioned them into a nation. For this, his people needed shared aspirations and common symbols, starting with the one object that had come to symbolize a country in the modern age, a flag.

The circumstances in which the Haitian flag first appeared are a matter of great importance to Haitians, who commemorate its creation each year on Flag Day (May 18), and the story has been told and retold countless times, each time with an added layer of fanciful details. According to the original version, which appeared in the nineteenth-century accounts of Thomas Madiou and Beaubrun Ardouin, the rebels initially kept their tricolor flags after defecting from the French army, publicizing their enmity simply by tearing off all regimental insignia. But after Pétion lost a flag in a December 1802 fight, the French used the fact that it was a tricolor as proof that the rebels did not want independence. Pétion urged Dessalines to provide a more fitting symbol for the rebel army, and in a dramatic gesture Dessalines cut the French tricolor in half with his saber, creating the blue-and-red flag that is still Haiti's today.[70]

Successive generations of historians embellished the story for nationalistic purposes. In 1850 the Haitian historian Saint-Rémy situated Dessalines' dramatic swashbuckling at the May 1803 Arcahaye conference (instead of three months earlier in previous accounts), thus transforming a rather mundane meeting with Maroon leaders from the west and south into an epic, foundational moment in Haitian history. Details later emerged about Catherine Flon, a Haitian Betsy Ross who sewed the torn strips of the French tricolor back together, and about the Vodou trance that had overwhelmed Dessalines as he performed his dramatic act. Madiou had briefly mentioned that a rebel captain named Laporte had been attacked as he sailed back from the Arcahaye conference, but new and improved versions specified that Laporte had chosen to scuttle his barge rather than surrender the newly created flag to the French enemy.[71] Although largely apocryphal, the story of Laporte's heroic death was enough to convince Hamilton Killick, the captain of the Haitian warship *Crête-à-Pierrot,* to wrap himself in the Haitian flag and go down with his ship when he was cornered by a German gunboat in 1902.[72]

Situating the creation of the flag at the Arcahaye conference served an important purpose in fostering racial unity. In colonial Saint-Domingue, where mixed-race individuals were sometimes known as *rouges,* the French tricolor's blue, white, and red had been reinterpreted as a metaphor for the colony's three main racial groups.[73] To Haitians, the birth of the bicolor flag thus paralleled the process by which *noirs* and *rouges,* no longer kept apart by the *blancs,* finally came together as one. For more than a century, the blue and red flag, complete with the inscription "l'union fait la force" (unity is strength), signified racial amity in a country too often divided by the subtle color gradations of one's skin.

The growth of the black nationalist movement known as *noirisme* in the twentieth century brought renewed scholarly attention to the creation of the Haitian flag, but it also turned a symbol of unity into a deeply divisive issue. In 1953 an explosive article appeared in the Port-au-Prince daily *Le Nouvelliste* that accused Madiou of having willfully misrepresented one crucial episode of the Arcahaye conference. Madiou had quoted a French naval report in a way that implied that the flag flying on Laporte's barge was blue and red. But the original source, it turned out, clearly described the flag as *black* and red. The falsification was highly significant, because after independence the (black) Dessalines had used a black-and-red flag, while his successor the (mixed-race) Pétion had adopted a blue-and-red flag. By misrepresenting the color of the flag that had flown at the Arcahaye conference, nineteenth-century (mixed-race) historians had brought legitimacy to Pétion's version of the flag, a lie that the (black) historians of the *noiriste* movement were eager to expose.[74] When François Duvalier (a.k.a. Papa Doc) won the presidency as a *noiriste* intellectual in 1957, he immediately adopted Dessalines' black-and-red flag to emphasize the role played by black generals in the Haitian Revolution. Duvalierist historians dutifully went to work trying to prove that Dessalines had created the flag without Pétion's input (allegedly with cloth cut from his daughters' dresses) and that all rebel flags were black and red.[75]

The black-and-red flag, now associated with the Duvalierist dictatorship, was abandoned with the fall of Papa Doc's son in 1986. The blue-and-red flag returned as Haiti's official flag, its two strips arranged horizontally so that no color could claim precedence by being nearer the pole, and new historical studies appeared to prove that the flag created at the Arcahaye conference had been blue and red after all. The central argument of the postrevisionist school was that the French captain who had sunk Laporte's barge had mistaken the flag's blue for black because the cloth was wet.[76]

Actual archival research paints a much blurrier picture. Contemporaries mentioned multiple iterations of the flag, many of them black and red (such as Laporte's), but some of them blue and red, white and blue (a secret code to Jamaican smugglers), red (to signify that no quarter would be given), and even—gasp—blue, white, and red.[77] Both the blue-and-red and the black-and-red flags were seen months before the Arcahaye conference, thus proving that no flag-making session took place there. As a general rule, Napoleonic officers were uninterested in the circumstances surrounding the creation of the symbols of Haitian nationhood, so mentions of the flag in contemporary documents were cursory and every additional detail, from Catherine Flon to Dessalines' daughters, is scurrilous.

These various controversies may seem pointless to a foreign audience, but symbols are central to a nation's sense of self, and the appearance of the Haitian flag does say something about the goals of the Dominguian rebels in the winter and spring of 1803. Unfortunately for patriotic Haitians, the lesson to be drawn from rebel insignia is that, far from defining themselves as enemies of France and the whites, they drew much of their symbolism and political agenda from revolutionary France itself.

The obvious, but often unmentioned, fact about the early Haitian flags is that they were all based on the French tricolor. Many rebels had once fought for England and Spain and now obtained their weapons from Jamaican and U.S. merchants, but using a modified Union Jack, Star Spangled Banner, or *rojigualda* never crossed anyone's mind, most likely because every foreign flag floating in the Caribbean was that of a slave-owning power. The French tricolor had come to represent the abolition of slavery after the emancipation law of 1794 and was revered for that reason; Bonaparte had even asked that regimental flags bear the sentence "brave blacks, remember that only France recognizes your liberty and equality" as a constant reminder that the tricolor stood for freedom.[78] For the rebels of 1803, the French tricolor was thus an apt symbol of their attachment to the revolutionary heritage, especially as they fought an aristocratic Rochambeau widely suspected of planning to bring the colony back to the days of the ancien régime.

The French captain's oft-cited report on the destruction of Laporte's barge also noted that the flag bore the inscription "libre ou mourir" (live free or die), which in the slightly modified version "la liberté ou la mort" (liberty or death) eventually became Dessalines' own motto.[79] Earlier rebels in revolutionary Saint-Domingue and Guadeloupe had used similar slogans, but these were hardly specific to slave revolts. Different versions of the same motto were commonly heard and seen in France and the United States during these countries' revolutions (starting with Patrick Henry's "give me liberty or give me death"), so the rebels' motto defined them as members of a Euro-American revolutionary tradition, not as anti-Western zealots.[80]

Another important symbol that now occupies the center of the Haitian flag is the country's coat of arms, which consists of an array of flags, cannon, and assorted military paraphernalia arranged symmetrically around a palm tree bearing a *bonnet phrygien* (liberty cap). In an attempt to put an Afro-Caribbean stamp on the design, some authors have traced its origins to the *vévé* (Vodou symbol) of the war spirit Ogou Feray, who is often associated with Dessalines, but the resemblance is far from striking. An alternate theory involving the phallic symbolism of the soaring tree is even less convincing. Other authors attribute the design to the beginning of Pétion's presidency in 1807, but it is in fact much older.[81]

Versions of the Haitian coat of arms actually appeared as early as 1790, and its main components are easily recognizable as standard Western allegories of liberty. The liberty cap at the focal point of the assemblage was worn by French revolutionaries (and, before them, Roman freedmen) to symbolize their emancipation from tyranny. Such a cap still graces Marianne's bust in thirty-six thousand French town halls today—as well as the seal of the U.S. Department of the Army, created in 1778. In the Franco-American pictorial tradition, the liberty cap usually appeared atop a liberty pole held by a Lady Liberty clad in classical garb. The triptych woman-pole-hat appeared on letterheads and coins used by Louverture, Pétion, and Christophe before and after independence, showing yet again the continuity in political imagery.[82]

The rest of the coat of arms is nearly identical to the letterhead of the French general Pierre Quantin, who was Dessalines' direct superior before his defection, so ironically Haiti's coat of arms most likely originated with a French general who had come with the Leclerc expedition.[83] The only notable difference between Quantin's letterhead and the current design is that freedom is now symbolized by a palm tree instead of a white woman. But planting trees of liberty had been a popular tradition at revolutionary festivals in France and Saint-Domingue, so this slight modification changes nothing of the fact that the Haitian coat of arms references multiple emblems of liberty used throughout the Atlantic world.

The rebels' embrace of French symbolism may seem incoherent for an army that was months away from bringing Haiti to independence. But the rebels were actually hesitant to reject a France that had brought emancipation as well as massacres and they did not immediately embrace formal independence as their objective. By borrowing freely from the French revolutionary tradition, rebel heraldry indicated that the rebels fought against a French army that had distanced itself from its revolutionary heritage, not France per se, and that their main wish was to retain the most important right they had acquired as French citizens: freedom.

The symbolism of the rebel insignia was further clarified by the rebels' speeches and letters in which they explained time and again—in elegant metropolitan French, not Kreyol or an African language—that they fought to preserve the French law of emancipation. Dessalines cited documents showing Rochambeau's support for slavery to justify the rebellion, and rebel officers regularly asked their men to take an oath to die rather than suffer being reenslaved.[84] Noting that the French tricolor flew at such ceremonies, a French noble concluded that the rebels were inspired by "these sentiments that are no longer fashionable with us, but that used to exalt us during the Revolution."[85] A French espionage report drafted on the eve of the Arcahaye conference similarly reported that a French naval bombardment had "hurt the rebels a lot, but they say that they do not mind, because they are willing to fight until extinction to preserve their freedom."[86]

Haitian authors often assume that black leaders began advocating independence during Louverture's heyday in 1801, or at the very latest when they defected from the French army in October 1802, but the rebels' rhetoric shows that it took many more months before they embraced that goal. When in October 1802 Dessalines wrote a letter to explain his decision to defect, he did not express any desire to declare independence, and instead emphasized that "I am French, a friend of my country and liberty."[87] During the French evacuation of Fort Liberté that same month, the rebel officer Toussaint Brave explained that he took over the town in the name of the French Republic (temporarily led astray, in his view, by the planter lobby).[88] "I have no doubt that the French *grande nation* will approve our decision" to rebel, Pierre Cangé also wrote. "We are not brigands, contrary to what our enemies the aristocrats pretend. . . . We are not waging a war to the death against whites as Rochambeau's faction claims, but a war of resistance against his oppression."[89] The rebels do not "consider themselves rebels at all," marveled a Polish officer. "They fight under the French colors and in the name of the French Republic. They accuse us of being rebels who desire the overthrow of the Republic; they proclaim us *émigrés* [counterrevolutionaries] and bandits."[90] "The French should be the ones who are called slaves!" boasted Dessalines. "They vanquished, only to cease being free."[91]

It took several months for the rebellion, which had begun with Dessalines' "I am French," to evolve into a genuine movement for national independence. Among the prisoners taken when Laporte's barge was sunk in May 1803 was an African-born sailor named Jean-Pierre. The interrogation report noted that "Dessalines was willing to make arrangements with us, but that Christophe was opposed, saying that we would always deceive them, and that we should fight until the French reembarked."[92] This fascinating document, which offers a rare window into the mind-set of the black rank and file, indicates that the Arcahaye conference had not been the place for virulent flag waving and weaving, but for a conversation on whether the rebels ought to sever all ties with France. Even more surprisingly, it suggests that Dessalines, the father of Haitian independence, was still hesitating at this late stage, twelve years into the revolution and six months before the rebel victory.

Independence only became the rebels' official goal in the summer and fall of 1803. By that point, it must have become clear that Bonaparte would never recall Rochambeau and that the French government tacitly supported his reactionary views. War with England also resumed, so the odds of a rebel victory improved markedly, and what had once seemed a radical, potentially suicidal idea now seemed within reach. Geffrard made references to "independence" during negotiations with the governors of Jamaica and Cuba in August, and that month Dessalines explained to a British admiral that "we would all prefer to die of a thousand tortures than bear the odious name of Frenchmen."[93] Even then, old habits died hard. After declaring independence in January 1804, an apparently distracted Dessalines awarded himself the title of "governor general" as if Saint-Domingue were still a French colony.[94]

~

The rebels' revolutionary agenda, loudly proclaimed in speeches, banners, songs, and letters, was well known to their French opponents, who listened in befuddlement as rebel forces attacked Jacmel to the sound of "onward, army of Moreau, onward!" in reference to the republican general Jean Moreau.[95] Despite the growing racial antagonism that marked the reign of Rochambeau, many soldiers fighting on the French and rebel sides were thus united by a common set of liberal political ideals. In Cap, French soldiers came close to overt mutiny when they threw down their arms and refused to risk their lives with the "colonial party" after fighting all over Europe "for the liberty of all men."[96] The veterans of Moreau's Army of the Rhine viewed Bonaparte and Rochambeau's embrace of right-wing causes with particular alarm. After going through the costly spring campaign and the ensuing epidemic, they had suffered staggering attrition rates and had become convinced that the expedition had been one vast conspiracy on Bonaparte's part to rid himself of his liberal critics.[97]

Aware of the political divide pitting republican soldiers against reactionary colonists, the rebels worked hard to enlist on their side not only Maroons and southerners but liberal whites as well. The "aristocrats" in Rochambeau's entourage "despise you, the *petits blancs,* as much as they despise us," Cangé warned the commander of Léogane, a white officer named Lacosse. "We recognize as comrades and brothers in arms all the whites who like liberty and equality. I promise them help and protection, and as proof of what I am telling you, you should know that several whites from Saint-Marc and Cap are with us, and the other day one fled from Port Républicain. . . . Long live liberty, equality, and General Moreau."[98] Cangé's appeal must have struck a chord, because in subsequent weeks Lacosse's superiors put him under close watch for fear that he might defect.[99]

Rumors of torture in rebel camps abounded, but the rebel army had a dire shortage of specialized troops and actually welcomed deserters with open arms. White workers manufactured cartridges; white gunners helped counteract the batteries defending French towns.[100] White converts could also be used to deceive French defenders already confused by the dizzying array of colored troops constantly switching sides. During an attack on Aquin, the rebel columns were led by uniformed whites and the garrison, thinking that the attackers were a friendly colonial unit under the command of white officers, opened the gates.[101]

Desertion eventually grew into a serious problem in the French army. Foreign units, whose commitment to Bonaparte's imperial project had always been wobbly, were particularly prone to it. Entire companies of the Polish demi-brigades left at once for the rebel army, where Dessalines nicknamed them the "negroes of Europe."[102] French officers also regularly spotted familiar faces in attacking rebel columns, and the rebels made frequent references to white Frenchmen who had joined the rebel cause.[103] Whites also collaborated with the rebels in Guadeloupe, where late in 1802 three whites loyal to revolutionary ideals masterminded the last major conspiracy against the French army.[104] Gabriel Véret, a French captain from Beauvais, joined the rebellion because he saw himself as "a soldier of liberty" and finished the revolution as an adjutant general in the rebel army.[105] Political idealism (along with lack of food) featured prominently in a letter sent by Corporal Alexandre Morand to his former unit in Bombarde, which was highly revealing of the average noncommissioned officer's general discontent. "I reached my destination safely and found the opposite of what I had been told," he wrote. "I found many of our comrades and came back to Bombarde specifically to let you know that we enjoy more freedom than in France and that we don't have to starve. . . . Don't listen to those who look down upon black troops and accuse them of massacring prisoners and deserters. I found that their army is well organized and disciplined and as for liberty they are less of a slave than we are."[106]

Morand's letter, in the approximate French spelling typical of his class, appeared below the heading "liberty, equality, or death" and epitomized the many similarities between French revolutionaries raised under the banner of "liberty, equality, fraternity" and a rebel army fighting for "liberty or death." The prevalence of desertion in French ranks also underlined that, as of early 1803, the war was as much about politics as it was about race and that it would have been possible for Bonaparte, even at this late stage, to find some common ground with the rebels by sharply disavowing Rochambeau's conduct. This Bonaparte chose not to do; in fact, after one year of military disasters in Saint-Domingue, he was about to abandon the colony to its fate altogether.

14

Echoes of Saint-Domingue

Louverture's Captivity and the Louisiana Purchase

In July 1802, the ship of the line *Le Héros* cast anchor in Brest after a twenty-five-day crossing from Cap. On board was the most famous of the Saint-Domingue exiles, Toussaint Louverture, whom Victoire Leclerc had deported on suspicions that he was planning to resume his rebellion. The voyage had been unpleasant for Louverture, who had been kept below decks with lowly sailors when such a prominent prisoner would normally have dined at the captain's table. His wife, Suzanne; sons Placide, Isaac, and Saint-Jean; and nieces Louise Chancy and Victorine Thusac had traveled on the same ship. However, it was not until Brest that, for the last time in his life, Louverture was allowed to see his family.[1] For a family man like Louverture, seeing loved ones in captivity was hard to bear, and he begged French authorities to spare his relatives as soon as he reached Brest. "If I faltered in my duty, I alone should be responsible for my conduct," he wrote Leclerc. "A fifty-three-year-old mother should deserve the indulgence of a generous and liberal nation," he wrote Napoléon Bonaparte.[2]

Leclerc had exiled Louverture without any evidence that could have formed the basis for a court-martial, so he spent the rest of the month in Brest as the government debated his fate. The Ministry of the Navy prepared a lengthy report outlining Louverture's disloyal conduct, but on Leclerc's advice Bonaparte concluded that a trial would only fan tensions in Saint-Domingue. Freeing Louverture was also out of the question, so he eventually decided that Louverture would simply be held prisoner without trial.[3]

Louverture's destination was the Fort de Joux in the Jura Mountains, an eastern location that lessened the risk of escape (most people tied to the colonial milieu lived in Paris or on the Atlantic seaboard). After what must have been a tearful adieu, Louverture left his family in Brest, his servant Mars Plaisir the only person allowed to follow him into captivity. Concerned that

Louverture might meet sympathizers on his way to prison, the minister of war specified that he would "leave Brest at night, travel in an enclosed carriage, never stop in a town of notable size," and speak to no one except his servant.[4] Many authors hold that Louverture slept at the Temple prison in downtown Paris, a stone's throw from Bonaparte's Tuileries Palace, but they must have mistaken him for another black captive as he never stopped in Paris.[5]

Locked inside his carriage as it sped through backcountry roads in the dead of night, Louverture did not see much of France until, one bright August day, the silhouette of the Fort de Joux finally rose in the distance. It was a medieval castle that had held many captives over its long history, most notably Berthe de Joux, who had spent the end of her life locked in a dungeon as punishment for cheating on her crusading husband. It was also a foreboding structure, with five successive layers of defenses, each gate closing behind Louverture like the lid of a tomb. He was held in the most protected area of the castle, a cell tucked behind the keep, his only opening to the world a small window that was made impassable by two sets of iron bars, bricks, wire netting, and storm shutters.[6] Aside from short visits to the next-door cell for his daily shave, Louverture never again crossed these doors alive.

For the once-mighty governor, the life of an impotent captive must have felt worse than death. Commanding was for him "an ecstasy, a need," his secretary had once noted. "For such a man, death must seem preferable to becoming a nobody. He said many times that he would rather sacrifice his own children than see his freedom taken away—and he loves them."[7] Being sequestered in the damp, dark cell, Louverture wrote in horror, felt like being "buried alive."[8]

Security was tight. The commander of the prison, Baïlle, assigned a squad of nineteen riflemen and officers to guard Louverture and instructed them to shoot unannounced visitors on sight. His work was closely supervised by the general commanding the region and the subprefect of Pontarlier, but even these security measures were not deemed enough: after hearing that two prisoners had managed to escape from Joux, the minister of war demanded that surveillance measures be doubled, and an apologetic Baïlle took away Louverture's knife and razor.[9] An officer then arrived from Paris with orders to confiscate Louverture's military uniform as well. He "refused, blamed the officer, and insulted him," remembered a guard. "Then all of a sudden he took off his jacket and threw it to the envoy, saying, 'here, take this to your master.'"[10]

Louverture's servant, Plaisir, fell victim to the new security measures.[11] He had been Louverture's last link to a bygone world, and a sense of loneliness overwhelmed the homesick prisoner during the melancholy months of fall. Even when Plaisir was still there, Louverture "often thought of death" and made "flattering speeches" about his wife and children, from whom he had received no news since they had parted ways in Brest.[12] After Plaisir's departure Louverture "spent most of his days looking through the small window," a guard noticed. "The poor man thought of his country, his children! He was devastated."[13] In September 1802, Louverture wrote to Suzanne of his "attachment to a wife I cherish" and urged his "children to behave well, with much wisdom and virtue. . . . I kiss you all tenderly." This was the last letter he ever sent his family.[14] Some books claim that Louverture was jailed next to his fellow Dominguians André Rigaud and Martial Besse, or even spent time with them, but they only reached Joux after his death and he never had any familiar company. Two other Caribbean exiles, Jean and Zamor Kina, did arrive in January 1803, but they were held on a different floor and it is unlikely that they ever met Louverture given the strict conditions under which they were kept.[15] Louverture, who had by then lost faith in the Catholic God and never asked for a priest while in captivity, was truly alone.

Baïlle's regimen was strict, but the more vexing regulations were directed by Paris, and he proved a humane jailer. He fed Louverture better than any other captive, gave him a generous daily allowance of two bottles of wine, and used his own funds to buy sugar for a man who, like all Creoles, had a sweet tooth. Baïlle also arranged for doctors from Pontarlier to make regular visits, provided Louverture with new clothes, and planned on giving him writing material and a secretary.[16] Forbidden from speaking to his guards, Louverture must have looked forward to Baïlle's daily visits and their freewheeling conversations on political matters. It was during one of these encounters that Louverture declared that he had "important" things to say to the French government.[17] Louverture probably meant that he wished to defend himself in person, but an ecstatic Bonaparte immediately sent his aide-de-camp, Marie-François Caffarelli, to the Fort de Joux to inquire about Louverture's secret "treasures," which Leclerc had never found.[18]

Caffarelli, a trusted aide whose Corsican siblings could be found throughout Bonaparte's administration, spent twelve days in Joux in frequent conversations with the prisoner. He expected Louverture to beg for forgiveness, but to his surprise he found a wily and combative man who managed to present his most questionable policies as good-faith attempts to further the interests of the metropolis. Even the disasters of the previous spring were other persons' fault, from the burning of Cap (Henri Christophe's mistake) to the outbreak of fighting (Leclerc's). Unable to force Louverture into a mea culpa, Caffarelli was no more successful when trying to get him to divulge the location of the family fortune.[19]

On September 27, a dejected Caffarelli prepared to return to Paris empty-handed except for a lengthy text that Louverture had dictated in preparation for Caffarelli's visit. The document is usually referred to as Louverture's memoirs (French *mémoires*), but the original manuscript actually bears the title *mémoire*, which in its singular form means "petition" or "memorandum" (in an accompanying letter, Louverture similarly described it as a "report").[20] Instead of a political testament or a tell-all insider account, one is thus left with a rather disappointing retelling of his recent behavior. Still hopeful that he would be brought to a court, Louverture never outlined his real views on such issues as slavery and independence, and instead carefully defended his conduct. In one passage he let out what sounded like genuine anger as he asked whether "my body's color interfered with my honor and my bravery?" But these seemingly heartfelt words were borrowed from a French adaptation of Shakespeare's *Othello* that Louverture had probably seen in Cap and were just another act of political theater.[21] The last sentences of his memoir, penned in his own hesitant hand and phonetic spelling, sounded more sincere as he begged Bonaparte to please "make a decision regarding my future. . . . I depend entirely on your justice and fairness."[22]

Neither the memoir nor the accompanying letter nor Caffarelli's own report elicited a response from Bonaparte, probably because Louverture had insisted that he was "ruined," and thus useless; Bonaparte rarely ever mentioned Louverture thereafter. His curiosity briefly peaked again in November, when one of the Caffarelli brothers (Joseph, the prefect of Brest) heard of a black woman who had seen cash being hidden on one of Louverture's plantations after the French landing. But Bonaparte's men never found her, and his excitement was short-lived. The only other person, Denis Decrès concluded, who probably knew where Louverture's money was hidden was his wife, Suzanne, but to Decrès' credit he never pressured her into talking.[23]

After entrusting his memoir to Caffarelli, Louverture waited anxiously for the first consul to contact him. No reply came, and as weeks passed Louverture wrote ever more plaintive letters asking for a public trial. "I beg you in the name of God and humanity to look favorably upon my request," he wrote on October 9, for "I am now crowned with thorns and paid with ungratefulness. . . . I am not educated, I know little, but my father . . . showed me the path to virtue and honesty." A postscript also begged Caffarelli to please "remind [Bonaparte] of my demands."[24] No reply came. Late in October, after a month-long wait, Louverture asked Baïlle for a secretary so that he could add to the memoir he had submitted to Caffarelli.[25] His request was rejected; instead, word came from Paris that the government no longer wished to receive any more letters from Louverture and that his ink and paper should be confiscated.[26]

Louverture's hope that he would be judged or pardoned was tragically misplaced. Enraged by daily accounts of massive losses in Saint-Domingue,

Bonaparte had long since concluded that Louverture was a traitor and a murderer who should consider himself lucky to even be alive. Louverture "was responsible for the death of 25,000 Frenchmen," wrote the minister of war. "He is an eminently guilty man who must feel how clement the government is." "Louverture has no rights others than those required by humanity," concurred Decrès. "If I were you," counseled Donatien de Rochambeau, "I would sentence him to forced labor in Brest. If he ever comes back to Saint-Domingue, I will have him hanged without trial."[27]

As nothing but sullen silence came from Paris, Louverture returned to a life of boredom and sorrow, his daily routine punctuated by visits from a doctor and a surgeon who stopped by regularly to pull out bad teeth. Even these visits were canceled when a mysterious defrocked priest managed to enter Louverture's cell by pretending that he was a doctor, and Paris expressed renewed concerns about an escape.[28] As winter descended on the Jura Mountains, Louverture began to complain of constant cold, fevers, and aches, but Baïlle understood that his career was at stake and that humanity was no longer the order of the day. "Since a negro's composition is wholly different from that of a European," he explained halfheartedly to Decrès, "I dispensed from sending in the doctors, whose help would be useless in his case."[29]

At Decrès' insistence, Louverture's cell was thrown upside down after the last scare to find anything that might buy his freedom. After being threatened with a body search, Louverture had to give away a large sum of cash. His valuable watch was also taken, per Decrès' instructions, leaving him with "one of those wooden clocks, of the cheapest kind, that are enough to tell the time." Decrès also specified that Louverture could no longer be addressed as "general" and that his boasts should be answered with "the deepest scorn" and reminders of his crimes.[30]

The search was a humbling experience that finally broke Louverture's indomitable will. "I have never been as humiliated as I was today," he complained to Baïlle in a letter written after the soldiers had left his cell. He had at first insisted on a receipt and told Baïlle that he would need his valuables "when he left the prison," but on second thought he concluded that he would never be freed. "The day I am executed," he gloomily wrote to Baïlle, "you will give [my valuables] to my wife and children."[31] October 22, 1802, was the day Louverture finally understood that he would never leave Joux alive.

For two weeks thereafter, Louverture was very agitated in his conversations with Baïlle, stomping his feet and "saying the most indecent things about General Leclerc" (who was coincidentally drawing his last breath around the same time).[32] This was the period in which word came from Paris that the government no longer wished to receive any more letters and that all his papers should be taken away. Again threatened with a body search, Louverture handed over three letters he had hidden in his pants and that were the last reminders of his treacherous capture the previous June.[33] Sullen and despondent, he declared that it was too cold and refused to leave his bed.[34] All he had to do now was to wait for death to take him to Guinea.

～

Bonaparte would not suffer the agony of exile until 1814, but the fall and winter of 1802 were still trying times for him. Leclerc's morose letters reached him at regular intervals, each more pessimistic than the last, their content made even more worrisome by the knowledge that the situation in Saint-Domingue had probably worsened in the time it had taken the letter to cross the Atlantic.[35] To lose dozens of promising generals, many of them personal acquaintances, and dozens of thousands of France's finest troops was deplorable; even worse was the knowledge that his favorite sister lived at the epicenter of the epidemic.

The growing uproar over the expedition's human toll exposed Bonaparte as a loser and a liar, neither of which pleased a man used to having his name sung in praise. In an effort to stem popular discontent, the government had initially denied the existence of a major outbreak of yellow fever, but enough sailors had returned with distressing accounts that by the end of 1802 it became impossible to ignore reality any longer. The new propaganda policy consisted in acknowledging that an epidemic had indeed broken out, while refusing to give precise casualty figures to avoid frightening the public.[36] But attentive readers of the *Moniteur* could easily suspect the magnitude of the disaster by noting that for lack of men several demi-brigades had been merged into one.[37]

In the opening days of 1803, Bonaparte learned that his brother-in-law was no more and that Saint-Domingue might be lost at any time. "I think it would be superfluous to dwell at length on the unpleasant feelings stirred by the latest news," Decrès wrote to Rochambeau in the euphemistic style of the courtier.[38] "Damn sugar, damn coffee, damn colonies!" Bonaparte actually burst out.[39] The special envoys sent after Leclerc's death reached Paris in rapid succession in following weeks, and Bonaparte and Decrès spent much of January assessing France's situation in the first major policy review since the fall of 1801. They eventually decided to continue committing resources to the colony, but Bonaparte's patience had reached the end of its tether, and he insisted on strict cost-cutting measures.[40] "Use public monies with the utmost economy," admonished Decrès. "Saint-Domingue has cost an awful lot to the Republic."[41]

Due to the penury of transports and the fear of disease, the next large expedition was not scheduled to reach Saint-Domingue until August 1803, and the few stopgap units earmarked for immediate departure were meant as so many sacrificial victims.[42] Even foreigners were now deemed too good; Bonaparte assimilated colonial service to a disciplinary measure and sent deserters, draft resisters, and political enemies whose Caribbean exile was an intriguing counterpoint to the simultaneous deportation of Dominguian rebels to France.[43] These units' poor quality made for a staggering death rate. Of 1,333 members of the colonial depot who arrived in Cap early in 1803, 229 died en route and another 546 headed to the hospital immediately upon their arrival, leaving only 42 percent of the force apt for service before combat and fevers took their share.[44]

Nearer isles also brought their share of bad news. Bonaparte had grown ever more frustrated by England's refusal to evacuate Malta as specified in the peace of Amiens, and by the end of February 1803 he was concerned enough about a possible resumption of hostilities to begin assembling a small fleet in Dunkirk.[45] On March 12, he publicly told the British ambassador that it would be "Malta or war" in a calculated attempt to create an international sensation.[46] Bonaparte needed at least two years of peace to rebuild his navy and hoped that England would back down, but his last-minute offers were rejected and in May England again declared war. The peace of Amiens had barely lasted a year.

Oblivious to the latest developments in Europe, Rochambeau sent envoy after envoy in the spring of 1803 to petition Paris for troops. Leclerc's secretary, Jacques de Norvins, his plans for fortune frustrated, left for France in March, but the first consul looked at the skeletal survivor as an unwelcome reminder of his disastrous colonial venture and kept him at arm's length. Unable to secure the prominent jobs to which his friendship with Leclerc had led him to aspire, Norvins settled for a disappointing career as a middling bureaucrat.[47] Rochambeau next sent his chief of staff Pierre Boyer, who was more likely to have the first consul's ear since he had served under him in Egypt and had been unusually close to his sister Pauline. But a British squadron captured his frigate within sight of Brest, and Boyer headed for England and captivity (his trademark brutality never left him: his exactions during the Peninsular War and the French conquest of Algeria again earned him the nickname of "Pierre le cruel").[48] The young Armand de Vanssay followed in July 1803, but he does not seem to have even obtained an audience.[49] Rochambeau continued to make plans for new envoys into the fall of 1803, but clearly the first consul had already made up his mind.[50]

For Bonaparte, the resumption of hostilities with England sealed the expedition's fate. Cautious optimism had been the norm until early 1803, but "the declaration of war," an advisor wrote in May, "wiped away our last delusions."[51] Bonaparte whisked a few last reinforcements before England could establish a full blockade, but these were subpar men from the colonial

Table 7.
Last French and foreign units to reach Saint-Domingue (April–June 1803).

Name of unit	Date of arrival	Troops who survived the crossing	Port of departure	Ship
89th demi-brigade of the line (2nd battalion)	April 13, 1803	399	Dunkirk	*Nécessité*
Colonial depot	April 15, 1803	130		*Lucie*
20th demi-brigade of the line (detachment)	April 17, 1803	327	Toulon	*Charles Honoré*
2nd and 3rd centennial companies (colonial depot)	April 18, 1803	235	Dunkirk	*Malicieuse* *Torche*
Foreign battalion (detachment)	April 18, 1803	194	Havre	*Justine*
89th demi-brigade of the line (2nd and 3rd battalions)	May 11, 1803	782	Dunkirk	*Nielly* *Moselle*
4th centennial company (colonial depot)	May 11, 1803	100	Dunkirk	*Nielly*
3rd colonial depot	May 11, 1803	134	Nantes	*Endymion*
5th colonial depot	May 12, 1803	60	Bordeaux	*Deux Amis*
6th colonial depot	May 25, 1803	130	Marseille	*Trois cousines*
Depot from various corps	June 8, 1803	18		*Infatigable*
5th colonial depot	June 9, 1803	121	Bordeaux	*Aimable*

2nd colonial depot	June 9, 1803	188	Havre	*Théobald*
6th colonial depot	June 9, 1803	361	Marseille	*Comète*
2nd colonial depot	June 9, 1803	127	Havre	*Sally*
3rd colonial depot	June 9, 1803	76	Nantes	*Nécessaire*
3rd colonial depot	June 9, 1803	332	Havre	*Mars*
1st centennial company	June 9, 1803	83	Dunkirk	
6th colonial depot	June 23, 1803	227	Marseille	*Bonne Mère*
6th colonial depot	June 24, 1803	248	Marseille	*Auguste*

Total: 4,272

Source: Armée de Saint-Domingue, "État général des troupes arrivées dans la colonie" (ca. July 1803), CC9/B23, Archives Nationales, Paris.

depot and the last two ships to reach Saint-Domingue lost 165 out of 640 troops in the crossing, a death rate higher than on most slave ships.[52] Shocked to learn that the colony had borrowed forty-two million francs from foreign lenders, Bonaparte also denounced all bills of exchange issued in Saint-Domingue.[53] Thereafter, the expedition of Saint-Domingue, which had dominated the news in 1801–2, largely disappeared from the columns of the *Moniteur* and from Bonaparte's correspondence.[54] The army of Saint-Domingue was on its own.

⁓

The ebb and flow of France's colonial fortunes was closely followed in the United States, whose Western territorial ambitions hinged on the fate of the Saint-Domingue expedition.[55] As early as 1801 there had been rumors that Bonaparte was seeking the retrocession of Louisiana from Spain, but it was the massive expedition of Saint-Domingue that brought the matter to the fore. "Every eye in the U.S.," Thomas Jefferson noted two months later, "is now fixed on this affair of Louisiana."[56] New Orleans was the main commercial outlet for the rapidly growing frontier states; given Leclerc's abrupt treatment of U.S. merchants in Cap, many Westerners and New Englanders were openly clamoring for a preemptive invasion of Louisiana rather than let the powerful Bonaparte take such a strategic port from enfeebled Spain.

Eager to solve the crisis via diplomacy, Jefferson decided in April 1802 to send an envoy to Paris. For this mission crucial to U.S. national security, he selected a French national, Pierre Du Pont de Nemours, whose son Victor, ironically, was simultaneously raising funds for the army of Saint-Domingue. Du Pont's instructions were dual: warn Bonaparte that a French takeover of Louisiana would "cost France . . . a war which will annihilate her on the ocean" and instruct the U.S. ambassador in Paris, David Livingston, to buy "the island of New Orleans and the Floridas" as an alternative to war.[57]

Jefferson's skillful use of the carrot and the stick and willingness to stretch the limits of executive power have led many U.S. historians to cite the Louisiana Purchase as his signal diplomatic achievement.[58] The reality was quite different; Jefferson's various diplomatic overtures, which also involved the U.S. ambassador to England and the French ambassador to the United States, may have been adroit, but they completely failed to sway Bonaparte. Although he met the first consul, Du Pont could not convince him to abandon his plans to take over Louisiana. Livingston, who labored under the added burden of being deaf and speaking no French, was even less fortunate. For one whole year he petitioned, begged, cajoled, threatened, and even tried to bribe the Bonapartes, yet never managed to convince Minister of Foreign Affairs Charles de Talleyrand to discuss a potential sale, or even to acknowledge that France had obtained Louisiana from Spain in the first place. "With respect to Louisiana," Livingston wrote in March 1803 after a most frustrating year, "I fear nothing will be done here."[59] Louisiana changed hands a month later.

Louisiana was not as much purchased by Jefferson as it was sold by Bonaparte, who dictated the tempo of negotiations according to an agenda all his own. As was suspected in the United States, in October 1800 he had secretly obtained from Spain the territory of Western Louisiana, which he planned to incorporate into a grand American empire spanning from Guiana to the edge of Canada. By June 1802, with Guadeloupe, Martinique, and Guiana back under French control and Saint-Domingue nearly pacified, his imperial vision seemed within reach, and he ordered Decrès to "take possession of Louisiana with the shortest possible delay with a secret expedition seemingly directed on Saint-Domingue."[60] Jefferson and Livingston's inability to make any headway during that period is hardly surprising.

To Jefferson, the only silver lining in this vexing business was that the French could not take Louisiana until they controlled Saint-Domingue, which might take some time as "the conquest of St. Domingo [Saint-Domingue] will not be short work. . . . St. Domingo delays their taking possession of Louisiana, and they are in the last distress for money for current purposes."[61] His analysis of the situation was correct, for in the end the fate of Louisiana— and, ultimately, the United States' continental ambitions—hinged more on the Maroon rebellion raging in the hills of Saint-Domingue than on Livingston's fruitless petitions. As the situation in Saint-Domingue grew increasingly dire over the summer of 1802, thousands of troops earmarked for Louisiana were rerouted to Cap, while Decrès expressed his inability to find enough transports for New Orleans given the strain of multiple deployments.[62] Delayed time and again, the Louisiana expedition was not ready to sail until January 1803, by which point winter had set in and the fleet, moored in Holland, found itself icebound. By the time the seas thawed in March, tensions with England were such that the expedition was quietly shelved. "To the deadly climate of St. Domingo, and to the courage and obstinate resistance made by its black inhabitants," later wrote Alexander Hamilton, "we are indebted for the obstacles which delayed the colonization of Louisiana."[63]

Had Leclerc quickly pacified Saint-Domingue, a large Louisiana expedition would probably have sailed in 1802, possibly sparking a war between France and the United States and rewriting the history of these two nations. Instead, Bonaparte reevaluated the much-delayed retrocession in light of new international developments. In January and February 1803, came news of Leclerc's death. With March came the likelihood of a new war with England, which shattered his colonial ambitions and increased France's financial needs. Convinced that Louisiana would soon be lost to a U.S. or British invasion, and that Louisiana without Saint-Domingue was not worth having in the first place, Bonaparte decided to make the best of a bad situation and sell the colony before it could be conquered. France could not keep Louisiana when British ships "dominate those seas, and our affairs in Saint-Domingue worsen every day since Leclerc's death," Bonaparte explained to his secretary of the treasury, François Barbé-Marbois, for whom "the bloody events playing out in Saint-Domingue were closely connected to the history of the Louisiana Purchase."[64]

Bonaparte announced his decision to sell Louisiana to Decrès and Barbé-Marbois on Easter Sunday, April 10, 1803. The latest envoy sent by Jefferson to buy New Orleans, James Monroe, was still on his way to Paris and his arrival thus had little to do with Bonaparte's change of mind. Jefferson's instructions to Monroe were also largely irrelevant, since he had called for the purchase of New Orleans and the Floridas, when France did not control the latter and Bonaparte refused to sell the former on its own. On the eleventh, Talleyrand told a dumbfounded Livingston that Bonaparte's intention was to sell the whole of Western Louisiana, and after thinking the matter over Livingston and Monroe took it upon themselves to accept Bonaparte's unexpected offer.[65] They spent the next few weeks haggling over a specific price, finally agreeing on a sum of sixty million francs, payable with a fifteen-year bond, plus the cancellation of debts owed since the Quasi-War, or fifteen million dollars overall. The sum represented thirteen cents an acre, but making such calculations would have been impossible at the time since the actual borders of Louisiana were unknown; in fact, none of the men who bought and sold the colony had ever been there.

The money could not have come at a better time for Bonaparte, whose poorly funded treasury had been laid bare by the costly expedition of Saint-Domingue. Already reduced to demanding tax advances from private bankers at a ruinous 12 percent rate, Barbé-Marbois was now tasked with financing a major war with England.[66] Strapped for cash, he immediately sold the United States' Louisiana debt to foreign banking firms, which exchanged sixty million francs worth of long-term U.S. bonds for fifty-two million francs of short-term notes and pocketed a quick eight-million-franc fee. As always, money ran thicker than patriotism; one of the two banks involved in the transaction was Baring's of London, which had no qualms about financing Bonaparte's upcoming war against its own countrymen.[67]

∾

During the bitter winter months of 1803, as each hour ticked by interminably on the cheap wooden clock specified by Decrès, Louverture had more important matters on his mind than the fate of Louisiana; he was in a battle for his life. The Fort de Joux, which Bonaparte had selected because it was located far from coastal areas, also happened to be situated in the heart of the Jura Mountains, the coldest region in France, where the average January temperature, even today, hovers just below freezing. For the elderly Creole, raised in a year-round summer, life in his frigid, clammy cell must have felt like a stone-cold hell.

Betrayed by one of his disciples, accused of rebellion against the empire, Louverture endured a slow, painful agony that to one of his later admirers bore an eerie resemblance to Jesus' own.[68] The next station of the cross, in this religious metaphor, was the departure of Baïlle, the prison director with whom Louverture had maintained cordial relations, and his replacement by Amiot in January 1803.[69] Amiot's reports made no mention of freewheeling conversations with the famous captive; instead, he made constant visits and searches, often in the cold of night, to ensure that the dying Louverture was not plotting an escape.[70]

Louverture's health worsened with each passing month. His head hurt constantly, as did his stomach; he was also plagued by a dry cough that would not go away.[71] The return of spring might have breathed new life into his shivering body, but Louverture was destined never to see the end of a European winter. At 11:30 a.m. on April 7, 1803, as he entered Louverture's cell to deliver his daily food allowance, Amiot found him sitting by the fireplace, his head leaning on the mantle, immobile. Doctors called in from nearby Pontarlier pronounced him dead a few hours later. An autopsy revealed that his lungs had filled with blood and concluded that he had died of pneumonia and apoplexy (a catchall term for internal hemorrhaging).[72]

In later years, stories surfaced that on Bonaparte's orders Amiot had purposely left Louverture alone and foodless for four full days in a deliberate attempt to kill him off, or that he had even poisoned him. But contemporary documents make no mention of any such plot, and Bonaparte's denial ("what would I have gained from murdering this negro?") was probably sincere.[73] Deep in the midst of the Louisiana negotiations and the nascent war with England, Bonaparte had more important things to do than to plot the death of his fallen nemesis. After his dreams of treasure evaporated in late 1802, Bonaparte never again mentioned Louverture in his correspondence; not even his death warranted a passing remark. The simple and sad truth is that Louverture died forgotten, of cold, old age, and sorrow, a month before his estimated sixtieth birthday.

In subsequent days, Louverture's few belongings were auctioned off and his body buried in the fort's chapel. The chapel was later destroyed in a renovation, so the exact location of his body remains a mystery to this day. Later claims that it had been transferred to Bordeaux led to several official Haitian demands for its repatriation, but the rumor was likely the work of a con artist trying to gather subscriptions for an imaginary mausoleum.[74] In 1983, France gave Haiti some soil from Joux to bring the issue to a symbolic end; his physical remains belong to the ages.[75]

Historical characters live on in people's memory, of course, but Louverture would have been pained to learn that his countrymen's view of his career was long unflattering. Nineteenth-century Haitian historians were surprisingly critical, and in 1884 the British consul in Haiti wrote of his surprise "to hear his memory so depreciated. I do not remember any Haytian having voluntarily spoken of him, though they never wearied of talking of Dessalines, Christophe, and Rigaud."[76] With a few exceptions, it took over a century before Louverture acquired his current reputation as one of Haiti's Founding Fathers. His low repute in Haiti stood in stark contrast with his high standing in the English-speaking world, where abolitionists lionized him as an example of the intellectual potential of enslaved blacks, and even partisans of slavery heralded him as a moderate whose record was far more appealing than Dessalines'. Aside from a short burst of hostile biographies published in 1802, French authors have generally heaped praise on their worthy adversary as well. Acrimonious debates on the bicentennial of the May 1802 law on slavery have even turned Louverture into something of a celebrity in France recently, where his reputation has soared just as Bonaparte's has sunk; a plaque now honors his memory in the Pantheon monument dedicated to France's great.[77]

Louverture's other legacy was his family. After his departure from Brest, his stepson Placide, who had fought on his side during the spring campaign, was sent to captivity in Belle Île, along with the black officer and former deputy Jean-Baptiste Belley. Louverture's wife, other sons, and nieces headed for Bayonne, then Agen, where Placide eventually joined them. The captivity of the family patriarch was hard to bear, especially since his family knew nothing of Louverture's fate and was not even notified of his death.[78] The death of the young Saint-Jean early in 1804 and that of his mother Suzanne in 1816 were two other blows.[79] But the Louverture family was generally treated with unexpected respect and even received a living allowance, which various French regimes paid until the death of Louverture's niece in 1871 (the Haitian government was less forthcoming; repeated efforts by Placide's descendants to obtain a pension or their inheritance proved unsuccessful).[80]

Many of the Louvertures' sorrows were self-inflicted. After Suzanne's death, her two sons, Placide and Isaac, waged a bitter family feud whose root cause, as often in the Haitian Revolution, was a financial dispute disguised as a racial row. In 1821, Isaac sued Placide to force him to stop using the family name on the grounds that he was merely Suzanne's mixed-race son.[81] Placide was indeed Louverture's stepson, but Louverture had always treated him as his own child and for Isaac to petition French courts at this late juncture had little to do with Placide's light skin and much to do with his intention to return to Haiti to recover the family estate. By emphasizing his direct filiation to Louverture, the avaricious Isaac simply sought to appropriate the entirety of his father's inheritance, along with the family's government pension. He prevailed, but the lawsuit forever split the family apart.[82]

Isaac's wife made a brief visit to collect his inheritance, but neither Isaac nor Placide ever returned to Haiti and the descendants of Haiti's most famous revolutionary hero are thus to be found in southwestern France (various Haitians also claim to descend from Louverture's ill-defined network of half-siblings and illegitimate children).[83] Saint-Jean and Isaac died without heirs, but Placide married a French noblewoman and begot a daughter, who herself had two girls. Placide's descendants, their slightly African features a distant reminder of their Haitian past, proudly recalled their ties to the famous Louverture well into the twentieth century, and in 1917 Louverture's great-great-grandchild, Jérôme Fontan, died fighting for France during World War I.[84]

15

New Enemy, New Partner

The British Navy at War

Summer 1803

Although rumors about a possible Franco-English war had reached him as early as March 1803, it was not until May that Donatien de Rochambeau, warned by Denis Decrès and governor of Jamaica George Nugent, fully realized that war was all but certain. Hostilities with England would make an already bad situation truly "desperate," he wrote back to Decrès in despair.[1] Besieged on land by the rebel army and at sea by British warships, the commanders of each town would ultimately have to choose between surrender and starvation. After thinking the matter over, Rochambeau proposed to return to France at once; he saw no reason to drag it out in Saint-Domingue with an army that would surely be defeated.[2] He informed his troops that they would likely "succumb entirely in the dual struggle they now have to wage" and pessimism about the expedition's chances was widespread ("THE COLONY IS LOST," a naval captain wrote Decrès in giant letters).[3]

Fighting England was so depressing a prospect that, despite a rash of British naval attacks, Rochambeau waited and dallied for weeks, hoping that the war scare might prove short-lived. Eager to maintain good relations with his Jamaican neighbors, he went out of his way to return runaway slaves to a British merchant and to free two British officers who had been taken hostage by the rebels.[4] It was not until July, after the Jamaican squadron had decimated his naval forces, that he finally yielded to reality and declared the colony in a state of siege.[5] Even then, wishful thinking remained the norm and rumors of imminent peace circled well into the fall, each more misguided than the next.[6]

Upon hearing that a war was imminent, an audacious commander might have chosen to strike the British before they could strengthen their defenses, but daring was not Rochambeau's forte. Back in November a French admiral had proposed to send the remnants of the expedition on a desperate death ride to Jamaica, a harebrained plan that might actually have succeeded since the entire British squadron had left the Caribbean for the hurricane season; but nothing came of it.[7] Rochambeau rejected similar suggestions in the spring of 1803 and did not even act on a tip that a richly laden merchant convoy was about to sail from Kingston.[8]

The might of the British navy was an obvious deterrent to any offensive plan, but Rochambeau's prudent stance also stemmed from his conservative political outlook. Contingency plans for an invasion of Jamaica had always been based on the premise that France would employ black colonial troops from Saint-Domingue and spark a slave revolt in Jamaica, a promising strategy at odds with the reactionary turn in French colonial thinking. Officers advocating an attack on Jamaica were thus often Republicans calling for a renewed embrace of emancipation, reconciliation with the rebels, and a joint war against England. This was an intriguing prospect, evocative of the period in early 1801 when Napoléon Bonaparte had hoped to ally himself with Toussaint Louverture, but it fell victim to the resurgence of the conservative faction under Rochambeau.

Forced to revise his military plans to take into account the fact that he was now fighting two enemies at once, Rochambeau simply decided to hold out in a defensive posture until Bonaparte's promised reinforcements reached Saint-Domingue.[9] Critics warned him that bottling up one's forces inside coastal cities was a poor strategy in a colony where controlling the countryside was the key to any lasting victory and garrisoned troops were subject to disease.[10] But he brushed aside such fears and issued orders to fortify the main towns. In June, having given up on his offensive ambitions in the west and south, he left Port Républicain and moved back to Cap, a major commercial center that offered easy access to the United States and a greater chance of surviving a British blockade (Cap was also located upwind from Cuba, which could easily be reached in the likely event of an evacuation).[11] Rochambeau wrote to the commanders of other French towns that they would soon be blockaded by British squadrons and that in the absence of further orders they should ration food and hold out until France sent help. He then abandoned them to their fate.[12]

A relief expedition was unlikely as long as the British navy dominated European waters, so Rochambeau's entire strategy banked on hopes that the new war, whose existence he had so long denied, would not last long. This was a risky proposition. Having fought in the last two wars with England, Rochambeau could not have ignored that they had lasted six and nine years apiece and that a similarly drawn-out conflict would condemn his troops to the certainty of famine and defeat. As it turned out, the latest outbreak of fighting would last until 1814 and Rochambeau's army would need to outlast a twelve-year siege against two enemies to have any hope of prevailing.

⁓

For John Thomas Duckworth, commander of the Jamaica squadron, the renewed war also struck a familiar note. Since entering the service in 1759 at age eleven, he had personally witnessed three Franco-English wars, all of which England had generally dominated on the seas. That the British navy was heavily favored to prevail again in the upcoming naval war can only have raised his spirits, since he stood to collect one-eighth of all the prize money collected by his squadron (in 1800, his share of a captured Spanish convoy had come to a princely 75,000 pounds sterling, or 1.8 million francs).[13] But high expectations for the Jamaica squadron, on whose strength Britain's colonies in the Greater Antilles relied almost exclusively for their safety, also placed a heavy burden on his shoulders. British triumphs had traditionally resulted from superior leadership, not larger fleets or better ships, so the outcome of the war in the Caribbean would depend largely on his ability to rise to the occasion.

Thankfully for Duckworth, as often in the Napoleonic era, misuse and neglect completely undermined his enemy's naval potential. Victoire Leclerc had enjoyed overwhelming naval superiority in early 1802, when two-thirds of the French navy had converged on Sámana before England could dispatch an equivalent force, but army and government policies had long since allowed the British to regain the upper hand. Most ships of the line had left for France during the spring campaign to pick up reinforcements, never to return because of maintenance problems or France's other strategic commitments. Remaining warships had been stripped of their naval guns and gunpowder to help strengthen land fortifications, or had been sent back to France in 1803 to prepare for a possible invasion of England, while the entire budget of the Saint-Domingue squadron sank to a paltry 1,160 francs.[14] By the spring of 1803 the French were down to three shopworn ships of the line in Cap and Cayes. The thirty-six smaller units in the fleet had enjoyed some recent successes against rebel barges, but they would be hopelessly outgunned against the seven ships of the line sent by Duckworth to blockade Saint-Domingue.[15]

The quality of her crew often counted as much as a ship's size in the age of sail, but there again army interference had cost the French navy dearly. Leclerc's refusal to send his ships on cruises during the epidemic of 1802 had left them so decimated by year's end that most could barely set sail, let alone maneuver and fight. By contrast, the famously tidy British ships had largely eliminated smallpox, typhoid, and scurvy with vaccination, cleanliness, and lime juice, and though two British captains died of yellow fever in 1803 frequent cruises limited the fevers' toll.[16] In Saint-Domingue, surviving sailors had often been assigned to shore duty and replaced by prisoners of color, a practice that continued throughout 1803 despite Rochambeau's talk of racial extermination.[17] The English navy faced its own manpower shortages, but it came first in the military pecking order and could always "press" (kidnap) able seamen if needed.

Astute leadership could have made the best of available naval resources, but the French navy's junior status left no room for independent thinking. The experienced commander of the Saint-Domingue squadron, Louis-René de Latouche-Tréville, was the rare seaman who could say that he had defeated Horatio Nelson in combat, but he was so thoroughly sidelined by Leclerc and Rochambeau that he could not even deploy his ships as he saw fit. Making matters worse, he fell hopelessly sick just as hostilities began and had to be repatriated to France in August 1803.[18] He was replaced by a minor officer, Henry Barré, who was unlikely to impose his views when those of a naval hero like Latouche had been ignored.[19] By contrast, Duckworth entertained cordial relations with the colony's governor and answered to no one but the British Admiralty.[20] His captains were a competent lot whose celebrated daring was reinforced by the knowledge that they would keep one-fourth of all prize money (French captains received a blanket pay raise for serving in a war zone, but in practice they were paid last if at all during the expedition).[21]

The outnumbered French ships could have pursued a variety of options—a surprise attack on Jamaica, commerce raiding in the Caribbean, or repatriation to France—but Rochambeau ordered them to stay put while he debated the likelihood of a Franco-British war. By contrast, Duckworth ordered his captains to seize French warships before he had even received instructions from the Admiralty.[22] Attacked by surprise before they knew that a war had been declared, many French ships did not even put up a fight. When the captain of the frigate *Embuscade* was fired upon near Gibraltar on his way back to Europe, his first reaction was to send an officer to inquire why the British were acting so hostilely. His ship was seized before he had made preparations for battle (by no less than the HMS *Victory*, which would soon make herself famous in these waters).[23] The *Franchise* was captured in similar circumstances near Brest.[24]

Duckworth's brazenness paid off. Half a dozen warships from the Saint-Domingue squadron surrendered in the last days of June, leaving the British free to ravage the colony's commerce at will.[25] In all, the Jamaica squadron captured fifty-eight merchantmen in the opening weeks of the war (June 25–August 10). These were most profitable times for the captain of the seventy-four-gun *Theseus*, who bagged fourteen prizes, or that of the eighteen-gun *Racoon*, who took ten.[26]

Awed by the British navy's seeming invincibility, many French captains thought of a battle as lost before it had even begun and mainly concerned themselves with finding a way to lose with honor. The captain of the frigate *Créole* was typical of this pervasive defeatism and explained to his superiors that she had been so poorly maintained and manned that he had had no other option but to strike his colors when faced with superior opposition.[27] Short on small naval units, Duckworth was pleased to note that the frigate was well built and the *Créole,* which had once transported Louverture into captivity, began a second career in the British navy under the command of the *Racoon's* lucky captain.[28]

Some French captains showed how much could have been accomplished with more proactive leadership. The most distinguished record of any naval officer during the expedition was that of Jean-Baptiste Philibert Willaumez, an experienced navigator who had twice explored the Pacific and fought in the wars of the American and French revolutions. Willaumez had come with the Rochefort squadron in 1802 and had served honorably since then, refusing to carry out the large-scale drownings ordered by his superiors.[29] By 1803 he was commanding the thirty-six-gun *Poursuivante,* an ill-maintained frigate whose keel had not been repaired since hitting bottom in European waters and whose crew consisted of 194 sailors, convalescents, and black prisoners when a ship of that size would normally have employed three hundred men.[30] But Willaumez made the best of difficult circumstances, and upon hearing that a war was likely he set sail for Cap with the corvette *Mignonne* so as to concentrate all naval units in a single spot.[31]

As Willaumez sailed by Môle Saint-Nicolas on June 28, his two ships encountered a vastly superior English squadron consisting of six ships of the line, two of which, the *Hercules* and the *Goliath,* pursued the *Poursuivante* while others gave chase to the *Mignonne.* The fight was grossly uneven: at close range, heavily armed ships of the line could sink a slender frigate or corvette with a single broadside, while a frigate's small-gauge cannon could do little against a two-decker's thick oak flanks. The *Mignonne* was soon in British hands, but Willaumez refused to strike his colors and used his ship's few advantages—speed, small draft, and maneuverability—to outdo his opponents. Putting on all sails at the risk of shattering the *Poursuivante's* badly damaged rigging, he headed for shallow areas where his bulky pursuers could not follow him, then made a sharp turn that put his ship perpendicular to the *Hercules.* Her cannon pointed in the wrong direction, the *Hercules* could do little as the frigate raked her exposed stern then entered the port of Môle. The modest Willaumez later wrote to Decrès to apologize for the fact that his ship had been quite damaged in the encounter, her hull having received thirty-five cannonballs and her rigging one hundred. But the *Poursuivante's* victory over the towering *Hercules* was one of the most superb feats of seamanship of the era, admired by English and French onlookers alike and immortalized by a large painting that for years hung in Decrès' office and is now in the French naval museum.[32]

Ever resourceful, Willaumez broke out of Môle a second time a month later and reached Santiago de Cuba, then Charleston, even though the *Poursuivante* came close to sinking after enduring a major storm. Hostile local authorities forced him to push to Georgetown, then Baltimore, where he chanced upon Jérôme Bonaparte while his battered ship finally received much-needed repairs. Bonaparte had sent his brother on several of the Caribbean expeditions in the hope that he would become a Napoléon of the seas, but Jérôme had absconded to the United States, where he declined Willaumez's offer to join his crew and instead eloped with the daughter of a local merchant. After the spring thaw Willaumez again eluded British cruisers outside the Chesapeake, crossed the Atlantic (capturing two British prizes on the way), and after breaking through one last British blockade reached Rochefort in May 1804, where Bonaparte awarded him a promotion and the Legion of Honor.[33]

Many frigate captains begged Rochambeau to let them follow Willaumez's example and escape to France before English squadrons could seal off the main ports. But he denied their requests (most likely because he needed fast frigates to sneak out in the eventuality of a defeat) and even asked that the captain of the *Télégraphe,* who had managed to save his ship from certain capture by leaving Port Républicain, be prosecuted for desertion.[34]

Keeping his ships of the line, which France would likely need for some climactic naval battle in Europe, made even less sense. The captain of the seventy-four-gun *Duquesne* asked to set sail as soon as war materialized, but Rochambeau withheld his authorization for several weeks, by which point a superior British squadron had established a blockade of Cap. Then, on the evening of July 24, Rochambeau ordered the *Duquesne* and another ship of the line (the *Duguay Trouin*) to leave at once with a large contingent of sick soldiers and civilian evacuees. The British squadron was far out at sea at the time, but the winds soon turned and by nighttime four British ships of the line and a frigate were pursuing the French ships as they sailed west along the northern coast of Saint-Domingue. In the darkness the *Duguay Trouin* made an abrupt turn and headed east to the open Atlantic and Europe. But the undermanned *Duquesne,* pursued by three British ships of the line and harassed by rebel coastal batteries, surrendered to the HMS *Vanguard* five leagues off Cuba after a daylong chase.[35]

The loss of a ship of the line like the *Duquesne,* which could easily have been averted by allowing it to leave a few weeks earlier, was a costly mistake, made slightly less disastrous by the fortunate escape of the *Duguay Trouin.* She made it to Cape Ortegal in Spain, where she miraculously escaped an even larger force that included the three-decker *Victory,* by throwing herself into the port of Ferol.[36] The ever-lucky *Duguay Trouin* was one of only four ships of the line to escape the disaster of Trafalgar two years later. Captured shortly thereafter, she was renamed HMS *Implacable* and served for a century and a half in the British navy, well into the age of dreadnoughts and aircraft carriers, and longer than any ship but the *Victory.* Given the fate of the rest of the Saint-Domingue squadron, it was only fitting that in the end she would fall victim to senseless bureaucratic stupidity: she was scuttled in 1949 as a cost-cutting measure and now lies on the channel's seafloor near the Isle of Wight.

⌒

It was in July 1803, on the heels of the unification of the rebel army, that Jean-Jacques Dessalines learned of England's entry into the war, a most welcome development that his men had been eagerly awaiting for months.[37] Dessalines knew that British naval support would make the rebel victory a quasi-certainty by allowing large-scale Anglo-American contraband while preventing the French from obtaining reinforcements and supplies. But such a close alliance, however desirable, was politically sensitive. In the 1790s his troops had fought off a lengthy British invasion designed to force them back into slavery, and they could legitimately be aghast by the proximity of a large plantation colony like Jamaica. As for the United States, the rebels could not forget that its southern states were home to almost one million slaves, some of them the property of the country's president.[38] Securing Anglo-American support without jeopardizing the liberty of his people would require careful diplomatic footwork on Dessalines' part.

In a clever, pragmatic attempt to secure vital help from unsavory partners, Dessalines chose to portray his regime in a moderate light and appeal to foreigners' mercantile instincts. Carefully eschewing all calls for a slave revolt overseas, he encouraged Dominguians to grow coffee for the export market and wrote to Thomas Jefferson that U.S. merchants would find "an immense harvest" in rebel warehouses.[39] Unwilling to upset southern voters and the French government (which had promised to help him buy the Floridas from Spain), Jefferson never officially replied to Dessalines' letter. But he also made no effort to prevent his countrymen from sailing to Saint-Domingue; U.S. smuggling to rebel-controlled areas soon became rampant, amounting to half of the total U.S. trade to the colony.[40]

The same day he wrote to Jefferson, Dessalines also wrote to Nugent to promise equally wondrous commercial opportunities to all Jamaican merchants who would come to sell arms.[41] Aware that as former slaves they labored against entrenched mistrust, the rebels tried hard to downplay any intent to export the slave revolt. "Come, come," the rebel officer François Capois-la-Mort wrote to Anglo-American merchants near Port-de-Paix. "We may be black, but we await you with open arms. . . . As long as our legitimate claim to freedom is not threatened, you will have nothing to fear from us."[42] In a clearly concerted effort, rebel commanders near Tiburon, Léogane, and Port Républicain also contacted British captains in the opening weeks of July to incite them to open trade relations.[43]

Nugent welcomed Dessalines' overtures because he viewed Rochambeau's army and the French refugee community in Kingston as greater security threats than the black rebels of Saint-Domingue.[44] Informed that it would be difficult to capture fortified French towns from the sea, he also concluded that aiding the rebels' land army with a naval blockade would be the most economical way to wage the war against France.[45] Soon, English-made weapons appeared with growing frequency in rebel hands, and by September some English captains were effectively mounting joint amphibious operations in close collaboration with the rebel army.[46]

English support for the rebels was never wholehearted, however. In keeping with the British doctrine of the balance of power, Duckworth and Nugent had long decided that a lengthy war resulting in "the utter destruction" of Saint-Domingue was in Jamaica's best interest, and they planned to abandon the rebels as soon as they grew too successful.[47] Racial prejudices also blurred the strategic picture. A few British captains openly embraced the rebel cause, notably the mixed-race captain of the HMS *Tartar*.[48] But Nugent and Duckworth felt the "greatest embarrassment in promoting the views of the Blacks against the Whites" and feared that the white planters of Saint-Domingue would be massacred in the event of a rebel victory.[49]

Probably aware of British reticence, Dessalines conducted his diplomatic activities through the intermediary of Nicolas Geffrard. As a mixed-race *ancien libre,* Geffrard was less objectionable than the African-born Dessalines (Masonic ties, which often bridged the gap between rebel officers and British captains, may also have been a factor in Geffrard's selection).[50] Geffrard, many of whose brethren had found refuge in Cuba after the War of the South, contacted the Spanish governor of Santiago to explain that "we intend not to disturb the tranquility of our neighbors, but instead to promote . . . links of commerce."[51] He also sent to Jamaica the mixed-race officer L. Dufour, who, judging by his elaborate French and taste for expensive clothes, was a European-educated *ancien libre.* Maria Nugent noted that her guest spoke in "good language" and was "not very dark"; in fact, she found him more agreeable than the French prisoners of war who visited her husband later that day and whom she studiously avoided because she could not forget the horrors they had committed in Saint-Domingue.[52] Dufour cleverly reassured Nugent that the rebels held no ambitions beyond Hispaniola and that their primary goal was to restore the plantation system.

Dufour's visit and another reassuring letter by Dessalines convinced Nugent to open formal negotiations, and on August 18 he and Duckworth wrote to Dessalines that "honored with your excellency's letters" they were sending two envoys to negotiate a commercial treaty.[53] Dessalines, whom they met in Gonaïves, offered trading privileges and made vague promises that he would not kill French planters after the war. But he adamantly rejected an oddly ambitious British demand that he give away the ports of Môle and Jérémie, a major concession that would likely have convinced the recently united rebel factions to overthrow him as a pawn of the slave-owning British.[54]

Dessalines never reached a treaty with the English (or the United States, or Spain), but a British blockade and large-scale smuggling were all that he needed. In fact, as his military position grew ever stronger, he was probably pleased for the British to limit themselves to indirect support because this left them unable to claim a share of the eventual victory (in later years, British boasts that they had single-handedly defeated Rochambeau's army always had a way of irking nationalistic Haitians).[55] Having secured tacit Anglo-American commercial and naval support, Dessalines could now continue his campaign with full arsenals and granaries; the starving soldiers of the expeditionary army could only wish that Rochambeau's and Bonaparte's diplomacy had been as astute.

16

Sodom and Gomorrah

Life in Besieged French Towns

In the spring of 1803, one of the last ships to bring reinforcements to the army of Saint-Domingue cast anchor in Port Républicain. Onboard was the unlikeliest person ever to serve in the expedition, the twelve-year-old Elie Brun-Lavainne.[1] Elie and his father had been visiting friends onboard a French warship waiting for deployment in Dunkirk when a sudden shift of wind had convinced the captain to set sail at once, forcing them to cross the Atlantic with little more than the shirts on their backs. They and other troops sent since the fall of 1802 numbered 12,100 individuals in all, boosting the size of the expeditionary army to 15,733 men by the end of spring (or something close to this number since the general staff remained unable to tabulate the number of available troops with any precision).[2] Late arrivals like the Brun-Lavainnes reached Saint-Domingue just as war with England resumed; marooned in the besieged towns along with the rest of the French army, they were destined to share the lot of the common soldier during the summer sieges: disease, hunger, and despair.

The hospital of La Providence had lost an average of 285 soldiers a month to various tropical ailments from October 1802 to February 1803, so everyone's abiding fear as the warm season approached was that a yellow fever epidemic as intense as the one that had ravaged the army in 1802 would strike again.[3] In preparation for this moment, army doctors contacted colleagues throughout the Caribbean to find a cure, the hospital complex of La Tortue was expanded, and in a step that Victoire Leclerc had never taken, Donatien de Rochambeau personally visited army hospitals to assess the treatment of the sick.[4] The first yellow fever cases appeared in March. Among the victims was Elie's father, forcing the orphaned child to fend for himself in an unfamiliar, war-torn city, where he sustained himself as a child drummer in the army band.[5]

In his correspondence, Rochambeau claimed that he lost two to three thousand men a month to yellow fever over the summer, but much of his army was actually immune by now and the monthly death toll in La Providence only averaged a mere eighty-six a month in the March–June period, lower than during the winter months.[6] By the fall of 1803 the number of patients was so low that many health officers were let go and the director of the health service, Joseph Hugonin's childhood friend Victor Bally, was allowed to return to France.[7] The expeditionary army did decline in size, from its March high of 15,733 men to 11,400 by August, but for other causes: Rochambeau's costly southern offensive; the capture of various troop transports by the British navy; and a new, terrifying enemy, hunger.[8]

Supplying the colony with sufficient food, a nagging difficulty before the sieges had even begun, became even more problematic once England entered the war. Like Leclerc, Rochambeau was under strict orders to displace foreign merchants to the benefit of French ones, but few French traders were visiting Saint-Domingue by the end of 1802 and in December he had granted foreigners most-favored-nation status to alleviate food shortages.[9] Even with preferential tariffs few foreign merchants had sailed to a colony that had no crops or cash to offer, and Rochambeau was forced to beg Spanish colonies for cattle and the United States for food.[10] Food prices were thus inordinately high by May 1803 and the urban poor often went hungry.[11] The outbreak of war made a bad situation worse as the British, as they had done during the Seven Years War, intercepted French merchantmen, then neutral ships as well, while rebel barges and raiding parties cut off most alternate supply sources.

For the more vulnerable of Saint-Domingue's inhabitants, the summer of 1803 was a long agony of shortages, hunger, and eventually famine. Daily rations were cut, then cut again; in Saint-Marc, the garrison was eventually reduced to a diet of dogs, cats, horses, leather, and cotton seeds, leaving soldiers so weakened that some succumbed at their post.[12] Persistent underfunding of the hospital system, compounded by corruption and the bane of private contractors, was as much the norm in 1803 as in 1802, and supply problems were felt most acutely in army hospitals. Even in the comparatively well-supplied city of Cap, patients were fed a "soupe économique" made of bread and rice mixed with water and that lacked essential vitamins and proteins. In a callous attempt to save money, bones picked up in the street and ground into a powder eventually replaced bread and rice as the main ingredients of the economical soup, whose twice-daily servings were the standard ration for patients and black domestics until the French evacuation.[13] Starvation, not sickness, was the single largest killer in hospitals that summer.[14]

The sieges struck a final blow to the morale of the army, which Rochambeau had already described early in 1803 as "weak and tired ... overwhelmed by disease and the fear of death."[15] The sole motive for hope had been the prospect of large reinforcements in the fall, but England's naval blockade dispelled the last delusions of victory, and despair was the norm thereafter. Of 250 foreigners and deserters sent from Le Havre among the last transports, two drowned themselves on purpose rather than serve in the colony.[16] The only person unaffected by the ambient distress was the young Elie Brun-Lavainne, whose strangely cheerful recollections of his childhood in besieged Port Républicain are testimony to children's ability to survive in the earthly hell fashioned by adults.

~

The naval war with England was the death knell of Saint-Domingue's once-thriving economy. At sea, insurance rates skyrocketed to 50 percent of the value of a ship's cargo as merchantmen were routinely intercepted. On land, rebel depredations reached yet another level and the fabled plantations of Saint-Domingue, already reeling from a yearlong insurrection, entered their final agony. Every scrap that remained was greedily appropriated by French officers, thus making the planters' ruin complete.

Jean-Baptiste Drouillard's itinerary was typical of the countless planters whose hopes of economic recovery were shattered that year. A Creole born in the western town of Croix-des-Bouquets, he had fled to the United States during the revolution, leaving his estates under the supervision of relatives. They had produced little in his absence, so Drouillard had headed back to the colony shortly after Leclerc's arrival to restore his sagging fortune. Within a few months his plantation was "rolling" again (a local expression for "producing"), and Drouillard was optimistic about the region's future, as were most planters in the west and south.[17] Despite the general rebellion in the north, exiles continued to head back to the quieter regions of the colony in steady numbers in the early months of Rochambeau's reign or to send legal stand-ins to take possession of their estates.[18]

The return of exiled planters like Drouillard in late 1802 was a welcome sign of colonial renewal, but as in Leclerc's time it also sparked intractable conflicts with the French officers who had leased their estates in their absence. Functioning plantations were in short supply given the ravages of the insurrection, and French officers generally viewed returning exiles as unwelcome competitors. In one of many similar cases, Admiral Latouche leased a small but intact estate in the southern town of Petit Trou, only to discover that its owners had recently returned to Saint-Domingue.[19] Ownership issues were also an important subtext to the conflict pitting French against colored officers in the south.[20]

Oblivious to the political consequences of their actions, Rochambeau's minions aggressively appropriated estates into early 1803—at which point they went up in flames. Angered by their financial losses, *anciens libres* in the west and south defected en masse and began ravaging their old estates, leaving these regions as devastated as the north by spring's end.[21] Drouillard's plantation near Port Républicain was among the victims as the rebels established a camp on a mountain dominating his estate, stole his mules, destroyed his house and the workers' quarters, then burned half his sugarcane fields.[22] So complete was the rebels' scorched-earth campaign that by June 1803 not a single refinery was functioning in a colony that had once provided Europe with half its sugar.[23] The administration in charge of sequestered estates (the *domaines*), which for a year had been the focus of all the dreams and ambitions of French officers, eventually had to be disbanded because there were not enough functioning plantations left to justify its existence.[24]

The colony's economic death spiral was equally hard on French commerce. Jean-Claude Sulauze, a Creole merchant born in Cap of immigrants from Provence, had welcomed Leclerc's arrival. As the colony recovered, he hoped, he would quickly amass a sizable fortune, settle the debts of his spendthrift father, and retire on the family estate in France. But the decline of the plantation sector cut deeply into the export business, and by early 1803 Sulauze found himself much poorer than he had been under Toussaint Louverture's rule.[25] He was not alone: after investing heavily in Saint-Domingue in 1802, many merchants on both sides of the Atlantic were ruined in the spring of 1803 when the last plantations went up in flames and England annihilated the French merchant fleet.[26]

After a year in which exiled Creoles and assorted upstarts had flocked to the colony by the thousands, 1803 thus saw a marked reversal in immigration trends as many civilians gave up on the colony for good. Rochambeau encouraged this process, seeing female civilians in besieged towns as "useless mouths" who would likely be massacred in the event of an evacuation (male planters could also leave by paying a bribe).[27] Like many others, Sulauze sailed for Philadelphia, where he acquired U.S. citizenship while his relatives put down new roots anywhere from Baltimore to St. Thomas and Bordeaux.[28] Drouillard settled in New Orleans, where he spent the rest of his life as a small-scale slave owner.[29] The lawyer Alfred de Laujon and the naturalist Michel-Étienne Descourtilz returned to France after eluding British squadrons, while Elie Brun-Lavainne found a spot on a ship overloaded with fleeing planters and reunited with his mother in France.[30] Even Rochambeau must have been quite pessimistic about the colony's long-term chances, because he secretly made plans to acquire estates in Cuba and Spanish Santo Domingo and exploit them with imported slaves.[31]

~

Planters and merchants were not the only ones with money problems. Having received little beyond promises of financial support from Paris, the army of Saint-Domingue had financed one year of a costly war primarily with local taxes and foreign loans. The demise of the colonial economy had ravaged the tax base by springtime; when Bonaparte denounced all bonds issued in Saint-Domingue as null and void in April, the colony's already tattered credit sank overnight and foreign loans dried up entirely. Forced to make drastic cuts, Rochambeau cracked down on fraudulent army rationing, slashed the colony's bloated bureaucracy, and delegated to private entrepreneurs such essential tasks as feeding the army, importing meat, caring for the sick, and transporting cannon.[32]

Money still had to be found, and cut off from traditional sources of income, Rochambeau increasingly resorted to extraordinary measures to finance the colonial treasury. The army imposed forced loans on U.S. merchants, and an incident in which the United States' de facto consul was told to "pay or *die*" led to a new spate of Franco-American disputes.[33] French nationals were just as likely to be amerced.[34]

Officially, taxes and forced loans served to finance public defense, but officers forbade civilian administrators from delving too deeply into the use of army funds. Even a special envoy sent by Bonaparte to audit the expedition's accounts was foiled when the colony's chief accountant left overseas, taking with him all ledgers.[35] Given the layers of secrecy surrounding army finances, planters and merchants suspected that the entire military structure was in fact a form of organized robbery for the benefit of an elite few. They were right: though Saint-Domingue's army was poor, its leaders were not. Corruption was systematic and ranged from stealing the assets of deceased individuals and deportees to selling army cannon and collecting bribes from departing planters in need of a passport.[36] A particularly bad offender was Louis d'Arbois in Jérémie, who in addition to the many cruelties he inflicted on people of color also collected hundreds of thousands of francs of forced loans and even killed individuals to steal their property.[37] "Some are burning, others are pillaging," a planter wrote in reference to rebels and French officers, while the colonial prefect was struck by the "near universal spirit of brigandage" in Rochambeau's entourage.[38] Brigandage must indeed have been universal, because the prefect himself was mentioned as an embezzler.[39]

Planters had initially regarded Rochambeau as a welcome change from the covetousness of the Leclerc era, but he proved as greedy as anyone else, his self-righteous proclamations against corruption notwithstanding. Like Leclerc, he doubled the salary of the captain general to 200,000 francs.[40] An account dated June 1803, at a time when the colonial treasury was mired in a severe financial crisis, showed that he had just paid himself an installment of 58,600 francs on his salary, along with 49,500 francs for unspecified "secret expenses."[41] Despite his reputation as a creature of the planter lobby, Rochambeau had no love lost on Creoles whom he saw as "hot-tempered, demanding, and turbulent" individuals whose only occupations were "getting rich and dying," and he had no qualms about pressing them for bribes.[42] Judging by his private accounts (which list all his assets down to the weight of the last silver spoon) Rochambeau made a sizable fortune in Saint-Domingue, accumulating paper assets of nearly 900,000 francs, which he sent to France in gold and bills of exchange through various intermediaries.[43] The sums vastly exceeded his salary; that many bills of exchange were signed by entrepreneurs to whom he had awarded generous army contracts is also ground for suspicion.[44] Like Rochambeau, many officers hurriedly sent their money back to France at the onset of war with England, their scattered shipments the last debris of a colony whose fabulous wealth had once earned it the nickname of Pearl of the Antilles.[45]

By the summer of 1803 the exploited colonists were looking back fondly to the days of the British occupation and Louverture's rule, when cultivators worked, order reigned, and taxes were low. In July, when the military commander of Port Républicain sent a civilian delegation to Jamaica to beg George Nugent to send some food to the besieged city, the envoys seized this opportunity to make another, more personal proposal: for England to reinvade Saint-Domingue. When Nugent refused to commit to such an unexpected request, the envoys explained that their second-best option was to ally themselves with the rebels against the hated French army and declare independence as a mixed-race Creole state.[46] However surprising it might sound, the plan made sense to colonists who longed for the more prosperous days that had preceded the French invasion. Their primary concern was to make money, whatever the party in power, and the rebels' leniency when the first French towns fell convinced many white civilians that Nicolas Geffrard and Jean-Jacques Dessalines might turn out to be merciful victors in Louverture's vein.

In the eyes of white colonists, the event that came to symbolize the French army's oppressive rule took place on October 25, 1803, when Rochambeau brusquely ordered the city of Cap to pay eight hundred thousand francs in the next two hours, allegedly so that he could pay his soldiers' salary. After several prominent merchants failed to deliver their apportioned share on time, Rochambeau chillingly announced that one of them, Jean-Baptiste Fédon, would be shot within the hour if he still refused to pay up (Rochambeau later accused him of being Dessalines' spy to justify his decision, but Fédon was more likely selected because the army owed him a large balance on a supply contract and he was close to several republican officers opposed to Rochambeau). Fédon's brother managed to deliver the funds to Rochambeau before the prescribed deadline, but the heroes of ancient Greek tragedies can do little when they labor against fate and the raison d'état. Rochambeau did not countermand his order in time, and Fédon was dragged to the outskirts of town and shot.[47]

Fédon's execution was hardly more barbaric than countless others performed under Rochambeau's reign, but for a prominent white merchant like him to be so callously executed sent a chill throughout the city. Echoes of his death resonated as far away as France, where his brother ceaselessly petitioned the French government for redress, and Fédon's murder was the only crime for which charges were ever brought against Rochambeau.[48] Following Fédon's death, three hundred civilians left the accursed city in a huff. By that time many of those who remained in Cap were secretly rooting, not for the French army, but for the rebels fighting for Saint-Domingue's independence.

～

Despite the daily spectacle of sickness and torture, there was something about the omnipresence of death that pushed contemporaries to enjoy life one last time, and the besieged cities of Saint-Domingue reeked of vice and lust. During his stay in Port Républicain, Rochambeau spent his time "giving balls and entertainment to the ladies" while soldiers, according to a local planter, "danced and delivered themselves to every kind of licentiousness, dissipation, and folly."[49] To the colonial prefect, Hector Daure, the city had become a new "Capua" where one forgot the drudgery of war in orgies worthy of decadent Rome.[50] Turning to the Orient for metaphors, other observers described Rochambeau's gaggle of mistresses as a "harem" or a "seraglio" that followed him from Cap to Port Républicain and back as he changed headquarters.[51] Even the twelve-year-old Brun-Lavainne, whose band was regularly summoned to serenade Rochambeau's mistresses, was taken aback by his superior's depravity.[52] That Rochambeau's wife had stayed in France may explain his penchant for debauchery; so had the wife and four daughters of the French officer Paul Valete, who penned a drinking song in Rochambeau's honor that brilliantly captured the spirit of the times.[53]

Je commence par notre hôte	I will start with our host
Dont les bacchiques vertus	Whose Bacchic virtues
Ont souvent mis à la côte	Often left panting
Tous ceux qui buvaient le plus.	Those who drank the most.
Il eut au moins dix véroles	He caught syphilis a good ten times
Douze chancres dix poulains.	Had twelve chancroids and ten buboes.
Célébrons les caprioles	Let's celebrate the rides
Qu'il fit à tant de putains.	He had on so many whores.

With Rochambeau's return to Cap in June 1803, the "Paris of the Antilles" became Saint-Domingue's new Sodom. Despite the desperate military situation, Rochambeau took time to sit for a portrait and organize lavish balls where he and his minions wooed their mistresses.[54] Gaming (particularly craps) was the rage, while a new theater rose from the ruins.[55] Between accounts of deadly skirmishes and oppressive decrees, the *Gazette Officielle de Saint-Domingue* wrote of parties and comedies, of marriages with beautiful Creoles, and of the detestable vogue of short-cropped hair among Parisian women.[56]

A city in which minuets competed with musket fire—Saint-Tropez in Stalingrad—was a perfect setting for a novelist like Mary Hassal, the Philadelphian romantic who described in vivid detail Saint-Domingue's dying days. Two of her books relate how Rochambeau organized a magnificent party on a warship that had been turned into an artificial tropical garden for the night, complete with dark retreats for gallant encounters. The main deck was a "scene of enchantment" in which black servants dressed as Turks and lovely Creole women swirled around "French officers, in their splendid uniforms, with their towering helmets and waving plumes." As Hassal's fictional stand-in, the young Clara Saint-Louis, stepped on the vessel, a smitten Rochambeau (an "exceedingly beautiful" man with "fine auburn hair" but a "short, Bacchus-like figure") soon leaned over to his neighbor to ask who was the beautiful newcomer.[57] "'Madame St. Louis,' was the reply. 'I thought, or am I in error, that she was an American?' 'You are not wrong,' replied St. Louis, 'but you know, general, that we are all here Americans.' 'Very true; but I mean a native of the United States. I have also heard that her husband is jealous. I hope his lovely wife has spirit enough not to suffer him to be so without cause.' 'I am the husband.'"

Because Hassal's books were novels based on real-life experiences, one can only wonder how much of such scenes owed to reality and to her imagination. Did Rochambeau really inherit from Pauline Bonaparte a bed whose canopy was "in the form of a shell, from which little cupids descend[ed]" toward a statue representing "silence, with a finger on its lips?"[58] Yes—probably. Hassal's novels occasionally resort to far-fetched dramatic ploys, but individual scenes closely match events found in the historical record and her portrayal of a polished, deviant Rochambeau rings true. Rochambeau, in real life as in her novels, sent officers to the front lines so that he could seduce their wives in their absence.[59] His refusal, in a novel, to grant a passport to Clara on the grounds that he only allowed "the old and the ugly" to leave Cap is reminiscent of the real Rochambeau's sharp wit.[60] And it was the real Rochambeau, not his fictional alter ego, who replied to desperate pleas for help from the commander of Môle with flighty letters relating "his nocturnal pleasures and his various exploits with women."[61]

The sentimental is often political, and Rochambeau's sexual trysts had important implications. The main complaint in the reports of the colonial prefect, Daure, was not that Rochambeau was spending his idle hours with "lost women," but that they had gained so much influence that they decided on "favors, promotions, even army matters."[62] Daure's tirade harked back to prerevolutionary fears that lascivious *mulâtresses* could have a nefarious influence over men of authority and was apparently grounded in fact.[63] Accusations of uxoriousness were also a covert way for Daure to denounce Rochambeau's abuses of power. In Bonaparte's thinking, the colonial prefect was supposed to be the captain general's equal, but like Leclerc, Rochambeau emasculated civilian authorities, took over their financial and logistical duties, jailed or killed critics, and even summarily deported Daure's first cousin.[64] All of this took place *before* the outbreak of the war with England, at which point Rochambeau declared a state of siege and suspended the functions of all civilian and judicial authorities.[65] A week later he sent Daure back to France in disgrace, and claiming for himself the authority to appoint all colonial administrators he hired and fired three colonial prefects in rapid succession. Many civilian administrators were also drafted into the army, an event that capped the wholesale militarization of colonial society.[66]

That Rochambeau also took over all police and judicial duties put him on a collision course with the colony's other civilian figure, Grand Judge Ludot, in a power struggle that, interestingly, was also expressed in sexual terms. The story began during Rochambeau's move to Port Républicain, when Ludot tried to seduce the wife of his subordinate, Judge Minuty, in a cabin of the *Duquesne*. She rejected his advances, only to find herself sharing a home in Port Républicain with her rightful husband and her putative lover because of a housing shortage. Ludot's insistence that she yield to his demands in order to advance her husband's career eventually convinced Minuty to complain to Rochambeau, who analyzed the situation not as a case of sexual harassment or wronged marital virtue but as an opportunity to secure his power. He fired Ludot (who, like Daure, was a vocal critic of Rochambeau's abuses of power) and sent him back to France. Minuty saved his marriage and earned the position of grand judge he had long coveted, while Rochambeau got a pliant official who immediately surrendered most of his judicial powers.[67] Like a late-imperial Roman tyrant, Rochambeau's authority over the colony was now as perverse as it was absolute, limited only by the fact that it was exerted over a minuscule territory rapidly shrinking into nonexistence.

⌒

Soldiers, colonists, and bureaucrats were not the only people dissatisfied with Rochambeau's dictatorial rule; many of his own officers were also convinced that his wrongheaded strategic choices and dissolute ways were responsible for the expedition's military downfall. Among Rochambeau's most vocal critics was Adjutant-Commandant Pierre Thouvenot, an officer who began the expedition as an enthusiastic supporter of white rule in Saint-Domingue and ended it advocating the overthrow of his superior.

In 1801 Thouvenot had sent a memoir to Bonaparte calling for the restoration of slavery (albeit under a strict regulatory system). He thus wholeheartedly supported the expedition, and, when finding himself at the heart of the northern insurgency in 1802, he expressed few reservations about a savage war that earned him money and a promotion to brigadier general.[68] It was during that time, however, that he expressed his first doubts about Rochambeau—then merely one of Leclerc's seconds—whose "despotism" was sapping public support for the French cause in the city of Saint-Marc.[69]

Months of fighting eventually took their toll, and Thouvenot's eagerness to fight the rebels did not last. By March 1803 he was writing of his disgust for a "frightful war" seemingly without end.[70] Convinced that he would never leave Saint-Domingue alive, he adopted two illegitimate children, wrote his will, and waited for death to do its part.[71] Unaware of Thouvenot's antipathy, Rochambeau made him chief of the general staff after Pierre Boyer was sent to France that month to seek reinforcements. In following weeks Thouvenot dutifully outlined his superior's aggressive policies, but he also added personal comments to his official reports to argue that a war of extermination was costly and amoral and that France would be best served allowing Saint-Domingue to become a free black republic while focusing its scant resources on another colony like Louisiana or Madagascar.[72] The outbreak of war with England only reinforced his belief that restoring slavery was a hopeless cause and he proposed a radical new strategy: make peace with the rebels and launch a joint attack on Jamaica.[73] When Rochambeau decided instead to barricade the army inside besieged cities, Thouvenot ruefully warned Decrès not to expect anything but bad news in the months to come. Daringly, he even expressed his sympathy for the French soldiers who chose to defect to the rebels rather than starve to death for a dubious cause.[74]

Thouvenot had always been very close to Bertrand Clauzel, a republican general who was next in line for the captain generalcy and whose policy of defending Cap by seeking the support of nearby Maroon groups he admired.[75] As their doubts about Rochambeau's military abilities grew, the two secretly began to discuss whether it might be possible to enroll one of Rochambeau's mistresses to influence his policies. Using a newly created Freemason lodge as their cover, they contacted various generals and officials, including the new colonial prefect, Magnytot, who was equally critical of Rochambeau's corrupt ways. Magnytot claimed that Bonaparte had empowered him to deport Rochambeau and conclude an alliance with the rebels (which was partly true, since Decrès was simultaneously considering this very step), and the officers' plot upped its ambitions to an outright exile of Rochambeau.[76]

Afraid of the risks facing them if they failed, the conspirators proceeded too slowly. A nervous Magnytot eventually revealed the plot to Rochambeau, and on September 9, Clauzel and Thouvenot were arrested and ordered deported.[77] Their plight must have stirred some sympathy in Cap while they awaited their departure, because in order to lessen their popularity among the troops Rochambeau immediately accused Clauzel and Thouvenot of hoarding flour destined for the army and of stealing a colleague's inheritance.[78] Hoping to rid himself of a cumbersome critic, Rochambeau eventually dispatched Clauzel on a leaky ship, which sank as expected near Florida—but without killing Clauzel, who made it to shore and ultimately France (Thouvenot left via Cuba and also reached France). The two generals were guilty of grave insubordination, but Bonaparte agreed with their basic analysis of the situation, and he took the unusual step of allowing them to resume their career in the French army.[79]

With the failure of the Clauzel-Thouvenot conspiracy, Rochambeau had now survived a yearlong insurgency, two epidemics, the opposition of the colonists, the criticisms of his bureaucracy, and a rebellion by his officers. There was only one enemy left with the means to defeat him: Dessalines and the rebel army.

17

Resolution

The Rebel Victory

As the war entered its final phase in July 1803, Jean-Jacques Dessalines faced a daunting task: to capture the ten main towns still under French occupation, four of them in the north, four in the west, and two in the south. Aware that the rebels always struggled against fortified positions, the French had dug themselves in deeply, but cleverly Dessalines turned their defensive strategy into an advantage.[1] Now that his enemy was divided and isolated, he planned to blockade each city with minimal forces until the garrison reached starvation. He would then concentrate the bulk of his forces on a single point, force the French to evacuate, and repeat the process until he had conquered the entire colony.[2] This was a simple, foolproof plan, which he proceeded to execute over the summer and fall of 1803 with the assistance of his British allies and, more surprisingly, that of many of the inhabitants of the besieged towns.

Leaving aside Tiburon, a small port located at the southwestern extremity of the colony that fell in early July, the first notable city to fall to the rebels was the southern town of Jérémie.[3] Its commander, Louis d'Arbois, who had abused and robbed Jérémians with unparalleled savagery, added cowardice to the list of his many crimes and left the town as soon as the English joined the war (captured at sea, he plotted to assassinate the captain taking him to Jamaica and later died in captivity).[4] His successor, Philibert Fressinet, tried to convince mixed-race defectors to return to the French fold, but given his predecessor's murderous record he was unsuccessful.[5] In fact, so unpopular was the French army in the city that Fressinet could barely hold on to his own force. Polish and even French troops were highly prone to desertion, as were the civilians who formed the national guard, and Fressinet estimated that he could only trust two hundred out of his twelve hundred troops. By mid-July, food supplies were low and the situation critical.[6] When Nicolas Geffrard encircled the city with three columns of colored and white rebels totaling four thousand men, Fressinet asked for a two-week truce and made preparations to evacuate to Cuba rather than face a hopeless siege.

The white civilians of Jérémie faced a life-changing choice: leave with the garrison and start their life anew overseas or remain under rebel rule. The de Bordes family of coffee planters was torn apart. Some, convinced that the rebels would massacre all whites, left for Philadelphia or Cuba; others, refusing to abandon a lifetime of work to put themselves at the mercy of English cruisers, decided to stay.[7] Étienne Chazotte, a planter and fierce Louverture critic who had helped the French capture Jérémie during the 1802 landings, had become so disappointed with the greed and ineffectualness of the French army that he too chose to stay. A longtime friend of mixed-race planters now serving in rebel ranks, as was common among southern colonists, he was convinced that he would suffer less under fellow Creoles than he had under his compatriots.[8]

On the night of August 3, Fressinet furtively evacuated Jérémie with 350 troops, most of whom were intercepted and sent to captivity in Jamaica. The rest of the French garrison stayed behind, including the sick and 160 Poles.[9] So did most of the colonists, who welcomed Geffrard with open arms and were treated with remarkable restraint.[10] "Therefore," wrote Chazotte (who obtained the contract to feed the new garrison), "the whites, although ruined, looked forward in the hope of a better prospect."[11]

According to the mixed-race historian Thomas Madiou, the rebels' merciful conduct toward the population of Jérémie was entirely of Geffrard's making and earned him many criticisms from Dessalines. In fact, Dessalines personally approved the policy and presented the siege as an attempt to "free [the town] from the French garrison" so as to incite other towns to surrender peacefully and reassure his British allies.[12] The uneventful takeover of Jérémie had the intended effect on French civilians, who could easily compare Jérémie's fate to that of Saint-Marc, a city north of Port Républicain that only surrendered on September 2 after exhausting all its food resources in a desperate defense. The French commander arranged with the British to evacuate the garrison, but the mixed-raced national guard, which had combated the rebels with singular vigor, was decimated by Dessalines as it tried to fight its way to Port Républicain.[13]

For the besieged French the main factor militating against a quick surrender was the rapacious treatment of fleeing garrisons at the hands of British squadrons. Tightly besieged by Geffrard, the city of Cayes ran out of food and fresh water in October, and its commander, Jean-Baptiste Brunet, capitulated to the British when he grew unsure of the loyalty of the grumbling civilians, colored guardsmen, and Moreauist French troops composing his garrison. Prize-hungry British crews meticulously searched through their captives' personal effects—including those of officers and female civilians, a practice considered dishonorable—and took everything of value.[14] An enterprising search party found a stash of cash hidden in the mattress of Brunet's wife, prompting him to threaten the captain of the HMS *Pique* with a duel to chastise him for this breach of gentlemanly behavior.[15]

Britain's role was ambiguous throughout. In Cayes the British greatly facilitated the rebel victory with a naval blockade, then helped the French escape, only to loot them mercilessly in the process and sell the weapons seized from the French back to the rebels.[16] In Saint-Marc and elsewhere, the British took sick French prisoners to Môle, ostensibly as an act of mercy, but probably also to overwhelm the starving port with useless mouths. After hastening the fall of Fort Liberté with a demonstration of naval power, the British intervened to free the French commander who had been taken hostage by the rebels, then transported the French garrison to Cap so that it could continue the war.[17] When it was Port-de-Paix's turn to fall in October, a British captain expressed his hope that the "brigands" would treat their French prisoners humanely, even as his own ship was blockading Cap to force the French garrison to surrender to the rebel army.[18]

The capture of most lesser towns left Dessalines free to focus his efforts on Port Républicain, where he arrived in late September with the artillery pieces seized in Saint-Marc to personally supervise the siege.[19] The town had been low on food since July, largely because corrupt pursers and officers had diverted funds earmarked for provisioning. The rebels had seized the town's main spring and pure water was also hard to find. Shortages were particularly hard on civilians, who could be found harvesting sugarcane in the outskirts of town, a sign of their desperation, since this was slave work and slave food. Hungry and oppressed, civilians made overtures to the British and to Dessalines and would have welcomed a prompt French evacuation, but out of a sense of personal honor the French commander, Jean Lavalette, refused to surrender until the situation was truly desperate. Many civilians thus chose to flee the starving city, some by ship to Cuba, others by land to rebel-controlled areas. The exodus ravaged the national guard and forced Lavalette to rely primarily on regular troops who lived on one-half, then one-third, then one-sixth of their normal ration; spent endless hours on guard duty; and occasionally killed themselves rather than endure any more of their ordeal.

Dessalines' arrival ushered in the siege's final phase. Vigorous as always, he tightened the blockade of Port Républicain, destroyed Fort Bizoton with artillery fire, and was preparing to do the same to the town itself when Lavalette finally prepared to evacuate. He was under orders to march to Santo Domingo, as the garrisons of Jacmel and Croix-des-Bouquets had done in similar circumstances.[20] But he concluded that hiking one hundred miles over mountains with a malnourished garrison while being pursued by 15,000 rebels was suicidal, and he capitulated to Dessalines on October 5. In exchange for receiving the large arsenal of Port Républicain intact, Dessalines allowed 1,100 soldiers, 400 sick, and 3,000 civilians to leave the town, most of whom made it past English warships to Santiago de Cuba. Encouraged by Dessalines' reassurances and the Jérémie precedent, the rest of the population remained in the city, where they were generally treated humanely. Dessalines' more radical lieutenants complained that his leniency greatly diminished the expected loot, but he thought it best to coddle the colonists if it could help sow dissention inside the last big town still under French rule: Cap Français, where the war of independence had begun, and where it was destined to end.

∾

The summer of 1803 was a strangely quiet one in Cap. Most houses had finally been rebuilt, the yellow fever epidemic was less intense than feared, and Rochambeau's taste for the good life made for a busy social schedule. The British blockade initially did not extend to U.S. merchants and food shortages were unknown at first.[21] Rebel barges seriously disrupted the cabotage trade for a time, until a French flotilla reopened the vital coastal link to Caracol and the cattle of Santo Domingo.[22] The sole reason for concern was the fate of other French towns, which, according to fragmentary reports, were starving and desperate. They would likely not last long, after which it would be Cap's turn to endure the pangs of hunger and the sting of battle.

Executions of rebels were comparatively few over the summer, but this relative leniency came too late to alter public opinion. Eager to find themselves on the right side of history, people of color fled from Cap every day despite strict security measures to prevent their defection. Last-minute rebels included the future Haitian president Jean-Pierre Boyer, who escaped in September 1803 with the help of a French officer.[23] "Joseph Godard, negro grandmaster of Vodou, and Apollon, also a negro," were not so lucky and ended their lives on a scaffold erected on Place Cluny after a failed escape attempt.[24]

The rebels' military pressure also eased temporarily. Before he was deported for plotting to overthrow Rochambeau, Bertrand Clauzel cultivated the goodwill of the few Maroon leaders Dessalines had not enlisted or killed.[25] He used as an intermediary the black brigadier chief Louis Labelinais, a former slave who remained on the French side until the very end of the expedition.[26] The plan paid off in July when the Maroon groups of Gagnet and Jacques Tellier helped disband the rebel camp of Jacques Romain near Cap, thus earning the city several months of relative calm.[27] Maroons also supplied the city with food and helped intercept defectors fleeing the city.[28] When subsequent attacks by Romain were again repulsed with the help of the Maroons, Dessalines decided to wait until he was done with Port Républicain before making one last push against Cap.[29]

The Maroons' military assistance had the unintended effect of giving the fractious inhabitants of Cap a few more months to fight among themselves. Many people urged Rochambeau to evacuate to Santo Domingo before Cap was too tightly surrounded, but faithful to a strategy that had failed everywhere else he insisted on holding out until the arrival of Bonaparte's nonexistent reinforcements.[30] In preparation for a lengthy siege, he ordered civilians to help strengthen fortifications and declare all their supplies or face immediate execution in a tone that did nothing to improve civilian-army relations.[31] Ever more obstinate and gruff, his unpopularity reached unprecedented levels. September saw the exile of Thouvenot and Clauzel; October was the month when Fédon was executed. By November, Rochambeau no longer dared to venture into the streets without a large personal guard for fear of being lynched.[32] A request that month that he be allowed to return to France (allegedly because of a bad stomach) was probably not unconnected to his unpopularity.[33]

So strong was the hatred of his countrymen that Rochambeau's friendliest exchanges during the siege of Cap were with Commodore John Loring, the commander of the British squadron blockading the city. In scenes seemingly drawn from the World War I classic *Grand Illusion,* Rochambeau and Loring spent most of the summer exchanging aristocratic niceties while their inferiors fought and starved one another. Rochambeau sent French wine, tropical fruit, fresh vegetables, and liqueurs to Loring, who replied with more modest shipments of Madeira wine and apologies that being on blockade duty left him few opportunities to purchase thank-you gifts.[34] In September, Rochambeau went as far as sending fresh water to a British ship of the line that would probably have been forced to abandon the blockade of Cap otherwise.[35]

It was Admiral John Duckworth who ruined the beginning of a beautiful friendship. Eager to "bring the business to conclusion," he sent orders from Kingston to tighten the blockade of Cap, where five British ships of the line were eventually stationed.[36] French ships were intercepted and searched with growing vigor, as were, eventually, U.S. ships as well. Ships repatriating the sick from other towns were exempt from the blockade, but these only added to supply problems. When in October the British dispersed the flotilla defending coastal areas from rebel barges, the French found themselves cut off from the cattle of Santo Domingo and Cap began to endure the familiar pattern of hunger and despair.[37]

To besiege a city and attack merchantmen was normal behavior in war, but direct British assistance to rebel barges came across as ungentlemanly behavior to Rochambeau, who fired off a sharp letter to Loring to express his "extreme displeasure" at this close an alliance with rebellious slaves.[38] The (all too founded) accusation smarted Loring, who replied angrily that it was too "malicious an assertion" to suggest that he had formed an alliance with "brigands."[39] There were no more exchanges of Madeira wine and French liqueurs thereafter, and Rochambeau was truly alone when in November Dessalines' combined forces set up camp outside Cap, eager to fire the opening shots of the last and largest battle of the Haitian Revolution.

∼

On November 15, 1803, the rebel army gathered at the Lenormand de Mézy plantation in Morne Rouge. Twelve years, three months, and one day earlier, plantation foremen had gathered on this very spot to plot the uprising that had marked the beginning of the Haitian Revolution, so the location brought a fitting sense of closure to a long and bloody conflict. Anxious to conquer Cap before the forces that had evacuated from Port Républicain could reinforce the city via Cuba, Dessalines had marched from the western province with the 3rd, 4th, 11th, and 20th demi-brigades. In Limbé they had joined up with the 9th, 21st, 22nd, 23rd, and 24th demi-brigades, which had come from as far away as Jacmel. After a lengthy delay due to torrential rains, they had marched together to Morne Rouge, where they had met the 1st, 2nd, 5th, and 17th demi-brigades, northern units that many times in prior months had faltered before the fortifications of Cap. In all, the rebel army totaled about fifteen thousand men drawn from all corners of Saint-Domingue.[40]

The army under Dessalines' command was one of the most magnificent forces ever assembled in the Caribbean. Its skills honed by twelve years of near-constant warfare, it included many veterans of English, French, and Spanish colonial units who had gone on to defeat the very armies that had trained them. Many went barefoot, their tattered clothes a hodgepodge of French and foreign uniforms; but these black Spartans lived off little and had guns and ammunition aplenty. Former slaves who had once believed their masters to be endowed with extraordinary powers had long since learned that theories of racial superiority were false. Confident in their capabilities, they were also willing to die to secure their freedom. "Dessalines sorti lan nord" (Dessalines is leaving for the north), they sang.[41]

Vini voué ca li porté	Come see what he's bringing
Ca li porté	What he's bringing
Li porté ouanga nouveau	He's bringing new magic
Ouanga nouveau	New magic

Dessalines, Vernet, Christophe, Romain, Clervaux, Cangé, Capois-la-Mort: to patriotic Haitians today, these proud names and their iron columns evoke glorious days when their ancestors banded together to throw off the yoke of French imperialism and give meaning to the national motto "unity makes strength." And yet, even on the eve of a decisive battle, old rivalries continued to complicate the revolutionary struggle. Nicolas Geffrard, whose assistance had been so decisive in the south, missed the last phase of the campaign because he had to put down an uprising by old partisans of Lamour Derance in the south. The rebel general Yayou was also diverted from the main army to stand guard by the mountains for fear that the Maroon groups of Gagnet and Jacques Tellier might assist the French, as they had done in recent encounters. Meanwhile, French and Polish defectors served as secretaries, engineers, and gunners in the rebel army, where they would provide crucial artillery support in the battle of Vertières.

The battlefield, as it appeared when the troops marched to their assigned positions on the morning of November 18, was a rolling plain dotted with a dozen blockhouses. These were purpose-built towers or modified plantation houses, typically situated atop a small prominence, whose second story held cannon and that could accommodate up to several hundred men. The French had not built a continuous palisade to link one blockhouse to another, so a daring enemy could theoretically force its way through the gaps. But blockhouses protected each other with interlocking fields of fire, and an attacking force would have to be inordinately brave and oblivious to casualties to succeed.[42] In all, the French had 2,700 regular troops, many of them sick with dysentery, and 500 national guardsmen of various colors (though hunger and desertion had greatly diminished the latter's numbers in recent weeks). Half the troops were stationed in outlying fortifications where they faced a rebel army that outnumbered them ten to one, while the rest guarded Cap itself—or more specifically its restive population, which effectively amounted to a second rebel force of uncertain allegiance.

As the battle began, Henri Christophe and Jacques Romain immediately headed for the hills above Cap while the main fighting focused on the blockhouses of Bréda and Vertières, whose three hundred French troops were the main obstacle separating the rebel army from the largest French city in the New World. Hoping to exploit the gaps between blockhouses, the rebels bypassed Bréda and headed directly for Vertières; but the two positions' combined fire dug frightful gaps into the advancing columns. A weaker assailant would likely have faltered, but the troops marched on to the sound of musket fire, the moans of the wounded, and their favorite battle hymn.[43]

Grenadiers, à l'assaut!	Onward, grenadiers!
Ça qui mouri zaffaire a yo,	Those who die it is their problem,
Gn'y a point papa,	We have no dad,
Gn'y a point maman!	We have no mom!
Grenadiers, a l'assaut!	Onward, grenadiers!
Ça qui mouri zaffaire a yo!	Those who die it is their problem!

Despite three courageous assaults, the rebels were still pinned before Vertières by the afternoon, their painful advance marked by hundreds of corpses projecting a lengthening shadow. It was at this point that the order came from Dessalines to seize the battery that the French had established on the hill of Charrier and whose guns dominated the battlefield. The path to Charrier went right by Vertières, where it funneled into an exposed, broken bridge swept by grapeshot, but the indomitable rebel officer, François Capois-la-Mort, personally led his troops under the eyes of Donatien de Rochambeau, who had come from Cap to observe the fighting in person. The courage of Capois particularly impressed him, and some accounts relate that a few French *bravos* fused from the captain general's position when Capois continued fighting after his horse was shot under him; a few days later Rochambeau sent his own horse as a reward for Capois's courage under fire.[44] After Augustin Clervaux and André Vernet were sent in support, the rebels finally broke through, seized Charrier, and set up artillery pieces with which they could respond to French fire in kind. Their efforts paid off when a crate of ammunition exploded inside Vertières, forcing French defenders to form an exposed square outside the blockhouse. The rebels had finally gained some momentum when an evening downpour and the falling night brought a sudden end to the battle.

On the evening of November 18, Dessalines trotted to Charrier to inspect the captured position. His troops had more than held their own in the type of pitched battle that was usually considered a European specialty, and Haitian revolutionaries always looked back on the battle of Vertières as their greatest victory. It was probably best, though, that the battlefield was plunged in darkness, for the view from Dessalines' position would have been gruesome. To liberate a small patch of soil, the rebels had lost about 1,200 men and 2,000 wounded to the French's 130 dead and 400 wounded. The French thought that Dessalines had access to black multitudes and could easily afford such losses, but the reality was that the lengthy revolution had nearly halved the colonial population and that Dessalines had tapped virtually every healthy man in Saint-Domingue for his final campaign.[45]

While Dessalines was visiting Charrier, the French garrison of Vertières evacuated the half-ruined position in the dead of night. With the other blockhouse at Bréda still surrounded by rebel forces, the road to Cap now lay open. It would have been technically feasible for the French to throw makeshift fortifications in the outskirts of town. But the British squadron was menacingly close to the shore batteries and the rebels had gained control of the hills overlooking Cap, so holding out any longer would have meant enduring a lengthy bombardment in an overcrowded city. This was more than the sick, hungry garrison and the fretful civilians could stomach. Estimating that he had fought long enough to safeguard his honor (and probably not unhappy to leave Saint-Domingue with his ill-gained fortune) Rochambeau concluded that the time had come to capitulate.

The close proximity of the rebels forced Rochambeau to treat directly with Dessalines himself, a controversial step that granted the rebel army de facto recognition as a legitimate adversary. At midnight a messenger reached Dessalines' camp with a demand for a cessation of hostilities, and an agreement was soon reached under which the French agreed to evacuate within ten days, leaving the city and its forts intact behind them, in exchange for a ceasefire (Rochambeau forgot to inquire about the fate of the French troops still huddled in Bréda, but Dessalines agreed on his own to let them march to Cap unscathed).[46] Louis-Mathieu Dembowski, an officer who had come with the 2nd Polish demi-brigade, was sent to the rebel camp as one of the hostages who would guarantee the faithful implementation of the agreement and returned with a sympathetic view of his enemy. "Despite their great savagery in all things, they treated me well," he wrote. "And even though we consider them ignorant, they reason well in their way. . . . These brave indigenes were simply aggravated by our barbaric actions."[47]

Hoping to leave Cap with his closest acolytes and the spoils of war, Rochambeau contacted his old friend Loring to request the right to leave directly for France with five hundred men and their luggage on board a frigate and a brig.[48] Unwilling to lose a likely windfall in prize money, the commodore refused and instead proposed to let the sick and the wounded escape captivity as long as Rochambeau reimbursed the value of the ships that would be needed for their evacuation.[49] This Rochambeau found "inadmissible" (why waste money on wasted men?), and after breaking off negotiations with Loring he began making plans to burn all French ships in the harbor and sneak out of Cap on a small vessel.[50] Both prospects angered Loring given the amount of money at stake. He ordered his ships to keep an eye out for blockade runners and issued a stern warning that if the French ever burned a single merchant ship his squadron would abandon all the troops that they captured on the nearest patch of land, where the rebels would likely massacre them.[51]

For ten days Rochambeau waited and hesitated. His inclination was to try to break through the British blockade, but contrary winds precluded his plan and the French were still in Cap on the twenty-eighth when Dessalines warned that the ceasefire was over.[52] He marched into town with two thousand of his finest troops the following day, and threatened with a bloodbath if he overstayed his welcome Rochambeau finally consented to Loring's stiff terms: the entire garrison of Cap, officers included, would be taken prisoner as it left Cap.[53] Loring also obtained Dessalines' grudging approval that he would not sink the departing French fleet as it passed by the forts of Cap, as had been his intention.[54]

After begging one last time for a few days' delay in the hope that better winds and a declining moon would give his fleet a fighting chance to elude the British, Rochambeau set sail at dawn on the thirtieth with 3,882 troops, administrators, and family members.[55] He sailed on the frigate *Surveillante,* the strongest and fastest in the fleet, and according to some accounts brought with him two of his paramours, a Mrs. Meignen and a Mrs. Parouty.[56] The rest of his army was spread between seventeen warships and merchantmen, including the small *Saint Nicolas* on which Gagnet, Labelinais, and thirty pro-French black officers and Maroon leaders had found a spot (for lack of room, the French left behind 500 sick and wounded and 1,200 of their Maroon allies). "We passed by Fort Picolet at 7 a.m.," a sailor on the *Surveillante* remembered: "The fort's parapets and bastions were covered with negroes; we also noticed a few whites. They had lit flintlocks in their hands and were ready to fire the cannon. A thousand voices drowned us under the worst invectives. 'Go, go, French brigands,' they said, 'go on the ocean, may it swallow you! Tonight we will drown the sick and wounded if you don't immediately give us the chiefs Labelinais and Gagnet, these traitors to their cause.'"[57]

Sailing in open daylight and light winds, the French were intercepted by the British squadron as soon as they left Cap, and the combined fleet headed for Jamaica. On the night of December 4, it passed by Môle Saint-Nicolas, the last city still in French hands in Saint-Domingue. Used primarily as a depot for the sick and convalescents, Môle overflowed with four thousand civilians and soldiers who had started eating horses and donkeys as early as July and were in a desperate situation.[58] As elsewhere, the population was diverse, and according to a French general ranged from "faithful mulattoes and negroes" to white colonists "who prefer to live under British than French rule" (another seven hundred whites served with the rebel forces besieging the city).[59] Upon seeing the convoy from Cap, the commander of Môle, Louis de Noailles (he of dog fame) embarked soldiers and willing civilians and set sail at once. His own ship went unnoticed in the jumble of warships and prizes and he made it to Cuba.[60] The rebels then took over Môle, completing a successful series of sieges that had finally brought them victory in their war of independence.

~

The evacuations of Cap and Môle brought an end to European rule in a colony long known as the "French part of Saint-Domingue" (the French still controlled the eastern, formerly Spanish part of Hispaniola, known as Santo Domingo). This was a time for celebration and Dessalines distributed 8 piasters to every one of his soldiers.[61] The day Rochambeau's army sailed from Cap, he and his main generals also issued a "preliminary declaration of independence" that marked the official beginning of Haiti's existence as an independent nation (Haitians use a second, more formal declaration issued on January 1, 1804 as the basis for their national holiday).[62] This often-overlooked document was primarily addressed to a French audience and informed white colonists that they could safely remain in Saint-Domingue as long as they forswore slavery. The promise was consistent with similar assurances given to the British, another proclamation issued on November 19, and the capitulation agreement signed with Rochambeau.[63] Dessalines reinforced its effect by summarily executing black soldiers convicted of robbing the houses of white civilians.[64]

Dessalines' reassurances had a great impact on the civilian population of Cap, which had received favorable reports on the fate of other colonists in Port Républicain and Jérémie. Unwilling to endure British captivity, the captain of the frigate *Vertu* doubled back as the rest of the French fleet left, and a few colonists returned from exile. In all, about 1,700 white civilians remained in Cap, as did a good part of the mixed-race population.[65] These numbers reflected a myriad individual choices. The merchant Hardivilliers stayed, probably because he had been one of the notables forced to pay tribute during the Fédon incident.[66] The decision of most French priests to remain in Saint-Domingue was consistent with their support for the rebels ever since the outbreak of the revolution.[67] Located in Montecristi on the Spanish border, Louis Dufaÿ was more hesitant and chose to hedge his bets. Writing to the French commander of Santiago, he carefully crossed out the words "liberty" and "equality" from his letterhead, leaving only "indivisibility of the Republic," to portray himself as a loyal French patriot with a conservative outlook. But he also wrote to the rebel generals Clervaux, Cangé, and Vernet, this time crossing out the reference to the French Republic and replacing it with the rebel motto "liberty or death" to remind his addressees that he was one of the French envoys who had brought Saint-Domingue's emancipation decree to Paris in 1794.[68] What happened to him is unclear.

In the near term, those who had the most to lose from the rebel takeover were France's Maroon allies, who stayed behind as their leaders sailed away. Their hatred of plantation work and independent spirit immediately put them at odds with Dessalines, and in subsequent months large groups of Maroons totaling 1,500 to 4,000 individuals battled his army in the areas of Dondon and Fort Liberté.[69] Little is known of their composition, but one group, which called itself the "Rochambeau army," clearly was one of France's former allies.[70] Tellier, the only prominent Maroon leader to have stayed behind with his followers, fought for a year until he was captured and shot on Dessalines' orders.[71] This made him the last member of France's multiracial army to fight and die in Saint-Domingue.

18

Liberty and Death

Haitian Independence

Independence brought to the fore Jean-Jacques Dessalines' secretary, Louis Boisrond-Tonnerre, one of those multifaceted figures so typical of the revolutionary era. A mixed-race southerner, he had witnessed firsthand the French exactions committed in early 1803 and had developed a strong hatred for the "monsters" who "in less than two years had managed to repeat the barbarity of the Spaniards against the Indians, the atrocities of the reign of Robespierre, and the cruel executions invented by Carrier."[1] Boisrond's reputation as a fanatical Francophobe is partly undeserved, however. Just like the nascent state of Haiti, he was as much France's offspring as he was its bitterest enemy. Born to a wealthy family of indigo planters, Boisrond had spent his early adulthood as a French-educated slave owner and had even managed to ensure that legal documents not describe him as a person of color. He had spent part of the revolution in France, where his uncle was a deputy in the Council of five hundred, and he owed his fiery nickname of Tonnerre (thunder), not to his exploits killing French soldiers, but to the French town of Tonnerre where he had lived.[2]

As the momentous year of 1803 came to a close, Boisrond followed Dessalines to the city of Gonaïves, where the victorious commander planned to issue a declaration of independence more elaborate than the one hastily drafted on November 29. The task of writing the document was initially entrusted to another secretary, Charéron, who proceeded to draft a lengthy exposé of the colony's grievances and rights modeled on the U.S. declaration of independence. But the document's legalistic tone displeased Dessalines, who enrolled Boisrond after the latter allegedly proposed to use "the skin of a white man as parchment, his skull as an ink pen, his blood as ink, and a bayonet for a nib."[3] The quote may be mythical, but Boisrond's ebullience was real. "I locked myself up in my room," he remembered, "drank two cups of coffee and three shots of rum, and the words came to me naturally."[4] He toiled all night, and at dawn on January 1, 1804, he was found asleep at his desk, his head resting on the document forever known as the Haitian declaration of independence.

Boisrond in tow, Dessalines and his generals proceeded to the place d'armes, where Dessalines warmed up the large crowd with an impassioned recounting of the horrors committed by the French army before Boisrond rose to read the declaration of independence itself.[5] Not surprisingly, the text made frequent references to the French atrocities that had pushed Boisrond into rebel ranks, but references to the Haitians' desire to be "free" were more vague. "We must, by one last act of national authority, secure forever a reign of freedom in the country of our birth," Boisrond exclaimed. "We must take away from the inhuman government that for too long kept our spirits in humiliating torpor any hope of enslaving us. We must live *independent or die*."[6] Depending on the context, the term "freedom" could potentially allude to slave emancipation, opposition to tyranny, or national independence; but Boisrond had owned slaves and served a military dictator, so freedom from French colonial rule was probably foremost in his mind. However strongly worded, his proclamation was in the end neither an emancipationist call to arms nor a political manifesto articulating the rights of men, but a narrowly focused declaration of independence that denounced French imperialism, not military rule nor the plantation system itself. The assembled generals then pledged to die rather than suffer recolonization, and 107 years of French rule in Saint-Domingue came to an official end.

Self-rule "in the country of our birth" was particularly meaningful for Creole *anciens libres* like Boisrond, who had always seen themselves as the only true citizens in a transient colony filled with French- and African-born immigrants who dreamed of returning overseas. Free people of color had often called themselves "Americans," while relegating their French compatriots to the status of "foreigners."[7] "You whites, France is your country, just like Africa is for blacks, and Saint-Domingue is for us," they also said.[8] In keeping with this nativist agenda, Boisrond dubbed the rebel army "indigenous army" in his declaration and argued that "the vastness of the seas separating us and the vengeful climate indicate clearly enough that [the French] are not our brothers and never will be." "One cannot question that we are, like the aborigenes of Haiti [the Tainos], the naturals or indigenes of our native country," a Haitian patriot later wrote to justify the Haitians' claim to self-government.[9]

The name Haiti, which made its first official appearance in the 1804 declaration of independence, was another way for Boisrond to draw a sharp distinction between Caribbean natives like himself and European imperialists.

Keeping the name "Saint-Domingue" or "Santo Domingo" would have offered no symbolic change to five hundred years of French and Spanish rule in
Hispaniola, but reviving the pre-Columbian term "Hayti" self-consciously
described the new state as an heir to the Tainos who had succumbed to exactions and disease within fifty years of the Spanish conquest. The black
and white ancestors of Haitian rebels like Boisrond had come long after the
Tainos' tragic end and were not biologically related to them, but cultivators
often found Taino artifacts when tilling the soil and they saw them as kindred
victims of European oppression.[10] For a time the rebels even called themselves "army of the Incas" and "true children of the sun" in a far-fetched attempt to represent all Amerindians from Haiti to Peru.[11]

And yet even as colonial Saint-Domingue turned into independent Haiti,
France's presence could not be fully erased. Cap Français was logically renamed Cap Haïtien, but Fort Liberté preserved its French name, probably
because it had been adopted during the French Revolution in reference to
emancipation. More strangely, Port Républicain reverted to the prerevolutionary, monarchist Port-au-Prince.[12] Haiti's place names, in the end, were a
hodgepodge of historical references, some referring to the Taino era (Haiti),
others to Spanish rule (Tiburon), Christianity (Saint-Marc), the ancien régime (Port-au-Prince), and the French Revolution (Fort Liberté).

"Barbarians," "vultures," "tigers": the Haitian declaration of independence was a document of extraordinary verbal violence, all of it directed
at France, yet none of the documents signed on January 1 were written in
Kreyol, the most widely understood language in the colony (or an African
language, which elite *anciens libres* like Boisrond never used).[13] Instead, Boisrond used a refined French peppered with references to *liberté* and French history, thus borrowing from the French cultural and political heritage to draft
the very document denouncing French imperialism. The new Haitian state
abandoned the French revolutionary calendar (as Toussaint Louverture had
done in his time), but its flag and coat of arms were both directly inspired by
French revolutionary iconography. A "Haitian hymn" composed in January
1804 by a certain "Ch . . ." (probably Henri Christophe or Charéron) similarly combined ardently anti-French lyrics with the language and rhyming
pattern of revolutionary battle hymns.[14]

Quoi? Tu te tais Peuple Indigène	What? You remain silent, indigenous people
Quand un Héros, par ses exploits,	When a Hero, through his exploits,
Vengeant ton nom, brisant ta chaîne,	Avenging your name, breaking your chains,
A jamais assure tes droits? (bis)	Protects your rights forever? (repeat)

Honneur à sa valeur guerrière!	Honor to his martial skills!
Gloire à ses efforts triomphants!	Glory to his triumphant efforts!
Offrons-lui nos coeurs, notre encens;	Let us offer him our hearts, our incense;
Chantons d'une voix mâle et fière,	Let us sing with a male and proud voice,
Sous ce bon Père unis	United under this benevolent Father
A jamais Réunis,	Forever United,
Vivons, mourons, ses vrais Enfans	Let us live and die as his true Children
(bis)	(repeat)
Libres, indépendans.	Free and independent.

The first national anthem of independent Haiti, it is worth noting, was meant to be sung to the tune of the French "La Marseillaise."

~

The second colony to achieve its independence in the Western Hemisphere and the only victorious slave revolt in world history, the young Haitian republic was a diplomatic oddity, bound, its neighbors feared, to use its considerable military potential to wreak havoc throughout the region. Such concerns were particularly prevalent in Cuba, which would remain Spanish until 1898 for fear that it would succumb to Haitian subversion if it dared break away from the metropolis. The southern United States, where laws to control the black population hardened considerably in the aftermath of the Haitian Revolution, also looked at the rebel republic with much angst. Even today, some historians claim that Dessalines, and before him Louverture, had a well-articulated plan to export the Haitian Revolution to foreign shores.[15]

Despite such overblown claims, for much of the nineteenth century slavery continued to expand in the New World with only minor interference from Haiti. Slaves from Brazil to Cuba and Venezuela heard of the Haitian Revolution, celebrated its achievements, and occasionally rebelled to fulfill its ideals, but they did so without any support from Haitian authorities.[16] As Louverture had done in 1799, and Nicolas Geffrard in 1803, Boisrond pledged in the declaration of independence to "leave our neighbors in peace" and announced that Haitians would not act as "revolutionary firebrands pretending to be the legislators of the Antilles." Dessalines made similar promises to a British envoy in early 1804, then again in an 1805 constitution, and remained largely true to his noninterventionist agenda.[17] The first rulers of independent Haiti occasionally attacked nearby Santo Domingo or offered asylum to a few Latin American revolutionaries seeking independence from Spain; but they never masterminded a slave revolt anywhere.[18]

Dessalines' decision not to spread the revolution overseas was largely tied to the continued risk of a French invasion. He ruled an infant state, isolated and vulnerable, whose long-term survival was far from assured when remnants of the Leclerc expedition could still be found in Cuba and Santo Domingo and Bonaparte could send a new army at any time. Preserving Haiti's independence would likely be impossible without the support of England, Spain, and the United States, all of them slave-owning powers, so Dessalines preferred not to anger potential allies with some ill-advised talk of general emancipation.

Convinced that a new French expedition was imminent, Dessalines spent much of the early months of independence preparing, not for a hemispheric slave uprising, but for an inevitable rematch with the French army. He kept a large army of about twenty thousand men on active duty, clearly not for overseas adventures since he built no navy beyond a handful of privateers and ordered the port of Môle razed to the ground.[19] No doubt inspired by the 1802 French invasion, when the rebels had failed to prevent a single landing but had inflicted debilitating losses on their enemy at Crête-à-Pierrot, he outlined a defensive strategy consisting in abandoning the coastal towns and immediately bringing the war to the favorable terrain of the interior. "As soon as the alarm gun sounds," a new constitution instructed, "the towns will disappear and the nation will rise."[20] In preparation for this moment, Dessalines ordered the coastal batteries dismantled and their guns transported to a dozen new inland mountain fortresses.[21] By the time Dessalines' and Christophe's wives arrived late in 1804 to celebrate the first anniversary of independence, Gonaïves was so thoroughly gutted that the first ladies had to sleep in a tent on the beach; the entire town had been reduced to a collection of thatch-roof huts. Meanwhile, Dessalines began work on a new capital on the Marchand plantation near Crête-à-Pierrot, where Polish transplants built a gunpowder manufacture while eight forts with names like Fin du Monde (world's end) rose amid fields of yams and plantains designed to ensure a long-term food supply.[22] Mountainous defensive structures remained the centerpiece of Haiti's national security strategy for several decades, and to this day the colossal ruins of the citadel of La Ferrière (inland from Cap) bear witness to early Haitians' fears of a new French expedition.

The main victim of the militarization of Haitian society, in the end, was not Jamaica's or Cuba's planter class but the Haitian population itself. The celebration of the male citizen-soldier excluded Haitian women from the public sphere, while the rest of the population financed an oversized security apparatus whose main objective over the following two centuries was to oppress its countrymen and preserve the privileges of its leaders, not to export revolutionary ideals. After yet another episode in which it overthrew the country's president, then failed to oppose any resistance to a U.S. invasion, the Haitian army was finally disbanded altogether in 1995, thus bringing an end to an institution that had once intimidated statesmen from Washington to Havana.[23]

5. Jean-Jacques Dessalines
frequently appeared as
a bloodthirsty brute
in French and Spanish
accounts. Manuel Lopez
Lopez, "Dessalines." In Juan
Lopez Cancelada. *Vida de
J. J. Dessalines, Gefe de los
negros de Santo Domingo.*
Mexico City: Mariano
de Zúñiga y Ontiveros,
1806: 72.

National independence and a defensive military posture, the two pillars
of the new Haitian state, were indissociable from a third, more vexing question: what should be done with Haiti's white inhabitants? Whites had occasionally supported the rebel cause, but they were also a daily reminder of the
country's former ties to France and a major security threat in the event of
another war. A decision on the matter could hardly be put off, since Dessalines planned on invading Santo Domingo at the earliest opportunity and he
could hardly leave behind him a population of uncertain allegiance.

Dessalines had repeatedly vowed that he would show mercy to the white
colonists who remained in Haiti, but he also had a long record of deceiving
his rivals until he was strong enough to crush them; his promises must thus be
analyzed with a critical eye. According to a French spy, as early as July 1803
Dessalines was telling his followers that he would slaughter all the whites of
Cap, "even nursing infants," after taking the town.[24] Promises he made that
year to white colonists, he later confessed, were a ploy to convince them to
remain in Haiti so that he could kill them all.[25] Similar assurances he gave

to British envoys were likely designed to secure their support, while his re-strained conduct after capturing Jérémie and Port Républicain was intended to prevent a drawn-out defense in other towns of the colony.

With the evacuation of Cap, Dessalines' need for British support and ci-vilian quiescence disappeared, and the first signs appeared that he might not hold true to his word. After promising Rochambeau that he would repatriate the sick and wounded French soldiers who had been left behind in Cap, he or-dered them drowned far at sea (as were the sick left in Môle) in retaliation for the mass drownings carried out by French troops. Eager to avenge the earlier crime of slavery, he also forced many whites to toil on his new fortresses and employed his former master as a servant. Many concerned colonists tried to leave Haiti, only to be denied a passport and told to await their fate.[26]

In this context, Boisrond's angry declaration of independence felt to many whites as their own eulogy. Not only did Boisrond remind his listeners of the horrific crimes committed by the French, he also argued that vengeance was a sacred duty for all Haitians who had lost family members. "Will you go down to your tomb without avenging them?" he intoned. "No, their bones would push yours away." Killing Frenchmen would have the added advan-tage of cementing the rebel victory. "Let us scare all those who would dare to ravish" our freedom, he said. "May they shudder when approaching our coasts . . . because of the terrible resolution that we will take to kill all French-born individuals who would sully the territory of liberty with their sacrile-gious presence." Technically, these vengeful words only applied to French-born citizens, not white Creoles, but the general tone of the declaration did not bode well for the new state's white inhabitants. That night, when Dessa-lines debated their fate with his generals, a few advocated a general massacre.[27]

Dessalines then headed to Port-au-Prince, where new fears arose about the loyalty of white Haitians. Many left surreptitiously on board foreign ships despite strict orders to remain in Haiti, and rumors abounded that the white colonists who had so promptly abandoned Louverture in 1802 were secretly rooting for France to intervene again.[28] After he was warned by Admiral John Duckworth that a new French expedition was imminent, Dessalines told his generals that they should not show "undue indulgence toward our ene-mies."[29] Soon after, he announced a vast investigation into the crimes com-mitted under Leclerc and Rochambeau, probably not to identify individual culprits (a daunting task with an estimated sixty thousand victims and no judicial system), but to convince Haitians that the white population teemed with murderers.[30]

By the middle of February, Dessalines concluded that after weeks of propa-ganda efforts the popular mood was ready for his long-delayed plans of ven-geance. He sent orders to Léogane, Jacmel, and Cayes to massacre local white inhabitants and spent several weeks in the southern region to oversee their implementation. Rich merchants and captured French privateers were executed at once, but resistance to Dessalines' comprehensive agenda proved stronger than he had anticipated. Despite his evocations of recent French atrocities, ties between white and mixed-race families were numerous in the area, and many individuals, though opposed to French rule in general, were unwilling to kill a French neighbor or stepbrother. Geffrard proved particularly reluctant and in Cayes executions dragged on for a month.[31] He also tacitly condoned the efforts of foreign merchants to smuggle out white victims, and a Scottish American merchant and Freemason named Duncan McIntosh managed to save dozens of fellow Masons by bribing sentinels.[32] In all, an estimated 120 of 500 whites in the town were spared or evacuated; the rest were put to death.[33]

Followed by a train of mules carrying the effects of Cayes' notables, Dessalines next marched to Jérémie, where he arrived on February 25.[34] Despite efforts at secrecy, rumors about his intentions had preceded him there. Étienne Chazotte, the merchant who had welcomed the rebel takeover with open arms in 1803, learned from a British resident that Haitian officers had resolved in a meeting "to permit but very few Frenchmen to remain on the island" and began to fear for his life.[35]

Probably angered by the resistance he had encountered in Cayes, Dessalines had brought with him outside troops to ensure that his orders would be strictly implemented and the killing was methodical. After demanding that all planters from rural areas gather in Jérémie, Dessalines assembled white males on the main square and separated them according to their trade. Doctors and a few merchants specializing in the U.S. trade were set aside; others were sent to prison. Dessalines promised that he would spare all those who paid protection money, but this was merely a trick to gather their riches more efficiently and two hundred of the captives were massacred in the prison when they attempted to revolt. The rest were taken to the outskirts of town to be decapitated or bayoneted (using guns would have alerted the population of other towns) and their bodies left in a pitiable pile "for the country Negroes, as Dessalines said, to look at their masters and no longer depend upon them."[36]

Geffrard had vouched for Chazotte, who found himself one of a dozen surviving Frenchmen in the town. After witnessing so much gore and theft, he was quite surprised when Dessalines summoned him and offered to pay for the goods soldiers had taken in his shop. Chazotte's good English had convinced Dessalines that he was a U.S. national, and eager to assuage foreign trading partners he assured Chazotte that "what he had done and I had witnessed was to revenge the wrongs Bonaparte had done to him and the colony.

But I love the Americans. . . . Write, write to your friends—let them send all these things; whatever may be the cost, I will pay them well."[37]

In following days, as his soldiers found several survivors who had been hidden by sympathetic Jérémians, an exasperated Dessalines insisted that local soldiers, particularly those of mixed racial ancestry, serve as executors to make it impossible for them to deny their involvement in the massacre. White women were also targeted at this stage and were often raped or pushed into forced marriages under threat of death. Dessalines finally offered amnesty to surviving whites—only to kill them as they got out of hiding—and left the town with eighty-seven mules laden with specie and silver plate. With the exception of a handful of individuals who had been spared for their skills or ties to local notables and an unspecified number of women, Jérémie's 450 white inhabitants were no more. U.S. merchants conspired to evacuate the few survivors in ensuing months, and Chazotte landed in Baltimore in June 1804.

The rest of Dessalines' campaign unfolded with remarkable similarity as he moved from Petit Goâve to Léogane and beyond. Everywhere, he reminded indecisive countrymen of French atrocities and forced the more reluctant to participate in executions. Everywhere, massacres were accompanied by plundering and sexual exactions. Everywhere, individuals with useful trades or personal ties to Dessalines and his officers were spared. Everywhere, foreign merchants smuggled potential victims out of the country. In Port-au-Prince, where isolated executions turned into a full-blown massacre with Dessalines' arrival on March 18, a British captain estimated the death toll at eight hundred, with fifty survivors.[38] Dessalines then headed for Cap, stopping in Arcahaye, Saint-Marc, and Gonaïves to oversee each town's massacre.[39] Popular opposition must have remained strong, because in order to justify his actions Dessalines published an old letter in which inhabitants of Jérémie had expressed their admiration for Rochambeau (his point was somewhat undermined by the fact that many of the signatories were foreign merchants and mixed-race individuals whom Dessalines had decided to spare).[40]

Christophe killed a few of Cap's notables on his own (primarily to steal their money), but it was not until Dessalines' arrival on April 18 that the general slaughter began in this city. The pattern was now familiar: financial requisitions, mass executions in the streets and outside of town, mercy for a few select individuals and all foreigners, searches, attempts to escape on board merchantmen or to Santo Domingo, and finally a pardon to lure the last survivors out of hiding.[41] Contemporaries put the death toll in the town at 3,000, but the figure was probably exaggerated since only 1,700 whites had remained in Cap after the French evacuation.[42]

In Cap as elsewhere, most white women and children survived the initial massacres, which were presented as retribution for slavery and French atrocities and targeted primarily planters and guardsmen. White and mixed-race women were instead abused sexually, probably in imitation of the planters' past exploitation of slave women. As the massacre in Cap reached its end, however, members of Dessalines' entourage told him that the white population would never be fully extirpated unless white women died as well, or "they w[ould] bear more Frenchmen."[43] On his orders most women were killed in the following days unless they agreed to marry officers of color.[44] In all, estimates about the total number of white colonists killed after independence range from three thousand to five thousand people.[45]

Contemporaries often attributed Dessalines' 1804 massacres to his violent personality, thus turning it into the irrational act of a psychopath, while his apologists blame popular pressure, his entourage, or even the British to exonerate him.[46] In fact, Dessalines' decision was a well-thought-out act whose rationale he outlined at length in an April 28 proclamation in which he announced that he had "avenged America." Front and center in his proclamation was payback for the crimes committed under Leclerc and Rochambeau, and more generally slavery and imperialism. Dessalines next cited security imperatives at a time when a French invasion was a distinct possibility. Last and most intriguingly, he presented the massacre as a form of nation building. "Your reconciliation had to be sealed in the blood of your executioners," he told black and mixed-race Haitians. "You suffered the same calamities, you struck your enemies with the same ardor, you faced the same punishment, so the same interests now make you inseparable."[47]

Left unmentioned in Dessalines' list of justifications were the important financial interests at stake. Scenes of looting marked every step of his northbound journey from Cayes to Cap, amply showing that appropriating the planters' wealth was a powerful motivator for the average soldier. The eagerness of officers of color to marry widowed white planters cannot have been unconnected to their wealth either. Dessalines also confiscated the estates of his victims and eventually decreed that land ownership in Haiti would be exclusively limited to Haitians, that is, people of color.[48] The nonownership clause, which drew on a long history of land disputes between colonial officers and white colonists, would remain a hallmark of all Haitian constitutions until it was abolished following a 1915 U.S. invasion.

"I do not care about the opinion that contemporary and future races will have about me," Dessalines concluded in his April 28 proclamation. The fact that he spent so much time justifying himself and protecting foreign nationals suggests that he did in fact care about public opinion; but the massacre shattered the reputation of the new Haitian state and that of black freedmen in general. Haitian folklore holds that what happens to a person on January 1 foreshadows the rest of the year; Dessalines' unfortunate New Year's resolution instantly gave Haiti a sulfurous reputation that it has, to a large extent, yet to shake. As a rebel colony led by former slaves, Haiti already labored against deeply entrenched racial prejudices, which could only have been overcome by adopting conciliatory policies. Instead, news of Haiti's independence was closely followed in Atlantic ports by accounts of mass executions, complete with horror stories of raped and disemboweled white women. The effect on most individuals was dramatic. As of February 1804, Étienne Dupusch, a white Dominguian exiled in Philadelphia, was sympathetic to the new re-gime because of the greed and despotism of the French expeditionary army. Two weeks later, after hearing of the first exactions against white civilians, he abruptly canceled plans to return to Cap and began describing Dessalines as a bloodthirsty monster.[49]

In later years, Haiti, which could have been the symbol of a successful postemancipation society, became a pariah state branded as a "nightmare on earth" whose history was "written in blood" (to use the titles of two histo-ries of Haiti).[50] By reinforcing the contemporary belief that the innate sav-ageness of black laborers could only be contained by strict social controls, the 1804 massacres gave a century worth of rhetorical ammunition to advocates of slavery in the U.S. South and beyond.[51] So controversial were the massacres that sympathetic historians of the revolution generally chose to ignore them altogether.[52]

Another victim of the massacres was Dessalines' alliance with the British. Early in 1804, a British diplomat named Edward Corbet twice visited Haiti to conclude a treaty of commerce and nonaggression.[53] British reluctance to fully recognize Haiti's sovereignty complicated negotiations, but an agree-ment was still within reach when Corbet heard rumors that a massacre was imminent in Jérémie, where the negotiations were taking place. Corbet "had it in contemplation to have made a representation to General Dessalines upon the subject," but after some hesitation he left for Jamaica on the HMS *Tartar* to seek further instructions.[54] By the time the *Tartar* returned on March 15, horrified sailors and negotiators realized that the massacre had already taken place. Even the *Tartar*'s mixed-race captain, John Perkins, who had sold much war contraband to the rebels in previous months, was moved by the "horrid" sight of rotting, mangled corpses and lost much of his admiration for the new regime.[55] Jamaica's governor, George Nugent, wrote Dessalines one last let-ter to salvage a commercial treaty, but aghast by the "cruelties committed by that ferocious chief" he began to express hopes that Dessalines would soon be overthrown.[56] The admiral who brought Nugent's last-chance letter landed in Cap in the midst of the city's massacre, thus shattering any chance of a British–Haitian alliance for good.[57] From that point on, British captains who had done so much to hasten the rebel victory focused their efforts on smuggling out white survivors while countenancing French privateering attacks on Haitian commerce.[58]

Whether exterminating individuals implicated in slavery and mass murder is morally justifiable is a complex ethical issue, one that remains open to this day; whether the 1804 massacres constitute a form of genocide is another difficult question. From a purely legal perspective, the events fulfill the criteria of present-day international law, but the term "massacre" or "pogrom" might be more fitting since a genocide implies that the victimized group was selected primarily on racial or religious grounds, when race was a secondary factor in 1804. The colonists were killed not because they were white, but because they were French (white foreigners were spared) and because they were land-owning planters whose assets were coveted by officers of color (many merchants, priests, craftsmen, widows, and doctors were spared). Support for or opposition to the colonists' death did not match racial lines either. The black Dessalines was among the hardliners, but so were his mixed-race aides-de-camp Boisrond, Chanlatte, and Bazelais, and in Jérémie Polish troops joined in the killing. Meanwhile, the black general, Christophe, and the former black mayor of Cap, César Télémaque, expressed their reservations, as did Dessalines' black wife Claire-Heureuse and much of the black population, which Dessalines constantly had to prod with proclamations.[59]

Contemporaries generally described the white population as virtually annihilated, and indeed to this day Haiti is the most ethnically African nation in the Caribbean; but a significant number of white individuals survived and lived on in the "black" republic. Dozens of British and American agents of foreign mercantile firms and hundreds of sailors could be seen in major ports. Like Chazotte, many of them were French nationals who had acquired foreign citizenship to save their lives, leading Dessalines to complain about the inordinate number of suspicious Swedes living in his country.[60] People with rare skills (from surgeons to boot makers) were also spared, so the person who printed Dessalines' vengeful proclamations in Cap was a Frenchman named Roux, whose name appears at the bottom of countless public documents from Louverture's time to Dessalines'.[61] In his April 28 proclamation, Dessalines also earmarked for special treatment "a handful of whites recommended by their religion and who pledged to live with us in the woods." This passage alluded to white priests like Delahaye and Corneille Brelle, who had supported the rebels since the 1791 uprising and remained in Haiti after independence.[62]

Among the white citizens of the "black" republic were many Polish defectors. Of the 5,200 Poles who sailed with the Leclerc expedition, 1,200 survived, 450 of whom remained in Haiti after independence.[63] Most Polish officers were eager to leave Haiti, but the rank and file were more hesitant;

a group of 160 Poles sent to Jamaica after independence asked to be repatriated to Haiti rather than enroll in the British army.[64] Dessalines viewed the Poles as fellow victims of imperialism and granted them full citizenship in a special clause of his 1805 constitution. Concentrated in a few towns like Casales, the Poles of Haiti gave birth to several generations of fair-skinned, blue-eyed Haitians. The community was still distinct enough in 1983 for Pope John Paul II to meet distant cousins during a state visit.[65]

The partial eradication of the white population made defining the requirements of Haitian citizenship particularly arduous. The Haitian Revolution had begun with the demands of white colonists for more colonial autonomy, so the new state could conceivably have adopted commitment to independence as the main standard for citizenship; Caribbean (and, temporarily, African) birth was another option. Instead, Dessalines declared that all Haitians would be known generically as "blacks," thus equating skin color with citizenship (to this day, a foreigner is described in Haitian Kreyol as a *blan,* or "white"). But Dessalines also granted full citizenship to Polish and German defectors, widows of white planters, and select male Frenchmen, thus tacitly admitting that Haiti's racial uniformity was a myth.[66]

The racial basis for citizenship and the habit of calling black Haitians *authentiques* were a source of legitimate concern for mixed-race individuals. Most were the children or grandchildren of white colonists; branding all white Frenchmen as traitors while using blackness as a standard for citizenship left them isolated in a country that was overwhelmingly black. The 1804 massacres, which Dessalines thought would unify the population of color, instead convinced many mixed-race individuals that they would be massacred next, prompting many to flee for Cuba in ensuing months.[67]

Dessalines' misguided racial agenda proved costly. A revolution waged in the name of racial equality gave birth to a country relegating certain races to second-class status. The only country in the world led by emancipated slaves was held as living proof that blacks could not govern themselves. And a war won by uniting most people of color into a single army gave its independence to a nation whose most glaring social characteristic has been a long history of conflict between its black and mixed-race citizenry.

~

In his April 28 proclamation, Dessalines insisted that he was "unlike [his] predecessor, the ex-general Louverture." Probably intended to capitalize on Louverture's unpopularity with the black rank and file, this passing swipe at the deceased statesman was wholly inaccurate. Dessalines spent the bulk of 1804 marching in Louverture's footsteps, a father figure he had successively served, betrayed, criticized, and now emulated. He began the year by declaring independence in a city, Gonaïves, that Louverture had once envisioned as his capital, in the heart of a province that Louverture had named after himself.[68] He also claimed the title of "governor general for life," which made no sense in a sovereign state but that had once been Louverture's.[69] Last and most importantly, he tried to maintain the export-based model he had inherited from Louverture (and, before him, France), thus keeping intact the economic and social structure of the new nation even as it obtained its political independence.

The Haitian Revolution damaged many plantation buildings, but it did not destroy the plantation system itself. Although rhetorically opposed to slavery, Dessalines was a rich landowner who maintained Louverture's cultivator system and forced laborers to remain on plantations after independence, so in the short term the revolution's sole effect was to transfer the ownership of surviving estates from white planters to officers of color.[70] The meaningless transition was a sobering letdown for a black population that had fought long and hard for individual freedom, and popular resistance to Dessalines' labor regulations was strong. As they had done in the days of slavery, laborers ran away (often to remote reaches of French-occupied Santo Domingo), forcing Dessalines to issue a law punishing emigration with the death penalty.[71]

Such harsh measures reflected Dessalines' demographic preoccupations. The new Haiti needed citizens (that is, soldiers and plantation laborers) but few could be found in the aftermath of a revolution that had killed half the population. Eager to repopulate his country, Dessalines offered U.S. merchants forty gourdes for every exiled Dominguian slave they brought back to Haiti and asked Nugent to repatriate the troops of color who had been taken to Jamaica.[72] Like Louverture, he also took the controversial step of asking British slave traders to sell some of their African cargo in Haiti, a plan that only fell through when the British government, facing growing domestic opposition to the slave trade, vetoed it.[73]

A number of individual deportees returned from France (most notably André Rigaud and Martial Besse, both of whom survived a stint in Fort de Joux), but overall the number of people who settled in Haiti under Dessalines was minimal.[74] Despite this setback, attempts to boost the country's population through immigration would remain an objective of subsequent Haitian regimes for over half a century, most notably in the 1820s, when President Jean-Pierre Boyer set up an immigration bureau in New York to encourage U.S. freedmen to settle in Haiti.[75] Culture shock, tropical diseases, and limited economic opportunities hampered such initiatives, and it was ultimately by natural growth that Haiti's population eventually recovered—so much so that the country is now severely overpopulated.

Dessalines' eagerness to preserve the plantation model had important political implications. To overcome popular resistance to forced labor, he decided to resort to military rule before independence had even been achieved, then formalized his dictatorship in an 1805 constitution.[76] The official, oddly racist justification for one-general rule was that a population of ex-slaves was not fit for self-government (the absence of checks and balances also facilitated massive corruption).[77] Dictatorship and embezzlement have remained two central features of the Haitian political scene ever since.

Eager to preserve Haiti as a plantation economy linked to Atlantic trading networks, Dessalines also strove to maintain the commercial links with the United States that Louverture had revived. U.S. merchants were shocked by the death of white colonists, but their primary purpose was commercial and they initially flocked to a country where the price of imports was high and coffee abundant.[78] Many of these merchants, surprisingly, were naturalized French citizens.[79] Among them was Antoine Laussat, once a French colonist (and the brother of the governor of Louisiana), now a Philadelphia merchant specializing in the Haitian trade.[80] Laussat was close to Louverture's former ambassador, Joseph Bunel, who also moved to Philadelphia after being persecuted by Leclerc. Bunel quickly renewed his commercial ties to Dessalines' regime, and in August 1804 set sail for Haiti. This and later voyages proved lucrative, and by 1807 he had settled permanently in Haiti. His wife Marie, though a black *ancien libre* close to the wives of many prominent Haitian generals, was reluctant to abandon the financially rewarding life she had made for herself in Philadelphia and only followed him three years later.[81]

Thomas Jefferson did little to interfere with U.S. trade to Haiti, so French privateers operating out of Cuba, Guadeloupe, and Santo Domingo took it upon themselves to prevent U.S. exports to a country they regarded as a rebel colony. As often before, controversies over the Haitian trade soon led to naval confrontations with armed U.S. merchantmen and a dangerously high state of Franco-American tensions.[82] Eager to appease France and the southern states, Jefferson eventually sponsored two laws that embargoed all U.S. trade to Haiti, but enforcement was lax and in the end it was Haiti's own economic decline that stamped out the foreign trade. By 1860, Haiti had become the United States' forty-sixth trading partner, down from second seventy years earlier and a striking reflection of the country's relative decline.[83]

Nonintervention overseas, Anglo-American trading links, forced labor, and military dictatorship: with the exception of formal independence, Dessalines' regime was closely modeled on that of Louverture, down to a constitutional clause allowing Dessalines to appoint his successor, and to a lesser extent on that of Leclerc.[84] Dessalines' relationship with white planters was more adversarial than had been the case under his predecessors, but even Louverture had advocated comprehensive massacres after the 1802 French landings. However stirring the words of the declaration of independence may have been, 1804 was to a large extent a period of continuity.

Did Dessalines remember Louverture's crowning moment, when he had presented his constitution to an adoring crowd in July 1801? Or was he moved into action by news that Bonaparte would soon become emperor of France? Six months after independence, Dessalines announced that he wanted to be crowned emperor of Haiti, and on October 8 he presided over a ceremony that replicated step for step the presentation of Louverture's constitution in Cap. Long before dawn, troops assembled on the Champ de Mars, followed an hour later by civilian and military authorities. Once everyone had gathered, the act nominating Dessalines as emperor was read, after which Louverture's former confessor, Corneille Brelle, officially crowned the former slave Jean-Jacques Dessalines as Emperor Jacques I to the sound of thunderous broadsides from the ships in the harbor. A formal Te Deum, a reception, and general rejoicing closed this memorable day, which to many participants must have had a strong feeling of déjà vu.[85]

Dessalines should have learned from Louverture's precedent not to trust the adulators surrounding him. A mere two years after his coronation, as he began taking steps to seize their plantations, Dessalines' own officers assassinated him. His violent death brought down a man generally considered in Haiti as the greatest of the revolutionary heroes. It also added one last item to the list of revolutionary practices that survived into postindependence Haiti: the army coup.

19

The Long Way Home

French Refugees and the Fall of Santo Domingo

1804–9

For the French veterans of the Leclerc expedition, Haiti's independence opened the last chapter in a long and often fatal personal journey. From Jamaica to Cuba, from Santo Domingo to the United States, Saint-Domingue's soldiers of misfortune spent years making their way back to France, often leaving behind an economic and cultural imprint that could still be felt decades later.

The single largest group of survivors was the garrison of Cap, which was intercepted at sea by the British as it evacuated and was immediately sent to Jamaica and captivity. The French deeply resented finding themselves at the mercy of the hated British, who had never defeated—or even fought—them on land during the expedition, while French officers complained that in violation of the capitulation agreement the British often seized their weapons. More to the point, the British performed a thorough search of their prisoners' abundant luggage, and many horrified officers saw the fruit of eighteen months of conscientious plundering disappear into the pockets of an English tar.[1]

Upon reaching Port Royal, the prisoners were welcomed by rotting corpses dangling within iron cages at the entrance to the port. These were the sailors of the HMS *Hermione,* who had been executed for participating in one of the most famous mutinies in the history of the British navy.[2] The grotesque scene was an apt harbinger of sufferings to come.

The individuals captured with the French army were white and black, male and female, young and old, but aside from civilian status the most relevant factor during captivity was military rank. Privates, noncommissioned officers, and their families (women included) were typically dispatched to pontoon ships.[3] These were derelict warships used to house prisoners of war during the revolutionary wars and whose reputation was notorious. Eaten through by worms, carrying fevers, overcrowded, and overheated, Jamaica's pontoon ships were among the worst of the era and came across as singularly hellish even to people who had survived the epidemic of 1802 and the 1803 sieges. So horrid were conditions on board Jamaican pontoons that Governor George Nugent was able to recruit 565 foreign soldiers, who preferred to enlist for a second round of duty in the Caribbean under a different uniform than endure another day of captivity.[4]

Prisoners were held below decks under heavy guard, and opportunities for escape were limited. A courageous cabin boy captured with the *Duquesne* jumped ship the day he arrived in Jamaica and apparently made it to shore and freedom, so British wardens fed circling sharks to discourage such initiatives thereafter.[5] Another reluctant prisoner was the sailor Jean-Baptiste Lemonnier-Delafosse, who was captured along with the garrison of Cap in November 1803. As a noncommissioned officer, Lemonnier was dispatched to the pontoons, but he quickly managed to be transferred to the hospital ship by pretending to be sick. Security was less strict there, and on "a beautiful, pitch-dark night made for lovers and prisoners" he slipped through a window and made it to shore, where he passed himself as an officer out on parole.[6]

The parole system was typical of the secluded world of honor and mutual respect in which officers of all nations lived during the revolutionary era. Paroled officers were allowed to live semifreely in their own rented house in Kingston as long as they made a formal pledge that they would not try to escape.[7] Their lives were accordingly far removed from the horrific world of the pontoons. The memoirs of Nugent's wife, Maria, even mention several instances in which her husband invited prominent French officers and their wives for dinner, and a particularly festive ball during which Philibert Fressinet "almost ma[d]e love to me."[8]

Jamaica was a plantation society similar to Saint-Domingue's, but relations between French exiles and the local population were often tense. Planters and merchants, Lemonnier noted, routinely incited their slaves to insult paroled French officers as "negroes of Bonaparte, valets of Rochambeau," and, of course, "frog eaters."[9] This poor reception stemmed from concerns that French evacuees would bring yellow fever to Jamaica or would initiate a slave revolt. Such concerns peaked around Christmas (a traditional time of revelry for slaves), then again in March 1804, when a rumor spread that Jean-Baptiste Brunet was plotting an uprising in collusion with Jamaica's Jewish community, which had also been involved in a 1799 French plot.[10]

Relations were particularly acrimonious with Donatien de Rochambeau, who was furious at the British for robbing him of what he had previously stolen in Saint-Domingue and regularly wrote incendiary letters to complain of various violations of the capitulation agreement.[11] Rochambeau also had a way of getting into fights with his own countrymen, who challenged him to duels no less than seventeen times in a single week because of his controversial record as captain general.[12] Eager to rid himself of the troublesome commander, Nugent sent him and his most disreputable associates to England within three weeks of their arrival in Jamaica.[13] Rochambeau's English exile was destined to be lengthy since Bonaparte, appalled by his colonial record, did not exchange him until 1811. He later rejoined the French army and died in combat near Leipzig in 1813, but his patriotic death was insufficient to reclaim his name: Rochambeau's horrendous reputation is one of the few consistent points in the various histories of the expedition, both French and Haitian.[14]

Concerned about a possible French uprising, Nugent quickly repatriated most officers and urged civilians to leave for Cuba or New Orleans, but evacuating the rest of the prisoners was bound to take more time.[15] Seven thousand prisoners, 5,500 of them in pontoon ships, crowded Kingston and Port Royal by the end of 1803.[16] Repatriating them at once was impossible for lack of warships, sailors, and guards, and since Nugent was wont to use private merchantmen due to the cost and risk of escape there were still 5,500 prisoners in Jamaica (4,400 of them on pontoons) as of March 1804.[17] According to the detailed statistics kept by British jailers, these numbers included 251 sailors, forty-nine men of color, twenty-two cabin boys, seven Jews, three dragoons, two women, and one vagrant, all of whom had been captured on the *Duquesne* nine months earlier.[18] Such delays often proved fatal; forty-eight of 209 evacuees from Jérémie had died by February 1804.[19] The wait also exasperated British captains, whose prizes could not be sold as long as they housed prisoners and daily lost value in the worm-infested waters of Port Royal.[20]

In April 1804 the arrival of a naval squadron from England finally gave Nugent an opportunity to dispatch a large number of prisoners, but the ships used for this purpose were in poor repair and the voyage far from pleasant. The *Duquesne* left in March, only to hit Morand Keys and return to Jamaica, then sail again with a nagging leak a month later. The *Créole* caught fire and exploded; the *Hardy* sank in Havana, as did the *Athenais* near St. Augustine, Florida; and the *Fanny* had to be rescued after spending five months wandering the Atlantic.[21] The medical student André Guimot was luckier and reached Plymouth safely in February 1804—if one can describe as "lucky" a journey spent in such squalor that it cost the lives of twenty French and fifteen British passengers.[22]

By November 1804, with the exception of a few hundred sailors, all French prisoners had left Jamaica, usually for an even lengthier bout of captivity in England.[23] Lemonnier had also evacuated—thrice. He first boarded a ship transporting civilians to Santiago de Cuba, only to be captured again when he enrolled on a French privateer. He left Jamaica a second time with a boatload of French officers in the fall of 1804, but refusing to endure captivity in England he jumped ship and swam to shore. A sympathetic planter arranged for him to leave one last time for Cuba, an island where Saint-Domingue exiles were particularly numerous.[24]

~

As seen through the eyes of Lemonnier and countless other French refugees, Cuba was a colonial backwater whose considerable economic potential was hampered by Spain's retrograde policies. Settled since the early days of the Spanish conquest, it held the most strategic port in the Western Hemisphere, Havana, and boasted a population of about four hundred thousand. But less than half that number were slaves, an unusually low proportion in a region where slaves often outnumbered freemen ten to one wherever sugar cultivation was possible and an indication of the primitive state of the plantation system.[25] The French viewed their Spanish hosts as equally backward culturally and often described them as lazy, fanatical Catholics addicted to gambling and smoking.[26]

The dislike was mutual. Afraid to see Haiti's revolutionary violence spread to Cuba, Governor Marques de Someruelos refused to admit people of color and tried to discourage other French refugees from landing in Cuba by claiming to have no food or insisting on lengthy quarantines.[27] Resistance proved futile; several waves of immigration pushed the French population in Cuba to between twenty and thirty thousand by 1804, two-thirds of them former slaves or free people of color.[28] People who had once been enslaved typically lost the benefits of the 1793 emancipation decree and became slaves once more, but the awkward transition seems to have gone surprisingly smoothly, possibly because French masters had brought their most devoted servants, or because slavery in Spanish colonies was considered comparatively mild.[29]

For all their faults the Saint-Domingue colonists were an entrepreneurial group that had managed in one century to turn a colonial backwater into the most prosperous colony in the Western Hemisphere. Their arrival radically transformed Cuba's eastern province, where they were most numerous. Finding themselves widowed and penniless, women who had never toiled a day learned to work for a living, while once-opulent colonists set out to restore their fortune from scratch. The French turned to privateering to seize slaves from passing merchantmen and switched their main focus from sugar to coffee, whose start-up costs were far smaller. With relatively small holdings of ten slaves per household, planters soon turned the hills around Santiago de

Cuba into a thriving area yielding three hundred thousand *arrobas* of coffee a year, up from eight thousand before their arrival. Cuba also benefited from the demise of Haiti as a major sugar producer, and over the following decades it became the Caribbean's new sugar powerhouse.[30]

The colonists also introduced their frivolous ways to an oft-austere Spanish culture. A new French quarter rose in Santiago de Cuba, its centerpiece a dance hall highly popular with the youth of the town. The French *belles* had long since lost their jewels, but they made up for their poverty with creativity; they attached small lightning bugs named *coejos* to their hair and went dancing surrounded by an emerald halo.[31] The French exiles' cultural imprint can still be witnessed in eastern Cuba to this day, where local clubs feature the *tumba francesa,* a form of quadrille imported by Dominguian slaves, who themselves had copied it from their aristocratic masters.[32]

For the French of Cuba, the Haitian war of independence did not end in January 1804. Rochambeau had been issuing letters of marque since the outbreak of the war with England, and many privateers used Cuban ports as a base despite the objections of Someruelos, who feared being dragged into a war with England.[33] British naval superiority hindered their activities at first, but after Haiti's independence the British came to conclude that French privateering might quell Dessalines' growing power, and with their tacit approval Cuba soon turned into a major nest of French privateers that wrought havoc on U.S. merchantmen headed for Haiti.[34]

In addition to civilian colonists, 1,500 French soldiers made it to Cuba, most of them members of the garrisons of Port-au-Prince and Môle Saint-Nicolas, which had eluded the British blockade with their commanders Jean Lavalette and Louis de Noailles.[35] Both generals were eager to continue the fight, and shortly after his arrival Noailles used his fluent English to deceive and board a British corvette in a surprise attack. He succeeded (a rare French naval victory in an era of English domination), but he was mortally wounded in the assault, his glorious death a slight corrective to a life forever tainted by his purchase of man-eating dogs during his previous stay in Cuba.[36]

Lavalette proved as energetic and ill fated as his colleague. After purchasing five vessels with prize money obtained from privateering ventures, he set sail from Havana in April 1804 to reinforce the French army in Santo Domingo.[37] To his troops, who had not been paid for eleven months and were hoping to finally return to France, he announced that they were instead headed back to Hispaniola and another round of fighting. "By taking them to Santo Domingo, I only offered them a continuation of their privations, a destructive climate, and the obligation to resume the campaign in Saint-Domingue as soon as feasible," Lavalette explained.[38]

Most of the troops traveling with Lavalette were from the elite 5th light demi-brigade, but two years of accumulated discontent reached their climax as the fleet neared the Bahamas and a storm broke out. The *Marianne* willfully lost ground in the hardening seas and, finding herself isolated, was soon captured by a British ship. The *Sans Pareil* went down, taking with her Lavalette and all but twenty-three survivors. The remaining ships were supposed to rendezvous in Puerto Rico on their way to Santo Domingo, but after witnessing Lavalette's death his troops decided to take their destiny in their own hands. The *Affricaine* left for Charleston, where it surrendered to a British privateer, while the *Habanera* and the *Dermide,* after wandering in the Atlantic long enough to claim that they had gotten lost in the storm, headed north for the Chesapeake. The French ambassador, Louis-André Pichon, saw through the ruse, but concerned that rerouting the discouraged soldiers to their proper destination would spark a mutiny he arranged for them to return to France at long last.[39]

Lemonnier was not on the ill-fated Lavalette squadron. He boarded a smaller detachment of two hundred French soldiers that left for Santo Domingo in December 1804. His safe arrival opened a new chapter in his eventful life, one that would last almost five years.[40]

~

Like Cuba, Santo Domingo came across to French refugees as both ancient and backward. Its capital (also named Santo Domingo) was the oldest continuously occupied European settlement in the Western Hemisphere and boasted elaborate fortifications and a half-ruined government house built by Christopher Columbus's son.[41] But the colony, though covering two-thirds of the surface of Hispaniola and some of its best lands, only produced a fraction of what its French neighbor had exported before the revolution. The French variously attributed Santo Domingo's economic underdevelopment to the laziness of its population, extensive racial miscegenation, or the nefarious influence of the monks.[42] Lemonnier was particularly struck by the excited processions of Holy Week, when statues of the saints were marched down the streets to the loud mourning wails of the population.[43]

The Spaniards had their own grievances regarding French ways. Short on cash, the French had once made plans to melt the silver altar ornaments of nunneries and monasteries, a sacrilegious idea that had raised a firestorm of opposition among religious orders.[44] Spaniards were also annoyed that their neighbor's frequent revolutionary upheavals always had a way of spilling into Spanish Santo Domingo. Settled by Spain, retroceded to France, invaded by Toussaint Louverture, then blockaded by England, the colony had seen enough masters in recent years for a local priest to improvise a mocking *quintilla*.[45]

Ayer Español nací.	Yesterday I was born a Spaniard.
A la tarde fui Francés.	In the evening I became French.
A la noche Etiope fui.	That night I was Ethiopian.
Hoy, dicen que soy Inglés:	Today, they say I am English:
No sé qué será de mí.	I do not know what will become of me.

Santo Domingo was under the leadership of François de Kerversau, who after doing so much to convince Bonaparte of Louverture's disloyalty had returned with the expedition in February 1802. He had been militarily successful, conquering the vast territory with a mere 450 French troops, then controlling it with 150 survivors of the yellow fever epidemic—so successful, in fact, that he was completely forgotten and left to his own devices.[46] Forced to make do with local resources, Kerversau drafted Spanish guardsmen, who proved highly unreliable and often deserted en masse whenever the rebels gained the upper hand. "Desertion is a disease that is endemic among the Spaniards of Santo Domingo," Kerversau noted in discouragement. "I have seen 600 or 700 men desert in three days' time, then return two weeks later. I made many threats, but always forgave in the end."[47]

It was the evacuation of Saint-Domingue that finally gave Santo Domingo strategic relevance. The garrisons of Jacmel and Croix-des-Bouquets evacuated to the Spanish part of Hispaniola, as did some of the troops present in Cuba, and the colony became the single largest concentration of French troops in the Greater Antilles. Among the newcomers was the garrison of the frontier town of Montecristi, which fled to the city of Santo Domingo after Dessalines threatened an attack.[48] The force was headed by Jean-Louis Ferrand, a general who imperiously demanded that the less senior Kerversau cede his overall command. Judging by a surviving portrait, Ferrand was short, balding, and unimpressive, but he must have had personal charisma because most troops promptly rallied to him, forcing Kerversau to depart for France.[49] As with many Saint-Domingue veterans, Kerversau's years of dutiful service brought few rewards. He was sent back to the Caribbean as prefect of Guadeloupe, only to be taken prisoner when the British seized that island and spend four years in captivity.[50]

Santo Domingo was the obvious starting point for a possible reconquest of Saint-Domingue, and it was not long before the Haitians, eager to remove a major threat to their national security, made their first move. They first targeted Santiago, which was taken and retaken twice in May 1804 as the population switched its support from one invader to the other.[51] But the massacre of most white Frenchmen in Haiti, followed by a menacing proclamation in which Dessalines threatened to do the same in Santo Domingo, quickly sapped local sympathy for the Haitian army.[52] Eager to fan racial fears, Ferrand cleverly presented his troops as the best rampart against "the anthropophagous Dessalines" while annulling some unpopular French decrees targeting the Catholic Church.[53] Spanish draftees defected one last time, Santiago remained in French hands, and sidetracked by the war against hostile Maroon groups Dessalines had to delay a full-blown invasion for another year.[54]

It was in January 1805, shortly after celebrating the first anniversary of Haiti's independence, that Dessalines renewed his calls for an invasion of Santo Domingo. The war, he told his countrymen, was indispensable because Ferrand was planning cross-border raids to take Haitians into slavery.[55] Whether this accusation was grounded in fact is uncertain, but it had the expected effect of whipping up popular support for an invasion (Louverture had used the same excuse to justify his 1801 invasion). More likely, Dessalines' primary objective was to destroy the last remnants of the Leclerc expedition and bring an end to privateering attacks launched from Spanish ports. According to some sources, he even planned to raze the city of Santo Domingo to the ground to secure his eastern border once and for all.

Dessalines attacked on February 25. He led the main column, which crossed Hispaniola's central mountains to attack Azua, while Henri Christophe led a second column that moved from Cap to Santiago on the northern coast. Carrying no cannon, the troops traveled at incredible speed over the difficult terrain and after throwing aside all opposition reached the city of Santo Domingo on March 6, where Nicolas Geffrard joined them with more troops from southern Haiti.

The combined Haitian army totaled up to twenty thousand men, but the French were well prepared for a siege. Santo Domingo was surrounded by a continuous stone wall fifteen feet high, which though ancient in design was effective against unsupported infantry and was hastily reinforced under Ferrand's supervision.[56] With the various forces repatriated to Santo Domingo, Ferrand commanded over a force of seven hundred French troops supplemented by two thousand French and Spanish militia. He sent away noncombatants on available ships, partly to save on food but also to convince remaining troops that no exile was possible.

Under the leadership of Alexandre Pétion, whose service in the French army had included a stint in the *génie* (military engineering), the Haitian army built an impressive series of earthen bastions. Frequent sorties failed to disrupt their work, and after twenty days the French were down to their last reserves while the Haitians, finally reinforced by artillery, made preparations for a mass attack. All night they danced the *calenda* to the sound of drums, while the French and Spanish troops huddled inside the city prepared themselves to die. Only a miracle, Lemonnier thought, could save him now.

A miracle was actually headed his direction. Bonaparte, whose dreams of colonial ventures had resurfaced, had recently sent a small fleet to the Caribbean.[57] In February 1805, it raided Dominica and proceeded northwest to the Greater Antilles, where on March 27 it reached Santo Domingo just as the Haitians prepared to attack. Overjoyed inhabitants rushed to the shore, while Dessalines, convinced that the French squadron was bound for undefended Haiti, lifted the siege and headed home. His invasion had failed; it would take another seventeen years before a Haitian army finally conquered Santo Domingo (atrocities committed during the 1805 retreat are one reason for the current animosity between Haiti and the Dominican Republic).[58]

Dessalines' failure to take the city of Santo Domingo was largely due to the absence of a British fleet, which during the 1803 sieges in Saint-Domingue had prevented the French from reinforcing and supplying their towns. Two British squadrons were sent to Santo Domingo in 1803 and 1805, but they imposed such a loose blockade that their Francophile commander regularly went to shore to have dinner with Ferrand.[59] Concerned by Dessalines' racial extremism, the British refrained from assisting his plans of invasion and even hoped that the French would hold out indefinitely so as to check his ambitions.[60] The British only began to view the French garrison of Santo Domingo as a threat in December 1805, when Bonaparte, after suffering a major setback at Trafalgar, dispatched two large squadrons to harass British commerce. One, led by (now Admiral) Philibert Willaumez, roamed the Atlantic for months but achieved little of substance; the other, under Corentin de Leissègues, stopped in Santo Domingo in January 1806 with five ships of the line and three smaller units.[61]

Contacts with France were rare and there was much celebrating as Leissègues' ships spent two weeks in Santo Domingo recovering from a recent storm. The *Diomède* was tipped over for careening; the 120-gun *Impérial* was outfitted for a large party; and many sailors were on shore early on February 6 when a corvette posted as a lookout fired several shots to warn that she had spotted unknown sails on the horizon. They belonged to the squadron of John Duckworth, former commander of the Jamaica squadron, and now at the head of seven ships of the line whose mission was to destroy any potential naval threat against Jamaica.

The French ships hurriedly set sail, some officers on the wrong ship, others desperately rowing from the shore to catch up with their vessel. The disorganized fleet headed west in a loose line, while Duckworth, clearly inspired by Horatio Nelson's recent triumph at Trafalgar, ordered his ships to attack the French line in two columns ahead. Afraid of being surrounded, Leissègues ordered his own ships to cut through the first enemy column, but several units lagged behind and the *Impérial* and the *Alexandre* faced the brunt of the British onslaught alone while the other ships were surrounded by the second English column. The inexperienced French crews fought bravely for three hours amid mounting casualties, but the disorderly French line could do little against a determined enemy (a naval melee favors veteran sailors who maneuver fast and fire accurately). The *Alexandre,* the *Brave,* and the *Jupiter* were captured in turn; the *Impérial* and the *Diomède* crashed into the coast to avoid being taken; and the morning of February 6, 1806, which had begun so brightly, cost the French navy five ships of the line in a matter of hours. The British had suffered minimal damage, making this naval battle, the largest of the Saint-Domingue expedition, a one-sided disaster. The French spent days trying to rescue sailors from the two wrecked ships (a difficult task on a rocky coast battered by choppy seas) until the British dispatched a party to capture the survivors and set the hulls on fire. The rest of the prizes, filled with hundreds of severely injured French sailors, headed for Jamaica and the dreaded rendezvous with the pontoon ships.[62]

After the destruction of Leissègues' fleet, the French troops marooned in Santo Domingo returned to their lonely routine, as did Lemonnier, now a first-class adjutant.[63] As one year followed another, Ferrand tried to develop the colony's plantations and made ambitious plans to build a port in strategic Sámana Bay.[64] He also sent agents provocateurs to foster ill will between Christophe and Pétion, who had established rival regimes in the north and west of Haiti after Dessalines' 1806 assassination.[65] The last survivors of the Leclerc expedition were otherwise forgotten in their tranquil corner of Hispaniola.

It took events in faraway Europe to upset this equilibrium. Bonaparte's 1808 invasion of Spain sparked a wave of anti-French sentiment throughout Latin America, and a year later the governor of Puerto Rico sent a force to Santo Domingo to expel the French garrison.[66] Hearing that thousands of Spanish rebels were massing in Seybo, Ferrand marched with a small column and, in a bout of overconfidence, attacked a vastly superior force on November 10, 1808. The uneven encounter quickly turned into a rout, and Ferrand, after isolating himself in a nearby wood, killed himself.[67]

Only twenty-eight survivors made it back to the city of Santo Domingo, which the Spanish rebels immediately besieged with the assistance of a British squadron. Ferrand's successor, General Barquier, led a determined resistance for months, but hunger eventually took its toll, and in July 1809 he capitulated to the British. The fall of Santo Domingo put a final end to French military presence in Hispaniola, more than seven years after Leclerc's massive fleet had first sighted Cape Sámana.[68] Along with 150 officers and 320 soldiers representing the last remnants of the expeditionary army, Lemonnier headed for Jamaica and yet another round of captivity. He was quickly granted parole and left for the United States, a frequent stopover for Saint-Domingue refugees as they slowly inched their way back to France.[69]

~

Lemonnier landed in Philadelphia, a city that throughout the revolutionary era served as a haven for French political refugees. Among them was Bonaparte's exiled rival, Jean Moreau, who confided to Lemonnier how distraught he had been to see so many close friends die in the Leclerc expedition.[70] The number of Saint-Domingue refugees in Philadelphia had been particularly large since the summer of 1793, when three thousand planters, free people of color, and slaves had arrived in the aftermath of the first burning of Cap (slavery was in the process of being abolished in Pennsylvania, so many of the slaves brought by French planters became indentured servants instead).[71] Most of these early exiles had returned to Saint-Domingue under Louverture and Leclerc, only to head back to Philadelphia during the colony's dying months.[72]

Although often destitute, white and free-colored Dominguian exiles participated actively in the economic and cultural life of Philadelphia, opening fencing schools, dance schools, and a charitable society.[73] During her stay in Philadelphia, Joseph Bunel's industrious black wife, Marie, acquired a farm outside of town and at least one servant.[74] Étienne Dupusch, the exiled French planter who had once thought of moving to independent Haiti, eventually changed his mind and, pleased with the probusiness environment prevalent in the United States, settled permanently in Philadelphia as a merchant and acquired U.S. citizenship.[75] Elizabeth Beauveau, the English-born wife of a French merchant from Cap, also settled in Philadelphia after her husband's death and opened a boarding house whose clients provided her with an income and a steady supply of husbands for her five daughters.[76] Among the boarders/grooms was the merchant Jean-Claude Sulauze, who after fleeing Jérémie acquired U.S. citizenship and went so quickly native that within two years he was corresponding with a younger brother in English.[77] Overall, the French Dominguians of Philadelphia founded some of the most prosperous business dynasties in town, but they quickly assimilated into the dominant Anglo-Saxon culture and were soon indistinguishable from the general population.[78]

The influence and distinctiveness of the French of New Orleans was more enduring, possibly because the local culture was very similar to Saint-Domingue (down to a penchant for gambling, impiety, and political corruption).[79] Few Dominguians were present in the city until Napoléon's invasion of Spain sparked a mass French exodus from Cuba and nine thousand exiles of all colors arrived at once in New Orleans in 1809, instantly doubling the population of the city. The U.S. abolition of the slave trade had become effective in 1808, but Congress temporarily lifted the ban to give the refugees the means to sustain themselves; the three thousand Dominguian slaves landed from Cuba were thus the last slaves ever imported legally into the United States.[80]

The Saint-Domingue immigrants gave *la Nouvelle Orléans* a marked French Creole character it kept for another fifty years. Notable exiles included Jean-Baptiste LeSueur Fontaine, who founded the city's first newspaper; Louis Moreau Lislet, who drafted Louisiana's Code Civil; Pierre Derbigny, who served as governor of Louisiana; James Pitot, the first mayor of U.S. New Orleans; and the composer Louis Moreau Gottschalk, whose pieces were often based on Caribbean themes he had heard from his Dominguian nanny. The 1809 migration particularly affected New Orleans's free-colored population, which became uniquely large and influential; the famous Supreme Court ruling *Plessy v. Ferguson,* for example, was initiated by Rodolphe Desdunes, a mixed-race New Orleanian descending from the in-laws of the naturalist Michel-Étienne Descourtilz.[81] Dominguian slaves also had a noted impact on the black culture of the city, from the *calenda* and *bamboula* of Congo Square to Louisiana Vodou. The rise of the Louisiana sugar industry during this period may also have been linked to the influx of Saint-Domingue planters.[82]

New Orleans's Dominguian exiles proved loyal to their adopted country, and few volunteered when French authorities arranged for their repatriation in 1810. Instead, battalions of French and mixed-race Dominguians played a distinguished role in the 1815 Battle of New Orleans—as did the famous Saint-Domingue corsair, Jean Lafitte, and veterans of the Leclerc expedition such as Pauline Bonaparte's former lover, Jean Humbert. The exiles' distinctiveness had ebbed by the 1840s, but in 1882 a New Orleans newspaper could still interview a frail near centenarian who spoke an odd mixture of French, English, and Kreyol. Marie-Françoise Similien, as was her name, had been born in Saint-Domingue during the time of the Haitian Revolution, had followed her owner to Santiago de Cuba, then migrated to New Orleans, where she had eventually acquired her freedom.[83]

Most of the French refugees in the United States eventually adapted to their new surroundings and assimilated so thoroughly into the general population that few French Americans nowadays are aware of their distant Dominguian ancestry. Those who still longed for the *douce France* could resort to a repatriation program organized by the French embassy and whose activities peaked in 1808–14.[84] Among the returnees was Lemonnier, who after a short stay in Philadelphia boarded a ship in November 1809 bound, at long last, for France.[85]

~

Lemonnier's arrival in La Rochelle was bittersweet. A British cruiser that intercepted his ship almost forced him back into captivity, while French authorities submitted him to a lengthy customs and medical inspection. Ensuing months were equally disappointing. Lemonnier received no recognition for his long colonial service, and getting the promotions he had earned in the Caribbean recognized proved an arduous process.[86] His experience was typical; the atrocities and corruption associated with the disastrous expedition gave a bad reputation to all its participants, whose careers were often sidetracked as a result.[87] Returning white colonists were better treated and obtained a government pension, which four thousand of them were still collecting in the 1820s.[88] One lucky refugee was the court clerk, Alfred de Laujon, who managed the rare feat of returning from Saint-Domingue alive and with ten thousand francs and later joined the government bureaucracy.[89]

Despite the loss of the remainder of France's Caribbean empire to a British offensive in 1808–10, debates continued to rage over the possible reconquest of a colony that the French still insisted on calling Saint-Domingue. Some, like Laujon, attributed the French defeat to unique factors like poor leadership and advocated a new expedition; others, including Lemonnier and Denis Decrès, viewed Saint-Domingue as hopelessly lost and called for a pragmatic alliance with the new Haiti.[90] Such debates were largely theoretical until 1814, when Bonaparte's first exile brought peace with England and reopened the seas of the Atlantic. The new regime, headed by Louis XVI's brother, Louis XVIII, was favorable to the planter milieu and named the former Saint-Domingue bureaucrat Victor Malouet as minister of the navy.

An unreconstructed product of the old empire, Malouet described Haitians as fellow monarchists who had rebelled against Bonaparte because they favored the cause of the Bourbons. His political analysis of the war of independence was delusional, but he immediately prepared a diplomatic mission to demand that Haiti return to the French fold. Upon perusing the envoys' secret instructions, Laujon was shocked to read that Malouet intended to restore slavery after recolonization had taken place. The French envoys met the rival leaders Pétion and Christophe in Port-au-Prince and Cap, both of whom predictably refused to forsake their country's independence. One envoy was even shot when Christophe came across a copy of the secret instructions in which Malouet made clear his intention to restore slavery.[91]

After the interlude of the Hundred Days, Louis XVIII returned to power and sent a second mission to Haiti, on which Laujon embarked as secretary. Louis XVIII was careful to express his opposition to slavery this time around, but a bizarre proclamation in which he announced his desire "to soothe the concerns some of the inhabitants of this island may have regarding their situation" by granting them the right to remain as a French colony indicated that he had yet to comprehend the depth of Haitians' commitment to independence.[92] Pétion treated the envoys well, but given Malouet's previous gaffe the population was extremely adversarial; Christophe lambasted Pétion for even meeting with the French envoys in the first place.

A prolonged period of subdued tensions followed. French merchants reopened trading links with Pétion's regime and Laujon returned to Haiti on commercial ventures six times in following years. But Christophe's northern kingdom remained irrevocably hostile.[93] It was the reunification of Haiti under Jean-Pierre Boyer in 1820 that opened the way for more diplomatic missions, during which France agreed to recognize Haiti as a sovereign nation as long as Haitians reimbursed the planters who had been dispossessed of their land. Further negotiations set the indemnity at 150 million francs (later reduced to 90 million) and in 1825 France finally recognized Haiti's independence, a full twenty-two years after it had been gained on the battlefield of Vertières.[94] Other nations quickly followed suit, but not the United States, which, torn apart by controversies over slavery, did not recognize the independence of its emancipated neighbor until 1862 and the Civil War.

The 1825 treaty led to normal diplomatic and economic relations between Haiti and France, but it has recently become a flashpoint for nationalistic Haitians who view the financial indemnity as the root cause of Haiti's economic problems in the nineteenth century and beyond. In 2003, as Haiti began to celebrate the bicentennial of its independence amid a mounting financial crisis, President Jean–Bertrand Aristide called on France to reimburse the money it had received from Haiti and pay reparations for the crime of slavery. Whether the 1825 indemnity is indeed responsible for every one of Haiti's economic ills today is far from certain; Aristide most likely revived old historical wounds to deflect popular anger at his own economic shortcomings toward the former colonial power. Either way, after adding penalties and compounding interest his U.S. lawyer sent France a startlingly large and precise bill for $21,685,155,571.48 in a move that further illustrated the way monetary gain and politics have often trumped race as the underlying issues of Haitian history.[95]

Conclusion

Saint-Domingue's war of independence is one of world history's most fascinating events. The total population of the colony on the eve of the Leclerc expedition was only equivalent to that of Omaha, Nebraska, today, but it encompassed a bewildering array of individuals, each with their own, extraordinary story. The lives of the main protagonists of the era seemed written by a gifted novelist, their character arc drawing from heroic archetypes dating back to antiquity. Toussaint Louverture and Jean-Jacques Dessalines were the classic man from the provinces who rises from obscurity to prominence through sheer ambition, only to become a victim of hubris and fall, Icarus-like, just as quickly as he has risen. Victoire Leclerc was the naive young man who embarks upon an epic quest that consumes and eventually destroys him. Donatien de Rochambeau was the incarnation of evil, the standard against which all the horrors committed in the conflict could be gauged.

The Haitian war of independence is a fantastic story, but it also was a fantastic waste of life and treasure. When launching the expedition, Bonaparte had hoped to achieve two objectives: to prevent the colony's slow slide toward independence and to restore France's colonial trade. Instead, the expedition hastened Haiti's independence and destroyed what remained of its plantations. Restoring slavery was probably not one of Bonaparte's immediate objectives, but the war also had the effect of shattering the planters' remaining hopes that they might one day recover their human chattel.

The cost to France, both human and financial, was substantial. Bonaparte was remarkably oblivious to the loss of human life, but one can only shudder at the long lists of casualties attributable to his failed colonial venture. Of the 43,800 soldiers sent to Saint-Domingue, only 7,000 made it to the pontoons of Jamaica. When taking into account later deaths in captivity as well as sailors and colonists, the total death toll hovered over 50,000—even more if one includes the many people of color who died fighting for France, not against it.[1] These losses dwarfed the 10,000 deaths that France had suffered earlier in the Haitian Revolution and represented a significant portion of the one million people (of all nations) who died during the Napoleonic wars in Europe.[2]

The expedition proved equally ruinous financially. Individual French officers occasionally amassed a fortune, but British sailors often looted them during the evacuation. One is hard-pressed to find many examples of French nationals who made any money during the expedition. Two shipments of sugar and cotton sent by Leclerc in the fall of 1802 may represent the sole item the French government ever placed in the "profit" column.[3] The list under the "loss" heading was far longer. After investing their last reserves in the Dominguian trade in 1802, French merchants were ruined when the colony collapsed in 1803, and the French colonial trade was wholly destroyed by the end of the Napoleonic era, by which time it averaged seven thousand tons a year, compared with one hundred thousand tons in 1789.[4] Overall, the expedition cost France 150 to 400 million francs and directly led to a grave banking crisis in 1805.[5] To these numbers must be added the large sums borrowed from Jamaica and Cuba and that were never reimbursed.

War is not a zero-sum game, and the victorious Haitians suffered even more in triumph than their vanquished foes did in defeat. Haitian rulers often exaggerated census numbers after independence for security reasons, but there is good reason to believe that the country's population, which had neared six hundred thousand in 1789, had dropped by half by 1804, and that the Leclerc expedition itself is responsible for the death of one hundred thousand Haitians.[6] The rebellious slaves of 1791 had pledged to live free or die; in the end, they did each in roughly equal numbers.

After declaring political independence, former colonies often fail to achieve economic independence and remain mired in a system of economic dependency based on low-tech exports of crops and minerals. Haiti did worse: it struggled to even preserve the plantation system it had inherited from colonial times. The rebels' scorched-earth tactics left most of the country's physical infrastructure in ruins by the time of its independence; the 1804 massacres did away with the white managerial class that had dominated the production of refined sugar; and attempts by Dessalines and his successors to maintain the cultivator system failed to overcome black laborers' hatred of plantation work. In 1826 the last oppressive labor code of Jean-Pierre Boyer fell flat and plantation laborers finally obtained full, unfettered labor freedom a full generation after independence.[7] Regrettably, Haiti was not able to match its social advances with economic gains. Coffee production declined markedly, while that of sugar ceased altogether.[8] Today, Haiti, the fabled Pearl of the Antilles, is the poorest country in the Western Hemisphere and a net importer of sugar.

~

To its contemporaries, the Haitian Revolution was the most astonishing event of its time. As echoes of the successful revolt reached every corner of the Western Hemisphere, Jamaican slaves sang songs about the rebel slaves of Haiti, Brazilian free-coloreds wore portraits of Dessalines, and U.S. blacks, sixty years away from their own emancipation, proudly pointed to the Haitians' achievements as a source of hope. From England to the United States, slavery's opponents and advocates repeatedly invoked the Haitian precedent to buttress their argument, while novelists from France to Germany used the revolution as a background for their works.[9]

These eventful years remain an important point of reference to this day. Haitians look back on the revolutionary era with understandable pride and celebrate the achievements of their greatest generation every year on January 1 (Independence Day), May 18 (Flag Day), and November 18 (the anniversary of Vertières).[10] Colonial struggles were long overlooked in French accounts of the revolutionary era, but public and scholarly interest has surged recently and Caribbean rebels like Toussaint Louverture and Guadeloupe's Louis Delgrès are now considered true national heroes in France, where both are honored with plaques in the national Pantheon.[11] Liberal circles from France to the United States also like to celebrate the revolution as a rare victory over racism, economic exploitation, and imperialism.[12]

How barefoot rebel slaves could overwhelm the best units in Bonaparte's army may be the most puzzling event of this era. To explain the French defeat, contemporaries often cited yellow fever's toll, Leclerc and Rochambeau's inadequate leadership, the British blockade, and Haitians' bravery under fire, itself a result of Bonaparte's alleged plans to restore slavery.[13] All of these explanations are consistent with the historical record, but one crucial factor is too often overlooked: that France lost the war primarily because it failed to keep on its side the many people of color who were long favorable to the ideals it embodied. Despite the popular view of the Haitian war of independence as a mass uprising of former slaves united in their hatred of French rule, when the conflict began much of the population of color sided with France against Louverture. It took many atrocities and political faux pas on the part of the expedition's leaders before people of color (and many whites) switched their allegiances, a process that was not completed (and even then partially) until July 1803, four months before the French evacuation.

More generally, race played a far smaller role in determining the behavior of revolutionary actors than is generally assumed. The inhabitants of Saint-Domingue's manifold society were complex individuals who based their actions on a wide variety of factors, starting with their economic interests, so the color of one's skin was merely one element of a person's profile, along with one's gender, nationality, family network, political ideas, and—crucially— social class. During the conflict, the most persistent divide pitted, not blacks against whites, but plantation laborers against plantation owners. Officers of color like Dessalines may have defeated French officers and white Creoles, but to the average cultivator or Maroon their victory only replaced one master with another.

For this reason, the term "Haitian Revolution," which is usually employed to describe the entire revolutionary era from 1791 to 1804, does not exactly fit the period of the Leclerc expedition in 1802–3. A revolution suggests a complete reordering of society, in which a previously oppressed class gains newfound political and economic importance. Little of that happened during this period. The reluctant, oppressed cultivators of 1801 remained cultivators in 1804, and the officers of color who had acquired plantations under Louverture kept them after eliminating the economic threat presented by French officers. For most rural inhabitants, the real change had taken place in 1791–93, when slaves had revolted and obtained their emancipation, or would take place in the first decades of the nineteenth century, when plantations were progressively dismantled and replaced with subsistence farms. What took place in the interim can only properly be described as a war of independence, during which the Creole elite, many whites included, embraced national sovereignty in reaction to the atrocities committed by the metropolitan army.

There is no questioning the worldwide appeal of these fascinating years; but if one focuses solely on the Haitian Revolution's actual political and diplomatic consequences, its impact was surprisingly limited.[14] People of African descent everywhere may have looked up to Haiti as a rallying point in the nineteenth century, but a surprisingly small number actually moved there despite campaigns by successive Haitian governments to promote their country as a haven for black freedmen. Neighboring slave powers may have lived in fear of revolutionary contagion, but Haitian leaders took no proactive step to export their revolution overseas. When slavery ended elsewhere in the Western Hemisphere in subsequent decades, it was because of purely local factors. Sadly, the Haitian Revolution did not even fully extinguish slavery in Haiti itself. Corvée (a forced labor tax) did not disappear until 1919, and child slavery in urban households (restavek) and indebted servitude on Dominican plantations remain a sad feature of Haitian life to this day.

Aside from independence, the one lasting legacy of the revolutionary era is that it shaped much of the culture of contemporary Haiti, which remains a predominantly rural, Creole society whose main features are derived from its dual African and French ancestry. Despite Dessalines' efforts, Maroon groups outlasted his reign, most notably in the form of an independent state established by Jean-Baptiste Perrier (a.k.a. Goman) in southern Haiti in 1806 and that was not defeated until 1820 (only to reappear as the so-called Piquet uprising of 1844–48).[15] Such heavily Africanized groups had an enduring influence on popular Haitian culture, from Vodou to oral folk traditions, and more generally the everyday life of the peasantry. Contemporary expectations for Haitian women are also eerily reminiscent of the roles they once played on the plantation.

Meanwhile, despite two centuries of independent rule, there remains a French cultural model whose enduring appeal among the Haitian elite is quite surprising given the two countries' troubled history. Haiti often comes across as a schizophrenic nation whose mixed-race elite looks up to French culture as superior, even as it lambastes France's imperial past, while black nationalists denounce their rivals as intrinsically foreign and unpatriotic, only to marry into light-skinned families whenever they get a chance. Haiti is the land of Vodou, folk tales, Kreyol, and *noirisme,* a cultural movement that celebrates Haiti's African heritage. But it is also a country where the most affluent citizens send their offspring to the *lycée français* of Port-au-Prince, where Haitian Kreyol was not recognized as an official language until the 1987 constitution, and where elite culture long consisted in imitating the latest literary trends from Paris, all of it in perfect French.

It is only fitting to end this book with Haiti's two leading nineteenth-century historians, Thomas Madiou and Beaubrun Ardouin, whose classical works were the first comprehensive studies of the revolutionary era, as well as a good illustration of elite Haitians' tortured attitude toward France. Both were committed nationalists who celebrated the deeds of their compatriots in glowing terms; and yet, revealingly, both chose to do so in the language of the former metropolis, all the while apologizing for the fact that living so far from "the hearth of our language" their French had been perverted by the "many idiocies" of Kreyol.[16] No example better encapsulates the tension between the appeal of the French cultural and political model and the rejection of the excesses of French imperialism that was at the heart of the revolutionary experience in Haiti.

Notes

ABBREVIATIONS

ADC	Archives Départementales du Calvados, Caen
ADG	Archives Départementales de la Guadeloupe, Basse Terre
ADGir	Archives Départementales de la Gironde, Bordeaux
AN	Archives Nationales, Paris
APS	American Philosophical Society, Philadelphia
BFV-FM	Fonds Montbret, Bibliothèque François Villon, Rouen
BNA	British National Archives, Kew
CAOM	Centre des Archives d'Outre-Mer, Aix-en-Provence
CN	Jean-Baptiste Vaillant, ed., *Correspondance de Napoléon Ier, publiée par ordre de l'empereur Napoléon III,* 32 vols. (Paris: Plon, 1858).
DHHAN	José Luciano Franco, ed., *Documentos para la historia de Haití en el Archivo Nacional* (Havana: Publicaciones del Archivo Nacional de Cuba, 1954).
HSP	Historical Society of Pennsylvania, Philadelphia
HU-KFC	Kurt Fisher Collection, Moorland-Springarn Research Center, Howard University, Washington, DC
LC-MD	Manuscript Division, Library of Congress, Washington, DC
LCP	Library Company, Philadelphia
LGC	Paul Roussier, ed., *Lettres du général Leclerc* (Paris: Société de l'histoire des colonies françaises, 1937).
LSU	Louisiana and Lower Mississippi Valley Collections, Louisiana State University Library, Baton Rouge
NARA-CP	National Archives Records Administration II, College Park
NARA-DC	National Archives Records Administration I, Washington, DC
NYPL-SC	New York Public Library (Schomburg Center), New York
SHD-DAT	Service Historique de la Défense (Département de l'Armée de Terre), Vincennes
SHD-DM	Service Historique de la Défense (Département de la Marine), Vincennes
UF-RP	Rochambeau Papers, University of Florida, Gainesville

INTRODUCTION

1. On Toussaint Louverture's presence in Sámana, see Louverture, *Mémoires du Général Toussaint l'Ouverture écrits par lui-même,* ed. St. Rémy (Paris: Pagnerre, 1853), 92; Lacroix Pamphile de Lacroix, *La révolution de Haïti* (1819; reprint, Paris: Karthala, 1995), 283; Antonio del Monte y Tejada, *Historia de Santo Domingo,* vol. 3 (Ciudad Trujillo: República Dominicana, 1952), 215.

2. Fritz Daguillard, "The True Likeness of Toussaint Louverture," *Américas* 55, no. 4 (2003): 50; Jacques Cauna, *Toussaint Louverture et l'indépendance d'Haïti* (Paris: Karthala, 2004), 41.

3. W. L. Whitfield to George Nugent (Dec. 5, 1801), CO 137/106, BNA.

4. Louverture to Members of the Central Assembly (Jan. 22, 1802), Reel 5, Sc. Micro R-2228, NYPL-SC.

5. Louverture to Simon Baptiste fils (Jan. 27, 1802), BB4 162, SHD-DM.

6. "État des troupes parties de France . . ." (ca. 1806), F/5B/67, AN.

7. Jean-Baptiste Lemonnier-Delafosse, *Seconde campagne de Saint-Domingue du 1 décembre 1803 au 15 juillet 1809* (Le Havre: Brindeau, 1846), 28.

8. Lacroix, *La révolution de Haïti,* 283.

CHAPTER 1

1. On the July 7 ceremony, see *Bulletin Officiel de Saint-Domingue,* no. 58 (July 8, 1801), CC9A/28, AN.

2. For the 1790 constitution, see "Décret de l'Assemblée Générale de la partie française de Saint-Domingue" (May 28, 1790), Folder 1A, HU-KFC.

3. Laurent Dubois, *Avengers of the New World: The Story of the Haitian Revolution* (Cambridge, MA: Harvard University Press, 2004), 22.

4. David Geggus, "The French Slave Trade: An Overview," *William and Mary Quarterly* 58, no. 1 (Jan. 2001): 125.

5. Antoine Métral, *Histoire de l'expédition des Français à Saint-Domingue sous le consulat de Napoléon Bonaparte* (1825; reprint, Paris: Karthala, 1985), 325; Toussaint Louverture, *Mémoires du Général Toussaint l'Ouverture écrits par lui-même,* ed. St. Rémy (Paris: Pagnerre, 1853), 98.

6. François de Kerversau, "Rapport sur la partie française de Saint-Domingue" (March 22, 1801), Box 2/66, UF-RP; Jacques Cauna, *Toussaint Louverture et l'indépendance d'Haïti* (Paris: Karthala, 2004), 86.

7. Jean Fouchard, *The Haitian Maroons: Liberty or Death* (1972; reprint, New York: Edward Blyden Press, 1981), 95; Louverture, *Mémoires,* 97.

8. David Geggus, "Toussaint Louverture and the Haitian Revolution," in *Profiles of Revolutionaries in Atlantic History,* ed. R. William Weisberger (New York: Columbia University Press, 2007), 115–35.

9. Gabriel Debien and Philip Wright, "Les colons de Saint-Domingue passés à la Jamaïque (1792–1835)," *Notes d'histoire coloniale* 168 (ca. 1976): 152–57; Alfred Nemours, *Histoire de la famille et de la descendance de Toussaint Louverture* (Port-au-Prince: Imprimerie de l'État, 1941), 4; Cauna, *Toussaint Louverture,* 198.

10. "Extrait des registres de l'Assemblée centrale de Saint-Domingue" (March 28, 1801), CO 137/106, BNA.

11. Thomas Madiou, *Histoire d'Haïti,* vol. 2 (Port-au-Prince: Courtois, 1847), 96.

12. Pierre Pluchon, *Toussaint Louverture* (Paris: Fayard, 1989), 364.

13. Louverture, "Arrêté" (July 14, 1801), CC9B/9, AN; Madiou, *Histoire,* vol. 2, 29, 75.

14. "Constitution de la colonie française de Saint-Domingue" (July 1801), CO 137/106, BNA.

15. Jean-Benoît Nadeau and Julie Barlow, *The Story of French* (New York: St. Martin's Press, 2006).

16. André Rigaud, [Speech] (Aug. 26, 1798), Folder "Hédouville Correspondence 1," Box 1, Sc MG 119, NYPL-SC.

17. Cauna, *Toussaint Louverture,* 61–67.

18. Thomas Gragnon-Lacoste, *Toussaint Louverture* (Paris: Durand, 1877), 216.

19. Louverture, "Règlement sur la culture" (Oct. 25, 1800), CC9B/9, AN.

20. Gabriel Debien, "A propos du trésor de Toussaint Louverture," *Revue de la société d'histoire et de géographie d'Haïti* 17, no. 62 (1946): 30–40.

21. Pamphile de Lacroix, *La révolution de Haïti* (1819; reprint, Paris: Karthala, 1995), 275.

22. Hilliard d'Auberteuil, *Considérations sur l'état présent de la colonie française de Saint-Domingue,* vol. 1 (Paris: Grangé, 1776), 88–111.

23. Francis Wimpffen, *A Voyage to Saint Domingo in the Years 1788, 1789, and 1790* (London: T. Cadell, 1797), 259.

24. John Iliffe, *Africans: The History of a Continent* (New York: Cambridge University Press, 1995), 64, 93, 137.

25. Robert Lacerte, "The Evolution of Land and Labor in the Haitian Revolution, 1791–1820," *Americas* 34, no. 4 (1978): 449; Marcel Dorigny, ed., *The Abolitions of Slavery: From Léger Félicité Sonthonax to Victor Schoelcher* (1995; reprint, New York: Berghahn, 2003), xii.

26. Jean Baptiste to Dupuis (July 22, 1800), Box 6:11, (Phi) 1602, HSP.

27. Philippe Roume, "Moyens proposé au gouvernement français . . . pour la réorganisation de cette colonie sans recourir aux voies de rigueur" (June 11, 1800), Roume Papers, LC-MD.

28. Louverture to Louis-André Pichon (July 3, 1801), CC9A/28, AN.

29. J. Hd., "La fécondité des anciens esclaves à Saint-Domingue, 1794–1801," *Population* 28, no. 6 (1973): 1208.

30. "Council minutes" (Nov. 19, 1799), CO 137/107, BNA; George Nugent to Duke of Portland (Sept. 5, 1801), CO 137/106, BNA.

31. Gordon Brown, *Toussaint's Clause: The Founding Fathers and the Haitian Revolution* (Jackson: University Press of Mississippi, 2005), 129–75.

32. Thomas Maitland and Louverture, "Convention secrète" (May 22, 1799), RG 59, M9/1, NARA-CP.

33. Debien and Pluchon, "Un plan d'invasion de la Jamaïque en 1799 et la politique anglo-américaine de Toussaint Louverture," *Revue de la société haïtienne d'histoire et de géographie* 36 (July 1978): 12.

34. W. L. Whitfield to John King (Jan. 17, 1801), CO 137/106, BNA.

35. "Mentions du gouvernement sur les colonies" (March 12, 1801), CC9B/18, AN.

36. Louverture, "Règlement sur la culture" (Oct. 25, 1800), CC9B/9, AN.

37. Gérard Barthélémy, Créoles, bossales: Conflit en Haïti (Petit Bourg: Ibis Rouge, 2000), 80, 96–106.

38. Whitfield to Edward Corbet (May 8, 1801), CO 137/105, BNA.

39. Michel-Étienne Descourtilz, Voyage d'un naturaliste en Haïti, 1799–1803 (1809; reprint, Paris: Plon, 1935), 166–73.

40. Gabriel Hédouville to Louverture (Aug. 8, 1798), CC9B/6, AN.

41. Madiou, Histoire, vol. 2, 106.

42. H. Castonnet des Fosses, La perte d'une colonie: La révolution de Saint-Domingue (Paris: Faivre, 1893), 250.

43. Louverture, Mémoires, 29.

44. Pluchon, Toussaint Louverture, 400–422.

45. Cauna, Toussaint Louverture, 69.

46. Debien, "Au Cap au temps de Toussaint Louverture (1798–1800)," Revue de la société haïtienne d'histoire de géographie et de géologie 124 (Nov. 1979): 8–20.

47. Étienne Dupusch, "Compte courant" (May 30, 1801), Box 6:6, (Phi) 1602, HSP; "Procès verbaux dressés par Corneille sur les habitations du citoyen Toussaint Louverture . . ." (June 1802), 7Yd284, SHD-DAT.

48. Louverture to Pichon (July 3, 1801), CC9A/28, AN.

49. "Loi sur les émigrés et sur leurs biens" (Aug. 6, 1801), CO 137/106, BNA.

50. Louverture, "Règlement" (May 14, 1800), Folder "Toussaint Louverture," Box 1, Sc MG 119, NYPL-SC.

51. Descourtilz, Voyage, i, 2–55.

52. Louverture, "Ordonnance" (Jan. 4, 1800), CC9B/9, AN; Descourtilz, Voyage, 105, 142, 152; Madiou, Histoire, vol. 2, 28, 79, 90.

53. Pichon to Pierre Forfait (June 3, 1801), CC9A/28, AN; Debien, Guillaume Mauviel, évêque constitutionnel de Saint-Domingue (Basse Terre: Société d'Histoire de la Guadeloupe, 1981), 17–26.

54. Kerversau, "Rapport sur la partie française"; Debien, Guillaume Mauviel, 37–42; Louis Dubroca, La vie de Toussaint Louverture, chef des noirs insurgés de Saint-Domingue (Paris: Dubroca, 1802), 14, 50.

55. Madison Smartt Bell, Toussaint Louverture: A Biography (New York: Pantheon Books, 2007), 288.

56. Descourtilz, Voyage, 224.

57. Louverture to Dupusch (May 28, 1801), Box 6:6, (Phi) 1602, HSP.

58. Lacroix, La révolution de Haïti, 243; Descourtilz, Voyage, 149; Alphonse de Lamartine, Toussaint Louverture (Paris: Levy, 1850), xvii.

59. Auberteuil, Considérations, vol. 2, 119.

60. Descourtilz, Voyage, 150, 156; Lacroix, La révolution de Haïti, 241.

61. Stewart King, Blue Coat or Powdered Wig: Free People of Color in Pre-Revolutionary Saint-Domingue (Athens: University of Georgia Press, 2001), 8, 10, 163–68.

62. Lacroix, La révolution de Haïti, 241.

63. Alfred Nemours, *Histoire de la famille et de la descendance de Toussaint Louverture* (Port-au-Prince: Imprimerie de l'État, 1941), 11.

64. Louis Dufaÿ to Louverture (Oct. 1796), Box 1:4, MG 140, NYPL-SC; Louverture to Bonaparte (July 16, 1801), in H. Pauléus Sannon, *Histoire de Toussaint Louverture,* vol. 3 (Port-au-Prince: Héraux, 1933), 19.

65. Bouillé [Malout] to Anon. (July 18, 1800), Folder 5410, F1716266, AN.

66. Cauna, *Toussaint Louverture,* 183–86, 260–63; Beaubrun Ardouin, *Études sur l'histoire d'Haïti, suivies de la vie du général J-M Borgella,* vol. 5 (Paris: Dézobry et Magdeleine, 1853–60), 198.

67. Descourtilz, *Voyage,* 30, 153; Madiou, *Histoire,* vol. 2, 105; Lacroix, *La révolution de Haïti,* 304.

68. Arlette Gautier, *Les sœurs de Solitude: La condition féminine dans l'esclavage aux Antilles du XVIIe au XIXe siècle* (Paris: Editions Caribéennes, 1985), 164, 179.

69. Pluchon, *Toussaint Louverture,* 549. On Louverture's suspicions about whites, see also Louverture to Hédouville (April 11, 1798), CC9B/6, AN.

70. Paul Louverture to Louverture (Feb. 4. 1802), Reel 5, Sc. Micro R-2228, NYPL-SC; Charles Belair to Louverture (April 1, 1802), ibid.

71. Louverture to Donatien de Rochambeau (July 8, 1796), Folder "Toussaint Louverture," Box 1, Sc MG 119, NYPL-SC.

72. Pascal to Louverture (April 12, 1799), Reel 5, Sc. Micro R-2228, NYPL-SC; [Pascal], "Mémoire secret," (ca. 1801), Reel 8, ibid.

73. Lacroix, *La révolution de Haïti,* 240.

74. Madame J. Michelet, *The Story of My Childhood* (1866; reprint, Boston: Little, Brown, 1867), 149–71.

75. Lacroix, *La révolution de Haïti,* 219; King, *Blue Coat,* 121, 168.

76. Marcus Rainsford, *An Historical Account of the Black Empire of Hayti* (London: Albion Press, 1805), 219.

77. Lacroix, *La révolution de Haïti,* 355; Cauna, *Toussaint Louverture,* 102.

78. Morin, "Réflexions . . . aux consuls de la république" (Aug. 13, 1800), 3, Reel 15, Sc. Micro R-2228, NYPL-SC.

79. Rainsford, *An Historical Account,* 244.

80. Guillaume Raynal, *Histoire philosophique et politique des établissements et du commerce des Européens dans les deux Indes,* vol. 4 (La Haye: 1774), 226; Kerversau, "Rapport sur la partie française."

81. Cauna, *Toussaint Louverture,* 112; Jean-Baptiste Lemonnier-Delafosse, *Seconde campagne de Saint-Domingue du 1er décembre 1803 au 15 juillet 1809* (Le Havre: Brindeau, 1846), 2; Rainsford, *An Historical Account,* 249; R. Lepelletier de Saint-Rémy, *Saint-Domingue: Étude et solution nouvelle de la question haïtienne* (Paris: Arthus Bertrand, 1846), 172.

82. Jean-Baptiste Michel, "Suite aux observations" (Jan. 26, 1801), CC9A/28, AN; Lacroix, *La révolution de Haïti,* 277.

83. Kerversau to Eustache Bruix (May 27, 1799), CC9/B23, AN; 1801 Constitution (art. 39).

84. On Charles de Vincent, see his officer file in 8Yd1825, SHD-DAT; Vincent,

"Précis des principaux événements de Saint-Domingue" (ca. Nov. 1801), MS. 619, BFV-FM; Vincent, *Observations . . . sur les deux premières notes rapportées dans une collection de mémoires pour servir à l'histoire de France sous Napoléon Ier* (Paris: Pélicier/Didot, 1824), 8–10; Christian Schneider, "Le colonel Vincent, officier du génie à Saint-Domingue," *Annales historiques de la révolution française* 329 (July 2002): 101–22.

85. Vincent to Forfait (June 17, 1800), CC9A/28, AN.

86. Castonnet, *La perte d'une colonie,* 253; Lacroix, *La révolution de Haïti,* 259.

87. Vincent, "Précis de mon dernier voyage à Saint-Domingue" (Feb. 9, 1802), AF/IV/1212, AN.

88. Louverture to Bonaparte (July 16, 1801), in Lemonnier, *Seconde campagne,* 286.

89. Tobias Lear to James Madison (July 27, 1801), 208 MI/2, AN.

90. Sannon, *Histoire de Toussaint Louverture,* vol. 3, 18–19.

91. Vincent to Louverture (July 18, 1801), Pièce 71, AF/IV/1212, AN; Vincent, *Observations,* 15.

92. Pichon to Charles de Talleyrand (Aug. 6, 1801), CC9/B21, AN.

93. Vincent to Louverture (Aug. 7, 1801), Box 2:1, MG 140, NYPL-SC. See also Vincent to Louverture (July 18, 1801), AF/IV/1212, AN.

94. *Gazette of the United States,* no. 3 (Aug. 17, 1801).

95. Kerversau to Bruix (June 13, 1800), CC9/B23, AN; Edward Stevens to Timothy Pickering (May 24, 1800), 208 MI/1, AN; Corbet to Earl of Balcarres (March 31, 1801), CO 137/105, BNA; Aimé Césaire, *Toussaint Louverture: La révolution française et le problème colonial* (Paris: Présence Africaine, 1981), 257; Roger Dorsinville, *Toussaint Louverture ou la vocation de la liberté* (Paris: Julliard, 1965), 187.

96. Louverture to Balcarres (Feb. 1, 1801), CO 137/105, BNA; Lear to Madison (July 17, 1801), 208 MI/2, AN.

97. Louverture, *Mémoires,* 48.

98. Louverture to Bonaparte (Aug. 25, 1801), in Sannon, *Histoire de Toussaint Louverture,* vol. 3, 21–22.

99. Gaston Nogérée to Louverture (Oct. 17, 1801), Box 1:5, MG 140, NYPL-SC; Pichon to Pascal (Oct. 27, 1801), BN08269/lot 107, UF-RP.

100. Lear to Madison (July 20, 1801), 208 MI/2, AN.

101. Lear to Madison (July 27, 1801), 208 MI/2, AN; Corbet to Balcarres (July 21, 1801), CO 137/105, BNA.

102. [Pascal], "Mémoire secret," (ca. 1801), Reel 8, Sc. Micro R-2228, NYPL-SC.

103. "Lois de la colonie française de Saint-Domingue," (ca. Aug. 1801), CO 137/106, BNA.

104. Roume to Jean-Louis Villatte and Étienne Laveaux (May 11, 1796), FM/F/3/200, CAOM.

105. Roume, "Discours" (July 18, 1799), CC9B/9, AN.

106. "Noticia relative a la situación militar de Santo Domingo" (April 14, 1800), DHHAN, 122.

107. Roume to Louverture (May 27, 1799), Roume Papers, LC-MD.

108. Maitland to Balcarres (June 17, 1799), CO 137/102, BNA.

109. Emilio Rodríguez Demorizi, *Cesión de Santo Domingo a Francia* (Ciudad

Trujillo: Impresora Dominicana, 1958), 560–64, 593–614; Louverture to Roume (April 22, 1801), BN08270/lot 132, UF-RP.

110. Vincent to Louverture (Aug. 7, 1801), Box 2:1, MG 140, NYPL-SC; Roume to Forfait (Oct. 11, 1801), BN08270/lot 132, UF-RP.

111. Pichon to Forfait (Sept. 30, 1801), CC9B/18, AN.

112. Roume to Forfait (Sept. 25, 1801), BN08270/lot 132, UF-RP.

113. Roume to Forfait (Dec. 2, 1801), BN08270/lot 132, UF-RP.

114. Nugent to Portland (Aug. 15, 1801), CO 137/106, BNA. Bunel stayed in Jamaica.

CHAPTER 2

1. Claude Wanquet, *La France et la première abolition de l'esclavage, 1794–1802: Le cas des colonies orientales Île de France (Maurice) et la Réunion* (Paris: Karthala, 1998), 529.

2. Beaubrun Ardouin, *Études sur l'histoire d'Haïti, suivies de la vie du général J-M Borgella,* vol. 4 (Paris: Dézobry et Magdeleine, 1853–60), 444; C. L. R. James, *The Black Jacobins: Toussaint L'Ouverture and the San Domingo Revolution* (1963; reprint, New York: Vintage Books, 1989), 270.

3. Emmanuel de Las Cases, *Mémorial de Sainte Hélène,* vol. 1 (Paris: Gallimard-La Pléiade, 1956), 769.

4. Barry O'Meara, *Napoléon en exil: Relation contenant les opinions et les réflexions de Napoléon sur les événements les plus importants de sa vie* (Paris: Garnier, 1897), 277.

5. Louis de Bourrienne, *Mémoires de M. de Bourrienne, ministre d'état,* vol. 4 (Paris: Ladvocat, 1829), 310.

6. Thomas Madiou, *Histoire d'Haïti,* vol. 2 (1847; reprint, Port-au-Prince: Fardin, 1981), 392; Ardouin, *Études,* vol. 4, 458–59; Thomas Ott, *The Haitian Revolution, 1789–1804* (Knoxville: University of Tennessee Press, 1973), 141; Wanquet, *La France et la première abolition,* 630.

7. Thomas Gragnon-Lacoste, *Toussaint Louverture* (Paris: Durand, 1877), 245. On the Beauharnais plantation, see Dossier 314, 73 J 115, ADGir.

8. Joséphine Bonaparte, *Memoirs,* vol. 1, ed. Léon Vallée (New York: Merrill and Baker, 1903), 194–205, 246; ibid., vol. 2, 27.

9. Joséphine Bonaparte, *Correspondance, 1782–1814,* ed. Bernard Chevallier et al. (Paris, Payot, 1996), 130.

10. Bureau of Colonies, "Rapport aux Consuls" (Dec. 3, 1799), CC9B/18, AN; Paul Alliot-Vauneuf to Daniel Lescallier (May 23, 1800), CC9A/27, AN; Yves Bénot, *La démence coloniale sous Napoléon* (Paris: La Découverte, 1992), 10, 50–54.

11. Louis Rallier to Pierre Forfait (Dec. 7, 1799), CC9A/23, AN; Léger-Félicité Sonthonax to Forfait (Dec. 8, 1799), CC9A/23, AN; Rallier, *Nouvelles observations sur Saint-Domingue* (Paris: Baudouin, ca. 1797), 15.

12. Louis Dubroca, *La vie de Toussaint Louverture, chef des noirs insurgés de Saint-Domingue* (Paris: Dubroca, 1802), 69.

13. Hilliard d'Auberteuil, *Considérations sur l'état présent de la colonie française de Saint-Domingue,* vol. 1 (Paris: Grangé, 1776), 132.

14. Paul François Page, *Traité d'économie politique et de commerce des colonies,* vol. 1 (Paris: Brochot, [1801–2]), 2, 223, 247.

15. Anon., *Histoire des désastres de Saint-Domingue* (Paris: Garnery, 1795), 20; M. J. La Neuville, *Le dernier cri de Saint-Domingue et des colonies* (Philadelphia: Bradford, 1800), 2; Charles Malenfant, *Des colonies, et particulièrement de celle de Saint-Domingue* (Paris: Audibert, 1814), i.

16. Pétiniaud to Directoire Exécutif (Nov. 28, 1798), CC9A/18, AN; Louis [Duteux?], "Réflexions sur les colonies françaises et principalement sur Saint-Domingue" (March 5, 1800), CC9A/27, AN; Alliot-Vauneuf to Lescallier (May 23, 1800), CC9A/27, AN; Guillois, "Réflexions sur l'état politique et commercial de Saint-Domingue" (ca. 1800), CC9C/1, AN; Louis Maury to Bonaparte (Sept. 29, 1801), CC9A/29, AN; Anon., "Vue ou plan sur la population, et repeuplement des blancs en l'île de Saint-Domingue" (ca. 1801), CC9A/30, AN; AF/IV/1212, AN; Wanquet, *La France et la première abolition,* 535, 557.

17. François de Kerversau to Eustache Bruix (Sept. 9, 1800), CC9/B23, AN; Huin and Augustin d'Hébécourt to Forfait (Nov. 1, 1800), CC9A/21, AN.

18. Pascal to Toussaint Louverture (April 12, 1799), Reel 5, Sc. Micro R–2228, NYPL-SC; Pierre Pluchon, *Toussaint Louverture* (Paris: Fayard, 1989), 364–67.

19. Laurent Dubois, *A Colony of Citizens: Revolution and Slave Emancipation in the French Caribbean, 1787–1804* (Chapel Hill: University of North Carolina Press, 2004), 289, 327, 351; Wanquet, *La France et la première abolition,* 630; Yves Bénot and Marcel Dorigny, *Rétablissement de l'esclavage dans les colonies françaises 1802: Ruptures et continuités de la politique coloniale française* (Paris: Maisonneuve-Larose, 2003), 9, 26, 63.

20. Pierre Malouet, *Mémoire sur l'esclavage des nègres dans lequel on discute les motifs proposés pour leur affranchissement, ceux qui s'y opposent, et les moyens praticables pour améliorer leur sort* (Neufchâtel, 1788); Malouet, *Mémoires de Malouet* (Paris: Plon, 1874), vol. 1, 31, 39–42; vol. 2, 264–68, 278–88.

21. Bénot, *La démence coloniale,* 47, 68; Marcel Dorigny and Bernard Gainot, eds., *La société des Amis des Noirs, 1788–1799: Contribution à l'histoire de l'abolition de l'esclavage* (Paris: UNESCO, 1998), 234, 304, 345; Joseph Fouché, *Memoirs,* vol. 1, ed. Léon Vallée (New York: Merrill and Baker, 1903), 181.

22. CN vol. 6, 28, 64, 227, 244, 458, 543.

23. Bénot, *La démence coloniale,* 46.

24. On Kerversau, see 8Yd743/1 and 8Yd743/2, SHD-DAT.

25. [White officer] to Mirdonday (June 13, 1799), CC9/B23, AN; Kerversau, "Rapport sur la partie française."

26. Kerversau to Bruix (May 29, 1799), CC9/B23, AN.

27. Kerversau to Bruix (June 13, 1800), CC9/B23, AN.

28. Kerversau to Louverture (Nov. 2, 1798), FP/49APC/1, CAOM; Kerversau to Bruix (Sept. 23, 1799), CC9/B23, AN.

29. Kerversau to Bruix (Feb. 9, 1799), CC9/B23, AN.

30. Kerversau to Bruix (Feb. 19, 1799), CC9/B23, AN.

31. Louverture to Kerversau (May 25, 1799), CC9A/21, AN; Kerversau to For-fait (Nov. 29, 1799), CC9A/23, AN.

32. Joaquin García to Mariano Urquijo (Oct. 26, 1799), in Emilio Rodríguez Demorizi, *Cesión de Santo Domingo a Francia* (Ciudad Trujillo: Impresora Domini-cana, 1958), 515.

33. García to Urquijo (Jan. 14, 1800), in Rodríguez Demorizi, *Cesión de Santo Domingo,* 540; Chanlatte to André Rigaud (May 27, 1800), DHHAN, 128; Chan-latte to French Government (June 9, 1800), in Emilio Rodríguez Demorizi, *La era de Francia en Santo Domingo: Contribución a su estudio* (Ciudad Trujillo: Editora del Caribe, 1955), 199–226; Chanlatte to Forfait (Sept. 21, 1800), CO 137/ 105, BNA.

34. "Procès-verbal de la prise de possession de la partie espagnole" (ca. late Jan. 1801), CO 137/106, BNA; Antonio del Monte y Tejada, *Historia de Santo Domingo,* vol. 3 (Ciudad Trujillo: República Dominicana, 1952), 210–13; Wendell Schaeffer, "The Delayed Cession of Spanish Santo Domingo to France, 1795–1801," *Hispanic American Historical Review* 29, no. 1 (1949): 46–68.

35. García to Roume (Nov. 24, 1800), in Rodríguez Demorizi, *Cesión de Santo Domingo,* 569.

36. Louverture to Pierre Agé (June 1, 1800), in Ardouin, *Études,* vol. 4, 171; Louverture to Inhabitants of Bani (Jan. 11, 1801), in Rodríguez Demorizi, *Cesión de Santo Domingo,* 616; François Chanlatte, *Considérations diverses sur Haïti* (Port-au-Prince: unspecified, July 1822), 14.

37. Somerset de Chair, ed., *Napoleon on Napoleon: An Autobiography of the Emperor* (London: Cassell, 1992), 177.

38. De Chair, *Napoleon on Napoleon,* 177.

39. P. L. Roederer, *Mémoires sur la Révolution, le Consulat, et l'Empire* (1840; re-print, Paris: Plon, 1942), 131.

40. O'Meara, *Napoléon en exil,* 276.

41. Philippe Girard, "Rêves d'Empire: French Plans of Expeditions in the South-ern United States and the Caribbean, 1789–1809," *Louisiana History* 48, no. 4 (2007): 389–412.

42. Bourrienne, *Mémoires,* vol. 4, 312.

43. Bonaparte to François Lequoy-Mongiraud (March 4, 1801), CN vol. 7, 78. See also "Instructions isolés . . ." (ca. Feb. 1801), Pièce 47, AF/IV/1212, AN.

44. Bonaparte to Louverture (March 4, 1801), HU-KFC.

45. Jean-Baptiste Lemonnier-Delafosse, *Seconde campagne de Saint-Domingue du 1 décembre 1803 au 15 juillet 1809* (Le Havre: Brindeau, 1846), 286.

46. Ministère de la Guerre, "Relevé de services" (ca. 1803), 7Yd284, SHD-DAT; Pluchon, *Toussaint Louverture,* 456; Bénot, *La démence coloniale,* 25.

47. CN vol. 7, 145, 202; Frederick Kagan, *The End of the Old Order: Napoleon and Europe, 1801–1805* (New York: Da Capo, 2007), 17–26.

48. Huin and d'Hébécourt to Louverture (Nov. 11, 1800), Folder D8, HU-KFC.

49. Bonaparte to Forfait (Oct. 25, 1800), CN vol. 6, 482.

50. "Extrait des registres de l'Assemblée centrale de Saint-Domingue" (March 28, 1801), CO 137/106, BNA.

51. Lemonnier, *Seconde campagne,* 284.

52. Jacques Cauna, *Toussaint Louverture et l'indépendance d'Haïti* (Paris: Karthala, 2004), 231.

53. Bénot, *La démence coloniale,* 25.

54. Bourrienne, *Mémoires,* vol. 3, 208, 222.

55. *Moniteur Universel* 23 (Oct. 15, 1801): 1.

56. De Chair, *Napoleon on Napoleon,* 175.

57. Pluchon, *Toussaint Louverture,* 389.

58. Kerversau, "Rapport sur la partie française"; Kerversau, "Compte-rendu de sa conduite à Saint-Domingue" (Sept. 15, 1801), CC9/B23, AN.

59. "Rapport du Général Kerversau," LGC, 23; Cauna, *Toussaint Louverture,* 157–61.

60. Bonaparte to Talleyrand (Sept. 17, 1801), in John Howard, ed., *Letters and Documents of Napoleon,* vol. 1 (New York: Oxford University Press, 1961), 500.

61. *Moniteur Universel* 204 (April 14, 1802): 3; Paul Butel, "Succès et déclin du commerce colonial français de la Révolution à la Restauration," *Revue économique* 40, no. 6 (1989): 1089.

62. N. A. M. Rodger, *The Command of the Ocean: A Naval History of Britain, 1649–1815* (New York: Norton, 2004), 465–71.

63. De Chair, *Napoleon on Napoleon,* 128.

64. Bourrienne, *Mémoires,* vol. 4, 181, 298.

65. Bonaparte, "Notes pour servir aux instructions à donner au capitaine général Leclerc" (Oct. 31, 1801), LGC, 263–74.

66. Claude Victor, "Mémoire abrégé de la Louisiane présenté au général Bonaparte . . ." (Aug. 3, 1802), AFIV/1211, AN; David Geggus and David Gaspar, eds., *A Turbulent Time: The French Revolution and the Greater Caribbean* (Bloomington: Indiana University Press, 1997), 204–25.

67. Bonaparte to Talleyrand (Oct. 15, 1801), CN vol. 7, 373.

68. Bénot, *La démence coloniale,* 9, 105–6, 128–39.

69. Jan Pachonski and Reuel Wilson, *Poland's Caribbean Tragedy: A Study of Polish Legions in the Haitian War of Independence, 1802–1803* (Boulder, CO: East European Monographs, 1986), 61; Claude Ribbe, *Le diable noir: Biographie du général Alexandre Dumas, père de l'écrivain* (Paris: Alphée, 2008).

70. Antoine Thibaudeau, *Mémoires sur le Consulat, 1799–1804* (Paris: Ponthieu, 1827), 120.

71. Bonaparte, "Notes pour servir aux instructions," 272.

72. Ardouin, *Études,* vol. 4, 449, 460, 467, 474; James, *Black Jacobins,* 275, 294; Wanquet, *La France et la première abolition,* 636; Bénot, *La démence coloniale,* 49.

73. O'Meara, *Napoléon en exil,* vol. 2, 247.

74. Bonaparte to Citizens of Saint-Domingue (Dec. 25, 1799), CN vol. 6, 42; ibid., 245, 572, 574.

75. Bonaparte, "Proclamation du Consul à tous les habitants de Saint-Domingue"

(Nov. 8, 1801), FM/F/3/202, CAOM; "Extrait des registres des délibérations des Consuls," *Moniteur Universel* 63 (Nov. 24, 1801): 1; Bonaparte to Talleyrand (Nov. 13, 1801), CN vol. 7, 406.

76. Bonaparte, "Notes pour servir aux instructions," 272; Madiou, *Histoire,* vol. 2, 135; H. Pauléus Sannon, *Histoire de Toussaint Louverture,* vol. 3 (Port-au-Prince: Héraux, 1933), 48.

77. "Marine et colonies—Budget" (1801–2), MS312/1, SHD-DM.

78. Juan Cole, *Napoleon's Egypt: Invading the Middle East* (New York: Palgrave, 2007), 10, 175.

79. Bénot and Dorigny, *Rétablissement de l'esclavage,* 13–28, 505–22.

80. Bonaparte, "Instructions . . . pour le Gen. Combis" (Jan. 14, 1801), CN vol. 6, 572.

81. Bonaparte to Forfait (March 9, 1801), CN vol. 7, 97; Wanquet, *La France et la première abolition,* 604.

82. Bonaparte to Denis Decrès (Oct. 7, 1801), CN vol. 7, 351.

83. Charles de Vincent to Alexandre Berthier (Sept. 24, 1801), 8Yd1825, SHD-DAT.

84. Bourrienne, *Mémoires,* vol. 4, 309.

85. Vincent, "Précis des principaux événements de Saint-Domingue" (ca. Nov. 1801), MS. 619, BFV-FM.

86. Wenda Parkinson, *"This Gilded African": Toussaint l'Ouverture* (New York: Quartet Books, 1978), 155. For similar expressions, see CN vol. 7, 640; Vincent, *Observations . . . sur les deux premières notes rapportées dans une collection de mémoires pour servir à l'histoire de France sous Napoléon Ier* (Paris: Pélicier/Didot, 1824), 19.

87. De Chair, *Napoleon on Napoleon,* 178.

88. Bénot, *La démence coloniale,* 65.

89. Vincent, "Précis des principaux événements."

90. Christian Schneider, "Le colonel Vincent, officier du génie à Saint-Domingue," *Annales historiques de la révolution française* 329 (July 2002): 120.

91. Vincent to Leclerc (Nov. 18, 1801), BN08270/lot 140, UF-RP. For Vincent's advice, see also Vincent, "Précis des principaux événements"; Vincent, "Nottes sur Saint-Domingue" (ca. Nov. 1801), Box 23/2307, UF-RP; Vincent, *Observations,* 13.

92. On Vincent's later life, see 8Yd1825, SHD-DAT; "Notes sur Keyserling, Razinvill, Oginski, Repnine . . ." (no date), MS. 619, BFV-FM; Vincent, *Observations,* 13; De Chair, *Napoleon on Napoleon,* 178.

CHAPTER 3

1. David Lawday, *Napoleon's Master: The Life of Prince Talleyrand* (New York: St. Martin's Press, 2006).

2. Michel-Étienne Descourtilz, *Voyage d'un naturaliste en Haïti* (1809; reprint, Paris: Plon, 1935), 100.

3. Ministry of Navy, "Rapport aux Consuls de la République" (Sept. 30, [1801]), CC9B/18, AN.

4. Douglas Egerton, "The Empire of Liberty Reconsidered," in *The Revolution of 1800: Democracy, Race, and the New Republic,* ed. James Horn, Jan Ellen Lewis, and Peter Onuf (Charlottesville: University of Virginia Press, 2002), 309–30.

5. Tim Matthewson, "Jefferson and Haiti," *Journal of Southern History* 61, no. 2 (1995): 213.

6. Gordon Brown, *Toussaint's Clause: The Founding Fathers and the Haitian Revolution* (Jackson: University Press of Mississippi, 2005), 195.

7. "Starving" (a misconception caused by poor translation) from Napoléon Bonaparte, "Notes pour servir aux instructions à donner au capitaine général Leclerc" (Oct. 31, 1801), LGC, 269.

8. James Madison to Robert Livingston (Sept. 28, 1801), RG 59, M28/5, NARA-CP.

9. Brown, *Toussaint's Clause,* 197.

10. Madison to Livingston (Sept. 28, 1801), RG 59, M28/5, NARA-CP.

11. Bonaparte, "Instructions pour le citoyen Lequoy-Mongiraud" (Jan. 14, 1801), CN vol. 6, 574.

12. Bonaparte to Charles de Talleyrand (Sept. 17, 1801), CN vol. 7, 323.

13. Bonaparte to Talleyrand (Oct. 21, 1801), CN vol. 7, 376.

14. Marcus Rainsford, *An Historical Account of the Black Empire of Hayti* (London: Albion Press, 1805), 264.

15. James Stephen, *The Crisis of the Sugar Colonies* (1802; reprint, New York: Negro University Press, 1969), 61–70, 85–90, 103.

16. CN vol. 7, 406. On British espionage, see Philippe d'Auvergne's reports in WO 1/923 and WO 1/924, BNA.

17. Claude Auguste and Marcel Auguste, *L'expédition Leclerc, 1801–1803* (Port-au-Prince: Henri Deschamps, 1985), 49.

18. [Robert Hobart?] to George Nugent (Nov. 18, 1801), CO 137/106, BNA.

19. Charles Cornwallis to Charles Jenkinson, Baron Hawkesbury (Nov. 13, 1801), PRO 30/11/264, BNA.

20. [Hobart?] to Nugent (Nov. 18, 1801), CO 137/106, BNA.

21. CN vol. 6, 28, 42, 64, 227, 458, 543, 590; ibid. vol. 7, 8, 81.

22. Bonaparte, "Arrêté" (May 4, 1801), CN vol. 7, 179.

23. Bonaparte, "Note pour l'organisation des troupes coloniales" (Oct. 7, 1801), CN vol. 7, 347.

24. "Rapport sur la composition du corps expéditionnaire" (Oct. 17, 1801), B7/1, SHD-DAT; Alexandre Berthier to Bonaparte (Oct. 24, 1801), B7/1, SHD-DAT; CN vol. 7, 366, 377–81.

25. CN vol. 7, 366; Auguste, *L'expédition Leclerc,* 52.

26. Livingston to [Madison?] (Jan. 13, 1802), RG 59, M34/10, NARA-CP; "Bordereau général des dépenses faites au port de Brest . . ." (Jan. 28, 1802), BB4 162, SHD-DM.

27. "État des troupes parties de France . . ." (ca. 1806), F/5B/67, AN.

28. Jean-Paul Bertaud, *The Army of the French Revolution: From Citizen-Soldiers to Instrument of Power* (1979; reprint, Princeton, NJ: Princeton University Press, 1988).

29. D'Auvergne to Hobart (April 13, 1802), WO 1/924, BNA; Antoine Métral, *Histoire de l'expédition des Français à Saint-Domingue sous le consulat de Napoléon Bonaparte* (1825; reprint, Paris: Karthala, 1985), 27; Jean-Baptiste Lemonnier-Delafosse, *Seconde campagne de Saint-Domingue du 1er décembre 1803 au 15 juillet 1809* (Le Havre: Brindeau, 1846), 276.

30. Bonaparte, "Arrêté" (Sept. 16, 1801), CN vol. 7, 322.

31. Adèle Foucher, *Victor Hugo raconté par Adèle* (Paris: Plon, 1985).

32. Berthier to Hondetot (Sept. 29, 1801), B7/1, SHD-DAT; Denis Decrès to Victoire Leclerc (March 18, 1802), CC9/B24, AN.

33. "Troupes expéditionnaires à Saint-Domingue" (July 19, 1802), B7/27, SHD-DAT; Georges Six, *Dictionnaire historique des généraux et amiraux français de la Révolution et de l'Empire* (Paris: Saffroy, 1934).

34. "État de situation des équipages et passagers embarqués sur l'armée navale . . ." (ca. Dec. 10, 1801), BB4 162, SHD-DM.

35. Hardÿ de Périni, *Correspondance intime du général Jean Hardÿ de 1798 à 1802* (Paris: Plon, 1901), 259.

36. Louis Bergeron, *France under Napoleon* (1972; reprint, Princeton, NJ: Princeton University Press, 1981), 104.

37. Charles Dugua, "Ordre du jour" (May 14, 1802), CC9/B22, AN.

38. Yves Bénot, *La démence coloniale sous Napoléon* (Paris: La Découverte, 1992), 93.

39. Decrès to Maritime Prefect of Havre (Oct. 19, 1801), R3674, ADC.

40. Richard Rhodes, *John James Audubon: The Making of an American* (New York: Knopf, 2004), 30.

41. [Lazare Carnot?], "Note sur l'expédition secrète projetée pour Saint-Domingue" (May 23, 1800), B7/1, SHD-DAT.

42. André Rigaud to Pierre Forfait (Aug. 24, 1801), 8Yd638, SHD-DAT.

43. Bonaparte to Berthier (Nov. 9, 1800), B7/2, SHD-DAT; Juan Cole, *Napoleon's Egypt: Invading the Middle East* (New York: Palgrave, 2007), 215, 219.

44. C. L. R. James, *The Black Jacobins: Toussaint L'Ouverture and the San Domingo Revolution* (1963; reprint, New York: Vintage Books, 1989), 235.

45. Decrès to [Berthier] (Oct. 28, 1801), 8Yd743/1, SHD-DAT; Alfred Nemours, *Histoire militaire de la guerre d'indépendance de Saint-Domingue,* vol. 2 (Paris: Berger-Levrault, 1925), 17.

46. Rigaud to Decrès (Nov. 5, 1801), BB4 162, SHD-DM.

47. On Villatte, see Métral, *Histoire de l'expédition,* 235. On Belley, see Marcel Dorigny and Bernard Gainot, eds., *La société des Amis des Noirs, 1788–1799: Contribution à l'histoire de l'abolition de l'esclavage* (Paris: UNESCO, 1998), 360. On Kayer, see Charles Mackenzie, *Notes on Haiti Made during a Residence in That Republic,* vol. 1 (1830; reprint, London: Frank Cass, 1971), 184. On Mentor, see Louis Dubroca, *La vie de Toussaint Louverture, chef des noirs insurgés de Saint-Domingue* (Paris: Dubroca, 1802), 67. On Léveillé, see Jean-Baptiste Léveillé to the Consuls of the Republic (Nov. 24, 1799), F/5B/38, AN; Anon., [Memoir on troops of color] (ca. 1801), Box 22/2194, UF-RP.

48. On Leclerc's name, see Curé Aubert, "Extrait des registres de baptême"

(June 25, 1786), 7Yd328, SHD-DAT. On his background, see Henry Mézière, *Le Général Leclerc et l'expédition de Saint-Domingue* (Paris: Tallandier, 1990).

49. Bergeron, *France under Napoleon,* 53, 58.

50. Christopher Hibbert, *Napoleon's Women* (New York: Norton, 2002), 60.

51. Bonaparte to Leclerc (July 1, 1802), CN vol. 7, 640.

52. CN vol. 7, 354, 379.

53. Mézière, *Le Général Leclerc,* 125.

54. Bonaparte to Leclerc (Oct. 30, 1801), CN vol. 7, 395; Bonaparte "Arrêté du Consul pour le traitement . . ." (Nov. 4, 1801), FM/F/3/202, CAOM.

55. "Marine et colonies—Budget" (1801–2), MS312/1, SHD-DM.

56. Nemours, *Histoire militaire,* vol. 2, 39.

57. Leclerc to Bonaparte (March 25, 1802), LGC, 116.

58. H. Pauléus Sannon, *Histoire de Toussaint Louverture,* vol. 3 (Port-au-Prince: Héraux, 1933), 39. See also Charles Malenfant, *Des colonies, et particulièrement de celle de Saint-Domingue* (Paris: Audibert: 1814), i.

59. Lemonnier, *Seconde campagne,* 3, 34; Hardÿ, *Correspondance,* 263.

60. Louis Tousard to Alexander Hamilton (Sept. 6, 1802), Tousard Papers, vol. 2, (Phi) 664, HSP; Bénot, *La démence coloniale,* 67.

61. "Procès verbal d'énumération et estimation des divers effets provenant de la succession du général en chef Leclerc" (Nov. 10, 1802), CC9/B23, AN; Rainsford, *An Historical Account,* 244.

62. Cavalier to Leclerc (Dec. 11, 1801), CC9B/19, AN. The unit never left.

63. CN vol. 7, 292, 375; Auguste, *L'expédition Leclerc,* 23.

64. Cole, *Napoleon's Egypt,* 36–48.

65. Thomas Madiou, *Histoire d'Haïti,* vol. 2 (Port-au-Prince: Courtois, 1847), 131.

66. Louis de Bourrienne, *Mémoires de M. de Bourrienne, ministre d'état,* vol. 4 (Paris: Ladvocat, 1829), 308.

67. Bonaparte, "Notes pour servir aux instructions," 272.

68. Rigaud to Decrès (Oct 24, 1801), Reel 1, Sc. Micro R-2228, NYPL-SC; [Pascal], "Mémoire secret" (ca. 1801), Reel 8, ibid.

69. Roume to Forfait (Sept. 25, 1801), BN08270 / lot 132, UF-RP.

70. Bonaparte to Leclerc (Nov. 19, 1801), CN vol. 7, 412.

71. Bonaparte, "Proclamation du Consul" (Nov. 8, 1801), FM/F/3/202, CAOM.

72. Bonaparte to Louverture (Nov. 18, 1801), CN vol. 7, 410.

73. Charles de Vincent, "Notes sur Saint-Domingue" (ca. Nov. 1801), Box 23/2307, UF-RP; Vincent to Leclerc (Nov. 20, 1801), BN08270 / lot 140, UF-RP.

74. Jacques Cauna, *Toussaint Louverture et l'indépendance d'Haïti* (Paris: Karthala, 2004), 207–44.

75. Métral, *Histoire de l'expédition,* 228.

76. Deborah Jenson, "From the Kidnapping(s) of the Louvertures to the Alleged Kidnapping of Aristide: Legacies of Slavery in the Post/Colonial World," *Yale French Studies* 107 (2005): 178.

77. Métral, *Histoire de l'expédition,* 229.

78. Jean-Marcel Humbert and Brunot Ponsonnet, eds., *Napoléon et la mer: Un rêve d'empire* (Paris: Seuil, 2004), 52.

79. Louis-Thomas Villaret de Joyeuse to Decrès (Oct. 23, 1801), BB4 161, SHD-DM.

80. Bonaparte, "Notes pour servir aux instructions," 268.

81. Hardÿ, *Correspondance,* 262, 263, 286.

82. Hibbert, *Napoleon's Women,* 60.

83. F. J. Jackson to Abbott (March 15, 1802), PRO 30/9/117, BNA.

CHAPTER 4

1. Donatien de Rochambeau, "Aperçu général sur les troubles des colonies françaises de l'Amérique" (ca. 1805), 64, 1M593, SHD-DAT; Kenneth Johnson, "Louis-Thomas Villaret de Joyeuse, Admiral and Colonial Administrator" (PhD diss., Florida State University, 2006), 175–83.

2. Jacques de Norvins, *Souvenirs d'un historien de Napoléon: Mémorial de J. de Norvins,* vol. 2 (Paris: Plon, 1896), 327.

3. Ships of the line from Brest transported 459 troops on average (with a maximum of 734 on the *Révolution*). "État des troupes de l'armée expéditionnaire . . ." (Feb. 20, 1802), BB4 162, SHD-DM.

4. Louis-Thomas Villaret de Joyeuse to Denis Decrès (Oct. 17, 1801), BB4 161, SHD-DM.

5. Villaret to Decrès (Oct. 21, 1801), BB4 161, SHD-DM.

6. Villaret to Decrès (Oct. 27, 1801), BB4 161, SHD-DM.

7. Joseph Caffarelli to Decrès (Nov. 12, 1801), BB4 162, SHD-DM.

8. Villaret to Decrès (Nov. 8, 1801), BB4 161, SHD-DM.

9. "État de situation des équipages et passagers . . ." (ca. Dec. 10, 1801), BB4 162, SHD-DM; [Untitled] (Dec. 1801–Feb. 1802), MS 373, SHD-DM.

10. [Villaret], "État des bouches à feu, armes, et munitions de guerre . . ." (Oct. 29, 1801), BB4 161, SHD-DM; Villaret to Decrès (Nov. 6, 1801), BB4 161, SHD DM.

11. 7Yd1173, SHD-DAT; Louis Bro to Jean-Louis Bro (Feb. 7–12, 1802), 82AP/1, AN.

12. Alfred de Laujon, *Souvenirs de trente années de voyages à Saint-Domingue, dans plusieurs colonies étrangères, et au continent d'Amérique,* vol. 2 (Paris: Schwartz and Gagnot, 1835), 221.

13. Clément, [Untitled] (ca. Dec. 1801), AF/IV/1325, AN; Bureau des Ports, "Extrait d'un état adressé par le commissaire en chef de l'armée navale" (Feb. 20, 1802), CC9B/23, AN.

14. Norvins, *Souvenirs,* vol. 2, 342.

15. Villaret to Decrès (Nov. 8, 1801), BB4 161, SHD-DM.

16. Norvins, *Souvenirs,* vol. 2, 306, 308.

17. Ibid., 316.

18. Ibid., 318.

19. André Nicolas Joseph Guimot and Louis Mathieu Dembowski, *Journal et voyage à Saint-Domingue* (Paris: Tesseidre, 1997), 44.

20. Karen Greene, "The Rise and Fall of a Revolutionary: The Political Career

of Louis-Marie Stanislas Fréron, Representative on Mission and Conventionnel, 1754–1802" (PhD diss., Florida State University, 2004), 184.

21. Villaret to Decrès (Nov. 20, 1801), BB4 161, SHD-DM.

22. "Ordre du jour" (Nov. 22, 1801), in "Analyse chronologique et alphabétique des ordres du jour," CC9/B23, AN.

23. Villaret to Decrès (Nov. 28, 1801), BB4 161, SHD-DM.

24. Jean-Baptiste Lemonnier-Delafosse, *Seconde campagne de Saint-Domingue du 1 décembre 1803 au 15 juillet 1809* (Le Havre: Brindeau, 1846), 2, 24, 35.

25. Villaret to Decrès (Dec. 10, 1801), BB4 161, SHD-DM.

26. Villaret to Napoléon Bonaparte (Dec. 14, 1801), AF/IV/1325, AN.

27. Lemonnier, *Seconde campagne,* vii, 26.

28. *Bulletin Officiel du Port Républicain,* no. 40 (Feb. 2, 1802), CC9A/32, AN.

29. Claude Auguste and Marcel Auguste, *L'expédition Leclerc, 1801–1803* (Port-au-Prince: Henri Deschamps, 1985), 62.

30. [Untitled] (Dec. 1801–Feb. 1802), MS 373, SHD-DM; Lemonnier, *Seconde campagne,* 26–27; Norvins, *Souvenirs,* vol. 2, 334.

31. Louis-René de Latouche-Tréville to Decrès (Feb. 4, 1802), CC9A/36, AN.

32. Federico Gravina to Decrès (Dec. 30, 1801), BB4 161, SHD-DM; Pierre Quérangal to Decrès (Jan. 8, 1802), BB4 164, SHD-DM; Villaret to Decrès (Feb. 10, 1802), CC9/B20, AN.

33. Somerset de Chair, ed., *Napoleon on Napoleon: An Autobiography of the Emperor* (London: Cassell, 1992), 179.

34. Norvins, *Souvenirs,* vol. 2, 339.

35. Auguste, *L'expédition Leclerc,* 98.

36. On the Atlantic crossing, see [Untitled] (Dec. 1801–Feb. 1802), MS 373, SHD-DM.

37. *Gazette of the United States,* no. 46 (Jan. 15, 1802).

38. Christophe Paulin de la Poix, *Mémoires du Chevalier de Fréminville* (Paris: Librairie Ancienne Champion, 1913), 30; Lemonnier, *Seconde campagne,* 28; Norvins, *Souvenirs,* vol. 2, 335.

39. "État des troupes embarquées à Cherbourg . . ." (ca. Jan. 13, 1802), BB4 161, SHD-DM; Fréminville, *Mémoires,* 13.

40. Honoré Ganteaume to Decrès (Feb. 17, 1802), in *Moniteur Universel* 182 (March 23, 1802): 729.

41. Andries Hartsinck to Decrès (Nov. 23, 1801), BB4 151, SHD-DM; Philibert Fressinet, "Mémoires sur la dernière expédition de Saint-Domingue" (1802 [probably May 1805]), 11, 1M593, SHD-DAT.

42. Charles de Linois to Decrès (Feb. 17, 1802), *Moniteur Universel* 182 (March 23, 1802): 729.

43. J. H. Thérèse Callamand to Dubois-Thainville (Feb. 5, 1802), BB4 160, SHD-DM; CN vol. 7, 616; http://www.piedsnoirs-aujourdhui.com/berbe0034.html.

44. On the Moyse uprising, see Law to Joseph Inginac (Oct. 26, 1801), CO 137/106, BNA; Silas Talbot to James Madison (Oct. 30, 1801), 208 MI/2, AN; Toussaint Louverture, "Récit des événements qui se sont passés dans la partie du

nord de Saint-Domingue" (Nov. 7, 1801), CO 137/106, BNA; "Extracts of letters," *Aurora* 3418 (Nov. 30, 1801): 2; [Painty?] to Médéric Moreau de Saint-Méry (Feb. 27, 1802), FM/F/3/202, CAOM; Thomas Madiou, *Histoire d'Haïti,* vol. 2 (Port-au-Prince: Courtois, 1847), 105.

45. Baptiste, "Notes sur la colonie de Saint-Domingue" (ca. 1801), CC9C/1, AN.

46. Pamphile de Lacroix, *La révolution de Haïti* (1819; reprint, Paris: Karthala, 1995), 275.

47. François de Kerversau, "Rapport sur la partie française de Saint-Domingue" (March 22, 1801), Box 2/66, UF-RP.

48. Philippe Roume to Pierre Forfait (Dec. 2, 1801), BN08270 / lot 132, UF-RP.

49. George Nugent to Duke of Portland (Nov. 7, 1801), CO 137/106, BNA.

50. "Extracts of letters," *Aurora* 3418 (Nov. 30, 1801): 2; W. L. Whitfield to Nugent (Dec. 5, 1801), CO 137/106, BNA.

51. Roume to Decrès (Feb. 3, 1802), BN08270 / lot 132, UF-RP.

52. Edward Corbet to [Anon.] (Nov. 16, 1801), CO 137/106, BNA.

53. Louverture, "Au nom de la colonie française de Saint-Domingue" (Nov. 25, 1801), Sc Micro R1527, NYPL-SC.

54. Louverture to Henri Christophe (July 24, 1801), Folder "Haiti–Historical Research 1/2," Box 1, Sc MG 714, NYPL-SC.

55. "Extracts of letters," *Aurora* 3418 (Nov. 30, 1801): 2.

56. Whitfield to John King (Jan. 17, 1801), CO 137/106, BNA.

57. Tobias Lear to James Madison (July 17, 1801), 208 MI/2, AN.

58. Louverture, "Aux officiers civils et militaires du Cap" (Sept. 15, 1801), in *Gazette of the United States,* no. 24 (Oct. 29, 1801).

59. Paul Louverture to Louverture (March 26, 1801), CO 137/105, BNA.

60. Louverture to Corbet (April 1, 1801), CO 137/105, BNA.

61. Nugent to Robert Hobart (Nov. 29, 1801), CO 137/106, BNA.

62. Silas Talbot to Madison (Nov. 9, 1801), 208 MI/2, AN.

63. Nugent to Hobart (Nov. 29, 1801), CO 137/106, BNA; *National Intelligencer and Washington Advertiser,* no. 168 (Nov. 30, 1801); Whitfield to Nugent (Dec. 5, 1801), CO 137/106, BNA.

64. Whitfield to Nugent (Dec. 9, 1801), CO 137/106, BNA.

65. Louverture, "Proclamation" (Dec. 20, 1801), in Nugent to Hobart (Jan. 19, 1802), CO 137/106, BNA.

66. Louverture to Colonial Assembly (Jan. 22, 1802), Reel 5, Sc. Micro R-2228, NYPL-SC.

67. Beaubrun Ardouin, *Études sur l'histoire d'Haïti, suivies de la vie du général J-M Borgella,* vol. 5 (Paris: Dézobry et Magdeleine, 1853–60), 13, 34; Auguste, *L'expédition Leclerc,* 84.

68. Allier to Victoire Leclerc (Feb. 8, 1802), in "Extrait de la correspondance concernant Toussaint Louverture" (ca. June 1802), CC9/B23, AN; Guillaume Mauviel, "Mémoires sur Saint-Domingue . . ." (May 24, 1806), 24, 1M599, SHD-DAT.

69. Corbet to William Molleson (Dec. 5, 1801), CO 137/106, BNA; Louver-

ture to Jean-Baptiste Dommage (Feb. 9, 1802), CC9B/19, AN; Gingembre Trop Fort to Joseph Casimir (Feb. 15, 1802), B7/2, SHD-DAT.

70. Roume to Louverture (July 8, 1800), Box 1:5, MG 140, NYPL-SC.

71. Louverture to Bartalie (Feb. 15, 1802), Reel 5, Sc. Micro R-2228, NYPL-SC.

72. Louverture to Soldiers of all ranks (April 26, 1801), CO 137/106, BNA; Descourtilz, *Voyage,* 171.

73. Vollée to Louverture (June 16, 1800), Reel 5, Sc. Micro R-2228, NYPL-SC. See also François de Kerversau to Victoire Leclerc (Feb. 13, 1802), 61 J 24, ADGir.

74. John D. Garrigus, "Catalyst or Catastrophe? Saint-Domingue's Free Men of Color and the Battle of Savannah, 1779–1782," *Revista/Review Interamericana* 22, nos. 1–2 (1992): 111; Stewart R. King, *Blue Coat or Powdered Wig: Free People of Color in Pre-Revolutionary Saint-Domingue* (Athens: University of Georgia Press, 2001), xv.

75. John Thornton, *Africa and Africans in the Making of the Atlantic World, 1400–1680* (New York: Cambridge University Press, 1992), 296.

76. Corbet to Molleson (Dec. 5, 1801), CO 137/106, BNA; Leclerc to Decrès (Feb. 9, 1802), CC9B/19, AN; Antonio del Monte y Tejada, *Historia de Santo Domingo,* vol. 3 (Ciudad Trujillo: República Dominicana, 1952), 214.

77. "Intérieur—Colonies," *Moniteur Universel* 248 (May 28, 1802): 2; Lacroix, *La révolution de Haïti,* 266–73; Madiou, *Histoire,* vol. 2, 109.

78. Louverture, "Arrêté" (Feb. 12, 1801), CC9B/9, AN; Municipal administration of Fort Liberté, "Procès-verbal relatif au corps de gendarmes" (Dec. 6, 1801), CC9C/25, AN.

79. H. Castonnet des Fosses, *La perte d'une colonie: La révolution de Saint-Domingue* (Paris: Faivre, 1893), 257.

80. André Vernet to Louverture (Jan. 29, 1802), Box 3/112, UF-RP; Peter Chazotte, *Historical Sketches of the Revolutions, and the Foreign and Civil Wars in the Island of St. Domingo* (New York: Applegate, 1840), 24.

81. Roume to Decrès (Feb. 3, 1802), BN08270 / lot 132, UF-RP; Auguste, *L'expédition Leclerc,* 82.

82. Louverture to Members of the Central Assembly (Jan. 2, 1802), Reel 5, Sc. Micro R-2228, NYPL-SC; Lear to Madison (Jan. 17, 1802), 208 MI/2, AN; Michel-Étienne Descourtilz, *Voyage d'un naturaliste en Haïti* (1809; reprint, Paris: Plon, 1935), 174.

83. Madiou, *Histoire,* vol. 2, 125.

84. André Rigaud to Decrès (Oct. 24, 1801), Reel 1, Sc. Micro R-2228, NYPL-SC.

85. Chazotte, *Historical Sketches,* 25.

86. Allier to Leclerc (Feb. 8, 1802), in "Extrait de la correspondance concernant Toussaint Louverture" (ca. June 1802), CC9/B23, AN.

87. Lacroix, *La révolution de Haïti,* 280.

88. Gilbert Guillermin, *Journal historique de la révolution de la partie de l'Est de Saint-Domingue, commencée le 10 août 1808* (Philadelphia: Lafourcade, 1810), vii.

CHAPTER 5

1. Jean-Baptiste Lemonnier-Delafosse, *Seconde campagne de Saint-Domingue du 1 décembre 1803 au 15 juillet 1809* (Le Havre: Brindeau, 1846), 31.

2. Louis-Thomas Villaret de Joyeuse to Denis Decrès (Feb. 10, 1802), CC9/B20, AN.

3. Victoire Leclerc to Decrès (Feb. 9, 1802), CC9B/19, AN.

4. Antoine Métral, *Histoire de l'expédition des Français à Saint-Domingue sous le consulat de Napoléon Bonaparte* (1825; reprint, Paris: Karthala, 1985), 232–33; Toussaint Louverture, *Mémoires du Général Toussaint l'Ouverture écrits par lui-même,* ed. St. Rémy (Paris: Pagnerre, 1853), 92.

5. Leclerc to Decrès (Feb. 9, 1802), CC9B/19, AN.

6. Administration of Fortifications, "Idées générales sur l'attaque de la ville du Cap . . ." (Jan. 30, 1802), B7/2, SHD-DAT.

7. Antonio del Monte y Tejada, *Historia de Santo Domingo,* vol. 3 (Ciudad Trujillo: República Dominicana, 1952), 215; Lemonnier, *Seconde campagne,* 80.

8. On the landing in Cap, see [Untitled] (Dec. 1801–Feb. 1802), MS 373, SHD-DM; "Délibérations de l'administration municipale du Cap (Feb. 5, 1802)," *Moniteur Universel* 212 (April 22, 1802): 1; Charles Dugua to Alexandre Berthier (Feb. 8, 1802), B7/2, SHD-DAT; Leclerc to Decrès (Feb. 9, 1802), CC9B/19, AN; Villaret to Decrès (Feb. 10, 1802), CC9/B20, AN; Tobias Lear to James Madison (Feb. 12, 1802), 208 MI/2, AN; [Edward Stevens?] to John Marshall (Feb. 28, 1802), 208 MI/2, AN; Alfred de Laujon, *Précis historique de la dernière expédition de Saint-Domingue* (Paris: Delafolie, ca. 1805), 14; Pamphile de Lacroix, *La révolution de Haïti* (1819; reprint, Paris: Karthala, 1995), 287; Louverture, *Mémoires,* 30; Lemonnier, *Seconde campagne,* 34, 78; Thomas Madiou, *Histoire d'Haïti,* vol. 2 (Port-au-Prince: Courtois, 1847), 137.

9. Hugh Cathcart to Thomas Maitland (Nov. 26, 1799), WO 1/74, BNA; Laujon, *Souvenirs de trente années de voyages à Saint-Domingue, dans plusieurs colonies étrangères, et au continent d'Amérique,* vol. 1 (Paris: Schwartz and Gagnot, 1835), 355; Hubert Cole, *Christophe, King of Haiti* (New York: Viking Press), 1967.

10. Dugua to Berthier (Feb. 8, 1802), B7/2, SHD-DAT; Villaret to Decrès (Feb. 10, 1802), CC9/B20, AN; Lear to [Unspecified] (Feb. 12, 1802), in *Aurora* 3507 (March 15, 1802): 2; [Stevens?] to Marshall (Feb. 28, 1802), 208 MI/2, AN. For Louverture's claims, see Louverture to Paul Louverture (Feb. 6, 1802), 61 J 24, ADGir; Louverture, *Mémoires,* 32.

11. "Compte-courant" (April 28, 1802), Box 6:7, (Phi) 1602, HSP.

12. Christophe, "Manifeste du roi" (Sept. 18, 1814), 20, RG 59 / MLR A1632, NARA-CP.

13. Lacroix, *La révolution de Haïti,* 288.

14. Leclerc to Decrès (Feb. 9, 1802), CC9B/19, AN. On the landing, see also Donatien de Rochambeau, "Aperçu général sur les troubles des colonies françaises de l'Amérique " (ca. 1805), 52, 1M593, SHD-DAT; Deseine and Courtois, "Mon

premier voyage sur mer . . ." (ca. 1809), 23, Reel 9, Sc. Micro R-2228, NYPL-SC; Lemonnier, *Seconde campagne,* 39.

15. Madiou, *Histoire,* vol. 2, 137; Jacques de Norvins, *Souvenirs d'un historien de Napoléon: Mémorial de J. de Norvins,* vol. 3 (Paris: Plon, 1896), 9.

16. "Délibérations de l'administration municipale du Cap."

17. [French officer], "Mémoire succint sur la guerre de Saint-Domingue" (1804), 5–16, 1M598, SHD-DAT.

18. Leclerc to Decrès (Feb. 9, 1802), CC9B/19, AN.

19. Madiou, *Histoire,* vol. 2, 222.

20. Louverture, *Mémoires,* 38; Hardÿ de Périni, *Correspondance intime du général Jean Hardÿ de 1798 à 1802* (Paris: Plon, 1901), 265.

21. Lear to [Madison?] (Feb. 12, 1802), B7/2, SHD-DAT.

22. Norvins, *Souvenirs,* vol. 2, 352; Laujon, *Souvenirs,* vol. 2, 229.

23. Beaubrun Ardouin, *Études sur l'histoire d'Haïti, suivies de la vie du général J-M Borgella,* vol. 5 (Paris: Dézobry et Magdeleine, 1853–60), 29.

24. Norvins, *Souvenirs,* vol. 2, 354.

25. Lear to [Madison?] (Feb. 12, 1802), B7/2, SHD-DAT; "Washington city," *Aurora* 3503 (March 10, 1802): 2.

26. Norvins, *Souvenirs,* vol. 2, 358.

27. Laujon, *Souvenirs,* vol. 2, 233.

28. Leclerc to Decrès (Feb. 9, 1802), CC9B/19, AN; Leclerc to Napoléon Bonaparte (Feb. 9, 1802), B7/26, SHD-DAT.

29. Paul Louverture to Louverture (Feb. 4, 1802), Reel 5, Sc. Micro R-2228, NYPL-SC; Joseph Maurillo to Sebastián Kindelán (Feb. 10, 1802), DHHAN, 146; Paul Louverture to Leclerc (Feb. 21, 1802), Box 1Ad./7, UF-RP; "Extrait d'une lettre de Santiago de Cuba" (ca. March 1802), BN08268 / lot 77, UF-RP; François de Kerversau to Decrès (Feb. 10, 1804), CC9A/37, AN; 61 J 24, ADGir; Tejada, *Historia de Santo Domingo,* vol. 3, 224.

30. Augustin Clervaux to Cabiro (Feb. 13, 1802), Reel 1, Sc. Micro R-2228, NYPL-SC; Clervaux to Charles Magon (Feb. 16, 1802), Folder 11C, HU-KFC; Gabriel Debien, *Guillaume Mauviel, évêque constitutionnel de Saint-Domingue* (Basse Terre: Société d'Histoire de la Guadeloupe, 1981), 37.

31. Pamphile Lacroix to Dugua (Feb. 8, 1802), B7/15, SHD-DAT. On the landing, see also Louis-René de Latouche-Tréville to Villaret (Feb. 6, 1802), CC9/B20, AN; Jean Boudet to Decrès (Feb. 8, 1802), CC9/B23, AN; [French civilian], "Journal of occurrences at Port-Républicain" (ca. Feb. 1802), in Edward Corbet to George Nugent (April 10, 1802), CO 137/108, BNA; Lacroix, *La révolution de Haïti,* 300.

32. "Extract from a letter," *Aurora* 3518 (March 29, 1802): 2; Lacroix, *La révolution de Haïti,* 304.

33. Alphonse de Lamartine, *Toussaint Louverture* (Paris: Levy, 1850), xxiv–xxviii.

34. Jacques Maurepas to Louverture (Feb. 14, 1802), 61 J 18, ADGir; Leclerc to Decrès (Feb. 15, 1802), B7/26, SHD-DAT; *Moniteur Universel* 182 (March 23, 1802): 728; Lacroix, *La révolution de Haïti,* 315; Madiou, *Histoire,* vol. 2, 176.

35. Lacroix, *La révolution de Haïti,* 319.

36. Villaret to Decrès (Feb. 19, 1802), CC9/B20, AN.

37. Leclerc to Decrès (Feb. 9, 1802), CC9B/19, AN; Leclerc to Bonaparte (Feb. 9, 1802), B7/26, SHD-DAT.

38. Métral, *Histoire de l'expédition,* 236. On the encounter, see also Jean-Baptiste Coisnon to Decrès (Feb. 20, 1802), in *Moniteur Universel* 212 (April 22, 1802): 1; Louverture, *Mémoires,* 43.

39. Bonaparte to Louverture (Nov. 18, 1801), CN vol. 7, 410.

40. Leclerc to Louverture (Feb. 12, 1802), B7/26, SHD-DAT.

41. Lacroix, *La révolution de Haïti,* 314.

42. "Notes sur l'expédition de Leclerc à Saint-Domingue et sur la famille Louverture," 10, 6APC/1, CAOM.

43. Lacroix, *La révolution de Haïti,* 314.

44. A. Charmant, *Haïti vivra-t-elle? Etude sur le préjugé des races: Race Noire, Race Jaune, Race Blanche et sur la doctrine de Monroe* (Havre: F. Le Roy, 1905), 147.

45. "Notes sur l'expédition de Leclerc," 10.

46. H. Pauléus Sannon, *Histoire de Toussaint Louverture,* vol. 3 (Port-au-Prince: Héraux, 1933), 59.

47. Lacroix to Dugua (Feb. 19, 1802), B7/15, SHD-DAT; Jean-Baptiste Dommage to Boudet (Feb. 26, 1802), Reel 1, Sc. Micro R-2228, NYPL-SC.

48. Leclerc to Decrès (Feb. 27, 1802), CC9B/19, AN.

49. "Récit succint des événements arrivés à Léogane et Jacmel" (Feb. 4–15, 1802), Box 3/114–15, UF-RP; Lacroix to Dugua (Feb. 19, 1802), B7/15, SHD-DAT.

50. Latouche to Villaret (Feb. 1802), BB4 161, SHD-DM; Boudet to [Philibert Willaumez] (Feb. 12, 1802), BB4 163, SHD-DM.

51. Lacroix to Dugua (Feb. 15, 1802), B7/15, SHD-DAT; Corbet to Nugent (Feb. 27, 1802), CO 137/107, BNA; "Extract of a letter from B. Dandrige," *Aurora* 3529 (April 9, 1802): 2; Lacroix, *La révolution de Haïti,* 303.

52. Lacroix to Vallabrigues (Feb. 15, 1802), B7/15, SHD-DAT.

53. "Récit succint des événements arrivés à Léogane et Jacmel." On Jacmel, see also "A sketch of occurrences at Jacmel," *Aurora* 3517 (March 27, 1802): 2; Louis Boisrond-Tonnerre, "Mémoire pour servir à l'histoire d'Hayti" (June 22, 1804), 8, CC9B/27, AN.

54. Jacques Cauna, ed., *Toussaint Louverture et l'indépendance d'Haïti* (Paris: Karthala, 2004), 223.

55. Army of Saint-Domingue, "État général des troupes arrivées dans la colonie" (ca. July 1803), CC9/B23, AN.

56. Charles de Linois to Decrès (Feb. 17, 1802), *Moniteur Universel* 182 (March 23, 1802): 729; Krohm to Decrès (April 20, 1802), BB4 164, SHD-DM; F. Teissedre, ed., *Souvenirs de marins du Premier Empire* (Paris: Teissedre, 1998), 99.

57. Philippe d'Auvergne to Henry Dundas (Sept. 2, 1800), WO 1/923, BNA.

58. Villaret to Decrès (Feb. 17, 1802), *Moniteur Universel* 182 (March 23, 1802): 728.

59. "Marine et colonies—Budget" (1801–2), 72–83, MS312/2, SHD-DM.

60. Clément to Decrès (March 22, 1802), BB4 162, SHD-DM.

61. Louis Bro to Jean-Louis Bro (Feb. 7–12, 1802), 82AP/1, AN.

62. Norvins, *Souvenirs,* vol. 2, 366.

63. Leclerc, "Proclamation aux habitants de Saint-Domingue" (Feb. 17, 1802), CC9B/19, AN.

64. Louverture, *Mémoires,* 112–22.

65. Lemonnicr, *Seconde campagne,* 47; Métral, *Histoire de l'expédition,* 245.

66. Sannon, *Histoire de Toussaint Louverture,* vol. 3, 69.

CHAPTER 6

1. Charles Paullin, *Commodore John Rodgers* (Cleveland: Arthur Clark, 1910), 73.

2. Edward Stevens to John Marshall (Feb. 28, 1802), 208 MI/2, AN; Tobias Lear to [Unspecified] (Feb. 12, 1802), *Aurora* 3507 (March 15, 1802): 2.

3. Victoire Leclerc to Denis Decrès (Feb. 9, 1802), CC9B/19, AN.

4. *Poulson's American Daily Advertiser,* no. 7697 (Aug. 13, 1801), 2; *Philadelphia Gazette,* no. 4241 (June 22, 1802), 2.

5. Lear to James Madison (March 22, 1802), 208 MI/2, AN.

6. Louis-Thomas Villaret de Joyeuse to Leclerc (Feb. 15, 1802), 135AP/1, doc. 1, AN; Leclerc, "Arrêté" (Feb. 17, 1802), CC9/B22, AN.

7. Leclerc to Decrès (Feb. 15, 1802), B7/26, SHD-DAT; Stevens to Marshall (Feb. 28, 1802), 208 MI/2, AN.

8. Reed and Forde to John Mitchell (June 4, 1801), (Phi) 541, HSP.

9. Stevens to Marshall (Feb. 28, 1802), 208 MI/2, AN; Pierre Boyer to Lear (March 20, 1802).

10. *Aurora* 3503 (March 10, 1802): 2.

11. *Aurora* 3516 (March 26, 1802): 2; Louis Tousard to Alexander Hamilton (Sept. 6, 1802), Tousard Papers, vol. 2, (Phi) 664, HSP.

12. Leclerc to François Watrin (Feb. 17, 1802), LGC, 97.

13. Victor du Pont de Nemours to Leclerc (March 20, 1802), B7/13, SHD-DAT.

14. Louis-André Pichon to [Charles de Talleyrand] (March 28, 1802), B7/13, SHD-DAT.

15. Pichon to Leclerc (March 1, 1802), BN08269 / lot 107, UF-RP; Pichon to Leclerc (March 30, 1802), B7/13, SHD-DAT.

16. "Aujourd'hui 5 brumaire an 10 . . ." (Oct. 27, 1801), Reel 6, Sc. Micro R-2228, NYPL-SC.

17. Charles Liot to Leclerc (March 11, 1802), BN08269 / lot 107, UF-RP.

18. Lear to Madison (April 11, 1802), 208 MI/2, AN; Ray Brighton, *The Checkered Career of Tobias Lear* (Portsmouth, NH: Portsmouth Marine Society, 1985), 192–210.

19. Leclerc to Lear (April 15, 1802?), 208 MI/1, AN.

20. John Rodgers to Madison (June 1802), Box 1:14, (Phi) 1208, HSP.

21. Madison to Robert Livingston (July 6, 1802), Microfilm M77/1, NARA-CP.

22. Boyer to Leclerc (March 12, 1802), 135AP/1, doc. 5, AN.

23. Leclerc to Decrès (May 4, 1802), B7/26, SHD-DAT.

24. Pichon to Leclerc (March 30, 1802), B7/13, SHD-DAT; Pichon to Leclerc (May 7, 1802), BN08269 / lot 107, UF-RP.

25. Leclerc to Napoléon Bonaparte (June 6, 1802), B7/26, SHD-DAT; Dolores Egger Labbe, ed., *The Louisiana Purchase Bicentennial Series in Louisiana History,* vol. 3 (Lafayette: Center for Louisiana Studies, 1998), 77.

26. David Geggus, *Slavery, War, and Revolution: The British Occupation of Saint-Domingue, 1793–1798* (Oxford: Clarendon Press, 1982), 171.

27. Leclerc to Bonaparte (Nov. 26, 1801), LGC, 54; Louis Antoine Fauvelet de Bourrienne, *Mémoires de M. de Bourrienne, ministre d'état,* vol. 4 (Paris: Ladvocat, 1829), 310.

28. Juan Cole, *Napoleon's Egypt: Invading the Middle East* (New York: Palgrave, 2007), 78.

29. Leclerc, "Arrêté" (Feb. 14, 1802), CC9/B22, AN; Leclerc, "Arrêté" (April 19, 1802), Box 4/262, UF-RP.

30. Leclerc to Bonaparte (April 1, 1802), B7/26, SHD-DAT.

31. "Marine et colonies—Budget" (1801–2), MS312/1 and /2, SHD-DM.

32. Decrès to Leclerc and Villaret (April 11, 1802), CC9/B22, AN.

33. Leclerc to Bonaparte (Oct. 7, 1802), LGC, 253.

34. François Lequoy Mongiraud to Leclerc (Feb. 24, 1802), BN08268 / lot 77, UF-RP.

35. On Havana, see Leclerc, [Drafts of letters] (ca. April 17, 1802), Box 4/247, UF-RP. On Veracruz, see Leclerc, "Instructions pour le capitaine de vaisseau Mayne" (April 17, 1802), Box 4/246, UF-RP. On Caracas, see Leclerc to Gov. of Caracas (April 25, 1802), Box 4/273, UF-RP. On Cartagena, see Jacques de Norvins, *Souvenirs d'un historien de Napoléon: Mémorial de J. de Norvins,* vol. 3 (Paris: Plon, 1896), 32. On Santiago, see Leclerc to Sebastián Kindelán (June 23, 1802), DHHAN, 148.

36. Lequoy to Marques de Someruelos (March 4, 1802), BN08268 / lot 77, UF-RP.

37. Guillaume Raynal, *Histoire philosophique et politique des établissements et du commerce des Européens dans les deux Indes,* vol. 3 (Amsterdam, 1773), 15; Bartolomc de Las Casas, *A Short Account of the Destruction of the Indies* (1559; reprint, Penguin Books: 1999), 120–25.

38. Gambart to Leclerc (March 27, 1802), Box 3/162, UF-RP.

39. Michel Descourtilz, "Plan d'organisation d'un lycée colonial" (April 1, 1802), B7/13, SHD-DAT; Leclerc to Jean-Antoine Chaptal (May 8, 1802), B7/26, SHD-DAT.

40. Leclerc, [Drafts of letters] (ca. April 17, 1802), Box 4/247, UF-RP; Norvins, *Souvenirs,* vol. 3, 24.

41. Malin to Decrès (Aug. 22, 1802), BB4 163, SHD-DM; [Leonora Sansay], *Zelica, the Creole,* vol. 1 (London: William Fearman, 1820), 161–63.

42. Leclerc to Chaptal (May 8, 1802), B7/26, SHD-DAT.

43. "Intérieur—Colonies," *Moniteur Universel* 248 (May 28, 1802): 2.

44. Joseph Caffarelli to Decrès (Nov. 22, 1802), CC9B/18, AN; Pamphile de Lacroix, *La révolution de Haïti* (1819; reprint, Paris: Karthala, 1995), 313, 356.

45. Leclerc to Bonaparte (April 1, 1802), B7/26, SHD-DAT; [White planter?], "Mémoire sur la colonie de Saint-Domingue" (1802), 1M594, SHD-DAT; Donatien de Rochambeau, "Aperçu général sur les troubles des colonies françaises" (ca. 1805), 54, 62, 1M593, SHD-DAT; Toussaint Louverture, *Mémoires du Général Toussaint l'Ouverture écrits par lui-même,* ed. St. Rémy (Paris: Pagnerre, 1853), 53, 94; Madiou, *Histoire,* vol. 2, 171, 202.

46. Alfred Nemours, *Histoire de la captivité et de la mort de Toussaint-Louverture* (Paris: Berger-Levrault, 1929), 245.

47. W. L. Whitfield to George Nugent (Dec. 16, 1801), CO 137/107, BNA; Anon., "Rapport—d'Hébécourt' (Jan.–Feb. 1803), B7/9, SHD-DAT.

48. Leclerc to Decrès (Feb. 9, 1802), CC9B/19, AN.

49. Jacques Cauna, ed., *Toussaint Louverture et l'indépendance d'Haïti* (Paris: Karthala, 2004), 200, 206.

50. Antoine Laussat to [Pierre Clément de] Laussat (July 1, 1802), CC9/B22, AN.

51. Gabriel Debien, "A propos du trésor de Toussaint Louverture," *Revue de la société d'histoire et de géographie d'Haïti* 17, no. 62 (July 1946): 35.

52. "Procès verbaux dressés par Corneille . . ." (June 1802), 7Yd284, SHD-DAT.

53. Alfred Nemours, *Histoire de la famille et de la descendance de Toussaint Louverture* (Port-au-Prince: Imprimerie de l'État, 1941), 187.

54. Thomas Gragnon-Lacoste, *Toussaint Louverture* (Paris: Durand, 1877), 378.

55. Hilliard d'Auberteuil, *Considérations sur l'état présent de la colonie française de Saint-Domingue,* vol. 1 (Paris: Grangé, 1776), 189; Gragnon, *Toussaint Louverture,* 216.

56. Philip Wright, ed., *Lady Nugent's Journal of Her Residence in Jamaica from 1801 to 1805* (Kingston: University of the West Indies Press, 2002), xviii.

57. George Campbell to Evan Nepean (Jan. 18, 1802), ADM 1/252, BNA; John Duckworth to Nepean (April 7, 1802), ADM 1/252, BNA.

58. Duckworth to Nepean (Feb. 19, 1802), ADM 1/252, BNA.

59. Nugent to [Robert Hobart] (July 10, 1802), CO 137/108, BNA.

60. Nugent to John Sullivan (Feb. 19, 1802), CO 137/106, BNA.

61. Nugent, *Journal,* 62, 72–97.

62. Villaret to Duckworth (Feb. 15, 1802), ADM 1/252, BNA; Leclerc to Nugent (Feb. 15, 1802), CO 137/107, BNA.

63. Villaret to Decrès (March 6, 1802), BB4 161, SHD-DM; Leclerc to Decrès (May 6, 1802), B7/26, SHD-DAT.

64. Decrès to Villaret (March 18, 1802), CC9/B24, AN.

65. R. Mends to Duckworth (April 1, 1802), ADM 1/252, BNA.

66. Duckworth to Nepean (April 4, 1802), ADM 1/252, BNA.

67. "Répartition faite par le général en chef . . ." (May 18, 1802), BB4 161, SHD-DM; "British naval force employed at Jamaica . . ." (ca. May 1802), BB4 161, SHD-DM.

68. Leclerc to Decrès (April 21, 1802), CC9B/19, AN.

69. Nugent, *Journal,* 1.

CHAPTER 7

1. Bureau des Ports, "Extrait d'un état adressé par le commissaire en chef de l'armée navale" (Feb. 20, 1802), CC9B/23, AN; Thomas Madiou, *Histoire d'Haïti,* vol. 2 (Port-au-Prince: Courtois, 1847), 182.

2. Pamphile Lacroix to Bruyère (Feb. 12, 1802), B7/15, SHD-DAT.

3. Hardÿ de Périni, *Correspondance intime du général Jean Hardÿ de 1798 à 1802* (Paris: Plon, 1901), 271.

4. Charles Esmangart to Donatien de Rochambeau (May 4, 1802), Box 1Ad./19, UF-RP.

5. Victoire Leclerc to Denis Decrès (Feb. 27, 1802), CC9B/19, AN; François de Kerversau to Augustin Clervaux (March 3, 1802), 61 J 23, ADGir; Charles Dugua to Alexandre Berthier (March 26, 1802), B7/3, SHD-DAT.

6. Alfred de Laujon, *Précis historique de la dernière expédition de Saint-Domingue* (Paris: Delafolie, ca. 1805), 53.

7. Hardÿ, *Correspondance,* 274.

8. Leclerc to Decrès (Feb. 27, 1802), CC9B/19, AN.

9. *Moniteur Universel* 182 (March 23, 1802): 729.

10. Leclerc to Decrès (Feb. 27, 1802), B7/26, SHD-DAT; Madiou, *Histoire,* vol. 2, 185.

11. Jacques Maurepas to Toissant Louverture (Feb. 19, 1802), 61 J 18, ADGir; Louis-Thomas Villaret de Joyeuse to Decrès (March 4, 1802), in "Extrait de la correspondance concernant Toussaint Louverture" (ca. June 1802), CC9/B23, AN.

12. Leclerc to Decrès (Feb. 27, 1802), B7/26, SHD-DAT; Rochambeau, "Aperçu général sur les troubles des colonies françaises" (ca. 1805), 58, 1M593, SHD-DAT; Toussaint Louverture, *Mémoires du Général Toussaint l'Ouverture écrits par lui-même,* ed. St. Rémy (Paris: Pagnerre, 1853), 49; Madiou, *Histoire,* vol. 2, 188–91.

13. Saint-Rémy, *Vie de Toussaint Louverture* (Paris: Moquet, 1850), 354.

14. Leclerc to Decrès (Feb. 27, 1802), CC9B/19, AN.

15. Ibid.

16. Jean-Baptiste Lemonnier-Delafosse, *Seconde campagne de Saint-Domingue du 1 décembre 1803 au 15 juillet 1809* (Le Havre: Brindeau, 1846), 287; Mathieu Dumas, *Précis des événements militaires,* vol. 8 (Paris: Treuttel and Würtz, 1819), 475.

17. Michel-Étienne Descourtilz, *Voyage d'un naturaliste en Haïti* (1809; reprint, Paris: Plon, 1935), 97.

18. Pamphile de Lacroix, *La révolution de Haïti* (1819; reprint, Paris: Karthala, 1995), 327.

19. Paul François Page, *Traité d'économie politique et de commerce des colonies,* vol. 2 (Paris: Brochot, 1802), 2.

20. Pierre Pluchon, *Toussaint Louverture* (Paris: Fayard, 1989), 488.

21. André Rigaud to Decrès (Oct. 28, 1801), Reel 1, Sc. Micro R-2228, NYPL-SC; Edmé-Étienne Desfourneaux to Leclerc (Feb. 21, 1802), 135AP/6, AN.

22. Lacroix to Louis d'Arbois (Feb. 10, 1802), B7/15, SHD-DAT.

23. Leclerc to Decrès (Feb. 27, 1802), B7/26, SHD-DAT; Dejean to Leclerc (July 19, 1802), BN08268 / lot 4, UF-RP.

24. Lemonnier, *Seconde campagne,* 36. See also Deseine and Courtois, "Mon premier voyage sur mer . . ." (ca. 1809), 27–31, Reel 9, Sc. Micro R–2228, NYPL-SC.

25. Dugua, "Ordre du jour" (April 21, 1802), B7/16, SHD-DAT.

26. "Bataillon allemand: Situation" (Oct. 14, 1802), B7/27, SHD-DAT.

27. Leclerc, "Ordre du jour" (Feb. 10, 1802), CC9B/19, AN.

28. Leclerc to Napoléon Bonaparte (Feb. 19, 1802), LGC, 101; Nicolas Bodard to Rochambeau (Jan. 24, 1803), Box 16/1563, UF-RP.

29. There were twelve heavy demi-brigades (8,294 men) and three light ones (3,029 men). "État des troupes de l'armée expéditionnaire . . ." (Feb. 20, 1802), BB4 162, SHD-DM.

30. Alexandre Dalton to [Unspecified] (March 26, 1802), B7/3, SHD-DAT.

31. Dugua to Berthier (March 26, 1802), B7/3, SHD-DAT.

32. John Thornton, *Africa and Africans in the Making of the Atlantic World, 1400–1680* (New York: Cambridge University Press, 1992), 102–25.

33. Marcus Rainsford, *An Historical Account of the Black Empire of Hayti* (London: Albion Press, 1805), 218.

34. H. Pauléus Sannon, *Histoire de Toussaint Louverture,* vol. 3 (Port-au-Prince: Héraux, 1933), 57.

35. Cercle des Philadelphes du Cap Français, *Recherches et observations sur les maladies épizootiques de Saint-Domingue* (Cap: Imprimerie Royale, 1788), 46, 48.

36. Antoine Métral, *Histoire de l'expédition des Français à Saint-Domingue sous le consulat de Napoléon Bonaparte* (1825; reprint, Paris: Karthala, 1985), 264.

37. David Geggus, "Sex, Ratio, Age, and Ethnicity in the Atlantic Slave Trade: Data from French Shipping and Plantation Records," *Journal of African History* 30, no. 1 (1989): 28–35; Thornton, *Africa and Africans,* 183; Geggus, "The French Slave Trade: An Overview," *William and Mary Quarterly* 58, no. 1 (2001): 123–30.

38. Chief of 1st Batallion of 19th light demi-brigade to Pierre Thouvenot (Feb. 23, 1802), B7/2, SHD-DAT.

39. Jean-Jacques Dessalines to Toussaint Louverture (Feb. 20, 1802), Reel 4, Sc. Micro R–2228, NYPL-SC.

40. Charles Belair to Louverture (April 1, 1802), Reel 5, Sc. Micro R–2228, NYPL-SC.

41. Louverture, [Untitled] (Nov. 25, 1801), CC9B/9, AN.

42. Edna Bay, *Wives of the Leopard: Gender, Politics, and Culture in the Kingdom of Dahomey* (Charlottesville: University of Virginia Press, 1998), 137.

43. Arlette Gautier, *Les sœurs de Solitude: La condition féminine dans l'esclavage aux Antilles du XVIIe au XIXe siècle* (Paris: Editions Caribéennes, 1985), 241–44; Judith Kafka, "Action, Reaction, and Interaction: Slave Women in Resistance in the South of Saint Domingue, 1793–94," *Slavery and Abolition* 18, no. 2 (1997): 57.

44. Gingembre Trop Fort, [Order] (Feb. 20, 1802), B7/2, SHD-DAT.

45. Leclerc, "Ordre du jour" (Feb. 10, 1802), CC9B/19, AN.

46. Leclerc to Decrès (Feb. 9, 1802), CC9B/19, AN; Leclerc to Bonaparte (April 1, 1802), B7/26, SHD-DAT.

47. "État nominatif des chefs de la colonie qui se sont soumis" (ca. March 1802), B7/2, SHD-DAT.

48. Alcindor and Bonaventure to Chief of Staff of Desfourneaux Division (Feb. 10, 1802), B7/2, SHD-DAT; Leclerc, "Le général en chef ordonne" (March 4, 1802), CC9/B22, AN.

49. Descourtilz, *Voyage,* 150.

50. On Gingembre, see B7/2 and /3, SHD-DAT.

51. Gingembre to Casimir (Feb. 28, 1802), B7/2, SHD-DAT.

52. Lacroix to Berthier (Oct. 10, 1801), 7Yd841/1, SHD-DAT.

53. 7Yd841/1 and /2, SHD-DAT; Lacroix, *La révolution de Haïti.*

54. Lacroix to Louis-René de Latouche-Tréville (Feb. 22, 1802), B7/15, SHD-DAT.

55. Lacroix to Pointe le Jeune (Feb. 14, 1802), B7/15, SHD-DAT.

56. Lacroix to Dugua (Feb. 19, 1802), B7/15, SHD-DAT.

57. Lacroix to Dugua (March 1, 1802), B7/15, SHD-DAT; Lacroix, *La révolution de Haïti,* 322.

58. Lacroix to Latouche (Feb. 22, 1802), B7/15, SHD-DAT; Lacroix, *La révolution de Haïti,* 323; Louverture, *Mémoires,* 61.

59. Lacroix, *La révolution de Haïti,* 306.

60. Descourtilz, *Voyage,* 179–207. The account is consistent with Madiou, *Histoire,* vol. 2, 209.

61. Descourtilz, *Voyage,* 179.

62. Dessalines to Louverture (May 6, 1802), Reel 4, Sc. Micro R-2228, NYPL-SC; Louverture, *Mémoires,* 58.

63. Beaubrun Ardouin, *Études sur l'histoire d'Haïti, suivies de la vie du général J-M Borgella,* vol. 5 (Paris: Dézobry et Magdeleine, 1853–60), 134.

64. Descourtilz, *Voyage,* 192.

65. Ibid., 198.

66. Madame Jules Michelet, *The Story of My Childhood* (1866; reprint, Boston: Little, Brown, 1867), 169.

67. Mr. Peyrac to Mrs. Peyrac (March 5, 1802), in Edward Corbet to George Nugent (April 4, 1802), CO 137/108, BNA; Lacroix, *La révolution de Haïti,* 344.

68. *Aurora* 3526 (April 7, 1802): 2; Jacques de Norvins, *Souvenirs d'un historien de Napoléon: Mémorial de J. de Norvins,* vol. 2 (Paris: Plon, 1896), 375–81; Lacroix, *La révolution de Haïti,* 328.

69. Pierre Boulle, *Race et esclavage dans la France de l'Ancien Régime* (Paris: Perrin, 2007); Sue Peabody and Tyler Stovall, eds., *The Color of Liberty: Histories of Race in France* (Durham, NC: Duke University Press, 2003), 2.

70. R. Mends to John Duckworth (April 1, 1802), ADM 1/252, BNA; Rochambeau, "Aperçu général," 64–66; Lacroix, *La révolution de Haïti,* 327.

71. Dessalines to Louverture (March 1, 1802), Reel 4, Sc. Micro R-2228, NYPL-SC.

72. Galbois to Rochambeau (April 5, 1802), Box 4/195, UF-RP.

73. Sonis to Leclerc (March 17, 1802), CC9A/30, AN; Leclerc to Decrès (March 26, 1802), 416AP/1, AN.

74. On the siege of Crête-à-Pierrot, see Leclerc to Decrès (March 26, 1802), 416AP/1, AN; Dugua to Berthier (March 26, 1802), B7/3, SHD-DAT; Louis Boisrond-Tonnerre, "Mémoire pour servir à l'histoire d'Hayti" (June 22, 1804),

12–18, CC9B/27, AN; Rochambeau, "Aperçu général," 60–66; Lacroix, *La révolution de Haïti*, 331–38; Descourtilz, *Voyage*, 208–15; Madiou, *Histoire*, vol. 2, 210–25.

75. Boisrond, "Mémoire," 14.

76. Descourtilz, *Voyage*, 212.

77. *Journal des officiers de santé de Saint-Domingue*, no. 2 (ca. Spring 1803): 125–28, Pcr J 7.5 60199.0.1, LCP.

78. Joseph Caffarelli to Decrès (Jan. 29, 1802), BB4 162, SHD-DM; Lacroix to [Coutelle?] (Feb. 24, 1802), B7/15, SHD-DAT; Gunther Rosenberg, *The Art of Warfare in the Age of Napoleon* (Bloomington: Indiana University Press, 1978), 230.

79. Saint-Rémy, *Vie de Toussaint Louverture*, 364.

80. Leclerc to Bonaparte (March 25, 1802), LGC, 116.

81. Dugua to Berthier (March 26, 1802), B7/3, SHD-DAT.

82. Lacroix, *La révolution de Haïti*, 333.

83. Dessalines to Louverture (March 14, 1802), in Cauna, *Toussaint Louverture*, 14.

84. Joan Dayan, *Haiti, History, and the Gods* (1995; reprint, Berkeley: University of California Press, 1998), 23.

85. Cauna, *Toussaint Louverture*, 14.

86. Lacroix, *La révolution de Haïti*, 333.

87. Ibid., 335.

88. Ibid., 332.

89. Henri Christophe to Louverture (March 19, 1802), Folder C14, HU-KFC; Cauna, *Toussaint Louverture*, 16.

90. *Minerve* 38 (April 10, 1802): 2, CO 137/108, BNA; Lacroix, *La révolution de Haïti*, 336.

91. Leclerc to Decrès (March 26, 1802), 416AP/1, AN.

92. Bourget to Jean Sulauze (March 17, 1802), Box 5:8, (Phi) 1602, HSP; Corbet to Nugent (April 6, 1802), CO 137/108, BNA; [Extracts of letters], *Aurora* 3526 (April 7, 1802): 2; Decrès to Leclerc (May 25, 1802), CC9/B24, AN.

93. Lacroix to Dugua (March 1, 1802), B7/15, SHD-DAT; Villaret to Decrès (April 4, 1802), BB4 161, SHD-DM.

94. Faure et al., "Copie de la déclaration du citoyen Barade Haut" (March 14, 1802), B7/3, SHD-DAT; Rochambeau, "Aperçu général," 67; Louverture, *Mémoires*, 52.

95. Latouche to Villaret (March 5, 1802), BB4 161, SHD-DM; Métral, *Histoire de l'expédition*, 291.

96. Delpech to Rochambeau (May 8, 1802), Box 5/333, UF-RP.

97. Bertrand Clauzel to Rochambeau (April 10, 1802), Box 4/216, UF-RP; Corbet to Nugent (April 23, 1802), CO 137/108, BNA.

98. Camas to Desfourneaux (March 16, 1802), B7/3, SHD-DAT; Boyer to Leclerc (March 19, 1802), 135AP/1, doc. 14, AN; Tobias Lear to James Madison (March 29, 1802), 208 MI/2, AN.

99. Jean Hardÿ to Leclerc (April 2, 1802), Box 3/173, UF-RP.

100. Hardÿ, *Correspondance*, 280, 286.

101. Madiou, *Histoire*, vol. 2, 242.

102. Christophe, "Manifeste du roi" (Sept. 18, 1814), 23, Publications on the independence of Haiti, RG 59 / MLR A1632, NARA-CP. On Christophe's submission, see also Boyer to Leclerc (March 22, 1802), 135AP/1, doc. 15, AN; Philibert Fressinet, "Mémoires sur la dernière expédition de Saint-Domingue" (1802 [probably May 1805]), 58, 1M593, SHD-DAT.

103. Leclerc to Inhabitants of Saint-Domingue (April 25, 1802), Box 4/277, UF-RP; Leclerc, "Le général en chef ordonne" (April 26, 1802), Box 4/281, UF-RP.

104. Baron de Vastey, *Political Remarks on Some French Works and Newspapers* (London, 1818), 177.

105. Armée de Saint-Domingue, "État général des troupes arrivées dans la colonie" (ca. July 1803), CC9/B23, AN.

106. "Notes sur l'expédition de Leclerc à Saint-Domingue et sur la famille Louverture," 23, 6APC/1, CAOM.

107. Leclerc to Decrès (April 1, 1802), CC9B/19, AN; Louverture, *Mémoires,* 63.

108. Leclerc to Decrès (May 6, 1802), B7/26, SHD-DAT.

109. [French officer], "Mémoire succint sur la guerre de Saint-Domingue" (1804), 30, 1M598, SHD-DAT.

110. Dessalines to Louverture (April 4, 1802), Reel 4, Sc. Micro R-2228, NYPL-SC; Dessalines to Louverture (May 5, 1802), Folder 23C, HU-KFC; Boisrond, "Mémoire," 19.

111. Leclerc to Louverture (May 1, 1802), in *Gazette du Port-Républicain* 66 (May 16, 1802), CO 137/108, BNA.

112. Leclerc to Decrès (April 9, 1802), B7/26, SHD-DAT; Leclerc to Bonaparte (May 7, 1802), LGC, 145.

113. Alphonse de Lamartine, *Toussaint Louverture* (Paris: Lévy, 1850), xx. On Louverture's arrival, see also *Gazette of the United States,* no. 89 (June 15, 1802); Fressinet, "Mémoires sur la dernière expédition," 64.

114. Norvins, *Souvenirs,* vol. 2, 395–96. See also Métral, *Histoire de l'expédition,* 287.

115. Paul Louverture to Louverture (May 29, 1802), 61 J 18 ADGir.

116. Norvins, *Souvenirs,* vol. 2, 364.

117. Leclerc to Bonaparte (May 7, 1802), LGC, 145.

118. Métral, *Histoire de l'expédition,* 295.

119. Leclerc, "Arrêté" (April 8, 1802), Box 4/208, UF-RP.

120. Leclerc to Louverture (May 5, 1802), Reel 5, Sc. Micro R-2228, NYPL-SC.

121. Hardÿ, *Correspondance,* 286, 289.

CHAPTER 8

1. Mary Hassal [Leonora Sansay], *Secret History; or, The Horrors of St. Domingo, in a Series of Letters, Written by a Lady at Cape François* (Philadelphia: Bradford and Inskeep, 1808), 1.

2. Hassal, *Secret History,* 20, 77. On women in Saint-Domingue, see also Arlette Gautier, *Les sœurs de Solitude: La condition féminine dans l'esclavage aux Antilles du XVIIe au XIXe siècle* (Paris: Editions Caribéennes, 1985); David Gaspar and

Darlene Clark Hine, eds., *More Than Chattel: Black Women and Slavery in the Americas* (Bloomington: Indiana University Press, 1996).

3. Hassal, *Secret History,* 77.

4. Doris Garraway, *The Libertine Colony: Creolization in the Early French Caribbean* (Durham, NC: Duke University Press, 2005), 37.

5. Hassal, *Secret History,* 7–12.

6. [Sansay], *Zelica, the Creole,* vol. 1 (London: William Fearman, 1820), 167.

7. Pierre Boyer, *Historique de ma vie,* vol. 1 (Paris: La Vouivre, 1999), 60.

8. Boyer to Victoire Leclerc (March 18, 1802), doc. 11, 135AP/1, AN.

9. Joan Dayan, *Haiti, History, and the Gods* (1995; reprint, Berkeley: University of California Press, 1998), 164–70.

10. [Hassal], *Laura,* vol. 1 (Philadelphia: Bradford and Inskeep, 1809), preface.

11. Hassal, *Secret History,* 36; Jacques de Norvins, *Souvenirs d'un historien de Napoléon: Mémorial de J. de Norvins* (Paris: Plon, 1896), vol. 2, 375; ibid., vol. 3, 11.

12. Inhabitants of Gros Morne, [Untitled] (July 23, 1802), B7/5, SHD-DAT.

13. Drouin to Donatien de Rochambeau (May 15, 1802), BN08268 / lot 39, UF-RP.

14. P. Panisse to Rochambeau (Dec. 18, 1802), Box 15/1448, UF-RP.

15. Pamela Scully and Diana Paton, eds., *Gender and Slave Emancipation in the Atlantic World* (Durham, NC: Duke University Press, 2005), 56–78.

16. Hassal, *Secret History,* 9, 38.

17. Norvins, *Souvenirs,* vol. 1, viii.

18. Louis d'Arbois to Pamphile Lacroix (Feb. 23, 1802), B7/2, SHD-DAT; Charles Dugua, "Ordre du jour" (April 15, 1802), B7/16, SHD-DAT; Leclerc, "Ordre du jour" (April 29, 1802), CC9/B22, AN.

19. [Raymond Labatut], [Mémoire] (April 25, 1803), BN08272 / lot 122, UF-RP; Antoine Laussat to Pierre Clément de Laussat (July 1, 1802), CC9/B22, AN.

20. Leclerc to Napoléon Bonaparte (March 5, 1802), B7/26, SHD-DAT.

21. Leclerc to Bonaparte (May 7, 1802), LGC, 145.

22. Dugua, "Ordre du jour" (May 14 1802), CC9/B22, AN; Dugua, "Ordre du jour" (May 15, 1802), B7/16, SHD-DAT; Leclerc, "Arrêté" (June 23, 1802), CC9/B26, AN; Hector Daure to Naudot (Nov. 8, 1802), B7/12, SHD-DAT.

23. On Paul Valete, see Box 6:2–4, (Phi) 1602, HSP.

24. Caroline and Laure Valete to Valete (ca. Jan. 27, 1802), Box 6:3, (Phi) 1602, HSP.

25. Barré Saint-Venant, *Des colonies modernes sous la zone torride, et particulièrement de celle de Saint-Domingue* (Paris: Brochot, 1802), 66, 96; Hilliard d'Auberteuil, *Considérations sur l'état présent de la colonie française de Saint-Domingue,* vol. 1 (Paris: Grangé, 1776), 72, 234.

26. Gambart to Leclerc (March 27, 1802), Box 3/162, UF-RP.

27. Lefebure to Rochambeau (ca. Spring 1802), Box 22/2240, UF-RP.

28. Leclerc, "Arrêté" (Feb. 17, 1802), CC9/B22, AN; Leclerc to Bonaparte (March 5, 1802), B7/26, SHD-DAT.

29. Administration des Domaines, "Récapitulation" (ca. 1802), 135AP/3, AN.

30. Administration des Domaines, "État de divers baux à ferme" (ca. Fall 1802), 135AP/3, AN.

31. Louis Clément de Rosières to Daure (ca. Sept. 1802), CC9A/36, AN.

32. Administration des Domaines, "Récapitulation" (ca. Sept. 1802), 135AP/3, AN.

33. Gambart to Leclerc (March 27, 1802), Box 3/162, UF-RP; Lenoir, "Mémoire sur la colonie de Saint-Domingue" (ca. 1803), 1M593, SHD-DAT.

34. Leclerc, "Arrêté" (July 17, 1802), CC9/B26, AN; Leclerc, "Arrêté" (Aug. 20, 1802), Box 10/843, UF-RP.

35. Lomelle Veuve Dodard to Rochambeau (April 19, 1802), Box 4/256, UF-RP.

36. Leclerc to Denis Decrès (May 4, 1802), B7/26, SHD-DAT.

37. Francis Wimpffen, *A Voyage to Saint Domingo in the Years 1788, 1789, and 1790* (London: T. Cadell, 1797), 259.

38. Saint-Venant, *Des colonies,* 193, 472.

39. Decrès to Leclerc (Sept. 16, 1802), CC9/B22, AN.

40. "Extrait des registres des délibérations" (July 5, 1802), CC9C/5, AN; Edward Corbet, "A general account of payments . . ." (July 5, 1802), CO 137/108, BNA; Paul Butel, "Succès et déclin du commerce colonial français de la Révolution à la Restauration," *Revue économique* 40, no. 6 (November 1989): 1087.

41. [French merchant] to Dominique Laxalde (May 16, 1802), Box 7:6, (Phi) 1602, HSP; St. Georges to Jean-Baptiste Drouillard (Aug. 12, 1802), Reel 1, Ms. 2590, LSU.

42. Leclerc, "Arrêté" (Feb. 15, 1802), CC9/B22, AN.

43. Jean-Antoine Chaptal to Merchants of Marseille (Feb. 1, 1803), F/12/549, AN; *Journal du Commerce* (March 31, 1802), CC9C/5, AN.

44. [Merchant in Cap] to Man and Foltz (Aug. 12, 1802), Box 7:6, (Phi) 1602, HSP.

45. Pierre Bénézech to Decrès (April 9, 1802), CC9A/29, AN.

46. Leclerc, "Proclamation" (May 12, 1802), CC9/B22, AN.

47. M. J. La Neuville, *Le dernier cri de Saint-Domingue et des colonies* (Philadelphia: Bradford, 1800), 27.

48. Louis-Thomas Villaret de Joyeuse to Decrès (Feb. 19, 1802), CC9/B20, AN; Auguste Bouvet de Cressé, ed., *Histoire de la catastrophe de Saint-Domingue* (Paris: Peytieux, 1824), 86.

49. Leclerc to Citizens of Saint-Domingue (Feb. 9, 1802), LGC, 74; François de Kerversau, [Proclamation] (Feb. 24, 1802), Log 1737.F, LCP.

50. John Lionard to Tobias Lear (April 8, 1802), 208 MI/2, AN.

51. Leclerc to Inhabitants of Saint-Domingue (April 25, 1802), Box 4/277, UF-RP.

52. Leclerc, "Règlement sur la culture" (ca. May 1802), Box 22/2239, UF-RP.

53. Joseph Idlinger to Leclerc (April 3, 1802), Box 3/185, UF-RP; Leclerc to Toussaint Louverture (May 3 [1], 1802), LGC, 132.

54. Leclerc to Decrès (May 4, 1802), B7/26, SHD-DAT.

55. Dugua, "Ordre du jour" (May 15, 1802), B7/16, SHD-DAT.

56. Leclerc to Bonaparte (July 6, 1802), LGC, 189.

57. Thomas Madiou, *Histoire d'Haïti,* vol. 2 (Port-au-Prince: Courtois, 1847), 268–70; Baron de Vastey, *Revolution and Civil Wars in Haiti* (1823; reprint, New York: Negro University Press, 1969), 29.

58. Joseph Bizouard, [Report to Leclerc] (June 13, 1802), Box 7/492, UF-RP.

59. Leclerc, "Le général en chef ordonne" (June 29, 1802), Box 7/564, UF-RP; Lenoir, "Mémoire sur la colonie."

60. Leclerc to Deraim (June 12, 1802), Box 7/489, UF-RP.

61. Leclerc to Decrès (May 6, 1802), LGC, 134.

62. Leclerc, "Ordonnance" (July 1, 1802), CC9/B26, AN; Bonaparte to Leclerc (July 1, 1802), CN vol. 7, 640.

63. Pierre Collette to Stanislas Foache (April 7, 1802), FP/92APC/16/43, CAOM.

64. Lacroix to Municipal Administration [of Port Républicain] (Feb. 12, 1802), B7/15, SHD-DAT.

65. Félix Carteau, *Soirées bermudiennes, ou entretiens sur les événemens qui ont opéré la ruine de la partie française de l'isle Saint-Domingue* (Bordeaux: Pellier-Lawalle, 1802), xxi–xxix.

66. Wimpffen, *A Voyage,* 269–74.

67. Hassal, *Secret History,* 34.

68. On Bonnet, see Guy-Joseph Bonnet, *Souvenirs historiques* (Paris: Durand, 1864). On free-coloreds, see Stewart King, *Blue Coat or Powdered Wig: Free People of Color in Pre-Revolutionary Saint-Domingue* (Athens: University of Georgia Press, 2001); John Garrigus, *Before Haiti: Race and Citizenship in French Saint-Domingue* (New York: Palgrave, 2006).

69. Carteau, *Soirées bermudiennes,* 152; La Neuville, *Dernier cri,* 11.

70. André Rigaud to Sebastián Kindelán (ca. Aug. 1800), DHHAN, 140.

71. Leclerc to Kindelán (Feb. 16, 1802), DHHAN, 147.

72. Bonnet, *Souvenirs,* 99–104.

73. 8Yd638, SHD-DAT; Louis Boisrond-Tonnerre, "Mémoire pour servir à l'histoire d'Hayti" (June 22, 1804), 25, CC9B/27, AN.

74. King, *Blue Coat or Powdered Wig,* 54.

75. Achille to Pierre Thouvenot (May 14, 1802), B7/4, SHD-DAT.

76. Leclerc to Bonaparte (June 6, 1802), B7/26, SHD-DAT.

77. Somerset de Chair, ed., *Napoleon on Napoleon: An Autobiography of the Emperor* (London: Cassell, 1992), 183.

78. Bonaparte to Leclerc (July 1, 1802), CN vol. 7, 640.

79. David Geggus and David Gaspar, eds., *A Turbulent Time: The French Revolution and the Greater Caribbean* (Bloomington: Indiana University Press, 1997), 1–50; Yves Bénot and Marcel Dorigny, *Rétablissement de l'esclavage dans les colonies françaises 1802: Ruptures et continuités de la politique coloniale française* (Paris: Maisonneuve-Larose, 2003), 69–94; Allyson Delnore, "Forced and Free Colonists: How French Elites Planned to Populate an Overseas Empire in the Age of Revolutions," *Proceedings and Selected Papers of the Consortium of the Revolutionary Era* (2006): 132–41.

80. Pamphile de Lacroix, *La révolution de Haïti* (1819; reprint, Paris: Karthala, 1995), 304.

81. On Idlinger, see Leclerc, [Decree] (July 14, 1802), Box 8/635, UF-RP. On Collet and Borgella, see Decrès, "Rapport aux Consuls" (Sept. 3, 1802), CC9A/32, AN. On Viard, see Leclerc to Decrès (July 18, 1802), LGC, 194. On Nogérée

and Lacour (who fled), see M. A. M. Andrieu to Rochambeau (June 26, 1802), BN08268 / lot 1, UF-RP. On d'Hébécourt, see Bureau des opérations militaires to Claude Régnier (April 2, 1803), B7/10, SHD-DAT.

82. Joseph Bunel to Bonaparte (July 7, 1803), CC9/B23, AN; Bunel Papers, (Phi) 1811, HSP.

83. Leclerc to Decrès (Aug. 25, 1802), CC9B/19, AN.

84. Claude Auguste and Marcel Auguste, *Les déportés de Saint-Domingue: Contribution à l'histoire de l'expédition française de Saint-Domingue, 1802–1803* (Sherbrooke, Quebec: Naaman, 1979), 46, 117–22.

85. [Sansay], *Zelica,* vol. 1, 211–15.

86. Edmé-Étienne Desfourneaux to Leclerc (March 16, 1802), 135AP/6, AN.

87. Andrieu to Jean-Baptiste Brunet (ca. May 14, 1802), BN08268 / lot 1, UF-RP.

88. Leclerc to Bonaparte (May 7, 1802), LGC, 145.

89. Pierre Thouvenot to Bertrand Clauzel (Aug. 23, 1802), B7/19, SHD-DAT; Auguste, *Les déportés,* 42, 57.

90. CN vol. 8, 260, 357; Auguste, *Les déportés,* 45–78; Michael D. Sibalis, "Les noirs en France sous Napoléon: L'enquête de 1807," in Bénot and Dorigny, *Rétablissement de l'esclavage,* 96–97.

91. Decrès to Rochambeau (Feb. 18, 1803), CC9/B22, AN.

92. "État des officiers, soldats, et individus quelconques partant pour France" (June 6, 1802), Box 6/464, UF-RP.

93. Francois Gachet, "Enquête sur les déportés, hommes de couleur de Saint-Domingue . . ." (May 2, 1803), B7/10, SHD-DAT.

94. Auguste, *Les déportés,* 47.

95. Paul Louverture to Louverture (June 5, 1802), Box 1Ad./25, UF-RP.

96. Pierre Pluchon, *Toussaint Louverture* (Paris: Fayard, 1989), 422.

97. Jean-Jacques Dessalines to Cila [Sylla] (May 22, 1802), Reel 4, Sc. Micro R-2228, NYPL-SC.

98. Achille Dampierre, "Rapport des opérations de la brigade de droite" (May 23, 1802), B7/4, SHD-DAT.

99. D'Esquidoux to Brunet (May 26, 1802), 135AP/6, AN.

100. Louverture to Jean-Pierre Fontaine (May 27, 1802), in *Moniteur Universel* 309 (July 28, 1802): 3.

101. Lacroix, *La révolution de Haïti,* 352.

102. Leclerc to Decrès (June 11, 1802), CC9B/19, AN.

103. Dessalines to Leclerc (May 22, 1802), Reel 4, Sc. Micro R-2228, NYPL-SC; Leclerc to Decrès (June 15, 1802), B7/26, SHD-DAT.

104. Esquidoux to Brunet (May 20, 1802), 135AP/6, AN.

105. Leclerc to Bonaparte (June 6, 1802), B7/26, SHD-DAT.

106. Brunet to Louverture (June 3, 1802), Folder 24C, HU-KFC.

107. Louverture to Brunet (June 5, 1802), 135AP/6, AN.

108. Brunet to Louverture (June 7, 1802), CC9B/18, AN.

109. Louverture, *Mémoires du Général Toussaint l'Ouverture écrits par lui-même,* ed. St. Rémy (Paris: Pagnerre, 1853), 73–82.

110. Lacroix, *La révolution de Haïti,* 354.

111. Brunet to Leclerc (June 7, 1802), 135AP/6, AN.

112. Brunet to Leclerc (June 19, 1802), Box 2:4, MG 140, NYPL-SC.

113. "Procès verbaux dressés par Corneille sur les habitations du citoyen Toussaint Louverture" (June 1802), 7Yd284, SHD-DAT; Louverture to Leclerc (July 18, 1802), Folder 3C, HU-KFC.

114. Brunet to Leclerc (June 9, 1802), Folder C25, HU-KFC.

115. Lacroix, *La révolution de Haïti,* 354. For different quotes, see George Nugent to John Sullivan (Aug. 12, 1802), CO 137/108, BNA; Vastey, *Revolution and Civil Wars,* 35.

116. Boyer, *Historique,* vol. 1, 62.

117. Brunet to Leclerc (June 9, 1802), Folder C25, HU-KFC; Louverture, *Mémoires,* 84.

118. "État des officiers, soldats, et individus quelconques partant pour France" (June 6, 1802), Box 6/464, UF-RP.

119. Leclerc to Bonaparte (June 11, 1802), LGC, 171; Leclerc to Decrès (July 6, 1802), B7/26, SHD-DAT.

120. Boyer, *Historique,* vol. 1, 62.

CHAPTER 9

1. *Journal des officiers de santé de Saint-Domingue,* no. 3 (Spring 1803): 134–42, Per J 7.5 60199.0.1, LCP.

2. *Journal des officiers,* no. 3, 143–51.

3. Ibid., 184–92; George Pinckard, *Notes on the West Indies,* vol. 2 (London: Longman, Hurst, Ress, Orme, 1806), vol. 2, 62, 119–30.

4. Alexandre Moreau de Jonnès, *Monographie historique et médicale de la fièvre jaune des Antilles* (Paris: Migneret, 1820), 7.

5. Charles de Vincent, "Précis des principaux événements de Saint-Domingue" (ca. Nov. 1801), MS. 619, BFV; Napoléon Bonaparte to Victoire Leclerc (Nov. 27, 1802), CN vol. 8, 142.

6. Moreau, *Monographie historique,* 1.

7. Renaux to Joseph Caffarelli (Dec. 28, 1801), B7/2, SHD-DAT; Caffarelli to Denis Decrès (Jan. 29, 1802), BB4 162, SHD-DM.

8. Leclerc to Hector Daure (Feb. 6, 1802), B7/14, SHD-DAT.

9. Decrès to Leclerc (March 18, 1802), CC9/B24, AN.

10. "Monthly return of the sick of his majesty's forces in Jamaica" (April 20, 1802), CO 137/108, BNA; James MacNamara to John Duckworth (April 26, 1802), ADM 1/252, BNA; George Nugent to John Sullivan (April 30, 1802), CO 137/108, BNA.

11. Leclerc to Decrès (May 8, 1802), CC9B/19, AN.

12. C. S. Cuynot, "Relation historique, topographique et médicale de Saint-Domingue en 1802 an 10" (ca. 1834), 3, Box 3:5, MG 140, NYPL-SC; Jean-Baptiste Lemonnier-Delafosse, *Seconde campagne de Saint-Domingue du 1 décembre 1803 au 15 juillet 1809* (Le Havre: Brindeau, 1846), 84.

13. Colonial Health Council to Leclerc (June 12, 1802), BN08270 / lot 141, UF-RP.

14. *Journal des officiers,* no. 3, 134–42.

15. *Journal des officiers,* no. 1, 11–16, 42; ibid., no. 2, 111–17; Cuynot, "Relation historique," 13, 18, 24; J. Vincent, *Dissertation sur la fièvre jaune . . .* (Paris: Didot, 1806), 23.

16. Leclerc to Decrès (June 6, 1802), B7/26, SHD-DAT.

17. Trabuc et al., "Journal de médecine, chirurgie, et histoire naturelle" (Jan. 18, 1803), CC9/B20, AN.

18. Gilbert, "Rapport du conseil de santé colonial" (May 31, 1802), BN08270 / lot 141, UF-RP.

19. Maillard to Police Commissar of Cap (Dec. 11, 1802), CC9B/10, AN; *Journal des officiers,* no. 1, 5.

20. Cuynot, "Relation historique," 4, 12, 19; Moreau, *Monographie,* 154, 171, 279; *Journal des officiers,* no. 1, 18–24; ibid., no. 3, 152–70.

21. *Journal des officiers,* no. 1, 29. On cures, see also ibid., no. 1, 30–41, 60; no. 2, 73–81; no. 3, 170–83.

22. Hilliard d'Auberteuil, *Considérations sur l'état présent de la colonie française de Saint-Domingue,* vol. 2 (Paris: Grangé, 1776), 73.

23. *Journal des officiers,* no. 2, 90, 93.

24. [Inspector of the colonial health service] to Jean-Baptiste Guillemain de Vaivres (Nov. 3, 1801), CC9A/28, AN.

25. Gilbert, "Rapport du conseil de santé colonial"; Antoine Moulut, "Mémoire . . ." (Sept. 2, 1802), Box 10/943, UF-RP; *Journal des officiers,* no. 1, 6–9; ibid., no. 3, 197–210; ibid., no. 4, 216–19.

26. Leclerc to Decrès (June 6, 1802), B7/26, SHD-DAT.

27. Colonial Health Council to Leclerc (June 12, 1802), BN08270 / lot 141, UF-RP.

28. Leclerc to Decrès (Feb. 15, 1802), B7/26, SHD-DAT.

29. W. L. Whitfield to Nugent (Aug. 26, 1802), CO 137/108, BNA.

30. Jean Hardÿ to Donatien de Rochambeau (May 16, 1802), Box 5/375, UF-RP; Jacques de Norvins, *Souvenirs d'un historien de Napoléon: Mémorial de J. de Norvins,* vol. 2 (Paris: Plon, 1896), 390.

31. Pierre Bénézech to Decrès (May 7, 1802), CC9B/20, AN.

32. Henriot to Bertrand (June 21, 1802), Box 7/532, UF-RP.

33. Maillard to Daure (Nov. 27, 1802), CC9B/10, AN.

34. Jean Humbert to Jean-Baptiste Brunet (Aug. 12, 1802), B7/6, SHD-DAT.

35. [Charles d'Hénin] to Cdt. of Station [of Fort Liberté?] (Sept. 16, 1802), B7/17, SHD-DAT.

36. Prévot to Rochambeau (June 12, 1802), BN08270 / lot 116, UF-RP.

37. Antoine Moulut, "Mémoire des ouvrages de fortifications . . ." (Nov. 24, 1802), Box 14/1351, UF-RP.

38. Charles Dugua, "Ordre du jour" (May 31, 1802), B7/16, SHD-DAT; Dugua, "Ordre du jour" (June 12, 1802), B7/16, SHD-DAT; Leclerc to Decrès (Sept. 26, 1802), Box 12/1098, UF-RP.

39. Bally et al. to Rochambeau (July 22, 1803), BN08271 / lot 122, UF-RP.

40. *Moniteur Universel* 103 (Jan. 3, 1802): 2.

41. Leclerc to Decrès (Feb. 9, 1802), CC9B/19, AN; *Moniteur Universel* 174 (March 15, 1802): 2.

42. Leclerc to Decrès (May 8, 1802), CC9B/19, AN; *Moniteur Universel* 264 (June 13, 1802): 3.

43. *Moniteur Universel* 297 (July 16, 1802): 1.

44. *Moniteur Universel* 350 (Sept. 7, 1802): 1; Gabriel Debien, "Autour de l'expédition de Saint-Domingue: Les espoirs d'une famille d'anciens planteurs, 1801–1804," *Notes d'histoire coloniale* 111 (1942): 80–82.

45. Michel Hector, ed., *La révolution française et Haïti: Filiations, ruptures, nouvelles dimensions,* vol. 2 (Port-au-Prince: Henri Deschamps, 1991), 356–66.

46. René Périn, *L'incendie du Cap, ou, le règne de Toussaint Louverture* (Paris: Marchands de nouveautés, 1802), 40.

47. Alain Pigeard, "La conscription sous le Premier Empire," *Revue du souvenir napoléonien* 420 (Oct.–Nov. 1998): 3–20.

48. Yves Bénot, *La démence coloniale sous Napoléon* (Paris: La Découverte, 1992), 94.

49. Philippe d'Auvergne to Robert Hobart (Aug. 2, 1802), WO 1/924, BNA.

50. Napoléon Bonaparte, "Décision" (March 19, 1802), CN vol. 7, 527; Delaborde to Alexandre Berthier (May 9, 1802), B7/4, SHD-DAT.

51. Rémi Monaque, "Les aspects maritimes de l'expédition de Saint-Domingue," *Revue Napoléon* 9 (Feb. 2002): 5–13.

52. CN vol. 7, 525, 540, 595, 596.

53. Decrès, "Rapport" (June 11, 1802), BB4 161, SHD-DM; Decrès to Leclerc (July 28, 1802), CC9/B22, AN.

54. Bonaparte to Decrès (March 29, 1802), CN vol. 7, 540.

55. Decrès to Berthier (June 5, 1802), B7/4, SHD-DAT; Bonaparte, "Décision" (July 29, 1802), CN vol. 7, 692.

56. Montalivet to Berthier (June 11, 1802), B7/5, SHD-DAT.

57. Leclerc to Bonaparte (June 6, 1802), B7/26, SHD-DAT.

58. L. Pellissier to Rochambeau (Sept. 7, 1802), Box 11/979, UF-RP; Christophe Paulin de la Poix, *Mémoires du Chevalier de Fréminville* (Paris: Champion, 1913), 27, 47; Debien, "Autour de l'expédition," 6.

59. F. Teissedre, ed., *Souvenirs de marins du Premier Empire* (Paris: Teissedre, 1998), 101.

60. Debien, "Autour de l'expédition," 39.

61. Fréminville, *Mémoires,* 35.

62. Ibid., 42; Thomas Madiou, *Histoire d'Haïti,* vol. 2 (Port-au-Prince: Courtois, 1847), 351.

63. Lemonnier, *Seconde campagne,* 84.

64. Louis-René de Latouche-Tréville to Decrès (Oct. 8, 1802), BB4 161, SHD-DM.

65. Teissedre, *Souvenirs,* 101.

66. Leclerc to Decrès (June 6, 1802), B7/26, SHD-DAT; Leclerc to Decrès

(July 12, 1802), CC9B/19, AN; Daure, "Compte-rendu de l'administration générale de Saint-Domingue" (late 1803), 3:66, CC9B/13, AN; Debien, "Autour de l'expédition," 64–69.

67. Rochambeau, "Aperçu général sur les troubles des colonies françaises de l'Amérique" (ca. 1805), 114, 1M593, SHD-DAT; J. Ho, "La mortalité des généraux et amiraux de la Révolution et de l'Empire," *Population* 26, no. 1 (1971): 146.

68. Debien, *Guillaume Mauviel, évêque constitutionnel de Saint-Domingue (1801–1805)* (Basse Terre: Société d'Histoire de la Guadeloupe, 1981), 47.

69. Philip Wright, ed., *Lady Nugent's Journal of Her Residence in Jamaica from 1801 to 1805* (Kingston: University of the West Indies Press, 2002), 117.

70. Krohm to Decrès (July 6, 1802), BB4 164, SHD-DM.

71. Raymond de Lacrosse to Leclerc (Nov. 15, 1802), Box 14/1335, UF-RP.

72. Jean Lavalette to Rochambeau (May 12, 1802), Box 5/357, UF-RP.

73. De Saon to Rochambeau (June 14, 1802), Box 7/495, UF-RP; Leclerc to Decrès (July 4, 1802), B7/26, SHD-DAT.

74. François de Kerversau to Pamphile Lacroix (Aug. 23, 1802), 7Yd841/1, SHD-DAT.

75. Fréminville, *Mémoires,* 51, 42.

76. R. Mends, "Narrative of a visit to Port-Républicain" (May 26, 1802), ADM 1/252, BNA; Norvins, *Souvenirs,* vol. 3, 26, 29.

77. Achille Dampierre to [Pierre Thouvenot] (May 10, 1802), B7/4, SHD-DAT.

78. Juan Cole, *Napoleon's Egypt: Invading the Middle East* (New York: Palgrave, 2007), 57, 111, 170, 175.

79. Leclerc to Decrès (Sept. 13, 1802), CC9B/19, AN.

80. Mends, "Narrative of a visit."

81. Leclerc to Decrès (July 4, 1802), B7/26, SHD-DAT.

82. Leclerc to Decrès (Aug. 2, 1802), B7/26, SHD-DAT.

83. Thouvenot to Dugua (Aug. 30, 1802), B7/20, SHD-DAT.

84. Dugua, "Ordre du jour" (Aug. 8, 1802), CC9/B23, AN.

85. Parnageon to Thouvenot (Aug. 23, 1802), B7/6, SHD-DAT.

86. Dugua, "Ordre du jour" (Feb. 15, 1802), CC9A/31, AN; Dugua, "Ordre du jour" (Aug. 8, 1802), CC9B/23, AN.

87. Dugua, "Ordre du jour" (July 11, 1802), CC9/B22, AN; Decrès to Leclerc (July 28, 1802), CC9/B22, AN; Leclerc to Decrès (Aug. 2, 1802), B7/26, SHD-AT.

88. *Journal des officiers,* no. 1, 9, 10.

89. Leclerc to Decrès (June 24, 1802), CC9B/19, AN; Daure, "Compte-rendu de l'administration," 85.

90. Fréminville, *Mémoires,* 55; Monaque, "Les aspects maritimes," 5–13.

91. Allemand to Decrès (Aug. 18, 1802), BB4 163, SHD-DM.

92. Fréminville, *Mémoires,* 65.

93. Teissedre, *Souvenirs,* 101.

94. Fréminville, *Mémoires,* 59.

95. Norvins, *Souvenirs,* vol. 3, 13–18, 43.

96. Debien, "Autour de l'expédition," 64–69.

97. Dugua, "Ordre du jour" (June 5, 1802), B7/16, SHD-DAT; Chief of staff of Clauzel division to Duilraux (June 13, 1802), CC9B/10, AN.

98. Daure to Dat (Nov. 16, 1802), B7/12, SHD-DAT; Michel-Étienne Descourtilz, *Voyage d'un naturaliste en Haïti* (1809; reprint, Paris: Plon, 1935), 219.

99. Latouche to Decrès (Oct. 6, 1802), BB4 161, SHD-DM.

100. Edmé-Étienne Desfourneaux to Rochambeau (Sept. 27, 1802), Box 12/1131, UF-RP; Déperonne to Desbureaux (Oct. 10, 1802), BN08269 / lot 103, UF-RP; "Station de Saint-Domingue—état de situation des bâtiments . . ." (Dec. 22, 1802), BB4 181, SHD-DM.

101. Gurin to Philibert Willaumez (Oct. 18, 1802), BB4 163, SHD-DM; Greban to Willaumez (April 19, 1803), BB4 183, SHD-DM.

102. Decrès to Leclerc (June 16, 1802), CC9/B24, AN; Latouche to Decrès (June 30, 1802), BB4 161, SHD-DM.

103. Latouche to Decrès (July 11, 1802), BB4 161, SHD-DM; Leclerc, "Ordre du jour" (July 15, 1802), CC9/B22, AN.

104. Latouche to Decrès (Oct. 8, 1802), BB4 161, SHD-DM.

105. Teissedre, *Souvenirs,* 8, 73–132.

106. Fréminville, *Mémoires,* xxv.

107. Debien, "Autour de l'expédition," 86–90.

108. Lacroix to Berthier (Sept. 26, [1802]), 7Yd841/1, SHD-DAT.

109. Jean Boudet to Rochambeau (Oct. 1, 1802), 135AP/1, AN.

110. Louis Bro to Marie Bro (May 3, 1802), 82AP/1, AN; ibid. (July 13, 1802); "État des services de Mr. Bro . . ." (ca. 1814), 7Yd1173, SHD-DAT.

111. Bonamy to Leclerc (June 11, 1802), B7/5, SHD-DAT; Leclerc to Decrès (June 11, 1802), B7/26, SHD-DAT; Leclerc, "Ordre du jour" (June 19, 1802), B7/5, SHD-DAT.

112. Leclerc to Bonaparte (June 6, 1802), B7/26, SHD-DAT; Leclerc to Decrès (June 6, 1802), CC9B/19, AN.

113. *Intelligencer and Washington Advertiser* no. 271 (Aug. 4, 1802).

114. Norvins, *Souvenirs,* vol. 3, 23.

115. Leclerc to Decrès (Sept. 17, 1803), CC9B/19, AN.

116. "État nominatif des officiers, sous-officiers et soldats morts au dit hôpital" (Sept. 1802–Feb. 1803), HOP/72, CAOM.

117. Stavelot to Rochambeau (Feb. 9, 1803), Box 16/1605, UF-RP.

118. Pierre Boyer to Thouvenot (April 8, 1803), B7/10, SHD-DAT.

119. Drew Gilpin Faust, *This Republic of Suffering: Death and the American Civil War* (New York: Knopf, 2008), 9.

120. Marie Eleonor Dies? to Rochambeau (Feb. 6, 1803), Box 16/1590, UF-RP.

121. Leclerc to Decrès (July 4, 1802), B7/26, SHD-DAT; Delplanque to Hénin (July 27, 1802), B7/17, SHD-DAT; Dugua, "Ordre du jour" (Aug. 25, 1802), B7/16, SHD-DAT.

122. Lacroix to Bertrand Clauzel (Oct. 3, 1802), B7/17, SHD-DAT; Latouche to Decrès (Oct. 6, 1802), BB4 161, SHD-DM; Leclerc to Decrès (Sept. 26, 1802), Box 12/1098, UF-RP.

123. Leclerc to Decrès (July 6, 1802), B7/26, SHD-DAT; Nugent, *Journal,* 118.

124. Leclerc to Bonaparte (Sept. 16, 1802), LGC, 228; Daure to Bonaparte (ca. Nov. 7, 1802), B7/8, SHD-DAT; Pamphile de Lacroix, *La révolution de Haïti* (1819; reprint, Paris: Karthala, 1995), 372.

125. "Compte-rendu du rapport du Général Rochambeau" (April 28, 1810), CC9A/46, AN; Daure, "Compte-rendu," 3:133, 146.

126. "Hôpital la Providence au Cap" (1802–3) and "Hôpital des Pères" (1802), DPPC/HOP/72, CAOM.

127. Leclerc to Decrès (Feb. 27, 1802), CC9B/19, AN; Leclerc to Decrès (April 21, 1802), B7/26, SHD-DAT; "Rapport des officiers de santé en chef . . ." (May 11, 1802), Box 5/351a, UF-RP.

128. LGC, 158, 228.

129. Kerversau to Lacroix (Sept. 27, [1802]), CC9/B23, AN.

130. Descourtilz, *Voyage,* 219; Delplanque to Mathieu (July 22, 1802), B7/17, SHD-DAT.

131. On Makandal, see Marquis Laurent de Rouvray, "Extrait d'un mémoire sur la création d'un corps de gens de couleur" (1779), DFC/XXXIII/Mémoires/3/doc. 10, CAOM; M. de C . . . , "Makandal, histoire véritable" (Sept. 15, 1787), *Mercure de France,* 21–28; Auberteuil, *Considérations,* vol. 1, 137.

CHAPTER 10

1. Victoire Leclerc to Napoléon Bonaparte (June 6, 1802), B7/26, SHD-DAT.

2. W. L. Whitfield to George Nugent (Aug. 26, 1802), CO 137/108, BNA; Naverrez to Denis Decrès (Feb. 21, 1803), CC9A/30, AN.

3. Madison Smartt Bell, *Toussaint Louverture: A Biography* (New York: Pantheon Books, 2007), 142, 197.

4. Grandet to Chief of staff of the division (July 22, 1802), B7/5, SHD-DAT.

5. Achille to Pierre Thouvenot (May 14, 1802), B7/4, SHD-DAT.

6. "Notice sur la division [Desfourneaux?]" (ca. Aug. 1802), B7/2, SHD-DAT.

7. Charles Dugua, "Ordre du jour" (June 1, 1802), B7/16, SHD-DAT.

8. Dugua to Donatien de Rochambeau (June 14, 1802), BN08268 / lot 1, UF-RP.

9. Leclerc, [Arrêté] (July 31, 1802), Box 9/732, UF-RP.

10. Chief of staff of Clauzel division to Jacques Maurepas, Henri Christophe, Augustin Clervaux (June 9, 1802), CC9B/10, AN.

11. Dugua to Rochambeau (June 12, 1802), BN08268 / lot 39, UF-RP; Inhabitants of Grande Ravine du Limbé to Bertrand Clauzel (June 18, 1802), B7/5, SHD-DAT.

12. Municipality of Baynet to Drouin (June 10, 1802), BN08268 / lot 39, UF-RP; David Troy to Rochambeau (July 24, 1802), Box 9/698, UF-RP.

13. Mathieu to [Clauzel] (June 18, 1802), B7/5, SHD-DAT.

14. Jean Michel to Rochambeau (July 8, 1802), BN08268 / lot 39, UF-RP; Jean-Pierre Lindor to Leclerc (ca. July 1802), Box 23/2243, UF-RP; Marie-Jeanne Rénoult to Leclerc (ca. July 1802), Box 23/2248, UF-RP.

15. Delplanque to Jean Boudet (June 25, 1802), B7/17, SHD-DAT.

16. Madière, "Rapport pour servir d'instructions . . ." (June 25, 1802), Box 8/624, UF-RP.

17. Louis d'Arbois to Charles Desbureaux (Aug. 11, 1802), 135AP/1, AN.

18. Leclerc to Jean-Baptiste Salme (April 27, 1802), B7/3, SHD-DAT.

19. Guillaume Mauviel, "Mémoires sur Saint-Domingue" (May 24, 1806), 37, 1M599, SHD-DAT; Thomas Madiou, *Histoire d'Haïti,* vol. 2 (Port-au-Prince: Courtois, 1847), 259.

20. Leclerc to Bonaparte (May 7, 1802), LGC, 145.

21. Yves Bénot and Marcel Dorigny, *Rétablissement de l'esclavage dans les colonies françaises 1802: Ruptures et continuités de la politique coloniale française* (Paris: Maisonneuve-Larose, 2003), 25.

22. Louis Dubroca, *La vie de Toussaint Louverture, chef des noirs insurgés de Saint-Domingue* (Paris: Dubroca, 1802), 44; Cousin d'Avallon, *Histoire de Toussaint Louverture, chef des noirs insurgés de cette colonie* (Paris: Pillot, 1802), 26–28, 83.

23. Paul François Page, *Traité d'économie politique et de commerce des colonies,* vol. 2 (Paris: Brochot, 1802), viii.

24. Barré Saint-Venant, *Des colonies modernes sous la zone torride, et particulièrement de celle de Saint-Domingue* (Paris: Brochot, 1802), xv; Félix Carteau, *Soirées bermudiennes, ou entretiens sur les événemens qui ont opéré la ruine de la partie française de l'isle Saint-Domingue* (Bordeaux: Pellier-Lawalle, 1802), xl; Bénot and Dorigny, *Rétablissement de l'esclavage,* 29–49.

25. Laurent Dubois, *A Colony of Citizens: Revolution and Slave Emancipation in the French Caribbean, 1787–1804* (Chapel Hill: University of North Carolina Press, 2004), 370.

26. Claude Wanquet, *La France et la première abolition de l'esclavage, 1794–1802: Le cas des colonies orientales Île de France (Maurice) et la Réunion* (Paris: Karthala, 1998), 645.

27. Decrès to Alexandre Berthier (May 13, 1802), CC9/B24, AN; Jacques Cauna, ed., *Toussaint Louverture et l'indépendance d'Haïti* (Paris: Karthala, 2004), 223.

28. Decrès to Leclerc (June 14, 1802), LGC, 284.

29. Somerset de Chair, ed., *Napoleon on Napoleon: An Autobiography of the Emperor* (London: Cassell, 1992), 184.

30. Bonaparte to Decrès (May 21, 1802), CN vol. 7, 596.

31. Decrès to Leclerc (June 14, 1802), CC9/B24, AN.

32. CN vol. 7, 661, 711.

33. Bonaparte to Leclerc (July 1, 1802), CN vol. 7, 640.

34. Bonaparte to Leclerc (Nov. 27, 1802), CN vol. 8, 142.

35. Leclerc to Decrès (July 6, 1802), B7/26, SHD-DAT.

36. Leclerc to Bonaparte (Oct. 7, 1802), LGC, 253.

37. Leclerc to Decrès (July 24, 1802), B7/26, SHD-DAT.

38. Philippe Roume to Henri Grégoire (Feb. 14, 1802), Roume Papers, LC; Wanquet, *La France et la première abolition,* 646.

39. Bonaparte to Decrès (July 13, 1802), CN vol. 7, 661.

40. Dubois, *A Colony of Citizens,* 359–411.

41. Leclerc to Raymond Lacrosse (April 18, 1802), Box 4/259, UF-RP.

42. Philippe Ménard, "Armée de la Guadeloupe—Situation de l'armée" (Sept. 11, 1802), 1 Mi 6 R1, ADG.

43. Bénot and Dorigny, Rétablissement de l'esclavage, 283–96.

44. Antoine Richepance to Decrès (July 8, 1802), 1 Mi 6 R1, ADG; John Duckworth to Evan Nepean (Aug. 7, 1802), ADM 1/252, BNA; Leclerc to Decrès (Aug. 25, 1802), LGC, 216; DHHAN, 148; Ramon de Castro to Leclerc (Oct. 30, 1802), Box 15/1461, UF-RP; James Madison to Robert Livingston (Feb. 7, 1803), Microfilm M77/1, NARA-CP.

45. Leclerc to Bonaparte (Aug. 6, 1802), B7/26, SHD-DAT.

46. Leclerc to Decrès (Sept. 27, 1802), CC9B/19, AN.

47. [British naval officer], "Observations made and information gained at Cap Français" (July 1802), ADM 1/252, BNA.

48. Alfred de Laujon, Souvenirs de trente années de voyages à Saint-Domingue, dans plusieurs colonies étrangères, et au continent d'Amérique, vol. 2 (Paris: Schwartz and Gagnot, 1835), 246.

49. Leclerc to Bonaparte (Aug. 6, 1802), B7/26, SHD-DAT.

50. Leclerc to Decrès (Aug. 6, 1802), B7/26, SHD-DAT.

51. Leclerc to Bonaparte (Sept. 16, 1802), LGC, 228.

52. Leclerc to Decrès (Aug. 9, 1802), CC9B/19, AN.

53. On Maroons, see Jean Fouchard, The Haitian Maroons: Liberty or Death (1972; reprint, New York: Edward Blyden Press, 1981); Carolyn Fick, The Making of Haiti: The Saint-Domingue Revolution from Below (Knoxville: University of Tennessee Press, 1990); David Geggus, "Le soulèvement d'août 1791 et ses liens avec le Vodou et le marronnage," in La révolution française et Haïti: Filiations, ruptures, nouvelles dimensions, vol. 1, ed. Michel Hector (Port-au-Prince: Henri Deschamps, 1991), 60–70.

54. Gamien, "Mémoire" (ca. 1780s), CC9C/1, AN.

55. Toussaint Louverture, "Règlement sur la culture" (Oct. 25, 1800), CC9B/9, AN.

56. C. L. R. James, The Black Jacobins: Toussaint L'Ouverture and the San Domingo Revolution (1963; reprint, New York: Vintage Books, 1989), 149, 337.

57. Hector, La révolution française et Haïti, 176.

58. John Thornton, Africa and Africans in the Making of the Atlantic World, 1400–1680 (New York: Cambridge University Press, 1992), 183–205.

59. Michel-Étienne Descourtilz, Voyage d'un naturaliste en Haïti (1809; reprint, Paris: Plon, 1935), 120.

60. Descourtilz, Voyage, 222; Charles Malenfant, Des colonies, et particulièrement de celle de Saint-Domingue (Paris: Audibert: 1814), 67.

61. On vodou, see Descourtilz, Voyage, 115; Madiou, Histoire, vol. 2, 28, 91, 322; Geggus, "Le soulèvement d'août 1791"; Joan Dayan, "Querying the Spirit: The Rules of the Haitian Lwa," in Colonial Saints: Discovering the Holy in the Americas, 1500–1800, ed. Allan Greer and Jodi Bilinkoff (New York: Routledge, 2003), 31–50.

62. Louis Boisrond-Tonnerre, "Mémoire pour servir à l'histoire d'Hayti" (June 22, 1804), 46, CC9B/27, AN.

63. Pamphile Lacroix to Clauzel (Oct. 11, 1802), B7/17, SHD-DAT.

64. Thouvenot to Julienne (Aug. 30, 1802), B7/20, SHD-DAT.

65. Hypolite Grandsaigne to Jean-Baptiste Brunet (Sept. 12, 1802), B7/7, SHD-DAT.

66. Joan Dayan, *Haiti, History, and the Gods* (1995; reprint, Berkeley: University of California Press, 1998), xvii.

67. Gérard Barthélémy, *Créoles, bossales: Conflit en Haïti* (Petit Bourg: Ibis Rouge, 2000), 183.

68. Louis Lamartinière to Jean Lavalette (Aug. 24, 1802), BN08268 / lot 1, UF-RP.

69. Jean-Jacques Dessalines to Brunet (Aug. 11, 1802), B7/6, SHD-DAT.

70. Thouvenot to Naverrez (Sept. 13, 1802), B7/20, SHD-DAT.

71. Puquet to Rochambeau (Aug. 16, 1802), Box 10/824, UF-RP; Grandsaigne to Brunet (Sept. 12, 1802), B7/7, SHD-DAT; Thornton, *Africa and Africans,* 296.

72. P. Panisse to Rochambeau (July 28, 1802), Box 9/719, UF-RP, Madiou, *Histoire,* vol. 2, 300, 319.

73. Magloire Ambroise to Lamour Dérance (Feb. 18, 1802), in Barthélémy, *Créoles, bossales,* 217.

74. Leclerc to Decrès (Aug. 25, 1802), B7/26, SHD-DAT.

75. Claude Auguste and Marcel Auguste, *L'expédition Leclerc, 1801–1803* (Port-au-Prince: Henri Deschamps, 1985), 188–91, 201–3, 236.

76. Louis-Thomas Villaret de Joyeuse to Decrès (March 4, 1802) in "Extrait de la correspondance concernant Toussaint Louverture" (ca. June 1802), CC9/B23, AN.

77. Dessalines to Cila [Sylla] (May 22, 1802), 135AP/6, AN.

78. Chief of staff of Clauzel division to Philibert Fressinet (June 25, 1802), CC9B/10, AN.

79. Pamphile de Lacroix, *La révolution de Haïti* (1819; reprint, Paris: Karthala, 1995), 366.

80. Whitfield to Nugent (July 26, 1802), CO 137/108, BNA; Lacroix, *La révolution de Haïti,* 323, 360.

81. Auguste, *L'expédition Leclerc,* 236.

82. "Contrôle nominatif des officiers du 1er bataillon de la 9ème demi-brigade coloniale" (June 20, 1802), B7/5, SHD-DAT; Makajoux to Thouvenot (July 29, 1802), B7/6, SHD-DAT.

83. [French officer], "Rapport de l'attaque et de la prise des retranchements du Mapou" (May 23, 1802), B7/4, SHD-DAT; Grandet to Thouvenot (June 20, 1802), B7/5, SHD-DAT; Dessalines to Brunet (Aug. 26, 1802), B7/6, SHD-DAT.

84. Grandet, "Journal des événements militaires . . ." (July 27, 1802), B7/5, SHD-DAT.

85. Jean-François Debelle to Leclerc (June 11, 1802), CC9A/29, AN.

86. Chief of staff of Clauzel division to Fressinet (June 11, 1802), CC9B/10, AN; "Réglement portant classification des délits et des peines" (July 29, 1802), CC9/B22, AN.

87. Desbureaux to Rochambeau (Aug. 27, 1802), Box 10/887, UF-RP; Grandet to Thouvenot (Aug. 16, 1802), B7/6, SHD-DAT.

88. Pierre Boyer to Brunet (July 24, 1802), B7/5, SHD-DAT.

89. Panisse to Rochambeau (Aug. 12, 1802), Box 9/798, UF-RP.

90. Thouvenot to Roy (Sept. 7, 1802), B7/20, SHD-DAT.

91. Boyer to Lachaise (Aug. 28, 1802), B7/6, SHD-DAT.

92. Leclerc, "Ordre du jour" (June 8, 1802), CC9A 31, AN; [Raymond Labatut], [Mémoire] (April 25, 1803), BN08272 / lot 122, UF-RP.

93. Leclerc to Decrès (Aug. 2, 1802), B7/26, SHD-DAT; Duckworth to Nepean (Aug. 29, 1802), ADM 1/252, BNA.

94. Boyer to Brunet (Aug. 11, 1802), B7/6, SHD-DAT; Madiou, *Histoire,* vol. 2, 290.

95. Boyer to Rochambeau (Aug. 12, 1802), Box 9/790, UF-RP; Thouvenot to Boyer (Aug. 26, 1802), B7/20, SHD-DAT.

96. Boyer, "Rapport des événements depuis le mois de Messidor an 10" (ca. Nov. 7, 1802), B7/8, SHD-DAT; Boyer to Brunet (Aug. 23, 1802), B7/6, SHD-DAT.

97. Alix to Leclerc (Oct. 18, 1802), Box 12/1195, UF-RP.

98. Brunet to Leclerc (July 22, 1802), 135AP/6, AN; Leclerc to Decrès (July 23, 1802), CC9B/19, AN; Lachaise to Thouvenot (July 23, 1802), B7/5, SHD-DAT.

99. Grandet to Thouvenot (June 20, 1802), B7/5, SHD-DAT; Chataigner to Clauzel (July 10, 1802), B7/5, SHD-DAT; Aussenac to Brunet (July 28, 1802), B7/5, SHD-DAT.

100. Panisse to Rochambeau (Aug. 26, 1802), Box 10/885, UF-RP.

101. Leclerc to Decrès (June 6, 1802; July 6, 1802; Aug. 25, 1802; Sept. 26, 1802), CC9B/19, AN.

102. Dugua, "Ordre du jour" (Sept. 10, 1802), B7/16, SHD-DAT.

103. Jean-Pierre Louverture to Leclerc (Sept. 14, 1802), B7/7, SHD-DAT; Thouvenot to Paul Louverture (Sept. 29, 1802), B7/20, SHD-DAT.

104. Leclerc to Bonaparte (Aug. 6, 1802), B7/26, SHD-DAT.

105. Chief of staff of Clauzel division to Duplanquis (July 5, 1802), CC9B/10, AN; Makajoux to Thouvenot (July 29, 1802), B7/6, SHD-DAT; Thouvenot to Dessalines (Aug. 11, 1802), B7/19, SHD-DAT.

106. Leclerc to Decrès (Aug. 25, 1802), B7/26, SHD-DAT.

107. Dessalines to Brunet (Aug. 11, 1802), B7/6, SHD-DAT.

108. Thouvenot to Clauzel (Aug. 13, 1802), B7/19, SHD-DAT.

109. Thouvenot to Dessalines (Aug. 11, 1802), B7/6, SHD-DAT.

110. Lachaise to Thouvenot (Aug. 12, 1802), B7/6, SHD-DAT.

111. [French officer], [Counter-intelligence report] (July 24, 1802), BN08270 / lot 116, UF-RP.

112. Dessalines to Brunet (Aug. 10, 1802), 135AP/6, AN.

113. Brunet to Dessalines (Aug. 16, 1802), 135AP/6, AN.

114. Pierre Quantin to Rochambeau (Sept. 9, 1802), Box 11/996, UF-RP.

115. Thouvenot to Clauzel (Aug. 23, 1802), B7/19, SHD-DAT; Brunet to Leclerc (Aug. 24, 1802), B7/20, SHD-DAT.

116. Leclerc to Bonaparte (Sept. 16, 1802), LGC, 228.

117. Descourtilz, *Voyage,* 221; Madiou, *Histoire,* vol. 2, 325, 358; Gérard Laurent, *Six études sur J. J. Dessalines* (Port-au-Prince: Les Presses Libres, 1950), 54–57.

CHAPTER 11

1. "Japanese" from Christophe Paulin de la Poix, *Mémoires du Chevalier de Fréminville* (Paris: Champion, 1913), 18. On Jablonowski's background, see 8Yd915, SHD-DAT; Jan Pachonski and Reuel Wilson, *Poland's Caribbean Tragedy: A Study of Polish Legions in the Haitian War of Independence, 1802–1803* (Boulder, CO: East European Monographs, 1986), 61.

2. Wladyslaw Jablonowski et al., [Copies of letters] (Dec. 23, 1801), 8Yd915, SHD-DAT.

3. Pierre Quantin to Donatien de Rochambeau (Aug. 1802), Box 10/901, UF-RP.

4. On the Belair uprising, see Faustin Répussard to Rochambeau (Aug. 21, 1802), BN08270 / lot 110, UF-RP; Jean-Jacques Dessalines to Victoire Leclerc (Sept. 1, 1802), Reel 4, Sc. Micro R-2228, NYPL-SC; François Pageot to Rochambeau (Sept. 9, 1802), Box 11/994, UF-RP; Répussard to Rochambeau (Sept. 10, 1802), BN08270 / lot 110, UF-RP.

5. Jean-Baptiste Brunet to Charles Belair (Aug. 26, 1802), B7/20, SHD-DAT.

6. Pierre Thouvenot to Charles Dugua (Aug. 25, 1802), B7/20, SHD-DAT.

7. Dessalines to Brunet (Aug. 26, 1802), B7/6, SHD-DAT.

8. Gérard Laurent, *Six études sur J. J. Dessalines* (Port-au-Prince: Les Presses Libres, 1950), 34–41; Jean Fouchard, *The Haitian Maroons: Liberty or Death* (1972; reprint, New York: Edward Blyden Press, 1981), 358.

9. Belair to Toussaint Louverture (April 26, 1802), Reel 5, Sc. Micro R-2228, NYPL-SC; Dessalines to Louverture (May 5, 1802), Folder 23C, HU-KFC.

10. Leclerc to Napoléon Bonaparte (Sept. 26, 1802), B7/26, SHD-DAT.

11. Dessalines to Leclerc (Sept. 10, 1802), Box 11/1000, UF-RP; *Moniteur Universel* 139 (Feb. 8, 1803): 4; Thomas Madiou, *Histoire d'Haïti,* vol. 2 (Port-au-Prince: Courtois, 1847), 329.

12. Mme Perrot to Rochambeau (Sept. 29, 1802), Box 12/1121, UF-RP.

13. Bonaparte to Denis Decrès (March 29, 1802), CN vol. 7, 540.

14. On the 3rd Polish demi-brigade, see Michaux to Decrès (April 28, 1802), BB4 162, SHD-DM; Michaux, "3ème Brigade polonaise—État nominatif" (May 18, 1802), B7/4, SHD-DAT; Council of the 86th demi-brigade to French Commissioner in Cartagena (July 8, 1802), B7/5, SHD-DAT; Pachonski and Wilson, *Poland,* 73–80.

15. Pachonski and Wilson, *Poland,* 82.

16. Piotroski to Alexandre Berthier (Oct. 24, 1803), B7/10, SHD-DAT.

17. Leclerc to Decrès (Sept. 13, 1802), CC9B/19, AN.

18. Boissy to [Unspecified] (Sept. 22, 1802), B7/7, SHD-DAT.

19. Naverrez to Brunet (Sept. 23, 1802), B7/7, SHD-DAT.

20. Thouvenot to Naverrez (Sept. 24, 1802), B7/20, SHD-DAT.

21. Thouvenot to Dugua (Sept. 24, 1802), B7/20, SHD-DAT; Sangoroski, "Rapport" (Sept. 26, 1802), B7/7, SHD-DAT.

22. Leclerc to Bonaparte (Sept. 16, 1802), LGC, 228.

23. Pachonski and Wilson, *Poland,* 90, 203.

24. Leclerc to Decrès (Sept. 13, 1802), CC9B/19, AN; Leclerc to Bonaparte (Sept. 16, 1802), LGC, 228.

25. Thouvenot to Roy (Sept. 1, 1802), B7/20, SHD-DAT.

26. Aussenac to Rochambeau (Aug. 11, 1802), Box 9/781, UF-RP.

27. Leclerc, "Arrêté" (April 10, 1802), CC9/B22, AN.

28. Répussard to Rochambeau (Sept. 10, 1802), BN08270 / lot 110, UF-RP.

29. Leclerc, "Arrêté" (Sept. 18, 1802), Box 11/1060, UF-RP.

30. Hector Daure to Decrès (Nov. 3, 1802), CC9/B20, AN.

31. Répussard to Rochambeau (Sept. 27, 1802), Box 12/1111, UF-RP; Quantin to Rochambeau (Oct. 24, 1802), Box 13/1241, UF-RP.

32. Pamphile Lacroix to his officers (Sept. 28, 1802), B7/17, SHD-DAT; Lacroix to Bertrand Clauzel (Oct. 3, 1802), B7/17, SHD-DAT.

33. Grandet to Thouvenot (Sept. 3, 1802), B7/7, SHD-DAT; Makajoux to Thouvenot (Sept. 6, 1802), B7/7, SHD-DAT.

34. Thouvenot to Naverrez (Sept. 13, 1802), B7/20, SHD-DAT.

35. Pageot to Rochambeau (Sept. 12, 1802), Box 11/1014, UF-RP; Hypolite Grandsaigne to Brunet (Sept. 12, 1802), B7/7, SHD-DAT; Maillard to Michel Claparède (Oct. 3, 1802), CC9B/10, AN.

36. Jacques de Norvins, *Souvenirs d'un historien de Napoléon: Mémorial de J. de Norvins,* vol. 3 (Paris: Plon, 1896), 34.

37. Chief of staff of Boudet Division to Bardet (Feb. 12, 1802), B7/15, SHD-DAT; *Gazette Officielle de Saint-Domingue,* no. 1 (June 26, 1802), CC9A/30, AN.

38. Thouvenot to Jolicoeur (Sept. 2, 1802), B7/20, SHD-DAT.

39. Charles Desbureaux, "Ordre du jour" (Sept. 9, 1802), Box 11/1043, UF-RP.

40. [Charles d'Hénin] to Jean Boudet (Sept. 11, 1802), B7/17, SHD-DAT; P. Panisse to Rochambeau (Sept. 27, 1802), Box 12/1110, UF-RP.

41. Leclerc to Decrès (Sept. 17, 1802), B7/26, SHD-DAT.

42. For the first recorded instance of mass drowning (eighty prisoners in Cap), see John Duckworth to Evan Nepean (Aug. 29, 1802), ADM 1/252, BNA.

43. George Nugent to John Sullivan (Nov. 12, 1802), CO 137/109, BNA.

44. Bonaparte to Leclerc (July 1, 1802), CN vol. 7, 640; Yves Bénot, *La démence coloniale sous Napoléon* (Paris: La Découverte, 1992), 88.

45. Montchoisy to Berthier (Aug. 9, 1802), B7/6, SHD-DAT.

46. Doris Kadish, "The Black Terror: Women's Responses to Slave Revolts in Haiti," *French Review* 68, no. 4 (1995): 671.

47. Decrès to Rochambeau (March 12, 1803), CC9/B22, AN.

48. Barré Saint-Venant, *Des colonies modernes sous la zone torride, et particulièrement de celle de Saint-Domingue* (Paris: Brochot, 1802), 165.

49. Paul Alliot-Vauneuf to Daniel Lescallier (May 23, 1800), CC9A/27, AN.

50. Paul François Page to Thouvenot (March 26, 1803), B7/9, SHD-DAT; Rochambeau to Decrès (May 15, 1803), CC9B/19, AN.

51. Lacroix to Inhabitants of Fort Dauphin (Sept. 30, 1802), B7/17, SHD-DAT.

52. J. M. Voisin to Thouvenot (Nov. 23, 1802), B7/8, SHD-DAT; Madiou, *Histoire,* vol. 2, 335.

53. CC9B/10, AN.

54. Pachonski and Wilson, *Poland,* 104–8.

55. Jean-Baptiste Lemonnier-Delafosse, *Seconde campagne de Saint-Domingue du 1 décembre 1803 au 15 juillet 1809* (Le Havre: Brindeau, 1846), 64; Madiou, *Histoire d'Haïti,* vol. 2 (1847; reprint, Port-au-Prince: Fardin, 1981), 393.

56. Madiou, *Histoire,* vol. 2 (1847), 353; Guy-Joseph Bonnet, *Souvenirs historiques* (Paris: Durand, 1864), 105.

57. [Hénin] to Achillaud (Sept. 5, 1802), B7/17, SHD-DAT.

58. Francis Wimpffen, *A Voyage to Saint Domingo in the Years 1788, 1789, and 1790* (London: T. Cadell, 1797), 134.

59. Devaux to Pierre Forfait (Dec. 2, 1799), CC9A/23, AN.

60. Nicolas Louis to Jacques Maurepas (Oct. 10, 1802), B7/8, SHD-DAT.

61. Leclerc to Bonaparte (Oct. 7, 1802), LGC, 253–60.

62. [Charles de Vincent], "Quelques observations fugitives sur les opérations de l'armée" (ca. 1804), Box 2:1, MG 140, NYPL-SC.

63. Panisse to Rochambeau (Sept. 27, 1802), Box 12/1110, UF-RP; Roy to Thouvenot (Oct. 6, 1802), B7/8, SHD-DAT; Lacroix to Clauzel (Sept. 29, 1802), B7/17, SHD-DAT.

64. Leclerc, "Proclamation" (Oct. 6, 1802), CC9A/30, AN.

65. Madiou, *Histoire,* vol. 2 (1847), 341, 350.

66. Daure to Bonaparte (ca. Nov. 7, 1802), B7/8, SHD-DAT; Alfred de Laujon, *Précis historique de la dernière expédition de Saint-Domingue* (Paris: Delafolie, ca. 1805), 122; Madiou, *Histoire,* vol. 2 (1847), 341–47.

67. Decrès to Leclerc (July 28, 1802), CC9/B22, AN.

68. Leclerc to Bonaparte (Sept. 26, 1802), B7/26, SHD-DAT.

69. Madiou, *Histoire,* vol. 2 (1847), 335.

70. Baron de Vastey, *Political Remarks on Some French Works and Newspapers* (London, 1818), 177.

71. Beaubrun Ardouin, *Études sur l'histoire d'Haïti, suivies de la vie du général J-M Borgella,* vol. 5 (Paris: Dézobry et Magdeleine, 1853–60), 295, 298, 344.

72. Baron to Brunet (Oct. 19, 1802), B7/8, SHD-DAT; Rochambeau to Decrès (Dec. 7, 1802), CC9B/19, AN.

73. Daure to Bonaparte (ca. Nov. 7, 1802), B7/8, SHD-DAT; Maillard, "Journal des opérations militaires" (ca. Nov. 9, 1802), Box 12/1173, UF-RP.

74. [French officer], "Mémoire succint sur la guerre de Saint-Domingue" (1804), 42, 1M598, SHD-DAT.

75. Norvins, *Souvenirs,* vol. 3, 36–38.

76. H. Pauléus Sannon, *Histoire de Toussaint Louverture,* vol. 3 (Port-au-Prince: Héraux, 1933), 151.

77. [Anon.], "Memorandum of intelligence obtained from St. Domingo" (ca. Nov. 1802), ADM 1/252, BNA.

78. Lemonnier, *Seconde campagne,* 7.

79. Bonnet, *Souvenirs historiques,* 111; Ardouin, *Études,* vol. 5, 301.

80. Alphonse de Lamartine, *Toussaint Louverture* (Paris: Lévy, 1850), xxiv–xxviii.

81. Pierre Boyer, "Rapport des événements depuis le mois de Messidor an 10" (ca. Nov. 7, 1802), B7/8, SHD-DAT.

82. Lacroix to Leclerc (Oct. 14, 1802), B7/17, SHD-DAT; Lemonnier, *Seconde campagne,* 49; André Nicolas Joseph Guimot and Louis Mathieu Dembowski, *Journal et voyage à Saint-Domingue* (Paris: Tesseidre, 1997), 68.

83. Fillette to Chief of Northern Division of the Right (Oct. 20, 1802), B7/8, SHD-DAT; Brunet to Leclerc (Oct. 21, 1802), Box 13/1214, UF-RP.

84. Clauzel to Thouvenot (Sept. 8, 1802), B7/7, SHD-DAT; Lamartine, *Toussaint Louverture,* xxiv.

85. Maurepas to Thouvenot (Oct. 23, 1802), B7/8, SHD-DAT; Louis Boisrond-Tonnerre, "Mémoire pour servir à l'histoire d'Hayti" (June 22, 1804), 32, CC9B/27, AN.

86. Henri Christophe, "Manifeste du roi" (Sept. 18, 1814), 11, Publications on the independence of Haiti, RG 59 / MLR A1632, NARA-CP.

87. Leclerc to Bonaparte (Sept. 26, 1802), B7/26, SHD-DAT.

88. Brunet to Leclerc (Sept. 30, 1802), Box 12/1125, UF-RP; Thouvenot to Dugua (Sept. 27, 1802), B7/20, SHD-DAT.

89. Madiou, *Histoire,* vol. 2 (1847), 334.

90. Leclerc to Clauzel (Oct. 2, 1802), Box 12/1137, UF-RP.

91. Dessalines to Brunet (Oct. 9, 1802), B7/8, SHD-DAT.

92. Dessalines to Brunet (Oct. 1802), B7/8, SHD-DAT.

93. CN vol. 8, 29, 30.

94. Brunet to Leclerc (Oct. 21, 1802), Box 13/1214, UF-RP; Boisrond, "Mémoire," 33; Madiou, *Histoire,* vol. 2 (1981), 341.

95. Philibert Fressinet to Rochambeau (Oct. 27, 1802), Box 13/1270, UF-RP; Boisrond, "Mémoire," 35.

96. Dessalines to Quantin (Oct. 24, 1802), Box 13/1238, UF-RP.

97. Louis-René de Latouche-Tréville to Philibert Willaumez (Oct. 16, 1802), BB4 163, SHD-DM.

98. Panisse to Rochambeau (Oct. 26, 1802), Box 13/1248, UF-RP; Grant Forbes to Tyrrell (Oct. 31, 1802), CO 137/109, BNA.

99. Desbureaux to Rochambeau (Sept. 8, 1802), Box 11/983, UF-RP; Joseph Bernard to Rochambeau (Oct. 4, 1802), Box 12/1147, UF-RP; Ministry of Navy, "Rapport au gouvernement" (Aug. 19, 1803), CC9/B22, AN.

100. Jacques Boyé to François de Kerversau (Oct. 24, 1802), no. 621, CC9B/11, AN.

101. Kerversau to Leclerc (Oct. 11, 1802), 61 J 24, ADGir.

102. Kerversau to Lacroix (Nov. 4, 1802), B7/8, SHD-DAT.

103. Kerversau to Lacroix (Nov. 16, 1802), B7/8, SHD-DAT.

104. Leclerc to Decrès (July 6, 1802), B7/26, SHD-DAT.

105. Leclerc to Marques de Someruelos (Oct. 11, 1802), Box 13/1220, UF-RP; Antoine Moralès to Lotter (Oct. 12, 1802), BN08269 / lot 103, UF-RP; Nugent to Leclerc (Oct. 17, 1802), CO 137/109, BNA.

106. Leclerc to Decrès (Sept. 26, 1802), B7/26, SHD-DAT.

107. Leclerc to Decrès (Sept. 17, 1802), CC9B/19, AN.

108. Leclerc to Bonaparte (Sept. 26, 1802), Box 12/1095, UF-RP.

109. Leclerc to Berthier (Oct. 7, 1802), Box 12/1159, UF-RP.

110. Leclerc to Bonaparte (Oct. 7, 1802), LGC, 260.

111. Leclerc to Bonaparte (Oct. 7, 1802), LGC, 253.

112. Girod-Chantrans, *Voyage d'un Suisse dans différentes colonies d'Amérique* (Neufchâtel: Société typographique, 1785), 136, 323.

113. Norvins, *Souvenirs,* vol. 3, 45.

114. Robert Vincent Remini, *The Battle of New Orleans: Andrew Jackson and America's First Military Victory* (1999; reprint, New York: Penguin, 2001), 120, 162, 184.

115. Corbet and [French planter], "Submission and afterward revolt of the blacks" (Jan. 28, 1803), CO 137/110, BNA.

116. Jeremy Popkin, *Facing Racial Revolution: Eyewitness Accounts of the Haitian Insurrection* (Chicago: University of Chicago Press, 2008), 319.

117. Norvins, *Souvenirs,* vol. 3, 42.

118. Daure to Louis-Thomas Villaret de Joyeuse (Nov. 11, 1802), B7/8, SHD-DAT.

119. E. Peyre, "Journal sur la maladie du général en chef" (Nov. 2, 1802), CC9B/20, AN.

120. Mary Hassal [Leonora Sansay], *Secret History; or, The Horrors of St. Domingo, in a Series of Letters, Written by a Lady at Cape François* (Philadelphia: Bradford and Inskeep, 1808), 17.

121. [British officer in Cap], "A few anecdotes not unworthy of noting" (ca. Nov. 1802), ADM 1/252, BNA.

122. Boyer, "Ordre du jour" (Oct. 25, 1802), CC9/B22, AN.

123. *Gazette Officielle de Saint-Domingue,* no. 38 (Nov. 3, 1802), CC9A/30, AN.

124. Daure, "Compte-rendu de l'administration générale" (late 1803), 200, CC9B/13, AN.

125. "État nominatif des militaires de toutes armes et autres, qui ont repassé en France. . . ." (Sept.18–Dec. 3, 1802), B7/9, SHD-DAT.

126. Daure to Boyé (Nov. 5, 1802), B7/8, SHD-DAT.

127. Latouche, "Instructions remises au capitaine du vaisseau le *Swiftsure*" (ca. Nov. 1802), CC9/B20, AN; Hubert to Honoré Ganteaume (Dec. 3, 1802), CC9/B21, AN; Fréminville, *Mémoires,* 84.

128. Decrès to Berthier (Jan. 7, 1803), B7/9, SHD-DAT, Bruguière to Berthier (Feb. 16, 1803), B7/9, SHD-DAT.

129. Boisrond, "Mémoire," 39; Madiou, *Histoire,* vol. 2 (1847), 259; Ardouin, *Études,* vol. 5, 310, 321; Somerset de Chair, ed., *Napoleon on Napoleon: An Autobiography of the Emperor* (London: Cassell, 1992), 182.

130. "Procès verbal d'énumération et estimation des divers effets provenant de la succession du général en chef Leclerc" (Nov. 10, 1802), CC9/B23, AN; Daure to Naudot (Nov. 8, 1802), B7/12, SHD-DAT; Gramont Chégaray to Leclerc (Nov. 24, [1800]), Box 2/61, UF-RP.

131. Steff to Napoléon III (April 23, 1862), 7Yd328, SHD-DAT.

132. "Contrat de mariage d'entre le Prince Borghese et Madame la Princesse Paulette Bonaparte" (Aug. 23, 1803), 400AP/79, AN.

CHAPTER 12

1. Hector Daure to Denis Decrès (ca. Nov. 3, 1802), B7/8, SHD-DAT.

2. Samuel Baynard, *History of the Supreme Council of the 33rd Degree . . . ,* vol. 1 (Boston: Supreme Council Ancient Scottish Rite, 1938), 92.

3. Deneuville to Donatien de Rochambeau (Aug. 14, 1802), Box 9/805, UF-RP.

4. Alexandre Berthier to Jean-Baptiste Bernadotte (Sept. 10, 1801), B7/1, SHD-DAT.

5. Rochambeau to Decrès (Dec. 11, 1802), CC9B/19, AN.

6. Pierre Thouvenot to Rochambeau (Jan. 4, 1803), Box 15/1490, UF-RP; Pascal Sabès to Rochambeau (Dec. 15, 1802), Box 15/1443, UF-RP.

7. John W. Lionard to Tobias Lear (April 8, 1802), 208 MI/2, AN; Wade Stubbs to L. Baury (June 4, 1803), Box 19/1917, UF-RP.

8. Rochambeau to Decrès (Jan. 1, 1803), in Bureau des Colonies, "Extrait de différentes lettres écrites," CC9A/34, AN.

9. Rochambeau and Daure, [Certificate of manumission] (Dec. 22, 1802), Box 1Ad./31, UF-RP.

10. Gorman to W. L. Whitfield (Jan. 5, 1803), CO 137/110, BNA.

11. Victoire Leclerc to Decrès (Aug. 6, 1802), B7/26, SHD-DAT; Guy-Joseph Bonnet, *Souvenirs historiques* (Paris: Durand, 1864), 115.

12. Daure to Decrès (Nov. 3, 1802), CC9/B20, AN.

13. *Moniteur Universel* 139 (Feb. 8, 1803): 3.

14. Daure to Decrès (Nov. 1, 1802), CC9/B20, AN; Daure, "Compte-rendu de l'administration générale" (late 1803), 15, 208, CC9B/27, AN.

15. "Extrait des lettres de Saint-Domingue du 10 au 18 Brumaire an XI" (ca. Nov. 9, 1802), CC9/B22, AN.

16. *Gazette of the United States,* no. 138 (Dec. 3, 1802).

17. Daure to Decrès (Nov. 3, 1802), CC9/B20, AN.

18. Gabriel Debien, "Autour de l'expédition de Saint-Domingue: Les espoirs d'une famille d'anciens planteurs, 1801–1804," *Notes d'histoire coloniale* 111 (1942): 61.

19. Daure, "Instructions pour le citoyen Abbé" (Nov. 9, 1802), 7Yd328, SHD-DAT; Daure to Jean-Baptiste Lacrosse (Nov. 11, 1802), B7/8, SHD-DAT; Daure to Louis-Thomas Villaret de Joyeuse (Nov. 11, 1802), B7/8, SHD-DAT; Pedro Claver to Rochambeau (Jan. 24, 1803), Box 16/1488, UF-RP.

20. Rochambeau to Decrès (Dec. 7, 1802), CC9B/19, AN.

21. Bellenger to Thouvenot (Nov. 2, 1802), B7/8, SHD-DAT; Louis Ferrand to Pierre Quantin (Feb. 26, 1803), B7/9, SHD-DAT; François Pageot to Rochambeau (May 12, 1803), Box 18/1859, UF-RP.

22. Quantin to Rochambeau (Nov. 1, 1802), Box 13/1283, UF-RP.

23. Jacques Boyé to Cdt. of the National Guard (Nov. 25, 1802), no. 759, CC9B/11, AN; Thouvenot to Berthier (March 9, 1803), B7/20, SHD-DAT.

24. Daure to Decrès (Nov. 3, 1802), CC9/B20, AN.

25. Rochambeau to Decrès (Dec. 14, 1802), CC9B/19, AN.

26. Berger to Rochambeau (Nov. 20, 1802), Box 14/1344, UF-RP.

27. Decrès to Leclerc (Nov. 3, 1802), CC9/B22, AN; Napoléon Bonaparte to Decrès (Nov. 23, 1802), CN vol. 8, 136; Decrès to Leclerc (Dec. 5, 1802), CC9/B22, AN.

28. Decrès to Rochambeau (Feb. 8, 1803), CC9/B22, AN.

29. "Armée de Saint-Domingue à l'époque du 1 Frimaire 11" (ca. Jan. 1803), B7/27, SHD-DAT.

30. Decrès to Leclerc (Dec. 5, 1802), CC9/B22, AN.

31. Rochambeau to Decrès (March 30, 1803), CC9A/34, AN.

32. Bonaparte to Decrès (Nov. 23, 1802), CN vol. 8, 136; Frédéric Berjaud, "Les Suisses au service de la France (1798–1805)," *Revue Napoléon* 9 (Feb. 2002): 76–83.

33. Pageot to Rochambeau (May 12, 1803), Box 18/1859, UF-RP.

34. Berthier to Decrès (Dec. 17, 1802), BB4 162, SHD-DM.

35. Jan Pachonski and Reuel Wilson, *Poland's Caribbean Tragedy: A Study of Polish Legions in the Haitian War of Independence, 1802–1803* (Boulder, CO: East European Monographs, 1986), 140. For the regimental rosters, see Xi82, SHD-DAT.

36. André Guimot and Louis Dembowski, *Journal et voyage à Saint-Domingue* (Paris: Tesseidre, 1997), 50.

37. Guimot and Dembowski, *Journal,* 66.

38. Ibid.

39. Alfred de Laujon, *Précis historique de la dernière expédition de Saint-Domingue* (Paris: Delafolie, ca. 1805), 180.

40. Maillard, "Journal des opérations militaires . . ." (Nov. 9, 1802), Box 12/1173, UF-RP; Brapatel to [Unspecified] (Nov. 11, 1802), B7/8, SHD-DAT.

41. Boyé to Berthier (Dec. 6, 1802), no. 897, CC9B/11, AN.

42. P. Panisse to Rochambeau (Nov. 22, 1802), Box 14/1359, UF-RP.

43. Philibert Fressinet to Rochambeau (Nov. 2, 1802), Box 13/1286, UF-RP. On Saint-Marc, see ibid., Box 13/1235, 1255, 1270, 1283.

44. Rochambeau, "Ordre du jour" (Dec. 29, 1802), CC9/B23, AN.

45. Jean-Baptiste Brunet to Rochambeau (Feb. 17, 1803), Box 16/1625a, UF-RP.

46. Grant Forbes to Tyrrell (Jan. 1, 1803), CO 137/110, BNA.

47. Boyé to Decrès and Berthier (Dec. 6, 1802), no. 891, CC9B/11, AN; Rochambeau, "Ordre du jour" (Jan. 18, 1803), B7/10, SHD-DAT; Thouvenot, "Ordre du jour" (April 23, 1803), CC9/B23, AN.

48. Pierre Quérangal to Louis-René de Latouche-Tréville (Jan. 9, 1803), BB4 182, SHD-DM.

49. Quérangal to Latouche (Jan. 7, 1803), BB4 182, SHD-DM; Rochambeau to Decrès (March 29, 1803), CC9A/33, AN.

50. Christophe Paulin de la Poix, *Mémoires du Chevalier de Fréminville* (Paris: Champion, 1913), 76.

51. Latouche to Rochambeau (Nov. 27, 1802), BN08269 / lot 103, UF-RP.

52. Council of notables of Môle to Thouvenot (Nov. 5, 1802), B7/8, SHD-DAT; Boyé to François Watrin (Nov. 18, 1802), no. 692, CC9B/11, AN; Marie Bunel to Rochambeau (Nov. 23, 1802), Box 14/1363, UF-RP.

53. Rochambeau to Decrès (Dec. 7, 1802), CC9B/19, AN.

54. Rochambeau to Decrès (Feb. 21, 1803), CC9B/19, AN.

55. Sabès to Rochambeau (Dec. 15, 1802), Box 15/1443, UF-RP.

56. Rochambeau to Decrès (Feb. 21, 1803), CC9B/19, AN.

57. Laurent Dubois, *Avengers of the New World: The Story of the Haitian Revolution* (Cambridge, MA: Harvard University Press, 2004), 146, 293.

58. Jean-Baptiste Lemonnier-Delafosse, *Seconde campagne de Saint-Domingue du 1 décembre 1803 au 15 juillet 1809* (Le Havre: Brindeau et compagnie, 1846), 69.

59. Louis Boisrond-Tonnerre, "Mémoire pour servir à l'histoire d'Hayti" (June 22, 1804), 42, CC9B/27, AN.

60. Thomas Madiou, *Histoire d'Haïti,* vol. 2 (1847; reprint, Port-au-Prince: Fardin, 1981), 390–93.

61. Charles Malenfant, *Des colonies, et particulièrement de celle de Saint-Domingue* (Paris: Audibert: 1814), 78.

62. Lemonnier, *Seconde campagne,* 70; Mary Hassal [Leonora Sansay], *Secret History; or, The Horrors of St. Domingo, in a Series of Letters, Written by a Lady at Cape François* (Philadelphia: Bradford and Inskeep, 1808), 99; [Sansay], *Zelica, the Creole,* vol. 3 (London: William Fearman, 1820), 165.

63. Madiou, *Histoire,* vol. 2, 391.

64. Lanchamp to Rochambeau (Nov. 27, 1802), Box 14/1383, UF-RP. For other balances, see ibid., Box 14/1389, /1489, /1494, /1650.

65. Rochambeau to Decrès (March 2, 1803), CC9B/19, AN.

66. Daure, "Instructions pour le Général Boyer" (ca. May 1803), CC9/B20, AN.

67. On Jamaica, see "Instructions pour le Commandant Morin" (May 5, 1803), 416AP/1, AN. On the United States, see Daure, "Instructions pour le citoyen Perrin" (Nov. 10, 1802), CC9/B20, AN. On Veracruz, see Lanchamp, "Instructions pour suivre les traces d'une négociation de traites sur la Veracruz" (ca. 1803), B7/12, SHD-DAT. On Havana, see Daure, "Instructions pour le citoyen Reynaud" (Dec. 6, 1802), BN08271 / lot 122, UF-RP; Jean Vermonnet to Rochambeau (Dec. 11, 1802), BN08269 / lot 103, UF-RP. On Cartagena, see François Pons to Rochambeau (Dec. 6, 1802), Box 14/1416, UF-RP; Leblond Plassan to Decrès (Dec. 12, 1802), BB4 163, SHD-DM. On Caracas, see Thouvenot to Lemoine Villaroy (April 18, 1803), B7/20, SHD-DAT; Roos to Rochambeau (Sept. 13, 1803), Box 20/2079, UF-RP.

68. Daure and Rochambeau, "Instructions pour le général de brigade Noailles" (Dec. 14, 1802), B7/9, SHD-DAT.

69. Alexandre Lindo, "Mémoire à consulter, adressé à M. Lapeyrère" (ca. Nov. 1802), Folder 109, Bunel Papers, (Phi) 1811, HSP.

70. George Nugent to Leclerc (Oct. 17, 1802), CO 137/109, BNA.

71. John Duckworth to Evan Nepean (March 5, 1803), ADM 1/253, BNA.

72. Nugent to John Sullivan (Dec. 26, 1802), CO 137/109, BNA; Philip Wright, ed. *Lady Nugent's Journal of Her Residence in Jamaica from 1801 to 1805* (Kingston: University of the West Indies Press, 2002), 138.

73. S[ullivan] to [Nugent] (Feb. 17, 1803), CO 137/109, BNA.

74. L. Pellissier to Rochambeau (March 13, 1803), Box 17/1725, UF-RP; Daure, "Compte-rendu," III, 76–93.

75. "Proceedings of a court martial held by virtue of a special commission . . ." (Dec. 16, 1799), CO 137/103, BNA; Hugh Cathcart to Earl of Balcarres (Dec. 21, 1799), WO 1/74, BNA.

76. Lindo to Rochambeau (March 10, 1803), Box 17/1710, UF-RP; Nugent, *Journal,* 99, 108, 144.

77. Pierre Morin to Daure (May 15, 1803), B7/12, SHD-DAT.

78. Louis de Noailles to Marques de Someruelos (Jan. 11, 1803), 416AP/1, AN.

79. Someruelos to Rochambeau (Jan. 4, 1803), B7/12, SHD-DAT; Vermonnet to Daure (Feb. 11, 1803), B7/13, SHD-DAT; Noailles to Rochambeau (Feb. 18, 1803), 416AP/1, AN.

80. Vermonnet to Daure (Feb. 28, 1803), B7/13, SHD-DAT.

81. Pons to Rochambeau (Dec. 6, 1802), Box 14/1416, UF-RP; David Geggus, ed., *The Impact of the Haitian Revolution in the Atlantic World* (Columbia: University of South Carolina Press, 2001), 178.

82. DHHAN, 237–59. On the Arango mission, see also Noailles to Daure (Feb. 22, 1803), 416AP/1, AN; Yves Bénot and Marcel Dorigny, *Rétablissement de l'esclavage dans les colonies françaises 1802: Ruptures et continuités de la politique coloniale française* (Paris: Maisonneuve-Larose, 2003), 320–23, 329–62.

83. Someruelos to Noailles (April 21, 1803), 416AP/1, AN; Daure and Francisco de Arango, [Convention] (May 15, 1803), B7/12, SHD-DAT.

84. Louis-André Pichon to Daure (March 17, 1803), Box 3:2, MG 140, NYPL-SC; Perrin to Rochambeau (Jan. 8, 1803), B7/13, SHD-DAT.

85. Lanchamp, "Montant des traites sur France tirées depuis le premier Vendémiaire" (April 20, 1803), Box 18/1804, UF-RP; Daure, "Compte-rendu," 76–93.

86. Pellissier to Rochambeau (May 15, 1803), Box 18/1869, UF-RP.

87. Noailles to Rochambeau (Dec. 30, 1802), 416AP/1, AN.

88. Lemonnier, *Seconde campagne,* 66; A. J. B. Bouvet de Cressé, ed., *Histoire de la catastrophe de Saint-Domingue* (Paris: Peytieux, 1824), 61.

89. Assistant prosecutor of the tribunal of Cap to Ludot (March 27, 1803), CC9/B21, AN; Madiou, *Histoire,* vol. 2, 390.

90. Thouvenot to Senneville (March 9, 1803), B7/20, SHD-DAT.

91. Thouvenot to Lespinasse (March 8, 1803), B7/20, SHD-DAT.

92. On the uprising in La Tortue, see Garnier to Pamphile Lacroix (Feb. 26, 1803), B7/9, SHD-DAT; [Raymond Labatut], [Mémoire] (April 25, 1803), BN08272 / lot 122, UF-RP; Boisrond, "Mémoire," 39.

93. On Lacroix, see 7Yd841/1 and /2, SHD-DAT; Rochambeau, "Aperçu général sur les troubles des colonies françaises de l'Amérique" (ca. 1805), 86, 1M593, SHD-DAT; Pamphile de Lacroix, *La révolution de Haïti* (1819; reprint, Paris: Karthala, 1995).

94. Boyé to Ramel (March 8, 1803), no. 2053, CC9B/11, AN.

95. Maillard to Boscu (March 9, 1803), no. 1086, CC9B/10, AN.

96. Lacroix, "Mémoire secret . . ." Pièce 68, AF/IV/1212, AN; Philippe-Albert de Lattre, *Campagne des Français à Saint-Domingue et réfutation des reproches faits au Capitaine-Général Rochambeau* (Paris: Locard, 1805), 171.

97. Bertrand Clauzel to Rochambeau (April 6, 1803), no. 1291, CC9B/10, AN.

98. Pierre Boyer to Decrès (Feb. 23, 1803), CC9A/36, AN.

99. Daure to Decrès (March 6, 1803), CC9/B20, AN; Daure to Decrès (March 20, 1803), CC9/B20, AN.

100. Madiou, *Histoire,* vol. 3, 12.

101. Lhermitte to Rochambeau (March 29, 1803), BN08269 / lot 103, UF-RP; Laujon, *Précis historique,* 167; Madiou, *Histoire,* vol. 3, 14.

102. Lhermitte to Rochambeau (April 8, 1803), BN08269 / lot 103, UF-RP.

103. Thouvenot to Brunet (March 29 [April 28?], 1803), B7/20, SHD-DAT.

104. Thouvenot to Berthier (May 10, 1803), B7/10, SHD-DAT.

105. [French officer], "Mémoire succint sur la guerre de Saint-Domingue" (1804), 41, 1M598, SHD-DAT.

106. Rochambeau, "Aperçu général," 85.

107. Noailles to Rochambeau (May 8, 1803), 416AP/1, AN; Vermonnet to Decrès (Aug. 8, 1803), CC9/B22, AN.

108. Boyé to Daure (July 3, 1803), no. 2667, CC9B/11, AN; Henry William Bayntun to Duckworth (June 30, 1803), ADM 1/253, BNA.

109. Nicolas Geffrard to Sebastián Kindelán (Sept. 14, 1803), DHHAN, 152.

110. Jean-Jacques Dessalines to British Minister (Sept. 2, 1803), CO 137/110, BNA.

111. Charles d'Hénin, "Conseil de Guerre" (Sept. 2, 1803), 135AP/3, AN.

112. Guillaume Mauviel, "Mémoires sur Saint-Domingue . . ." (May 24, 1806), 88, 1M599, SHD-DAT; Laujon, *Précis historique,* 142.

113. Brunet to Thouvenot (Feb. 4, 1803), B7/9, SHD-DAT.

114. C. E. P. Wante to Rochambeau (March 6, 1803), Box 2:1, MG 140, NYPL-SC.

CHAPTER 13

1. On Jean-Jacques Dessalines, see [Anon.], "Portrait de Dessalines" (1804?), Box 1:2, MG 140, NYPL-SC; [French officer], *Notice historique sur les désastres de Saint-Domingue pendant l'an XI et l'an XII, par un officier français détenu par Dessalines* (Paris: Pillot, ca. 1804), 25; [Tussac], *Cri des colons contre un ouvrage de M. l'évêque et sénateur Grégoire, ayant pour titre De la littérature des nègres* (Paris: Delaunay, 1810), 229; Antonio del Monte y Tejada, *Historia de Santo Domingo,* vol. 3 (Ciudad Trujillo: República Dominicana, 1952), 246.

2. Hector Daure to Denis Decrès (Nov. 16, 1802), CC9/B20, AN.

3. Pierre Boyer to Alexandre Berthier (March 11, 1803), B7/9, SHD-DAT.

4. Victoire Leclerc to Napoléon Bonaparte (Sept. 16, 1802), LGC, 228.

5. Louis-René de Latouche-Tréville to Decrès (Jan. 23, 1803), BB4 181, SHD-DM; Thomas Madiou, *Histoire d'Haïti,* vol. 2 (1847; reprint, Port-au-Prince: Fardin, 1981), 355, 360.

6. Pierre Thouvenot to Decrès (Aug. 26, 1803), B7/20, SHD-DAT.

7. Madiou, *Histoire d'Haïti,* vol. 2, 339.

8. [Spying report on the rebel army] (ca. Jan. 1803), Box 23/2268, UF-RP; Madiou, *Histoire,* vol. 2, 378.

9. Louis Labelinaye to Donatien de Rochambeau (Jan. 28, 1803), Box 16/1570, UF-RP.

10. Lerat de Magnytot to Decrès (Aug. 19, 1803), CC9/B20, AN; Dessalines to John Loring (Sept. 16, 1803), ADM 1/253, BNA.

11. Thouvenot to Decrès (Aug. 26, 1803), B7/20, SHD-DAT.

12. Nicolas Geffrard to Sebastián Kindelán (Sept. 14, 1803), DHHAN, 152; Guillaume Mauviel, "Mémoires sur Saint-Domingue . . ." (May 24, 1806), 102, 1M599, SHD-DAT; Guy-Joseph Bonnet, *Souvenirs historiques* (Paris: Durand, 1864), 104.

13. *Affiches Américaines de Saint-Domingue* 52 (June 29, 1803), B7/10, SHD-DAT.

14. Louis Boisrond-Tonnerre, "Mémoire pour servir à l'histoire d'Hayti" (June 22, 1804), 40, CC9B/27, AN; Beaubrun Ardouin, *Études sur l'histoire d'Haïti, suivies de la vie du général J-M Borgella,* vol. 5 (Paris: Dézobry et Magdeleine, 1853–60), 354.

15. Berger to Leclerc (Nov. 6, 1802), Box 13/1304, UF-RP; "État nominatif des militaires de toute arme et autres, qui ont repassé en France" (Dec. 3, 1802), Reel 6, Sc. Micro R-2228, NYPL-SC.

16. Thouvenot to Jean-Baptiste Brunet (March 29, 1803), B7/20, SHD-DAT.

17. Bonaparte, "Décision" (Dec. 16, 1803), CN vol. 9, 193.

18. Berger to Rochambeau (Dec. 2, 1802), Box 14/1397, UF-RP; Bonnet, *Souvenirs,* 117.

19. Rochambeau to Decrès (April 28, 1803), CC9A/34, AN.

20. Thouvenot to Paul François Page (May 8, 1803), B7/20, SHD-DAT.

21. Rochambeau to Decrès (May 15, 1803), CC9B/19, AN.

22. Rochambeau, "Aperçu général sur les troubles des colonies françaises de l'Amérique . . ." (ca. 1805), 1, 1M593, SHD-DAT.

23. Rochambeau, "Arrêté" (Nov. 23, 1802), CC9/B22, AN; Joseph-Antoine Idlinger, "Bail" (Dec. 23, 1802), 135AP/3, AN.

24. Ludot to Rochambeau (Jan. 20, 1803), Box 15/1545, UF-RP.

25. Nérette to Rochambeau (Jan. 14, 1803), Box 15/1513, UF-RP; Le Charpentier to Rochambeau (Jan. 17, 1803), Box 15/1525, UF-RP.

26. Dieudonné Jambon to Rochambeau (Jan. 18, 1803), Box 15/1532, UF-RP; Boyé to Ludot (May 8, 1803), no. 2531, CC9B/11, AN.

27. Hautière to Thouvenot (Nov. 22, 1802), B7/8, SHD-DAT.

28. Boisrond, "Mémoire," 44; Madiou, *Histoire,* vol. 2, 366, 386, 402.

29. Baptiste B. to Alexandre Pétion (Jan. 19, 1803), Box 15/1537b, UF-RP; [Chapelle], "Note confidentielle remise au Général Dejean" (ca. May 1803), B7/10, SHD-DAT.

30. Dessalines, "Aux hommes de couleurs habitant la partie ci-devant espagnole" (Dec. 27, 1802), CC9A/32, AN.

31. Bonnet, *Souvenirs,* 116–19; Madiou, *Histoire,* vol. 2, 399–402.

32. H. Pauléus Sannon, *Histoire de Toussaint Louverture,* vol. 3 (Port-au-Prince: Héraux, 1933), 147.

33. Boyer, "Ordre du jour" (March 27, 1803), CC9/B22, AN; Boisrond, "Mémoire," 46–48.

34. Magloire Ambroise to Lamour Dérance (Feb. 18, 1802), in Gérard Barthélémy, *Créoles, bossales: Conflit en Haïti* (Petit Bourg: Ibis Rouge, 2000), 217.

35. Alfred de Laujon, *Précis historique de la dernière expédition de Saint-Domingue* (Paris: Delafolie, ca. 1805), 185.

36. Brunet to Rochambeau (Feb. 17, 1803), Box 16/1625a, UF-RP.

37. Madiou, *Histoire,* vol. 2, 345, 374, 407; ibid., vol. 3, 29.

38. Laujon, *Précis,* 196.

39. Ardouin, *Études,* vol. 5, 408.

40. François de Kerversau to Decrès (Feb. 10, 1804), CC9/B23, AN.

41. Madiou, *Histoire,* vol. 3, 43.

42. Philibert Fressinet to Férou (July 9, 1803), in Sannon, *Histoire de Toussaint Louverture,* vol. 3, 169.

43. Dessalines to Fressinet (July 13, 1803), B7/10, SHD-DAT.

44. Madiou, *Histoire,* vol. 3, 43.

45. Boisrond, "Mémoire," 49; Bonnet, *Souvenirs,* 118.

46. Robbe to Rochambeau (Oct. 19, 1802), Box 13/1207, UF-RP.

47. Fressinet to Rochambeau (Feb. 17, 1803), Box 16/1623, UF-RP; Boyer to Decrès (March 10, 1803), CC9A/34, AN.

48. Brunet to Rochambeau (Feb. 17, 1803), Box 16/1625a, UF-RP; Thouvenot, "Ordre du jour" (April 23, 1803), CC9/B23, AN; Madiou, *Histoire,* vol. 2, 410.

49. Edward Corbet to George Nugent (Jan. 25, 1804), CO 137/111, BNA.

50. Naverrez to Decrès (Feb. 21, 1803), CC9A/30, AN.

51. Francisco de Arango, "Comisión de Arango en Santo Domingo" (July 17, 1803), DHHAN, 237–59.

52. François Pageot to Rochambeau (Nov. 26, 1802), Box 14/1375, UF-RP; Pageot to Rochambeau (March 11, 1803), Box 17/1715, UF-RP.

53. "Rapport d'espionnage" (May 3, 1803), 135AP/3, AN; Latouche to Decrès (May 20, 1803), CC9/B20, AN; Madiou, *Histoire,* vol. 2, 397, 406.

54. Joan Dayan, *Haiti, History, and the Gods* (1995; reprint, Berkeley: University of California Press, 1998), 33, 41.

55. Makajoux to Thouvenot (Sept. 6, 1802), B7/7, SHD-DAT; Fressinet, "Mémoires sur la dernière expédition de Saint-Domingue" (1802 [probably May 1805]), 59, 1M593, SHD-DAT.

56. Pascal Sabès to Rochambeau (Feb. 20, 1803), 135AP/3, AN.

57. Council of notables of Môle to Thouvenot (Nov. 5, 1802), B7/8, SHD-DAT; Rochambeau, "Arrêté" (Jan. 4, 1803), CC9/B22, AN.

58. Sabès to Rochambeau (Feb. 20, 1803), 135AP/3, AN; ibid. (March 5, 1803).

59. Boyé to Sabès (Dec. 17, 1802), no. 1034, CC9B/11, AN.

60. Thouvenot, "Ordre du jour" (April 30, 1803), CC9A/34, AN; Jean-Baptiste Lemonnier-Delafosse, *Seconde campagne de Saint-Domingue du 1er décembre 1803 au 15 juillet 1809* (Le Havre: Brindeau, 1846), 68; Madiou, *Histoire,* vol. 2, 392.

61. Brunet to Rochambeau (March 9, 1803), Box 17/1705, UF-RP.

62. Latouche to Decrès (March 27, 1803), BB4 181, SHD-DM; Latouche to Nugent (May 2, 1803), CO 137/110, BNA.

63. Naverrez to Decrès (Feb. 21, 1803), CC9A/30, AN.

64. Jean-Baptiste Daoust?, "Rapport de l'expédition . . ." (Oct. 21, 1802), Folder C48, HU-KFC; Fressinet to Brunet (Jan. 17, 1803), Box 15/1524, UF-RP; Madiou, *Histoire,* vol. 2, 399–406.

65. *Gazette of the United States,* no. 127 (Oct. 26, 1802).

66. Joseph Bunel to Dessalines (Oct. 9, 1803), B7/10, SHD-DAT.

67. Thouvenot to Marêt (March 8, 1803), B7/20, SHD-DAT; Thouvenot to Boyer (April 7, 1803), B7/10, SHD-DAT.

68. John Duckworth to Evan Nepean (March 27, 1803), ADM 1/253, BNA; Lenoir, "Faits relatifs au séjour de la corvette *La Surinam . . .*" (May 7, 1803), BB4 181, SHD-DM; "Rapport de l'Enseigne de Vaisseau Babron . . ." (ca. July 17, 1803), Folder C4, HU-KFC; Ardouin, *Études,* vol. 6, 82.

69. Boyer to Berthier (March 11, 1803), B7/9, SHD-DAT.

70. Madiou, *Histoire,* vol. 2, 346, 408; Ardouin, *Études,* vol. 5, 386–88, 405.

71. Saint-Rémy, *Vie de Toussaint Louverture* (Paris: Moquet, 1850); Sannon, *Histoire de Toussaint Louverture,* vol. 3, 175; Fortuna Guéry, *Témoignages* (Port-au-Prince: Henri Deschamps, 1950), 89–95; Dayan, *Haiti, History, and the Gods,* 3, 52.

72. Wiener Fleurimond, *Haïti 1804–2004: Le bicentenaire d'une révolution oubliée* (Paris: l'Harmattan, 2005), 94.

73. Marcel Dorigny, ed., *The Abolitions of Slavery: From Léger Félicité Sonthonax to Victor Schoelcher, 1793, 1794, 1848* (1995; reprint, New York: Berghahn, 2003), 169.

74. Claude Auguste and Marcel Auguste, *Pour le drapeau: Contribution à la recherche sur les couleurs haïtiennes* ([Québec: Namaan?], 1982), 42; Laurore Saint-Juste, *Les couleurs du drapeau national* (Port-au-Prince: L'imprimeur II, 1988), 6.

75. Hénock Trouillot, *Le drapeau bleu et rouge: Une mystification historique* (Port-au-Prince: Théodore, 1958); Aubourg, Michel. *Le drapeau desslinien: contribution à la h'istoire d'Haïti* (Port-au-Prince: Théodore, 1958).

76. Odette Roy Fombrun, *Le drapeau et les armes de la république d'Haïti* (Port-au-Prince: Deschamps, 1987), 20, 24, 33.

77. Pageot to Brunet (7 Vent. 11 [Feb. 26, 1803]), Box 16/1657a, UF-RP; Henry William Bayntun to Duckworth (May 15, 1803), ADM 1/253, BNA; Latouche to Decrès (May 20, 1803), CC9/B20, AN; Charles d'Hénin, "Mémoire historique et politique" (July–Aug. 1803), 11, Box 19/2016, UF-RP; Corbet to Nugent (Jan. 25, 1804), CO 137/111, BNA.

78. Bonaparte, "Arrêté" (Dec. 25, 1799), CN vol. 6, 42. Louverture did not comply.

79. Latouche to Decrès (May 20, 1803), CC9/B20, AN.

80. Michel Hector, ed., *La révolution française et Haïti: Filiations, ruptures, nouvelles dimensions,* vol. 1 (Port-au-Prince: Henri Deschamps, 1991), 188.

81. Sannon, *Histoire de Toussaint Louverture,* vol. 3, 174; Mimi Sheller, "Sword-Bearing Citizens: Militarism and Manhood in Nineteenth-Century Haiti," *Plantation Society in the Americas* 4, nos. 2–3 (1997): 244.

82. Louverture, [Passport] (1799–1800), Papers of Toussaint Louverture, LC-MD;

Pétion, "Ordre du jour" (March 16, 1814), Publications on the independence of Haiti, RG 59 / MLR A1632, NARA-CP; Dorigny, *The Abolitions of Slavery,* 217.

83. Pierre Quantin to Rochambeau (Oct. 24, 1802), Box 13/1241, UF-RP.

84. Dessalines to Generals of the indigenous army (April 1, 1804), CO 137/111, BNA.

85. Hénin, "Mémoire historique et politique sur la situation actuelle de la colonie" (July–Aug. 1803), 12, Box 19/2016, UF-RP.

86. "Rapport d'espionnage" (May 3, 1803), 135AP/3, AN.

87. Dessalines to Quantin (Oct. 24, 1802), Box 13/1238, UF-RP.

88. [British officer], "A few anecdotes not unworthy of noting" (ca. Nov. 1802), ADM 1/252, BNA.

89. Pierre Cangé to Delpech (Nov. 13, 1802), Box 14/1331, UF-RP; Cangé to Lacosse (Jan. 3, 1803), Box 15/1488, UF-RP.

90. Jan Pachonski and Reuel Wilson, *Poland's Caribbean Tragedy: A Study of Polish Legions in the Haitian War of Independence, 1802–1803* (Boulder, CO: East European Monographs, 1986), 203.

91. Dessalines, "Proclamation" (Jan. 1, 1804), AB/XIX/3302/15, AN.

92. Latouche to Decrès (May 20, 1803), CC9/B20, AN.

93. Nugent to Robert Hobart (Aug. 9, 1803), CO 137/110, BNA; Dessalines to Duckworth (Aug. 13, 1803), ADM 1/253, BNA; Geffrard to Kindelán (Sept. 14, 1803), DHHAN, 152.

94. "Nomination de l'empereur d'Hayiti" (Jan. 25, 1804), CC9/B21, AN.

95. Brunet to Rochambeau (Feb. 17, 1803), Box 16/1625a, UF-RP.

96. Madiou, *Histoire d'Haïti,* vol. 3, 40.

97. De Constard, "Détail des événements . . ." (ca. 1830), CC9/B23, AN.

98. Cangé to Lacosse (Jan. 3, 1803), Box 15/1488, UF-RP. See also François Capois-la-Mort to all white soldiers (Aug. 16, 1803), 61 J 18, ADGir.

99. Brunet to Rochambeau (Jan. 7, 1803), Box 15/1497, UF-RP.

100. Dessalines to Quantin (Oct. 24, 1802), Box 13/1238, UF-RP; Latouche to Decrès (May 20, 1803), CC9/B20, AN.

101. Latouche to Decrès (Nov. 9, 1802), CC9/B20, AN.

102. Peter Chazotte, *Historical Sketches of the Revolutions, and the Foreign and Civil Wars in the Island of St. Domingo* (New York: Applegate, 1840), 56.

103. Dessalines to Quantin (Oct. 24, 1802), Box 13/1238, UF-RP; Cangé to Delpech (Nov. 13, 1802), Box 14/1331, UF-RP; [List of suspects] (ca. 1802), Box 23/2244, UF-RP.

104. Philippe Ménard to Decrès (Nov. 16, 1802), 1 Mi 6 R1, ADG.

105. Ardouin, *Études,* vol. 5, 293.

106. Alexandre Morand to his ex-brothers in arms (Sept. 29, 1803), B7/10, SHD-DAT.

CHAPTER 14

1. W. L. Whitfield to George Nugent (July 26, 1802), CO 137/108, BNA; Philippe d'Auvergne to Robert Hobart (Aug. 2, 1802), WO 1/924, BNA; Tous-

saint Louverture, *Mémoires du Général Toussaint l'Ouverture écrits par lui-même,* ed. St. Rémy (Paris: Pagnerre, 1853), 84.

2. Louverture to Victoire Leclerc (July 18, 1802), Folder 3C, HU-KFC; Louverture to Napoléon Bonaparte (July 20, 1802), Dossier 1, AF/IV/1212, AN.

3. "Rapport aux consuls concernant Toussaint Louverture" (July 23, 1802), CC9/B23, AN; Bonaparte, "Décret" (July 23, 1802), CN vol. 7, 676.

4. Alexandre Berthier, "Rapport fait au premier consul" (Aug. 1, 1802), B7/6, SHD-DAT.

5. Fernand Clamettes, ed., *Mémoires du général Bon. Thiébault,* vol. 3 (Paris: Plon, 1893–95), 301; Pierre Pluchon, *Toussaint Louverture* (Paris: Fayard, 1989), 522.

6. Baïlle to Denis Decrès (Sept. 28, 1802), CC9B/18, AN; Louis Martin, *Le château de Joux de ses origines à nos jours* (Pontarlier: Syndicat d'Initiative, 1973).

7. [Pascal], "Mémoire secret," (ca. 1801), Reel 8, Sc. Micro R-2228, NYPL-SC.

8. Louverture, *Mémoires,* 87.

9. Baïlle, "Copie de la consigne du poste du donjon du château de Joux" (Aug. 24, 1802), B7/6, SHD-DAT; Baïlle to Jean-François Menard (Aug. 27, 1802), B7/6, SHD-DAT; Alfred Nemours, *Histoire de la captivité et de la mort de Toussaint Louverture: Notre pélerinage au fort de Joux* (Paris: Berger Levrault, 1929), 26.

10. Pluchon, *Toussaint Louverture,* 541.

11. Berthier to Menard (Aug. 31, 1802), B7/6, SHD-DAT.

12. Thomas Gragnon-Lacoste, *Toussaint Louverture* (Paris: Durand, 1877), 364.

13. Pluchon, *Toussaint Louverture,* 541.

14. Sannon, *Histoire de Toussaint Louverture,* vol. 3, 162.

15. Nogaret to Claude Régnier (April 30, 1803), Reel 1, Sc. Micro R-2228, NYPL-SC; Régnier to Decrès (May 14, 1803), 8Yd638, SHD-DAT; David Geggus, "Slave, Soldier, Rebel: The Strange Career of Jean Kina," *Notes d'histoire coloniale* 20 (1980).

16. Sannon, *Histoire de Toussaint Louverture,* vol. 3, 157–65.

17. Baïlle to Menard (Aug. 27, 1802), B7/6, SHD-DAT.

18. Bonaparte to Marie-François Caffarelli (Sept. 9, 1802), CN vol. 8, 39.

19. Nemours, *Histoire de la captivité,* 72–89, 241–49.

20. Louverture to Bonaparte (Sept. 17, 1802), Dossier 1, AF/IV/1213, AN.

21. Jean-François Ducis, *Oeuvres,* vol. 2 (Paris: Didot aîné, 1819), 190.

22. "Mémoire par le général Toussaint Louverture" (ca. Sept. 1802), Dossier 1, AF/IV/1213, AN.

23. Joseph Caffarelli to Decrès (Nov. 22, 1802), CC9B/18, AN.

24. Louverture to Bonaparte (Oct. 9, 1802), Dossier 1, AF/IV/1213, AN.

25. Menard to Berthier (Oct. 22, 1802), B7/8, SHD-DAT.

26. Baïlle to Decrès (Nov. 6, 1802), CC9B/18, AN.

27. Berthier to Menard (Oct. 22, 1802), B7/8, SHD-DAT; [Decrès] to Baïlle (Oct. 27, 1802), CC9B/18, AN; Donatien de Rochambeau to Decrès (Dec. 7, 1802), CC9B/19, AN.

28. Menard to Berthier (Oct. 15, 1802), B7/8, SHD-DAT.

29. Baïlle to Decrès (Oct. 30, 1802), CC9B/18, AN.

30. [Decrès] to Baïlle (Oct. 27, 1802), CC9B/18, AN.

31. Menard to Berthier (Oct. 22, 1802), B7/8, SHD-DAT; Louverture to Baïlle (ca. Oct. 22, 1802), CC9B/18, AN.

32. Baïlle to Decrès (Nov. 6, 1802), CC9B/18, AN.

33. Baïlle to Decrès (Nov. 18, 1802), CC9B/18, AN; Amiot to Comte du Poul (Aug. 24, 1814), 7Yd284, SHD-DAT.

34. Baïlle to Decrès (Nov. 14, 1802), CC9B/18, AN.

35. Victoire Leclerc to Bonaparte (Oct. 7, 1802), LGC, 253.

36. Jean Boudet to Rochambeau (Feb. 2, 1803), Box 16/1579, UF-RP; *Moniteur Universel* 154 (Feb. 23, 1803): 1.

37. *Moniteur Universel* 139 (Feb. 8, 1803): 3.

38. Decrès to Rochambeau (Feb. 8, 1803), CC9/B22, AN.

39. Alexander DeConde, *This Affair of Louisiana* (New York: Scribners, 1976), 151.

40. Bonaparte, "Arrêté du gouvernment sur les fonds attribués aux [armées?] de la colonie" (March 5, 1803), FM/F/3/202, CAOM.

41. Decrès to Hector Daure (Feb. 8, 1803), CC9/B22, AN.

42. Bureau of Ports, "Rapport au Premier Consul" (Feb. 25, 1803), BB4 181, SHD-DM.

43. Bonaparte, "Note relative aux déserteurs des dépôts coloniaux" (Jan. 7, 1803), CN vol. 8, 208; Decrès to Rochambeau (Feb. 17, 1803), CC9/B22, AN.

44. Maillard, "Notice des dépôts coloniaux débarqués au Cap" (ca. March 1803), 135AP/1, AN.

45. CN vol. 8, 114, 288, 304.

46. Robert Livingston to Thomas Jefferson (March 12, 1803), Microfilm M34/10, NARA-CP.

47. Jacques de Norvins, *Souvenirs d'un historien de Napoléon: Mémorial de J. de Norvins,* vol. 1 (Paris: Plon, 1896), ix–xv; ibid., vol. 3, 56–70.

48. Daure, "Instructions pour le Général Boyer" (ca. April 1803), CC9/B20, AN; Pierre Boyer, *Historique de ma vie,* vol. 1 (Paris: La Vouivre, 1999), i–xvi, 67, 75–88.

49. Gabriel Debien, "Autour de l'expédition de Saint-Domingue: Les espoirs d'une famille d'anciens planteurs, 1801–1804," *Notes d'histoire coloniale* 111 (1942): 86–90.

50. Jean-François de La Poype to Rochambeau (Aug. 10, 1803), Box 20/2026, UF-RP.

51. [Chapelle], "Note confidentielle remise au Général Dejean" (ca. May 1803), B7/10, SHD-DAT.

52. CN vol. 8, 314, 319; Armée de Saint-Domingue, "État général des troupes arrivées dans la colonie" (ca. July 1803), CC9/B23, AN.

53. *Affiches Américaines de Saint-Domingue* 52 (June 29, 1803), B7/10, SHD-DAT.

54. Michel Hector, ed., *La révolution française et Haïti: Filiations, ruptures, nouvelles dimensions,* vol. 2 (Port-au-Prince: Henri Deschamps, 1991), 366–72.

55. On the Louisiana Purchase, see DeConde, *This Affair of Louisiana,* 91–175; Dolores Egger Labbe, ed., *The Louisiana Purchase Bicentennial Series in Louisiana History,* vol. 3 (Lafayette: Center for Louisiana Studies, 1998), 20–86; Jon Kukla, *A*

Wilderness So Immense: The Louisiana Purchase and the Destiny of America (New York: Knopf, 2003), 216–83.

56. DeConde, *This Affair of Louisiana,* 114.

57. Kukla, *A Wilderness So Immense,* 230, 232.

58. Labbe, *The Louisiana Purchase,* vol. 3, 20–51; DeConde, *This Affair of Louisiana,* ix, 155.

59. Labbe, *The Louisiana Purchase,* vol. 3, 29.

60. Bonaparte to Decrès (June 4, 1802), CN vol. 7, 617.

61. Labbe, *The Louisiana Purchase,* vol. 3, 25; Gordon Brown, *Toussaint's Clause: The Founding Fathers and the Haitian Revolution* (Jackson: University Press of Mississippi, 2005), 224.

62. Bonaparte to Decrès (Dec. 19, 1802), CN vol. 8, 184.

63. Brown, *Toussaint's Clause,* 228.

64. Yves Bénot and Marcel Dorigny, *Rétablissement de l'esclavage dans les colonies françaises 1802: Ruptures et continuités de la politique coloniale française* (Paris: Maisonneuve-Larose, 2003), 460, 461.

65. Livingston to James Madison (April 11, 1803), Microfilm M34/10, NARA-CP.

66. Bonaparte to François Barbé-Marbois (Dec. 2, 1802), CN vol. 8, 154; Guy Antonetti, *Les ministres des finances de la Révolution française au second empire,* vol. 1 (Paris: Documentation Française, 2007).

67. "Engagement soucrit par M. Alex Baring . . ." (May 2, 1803), Louisiana miscellany, Box 15, LC-MD.

68. Nemours, *Histoire de la captivité,* 23.

69. Amiot to Decrès (Jan. 3, 1803), CC9B/18, AN.

70. Nemours, *Histoire de la captivité,* 49.

71. Ménard to Berthier (March 7, 1803), B7/9, SHD-DAT.

72. Amiot to Decrès (April 9, 1803), CC9B/18, AN; Alfred Nemours, *Histoire de la famille et de la descendance de Toussaint Louverture* (Port-au-Prince: Imprimerie de l'État, 1941), 235.

73. Barry O'Meara, *Napoléon en exil: Relation contenant les opinions et les réflexions de Napoléon sur les événements les plus importants de sa vie,* vol. 2 (Paris: Garnier, 1897), 276.

74. Nemours, *Histoire de la captivité,* 18, 116, 140–64; Gragnon-Lacoste, *Toussaint Louverture,* 385.

75. Musée du Panthéon National, Toussaint Louverture (Port au Prince: Henri Deschamps, [1983]), 9.

76. Spenser St. John, *Hayti or the Black Republic* (1884; reprint, London: Frank Cass, 1971), 70.

77. Laurent Dubois, *A Colony of Citizens: Revolution and Slave Emancipation in the French Caribbean, 1787–1804* (Chapel Hill: University of North Carolina Press, 2004), 423.

78. Isaac Louverture to Decrès (June 9, 1803), CC9B/18, AN.

79. Nemours, *Histoire de la famille,* 239.

80. Gabrielle Fontan to [Nemours] (Oct. 25, 1929), Sc Micro R1527, NYPL-SC; Nemours, *Histoire de la famille,* 27–44.

81. Isaac Louverture to [Chandordy] (Oct. 10, 1821), 6APC/1, CAOM; Nemours, *Histoire de la famille,* 184, 212.

82. Nemours, *Histoire de la famille,* 176.

83. Louise Louverture to Isaac Louverture (April 6, 1822), 6APC/1, CAOM; Nemours, *Histoire de la famille,* 101; Cauna, *Toussaint Louverture,* 182–86.

84. Fontan to Nemours (Jan. 28, 1930), Sc Micro R1527, NYPL-SC; Nemours, *Histoire de la famille,* 85–101.

CHAPTER 15

1. Donatien de Rochambeau to Denis Decrès (May 15, 1803), CC9B/19, AN.

2. Rochambeau to Decrès (May 20, 1803), CC9B/19, AN.

3. Rochambeau, "Ordre du jour" (July 9, 1803), CC9/B22, AN; Morel-Beaulieu to Decrès (June 28, 1803), CC9/B20, AN.

4. John Duckworth to Rochambeau (May 13, 1803), Box 18/1860, UF-RP; Wade Stubbs to L. Baury (June 4, 1803), Box 19/1917, UF-RP.

5. Rochambeau, "Arrêté" (July 6, 1803), B7/10, SHD-DAT.

6. Henri Barré to Rochambeau (Sept. 27, 1803), BN08269 / lot 103, UF-RP; Alfred de Laujon, *Précis historique de la dernière expédition de Saint-Domingue* (Paris: Delafolie, ca. 1805), 208.

7. Louis-René de Latouche-Tréville to Decrès (Nov. 9, 1802), CC9/B20, AN; Duckworth to Evan Nepean (Nov. 16, 1802), ADM 1/252, BNA.

8. L. Pellissier to Rochambeau (May 15, 1803), Box 18/1869, UF-RP; Pierre Thouvenot to Bertrand Clauzel (May 16, 1803), B7/10, SHD-DAT; Thouvenot to Decrès (May 21, 1803), B7/20, SHD-DAT.

9. Rochambeau to Decrès (June 4, 1803), CC9B/19, AN.

10. Hector Daure to Decrès (March 6, 1803), CC9/B20, AN; Latouche to Decrès (May 15, 1803), BB4 181, SHD-DM.

11. Rochambeau, "Aperçu général sur les troubles des colonies françaises de l'Amérique" (ca. 1805), 94, 1M593, SHD-DAT.

12. Rochambeau to Decrès (July 9, 1803), CC9B/19, AN.

13. N. A. M. Rodger, *The Command of the Ocean: A Naval History of Britain, 1649–1815* (New York: Norton, 2004), 522–24.

14. Rochambeau to Decrès (May 11, 1803), CC9A/34, AN; Barré to Decrès (Aug. 12, 1803), CC9/B20, AN.

15. [Latouche], "État des bâtiments de la station" (April 21, 1803), BB4 181, SHD-DM; Jean-Louis Bargeau, "A bord de la corvette *La Mignonne* . . ." (June 28, 1803), BB4 182, SHD-DM.

16. Philip Wright, ed., *Lady Nugent's Journal of Her Residence in Jamaica from 1801 to 1805* (Kingston: University of the West Indies Press, 2002), 176, 185; Rodger, *The Command of the Ocean,* 485, 503.

17. Jacques Boyé to Latouche (May 21, 1803), no. 2667, CC9B/11, AN.

13. Bally to Rochambeau (Oct. 13, 1803), BN08271 / lot 122, UF-RP.

14. Thouvenot to Decrès (Aug. 14, 1803), B7/20, SHD-DAT.

15. Rochambeau to Decrès (March 2, 1803), CC9A/34, AN.

16. Pierre Quérangal to Decrès (June 14, 1803), BB4 182, SHD-DM.

17. Drouillard family papers, Ms. 2590, Reel 1, LSU.

18. "État des levées de sequestre" (ca. June 19, 1803), Reel 6, Sc. Micro R-2228, NYPL-SC.

19. Louis-René de Latouche-Tréville to Rochambeau (Jan. 22, 1803), BN08269 / lot 103, UF-RP.

20. Ludot to Rochambeau (Jan. 20, 1803), Box 15/1545, UF-RP.

21. Michot to Guillaubel (March 7, 1803), dossier 27, 195MI, AN.

22. Jean-Baptiste Drouillard to Popote (May 13, 1803), Reel 1, Ms. 2590, LSU.

23. [Troude], "Demandes/réponses" (July 31, 1803), BB4 182, SHD-DM.

24. Rochambeau, "Arrêté" (May 1803), BN08271 / lot 122, UF-RP.

25. Box 5:9, (Phi) 1602, HSP.

26. Lemesle Haudaudine to Dominique Laxalde (June 14, 1803), Box 7:5, (Phi) 1602, HSP.

27. Thouvenot to Decrès (May 21, 1803), B7/20, SHD-DAT.

28. Clerk Caldwell, "Be it remembered . . ." (May 19, 1804), Box 5:12, (Phi) 1602, HSP.

29. F. Duplessis, "Je soussigné . . ." (Sept. 30, 1805), Reel 1, Ms. 2590, LSU.

30. Alfred de Laujon, *Souvenirs de trente années de voyages à Saint-Domingue, dans plusieurs colonies étrangères, et au continent d'Amérique,* vol. 2 (Paris: Schwartz and Gagnot, 1835), 253; Michel-Étienne Descourtilz, *Voyage d'un naturaliste en Haïti* (1809; reprint, Paris: Plon, 1935), xviii, 225; Popkin, *Facing Racial Revolution,* 335.

31. Jean Vermonnet to Daure (Dec. 30, 1802), B7/12, SHD-DAT; François Lequoy-Mongiraud to Rochambeau (Feb. 14, 1803), Box 16/1613, UF-RP.

32. Rochambeau, "Ordre du jour" (April 30, 1803), B7/10, SHD-DAT; Jean-Marie Voisin, "Récapitulation générale des sommes résultantes . . ." (July 29, 1803), BN08271 / lot 122, UF-RP; Daure, "Compte-rendu de l'administration générale" (late 1803), 115–37, CC9B/27, AN.

33. Madison to Louis-André Pichon (May 20, 1803), Microfilm M40/12, NARA-CP; Unite Dodge to Rochambeau (Nov. 2, 1803), Box 21/2163, UF-RP.

34. P. C. E. Parade to Decrès (Oct. 2, 1803), CC9/B22, AN.

35. Voisin to Decrès (May 11, 1803), CC9/B22, AN; Richelle to Rochambeau (Nov. 1, 1803), Box 21/2162, UF-RP.

36. Ludot to Decrès (Feb. 11, 1803), CC9/B21, AN; [Chapelle], "Note confidentielle remise au Général Dejean" (ca. May 1803), B7/10, SHD-DAT.

37. Ministry of Navy, "Rapport au gouvernement" (Aug. 19, 1803), CC9/B22, AN.

38. Debien, "Vers la fin de l'expédition," 100; Magnytot to Napoléon Bonaparte (Aug. 13, 1803), BB4 181, SHD-DM.

39. "Administration de Magnytot préfet . . ." (ca. Nov. 7, 1803), B7/13, SHD-DAT.

40. Rochambeau, "Arrêté" (Nov. 25, 1802), CC9A 31, AN.

41. Lanchamp, "Bordereau des sommes payées sur le fonds de réserve" (June 2, 1803), Box 19/1906, UF-RP.

42. Rochambeau to Decrès (Dec. 11, 1802), CC9B/19, AN.

43. Rochambeau, "Affaires relatives à Saint-Domingue" (1802–3), BN08270 / lot 131, UF-RP.

44. Magnytot, "Observations sur le marché passé avec le citoyen Dat" (Oct. 15, 1803), BN08271 / lot 122, UF-RP.

45. Pascal Sabès to his wife (March 7, 1803), Box 17/1699, UF-RP; Joseph Bizouard to Rochambeau (Sept. 23, 1803), Box 20/2096, UF-RP.

46. George Nugent to Robert Hobart (Aug. 9, 1803), CO 137/110, BNA.

47. Hardivilliers to Stanislas Foache (Oct. 26, 1803), FP/92APC/16/43, CAOM; Rochambeau to Decrès (Nov. 1, 1803), CC9A/53, AN; Philippe de Lattre, *Campagne des Français à Saint-Domingue et réfutation des reproches faits au Capitaine-Général Rochambeau* (Paris: Locard, 1805), 121–32; Rochambeau, "Aperçu général," 104–15; François Pageot, [Testimony] (July 20, 1822), CC9A/53, AN.

48. "Affaire Rochambeau" (ca. 1805), BB/3/27 no. 24, AN; Barthélémy Fédon, *Réclamations de M. Bmy Fédon contre un ouvrage intitulé Campagnes de Français à Saint-Domingue, et réfutation des reproches faits au capitaine-général Rochambeau* (Paris: Brasseur, 1805), 5–32.

49. John Duckworth to Evan Nepean (May 21, 1803), ADM 1/253, BNA.

50. Daure, "Rapport confidentiel sur l'état de la colonie" (ca. May 1803), CC9A/36, AN.

51. Lacroze, "Mémoire contenant un aperçu succint . . ." (1804), CC9/B23, AN; Jacques de Norvins, *Souvenirs d'un historien de Napoléon: Mémorial de J. de Norvins,* vol. 3 (Paris: Plon, 1896), 47.

52. Popkin, *Facing Racial Revolution,* 332.

53. Paul Valete, [Song] (ca. 1803), Box 6:2, (Phi) 1602, HSP.

54. Henri Darré to Rochambeau (July 26, 1803), Box 19/2008, UF-RP; "Administration de Magnytot préfet . . ." (ca. Nov. 7, 1803), B7/13, SHD-DAT.

55. Laujon, *Souvenirs,* vol. 1, 330; Debien, "Vers la fin de l'expédition," 115.

56. *Gazette Officielle de Saint-Domingue,* no. 59 (July 23, 1803), CC9A/36, AN; ibid., no. 60 (July 27, 1803); ibid., no. 70 (Aug. 31, 1803).

57. [Leonora Sansay], *Zelica, the Creole,* vol. 2 (London: William Fearman, 1820), 79, 83, 89. See also Mary Hassal, *Secret History; or, The Horrors of St. Domingo, in a Series of Letters, Written by a Lady at Cape François* (Philadelphia: Bradford and Inskeep, 1808), 23, 29, 31.

58. Hassal, *Secret History,* 51.

59. Lacroze, "Mémoire."

60. Ministry of Navy, "Rapport au gouvernement" (Aug. 10, 1803), CC9/B22, AN; Hassal, *Secret History,* 103.

61. Anon., "Saint-Domingue—1803" (ca. Dec. 1803), B7/10, SHD-DAT.

62. Daure, "Rapport confidentiel."

63. Aimé Merceron to Daure (Sept. 28, 1803), B7/10, SHD-DAT.

64. Daure to Rochambeau (Feb. 22, [1803]), Reel 1, Sc. Micro R-2228, NYPL-SC; Daure to Decrès (May 6, 1803), CC9A/36, AN.

65. Rochambeau, "Arrêté" (July 6, 1803), B7/10, SHD-DAT.

66. Sabès to Henri Perroud (July 26, 1803), Folder C38, HU-KFC. The prefects were Tirol, Magnytot, and Perroud.

67. Ludot to Decrès (May 9, 1803), CC9/B21, AN; Ludot to Rochambeau (June 25, 1803), Box 19/1953, UF-RP; Jean-François Minuty to Decrès (June 29, 1803), CC9/B21, AN; Rochambeau, "Ordre du jour" (Aug. 14, 1803), CC9/B22, AN.

68. Thouvenot, "Mémoire sur la marine et les colonies" (May 8, 1801), Box 2/69, UF-RP; Thouvenot to Jean-Jacques Dessalines (Aug. 23, 1802), B7/19, SHD-DAT.

69. Thouvenot to Bertrand Clauzel (Aug. 27, 1802), B7/20, SHD-DAT.

70. Thouvenot to Edouard Henry (March 18, 1803), B7/20, SHD-DAT.

71. Thouvenot, [Living will] (April 18, 1803), B7/20, SHD-DAT.

72. Thouvenot to Paul François Page (May 8, 1803), B7/20, SHD-DAT; Thouvenot, "Notes" (May 11, 1803), B7/20, SHD-DAT.

73. Thouvenot to Clauzel (May 16, 1803), B7/10, SHD-DAT.

74. Thouvenot to Decrès (Aug. 18, 1803), B7/20, SHD-DAT; Thouvenot to Decrès (Aug. 22, 1803), B7/20, SHD-DAT.

75. Thouvenot to Decrès (Aug. 26, 1803), B7/20, SHD-DAT.

76. Merceron to Bréchon (July 12, 1803), 416AP/1, AN; Magnytot to Decrès (Aug. 13, 1803), CC9/B22, AN; Poterat, "Mémoire sur la colonie de Saint-Domingue" (Sept. 8, 1803), CC9A/35, AN.

77. Magnytot to Bonaparte (Aug. 13, 1803), BB4 181, SHD-DM; Clauzel to Barré (Sept. 14, 1803), B7/10, SHD-DAT; Thouvenot to Rochambeau (Sept. 15, 1803), B7/10, SHD-DAT; Merceron to Daure (Sept. 28, 1803), B7/10, SHD-DAT; Rochambeau, "Aperçu général," 35; Norvins, *Souvenirs,* vol. 3, 50.

78. Rochambeau to Decrès (Sept. 24, 1803), CC9B/19, AN.

79. "Compte-rendu du rapport du Général Rochambeau" (April 28, 1810), CC9A/46, AN; Claude Auguste and Marcel Auguste, *L'expédition Leclerc, 1801–1803* (Port-au-Prince: Henri Deschamps, 1985), 299.

CHAPTER 17

1. Donatien de Rochambeau to Denis Decrès (March 14, 1803), CC9A/33, AN.

2. Jean-Jacques Dessalines to John Duckworth (Aug. 13, 1803), ADM 1/253, BNA.

3. On Tiburon, see John Bligh to Duckworth (July 10, 1803), ADM 1/253, BNA.

4. Duckworth to Evan Nepean (Oct. 25, 1803), ADM 1/253, BNA.

5. Philibert Fressinet to Férou (July 9, 1803), in H. Pauléus Sannon, *Histoire de Toussaint Louverture,* vol. 3 (Port-au-Prince: Héraux, 1933), 169.

6. Fressinet, "Journal—Évacuation de Jérémie" (Oct. 28, 1803), B7/10, SHD-DAT; Gabriel Debien and Philip Wright, "Les colons de Saint-Domingue passés à la Jamaïque," *Notes d'histoire coloniale* 168 (ca. 1976): 158.

7. Folder 9, B:13, De Bordes family papers, Mss. 2246, LSU.

8. Peter Chazotte, *Historical Sketches of the Revolutions, and the Foreign and Civil Wars in the Island of St. Domingo* (New York: Applegate, 1840), 35.

9. Bénard to Rochambeau (Aug. 6, 1803), BN08272 / lot 122, UF-RP; Berger, [Report] (Aug. 20, 1803), Box 20/2045, UF-RP; Fressinet, "Journal"; Fressinet, "Mémoire adressé . . . [au] Maréchal Berthier . . ." (May 5, 1805), 1M593, SHD-DAT.

10. A. de Raymond to Madame Veuve Lavalette (Aug. 12, 1803), Folder 9, B:13, Mss. 2246, LSU.

11. Chazotte, *Historical Sketches,* 37.

12. Dessalines, "Extrait du journal tenu pendant l'expédition entreprise contre le Port-au-Prince" (Oct. 17, 1803), CC9/B20, AN; Thomas Madiou, *Histoire d'Haïti,* vol. 3 (1847; reprint, Port-au-Prince: Fardin, 1981), 53.

13. Charles d'Hénin, "Conseil de Guerre," (Sept. 2, 1803), 135AP/3, AN; Alfred de Laujon, *Précis historique de la dernière expédition de Saint-Domingue* (Paris: Delafolie, ca. 1805), 204, 221.

14. "Articles of capitulation . . ." (Oct. 12, 1803), ADM 1/253, BNA; Lefebvre, "Journal du siège . . ." (Dec. 1, 1803), BN08268 / lot 76, UF-RP; Débuour, "Précis des événements militaires . . ." (Sept. 17, 1804), CC9A/35, AN; De Constard, "Détail des événements arrivés à Saint-Domingue . . ." (ca. 1830), CC9/B23, AN.

15. Edward Bust, [Account] (ca. Dec. 1803), ADM 1/253, BNA; Jean-Baptiste Brunet, "Copie du détail des événements . . ." (ca. Oct. 1803), CC9A/35, AN; John Loring et al., [Enquiry report] (Dec. 14, 1803), ADM 1/253, BNA.

16. Duckworth to Nepean (March 4, 1804), ADM 1/254, BNA.

17. Corvinus to Rochambeau (Sept. 7, 1803), Box 20/2073, UF-RP; Henri Barré to Rochambeau (Sept. 9, 1803), BN08269 / lot 103, UF-RP; Jean-Baptiste Lemonnier-Delafosse, *Seconde campagne de Saint-Domingue du 1 décembre 1803 au 15 juillet 1809* (Le Havre: Brindeau, 1846), 54.

18. Loring to Rochambeau (Oct. 10, 1803), Box 21/2122, UF-RP.

19. On the siege of Port Républicain, see [Anon.] to Hector Daure (July 28, 1803), 416AP/1, AN; George Nugent to Robert Hobart (Aug. 9, 1803), CO 137/110, BNA; [Minutes of War Council] (Oct. 5, 1803), B7/10, SHD-DAT; Commissaire Colbert, "Réponse . . ." (ca. Oct. 1803), CC9/B21, AN; Dessalines, "Extrait du journal"; Duckworth to Nepean (Oct. 24, 1803), ADM 1/253, BNA; Guy-Joseph Bonnet, *Souvenirs historiques* (Paris: Durand, 1864), 122.

20. François Pageot to Rochambeau (ca. Sept. 18, 1803), Box 21/2142, UF-RP; P. C. E. Parade to Decrès (Oct. 2, 1803), CC9/B22, AN.

21. Pierre Thouvenot to Decrès (Aug. 14, 1803), B7/20, SHD-DAT.

22. Barré to Bonaparte (Sept. 30, 1803), AF/IV/1325, AN; [Auguste Marie Duquesne], "Journal de la flotille . . ." (ca. Nov. 12, 1803), BN08269 / lot 103, UF-RP.

23. Pascal Sabès, [Order] (July 5, 1803), BN08268 / lot 14, UF-RP; Beaubrun Ardouin, *Études sur l'histoire d'Haïti, suivies de la vie du général J-M Borgella,* vol. 5 (Paris: Dézobry et Magdeleine, 1853–60), 328.

24. Gt. Néraud to Rochambeau (Sept. 6, 1803), BN08268 / lot 14, UF-RP.

25. Bertrand Clauzel to Rochambeau (March 30, 1803), no. 1241, CC9B/10, AN.

26. Delplanque to Jean Boudet (June 25, 1802), B7/17, SHD-DAT; Louis Labelinaye to Rochambeau (Jan. 28, 1803), Box 16/1570, UF-RP.

27. Thouvenot, "Ordre du jour" (July 27, 1803), CC9/B22, AN; [French officer], "Mémoire succinct sur la guerre de Saint-Domingue" (1804), 58, 65–67, 1M598, SHD-DAT.

28. Thouvenot to Decrès (Aug. 26, 1803), B7/20, SHD-DAT; Néraud to Rochambeau (Sept. 11, 1803), BN08268 / lot 14, UF-RP.

29. Dessalines to Loring (Sept. 16, 1803), ADM 1/253, BNA; Barré to Decrès (Sept. 30, 1803), CC9/B20, AN.

30. "Compte-rendu du rapport du Général Rochambeau . . ." (April 28, 1810), CC9A/46, AN.

31. Néraud to Rochambeau (Oct. 1, 1803), BN08268 / lot 14, UF-RP; Moulut, "Mémoire abrégé sur les fortifications du Cap . . . ," Article 14/3, SHD-DM; Victor Bally to Rochambeau (Nov. 15, 1803), BN08271 / lot 122, UF-RP.

32. Piécourt to [Unspecified] (Nov. 22, 1803), B7/6, SHD-DAT.

33. Rochambeau to Decrès (Nov. 2, 1803), CC9B/19, AN.

34. Loring to Rochambeau (Sept. 29, 1803), Box 20/2105, UF-RP.

35. Barré to Rochambeau (Sept. 17, 1803), BN08269 / lot 103, UF-RP.

36. Duckworth to Nepean (July 19, 1803), ADM 1/253, BNA.

37. Barré to Rochambeau (Aug. 18, 1803), BN08269 / lot 103, UF-RP; Barré to Rochambeau (Sept. 3, 1803), BN08269 / lot 103, UF-RP; Duckworth to Nepean (Nov. 30, 1803), ADM 1/253, BNA.

38. Rochambeau to Loring (Oct. 21, 1803), ADM 1/253, BNA.

39. Loring to Rochambeau (Oct. 25, 1803), ADM 1/253, BNA.

40. On the battle of Vertières, see Sabron, "Précis des opérations maritimes . . ." (ca. Dec. 1803), CC9/B20, AN; [French officer], "Mémoire succinct," 72–88; Dessalines, "Journal de la campagne du nord" (Dec. 2, 1803), CC9/B20, AN; Rochambeau, "Aperçu général sur les troubles des colonies françaises de l'Amérique" (ca. 1805), 105–8, 1M593, SHD-DAT; Madiou, *Histoire,* vol. 3, 75–82.

41. Joan Dayan, *Haiti, History, and the Gods* (1995; reprint, Berkeley: University of California Press, 1998), 40.

42. Moulut, "Mémoire abrégé sur les fortifications du Cap . . ." (Nov. 2, 1803), Article 14/3, SHD-DM.

43. Lemonnier, *Seconde campagne,* 85.

44. Jacques Boyé to Dessalines (Nov. 22, 1803), CC9/B20, AN.

45. Edward Corbet to Nugent (Jan. 25, 1804), CO 137/111, BNA.

46. French and indigenous armies, [Capitulation of Cap] (Nov. 19, 1803), ADM 1/253, BNA; J. Pegot to Dessalines (Nov. 19, 1803), CC9/B21, AN.

47. André Guimot and Louis Dembowski, *Journal et voyage à Saint-Domingue* (Paris: Tesseidre, 1997), 132.

48. Rochambeau to Loring (Nov. 19, 1803), ADM 1/253, BNA.

49. Loring to Rochambeau (Nov. 19, 1803), Box 21/2176, UF-RP.

50. Rochambeau to Loring (Nov. 20, 1803), ADM 1/253, BNA.

51. Loring to Rochambeau (Nov. 21, 1803), Box 21/2178, UF-RP; Loring to Duckworth (Nov. 23, 1803), ADM 1/253, BNA.

52. Dessalines to Loring (Nov. 28, 1803), ADM 1/253, BNA.

53. "Copie de l'accord pour l'évacuation du Cap" (Nov. 30, 1803), CC9A/33, AN.

54. Duckworth to Nepean (Dec. 15, 1803), ADM 1/253, BNA.

55. Sabron, "Précis des opérations maritimes."

56. Debien and Wright, "Les colons de Saint-Domingue passés à la Jamaïque," 160.

57. Sabron, "Précis des opérations maritimes."

58. Jean-François de La Poype to Rochambeau (July 17, 1803), Box 19/1986, UF-RP; Louis de Noailles to Alexandre Berthier (Nov. 2, 1803), B7/10, SHD-DAT.

59. La Poype to Rochambeau (Aug. 6, 1803), Box 20/2024, UF-RP.

60. Noailles to Decrès (Dec. 19, 1803), CC9B/19, AN.

61. Madiou, Histoire, vol. 3, 101.

62. Dessalines, Augustin Clervaux, Henri Christophe, "Déclaration préliminaire d'indépendance" (Nov. 29, 1803), B7/11, SHD-DAT.

63. Hugh Cathcart and James Walker, [Account of their mission to Dessalines] (Aug. 27–30, 1803), CO 137/110, BNA; Dessalines, "Aux citoyens de la ville du Cap" (Nov. 19, 1803), CC9/B21, AN; French and indigenous armies, [Capitulation of Cap] (Nov. 19, 1803), ADM 1/253, BNA.

64. [French officer], Notice historique sur les désastres de Saint-Domingue pendant l'an XI et l'an XII, par un officier français détenu par Dessalines (Paris: Pillot, ca. 1804), 30.

65. Sabron, "Précis des opérations maritimes"; Laujon, Précis historique, 223; Étienne Dupusch to Chicon St. Bris (Feb. 20, 1804), Box 5:15, (Phi) 1602, HSP.

66. Philippe de Lattre, Campagne des Français à Saint-Domingue et réfutation des reproches faits au Capitaine-Général Rochambeau (Paris: Locard, 1805), 151.

67. Debien, Guillaume Mauviel, évêque constitutionnel de Saint-Domingue (Basse Terre: Société d'Histoire de la Guadeloupe, 1981), 69–73.

68. Louis Dufaÿ to [Louis Ferrand] (ca. Nov. 1803), CC9/B21, AN; Dufaÿ to Clervaux (Dec. 26, 1803), CC9/B21, AN.

69. Corbet to Nugent (Jan. 25, 1804), CO 137/111, BNA; Nugent to Earl Camden (Oct. 12, 1804), CO 137/112, BNA.

70. La Chevardière to Decrès (May 22, 1804), CC9/B21, AN.

71. "Déclaration que fait le sieur Beaumont . . ." (ca. Dec. 1804), 1M593, SHD-DAT.

CHAPTER 18

1. Louis Boisrond-Tonnerre, "Mémoire pour servir à l'histoire d'Hayti" (June 22, 1804), 1, CC9B/27, AN.

2. John Garrigus, Before Haiti: Race and Citizenship in French Saint-Domingue (New York: Palgrave, 2006), 71, 188, 308.

3. Beaubrun Ardouin, Études sur l'histoire d'Haïti, suivies de la vie du général J-M Borgella, vol. 6 (Paris: Dézobry et Magdeleine, 1853–60), 23–25.

4. Guy-Joseph Bonnet, Souvenirs historiques (Paris: Durand, 1864), 128.

5. Thomas Madiou, *Histoire d'Haïti,* vol. 3 (1847; reprint, Port-au-Prince: Fardin, 1981), 103.

6. Jean-Jacques Dessalines [Boisrond], "Proclamation" (Jan. 1, 1804), AB/XIX/3302/15, AN.

7. Jacques Tourreaux et al. to Alexandre Berthier (March 1, 1803), B7/9, SHD-DAT; Toussaint Louverture, "Au nom de la colonie française de Saint-Domingue" (Nov. 25, 1801), Sc Micro R1527, NYPL-SC; Garrigus, "Colour, Class, and Identity on the Eve of the Haitian Revolution: Saint-Domingue's Free Coloured Elite as Colons Américains," *Slavery and Abolition* 17, no. 1 (1996): 38.

8. M. J. La Neuville, *Le dernier cri de Saint-Domingue et des colonies* (Philadelphia: Bradford, 1800), 9.

9. Desrivieres Chanlatte, "Situation d'Hayti à l'égard de la France" (1814), Publications on the independence of Haiti, RG 59 / MLR A1632, NARA-CP.

10. Du Simitière, [Untitled] (1773), 968.F.5, Du Simitière Collection, LCP; Dessalines to British Minister (Sept. 2, 1803), CO 137/110, BNA.

11. Donatien de Rochambeau to Denis Decrès (Aug. 31, 1803), CC9A/34, AN; Julien Prévost, *Relations des glorieux événements qui ont porté leurs majestés royales sur le trône d'Hayti* (Cap: P. Roux, 1811), xxii.

12. Jonathan Brown, *History and Present Condition of St. Domingo,* vol. 2 (Philadelphia: William Marshall, 1837), 141.

13. Albert Valdman, "Haitian Creole at the Dawn of Independence," *Yale French Studies* 107 (2005): 148–59.

14. "Hymne haytiène" (ca. late Jan. 1804), in Dessalines, "Journal de la campagne du Nord" (Dec. 2, 1802), CO 137/111, BNA.

15. Yves Bénot and Marcel Dorigny, *Rétablissement de l'esclavage dans les colonies françaises 1802: Ruptures et continuités de la politique coloniale française* (Paris: Maisonneuve-Larose, 2003), 327, 395; Alfred Hunt, *Haiti's Influence on Antebellum America: Slumbering Volcano in the Caribbean* (Baton Rouge: Louisiana State University Press, 1988), 108–16; Michel Hector, ed., *La révolution française et Haïti: Filiations, ruptures, nouvelles dimensions,* vol. 2 (Port-au-Prince: Henri Deschamps, 1991), 186–99.

16. David Geggus, ed., *The Impact of the Haitian Revolution in the Atlantic World* (Columbia: University of South Carolina Press, 2001), 10–14.

17. Thomas Maitland and Louverture, "Convention secrète" (May 22, 1799), Microfilm M9/1, NARA-CP; Nicolas Geffrard to Sebastián Kindelán (Sept. 14, 1803), DHHAN, 152; "Conventions à arrêter . . ." (ca. Jan. 25, 1804), CO 137/111, BNA; May 20, 1805 constitution (art. 36).

18. Darién Davis, ed., *Beyond Slavery: The Multilayered Legacy of Africans in Latin America and the Caribbean* (New York: Rowman and Littlefield, 2007), 31.

19. Corbet to Nugent (Feb. 16, 1804), CO 137/111, BNA; Déclaration que fait le sieur Beaumont . . ." (ca. Dec. 1804), 1M593, SHD-DAT.

20. May 20, 1805 constitution (art. 28).

21. "Déclaration que fait le sieur Beaumont . . ." (ca. Dec. 1804), 1M593, SHD-DAT; Roulet, "Aperçu sur la position actuelle de l'île de Saint-Domingue"

(May 12, 1806), B7/11, SHD-DAT; Guillaume Mauviel, "Mémoires sur Saint-Domingue . . ." (May 24, 1806), 93–95, 1M599, SHD-DAT.

22. Madiou, *Histoire,* vol. 2, 377; ibid., vol. 3, 165.

23. Philippe Girard, *Clinton in Haiti: The 1994 US Invasion of Haiti* (New York: Palgrave, 2004), 125.

24. "Rapport d'espionnage" (July 12, 1803), 135AP/3, AN.

25. W. L. Whitfield to Nugent (March 22, 1804), CO 137/111, BNA.

26. Corbet to Nugent (ca. Jan. 1804), CO 137/111, BNA; Étienne Dupusch to Chicon St. Bris (Feb. 20, 1804), Box 5:15, (Phi) 1602, HSP; Vidal to Noos (March 20, 1804), CC9/B21, AN; Antoine Frinquier, "Relation des événements du Cap . . ." (ca. May 1804), 1M597, SHD-DAT; Madiou, *Histoire,* vol. 3, 122.

27. Madiou, *Histoire,* vol. 3, 107.

28. Ibid., 113.

29. Dessalines to John Duckworth (Feb. 12, 1804), ADM 1/254, BNA; Dessalines to civilian and military authorities (Feb. 15, 1804), CC9/B21, AN.

30. Dessalines, "Proclamation" (Feb. 29, 1804), CC9B/18, AN.

31. On the massacre in Cayes, see *Gazette of the United States,* no. 281 (April 27, 1804); Madiou, *Histoire,* vol. 3, 114. On Jacmel, see Jacob Ritter, "Autobiography" (March 12, 1836), 38–43, (Phi) Am.1305, HSP.

32. Jean Butler, *Tribut de reconnaissance: Collection des différents discours et pièces de poésie . . .* (Baltimore: Coale and Thomas, 1809), 10–16, 23.

33. *Gazette de Philadelphie* (April 30, 1804), CC9B/18, AN; Lacroze, "Mémoire contenant un aperçu succinct des événements . . ." (1804), CC9/B23, AN.

34. On the massacre in Jérémie, see John Perkins to Duckworth (March 17, 1804), ADM 1/254, BNA; Whitfield to Nugent (March 22, 1804), CO 137/111, BNA; Corbet to Nugent (May 10, 1804), CO 137/111, BNA; Madiou, *Histoire,* vol. 3, 114.

35. Chazotte, *Historical Sketches,* 39.

36. Ibid., 48.

37. Ibid., 53.

38. On the massacre in Port-au-Prince, see Jean Lavalette to Berthier (Feb. 28, 1804), B7/11, SHD-DAT; [Sutherland?], [Account] (March 24, 1804), CO 137/111, BNA; Perkins to Duckworth (April 8, 1804), ADM 1/254, BNA; [Jean Guon?], "Lettre de G . . ." (ca. 1804), Dossier 153, 73 J 114, ADGir; Bonnet, *Souvenirs,* 129.

39. Madiou, *Histoire,* vol. 3, 120.

40. Dessalines to Generals of the indigenous army (April 1, 1804), CO 137/111, BNA.

41. Antoine Frinquier, "Relation des événements du Cap Français . . ." (ca. May 1804), 14–23, 1M597, SHD-DAT.

42. James Richard Dacres to Duckworth (May 15, 1804), ADM 1/254, BNA.

43. Madiou, *Histoire,* vol. 3, 122–24.

44. Mauviel to Jean Portalis (ca. 1804), F/19/6212, AN; Ardouin, *Études,* vol. 6, 64.

45. Jean-Marie Garlaud to Decrès (June 15, 1804), CC9/B22, AN; Madiou, *Histoire,* vol. 3, 127.

46. [French officer], *Notice historique sur les désastres de Saint-Domingue pendant l'an XI et l'an XII* (Paris: Pillot, ca. 1804), 25; Hénock Trouillot, *Dessalines ou la tragédie post-coloniale* (Port-au-Prince: Panorama, 1966), 2; Bonnet, *Souvenirs,* 129; C. L. R. James, *The Black Jacobins: Toussaint L'Ouverture and the San Domingo Revolution* (1963; reprint, New York: Vintage Books, 1989), 371.

47. Dessalines, "Proclamation" (April 28, 1804), AB/XIX/3302/15, AN.

48. Hugh Cathcart and James Walker, [Account of their mission to Dessalines] (Aug. 27–30, 1803), CO 137/110, BNA; Corbet to Nugent (June 4, 1804), CO 137/111, BNA.

49. Dupusch to Dubourg (Feb. 7, 1804), Box 5:15, (Phi) 1602, HSP; Dupusch to Chicon St. Bris (Feb. 20, 1804), ibid.

50. Michael Heinl et al., *Written in Blood: The Story of the Haitian People, 1492–1995* (New York: University Press of America, 1996); Herbert Gold, *Best Nightmare on Earth: A Life in Haiti* (New York: Simon and Schuster, 1991).

51. Hunt, *Haiti's Influence,* 2, 122–63.

52. Marcus Rainsford, *An Historical Account of the Black Empire of Hayti* (London: Albion Press, 1805), 354; Baron de Vastey, *Revolution and Civil Wars in Haiti* (1823; reprint, New York: Negro University Press, 1969), 43; Civique de Gastine, *Histoire de la république d'Haïti ou Saint-Domingue, l'esclavage et les colons* (Paris: Plancher, 1819), 231.

53. Corbet to Nugent (Jan. 25, 1804), CO 137/111, BNA; Corbet to Nugent (Feb. 16, 1804), CO 137/111, BNA.

54. Corbet to Nugent (Feb. 29, 1804), CO 137/111, BNA.

55. Perkins to Duckworth (March 17, 1804), ADM 1/254, BNA.

56. Nugent to John Sullivan (March 8, 1804), CO 137/111, BNA.

57. Dacres to Duckworth (May 15, 1804), ADM 1/254, BNA.

58. Duckworth to William Morsden (April 15, 1804), ADM 1/254, BNA; Dacres to Duckworth (May 19, 1804), ADM 1/254, BNA.

59. [Anon.], "Portrait de Dessalines" (1804?), Box 1:2, MG 140, NYPL-SC; Corbet to Nugent (May 10, 1804), CO 137/111, BNA; G. Hallam to [Unspecified] (July 1, 1804), WO 1/75, BNA; Madiou, *Histoire,* vol. 3, 122.

60. Madiou, *Histoire,* vol. 3, 121.

61. Frinquier, "Relation des événements," 16; Mauviel, "Mémoires," 55.

62. Mauviel, "Mémoires," 138, 209; Charles Mackenzie, *Notes on Haiti Made during a Residence in That Republic,* vol. 1 (1830; reprint, London: Frank Cass, 1971), 183.

63. Sabron, "Précis des opérations maritimes . . ." (ca. Dec. 1803), CC9/B20, AN; Jan Pachonski and Reuel Wilson, *Poland's Caribbean Tragedy: A Study of Polish Legions in the Haitian War of Independence, 1802–1803* (Boulder, CO: East European Monographs, 1986), 311.

64. Dessalines to Nugent (May 13, 1804), CO 137/111, BNA; Nugent to Robert Hobart (June 10, 1804), CO 137/111, BNA.

65. Riccardo Orizio, *Lost White Tribes: Journeys among the Forgotten* (London: Secker and Warburg, 2000).

66. Dessalines, [Blank form of naturalization] (ca. April 1804), ADM 1/254,

BNA; Sibylle Fischer, *Modernity Disavowed: Haiti and the Cultures of Slavery in the Age of Revolution* (Durham, NC: Duke University Press, 2004), 232.

67. Corbet to Nugent (June 7, 1804), CO 137/111, BNA; Kindelán to [Marques de Someruelos?] (July 30, 1804), DHHAN, 158; Bonnet, *Souvenirs,* 132.

68. "Lois de la colonie française de Saint-Domingue" (ca. Aug. 1801), CO 137/106, BNA; Louis-André Pichon to Pierre Forfait (Sept. 30, 1801), CC9B/18, AN.

69. Dessalines et al., "Armée indigène: Liberté ou la mort" (Jan. 1, 1804), CC9/B20, AN.

70. Mauviel, "Mémoires," 56; Mackenzie, *Notes,* vol. 1, 95; Ardouin, *Études,* vol. 6, 84.

71. May 20, 1805 constitution (art. 7).

72. Dessalines, "Arrêté" (Jan. 14, 1804), AB/XIX/3302/15, AN; Nugent to Hobart (June 10, 1804), CO 137/111, BNA.

73. Corbet to Nugent (Jan. 25, 1804), CO 137/111, BNA; Dessalines to Corbet (Feb. 27, 1804), CO 137/111, BNA; [Earl Camden] to Nugent (Aug. 1, 1804), CO 137/112, BNA.

74. Claude Auguste and Marcel Auguste, *Les déportés de Saint-Domingue: Contribution à l'histoire de l'expédition française de Saint-Domingue, 1802–1803* (Sherbrooke, Quebec: Naaman, 1979), 111–27.

75. Loring Dewey, *Correspondence Relative to the Emigration to Hayti of the Free People of Colour in the United States* (New York: Mahlon Day, 1824), 1, 29–31; Chris Dixon, *African America and Haiti* (Westport, CT: Greenwood Press, 2000); Prince Saunders, *Haytian Papers* (1818; reprint, Philadelphia: Rhistoric Publications, 1969), 3–19.

76. Cathcart and Walker, [Account of their mission to Dessalines]; May 20, 1805 constitution (art. 15–17).

77. Vastey, *Revolution and Civil Wars,* 43, 50; Madiou, *Histoire,* vol. 3, 156, 161.

78. *Gazette of the United States,* no. 281 (April 27, 1804); Ritter, "Autobiography," 38–43.

79. Maurice Lubin, "Les premiers rapports de la nation haïtienne avec l'étranger," *Journal of Inter-American Studies* 10, no. 2 (1968): 292.

80. André Vernet to Antoine Laussat (June 15, 1805), Folder "André Vernet," Box 1, Sc MG 119, NYPL-SC.

81. Philippe Girard, "Trading Races: Joseph and Marie Bunel, a Diplomat and a Merchant in Revolutionary Saint-Domingue and Philadelphia," *Journal of the Early Republic* 30 (Fall 2010): 370–76.

82. Tim Matthewson, "Jefferson and the Nonrecognition of Haiti," *Proceedings of the American Philosophical Society* 40, no. 1 (1996): 26.

83. B. Taylor to Reed and Forde (Jan. 7, 1806), Reed and Forde correspondence 1806–29, (Phi) 541, HSP; Gordon Brown, *Toussaint's Clause: The Founding Fathers and the Haitian Revolution* (Jackson: University Press of Mississippi, 2005), 293.

84. May 20, 1805 constitution (art. 26).

85. "Nomination de l'empereur d'Hayti" (Jan. [Sept.] 25, 1804), CC9/B21, AN; Madiou, *Histoire,* vol. 3, 150–60.

CHAPTER 19

1. John Duckworth to Evan Nepean (Dec. 19, 1803), ADM 1/253, BNA; Donatien de Rochambeau to Denis Decrès (Dec. 21, 1803), CC9A/35, AN.

2. Jean-Baptiste Lemonnier-Delafosse, *Seconde campagne de Saint-Domingue du 1 décembre 1803 au 15 juillet 1809* (Le Havre: Brindeau, 1846), 93.

3. "Jamaica—French prisoners between 1 Oct. and 30 Nov. 1803" (Nov. 30, 1803), ADM 103/194, BNA; John Bligh, "Report of the prisoners of war" (March 24, 1804), ADM 1/254, BNA.

4. George Nugent to Robert Hobart (March 10, 1804), CO 137/111, BNA.

5. "Jamaica—French prisoners between 25 June and 30 Sept. 1803" (Nov. 1803), ADM 103/193, BNA; Lemonnier, *Seconde campagne,* 96.

6. Lemonnier, *Seconde campagne,* 100.

7. André Guimot and Louis Dembowski, *Journal et voyage à Saint-Domingue* (Paris: Tesseidre, 1997), 153.

8. Philip Wright, ed. *Lady Nugent's Journal of Her Residence in Jamaica from 1801 to 1805* (Kingston: University of the West Indies Press, 2002), 180.

9. Lemonnier, *Seconde campagne,* 101.

10. Duckworth to William Morsden (April 29, 1804), ADM 1/254, BNA; Nugent, *Journal,* 171, 187.

11. Rochambeau to Decrès ([Dec.?] 6, 1803), CC9A/33, AN; Duckworth to Nepean (Dec. 19, 1803), ADM 1/253, BNA.

12. Gabriel Debien and Wright, "Les colons de Saint-Domingue passés à la Jamaïque (1792–1835)," *Notes d'histoire coloniale* 168 (ca. 1976): 162.

13. Duckworth to Nepean (Dec. 20, 1803), ADM 1/253, BNA.

14. M. de Clermont-Tonnerre to Louis XVIII (Nov. 16, 1822), CC9A/53, AN.

15. Debien and Wright, "Les colons de Saint-Domingue," 171, 173, 182.

16. Nugent to Hobart (Dec. 19, 1803), CO 137/110, BNA.

17. Duckworth to Nepean (Oct. 31, 1803), ADM 1/253, BNA; "An account of French Prisoners of War on Parole, at Kingston and Spanishtown" (ca. March 6, 1804), CO 137/111, BNA.

18. "Jamaica—French prisoners between 25 June and 30 Sept. 1803" (Nov. 1803), ADM 103/193, BNA.

19. "General entry book of French prisoners of war at Jamaica on 1 Dec. 1803" (ca. April 1804), ADM 103/195, BNA.

20. Duckworth to Morsden (July 12, 1804), ADM 1/254, BNA.

21. On the *Duquesne,* see Duckworth to Morsden (May 20, 1804), ADM 1/254, BNA. On the *Créole,* see Guimot and Dembowski, *Journal,* 116. On the *Hardy,* see William Brown to Marques de Someruelos (Sept. 22, 1804), ADM 1/254, BNA. On the *Athenais,* see H. Moore to Duckworth (Dec. 7, 1804), ADM 1/255, BNA. On the *Fanny,* see Gallier-Labrosse to Decrès (March 4, 1805), BB4/209, SHD-DM.

22. Guimot and Dembowski, *Journal,* 110–23.

23. Nugent to Earl Camden (Nov. 16, 1804), CO 137/112, BNA.

24. Lemonnier, *Seconde campagne,* 102.

25. William Lux, "French colonization in Cuba, 1791–1806," *Americas* 29, no. 1 (1972): 57–61.

26. Pierre Collette to Stanislas Foache (Nov. 16, 1804), FP/92APC/16/43, CAOM; Guimot and Dembowski, *Journal,* 160.

27. DHHAN, 151, 156.

28. Lanchamp to Hector Daure (Feb. 25, 1804), B7/12, SHD-DAT; Jean-Marie Garlaud to Decrès (26 Prai. 12 [June 15, 1804]), CC9/B22, AN; Darién Davis, ed., *Beyond Slavery: The Multilayered Legacy of Africans in Latin America and the Caribbean* (New York: Rowman and Littlefield, 2007), 27.

29. Yves Bénot and Marcel Dorigny, *Rétablissement de l'esclavage dans les colonies françaises 1802: Ruptures et continuités de la politique coloniale française* (Paris: Maisonneuve-Larose, 2003), 350.

30. [List of slaves in Santiago] (July 20, 1807), Folder 9, B:13, Mss. 2246, LSU; Debien, "De Saint-Domingue à Cuba avec une famille de réfugiés, les Tornézy," *Notes d'histoire coloniale* 74 (1964): 19; Lux, "French colonization in Cuba," 57–61.

31. Lemonnier, *Seconde campagne,* 102.

32. Céline Lison, "Dernières notes de l'histoire française à Cuba," *National Geographic France* (July 2003): 2–15.

33. Rochambeau, "Lettre de marque . . ." (July 22, 1803), CC9C/20, AN; Someruelos to [Sebastián Kindelán?] (Sept. 22, 1803), DHHAN, 154; Duckworth to Nepean (Jan. 15, 1804), ADM 1/254, BNA.

34. Nugent to Hobart (March 11, 1804), CO 137/111, BNA; James Madison to [Someruelos] (May 5, 1804), Microfilm M78/1, NARA-CP.

35. Dusaulchoix to Decrès (Feb. 28, 1804), CC9/B20, AN.

36. Deshayes to Decrès (Jan. 31, 1804), BB4/209, SHD-DM; J. R. Fitzgerald to Hugh Cathcart (Feb. 23, 1804), CO 137/111, BNA.

37. Jean Lavalette to Decrès (Feb. 22, 1804), CC9B/19, AN; Lavalette, "État de situation des troupes françaises . . ." (April 10, 1804), B7/27, SHD-DAT.

38. Lavalette to Alexandre Berthier (April 10, 1804), B7/11, SHD-DAT.

39. [Ministry of Navy?], "Sommaire de trois lettres écrites de Norfolk . . ." (April 28, 1804), CC9/B22, AN; Marchand to Berthier (May 4, 1804), B7/11, SHD-DAT; Commissar of Commercial Relations to James Simon (May 5, 1804), Microfilm M179/20, NARA-CP; Louis-André Pichon to Decrès (May 26, 1804), CC9B/18, AN; Castet to Decrès (Sept. 1, 1804), BB4 208, SHD-DM.

40. Lemonnier, *Seconde campagne,* 107.

41. Dorvo-Soulastre, *Voyage par terre de Santo-Domingo . . . au Cap Français* (Paris: Chaumerot, 1809), 21.

42. C. Robbin, *Voyages dans l'intérieur de la Louisiane, de la Floride occidentale, et dans les îles de la Martinique et de Saint-Domingue,* vol. 1 (Paris: Buisson, 1807), 276–83; Dorvo, *Voyage,* 5–16, 23–28; Gilbert Guillermin, *Journal historique de la révolution de la partie de l'Est de Saint-Domingue, commencée le 10 août 1808* (Philadelphia: Lafourcade, 1810), 272; Emilio Rodríguez Demorizi, *La era de Francia en Santo Domingo: Contribución a su estudio* (Ciudad Trujillo: Editora del Caribe, 1955), 109–98.

43. Lemonnier, *Seconde campagne,* 157.

44. François de Kerversau to [Daure?] (Sept. 16, 1802), Folder "French Colonial Administration," Box 1, Sc MG 119, NYPL-SC; Guillaume Mauviel to Rochambeau (May 4, 1803), BN08268 / lot 16, UF-RP.

45. Antonio del Monte y Tejada, *Historia de Santo Domingo,* vol. 3 (Ciudad Trujillo: República Dominicana, 1952), 237.

46. Kerversau to Decrès (Feb. 10, 1804), CC9/B23, AN.

47. Kerversau to Rochambeau (May 7, 1803), 135AP/1, AN.

48. Louis Ferrand to Kerversau (Dec. 12, 1803), B7/10, SHD-DAT.

49. Ferrand to Barquier (Dec. 20, 1803), B7/10, SHD-DAT; Valdony and L. C. Miquel to Berthier (May 21, 1804), B7/11, SHD-DAT.

50. 8Yd743/1, SHD-DAT.

51. Urbain Devaux, "Précis des opérations . . ." (ca. Jan. 1805), 1M593, SHD-DAT; Monte, *Historia,* vol. 3, 239–45.

52. Jean-Jacques Dessalines, "Proclamation aux habitants de la partie espagnole" (May 8, 1804), AB/XIX/3302/15, AN.

53. Ferrand, "Proclamación a los vecinos del departamento del Cibao" (June 14, 1804), B7/11, SHD-DAT; Ferrand and François Dubuisson, "Decreto" (April 10, 1804), F/19/6212, AN.

54. La Chevardière to Decrès (May 22, 1804), CC9/B21, AN.

55. On the 1805 invasion, see Ferrand to Decrès (April 10, 1805), B7/11, SHD-DAT; Thomas Madiou, *Histoire d'Haïti,* vol. 3 (1847; reprint, Port-au-Prince: Fardin, 1981), 168–86; Lemonnier, *Seconde campagne,* 121, 126–43.

56. Miguel Feriet, "Mémoire relatif à la direction de Santo Domingo" (Jan. 30, 1803), B7/9, SHD-DAT.

57. Napoléon Bonaparte to Decrès (Sept. 29, 1804), CN vol. 9, 693; James Richard Dacres to Morsden (March 9, 1805), ADM 1/255, BNA.

58. Beaubrun Ardouin, *Études sur l'histoire d'Haïti, suivies de la vie du général J-M Borgella,* vol. 6 (Paris: Dézobry et Magdeleine, 1853–60), 139.

59. James Walker to Ferrand (Dec. 23, 1803), CO 137/111, BNA; Edward Corbet to Nugent (June 2, 1804), CO 137/111, BNA; Lemonnier, *Seconde campagne,* 156.

60. Nugent to Hobart (March 11, 1804), CO 137/111, BNA.

61. On the battle of Santo Domingo, see "Combat de l'Amiral Leissègues" (Feb. 7, 1806), BB4 251, SHD-DM; Henry, "Rapport sur le combat, mise à la côte et reddition du vaisseau de sa majesté *Diomède* . . ." (Feb. 19, 1806), BB4 251, SHD-DM; Garreau, "Rapport fait à son excellence le Ministre de la Marine . . ." (ca. March 1806), BB4 251, SHD-DM; Corentin de Leissègues to Decrès (April 8, 1806), BB4 251, SHD-DM; Duckworth, "A Journal of the proceedings . . ." (Nov. 29, 1805–March 18, 1806), ADM 50/41, BNA; Lemonnier, *Seconde campagne,* 162.

62. "General entry book of French parole prisoners of war" (ca. April 1806), ADM 103/576, BNA.

63. Lemonnier, *Seconde campagne,* 155.

64. Bron, "Mémoire relatif au projet du port Napoléon" (June 3, 1806), Article 14/4, SHD-DM; Guillermin, *Journal,* 2, 5.

65. Yves Bénot, *La démence coloniale sous Napoléon* (Paris: La Découverte, 1992), 124.

66. Juan Sanchez Ramirez to Barquier (Nov. 17, 1808), B7/11, SHD-DAT.

67. Monte, *Historia,* vol. 3, 268, 301–25; Lemonnier, *Seconde campagne,* 193–222; Guillermin, *Journal,* 35–53.

68. Barquier to Jean Ernouf (April 24, 1809), B7/18, SHD-DAT; Guillermin, *Journal,* 56–250.

69. Lemonnier, *Seconde campagne,* 273–75.

70. Lemonnier, *Seconde campagne,* 276.

71. Catherine Hébert, "The French Element in Pennsylvania in the 1790s: The Francophone Immigrants' Impact," *Pennsylvania Magazine of History and Biography* 108, no. 4 (1984): 451–66; David Geggus, ed., *The Impact of the Haitian Revolution in the Atlantic World* (Columbia: University of South Carolina Press, 2001), 193–204.

72. Pichon to Decrès (Sept. 3, 1804), CC9B/18, AN.

73. *Aurora* 3708 (Nov. 4, 1802); "Projet d'une société de bienfaisance" (ca. 1804), Box 16:1, MSS141, HSP.

74. Joseph B[unel] to Marie Bunel (ca. 1808?), Folder 109, Bunel Papers, (Phi) 1811, HSP.

75. Étienne Dupusch to Jean-Baptiste Marcq (Feb. 7, 1804), Box 5:15, (Phi) 1602, HSP.

76. Katherine Gallup, "Borie Family Papers Finding Aid" (Philadelphia: Historical Society of Pennsylvania, 2006), 1.

77. Fanfan Sulauze to Jean Sulauze (Jan. 29, 1805), Box 5:8, (Phi) 1602, HSP.

78. Alfred Hunt, *Haiti's Influence on Antebellum America: Slumbering Volcano in the Caribbean* (Baton Rouge: Louisiana State University Press, 1988), 45.

79. Robbin, *Voyages,* vol. 2, 118–25.

80. Dolores Egger Labbe, ed., *The Louisiana Purchase Bicentennial Series in Louisiana History,* vol. 3 (Lafayette: Center for Louisiana Studies, 1998), 82, 251–78.

81. Rodolphe Desdunes, *Our People and Our History: Fifty Creole Portraits* (1911; reprint, Baton Rouge: Louisiana State University Press, 2001); Dana Kress, "Pierre-Aristide Desdunes, Les Cenelles, and the Challenge of Nineteenth-Century Creole Literature," *Southern Quarterly* 44, no. 3 (2007): 42–67.

82. Geggus, *The Impact of the Haitian Revolution,* 211, 221; Hunt, *Haiti's Influence,* 62; Robbin, *Voyages,* vol. 2, 223–26.

83. "Old Mamie," *Times-Democrat* (Sept. 10, 1882): 16.

84. French Embassy, "État général des sommes dépensées . . ." (June 30, 1808), CC9C/5, AN.

85. Lemonnier, *Seconde campagne,* 277.

86. Ibid., 277–82.

87. Solinger to Daure (July 9, 1804), 416AP/1, AN; Debien, "De Saint-Domingue à Cuba," 22–25.

88. Ministry of the Interior, "Bases de règlement de secours aux colons . . ." (1821), CC9C/5, AN.

89. Alfred de Laujon, *Souvenirs de trente années de voyages à Saint-Domingue, dans plusieurs colonies étrangères, et au continent d'Amérique,* vol. 2 (Paris: Schwartz and Gagnot, 1835), 253–75.

90. Decrès, "De Saint-Domingue" (Aug. 9, 1806), Dossier 8, AF/IV/1213, AN; Laujon, *Précis historique de la dernière expédition de Saint-Domingue* (Paris: Delafolie, ca. 1805), 231; Lemonnier, *Seconde campagne,* 19.

91. F. Desrivieres Chanlatte, "Situation d'Hayti à l'égard de la France . . ." (1814), Publications on the independence of Haiti, RG 59 / MLR A1632, NARA-CP; *Gazette royale d'Hayti,* no. 5 (June 29, 1815), LCP; Bénot and Dorigny, *Rétablissement de l'esclavage,* 222; Laujon, *Souvenirs,* vol. 2, 285.

92. Chanlatte, *Almanach républicain* (Port-au-Prince: Imprimerie du Gouvernment, 1818), 48. On the 1816 mission, see also Comte du Bouchage, "Extrait des instructions approuvées par Sa Majesté" (July 17, 1816), Sc Micro R1527, NYPL-SC; Laujon, *Souvenirs,* vol. 2, 286–306; Bénot and Dorigny, *Rétablissement de l'esclavage,* 222.

93. Laujon, *Souvenirs,* vol. 2, 323–437.

94. Bénot and Dorigny, *Rétablissement de l'esclavage,* 221–37.

95. Philippe Girard, *Paradise Lost: Haiti's Tumultuous Journey from Pearl of the Caribbean to Third World Hot Spot* (New York: Palgrave, 2005), 191.

CONCLUSION

1. HOP 82 and 83, CAOM; Pamphile de Lacroix, *La révolution de Haïti* (1819; reprint, Paris: Karthala, 1995), 431, 434; Pierre Pluchon, *Toussaint Louverture* (Paris: Fayard, 1989), 514.

2. Louis Bergeron, *France under Napoleon* (1972; reprint, Princeton, NJ: Princeton University Press, 1981), 113, 118.

3. Victoire Leclerc to Denis Decrès (Sept. 26, 1802), B7/26, SHD-DAT; Gramont Chégaray to Leclerc (Oct. 27, 1802), Box 2/61, UF-RP.

4. Marcel Dorigny, ed., *The Abolitions of Slavery: From Léger Félicité Sonthonax to Victor Schoelcher, 1793, 1794, 1848* (1995; reprint, New York: Berghahn, 2003), 237–45.

5. François Dubuisson to Decrès (June 27, 1804), CC9A/36, AN; Alfred de Laujon, *Souvenirs de trente années de voyages à Saint-Domingue, dans plusieurs colonies étrangères, et au continent d'Amérique,* vol. 2 (Paris: Schwartz and Gagnot, 1835), 278; Alain Plessis, "La Révolution et les banques en France: De la Caisse d'Escompte à la Banque de France," *Revue Économique* 40, no. 6 (Nov. 1989): 1010.

6. [John Duckworth?], "A short sketch of the situation and mutation of the negroes in Saint-Domingue . . ." (ca. Sept. 10, 1803), ADM 1/253, BNA; Francisco de Arango, "Comisión de Arango en Santo Domingo" (July 17, 1803), DHHAN, 237–59; Charles Mackenzie, *Notes on Haiti Made during a Residence in That Republic,* vol. 2 (1830; reprint, London: Frank Cass, 1971), 110–21.

7. Robert Lacerte, "The Evolution of Land and Labor in the Haitian Revolution, 1791–1820," *Americas* 34, no. 4 (April 1978): 456–58.

8. Robert Sutherland to William Faulkner [Zawkener?] (Oct. 1, 1806), WO 1/75, BNA; [Tournès?] "Evaluation des produits de Saint-Domingue aux prix actuels" (1814?), CC9A/53, AN; Mackenzie, *Notes,* vol. 1, 39.

9. David Geggus, ed., *The Impact of the Haitian Revolution in the Atlantic World* (Columbia: University of South Carolina Press, 2001), x, xv, 3; Yves Bénot and Marcel Dorigny, *Rétablissement de l'esclavage dans les colonies françaises 1802: Ruptures et continuités de la politique coloniale française* (Paris: Maisonneuve-Larose, 2003), 159, 395; Dorigny, *The Abolitions of Slavery*, 272–79; Michel Hector, ed., *La révolution française et Haïti: Filiations, ruptures, nouvelles dimensions,* vol. 2 (Port-au-Prince: Henri Deschamps, 1991), 375–83.

10. Mackenzie, *Notes,* vol. 1, 18, 21; Fortuna Guéry, *Témoignages* (Port-au-Prince: Henri Deschamps, 1950), 5.

11. Hector, *La révolution française,* 348–57; Laurent Dubois, *A Colony of Citizens: Revolution and Slave Emancipation in the French Caribbean, 1787–1804* (Chapel Hill: University of North Carolina Press, 2004), 408, 423.

12. Pat Chin et al., eds., *Haiti, a Slave Revolution: 200 Years after 1804* (New York: International Action Center, 2004), v.

13. Henri Barré to Decrès (19 Flor. 12 [May 9, 1804]), CC9/B20, AN; Guillaume Mauviel, "Mémoires sur Saint-Domingue . . ." (May 24, 1806), 40–50, 1M599, SHD-DAT; Somerset de Chair, ed., *Napoleon on Napoleon: An Autobiography of the Emperor* (London: Cassell, 1992), 182, 184; Philippe de Lattre, *Campagne des Français à Saint-Domingue et réfutation des reproches faits au Capitaine-Général Rochambeau* (Paris: Locard, 1805), 75–82.

14. Geggus, *The Impact of the Haitian Revolution,* 10–14, 247–50.

15. Bénot and Dorigny, *Rétablissement de l'esclavage,* 180, 191–95.

16. Thomas Madiou, *Histoire d'Haïti,* vol. 1 (Port-au-Prince: Courtois, 1847), viii. See also Beaubrun Ardouin, *Études sur l'histoire d'Haïti, suivies de la vie du général J-M Borgella,* vol. 1 (Paris: Dézobry et Magdeleine, 1853–60), 9.

Glossary of French and Kreyol Terms

ancien libre: Person who was free prior to the 1793 decree of emancipation.

ancien régime: Prerevolutionary era (before 1789).

Congo: Person born in Africa (not necessarily the modern-day Congo); a.k.a. *bossale, africain.*

Creole: Person (of any color) born in the Caribbean; more generally, mixture of European and African influences in the New World (for the Creole language, see Kreyol).

cultivateur: Farm laborer forced to remain on plantations after the abolition of slavery.

demi-brigade: Basic unit of the French army (similar to a division).

domaines: Administration in charge of managing the estates of exiled *émigrés.*

émigré: Person, often of aristocratic descent, who fled France during the Revolution.

exclusif: Mercantilist trade system that gave French merchants privileged access to French colonies.

grand blanc: Upper-class white colonist (usually a slave-owning planter).

Kreyol: Afro-French language of Haiti.

loa (a.k.a. *lwa*): Vodou spirit.

marchande: Female market seller (usually a woman of color).

marron (a.k.a. *mawon,* Maroon): Runaway plantation laborer.

morne: Steep hill.

mulâtre: Mulatto (feminine: *mulâtresse*).

nouveau libre: Person freed by the 1793 decree of emancipation.

petit blanc: Poor white colonist (derogatory).

Vodou (a.k.a. *Vodun* or voodoo): Afro-Christian religion of Haiti.

Bibliographic Essay

The Haitian Revolution has received little of the scholarly attention showered on its more famous French and American counterparts. That Haiti's cash-strapped university lacks the resources to finance much historical research partly explains this historiographical gap. French academics are better financed, but until recently they were more eager to study the Napoleonic triumphs of Marengo, Austerlitz, and Wagram (won in the name of liberty and equality) than the disastrous expedition of Saint-Domingue (lost in the name of racism and imperialism), even though the expedition cost more French lives than these three battles combined and should rightfully have received far more attention than it has. The current boom in Atlantic history is bringing some U.S. scholars to the fray, but researching Haiti's past is an arduous task. The accidents of history have dispersed crucial documents to a dozen major archival deposits, and the prospect of traveling thousands of miles to read dozens of thousands of pages of documents written in four languages is enough to frighten the most daring scholar. Until some recent improvements, the literature on the Haitian war of independence was thus scant and often based on slim archival research.

Nineteenth-century Western accounts are rarely worth reading. Alternatively glowing (when written by abolitionists) or disparaging (when written by slavery's apologists), they reveal more about their author's political views than about the subject they cover. For anti-Haitian works, see Louis Dubroca, *La vie de Toussaint Louverture, chef des noirs insurgés de Saint-Domingue* (Paris: Dubroca, 1802); Jonathan Brown, *History and Present Condition of St. Domingo*, 2 vols. (Philadelphia: William Marshall, 1837); R. Lepelletier de Saint-Rémy, *Saint-Domingue: Étude et solution nouvelle de la question haïtienne* (Paris: Arthus Bertrand, 1846); H. Castonnet des Fosses, *La perte d'une colonie: La révolution de Saint-Domingue* (Paris: Faivre, 1893). On the laudatory side, see Marcus Rainsford, *An Historical Account of the Black Empire of Hayti* (London: Albion Press, 1805); John Beard, *The Life of Toussaint L'Ouverture: The Negro Patriot of Hayti* (London, 1853); Thomas Gragnon-Lacoste, *Toussaint Louverture* (Paris: Durand, 1877); Victor Schoelcher, *Vie de Toussaint Louverture* (Paris: Ollendorf, 1889). Several books presented as works of history were largely fictional, including René Périn, *L'incendie du Cap;*

ou, Le règne de Toussaint Louverture (Paris: Marchands de nouveautés, 1802); Mary Hassal [Leonora Sansay], *Secret History; or, The Horrors of St. Domingo, in a Series of Letters, Written by a Lady at Cape François* (Philadelphia: Bradford and Inskeep, 1808); Anatolii Vinogradov, *The Black Consul* (New York: Viking Press, 1935). One is better served reading memoirs written by veterans of the Leclerc expedition, such as Pamphile de Lacroix and Louis Boisrond-Tonnerre, who were also biased but at least knew their subject. For French veterans, see Alfred de Laujon, *Précis historique de la dernière expédition de Saint-Domingue* (Paris: Delafolie, ca. 1805); Michel-Étienne Descourtilz, *Voyage d'un naturaliste en Haïti, 1799–1803* (1809; reprint, Paris: Plon, 1935); Pamphile de Lacroix, *La révolution de Haïti* (1819; reprint, Paris: Karthala, 1995); Jean-Baptiste Lemonnier-Delafosse, *Seconde campagne de Saint-Domingue du 1 décembre 1803 au 15 juillet 1809* (Le Havre: Brindeau, 1846); Jacques de Norvins, *Souvenirs d'un historien de Napoléon: Mémorial de J. de Norvins,* 3 vols. (Paris: Plon, 1896); Christophe Paulin de la Poix, *Mémoires du Chevalier de Fréminville* (Paris: Librairie Ancienne Champion, 1913). For Haitian memoirs, see Auguste Bouvet de Cressé, ed., *Histoire de la catastrophe de Saint-Domingue* (Paris: Peytieux, 1824); Antoine Métral, *Histoire de l'expédition des Français à Saint-Domingue sous le consulat de Napoléon Bonaparte (1802–1803), suivie des mémoires et notes d'Isaac l'Ouverture* (1825; reprint, Paris: Karthala, 1985); Toussaint Louverture, *Mémoires du Général Toussaint l'Ouverture écrits par lui-même,* ed. St. Rémy (Paris: Pagnerre, 1853). Thomas Madiou and Beaubrun Ardouin, who drew from oral histories of revolutionary veterans, produced more valuable accounts, but both—especially Ardouin—tended to exaggerate the role of fellow mixed-race individuals: Thomas Madiou, *Histoire d'Haïti,* 3 vols. (Port-au-Prince: Courtois, 1847); Beaubrun Ardouin, *Études sur l'histoire d'Haïti, suivies de la vie du général J-M Borgella,* 11 vols. (Paris: Dézobry et Magdeleine, 1853–60).

More recent Haitian historians such as the Augustes have occasionally produced works of quality based on primary research, but many content themselves with rehashing Madiou's and Ardouin's old histories, often with a strong anti-colonialist tone that leads them to overlook the attractiveness of the French republican ideals to their ancestors. For good Haitian histories, see H. Pauléus Sannon, *Histoire de Toussaint Louverture,* 3 vols. (Port-au-Prince: Héraux, 1920–33); Alfred Nemours, *Histoire militaire de la guerre d'indépendance de Saint-Domingue,* 2 vols. (Paris: Berger-Levrault, 1925); Claude Auguste and Marcel Auguste, *L'expédition Leclerc, 1801–1803* (Port-au-Prince: Henri Deschamps, 1985). For nationalist works, see Faine Scharon, *Toussaint Louverture et la révolution de Saint-Domingue,* 2 vols. (Port-au-Prince: Imprimerie de l'État, 1957); Roger Dorsinville, *Toussaint Louverture ou la vocation de la liberté* (Paris: Julliard, 1965); Berthony Dupont, *Jean-Jacques Dessalines: Itinéraire d'un révolutionnaire* (Paris: L'Harmattan, 2006). Their works have found an echo in France, where the current controversy over France's imperial past has led to various one-sided indictments of Napoléon Bonaparte's colonial policies: Aimé Césaire, *Toussaint Louverture: La révolution française et le problème colonial* (Paris: Présence Africaine, 1981); Yves Bénot, *La démence coloniale sous Napoléon* (Paris: La Découverte, 1992); Claude Ribbe, *Le crime de Napoléon* (Paris: Privé, 2005); Alain Foix, *Toussaint Louverture* (Paris: Gallimard, 2007). Similarly, the English-language literature was long dominated by C. L. R. James, *The Black Jacobins: Toussaint L'Ouverture and the San Domingo Revolution* (1938; reprint, New York: Vintage Books, 1989), which was more notable for its political passion than the diligence of its research. Some more recent summaries of the Haitian Revolution are more balanced and scholarly but are based on limited original archival research: Thomas Ott, *The Haitian Revolution, 1789–1804* (Knoxville: University of Tennessee Press, 1973); Laurent Dubois, *Avengers of the New World: The Story of the Haitian Revolution* (Cambridge, MA: Harvard University Press, 2004); Madison Smartt Bell, *Toussaint Louverture: A Biography* (New York: Pantheon Books, 2007).

Starting with Gabriel Debien, a new generation of French historians finally began applying the rigorous standards of the historical craft to the history of Saint-Domingue in works such as Pierre Pluchon, *Toussaint Louverture* (Paris: Fayard, 1989); and Jacques Cauna, *Toussaint Louverture et l'indépendance d'Haïti* (Paris: Karthala, 2004). This approach is starting to filter into the English-language historiography, notably in the meticulous work of David Geggus, *Slavery, War, and Revolution: The British Occupation of Saint-Domingue, 1793–1798* (Oxford: Clarendon Press, 1982); Jan Pachonski and Reuel Wilson, *Poland's Caribbean Tragedy: A Study of Polish Legions in the Haitian War of Independence, 1802–1803* (Boulder, CO: East European Monographs, 1986); Carolyn Fick, *The Making of Haiti: The Saint Domingue Revolution from Below* (Knoxville: University of Tennessee Press, 1990); Gordon Brown, *Toussaint's Clause: The Founding Fathers and the Haitian Revolution* (Jackson: University Press of Mississippi, 2005); Jeremy Popkin, *You Are All Free: The Haitian Revolution and the Abolition of Slavery* (New York: Cambridge University Press, 2010). Their collective efforts have added much complexity to a story long presented as a Manichaean fight between black Haitian freedom fighters and white, racist French imperialists. Saint-Domingue, it increasingly appears, was a social kaleidoscope whose inhabitants' lives were shaped by a variety of factors, race among many others. This book, to a large extent, belongs to this school of thought.

The Slaves Who Defeated Napoléon draws on the findings of earlier generations of scholars, but it mostly relies on primary research conducted in twenty different archives and research libraries in France, Britain, and the United States (Haiti's archives have been largely destroyed or sold off). On archival sources, see Conseil International des Archives, *Guide des sources de l'histoire d'Haïti . . . dans les archives françaises* (Vincennes: Service Historique de la Défense), SHD-DAT; Joseph Boromé, "Toussaint Louverture: A Finding List of His Letters and Documents in Archives and Collections (Public and Private) of Europe and America," Box 1, Sc MG 714, NYPL-SC; David Geggus, "Unexploited Sources for the History of the Haitian Revolution," *Latin American Research Review* 18, no. 1 (1983), 95–103.

French government documents proved most useful. The Centre des Archives d'Outremer in Aix-en-Provence holds three large collections on revolutionary Haiti (the CC9A, B, and C), each of them containing twenty-five to fifty-three boxes, and which together form the single richest source on the expedition. These are available in microfilm format at the Archives Nationales in Paris, which also house important documents on topics like Toussaint Louverture's capture (135AP/6) and captivity (AF/IV/1213), colonial lobbying (AF/IV/1211), and specific individuals such as the colonial prefect Hector Daure (416AP). The Service Historique de l'Armée de Terre in Vincennes has twenty-seven boxes on the military aspects of the Saint-Domingue expedition (B7 series), the personal files of officers like Louverture (7yd328), and important memoirs by Donatien de Rochambeau and others (1M593). The expedition's naval dimension can be studied at the Départment de la Marine next door (BB4 series). Yet another crucial deposit is the University of Florida in Gainesville, which holds twenty-four boxes in its Rochambeau collection, along with five microfilm reels of now-lost original documents once housed in Haiti (BN08268 to BN08272).

Foreign governmental archives were also consulted to underline the international implications of the expedition. Jamaican authorities' correspondence with Louverture and Victoire Leclerc can be found at the British National Archives in Kew (CO 137, ADM 1, and WO 1). The United States' own role in the expedition can be retraced through the reports of its consuls in Cap, now preserved at the National Archives in College Park (Record Group 59, particularly M9/1–4), and its naval captains, found at the archives' Washington, DC, location (Record Group 45, particularly M625). Relevant Cuban and Dominican documents—such as José Luciano Franco, ed., *Documentos para la historia de Haití en el Archivo Nacional* (Havana: Publicaciones del Archivo Nacional de Cuba, 1954); Emilio Rodríguez Demorizi, ed., *La era de Francia en Santo Domingo* (Ciudad Trujillo: Impresora Dominicana, 1955)—are available in printed form.

A scholar's Atlantic *grand tour* cannot be complete without a visit to deposits that retrace Saint-Domingue's commercial ties and the human migrations that accompanied the revolutionary era. The papers of various exiled merchants and planters like Marie Bunel are at the Historical Society of Pennsylvania in Philadelphia (Phi 1811) and Louisiana State University (Mss 2590). The massive papers of the French banker, Stephen Girard, are at the American Philosophical Society in Philadelphia. The Archives Départementales du Calvados in Caen shed some light on French commerce (R3674).

Finally, one should mention disparate deposits that highlight various individuals and events connected with the expedition. Letters by Louverture and the French agent Philippe Roume are available at the Library of Congress, while the Bibliothèque François Villon in Rouen owns an interesting memoir by Charles de Vincent (MS 619). The simultaneous Richepance expedition can be studied at the Archives Départementales of Guadeloupe (1 Mi 6). Last, but not least, a smorgasbord of Haitian government papers were bought by the Austrian ethnologist Kurt Fisher, whose collection is now split between Howard University and the Schomburg Center of the New York Public Library; the equally diverse

Marcel Chatillon collection at the Archives de la Gironde in Bordeaux is also worth a look (61 J), as is the West Indies Collection of the Boston Public Library. Many papers related to Louverture's captivity are in the Nemours collection of the University of Puerto Rico–Rio Piedras. Others related to his arrest were sold by the Philippe Rouillac auction house as part of the Vente Rochambeau (lot 215 and 224 notably).

As for printed memoirs, contemporary pamphlets, and hard-to-find secondary sources, the collections of the Library Company of Philadelphia, the Bibliothèque Martial Lapeyre in Paris, and the Bibliothèque Nationale in Paris are the best starting points.

Index